41: *Afro-American Poets Since 1955*, edited by Trudier Harris and Thadious M. Davis (1985)

42: *American Writers for Children Before 1900*, edited by Glenn E. Estes (1985)

43: *American Newspaper Journalists, 1690-1872*, edited by Perry J. Ashley (1986)

44: *American Screenwriters*, Second Series, edited by Randall Clark, Robert E. Morsberger, and Stephen O. Lesser (1986)

45: *American Poets, 1880-1945*, First Series, edited by Peter Quartermain (1986)

46: *American Literary Publishing Houses, 1900-1980: Trade and Paperback*, edited by Peter Dzwonkoski (1986)

47: *American Historians, 1866-1912*, edited by Clyde N. Wilson (1986)

48: *American Poets, 1880-1945*, Second Series, edited by Peter Quartermain (1986)

49: *American Literary Publishing Houses, 1638-1899*, 2 parts, edited by Peter Dzwonkoski (1986)

50: *Afro-American Writers Before the Harlem Renaissance*, edited by Trudier Harris (1986)

51: *Afro-American Writers from the Harlem Renaissance to 1940*, edited by Trudier Harris (1987)

52: *American Writers for Children Since 1960: Fiction*, edited by Glenn E. Estes (1986)

53: *Canadian Writers Since 1960*, First Series, edited by W. H. New (1986)

54: *American Poets, 1880-1945*, Third Series, 2 parts, edited by Peter Quartermain (1987)

55: *Victorian Prose Writers Before 1867*, edited by William B. Thesing (1987)

56: *German Fiction Writers, 1914-1945*, edited by James Hardin (1987)

57: *Victorian Prose Writers After 1867*, edited by William B. Thesing (1987)

58: *Jacobean and Caroline Dramatists*, edited by Fredson Bowers (1987)

59: *American Literary Critics and Scholars, 1800-1850*, edited by John W. Rathbun and Monica M. Grecu (1987)

60: *Canadian Writers Since 1960*, Second Series, edited by W. H. New (1987)

61: *American Writers for Children Since 1960: Poets, Illustrators, and Nonfiction Authors*, edited by Glenn E. Estes (1987)

62: *Elizabethan Dramatists*, edited by Fredson Bowers (1987)

63: *Modern American Critics, 1920-1955*, edited by Gregory S. Jay (1988)

64: *American Literary Critics and Scholars, 1850-1880*, edited by John W. Rathbun and Monica M. Grecu (1988)

65: *French Novelists, 1900-1930*, edited by Catharine Savage Brosman (1988)

66: *German Fiction Writers, 1885-1913*, 2 parts, edited by James Hardin (1988)

67: *Modern American Critics Since 1955*, edited by Gregory S. Jay (1988)

68: *Canadian Writers, 1920-1959*, First Series, edited by W. H. New (1988)

69: *Contemporary German Fiction Writers*, First Series, edited by Wolfgang D. Elfe and James Hardin (1988)

70: *British Mystery Writers, 1860-1919*, edited by Bernard Benstock and Thomas F. Staley (1988)

71: *American Literary Critics and Scholars, 1880-1900*, edited by John W. Rathbun and Monica M. Grecu (1988)

72: *French Novelists, 1930-1960*, edited by Catharine Savage Brosman (1988)

73: *American Magazine Journalists, 1741-1850*, edited by Sam G. Riley (1988)

74: *American Short-Story Writers Before 1880*, edited by Bobby Ellen Kimbel, with the assistance of William E. Grant (1988)

75: *Contemporary German Fiction Writers*, Second Series, edited by Wolfgang D. Elfe and James Hardin (1988)

76: *Afro-American Writers, 1940-1955*, edited by Trudier Harris (1988)

77: *British Mystery Writers, 1920-1939*, edited by Bernard Benstock and Thomas F. Staley (1988)

78: *American Short-Story Writers, 1880-1910*, edited by Bobby Ellen Kimbel, with the assistance of William E. Grant (1988)

79: *American Magazine Journalists, 1850-1900*, edited by Sam G. Riley (1988)

(Continued on back endsheets)

Dictionary of Literary Biography • Volume One Hundred Eleven

American Literary Biographers
Second Series

Dictionary of Literary Biography • Volume One Hundred Eleven

American Literary Biographers
Second Series

Edited by
Steven Serafin 9597
Hunter College of The City University of New York

A Bruccoli Clark Layman Book
Gale Research Inc.
Detroit, London

Printed in the United States of America

Published simultaneously in the United Kingdom
by Gale Research International Limited
(An affiliated company of Gale Research Inc.)

The paper used in this publication meets the minimum requirements
of American National Standard for Information Sciences—Permanence
Paper for Printed Library Materials, ANSI Z39.48-1984. ∞™

ISBN 0-8103-4591-9
91-26672 CIP

Contents

Plan of the Series

. . . Almost the most prodigious asset of a country, and perhaps its most precious possession, is its native literary product—when that product is fine and noble and enduring.

Mark Twain*

The advisory board, the editors, and the publisher of the *Dictionary of Literary Biography* are joined in endorsing Mark Twain's declaration. The literature of a nation provides an inexhaustible resource of permanent worth. We intend to make literature and its creators better understood and more accessible to students and the reading public, while satisfying the standards of teachers and scholars.

To meet these requirements, *literary biography* has been construed in terms of the author's achievement. The most important thing about a writer is his writing. Accordingly, the entries in *DLB* are career biographies, tracing the development of the author's canon and the evolution of his reputation.

The purpose of *DLB* is not only to provide reliable information in a convenient format but also to place the figures in the larger perspective of literary history and to offer appraisals of their accomplishments by qualified scholars.

The publication plan for *DLB* resulted from two years of preparation. The project was proposed to Bruccoli Clark by Frederick G. Ruffner, president of the Gale Research Company, in November 1975. After specimen entries were prepared and typeset, an advisory board was formed to refine the entry format and develop the series rationale. In meetings held during 1976, the publisher, series editors, and advisory board approved the scheme for a comprehensive biographical dictionary of persons who contributed to North American literature. Editorial work on the first volume began in January 1977, and it was published in 1978. In order to make *DLB* more than a reference tool and to compile volumes that individually have claim to status as lit-

erary history, it was decided to organize volumes by topic, period, or genre. Each of these freestanding volumes provides a biographical-bibliographical guide and overview for a particular area of literature. We are convinced that this organization—as opposed to a single alphabet method—constitutes a valuable innovation in the presentation of reference material. The volume plan necessarily requires many decisions for the placement and treatment of authors who might properly be included in two or three volumes. In some instances a major figure will be included in separate volumes, but with different entries emphasizing the aspect of his career appropriate to each volume. Ernest Hemingway, for example, is represented in *American Writers in Paris, 1920-1939* by an entry focusing on his expatriate apprenticeship; he is also in *American Novelists, 1910-1945* with an entry surveying his entire career. Each volume includes a cumulative index of subject authors and articles. Comprehensive indexes to the entire series are planned.

With volume ten in 1982 it was decided to enlarge the scope of *DLB*. By the end of 1986 twenty-one volumes treating British literature had been published, and volumes for Commonwealth and Modern European literature were in progress. The series has been further augmented by the *DLB Yearbooks* (since 1981) which update published entries and add new entries to keep the *DLB* current with contemporary activity. There have also been *DLB Documentary Series* volumes which provide biographical and critical source materials for figures whose work is judged to have particular interest for students. One of these companion volumes is entirely devoted to Tennessee Williams.

We define literature as the *intellectual commerce of a nation:* not merely as belles lettres but as that ample and complex process by which ideas are generated, shaped, and transmitted. *DLB* entries are not limited to "creative writers" but extend to other figures who in their time and in their way influenced the mind of a people. Thus the series encompasses historians, journalists, publishers, and screenwriters. By this means readers of *DLB* may be aided to perceive litera-

*From an unpublished section of Mark Twain's autobiography, copyright © by the Mark Twain Company.

ture not as cult scripture in the keeping of intellectual high priests but firmly positioned at the center of a nation's life.

DLB includes the major writers appropriate to each volume and those standing in the ranks immediately behind them. Scholarly and critical counsel has been sought in deciding which minor figures to include and how full their entries should be. Wherever possible, useful references are made to figures who do not warrant separate entries.

Each *DLB* volume has a volume editor responsible for planning the volume, selecting the figures for inclusion, and assigning the entries. Volume editors are also responsible for preparing, where appropriate, appendices surveying the major periodicals and literary and intellectual movements for their volumes, as well as lists of further readings. Work on the series as a whole is coordinated at the Bruccoli Clark Layman editorial center in Columbia, South Carolina, where the editorial staff is responsible for accuracy of the published volumes.

One feature that distinguishes *DLB* is the illustration policy–its concern with the iconography of literature. Just as an author is influenced by his surroundings, so is the reader's understanding of the author enhanced by a knowledge of his environment. Therefore *DLB* volumes include not only drawings, paintings, and photographs of authors, often depicting them at various stages in their careers, but also illustrations of their families and places where they lived. Title pages are regularly reproduced in facsimile along with dust jackets for modern authors. The dust jackets are a special feature of *DLB* because they often document better than anything else the way in which an author's work was perceived in its own time. Specimens of the writers' manuscripts are included when feasible.

Samuel Johnson rightly decreed that "The chief glory of every people arises from its authors." The purpose of the *Dictionary of Literary Biography* is to compile literary history in the surest way available to us–by accurate and comprehensive treatment of the lives and work of those who contributed to it.

The *DLB* Advisory Board

Foreword

The development of biography as a distinctive mode of literary expression reflects the emergence of the genre as a vital and necessary presence within contemporary literature. Merging historical scholarship with social and cultural inquiry, biography appeals to both the general and the specialized reader. One of the most widely read and accessible forms of literature, biography constitutes a bold and innovative literary activity. There is now considerable interest in the evolution of biography as an art form and the role of the biographer within the biographical process. The study of the literary properties of biography has generated unprecedented critical discussion as well as analysis and evaluation of the genre.

Responding to the popularity of biography within contemporary culture, James F. Veninga in his preface to *The Biographer's Craft: Life Histories and Humanism* (1983) emphasizes the role biography has assumed for readers: "We want to know the private lives of public people, and we want to know the lives of 'common' men and women—people like ourselves—who have struggled with the possibilities and limitations of life." The traditional objective of the biographer has been to shape a person from the past into the present, or more literally to evoke a person into being. Through biography readers seek in others a better understanding of themselves. "In this age of Freud and his intellectual descendants," Veninga adds, "we crave insight, if not wisdom, in the business of living." In his introduction to *Biography: Fiction, Fact and Form* (1984) Ira Bruce Nadel refers to biography as "a literary process as well as a historical product," observing that the narrative of a biography frames the subject and affects the reader's vision, providing "a greater awareness of the complexity and richness of biographical form." In effect, the biographer acts as a medium through which readers can engage the subject. When the subject of a biography is a literary figure, the process is compounded by a multiplicity of purpose. The literary biographer attempts not only to re-create the life of a writer, but to examine the life in relation to the writer's body of work as well as the period in which he or she lived.

There is in biography a strong correlation with the social sciences—psychology, sociology, anthropology—and in literary biography this correlation is affected by the changing ideology of literary criticism. As noted by Gail Porter Mandell in the introduction to her *Life into Art: Conversations with Seven Contemporary Biographers* (1991), "The illumination of the inner life of the subject is a peculiarly contemporary aim of biography, indebted ultimately to psychoanalytic theory." In literary biography the text serves as a means to enter the subjective world of the author: "the biographer," Mandell claims, "aims to present the subject as he or she might know him or herself, using the written word as the link between inner and outer realities."

American Literary Biographers, Second Series, studies the lives of contemporary American biographers recognized predominantly as writers on literary subjects and examines both the theory and practice of their profession. Representative of the artistic growth and development of the genre within the second half of the twentieth century, the biographers included in this volume have contributed to the reputation of American literary biography established by the work of individuals such as Edwin H. Cady, Leslie A. Marchand, Edgar Johnson, Leon Edel, Richard Ellmann, Frederick A. Pottle, Gay Wilson Allen, and Walter Jackson Bate, among many others. Contemporary literary biographers continue to explore the limits of the genre and to expand the creative possibilities of their art. Although the nature of literary biography remains relatively consistent for most of its practitioners, there is today more diversity in relation to a biographer's motivation, methodology, application of narrative technique, and compositional strategy. This diversity has enabled biography to generate more widespread appeal as well as critical recognition.

Similar to their predecessors, the biographers included in the Second Series have written on a wide spectrum of literary subjects, historical as well as modern, the celebrated as well as the obscure. Unrestricted by national boundaries, ethnicity, or gender, American literary biographers have succeeded in re-creating lives from Geoffrey Chaucer's to Robert Penn Warren's. In fact, how a biographer comes to his or her subject is often an intricate as well as intriguing aspect of the biographical process. The image of one writer being drawn to another is indeed accurate for many biographers—Walter Harding to Henry Thoreau, Richard S. Kennedy to Thomas Wolfe, Maynard Mack to Alexander Pope, Ernest Samuels to Henry Adams, Stephen E. Whicher to Ralph Waldo Emerson, Virginia Spencer Carr to Carson McCullers—but for others the choice was more aptly the result of circumstance—Richard B. Sewall, for example, reluctantly accepting his role as biographer of Emily Dickinson, or Jackson J. Benson almost accidently becoming the authorized biographer of John Steinbeck. Some biographies, such as Joseph Blotner's two-volume *Faulkner: A Biography* (1974), are written during a period of popular as well as scholarly interest in a subject, or at a time coinciding with overdue critical recognition for the subject, as was the case with Scott Donaldson's *John Cheever: A Biography* (1988). There are others that result from the biographer's determination to redeem a subject's reputation—Benson's *The True Adventures of John Steinbeck, Writer* (1984), Millicent Bell's *Marquand: An American Life* (1979), Paul Mariani's *William Carlos Williams: A New World Naked* (1981), Jay Martin's *Conrad Aiken: A Life of His Art* (1962), and Frank MacShane's *Into Eternity: The Life of James Jones, American Writer* (1985). Some biographies are written to revise an existing interpretation of the subject—R. W. B. Lewis's *Edith Wharton: A Biography* (1975), Jean Strouse's *Alice James: A Biography* (1980), James R. Mellow's *Invented Lives: F. Scott and Zelda Fitzgerald* (1984), and, perhaps

most notably, William H. Pritchard's *Frost: A Literary Life Reconsidered* (1984). Often one venture into biography leads to another, as it did for Stanley Weintraub, who has said that writing *Beardsley: A Biography* (1967) initiated the writing of *Whistler: A Biography* (1974), which, in turn, inspired *Four Rosettis: A Victorian Biography* (1977) and *The London Yankees: Portraits of American Writers and Artists in England, 1894-1914* (1979). All biographers sense a need that a life be written, and what the biographer discovers is ultimately what he or she shares with the reader.

American Literary Biographers, Second Series, examines the process of literary biography by investigating the literary techniques and strategies utilized by its practitioners. As a result, one comes to realize the artistry of the biographer in presenting the life and literary career of his or her subject. In essence, readers gain through one art form access to another. The biographer provides insight as well as understanding, but the biographical process offers both speculation and unlimited possibility. As Richard Ellmann says in *Literary Biography* (1971):

> we cannot know completely the intricacies with which any mind negotiates with its surroundings to produce literature. The controlled seething out of which great works come is not likely to yield all its secrets. Yet at moments, in glimpses, biographers seem to be close to it, and the effort to come close, to make out of apparently haphazard circumstances a plotted circle, to know another person who has lived as well as we know a character in fiction, and better than we know ourselves, is not frivolous. It may even be, for reader as for writer, an essential part of experience.

—*Steven Serafin*

Acknowledgments

This book was produced by Bruccoli Clark Layman, Inc. Karen L. Rood is senior editor for the *Dictionary of Literary Biography* series. Jack Turner was the in-house editor.

Production coordinator is James W. Hipp. Projects manager is Charles D. Brower. Photography editors are Edward Scott and Timothy C. Lundy. Permissions editor is Jean W. Ross. Layout and graphics supervisor is Penney L. Haughton. Copyediting supervisor is Bill Adams. Typesetting supervisor is Kathleen M. Flanagan. Systems manager is George F. Dodge. Charles Lee Egleston is editorial associate. The production staff includes Rowena Betts, Teresa Chaney, Patricia Coate, Gail Crouch, Margaret McGinty Cureton, Sarah A. Estes, Robert Fowler, Mary L. Goodwin, Cynthia Hallman, Ellen McCracken, Kathy Lawler Merlette, Catherine A. Murray, John Myrick, Pamela D. Norton, Cathy J. Reese, Laurrè Sinckler-Reeder, Maxine K. Smalls, Teri C. Sperry, and Betsy L. Weinberg.

Walter W. Ross, Timothy D. Tebalt, and Henry Cunningham did library research. They were assisted by the following librarians at the Thomas Cooper Library of the University of South Carolina: Jens Holley and the interlibrary-loan staff; reference librarians Gwen Baxter, Daniel Boice, Faye Chadwell, Jo Cottingham, Cathy Eckman, Rhonda Felder, Gary Geer, Jackie Kinder, Laurie Preston, Jean Rhyne, Carol Tobin, Virginia Weathers, and Connie Widney; circulation-department head Thomas Marcil; and acquisitions-searching supervisor David Haggard.

The editor expresses his appreciation to Jason Berner and Geneviève Trousereau for their editorial assistance.

Dictionary of Literary Biography • Volume One Hundred Eleven

American Literary Biographers
Second Series

Dictionary of Literary Biography

Herschel C. Baker
(8 November 1914 - 2 February 1990)

Robert G. Blake
Elon College

BOOKS: *John Philip Kemble: The Actor in His Theatre* (Cambridge, Mass.: Harvard University Press, 1942);

The Dignity of Man: Studies in the Persistence of an Idea (Cambridge, Mass.: Harvard University Press, 1947); republished as *The Image of Man: A Study of the Idea of Human Dignity in Classical Antiquity, the Middle Ages, and the Renaissance* (New York: Harper & Row, 1961);

The Wars of Truth: Studies in the Decay of Christian Humanism in the Earlier Seventeenth Century (Cambridge, Mass.: Harvard University Press, 1952; London & New York: Staples, 1952);

Hyder Edward Rollins: A Bibliography (Cambridge, Mass.: Harvard University Press, 1960);

William Hazlitt (Cambridge, Mass.: Harvard University Press / London: Oxford University Press, 1962);

The Race of Time: Three Lectures on Renaissance Historiography (Toronto: University of Toronto Press, 1967).

OTHER: *The Renaissance in England: Non-Dramatic Prose and Verse of the Sixteenth Century*, edited by Baker and Hyder E. Rollins (Boston: Heath, 1954);

Critical Approaches to Six Major English Works: Beowulf through Paradise Lost, edited by Baker and R. M. Lumiansky (Philadelphia: University of Pennsylvania Press, 1968);

Four Essays on Romance, edited by Baker (Cambridge, Mass.: Harvard University Press, 1971);

William Shakespeare, *Twelfth Night; or What You Will*, edited by Baker (New York: New American Library, 1972);

"Histories," edited by Baker, in *The Riverside Shakespeare*, general editor G. Blakemore Evans (Boston: Houghton Mifflin, 1974);

The Later Renaissance in England: Nondramatic Verse and Prose, 1600-1660, edited by Baker (Boston: Houghton Mifflin, 1975).

Herschel C. Baker established his reputation as an intellectual historian, editor, biographer, and teacher. His writings range over the spectrum of history and literature from pre-Socratic Greece to nineteenth-century England; and, as was his teaching, they are informed by urbane wit and good humor. A 13 November 1990 memorial minute of the Harvard faculty refers to Baker as a "versatile humanist and Renaissance scholar in the Harvard tradition of George Lyman Kittredge and Hyder E. Rollins." To Rollins he dedicated his first work of intellectual history, *The Dignity of Man: Studies in the Persistence of an Idea* (1947), and edited with him *The Renaissance in England: Non-Dramatic Prose and Verse of the Sixteenth Century* (1954).

Born in Cleburne, Texas, on 8 November 1914 to Tyler Alexander Baker and Mae Waples Deffenbach Baker, Herschel Clay Baker attended Southern Methodist University, where he wrote the music for several amateur operas. He graduated in 1935 with both Mus.B. and A.B. degrees, early displaying the eclecticism and versatility that would distinguish his professional career. In 1936 he received his A.M. degree and three

Herschel C. Baker, 1967 (Harvard University News Office)

years later his Ph.D., both from Harvard University. His dissertation on John Philip Kemble was published in 1942 by Harvard University Press as *John Philip Kemble: The Actor in His Theatre.*

On 7 September 1939 Baker married Mary Barbara Morris (they were to have three children), and in that same year he joined the faculty of the University of Texas at Austin as an instructor of English. He taught there for seven years, attaining the rank of assistant professor. In 1946 he took a position as assistant professor of English at Harvard, where he was to remain for the rest of his professional life. In 1949 Baker was promoted to associate professor. He chaired the English department from 1952 to 1957 and again from 1965 to 1967. At the beginning of his first term as chair he published *The Wars of Truth: Studies in the Decay of Christian Humanism in the Earlier Seventeenth Century* (1952).

In 1960 he published *Hyder Edward Rollins: A Bibliography*, a tribute to his mentor. Aided by a

Guggenheim Fellowship and relieved temporarily from the burdens of administration, in 1962 Baker published *William Hazlitt*, which earned him the Harvard University Press Faculty Prize, an award to the member of the Harvard faculty who wrote the most outstanding book in the previous year. *The Race of Time*, a collection of his Alexander Lectures on Renaissance historiography at the University of Toronto, was published in 1967. The remainder of Baker's publications are volumes he edited, the most important being the last, *The Later Renaissance in England: Nondramatic Verse and Prose, 1600-1660* (1975). In recognition of his publications and teaching, Baker was named Francis Lee Higginson Professor of English Literature in 1967 and professor emeritus in 1984.

Baker's two biographies, *John Philip Kemble* and *William Hazlitt*, published twenty years apart, have as their subjects men, different in many ways, whose lives also share striking similarities.

Both men at one time were embarrassed by their attempted seduction of a woman: Kemble by forcing himself on the celebrated beauty Mrs. Marie Thérèse DeCamp, for which he had to apologize publicly; and the youthful Hazlitt for manhandling a young countrywoman at Keswick, an episode that would dog him for years. Both men underwent periods of problem drinking; both were jailed—the young, impecunious Kemble for stealing a suit, and Hazlitt in the last year of his life (unjustly) for debts of the publisher of his life of Napoleon—and, most important, both had to surmount major obstacles to achieve success, which for the two took very different forms.

Kemble emerged from the penurious life of a strolling player to become manager of the Drury Lane theater, only to be frustrated by the business ineptitude of Richard Brinsley Sheridan ("Sheri"), and later, as manager of the Covent Garden theaters, to be undermined financially and artistically by Thomas Harris, the tyrannical major patentee. Although the dominant actor of his age, Kemble throughout his stage career was confronted by rivals and prima donnas, and near the end of his professional life he was publicly humiliated by the "Old Price Riots" of 1809 (a protest over increased theater-admission prices)—according to Baker certainly the most harrowing attack any great English actor has ever had to endure.

Hazlitt's difficulties were the result of his disagreeable personality and intransigent liberal political views in an age that turned out to be unreceptive to them. In response to his vituperative attacks on his many enemies, Hazlitt was the object of numerous castigations in the savage periodical wars of the early nineteenth century, when literature and politics were inextricably intertwined. Unlike Kemble, Hazlitt cared nothing for social standing, and except for Charles and Mary Lamb and a few others he had no friends; he never attained any degree of financial security.

Both biographies are characterized by an authoritative grasp of detail, born of meticulous research. As a doctoral dissertation *John Philip Kemble* was written for the cognoscenti; consequently references and chronologies—even in the published version—may not always be clear to the general reader. Further, there is little of that effort to understand the inner man that one has come to expect from such full-scale biographies as Baker's *William Hazlitt*. However, his densely factual study of Kemble succeeds in presenting the progress of Kemble's career from his degrading beginnings as a strolling player in 1776 to his stage tri-

umphs at Drury Lane and Covent Garden as the premier actor of the English stage, and his triumphal reception in Paris.

John Philip Kemble consists of a prologue and sixteen chapters, each headed by an epigraph. The focus of the prologue is Kemble's father, Roger, a strolling player who never achieved fame and who forbade his children to pursue stage careers. He quickly drops from view, and Baker says only that he was granted a gentleman's coat of arms in 1792, died while his well-known son was touring Spain, and left a respectable inheritance.

Although Baker's chronicling of Kemble's dramatic seasons at Drury Lane and Covent Garden over a long career threatens to become tedious, he does enliven his narrative with anecdotes about the actor that stand in stark contrast to the image of the austere, classical tragedian that Kemble presented to the public; thus Baker suggests the man's multidimensionality without trying to get inside his psyche. For example, in 1776 Kemble, in dire financial straits, fell in with a fellow stroller with the stage name of Carleton (John Boles Watson), and their antics remind one of those of the Duke and Dauphin in *Huckleberry Finn*. Once, Kemble passed himself off as a Methodist preacher with Carleton as his clerk, and at Tewkesbury they took in a large collection. While playing *All for Love* in Dublin early in his career, Kemble saw an old man with a listening trumpet in his ear leaning over the upper boxes. Unable to restrain himself, Kemble broke into uncontrollable laughter—this from the actor who was to become the punctilious manager of Drury Lane and the terror of his fellow players for the slightest breach of stage decorum. Many of Baker's anecdotes center on Kemble's drinking. He was a prodigious drinker even in a period known for its intemperance: "He drank early and he drank late, alone and in company, among the vegetable peddlers of Covent Garden or in the drawing room of a duchess." Drunk, Kemble was loud, argumentative, full of self-praise, and generally obnoxious. Once during a prolonged drinking bout, he threw a decanter at Sheridan, but the episode ended amicably.

Baker is at his best when discussing the nature of Kemble's acting, the condition of the theatrical scene in London when Kemble arrived from the provinces, and such social phenomena as the uncanny but short-lived success of the boy actor Master Betty ("the Infant Roscius") and the OP Riots.

Baker calls Kemble "the first great producer." He strove for historical accuracy in scenic design and costuming, and he was enamored of lavish productions and spectacle. He made William Shakespeare's works the centerpieces of Drury Lane and Covent Garden. Kemble became "the official voice of the national poet—the arbiter, *par excellence*, of Shakespeare on the stage." In twenty-nine years as a stage manager he undertook twenty-five Shakespeare revivals. They ranged in quality from the then-acclaimed *Lear* on 21 January 1788 (Nahum Tate's sentimental version) to the ridiculous operatic version of *The Tempest*, based on John Dryden's 1667 mélange. Baker summarizes this absurd deformation of Shakespeare and remarks that the "monstrosity pleased the town." Kemble's revisions of existing plays, including Shakespeare's, were generally made for brevity and speed of action. He was careful to excise any "indecent" language to please the duplicitous morality of the period.

Despite his many problems, or perhaps because of them, there is something heroic about a man who, suffering from the breathing difficulties of asthma and working for owners who declined to grant him much artistic latitude, imposed his grand style of acting on an entire generation of playgoers who had grown accustomed to the colorful David Garrick. Baker, who refuses to pass judgment on the morality of his subjects, writes of Kemble: "His last entrance was his best one." Thirty-four years after his London debut, he played Coriolanus to a sold-out Covent Garden and received a five-minute ovation before speaking a line.

His career over, he took his leave of his beloved London and Edinburgh and, with his wife, Priscilla, lived out his final days at Lausanne, Switzerland, where he died on 26 February 1823. He was buried in the foreign cemetery just outside Lausanne.

Although the Kemble study is valuable (it has yet to be superseded), *William Hazlitt* is of a different magnitude. It consists of three parts: "Beginnings," "The Middle Years," and "The Later Years." Explanatory notes appear at the bottom of many pages—for example, details of William Godwin's eviction from his house on Skinner Street and the intervention of Samuel Rogers to secure a sinecure for him in 1832, when the Whigs returned to power; consequently, Godwin, the apostle of anarchy, lived out his last days as a "Yeoman Usher of the Exchequer in a snug little house in New Palace Yard." Baker's book is enlivened by portraits of such notables of the period as Samuel Taylor Coleridge, William Wordsworth, Charles Lamb, and Godwin, as well as six holographs, most of which were taken from Benjamin Robert Haydon's *Diary* (published in five volumes, 1960-1963), "one of the most fascinating records of the age," according to Baker.

William Hazlitt is more an intellectual biography than a chronological account of his life. Much of Hazlitt's childhood is clothed in mystery, almost nothing is known about his second wife and marriage, and he did not divulge his religious beliefs. In the preface Baker says his intent was "to place Hazlitt in his literary, political, and psychological milieu, and to trace the development and expression of his main ideas, relating them to the facts of his career in so far as these are known or can be ascertained."

Baker begins the biography by discussing the political environment in which Hazlitt grew up. Born on 10 April 1776 to a Unitarian minister, Hazlitt was barred from attending the universities. In 1793 his father sent him to Hackney, one of the many Dissenting academies of the time. While there Hazlitt's faith was undermined, and for reasons that are not entirely clear, he returned home much to his father's disappointment. At home Hazlitt tried to write an essay on benevolence, but the words refused to come, causing him to weep in frustration. In eight years he managed to write eight pages. Not until 1805 did the essay appear as the anonymous *An Essay on the Principles of Human Action*, a poorly received and unoriginal little work that nonetheless remained Hazlitt's favorite of all his writing.

Hazlitt arrived at maturity when the reactions against reform were in full swing. The writings of Edmund Burke and the draconian domestic policies of William Pitt had won the day over the efforts of such Dissenters as Richard Price, Joseph Priestley, and William Godwin. The broad assault on reform served to strengthen Hazlitt's liberal convictions and furnished him with a theme as a writer. All his life he "showed the moral vigor of Dissent in an age when Dissent itself had ceased to count for very much." His unwavering championing of individual liberty together with his acerbic personality made him many enemies. Thomas De Quincey, who despised him as an ignorant malcontent, "thought his habit of keeping one hand in his waistcoat gave him the look of a villain searching for a hidden dagger."

It is perhaps paradoxical that Hazlitt constructed an ethical system based on benevolence

Frontispiece and title page for the book that won the Harvard University Press Faculty Prize in 1963

and yet displayed so little of it in his personal life. His anonymous *Characteristics: In the Manner of Rouchefoucault's Maxims* (1823) is a bitter indictment of mankind's sins and weaknesses. From what is known, Hazlitt was a poor husband and father and a notorious womanizer who held women in contempt. His cheating of Haydon in a loan transaction was malicious. "This is the meanest thing Hazlitt ever did," Haydon wrote in his diary. Baker remarks with characteristic wit, "Although a man is not upon his oath in lapidary inscriptions, as Johnson said, we may none the less rejoice that Haydon was not called upon for composing Hazlitt's epitaph."

In "The Middle Years," the longest and, from a literary viewpoint, the most interesting part of Baker's book, he shifts from a panoramic view of England during the tumultuous period of Godwin and Thomas Malthus to a close examination of Hazlitt's mind and development as a writer, from the 1805 essay on benevolence to the vituperative *Letter to William Gifford, Esq.* (1819), so admired by John Keats. Much of Hazlitt's writing during this period was hackwork for periodicals. He wrote for the *Examiner*, the

powerful *Edinburgh Review*, and the *London Magazine*, among others; and as his political passions heated up, he attacked the writings of Robert Southey, Wordsworth, and Coleridge in words as vicious as any to be found in the dreadful periodical quarrels of the period. Baker's meticulous account of these scurrilous attacks and counterattacks, which tragically resulted in the death in a duel of John Scott, the brilliant editor of the *London Magazine*, is as fascinating as anything in *William Hazlitt*. Other segments of particular interest in "The Middle Years" include the vivid word portrait of Haydon, a boisterous, confident, gregarious man bigger than life, whose painting "Christ's Triumphal Entry into Jerusalem" required a six-hundred-pound frame; the analysis of Hazlitt's *Characters of Shakespear's Plays* (1817), an uneven, ill-informed work that contains all Hazlitt had to say about the art of drama; and the detailed account of his 1818-1819 lectures on English literature, which secured his reputation as a critic.

The most uneven of the great critics, Hazlitt was at his best only when writing appreciatively, as in his essays on *Othello* and *Macbeth*. His knowledge of English literature was spotty and his judgments highly opinionated. He was sadly lacking in scholarship. He was unfair to Sir Philip Sidney and William Cowper, and he did not understand John Donne. It is doubtful that he understood Samuel Johnson, since he censured his style as being artificial and pompous and accused that great moralist of a timidity of intellect that blighted everything he touched. On the positive side, Hazlitt knew Shakespeare by heart; he had read through Edmund Spenser's writings; he liked the works of Geoffrey Chaucer; and he was intimately familiar with the eighteenth-century novelists and playwrights.

Among his contemporaries Hazlitt discounted Southey's writings as inconsequential, and he deplored Coleridge's unfulfilled genius. He recognized the genius of Keats but was not always judicious in evaluating his poetry, and he contributed to the canard that Keats died as a result of hostile reviews. Hazlitt regarded Wordsworth as the greatest living poet, whose work suffered from massive egotism. Hazlitt's castigation of Wordsworth's subjectivity and monumental self-esteem is curious coming from one who idolized Jean-Jacques Rousseau, whose study of Shakespeare is so subjective that Baker concludes Hazlitt was sometimes more interested in examining his own reactions than the plays, and whose essays are often as self-centered and rooted in his personal past as much of Wordsworth's poetry. In fact, the extensive passages Baker quotes from some of Hazlitt's late essays could almost be taken as prose transcriptions from Wordsworth's *Prelude* (1850). Hazlitt's critical values were based on a commitment to concrete facts and feelings and the moral value of the imagination. It is unfortunate that he so often allowed his values to be compromised by partisan politics.

Hazlitt's last years were extraordinarily creative, but they were marred by his bitter belief that life held "nothing worth obtaining" and by his obsession with Sarah Walker, which nearly drove him mad and which Baker chronicles in minute detail. Hazlitt's embarrassingly personal rev-

elation that he was a spurned lover in *Liber Amoris* (1823), although published anonymously, did great harm to his already damaged reputation. His voluminous *The Life of Napoleon Buonaparte* (four volumes, 1828-1830), which he planned as his masterpiece, was largely ignored and bears out Baker's contention that Hazlitt, despite the greatness of his talent, was incapable of creating larger structures that demanded consecutive thinking and organization. The majority of Hazlitt's "books" are collections of shorter pieces he had written.

Hazlitt died on 18 September 1830. When he was buried five days later, Lamb and P. G. Patmore were the only mourners.

William Hazlitt is more than a biography of a thoroughly disagreeable genius. It is a powerful evocation of the Romantic period, filled with scores of vivid profiles of persons from various walks of life who touched Hazlitt in some way. Unforgettable—to name but a few—are the verbal portraits of the emotionally cold Godwin, of James Northcote, the ancient painter whose talk was "like hearing one of Titan's faces speak," of Wordsworth, who comes across as mean spirited and spiteful, and of the aging Coleridge, seen as a majestic ruin. So thoroughly researched and so rich in detail, Baker's study will likely remain definitive unless important new evidence about Hazlitt is uncovered.

Baker was a respected member of the Harvard community as a scholar, teacher, and faculty leader. In addition to chairing the English department, he served on the Board of Freshman Advisors from 1946 to 1948 and was a member of the Board of Syndics at the Harvard University Press (from 1961 to 1963 and from 1967 to 1968). In recognition of his scholarship he was awarded two Guggenheim Fellowships (in 1957 and 1963) and honorary degrees from Southern Methodist University (1966) and the University of Vermont (1967). After a long struggle with Parkinson's disease, Herschel C. Baker died at his home in Belmont, Massachusetts, on 2 February 1990, leaving his wife, Barbara, and three children.

Millicent Bell

(14 October 1919 -   )

Margaret Carter
Bradley University

BOOKS: *Hawthorne's View of the Artist* (Albany: State University of New York Press, 1962);

The Jargon Idea (Providence, R.I.: Brown University Press, 1963);

Edith Wharton and Henry James: The Story of Their Friendship (New York: Braziller, 1965; London: Owen, 1966);

Marquand: An American Life (Boston: Little, Brown, 1979).

OTHER: "Adams' *Esther*: The Morality of Taste," in *Critical Essays on Henry Adams*, edited by Earl N. Harbert (Boston: G. K. Hall, 1981), pp. 104-114;

"A Farewell to Arms: Pseudoautobiography and Personal Metaphor," in *Ernest Hemingway: The Writer in Context*, edited by James Nagel (Madison: University of Wisconsin Press, 1984), pp. 107-128;

"*The Turn of the Screw* and the 'Recherche de L'Absolu,'" in *Henry James: Fiction as History*, edited by Ian F. A. Bell (London: Vision, 1984; Totowa, N.J.: Barnes & Noble, 1985), pp. 65-81;

"Huckleberry Finn and the Sleights of the Imagination," in *One Hundred Years of Huckleberry Finn*, edited by Robert Sattlemeyer and J. Donald Crowley (Columbia: University of Missouri Press, 1985), pp. 128-145.

SELECTED PERIODICAL PUBLICATIONS—
UNCOLLECTED: "The Fallacy of the Fall in *Paradise Lost*," *PMLA*, 68 (September 1953): 863-883;

"The Dream of Being Possessed and Possessing: Henry James's *The Wings of the Dove*," *Massachusetts Review*, 10 (Winter 1969): 97-114;

"The Message of D. H. Lawrence," *New Republic*, 171 (20 July 1974): 17-21;

"Jamesian Being," *Virginia Quarterly Review*, 52 (Winter 1976): 115-132;

"Portrait of the Artist as a Young Woman," *Virginia Quarterly Review*, 52 (Autumn 1976): 670-686;

"'Art Makes Life,'" *Revue Francaise d'Etudes Americaines*, 14 (7 May 1982): 211-223;

"Henry James and the Fiction of Autobiography," *Southern Review*, 18 (Summer 1982): 463-479;

"Female Regional Writing: An American Tradition," *Revue Francaise d'Etudes Americaines*, 30 (11 November 1986): 469-480;

"What Happened in the Cave?," *Partisan Review*, 53 (Winter 1986): 103-110;

"*The Aspern Papers*: The Unvisitable Past," *Henry James Review*, 10 (Spring 1989): 120-127.

Millicent Bell has written widely acclaimed literary and biographical studies of nineteenth- and twentieth-century English and American novelists. Her major works include a study of Nathaniel Hawthorne's view of the artist's vocation and a detailed account of the twelve-year personal and literary friendship of Edith Wharton and Henry James. Bell's most impressive work is her definitive biography of John P. Marquand, the immensely successful American fiction writer of the mid twentieth century. It is a meticulously researched and penetrating analysis of the relationship between Marquand's personal life and his novels. Bell's scrupulous biographical method and graceful narrative style make her works valuable and readable both for the general audience and for specialists in American biographical and cultural studies.

Born on 14 October 1919 in New York City, Millicent Lang Bell graduated with an A.B. in English from New York University in 1942 and earned her M.A. in 1951 and her Ph.D. in 1955 from Brown University. From 1943 to 1948 she worked as a journalist and editor in Savannah, Toledo, Chicago, and New York. She began her teaching career in the English department at Brown University in 1955. In 1962 she published her first book, *Hawthorne's View of the Artist*. In this work, Bell employs literary and biographical analysis to show that Hawthorne was profoundly

Millicent Bell in 1983 (Boston University Photo Services)

troubled by the often conflicting practical and aesthetic problems of the artist's vocation.

Through her close study of Hawthorne's
life and his notebooks, letters, and fiction, Bell
concludes that Hawthorne's views on art and artists were deeply divided. His consciously expressed opinions reflected the prevailing Romantic, transcendental views of Ralph Waldo Emerson, which held that the artist is an individual endowed with extraordinary insight beneficial to society.

In the patterns of Hawthorne's fiction, however, Bell finds evidence of a contradictory view
of art and artists, which she calls negative Romanticism. Hawthorne portrays the artist as a vaga-
bond or outcast whose special powers are closer
to those of the Gothic figure of evil than those of
the ideal artist. In Hawthorne's novels—for example, *The House of Seven Gables* (1851) and *The Marble Faun* (1860)—works of art are imbued with
dark magical powers. Bell concludes that Haw-

thorne used an admixture of Romantic thought
to uncover its dangerously distorted view of the
artist's vocation, and thus in his most important
judgments he was an anti-Romantic.

Bell's work on Hawthorne received considerable critical attention. Arlin Turner in *Nineteenth
Century Fiction* (March 1963) called it "the fullest
survey yet published of Hawthorne's treatment
of the artist." In *American Literature* (March 1963)
Richard Harter Fogle wrote that the book was
"well-focused, thoughtful, and unusually well-
written." Although he questioned some of Bell's
arguments, he praised "the vitality and the significance of the issues raised," emphasizing their
value for evoking debate.

In 1963 Bell joined the English department
at Boston University, and two years later she published her first major biographical work, *Edith
Wharton and Henry James: The Story of Their Friendship*. The book is broader in scope than its title
might suggest. Part 1, "The Personal Relation,"

places James and Wharton in their social milieu and tells of their close friendship from 1903 until James's death in 1916. Part 2, "The Literary Relation," provides a critical assessment of Wharton's novels and the extent of James's influence on them. There is also an appendix, "Lady into Author: Edith Wharton and the House of Scribner," that traces Wharton's shrewd business dealings with her publishers.

Bell provides the first detailed account of the relationship between James and Wharton. Previously published correspondence and biographies, along with Wharton's autobiography, *A Backward Glance* (1934), mention their association but give only glimpses of their personal relationship. In compiling her account, Bell drew information from James's unpublished correspondence to Wharton and their friends, correspondence within their circle, and unpublished portions of Wharton's notebook diary. Bell weaves extensive quotations from these sources, detailed biographical information, and her own judicious inferences into a narrative that reads like a novel yet has the veracity of a historical document.

In tracing the origins of the Wharton-James friendship, Bell shows that they had similar backgrounds and interests. Although twenty years apart they had both grown up in genteel Old New York and spent their summers at Newport. They had mutual friends in the literary and social worlds of the American East Coast and Europe. As an aspiring young author, Wharton was eager to meet the great man of letters, although she had some reservations about his fiction. James was curious about this young woman writer who was publishing short stories said to reflect his influence, although he apparently did not remember their first social introduction. Bell shows that his interest in becoming acquainted was piqued by reading Wharton's first novel, *The Valley of Decision* (1902); once they conversed, he became fascinated by her strong determination to escape the dull philistinism of her American circle.

Bell vividly evokes the quality and tone of the Wharton-James friendship. She shows that although the two were probably never romantically involved, they shared a remarkable intellectual and emotional relationship. James became deeply absorbed in Wharton's struggle for self-development in the European milieu.

Bell's account shows a more sympathetic and gentle side of James than is usually realized; yet it also emphasizes the intellectual detachment

and ironic humor that colored the writers' attitudes toward each other. James, in particular, made elaborate jokes at Wharton's expense. Bell uses these jokes, which were excised from Percy Lubbock's earlier collection of James's correspondence, *The Letters of Henry James* (1920), to show that Wharton's prodigious zest for cultural travel and her extravagant expenditures of energy and money both amused and shocked James. Bell's own occasionally ironic view of Wharton's adventures is evident in her extensive quoting of James's imaginative metaphors to describe Wharton's way of life. He called her "the golden eagle" (while he was "the poor worm") and "the whirling princess," "the great and glorious pendulum" swinging from country to country, and "the historic ravager." In a phrase reminiscent of his own fiction, he described her Parisian life as "the dance on the Aubusson carpet."

Bell pays minute attention to the Wharton-James exchange of visits; they were terminated by James's ill health and the outbreak of World War I. In brief scenes she depicts the two sharing a literary conversation or a beautiful landscape. James took great pleasure in traveling in Wharton's luxurious motorcar. Bell suggests that their motor tour of the Berkshire country provided the stimulus for *The American Scene*, written after his 1904 visit to The Mount, the Whartons' splendid American home. A few years later the friends shared a motor tour of France that inspired Wharton's *A Motor Flight Through France* (1908).

Bell concludes "The Personal Relation" with evidence of the friends' intense intellectual and emotional engagement in the Allied war effort. Although they did not see each other again, James was experiencing Wharton's activities vicariously. His letters show that he humbly admired the energy with which she set up a Red Cross workroom for women in her Paris arrondissement and toured military hospitals in the war zone. He told Wharton that he yearned to participate in the war effort, and at the time of his death he was collaborating with her on a project to help Belgian refugee agencies.

In the second part of the Wharton-James account, Bell traces the evolution of Wharton's literary career. Early on, James advised his friend to seek inspiration in her native land, or in England as next best. When Wharton persisted in cultivating friends in Parisian society and following her own artistic bent, James grew resigned to their fundamental literary differences. Throughout her ca-

Dust jacket for Bell's 1965 book, the first detailed examination of the personal and literary relationship between Wharton and James

reer, Wharton resented the critics' assumption that she was the great man's disciple.

Bell says that traces of James's influence are more or less apparent in all of Wharton's fiction, citing *The Reef* (1912) as the most Jamesian of her novels. In *The Reef* Wharton focuses on James's favorite subject, the moral conflicts caused when American innocence encounters European experience. In her major novels, *The House of Mirth* (1905), *Ethan Frome* (1911), and *The Age of Innocence* (1920), however, Wharton's real interest lies in delineating the outer flow of events rather than analyzing the inner moral life.

Bell's final assessment is that Wharton's fiction differs markedly from James's in technique and style. James concentrated upon artistic form, carefully controlling plot and point of view through a central consciousness chosen for its moral imagination. Wharton was more interested in social criticism, for which she believed that a shifting or authorial point of view and an epi-

sodic structure were more useful.

Bell's study of the Wharton-James friendship was well received by the critics. Wayne Andrews wrote in *Harper's* (May 1965) that "Bell comes close to the final word on the relationship between Henry James and Edith Wharton." Andrews found that Bell's sympathy for the two writers "is apparent on every page." Francis Biddle in the *Sewanee Review* (Summer 1967) described the book as "a delightful and understanding account of their intimacy." In the *New Republic* (29 May 1965) Joseph L. Featherstone praised Bell's "wise and careful exploration" of the friendship. Edward Stone in *American Literature* (January 1966) praised Bell for bringing "scholarly and critical techniques to bear on the old charges of professional discipleship." Arthur Mizener in the *New York Times* (18 April 1965) found "wholly convincing" Bell's argument that Wharton was not a disciple of James "except in the very general sense that she too believed in making novels constructed works of art."

In 1971 Bell was the recipient of a Guggenheim Fellowship. From 1977 to 1978 she held a Hays-Fulbright Chair in Belgium. Then in 1979, after years of research, she published *Marquand: An American Life*, a detailed and thoroughly documented biography of the man who was hailed by *Life* magazine in 1943 as the most successful novelist in the United States. During his lifetime Marquand sold over a hundred short stories and serials, primarily to the *Saturday Evening Post*, and published twelve novels about the lives of the New England upper class. When he died in 1960, his estate amounted to over a million dollars. Yet he never received the critical recognition given to such contemporaries as Ernest Hemingway, F. Scott Fitzgerald, and Sinclair Lewis.

Bell's purpose is to show that both Marquand's life and his fiction, with its autobiographical themes, provide valuable insights into the American experience. She contends that Marquand's sentimental attachment to his ancestral origins and his obsessive pursuit of material success as a means to social prestige are metonymies for the American dream. Marquand both believed in and criticized this dream, shaping his life by it yet satirizing it in his fiction.

Bell faced the challenging task of distinguishing Marquand's self-image, shown in his spoken and written accounts of his experience, from the image put forth by independent sources. A large amount of material was available to her not only in his autobiographical fiction but also in the papers placed at her disposal by his survivors—his private papers and manuscripts; the correspondence and accounts of his five children, his close friends, and associates; and family histories. She succeeds in integrating this documentation into a full and compassionate, yet objective, account of Marquand's public successes and private failures.

As a leitmotif Bell uses Marquand's lifelong discontent. In his youth he sought to identify with his well-connected ancestors and their home at Curzon's Mill in Newburyport, the small Massachusetts shipping center founded in pre-Revolutionary days. He felt disgraced, however, when his father's business failed and the family moved to Rye, New York. He was humiliated by having to go to a public high school instead of an exclusive prep school and by only being able to attend Harvard by means of a science scholarship. Although he wrote for the *Harvard Lampoon* and did well enough in chemistry to graduate in

three years, he felt excluded from his rightful place as a privileged Harvard man.

Bell shows that Marquand's sense of exclusion was an important factor in his choice of wives and the failure of his two marriages. Both of his wives came from aristocratic New England families; yet the marriages ended in divorce on grounds of incompatibility. He sought companionship and understanding in affairs with three women he did not marry. His relationships with his five children were also damaged by his drive for wealth and recognition. Although he eventually became the sole owner of Curzon's Mill and, as Bell describes him, the Squire of Newburyport, Marquand never overcame his deeply buried resentments.

Bell carefully traces the development of Marquand's success in writing commercial fiction during the golden age of the popular magazines. She attributes his technical competence to his brief stints as a writer for the *Boston Evening Transcript* magazine department, the *New York Tribune*, and the J. Walter Thompson advertising agency. At the advertising firm, he became fascinated with the American obsession for buying and selling, which he later satirized in his novels.

According to Bell, Marquand turned to the *Saturday Evening Post* in order to make money fast. She notes that although he quickly mastered the short-story formula, even his most commercial stories are enhanced by his remarkable faculty for observation and expression of authentic detail.

A particularly valuable feature of Bell's biography is her chronicle of Marquand's transition from slick-magazine romances to the satiric novel of manners in the mode of Anthony Trollope, Edith Wharton, and the later John Cheever and John Updike. Although Marquand was proud of his short stories, he began to worry that magazine publishing stifled his skills and spoiled his chance for serious literary recognition. Bell shows that these concerns spurred his changeover, aided by his sense of being at a dead end after his first divorce, the increasingly stringent restrictions of the magazine editors, and the federal income tax bite into his yearly income.

Bell reveals the parallels between Marquand's life and his novels. She credits his ambivalent perspective on the New England aristocracy as the major cause for his success as a satirical novelist. As his first novel, *The Late George Apley* (1937), shows, Marquand possessed both the insider's appreciative understanding and the outsid-

Dust jacket for the book that won the Laurence L. Winship Award in 1980

er's satirical criticism of upper-class morals and manners. Apley is a representative Boston Brahmin living within the circles Marquand had observed so closely—the clubs, the social and civic activities, and the family. The novel's verisimilitude convinced some readers that it was a true biography.

According to Bell the popular reception of *The Late George Apley* and his next two novels secured Marquand's fame as a novelist of regional traditions. The narrator-hero of his second novel, *Wickford Point* (1939), is a popular writer who resents the condescension of the literary establishment. The hero of *H. M. Pulham, Esquire* (1941) is depicted returning to his twenty-fifth Harvard reunion, a plot based on Marquand's ironic and resentful memories of his own twenty-fifth reunion. Bell shows that Marquand's novels about World War II also demonstrate his need to write autobiographically. Although he wrote more about the war years than any other novelist of his generation, he did not attempt any battle scenes. His four war novels—*So Little Time* (1943), *Repent in Haste* (1945), *B. F.'s Daughter* (1946), and *Melville Goodwin, USA* (1951)—depict American daily life during the war from the civilian's point of view.

Bell gives a carefully balanced view of Marquand's attitudes toward women, as reflected in his marital and extramarital relationships and in his fiction. All of his novels deal with the nature of female authority in the middle- or upper-class American marriage. Bell believes that he thought American women were frustrated by the conflicting traditions of sex discrimination and mother worship; hence they tried to dominate their husbands. Bell claims that Marquand's last novel, *Women and Thomas Harrow* (1958), written after his bitter second divorce, includes his most misogynistic view of women.

Bell's sensitive handling of Marquand's final years evokes a sense of collapse underneath his restless activity and bitterness. Although he continued to be at the top of the competitive book market and to shape American reading tastes, both through his novels and his decisions as a Book-of-the-Month-Club judge, he resented the critics' continued failure to take his work seriously. Bell describes the minutiae of his daily routine, alone in his Pinehurst, North Carolina, retreat: his work on a new novel, plans for a cruise among the Greek islands, and talk of supporting John F. Kennedy for president in the fall. She explains that, although his death was very sudden, he seemed to be anticipating the end. He died in his sleep during the night of 16 July 1960, at the age of sixty-six. The final paragraph of Bell's book quietly closes the story with Marquand's daughter Ferry's memory of flying from Phoenix, with her brother Timmy and their mother, to the funeral.

Marquand: An American Life was awarded the Laurence L. Winship Award in 1980. Bell received high praise from the critics for her impressive scholarship and objectivity, as well as her skillful tracing of the relationships between Marquand's life and his fiction. Peter S. Prescott of *Newsweek* (29 October 1979) wrote, "In Millicent Bell, he has found his ideal biographer. Clear-eyed but compassionate, adroit at tracing autobiographical themes throughout his fiction, Bell makes no exaggerated claims for her subject; nevertheless, she has convincingly demonstrated that serious readers may no longer dismiss his work." John Brooks in the *Chicago Tribune* (7 October 1979) called Bell's book "a first-rate biography, which does much more than give the facts behind his bitter-sweet stories of unhappy Ameri-

can aristocrats: It tells the dramatic tale of how his life, for the most part a Marquand novel itself, ended up something else—not satire, but tragedy." In the *New York Times Book Review* (30 September 1979) Jay Martin noted that "Mrs. Bell's portrait is the kind of complex book that Marquand always tried and failed to write."

In the years following the publication of the Marquand biography, Bell continued to teach at Boston University, until her retirement in 1990, and to write scholarly articles on American and British fiction writers for French and American journals. Her studies of American writers have secured her a reputation for writing literary biography and criticism of the highest order. Her books are notable for their scholarly research, literary judgment, and imaginative narrative style. Because of her sensitive engagement with her subject matter, Bell provides her readers with a vivid sense of the writer's personal and literary life and its roots in American tradition.

Jackson J. Benson

(2 September 1930 -   )

Warren French
University of Wales, Swansea

BOOKS: *Hemingway: The Writer's Art of Self-Defense* (Minneapolis: University of Minnesota Press, 1969; London: Oxford University Press, 1969);

The True Adventures of John Steinbeck, Writer (New York: Viking, 1984; London: Heinemann, 1984);

Looking for Steinbeck's Ghost (Norman & London: University of Oklahoma Press, 1988).

OTHER: *Hemingway in Our Time*, edited by Benson and Richard Astro (Corvallis: Oregon State University Press, 1974);

The Short Stories of Ernest Hemingway: Critical Essays, edited by Benson (Durham, N.C.: Duke University Press, 1975);

The Fiction of Bernard Malamud, edited by Benson and Astro (Corvallis: Oregon State University Press, 1977);

"John Steinbeck," in *Dictionary of American Biography*, Supplement 8 (New York: Scribners, 1988), pp. 624-627;

The Short Novels of John Steinbeck: Critical Essays, edited by Benson (Durham, N.C. & London: Duke University Press, 1990);

New Critical Approaches to the Short Stories of Ernest Hemingway, edited by Benson (Durham, N.C.: Duke University Press, 1991).

SELECTED PERIODICAL PUBLICATIONS—
UNCOLLECTED: "Literary Allusions and the Private Irony of Ernest Hemingway," *Pacific Coast Philology*, 2 (April 1969): 24-29;

"Patterns of Connection and Their Development in Hemingway's *In Our Time*," *Rendezvous*, Special Hemingway issue, 5 (Winter 1970): 37-52;

"Quentin Compson: Self-Portrait of a Young Artist's Emotions," *Twentieth Century Literature*, 17 (July 1971): 143-159;

"The Background of *The Grapes of Wrath*," *Journal of Modern Literature*, 5 (April 1976): 151-232;

"Environment as Meaning: John Steinbeck and the Great Central Valley," *Steinbeck Quarterly*, 10 (Winter 1977): 12-20;

"John Steinbeck's *Cannery Row:* A Reconsideration," *Western American Literature*, 12 (May 1977): 11-40;

"John Steinbeck: The Novelist as Scientist," *Novel: A Forum on Fiction*, 10 (Spring 1977): 248-264;

"John Steinbeck and Farm Labor Unionization: The Background of *In Dubious Battle*," by Benson and Anne Loftis, *American Literature*, 52 (May 1980): 194-223;

"John and Kate: A Tale of Two Artists," *Stanford Magazine*, 13 (Spring 1985): 42-49;

"Down for the Count: Posthumous and Revisionist Hemingway," *Resources for American Literary Study*, 15 (Spring 1985): 17-29;

"Steinbeck: A Defense of Biographical Criticism," *College Literature*, 16 (Spring 1989): 107-116;

"Ernest Hemingway: The Life as Fiction and the Fiction as Life," *American Literature*, 61 (October 1989): 345-358.

Espied on a bookshelf, Jackson J. Benson's weighty account of John Steinbeck looks suspiciously like one of those terribly long biographies that Steinbeck's sister Elizabeth Ainsworth found impossible to read; but the title, *The True Adventures of John Steinbeck, Writer* (1984), gives one the feeling that this tome may yet prove to be an engrossing experience. And indeed it is, because an adventurer is precisely what Steinbeck was. His life was a quest like that of the legendary King Arthur, whose exploits Steinbeck admired from childhood and whose story he spent many years trying to reinvigorate for a new generation. Benson was the right choice to chronicle the adventures of this belated knight-errant, because Benson himself is one of those rare figures Richard Altick honored in *The Scholar Adventurers* (1951) as combining the adventurer's creative imagination with scholarly devotion to an unremitting search for truth in the minutest detail.

Jackson J. Benson (photograph by Reginald Castro)

Yet Benson was a reluctant biographer, becoming one at last only because Steinbeck's sister just took it for granted that Benson, once her polite but inquisitive visitor, would devote himself to her brother's memory. When Benson's mother-in-law introduced him in 1969 to her friend Elizabeth Ainsworth, he had no intention of spending fifteen years researching and writing a biography; but, as he explains in *Looking for Steinbeck's Ghost* (1988), his recital of his own adventures trying to reconstruct Steinbeck's, "I just drifted into the job of becoming an authorized biographer."

Benson, however, had long felt a special affinity for Steinbeck because they were both third-generation, middle-class northern Californians of half English-Irish and half German descent.

Benson was born in San Francisco on 2 September 1930 to William Alexander and Freda Sperling Benson. During his early years he had unusual opportunities for becoming familiar with his native region, from the seacoast to the fruitful inner valleys that Steinbeck had staked out as his country in the novels upon which his international reputation would be based. As Benson was growing up during the Depression, his parents were separated by the necessity of providing adequate support for the family. His mother worked, he recalls, as "the home economics editor for a farm paper, the *Pacific Rural Press*, and part of her job was to go to farming communities and give cooking demonstrations" (*Looking for Steinbeck's Ghost*). He sometimes accompanied her and watched her dealing tactfully with skeptical

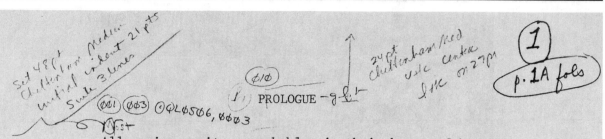

PROLOGUE

~~All~~ serious writers ~~probably~~, in their heart of hearts,
have some concern for ~~a possible~~ artistic immortality. But I
~~don't think that~~ Steinbeck really cared about it much one way
or the other. His perspective was too broad, and his sense of
self-importance too small. What he cared about was ~~the~~ writing
itself. He didn't write for fame, although occasionally he enjoyed being famous; he didn't write for money, although there
were times when he needed money; he wrote because he loved to
write, ~~He not only loved to write,~~ he was addicted to it. ~~He
existed as writer, not as Writer.~~

If you understand his writing habit, then a good many things
about ~~the shape of~~ his career become understandable. He loved
the words, the shape, the sound, the history of meaning; he delighted in the magical properties of language; he even got sat-
isfaction from the touch of pencil and paper. Behind nearly
everything that he wrote, ~~whether serious or trivial,~~ there is
a man enjoying himself, surprised and delighted that words work
the way they do. In Cannery Row he articulated that joy: ~~that
was with him as he wrote.~~

The word is a symbol and a delight which sucks up men and scenes,
trees, plants, factories, and Pekinese. Then the Thing becomes
the Word and back to Thing again, but warped and woven into a

11

Pages from the setting copy for The True Adventures of John Steinbeck, Writer, *with corrections by Benson and notations
in another hand (by permission of Jackson J. Benson; courtesy of the Steinbeck Archives of the Salinas Public Library,
Salinas, California)*

xii 1E

p. 1F fols.

A sense of fun, a probing curiosity, and a capacity for
wonder--all of these are qualities that we associate with childhood, and there was a good deal of the child in Steinbeck
throughout his life. He was a big man who took great delight in
small things. He never got too old so as to take things for
granted or to accept the unacceptable. The child in Steinbeck,
as the child in Twain, was very often the writer's best part.

The childish sense of wonder was also present in his feeling that
The act of writing for him was a sort of miraculous thing,
and I think he thought it was sort of a miracle that he could
spend his life doing it. It was both heaven and hell, the
source of great fun and the cause of terrible suffering. At the
end he tended to think of himself as a failure, and in this he
was his own harshest critic. Of course he wasn't--it was just
that he was never, ever satisfied with what he had done. About
being a writer, he once wrote,

A writer out of loneliness is trying to communicate like a distant star sending signals. He isn't telling or teaching or
ordering. Rather he seeks to establish a relationship of meaning,
of feeling, of observing. We are lonesome animals. We spend
all life trying to be less lonesome. One of our ancient methods
is to tell a story begging the listener to say--and to feel--

"Yes, that's the way it is, or at least that's the way I
feel it. You're not as alone as you thought."

It is so hard to be clear. Only a fool is wilfully

THE TRUE ADVENTURES OF
John Steinbeck,
WRITER

A Biography by Jackson J. Benson

Dust jacket for the biography with which Benson hoped to spark a revaluation of Steinbeck's fiction

audiences of farm wives. He cannot remember hearing anything about the migrant laborers, immortalized in Steinbeck's *Of Mice and Men* (1937) and *The Grapes of Wrath* (1939), who were causing problems in the region; the mention of Steinbeck's name, however, upset the editor of his mother's paper. During this period Benson's father was constable of a small lumber town. After the family's reunion, annual vacation trips made Benson familiar with the San Joaquin Valley and the Sierra Nevada.

Benson gained his first taste for serious American fiction when he picked some of Steinbeck's novels off the shelves of a public library without any knowledge about the author. "These works made a great impression," he reports in *Looking for Steinbeck's Ghost*, "because they were my own discovery. I never read them in school . . . nor had anyone recommended them

to me. . . . Reading Steinbeck's books changed my sense of literature." This discovery also helped him endure his high school years: "there were people I liked in high school, but my overall impression is of a time in my life when I was confined, subject to standards of approval and popularity that I couldn't meet, and at the mercy of gangs of other students who, through intimidation or disruptions, made my life miserable." Certainly he could empathize with the characters in Steinbeck's works, from *The Pastures of Heaven* (1932) to *The Grapes of Wrath*, whose even more heartrending experiences with intimidation and disruption helped him endure this intellectually impoverished environment well enough to garner the grades to enter Stanford University.

There he was most interested—as Steinbeck had been earlier—in the creative-writing courses, although he did not find even the distinguished university a magical improvement over high school. "The rest of the curriculum," he says in his introduction to *Hemingway in Our Time* (1974), "was a charade that I was willing to endure for the sake of somehow improving my low standing with my parents and with the world in general. But creative writing was something I would do for myself," although his instructors made him feel that even this activity was not supposed to be fun. "By the time I got to college," he goes on, "I came to realize that the best way to get along with one's English teachers was to suppress any enthusiasm one might have for literature or for life. . . . I remember distinctly any number of fellow students in my freshman and sophomore classes who were unwise to gush about something they had read and who were promptly led to the rock-throwing wall. The climate of education itself was stoic, Hemingwayesque; the worst sin of all was to be a Romantic."

Benson earned his B.A. from Stanford in 1952 (Steinbeck had left without one) and his M.A. at what was then San Francisco State College, famed for its creative-writing program, in 1956. That year he began his teaching career as an instructor at Orange Coast College in Costa Mesa, California. On 26 November 1960 he married Sue Ellen Beck, and they were to have two daughters, Katrina Adele and Belinda Sue. He was promoted to associate professor in 1962. Receiving his Ph.D. from the University of Southern California in 1966, he moved to San Diego State University as an assistant professor. He became an associate professor in 1969 and a full professor in 1971.

Although Benson thought of himself as essentially a literary critic, his dissertation showed a leaning toward biography which became more accentuated as he developed it into a book. The dissertation, "Ernest Hemingway and the Doctrine of True Emotion," describes two interconnected patterns that may be perceived in the novelist's lifelong quest for "true emotion." One is a movement from an attack upon what Hemingway considers false emotional values in life and literature toward an affirmation of values he feels are true; the other movement is from a protagonist's honest commitment to self, to commitment to another, and then to mankind. Both movements parallel "a struggle of Hemingway the writer to learn to communicate felt experience truly." In the book version of the dissertation, *Hemingway: The Writer's Art of Self-Defense* (1969), Benson ar-

gues that the main influences on these patterns in Hemingway's life and work are to be found in his early environment, especially his relationships with the members of his family.

Having probably made as much as he could of his Hemingway research at a time when Carlos Baker's official biography, *Ernest Hemingway: A Life Story* (1969), dominated the market, Benson turned his thoughts to "saving" Steinbeck's novels from the scorn of the critics and academics who considered them beneath notice. The distaste for Steinbeck can be traced back to a passing mention of *The Grapes of Wrath* in an article by Lionel Trilling in the *Kenyon Review* (Autumn 1942). Arguing that the novel "cockers-up the self-righteousness of the liberal middle class" because "it is so easy to feel virtuous in our love for such *good* poor people," Trilling concedes that "it is conceivable that books like Steinbeck's have an immediate useful effect by rallying people to the right side [but] ultimately they leave hollowness and confusion." Meanwhile, Harry T. Moore, Steinbeck's first champion, had lost patience with the same novel because the author seemed to be diluting with too much sentimentality the apocalyptic vision that had attracted Moore to Steinbeck during the Depression. A small group led by Japanese-born Shakespeare scholar Tetsumaro Hayashi had organized a society and launched a journal at Ball State University to promote Steinbeck's work; yet when Benson set forth on his redemptive mission, shortly after the novelist's death, Steinbeck's reputation was at its lowest point because of his loyalty to President Lyndon Johnson, who was under attack from nearly every other prominent writer as a result of his commitment to the American presence in Vietnam. Only those closest to Steinbeck still believed in the quality of his work, and they—especially Steinbeck's widow, Elaine—subjected Benson to the closest scrutiny before approving his undertaking.

Benson had no idea how Herculean a task it would prove: "the project could have occupied the full attention of a team of researchers over several years, and there are a few literary scholars around the country who indeed have teams of graduate assistants paid for by their universities or through grants. There was many a time I wished for that kind of help" (*Looking for Steinbeck's Ghost*). He could especially have used help in transcribing many taped interviews and in devising a methodology for locating individual items among the mass of materials that began to crowd his family out of their home. He did receive some planning grants in 1970 and 1971, the National Endowment for the Humanities provided him a year's fellowship in 1978, and the Viking Press (which had been for many years Steinbeck's own publisher) gave him an advance; but Benson had to finance most of the project himself.

The impressive book that finally appeared was a drastically reduced version of Benson's original conception. In one of the most intriguing passages in *Looking for Steinbeck's Ghost*, he describes his initial plan, which would surely have resulted in a stunning innovation in a genre bound by many traditional rules: "I wanted not just to write an ordinary biography but also to create a new art form. Like so many who had gotten into trouble before me, I was inspired by John Dos Passos's technique in *U.S.A.*, where he interspersed various materials—newspaper headlines, popular-song fragments, and small biographies—into his narrative.... I followed this plan as I traced John's life and times through his childhood into young adulthood and ended up with 360 pages." When it became clear that Benson would never be able to finish the book at this rate, he cut what he had already assembled back to only 57 pages. The original plan would have led to quite a production, a cross between Lois and Alan Gordon's 700-page folio, *American Chronicle: Seven Decades in American Life, 1920-1989* (1990), and the inventory of the boxcar load of personal papers that Indiana University acquired from the Upton Sinclair estate. It would have been the size of a big-city telephone book. The ambition was worthy of one adventurer's tribute to another.

Benson's wise compromise with his dream, however, did not end his troubles. Even after fourteen years of research and writing, he found that there were still cuts to be made at the behest of the publishers and Steinbeck's family. Publication, originally planned for 1 July 1983, had to be delayed until 16 January 1984 as Benson worked feverishly to make the text acceptable to everyone involved.

There were more than a hundred reviews of the book, most of which were positive. Most gratifying was a rave review on the front page of the *New York Times Book Review* (22 January 1984), in which the California literary historian Kevin Starr describes Benson's book as "an important American life well told." Steinbeck, Starr continues, "lived a full American life—with its

promises and its paradoxes, its stimuli and temptations—with appetite and bravery. And Mr. Benson has told the story with a narrative force that in itself is the highest compliment he can pay to his subject." A front-page review in the *Washington Post Book World* (1 January 1984) proclaimed that "Benson works on an epic scale, building in slow and stately rhythms toward his climaxes, which he relates with great feeling for emotional nuance and historical precision." In the *Chicago Tribune Book World* (15 January 1984) Clancy Sigal said that he found himself "almost in tears at the end of Benson's long journey through Steinbeck's life." Ian Hamilton reported in the *Sunday Times* (London) that "Steinbeck would have been surprised, and much relieved to find his life in hands that are both respectful and fastidious" (8 April 1984). Stephen Fender in the *Times Literary Supplement* (13 April 1984) had some reservations but concluded that "the result is a book with which one may argue and even disagree, but not easily dispense." An anonymous reviewer in the *Library Journal* (July 1983) reported that "Benson captures vividly the agony of this admirably tough-minded yet chronically sentimental man's dedication to his craft. Like many of Steinbeck's novels, this biography engages us emotionally."

The biography received the P.E.N. Los Angeles Center Award for the best nonfiction book by a southern California writer in 1984. Benson was elected to the Phi Kappa Phi Honor Society at San Diego State University and received the Alumni and Associates Outstanding Faculty Contribution Award from that school and the 1985 Meritorious Performance and Professional Promise Award from the California state universities system. Benson describes in *Looking for Steinbeck's Ghost* an honor that he found most gratifying: "I was invited to give a talk on Steinbeck at the dedication of the Steinbeck Collection at Stanford University. I had been of some help to the library in acquiring parts of the collection. The invitation had come not from the university itself but from the Associates of the Stanford University Libraries—still, it was an exciting thing for me, an indifferent scholar and obscure student there, to go back to my own university and, after an introduction by Pulitzer Prize winner F. Scott Momaday, to give a speech to a filled auditorium."

After completing his gargantuan project, Benson felt for a while that he had had enough of Steinbeck. Fortunately for admirers of Steinbeck and his biographer and for anyone inter-

Benson circa 1984 (photograph by Stan Honda)

ested in a behind-the-scenes account of such a venture, Benson still felt an urge to set down the record of his quest. *Looking for Steinbeck's Ghost* is in many ways even more fascinating than the biography itself.

In writing a formal account of another person's life—especially a person the biographer has not known personally and whose life and works have been controversial—one is under constraints. Accuracy in the minutest detail necessarily entails some tedious passages. The interests and feelings of many others must be constantly contemplated in shaping the text. There are always gaps in the account because of the things one could not discover (and Benson discusses these gaps candidly and entertainingly). When writing about one's own adventures, one knows the whole story as no one else can, and one can keep control of what one tells and how one tells it. Perhaps the most remarkable thing about *Looking for Steinbeck's Ghost* is that the reader comes

not only to know the writer behind the biography and to learn something about the perils of biographical investigation but also gets to know the subject of the original biography even better than from the more detailed chronicle. By focusing on himself, Benson is able to relate incidents omitted from the biography as too trivial or idiosyncratic but which present Steinbeck more vividly and understandably than he ever presented himself to the public. It is a thoroughly captivating work that may depend on Steinbeck for its existence but not for its success.

Since editing a collection of essays by other critics about Steinbeck's short fiction (1990), Benson plans no further work on the author that he spent so much of his life getting to know. The voluminous files that threatened to drive the Benson family out of their home are now stored at Stanford. Benson is collecting material for a short biographical and critical introduction to Wallace Stegner, another California author associated with Stanford. The Stegner book, for a series on western writers, was to have been compiled principally from published sources, but Benson has decided to make it a firsthand account based on interviews with Stegner and his family, friends, and colleagues. Benson is thinking about partially retiring early from teaching to be free to devote more time to other projects.

In *Looking for Steinbeck's Ghost* Benson discusses many things he has in common with Steinbeck. One thing that the two Californians share

is their character as adventurers. Such questers are described in Alfred, Lord Tennyson's "Ulysses" (1842), which Steinbeck asked to be read at his funeral:

> I cannot rest from travel . . .
> For always roaming with a hungry heart
> Much have I seen and known. . . .
> Yet all experience is an arch where through
> Gleams that untravelled world, whose margin fades
> For ever and for ever when I move.

Joseph Blotner
(21 June 1923 -   )

Joseph Millichap
Western Kentucky University

BOOKS: *The Political Novel* (Garden City, N.Y.: Doubleday, 1955);

Fundamentals of Technical Writing (Princeton: RCA Laboratories, 1956);

The Fiction of J. D. Salinger, by Blotner and Frederick L. Gwynn (Pittsburgh: University of Pittsburgh Press, 1959; London: Spearman, 1960);

The Modern American Political Novel: 1900-1960 (Austin & London: University of Texas Press, 1966);

Faulkner: A Biography (2 volumes, New York: Random House, 1974; London: Chatto & Windus, 1974; revised edition, 1 volume, New York: Random House, 1984);

Robert Penn Warren (New York: Random House, forthcoming, 1992).

OTHER: *Faulkner in the University: Class Conferences at the University of Virginia, 1957-1958*, edited by Blotner and Frederick L. Gwynn (Charlottesville: University of Virginia Press, 1959);

William Faulkner's Library: A Catalogue, edited by Blotner (Charlottesville: University of Virginia Press, 1964);

"Faulkner in Hollywood," in *Man and the Movies*, edited by W. R. Robinson (Baton Rouge: Louisiana State University Press, 1967), pp. 261-303;

Selected Letters of William Faulkner, edited by Blotner (New York: Random House, 1977); London: Scolar Press, 1977);

Uncollected Stories of William Faulkner, edited by Blotner (New York: Random House, 1979; London: Chatto & Windus, 1980);

William Faulkner, *Mississippi Poems*, edited by Blotner (Oxford, Miss.: Yoknapatawpha Press, 1979);

"Did You See Him Plain?," in *Fifty Years of Yoknapatawpha: Faulkner and Yoknapatawpha, 1979*, edited by Doreen Fowler and Ann J. Abadie (Jackson: University Press of Mississippi, 1980), pp. 3-22;

Faulkner, *Helen: A Courtship; and, Mississippi Poems*, edited by Blotner (New Orleans: Tulane University Press, 1981);

"From the World to Jefferson," in *Faulkner: International Perspectives: Faulkner and Yoknapatawpha, 1982*, edited by Fowler and Abadie (Jackson: University Press of Mississippi, 1984), pp. 298-317;

Joseph Blotner delivering the annual Robert Penn Warren Lecture at Western Kentucky University, 1989
(photograph by David Stephenson)

Faulkner, *Novels, 1930-1935*, edited by Blotner and Noel Polk (New York: Literary Classics of the United States, 1985);

"William Faulkner: Life and Art," in *Faulkner and Women: Faulkner and Yoknapatawpha, 1985*, edited by Fowler and Abadie (Jackson: University Press of Mississippi, 1986), pp. 3-20;

William Faulkner Manuscripts Series, 8 volumes to date, edited by Blotner and others (New York: Garland, 1987-   );

"Faulkner's Religious Sensibility," in *The Incarnate Imagination*, edited by Ingrid H. Shafer (Bowling Green, Ohio: Bowling Green University, 1988), pp. 185-196;

"On Having Known One's Subject," in *Leon Edel and Literary Art*, edited by Lyall H. Powers (Ann Arbor, Mich.: UMI Research Press, 1988), pp. 55-62.

SELECTED PERIODICAL PUBLICATIONS—
UNCOLLECTED: "Mythic Patterns in *To the Lighthouse*," *PMLA*, 71 (September 1956): 547-562;

"The Faulkners and the Fictional Families," *Geor-*

gia Review, 30 (Fall 1976): 572-592;

"The Artist as Social Critic: William Faulkner," *National Forum*, 9 (Fall 1980): 3-5;

"Faulkner in the Soviet Union," *Michigan Quarterly Review*, 24 (Summer 1985): 461-476;

"Faulkner's Last Days," by Blotner and Chester A. McLarty, *American Literature*, 57 (December 1985): 641-649;

"Faulkner and the Military: Introductory Address at the West Point Symposium," *Faulkner Journal*, 2 (Spring 1987): 4-11.

Joseph Blotner is one of America's most respected literary biographers, best known for his monumental *Faulkner: A Biography* (1974), but he is also a scholar, editor, and critic of considerable reputation. His distinguished academic career includes positions at some of America's finest universities. He has been a visiting professor both in America and abroad, and he has held many prestigious fellowships and advisory positions. Having recently finished the authorized biography of Robert Penn Warren, Blotner is a biographer and scholar-critic who, in a sense, writes biographies of literary works as much as of literary artists. As he has said himself, his emphasis falls more on the works than on the lives of his subjects. Like his subjects, Faulkner and Warren, Blotner is reserved in manner and reticent about his own life and work; he would prefer to talk about biographies and criticism by others he admires than to discuss his own efforts in either genre. Perhaps it was these characteristics, the sense that their life stories would be safe with this scholar and gentleman, that drew his subjects to Blotner. Like them, Blotner seems to have lived most fully in his books, projecting his commitment and energy into his work.

Joseph Leo Blotner was born on 21 June 1923 in Plainfield, New Jersey, to Joseph and Johanna Slattery Blotner. He grew up in Scotch Plains, New Jersey. In 1941 he entered Drew University, a small but distinguished Methodist institution in nearby Madison. He enlisted in the Army Air Corps in 1942 and served in Europe with the Eighteenth Air Force, winning the Air Medal and spending seven months as a German prisoner of war before his discharge in 1945 with the rank of first lieutenant.

After returning to Drew, Blotner married Yvonne Wright on 24 August 1946. They have three daughters: Tracy, Pamela, and Nancy. After graduating from Drew in 1947, Blotner took his M.A. at Northwestern University in the same year and his Ph.D. from the University of Pennsylvania in 1951. While finishing his doctorate he worked as an assistant instructor at Penn and as a technical writer at the Radio Corporation of America's Research Laboratories in Princeton. He became an instructor of English at the University of Idaho in 1953. These years of intellectual formation were precisely those in which Faulkner's literary reputation was established, as much by Warren as by anyone else. In his review in the *New Republic* (12 August 1946) of Malcolm Cowley's *The Portable Faulkner* (1946) Warren credits Faulkner's new popularity to the tragic sense of modern life brought back to America by veterans of the war.

Blotner's first book, *The Political Novel* (1955), finds disillusionment with American politics to be the major motif of American political fiction. This and other publications led to his appointment as assistant professor at the University of Virginia in 1955. In 1957 Faulkner was invited to lecture there, and Blotner and Frederick L. Gwynn became coordinators of his activities.

Faulkner's talks, edited by the two young professors, were published in 1959 as *Faulkner in the University*. The book contains Faulkner's most penetrating assessments of his own work, and it has proved a valuable resource since its publication. That same year, Blotner and Gwynn published a book on J. D. Salinger, another observer of postwar alienation. On the strength of these works Blotner was promoted to associate professor in 1961. The friendship with Faulkner formed at Virginia led to Blotner's appointment as his authorized biographer after the writer's death in 1962. *The Modern American Political Novel: 1900-1960* was published in 1966. A thorough reworking of Blotner's first book, this study traces archetypal patterns of quest and corruption in American politics. Blotner finds Warren's *All the King's Men* (1946) the finest modern American political novel.

At the same time he was completing his book on the political novel, Blotner was starting on his major work, the two-volume Faulkner biography. When he began the project, Blotner has said, he sought the help of his models: "In terms of other biographers [I turned to] the ones who were kind to me personally and the ones whom I admire, people like Dick Ellmann. He was one of the first to help me. And then Larry Thompson, Mark Schorer, and Carlos Baker. So those four very distinguished people older than I were awfully nice to me, and I respect them and admire their work. If you look at those four I think they represent a kind of spectrum. First you see the kind of thing that Dick Ellmann does with his probing and probing. I admire Larry's thoroughness greatly, and his basic loyalty to the work. I like Mark a lot, and I thought he did a conscientious job, but that was a case of somebody who got into a project that I think he later regretted, but did the best he could. And then Carlos, who was doing such a conscientious job of trying to get everything in, which I admired, that people criticized him for it, and said that he did not provide enough fundamental insight into Hemingway's strange personality. I think that's a 'bum rap'.... I recall, once while I was still at the University of Virginia, [Leon] Edel came and gave a lecture and we had a chance for a brief conversation; he was very nice to me. He gave me some advice, and I remember his saying that the biographer should use the devices of the novelist; the biographer should not handcuff himself, so to speak, to any kind of rigidity, especially with respect to chronology. I remember Edel saying that

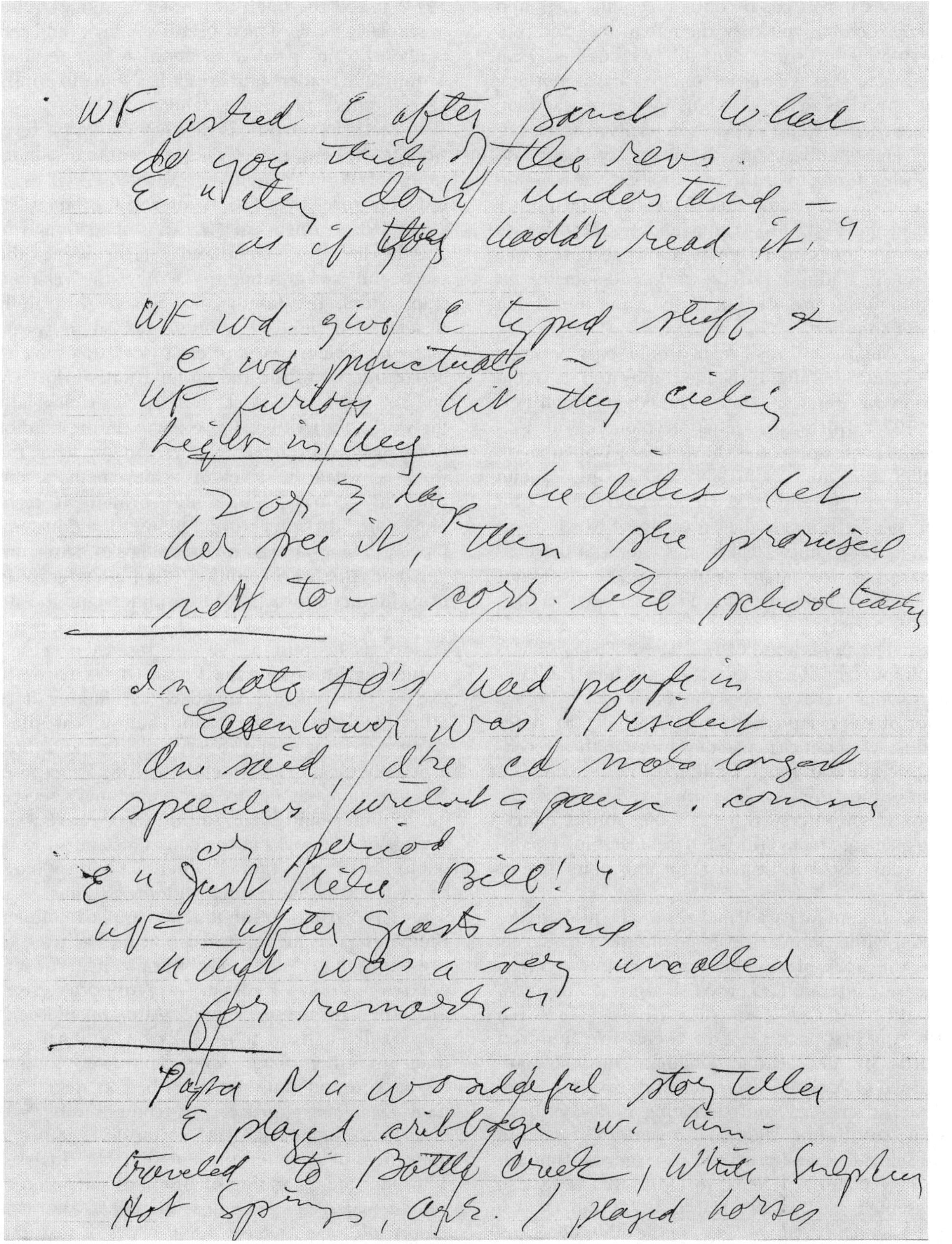

WF asked E after [Sanct] what
do you think of the revs.
E writer don't understand —
as if they hadn't read it."

WF wd. give E typed stuff &
E wd punctuate —
WF furious hd they [circling]
[begin in]...

2 or 3 days he didn't let
her see it, then she promised
not to — sort. like [schoolteach]

In late 40's had people in
[Eisenhower] was President
An said, d'ke ed [make] longest
speeches [without] a pause. comma
or period
E " just like Bill! "
WF after guests home
" that was a very uncalled
for remark. "

Papa N a wonderful storyteller
E played cribbage w. him —
traveled to Battle Creek, White [Sulphur]
Hot Springs, Ark. / played horses

Page from Blotner's 29 April 1968 notes on an interview with William Faulkner's wife, Estelle (by permission of Joseph Blotner; from the Brodsky Collection, Southeast Missouri State University)

it was as if you could conflate certain times and events, because you knew them to be true and representative of some dynamic in the life. That made me feel a little bit uneasy. I was nothing like the veteran he was, but my stance was that, yes, we use novelist's devices in terms of scene setting and flashbacks, but I felt uneasy about taking what I took to be the kind of liberty he was suggesting. At the same time I couldn't but admire the elegance of his writing and his devotion to [Henry] James, and I guess that's the fairest way to put it. I admire [Edel's] work, and some of his techniques, certainly, but at the same time I felt closer to others."

Almost a dozen years would pass between the commissioning of the biography and its publication by Random House, Faulkner's publisher, in 1974. During its gestation Blotner was Fulbright professor at the University of Copenhagen (1958-1959 and 1963-1964) and a Guggenheim fellow in 1965 and 1968. He moved from the University of Virginia to the University of North Carolina in 1968; since 1971 he has taught at the University of Michigan. Aspects of his Faulkner study were published during these years as articles and essays.

The publication of *Faulkner: A Biography* was an important literary event. By this time Faulkner was widely recognized as the major American author of the twentieth century. A whole "Faulkner industry" of criticism had developed in the preceding decades, although Faulkner's life remained in dim outline even for his closest readers. Blotner's book was a watershed for Faulkner studies, marking a change from criticism to scholarship. The biography also constituted a turning point for its genre.

In general, academic reviewers praised the book, while popular reviewers attacked it. Rarely has the work of an American academic received the wide attention accorded *Faulkner: A Biography*. In the *New York Times Book Review* (17 March 1974) a first-page piece of twenty-five hundred words by the acerbic Jonathan Yardley complained of "doggedly researched discoveries," "pedestrian writing," and "irritating non-sequiturs," while still finding the book "a work of scope and usefulness" that "provides a staggering amount of new material." Negative judgments were also presented in *Time* (25 March 1974) and the *Library Journal* (1 April 1974). On the other hand, academic reviewers such as Richard P. Adams in *American Literature* (November 1974) and Carlos Baker in the *Virginia Quarterly Review* (Summer

1974) found the book to be of the highest value in scholarly terms. The consensus today would certainly echo this positive position, as a generation of Faulkner readers and critics has come to appreciate Blotner's prodigious scholarship.

Blotner's purpose is clearly stated in his foreword to the biography: "This is meant to be a biography of William Faulkner's works as well as of their creator." In a recent interview Blotner has expanded on this idea: "My first obligation is to get the life story right and set the scene, the place, the background, the writer, the relationships within the family and outside the family that molded him. I go on to do, so to speak, many mini-biographies of each work that have to be considered within the larger framework. I relate the life to the work; besides describing how the works got written. I also try to do the kind of thing you do in a book review, to say what the work is, what the level of achievement is and what its central themes and prominent techniques are." In other words, Blotner is a critic employing a biographical methodology to better understand the works, rather than a biographer using literary criticism to better understand the author behind the works. Still, Blotner's work is not critical, as he puts it, "in the restricted sense." Rather, as he says in the foreword, he tried "to use a developmental approach . . . linking it to other elements in the canon and in the life." Blotner did not intend to write a "life," and most especially he did not intend to write an exposé. His intention was not to reveal Faulkner's secrets but to understand them, to find the creative wellsprings of the works in the conscious and subconscious life of the writer. Blotner is a literary biographer, not the biographer of a literary star.

This basic commitment implies others. Blotner says in his foreword that he has tried to present Faulkner's life "as fully as possible" for several reasons. First, Faulkner was "America's greatest writer of prose fiction." Also, in Blotner's view Faulkner drew more fully on regional lore than any other major American writer, so that his background must be described in detail. Finally, Faulkner's process of composition "was often exceedingly complex," again necessitating a great deal of complex presentation and analysis. Thus, an understanding of Blotner's purpose negates a major charge against the book—that it is simply too long. Indeed, 1,846 pages of text and 396 pages of apparatus prove daunting even to the most interested reader. On the other hand, one must consider the book's subjects—an ob-

Dust jackets for the work that Blotner calls "a biography of William Faulkner's works as well as of their creator"

scure and complicated life and a voluminous and complex canon. When one remembers the thousands of pages that comprise the chronicle of Yoknapatawpha, Blotner's biography of its author assumes its proper scale.

Certain critics complained that Blotner's narrative was burdened with a "dogged" chronological order—unlike the works of his subject, who often telescoped time in a daring manner learned from the modernists. But the very thought of Faulkner's life and works presented in stream-of-consciousness style should be enough to make any reader grateful to the biographer who ordered this complexity chronologically.

Another criticism of the book is that it lacks a critical consistency. Blotner admits that his critical approach is varied: "My method is to get the life straight and within that picture to analyze works in a kind of eclectic way that uses whatever will help to open them up." He eschews heavily ideological approaches, whether Marxist or Freudian; he prefers traditional historical approaches, explication of texts in the New Critical manner,

and the analysis of cultural myth. What emerges is perhaps more widely accepted at present than it was in 1974. Blotner thinks so: "I suppose I would think of myself in this current term as a New Historicist, sort of; just like my colleague, James Wynn, who has published a biography of Dryden. He does an enormous amount of research, sets the scene with great care, and relates Dryden to all the pieces of the picture. I guess I fit in that tradition." Blotner also admits other influences: "For instance I did an essay on Virginia Woolf called 'Mythic Patterns in *To the Lighthouse*.' And in that I used myth criticism, but I also alluded to the kinds of things that a Freudian would pick up in the novel. So like most people I've tried to do different kinds of things, but I see myself as kind of a mainstream biographer."

Blotner's book on the American political novel employs a mythic framework that informs his life of Faulkner as well. He emphasizes a Jungian view of psychological development: youth, apprenticeship, maturity, midlife struggles, acclaim, and reconciliation. Patterns for the writer's career

492

65 FOOTNOTES — 6

Page Line

512 26 ← ——— 37 ——— For some reason Old Ash, the cook, had been replaced by Simon, though
he gave the same wake-up call, "Raise up and get your four-o'clock coffee!"
remained the same:

"Race at Morning," The Saturday Evening Post, CCXXVII (March 5, 1955), pp. 26, and 106,
in BW, pp. 175-198.

513 6 ESP, p. 193. 38 "Race at Morning," pp. 104, and 106. Essays, Speeches and Public Letters,
p. 193.

593 17 ← ——— 38A ——— Jay B. Julien to RH, 26 Nov. 1954.
39
Marianne Roney to Saxe Commins, 8 September 1954; courtesy of RH;

514 1 Harvey Breit, "In and Out of Books," The New York Times Book Review, 17 October
NYT
1954; interview, Miss Barbara Cohen, 8 September 1954.
23 Feb. 67

514 14 ← ——— 40 ——— Saxe Commins to Prof. Carvel Collins, 5 October 1954.
SC to

514 21 I: ← Interview, Harry Kurnitz, 8 January 1964.
41

515 8 ← ——— 42 ——— Courtesy of Mrs. Dorothy Commins, and the Princeton University Library;
Saxe
"By the People," Mademoiselle, October, 1955, p. 138. Colonel Devries' feat of
heroism may have owed something to a similar one of Bob Haas, who, as a Captain,
RKH,
had rescued one of his enlisted men by going out into No-man's Land despite an
artillery barrage.

515 30 ← ——— 43 ——— Ibid., pp. 86, and 138. There were echoes of other stories here, as
when Ratliff imagined a dog in the thicket recognizing the odor of the fyce Grier
and Bookwright contested for in "Shingles for the Lord." There were also aphorisms WF
Faulkner had used himself or given before to characters, such as Stevens here
remarking, "The United States, America--the greatest country in the world, if we
can just keep on affording it." (P. 138.) Faulkner view of the uses of "politics
WF's
and political office" remained unchanged: "our national refuge for our incompetents
who have failed at everything else to make a living for themselves and their
families." (P. 134.)

Page from the corrected typescript with editorial markings for Faulkner, *volume one (1974), showing corrections by Blotner and in another hand (by permission of Joseph Blotner; from the Brodsky Collection, Southeast Missouri State University)*

From reviews of the two-volume edition of
Faulkner: A Biography

"As a literary biography, it is a masterpiece. It gives us the man, his career, his time and place, in utterly authoritative fashion; it is written beautifully; it pulls no punches, and is altogether worthy of its subject...For as long as people will be reading Faulkner's fiction and wondering about the man who wrote it, they will be turning to this fine biography to find answers."
—Louis D. Rubin, Jr., *Charlotte Observer*

"This is an overbrimming book, indispensable for anyone interested in the life and works of our greatest contemporary novelist."
—Malcolm Cowley, *Chicago Tribune*

"Blotner has written an old-fashioned biography, free of 'interpretation' and analytic cant, which allows us to draw our own conclusions about a truly exemplary life."
—Charles Newman, *Harper's* Magazine

"Steadily chronological, the lengthy account minutely records the great Mississippian's life from birth to death, with ample note at every stage of his associations and all kinds of activities, not just his career as fictionist..."
—Warren Beck, *Milwaukee Journal*

"A staggering amount of new material about the personal life of the man whom [Blotner] calls—quite properly, in my view—'America's greatest writer of prose fiction.'"
—Jonathan Yardley, *The New York Times Book Review*

"Blotner is sympathetic, his study comprehensive and objective. What can surely be said of the two volumes is that they are and likely will remain crucial source material for any future critical assessment of Faulkner..."
—Robert Kirsch, *Los Angeles Times*

"This is the sort of biography William Faulkner would have approved. It is as much a biography of the work as of the man. Blotner clarifies interrelationships between life and art by showing how much Faulkner borrowed from life and nevertheless managed to transform it..."
—Panthea Broughton, *Chicago Sun Times*

194-50413-5

FAULKNER:
JOSEPH BLOTNER
A BIOGRAPHY
ONE-VOLUME EDITION

RANDOM HOUSE

FAULKNER
A BIOGRAPHY • ONE-VOLUME EDITION

BY JOSEPH BLOTNER
REVISED • UPDATED • CONDENSED

Dust jacket for the 1984, one-volume edition of Blotner's biography of Faulkner, in which he includes data omitted from the 1974 edition

could fit as well for others, including the biographer himself. For as much as Blotner is interested in the great writer, he also views Faulkner as a great man. The last thing Blotner says in his foreword is: "the narrative will perhaps reveal more clearly how [Faulkner] seems to me as a man. I cannot hope to look upon his like again."

Other connections exist between Blotner's major critical work and his major biographical book. Both are concerned with politics. As Blotner puts it: "With respect to Faulkner and politics, that was something that I just worked my way toward when I came to the 1950s and the Civil Rights crisis. It became interesting to me to see a man of Faulkner's age and background and inheritance, who was, for that time and place, assuming the stance of not just a moderate, but practically a liberal, and you remember the abuse he got for the stance that he took trying to position himself between the NAACP and the White Citizens groups. So anything I had in my baggage, from studying the political books, was useful to me in terms of trying to accurately represent Faulkner's stance." Most striking is Blotner's inter-

est in a "man" rather than a writer—even a great writer—of a certain time and place. Blotner is interested in the tensions between the writer and the man, the man and the work.

It is exactly at this point that one can find a problem in Blotner's biography: his scholarly, liberal, and humane viewpoint results in his Faulkner taking on this cast as well. The biographer knew personally the Faulkner he calls "The Public Man." His Faulkner tends to be the great writer after the 1949 Nobel Prize address, the Faulkner of *A Fable* (1954) and *The Reivers* (1962), rather than that of *The Sound and the Fury* (1929) or *Sanctuary* (1931). Although Blotner is too astute not to posit this public persona as only one among many, he naturally emphasizes this final "Faulkner in the university," so that the picture of the other Faulkners becomes somewhat less focused. In particular, focusing proves a problem in the exploration of what one might call the "darkest Faulkner": Faulkner in relation to blacks and women, Faulkner with modes of surrealism and Gothicism (including his own "family romance" in the Freudian sense), and, most important, Faulkner's excessive drinking and womanizing.

Certainly, the Faulkner biography is the central work of Blotner's career. Yet for a decade after its publication he produced other Faulkner material of almost equal importance. His edition of the *Selected Letters of William Faulkner* appeared in 1977, almost like an appendix to the biography. Blotner's main purpose in editing the correspondence was "to provide a deeper understanding of the artist," and in this the collection succeeds admirably. Cowley complained in the *New Republic* (12 March 1977) that the best letters had been published by James Meriwether in 1965; others, such as Walter Clemons in *Newsweek* (7 February 1977), were disappointed by the lack of "intimate tidbits," but Faulkner scholars acknowledged their debt to Blotner for his careful editing, just as they did for his *Uncollected Stories of William Faulkner* (1979) and his edition of Faulkner's *Mississippi Poems* (1979).

To a great extent Blotner corrected the problems with his Faulkner biography in the revised, updated, and condensed one-volume edition of 1984. Some difficulties of both personal consideration and legal liability had disappeared in the decade following the publication of the two-volume biography, so that Blotner was able to say more about Faulkner's women. He also was able to take advantage of insights by other Faulkner scholars, critics, and biographers. In fact, Blotner seems to have reacted to the reviews of his earlier work and to have met the objections of his critics at almost every point. The single-volume *Faulkner* is a pleasure to read. It retains the strong points of the longer work while skillfully reshaping the materials to reveal more clearly the career patterns of the man and the writer. Certainly, the 1984 biography is much more accessible for the general reader, and it remains the single best introduction to Faulkner among the hundreds published.

In 1986 Blotner began a new project. As he puts it, he had said what he had to say about Faulkner. He considered several new critical and biographical subjects, notably his friend Eudora Welty. It is probably a good indication of Blotner's primary commitments that he chose to enter a five-year contract for the authorized biography of Robert Penn Warren. Warren—who died in 1989—was, like Faulkner, a complex and contradictory modernist, regional yet universal, traditional yet innovative, harsh yet hopeful in vision. Perhaps this choice of subject demonstrates similar traits in the biographer, an academic essaying a bold new work at a time of life when many are considering the comforts of retirement.

Blotner attributes his decision to begin the Warren biography to the example of his friend Ellmann, who, late in his career, wrote a biography of Oscar Wilde. After securing Warren's consent to begin the new project, Blotner tried to see as many people as possible who had known Warren over the years. He trailed Warren from Kentucky to Tennessee to Louisiana to Connecticut and finally to Europe. Warren wrote voluminous correspondence, so Blotner worked with the vast collection of his letters at Yale's Beinecke Library as well as with materials at Louisiana State University, Vanderbilt University, the University of Kentucky, and the Center for the Study of Robert Penn Warren at Western Kentucky University.

All of this activity Blotner calls the "gathering phase." Next he spent a year in what he considers "the reviewing and assimilating phase," ordering his materials for the final "writing phase." With the support of a National Endowment for the Humanities Fellowship, Blotner projected "a single good solid volume" for 1992 publication. Blotner calls it "the story . . . of the life of the mind and the pursuit of perfection in art."

It seems clear that Faulkner is the great American fictionist of the modernist period; it seems just as clear that Blotner is the great chronicler of this enigmatic genius. As biographer, editor, scholar, and critic, Blotner has done more than anyone else to elucidate Faulkner's dark complexities. At the same time, he has made a distinct contribution to the art of biography: his particular combination of scholarship and criticism, especially his eclectic selection of critical/biographical approaches, creates a model for future biographers.

Frank Brady

(3 November 1924 - 2 September 1986)

John C. Ward
Centre College

BOOKS: *Boswell's Political Career* (New Haven & London: Yale University Press, 1965);

James Boswell: The Later Years, 1769-1795 (New York: McGraw-Hill, 1984; London: Heinemann, 1984);

Mickle, Boswell, and Garrick and "The Siege of Marseilles" (Hamden, Conn.: Archon Books, 1987).

OTHER: *Boswell on the Grand Tour: Italy, Corsica, and France, 1765-1766*, edited by Brady and Frederick A. Pottle (New York: McGraw-Hill, 1955; London: Heinemann, 1956);

Boswell in Search of a Wife, 1766-1769, edited by Brady and Pottle (New York: McGraw-Hill, 1956; London: Heinemann, 1957);

English Prose and Poetry, 1660-1800: A Selection, edited by Brady and Martin Price (New York: Holt, Rinehart & Winston, 1961);

Alexander Pope, *An Essay on Man*, edited by Brady (Indianapolis: Bobbs-Merrill, 1965);

James Boswell, *The Life of Samuel Johnson*, edited and abridged by Brady (New York: New American Library, 1968; London: New English Library, 1968);

Twentieth Century Interpretations of Gulliver's Travels: A Collection of Critical Essays, edited by Brady (Englewood Cliffs, N.J.: Prentice-Hall, 1968);

"The Strategies of Biography and Some Eighteenth-Century Examples," in *Literary Theory and Structure: Essays in Honor of William K. Wimsatt*, edited by Brady, Price, and John Palmer (New Haven: Yale University Press, 1973), pp. 245-265; reprinted in *Dr. Samuel Johnson and James Boswell*, edited by Harold Bloom (New York: Chelsea House, 1986), pp. 133-147;

"Fact and Factuality in Literature," in *Directions in Literary Criticism: Contemporary Approaches to Literature*, edited by Stanley Weintraub and Philip Young (University Park: Pennsylvania State University Press, 1973), pp. 93-111;

Poetry: Past and Present, edited by Brady and Price (New York: Harcourt Brace Jovanovich, 1974);

Samuel Johnson: Selected Poetry and Prose, edited by Brady and W. K. Wimsatt (Berkeley: University of California Press, 1977);

"Boswell's London Journal: The Question of Memorial and Imaginative Modes," in *Literature and Society: The Lawrence Henry Gipson Symposium, 1978*, edited by Jan Fergus (Bethlehem, Pa.: Gipson Institute, 1981);

"Johnson as a Public Figure," in *Johnson after Two Hundred Years*, edited by Paul J. Korshin (Philadelphia: University of Pennsylvania Press, 1986), pp. 43-54;

Boswell: The Great Biographer, 1789-1795, edited by Brady and Marlies K. Danziger (New York: McGraw-Hill, 1989; London: Heinemann, 1989).

SELECTED PERIODICAL PUBLICATIONS—UNCOLLECTED: "Recent Studies in Restoration and Eighteenth-Century," *Studies in English Literature*, 8 (1968): 551-572;

"Boswell's Self-Presentation and His Critics," *Studies in English Literature*, 12 (1972): 545-555.

Frank Brady's reputation in the field of literary biography rests on *James Boswell: The Later Years, 1769-1795* (1984); on his skillful editing of several volumes of Boswell's journals; and on his thirty years of work on the Yale edition of Boswell's papers. He completed the biography of Boswell that his colleague and mentor Frederick A. Pottle had begun with *James Boswell: The Early Years, 1740-1769* (1966), and Brady collaborated with Pottle on many other editorial and scholarly tasks. Throughout his career Brady was devoted to organizing, preserving, and presenting Boswell's writings and to protecting Boswell's reputation against attacks by critics. Brady did all his research with scrupulous care, and the scholarly community will always be indebted to him for his efforts.

Frank Brady (Boswell Collection, Sterling Library, Yale University)

Brady was born in Brookline, Massachusetts, on 3 November 1924 to Francis Anthony Brady and Alma Ranger Brady. World War II interrupted his studies at Dartmouth College; he served in the United States Army Quartermaster Corps from 1943 to 1946, achieving the rank of first lieutenant. He graduated from Dartmouth magna cum laude and Phi Beta Kappa in 1948 and went to Yale University, where he earned his M.A. in 1949. He began teaching at Yale as an instructor in 1951 while continuing to work on his Ph.D. in English, which he received in 1952.

The hallmarks of Brady's style and preoccupations are evident in *Boswell on the Grand Tour: Italy, Corsica, and France: 1765-1766* (1955), which he and Pottle edited. Brady's introduction begins: "James Boswell's main concerns during the period of his life covered by this volume were sex, religion, and politics—the three subjects of conversation forbidden in polite society." Boswell's candor and unapologetic completeness in his journal entries are matched by Brady's forthrightness; these are not polite journals, but they reveal the man and his age in extraordinary detail. Later in the introduction Brady compares Boswell to James

Joyce, emphasizing the art of the journal and implying that Boswell's eye for detail is like that of the great twentieth-century novelist. Furthermore, Boswell, like Joyce, is not constrained by convention; the narrative offers the bawdy and the unflattering as it presents the whole range of human experience. From the beginning of his career as editor, Brady admires Boswell's modern, shameless, and untrammeled genius.

Brady was promoted to assistant professor in 1956. In 1960 he left Yale to become an associate professor at his alma mater, and in 1963 he joined the English faculty at Pennsylvania State University as a full professor. A revised version of his dissertation was published in 1965 as *Boswell's Political Career*.

Also in 1965 Pottle began to plan for the second volume of his biography of Boswell and invited Brady to collaborate on it. The two worked together for a short period, but increasingly the task fell to Brady alone.

After enjoying a Guggenheim Fellowship (1966-1967), Brady left Pennsylvania State University to become Distinguished Professor of English in the Graduate School and at Hunter College,

Dust jacket for Brady's 1984 book, written as a companion to Frederick A. Pottle's James Boswell:
The Early Years, 1740-1769 *(1966)*

City University of New York; he directed the graduate program from 1969 to 1972. In 1972 he was appointed to the editorial committee of the Yale Editions of the Private Papers of James Boswell; he was selected to chair the committee in 1979.

While working through Pottle's notes and outlines throughout the late 1960s and early 1970s Brady wrote a series of theoretical articles explaining his plan for the writing of Boswell's life. Sounding a recurring note, Brady is critical in "Boswell's Self-Presentation and His Critics" (1972) of those in the academic and literary communities who dismiss Boswell because of his sexual behavior or the apparent lack of self-knowledge and moral consistency with which he acted and with which he later evaluated his actions in his journals. To allow a judgment of an author's moral and personal standards to affect the evaluation of that author's artistic accomplishment seems to Brady a mistake. In "Fact and Factu-

ality in Literature" (1973) Brady addresses the problem of how and whether to distinguish between the facts and fictionalized or imagined reality, concluding, "The imaginative orders the factual; the factual sustains the imaginative. They are inextricably connected." Brady's extraordinarily wide reading is evident in the essay, and demonstrates the catholicity of his taste. Finally, in "The Strategies of Biography and Some Eighteenth-Century Examples" (1973) Brady emphasizes the interplay between artistic genres and biographical form in biographies written in the eighteenth century. Brady defends a certain artistic license, arguing for the appropriateness of using generic models such as the epic, the mock epic, and the novel to inform and shape biographical narratives. Here Brady makes his strongest case for innovations in the biographical mode, such as deliberate omissions, alteration of time sequences, and other devices that might convey more forcefully the personality of the subject.

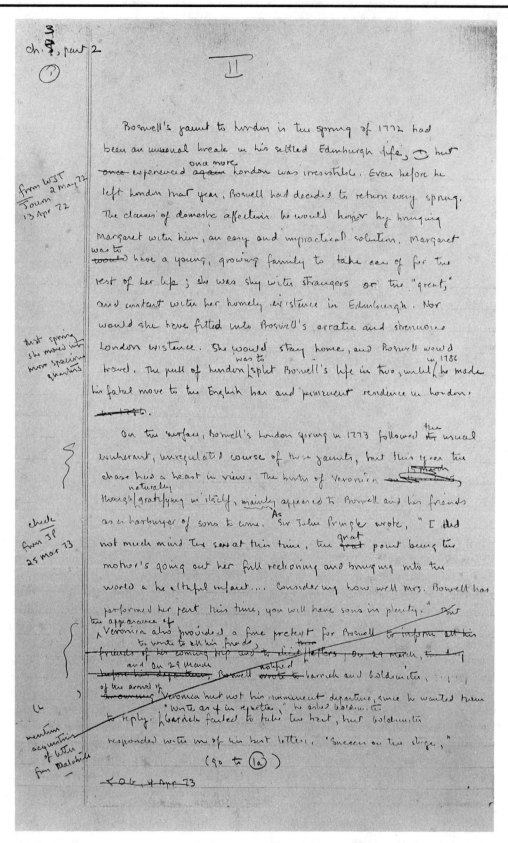

Pages from an early draft for James Boswell: The Later Years, 1769-1795 *(by permission of the Estate of Frank Brady; Yale Boswell Editions, Sterling Library, Yale University)*

(12)

But the emergence of Veronica provided Boswell with a fine pretext to flatten his archives with the correspondence of the famous. ~~On 22 March he wrote to Garrick and to Goldsmith announcing the arrival of Veronica and his hope of~~ coming to London that spring, but saying nothing ~~of his imminent departure.~~ On 29 March he wrote to Goldsmith:

You must know that my wife was safely delivered of a daughter, the very evening that <u>She Stoops to Conquer</u> first appeared. I am fond of the coincidence. My little daughter is a fine healthy, lively child and, I flatter myself, shall be blessed with the disposition of your comic muse. She has nothing of that wretched whining and crying which we see children so often have; nothing of the <u>comédie larmoyante</u>, ~~#~~ (that "sentimental comedy," which <u>She Stoops to Conquer</u> did so much to displace). But ~~Boswell~~ instead of mentioning his imminent departure, Boswell ~~his imminent departure, instead to~~ added: "Pray write directly. Write as in repartee."

Goldsmith's reply, one of the best of his few surviving letters, is famous in Boswell annals as the first document which Colonel Isham acquired from Boswell's descendant Lord Talbot de Malahide in 1926. "Success on the stage," Goldsmith told Boswell ~~is in this letter~~, is

Lee Morgan "Boswell's Portrait of Goldsmith,"
<u>Studies in Honor of John C. Hedges and Alwin Thaler</u>,
(Univ. of Tenn. Press, 1961) eds. R. B. Davis and J. L. Lievsay
67-76

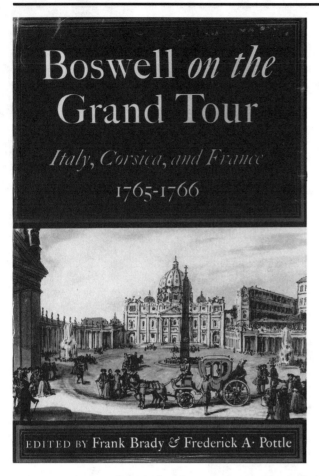
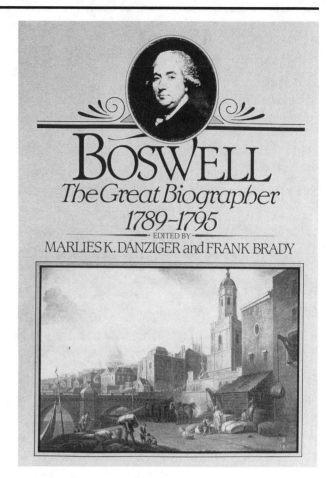

Dust jackets for two volumes of Boswell's journals published in the Yale Boswell Editions

At first glance, his best-known and most valuable work, *James Boswell: The Later Years*, does not demonstrate that spirit of innovation; it seems to be a continuation of Pottle's style in the earlier volume. Indeed, as Brady notes in his introduction, much of the material in the early chapters is Pottle's work. But gradually Brady's voice and concerns surface. Patricia Meyer Spacks points out that Brady faced a daunting task: "Since Boswell himself wrote a biography of unchallengeable greatness, his biographer in effect enters a kind of competition with his subject—a curious moral and psychological position." Brady, in fact, had a double challenge, for he had to emulate and, if possible, surpass the accomplishment of Pottle and do Boswell's example justice as well.

Brady solves this problem of the "anxiety of influence" by befriending, not competing; he invites the reader to identify with Boswell, to sympathize, to understand, and to forgive. Richard B. Schwartz comments approvingly on this tendency: "Since all of us have experienced these sorts of frustrations to some degree, Boswell

stands as a sad but powerful model of what it means, in part, to be human. This Brady portrays eloquently and convincingly. He asks us to love the sinner and regret rather than hate the sin."

Pottle's and Brady's biographies of Boswell are filled with episodes and journal entries that reveal Boswell's ambitions, anxieties, concerns for himself, sexual activities, and his awareness of failure. Brady writes, "It would be intolerably tedious to record Boswell's wretched and endless fits of irresolution if he did not draw us into his alternations of pleasure and misery until they acquire some of the familiarity and obsessiveness of our own. . . ." Depending so heavily on the voluminous journal materials in the Yale collection, Brady seems obliged to adopt Boswell's view of his own career; a friendly alliance is established between biographer and subject that is reminiscent of Boswell's relationship with Johnson. In his own biography of Johnson (1791), Boswell hurries through the narrative describing Johnson's career before their fateful meeting in 1763, then takes extraordinary care in reporting the events and conversations in which he himself participated. In effect, Boswell's journals gave Brady the chance to observe Boswell as closely as Boswell had observed Johnson.

The disadvantages of friendly feelings toward one's subject in a biography must be evident; friendship invites a certain shading of the record, and Brady falls victim to this temptation in two ways. First, he takes Boswell's part against his contemporary and twentieth-century foes. Howard D. Weinbrot, in the annual review of eighteenth-century scholarship in *Studies in English Literature* (Summer 1985), admires Brady's thoroughness but complains, "Whether or not the anti-Boswellians are right, they are not bizarre, ludicrous, uninformed, unworthy of being dignified by mention, profoundly ignorant, sibling rivals, insecure, and, among other insults Brady offers, as writers, anachronistically not 'good enough to tie his shoe-laces.' " Second, by befriending Boswell, Brady chooses to slight some problems in Boswell's life that invite serious consideration. For example, Boswell returned again and again to prostitutes, contracting the expectable gonorrhea, and his motives remain obscure; no one has been in a better position to explore Boswell's self-destructive tendencies than Brady. But the pathology and psychology of this topic have their principal treatment in William Ober's provocative *Boswell's Clap and Other Essays: Medical Analyses of Literary Men's Afflictions* (1979). It is evident from Ober's account that Boswell knowingly precipitated his own death by continuing to indulge in sexual relations with prostitutes in London; his compulsion to do so cannot be explained by the pleasure-seeking of the youthful Boswell or the sexual athleticism of the proud middle-aged man.

Nevertheless, Brady's record remains the most useful, complete, readable, and sympathetic treatment of Boswell's later years. No one again is likely to have the resources, the commitment, the professional support, and the affection that Brady brought to his subject. Brady died of cancer on 2 September 1986.

References:

Irvin Ehrenpreis, "The Seductive Journalist," *New York Review of Books* (28 March 1985): 3-6;

Richard B. Schwartz, "A Rake's Progress," *Sewanee Review*, 93 (Winter 1985): xxii-xxvi;

Patricia Meyer Spacks, "Interpreted Lives," *Georgia Review*, 39 (Spring 1985): 182-187;

John Ward, "Brady's Boswell: Enthusiastic Indiscretions," *Kenyon Review*, 7 (Fall 1985): 125-129;

Howard D. Weinbrot, "Recent Studies in the Restoration and Eighteenth Century," *Studies in English Literature*, 25 (Summer 1985): 671-717.

Virginia Spencer Carr

(21 July 1929 -   )

Lenemaja Friedman
Columbus College

BOOKS: *The Lonely Hunter: A Biography of Carson McCullers* (Garden City, N.Y.: Doubleday, 1975; London: Owen, 1977);

Dos Passos: A Life (Garden City, N.Y.: Doubleday, 1984);

Understanding Carson McCullers (Columbia: University of South Carolina Press, 1989).

OTHER: "Carson McCullers," in *Bibliographical Guide to the Study of Southern Literature*, edited by Louis D. Rubin, Jr. (Baton Rouge: Louisiana State University Press, 1969), p. 243;

"Tennessee Williams: An Aside," in *On Broadway*, edited by William and Jane Stott (Austin: University of Texas Press, 1978), pp. 334-335;

"Carson McCullers," by Carr and Joseph R. Millichap, in *American Women Writers: Fifteen Bibliographical Essays*, edited by Maurice Duke, Jackson R. Bryer, and M. Thomas Inge (Westport, Conn.: Greenwood Press, 1983), pp. 297-319;

"Dos Passos as Playwright and Artist: New Opportunities for Research," in *Resources for American Literary Study*, edited by Duke, Bryer, and Inge (Westport, Conn.: Greenwood Press, 1984), pp. 207-214;

"Carson McCullers," in *Fifty Southern Writers After 1900: A Bio-Bibliographical Sourcebook*, edited by Robert Bain and Joseph M. Flora (Westport, Conn.: Greenwood Press, 1986), pp. 301-312;

Carson McCullers, *Collected Stories*, introduction by Carr (Boston: Houghton Mifflin, 1987);

"Fiction: The 1930s to the 1960s," in *American Literary Scholarship: An Annual*, edited by David Nordloh (Durham: Duke University Press, 1987), pp. 259-282;

"Fiction: The 1930s to the 1960s," in *American Literary Scholarship: An Annual*, edited by James Woodress (Durham: Duke University Press, 1988), pp. 262-291.

SELECTED PERIODICAL PUBLICATIONS—
UNCOLLECTED: "Iron Butterfly or Wounded Sparrow: The Enigma of Carson McCullers," *South Atlantic Bulletin* (January 1973): 52;

"Biography: Essay Reviews on Elizabeth Frank's *Louise Bogan: A Portrait* and Donald Spoto's *The Kindness of Strangers: The Life of Tennessee Williams*," *America*, 153 (31 August 1985): 106-109;

"Carson McCullers, Novelist Turned Playwright," *Southern Quarterly*, 25 (Spring 1987): 37-52.

Virginia Spencer Carr has received international recognition as a biographer of Carson McCullers and John Dos Passos. Scholars and lay readers alike agree that her work sets a high standard for biographical writing, and it is a tribute to Carr's versatility that she has successfully written the stories of two important literary figures of the twentieth century whose lives, temperaments, convictions, techniques, and themes are quite different. McCullers led a restricted life because of ill health, had limited formal education, little worldly experience, and was an intuitive writer. Dos Passos was a highly educated world traveler, a rugged individualist who was at home everywhere. McCullers remained provincial, temperamental, self-indulgent, and heavily dependent on her mother, husband, and friends for her emotional and physical nurturing. Moreover, she was afflicted throughout her life with a painful sense of loneliness and isolation. Dos Passos was a devoted husband and father, a kind and much-admired man whose nobility of spirit and zest for life sustained him until his death at seventy-four. Both remained strong, principled fighters and champions of the underdog, and neither ever stopped writing for long—their work was vital to their existence.

Carr's first book, *The Lonely Hunter: A Biography of Carson McCullers* (1975), was nominated for a Pulitzer Prize and a National Book Award and won the Francis Butler Simkins Prize of the South-

Virginia Spencer Carr (photograph by Katharine Gamble Scranton)

ern Historical Association and Longwood College, Virginia (awarded to a single recipient every two years) "in recognition of distinguished writing in Southern history." The introduction to *The Lonely Hunter* was written by Tennessee Williams, whom Carr met in 1971 and whose cooperation proved vital to her McCullers research. Her second book, *Dos Passos: A Life* (1984), was also nominated for a Pulitzer Prize, and it received the Dixie Council of Authors and Journalists Prize for the "best book of nonfiction" published in 1984-1985. It, too, was highly acclaimed and well reviewed across the country.

Carr, who has had three fellowships at Yaddo Artists Colony, is involved presently in several literary projects including biographies of Williams and Paul Bowles. She also has a novel in progress that is set in Poland during the years in which she was a Fulbright Professor of American

Literature (1980-1981). Since 1985 she has been chairman of the Department of English at Georgia State University, where she holds the rank of professor and teaches graduate and undergraduate courses in twentieth-century American literature, Southern literature, and biography. In addition to her numerous professional affiliations as a scholar and teacher, she is a member of the Author's Guild and PEN-American Center. On 6 May 1987, Carr was awarded the honorary Doctor of Humane Letters degree by Lynchburg College in Lynchburg, Virginia, "in recognition of her distinguished attainments."

Carr grew up as Virginia Claire Spencer, the only girl among four brothers in West Palm Beach, Florida, where she was born on 21 July 1929, the fourth child of Louis Perry and Wilma Bell Spencer. According to Virginia's brother Donald, "she could do anything we could do—

and sometimes better. She bought a horse, a two-year-old stallion, when she was thirteen with money earned from babysitting and broke him herself. As children, when we had our neighborhood carnivals and 'midways' on the vacant lot across the street, Virginia—who was six or seven at the time—was usually billed as the snake charmer. She caught her own snakes, the harmless green snake variety, and her 'act' was to let them crawl over her and in and out of her sleeves and in her hair" (unpublished interview, 24 February 1989).

Carr's father, an electrical engineer, went into business for himself in the early 1920s. For a time he operated a large chicken ranch (until it was destroyed in the 1928 hurricane), then a tire company (which failed during the Depression). Carr's mother sold magazine subscriptions over the telephone and made doughnuts for her children to sell in the neighborhood to help the family weather the Depression. In 1939 Wilma Spencer went to work as a news and feature writer for the *Palm Beach Daily News*, and for twenty-nine years she was its society editor. She also wrote poetry and short fiction and took creative-writing courses at Columbia University for three summers after her youngest child finished high school. Wilma's slim volume of little-known facts about Palm Beach and its various residents (entitled *Did you Know?*) was published in 1965, and a decade later her *Palm Beach, A Century of Heritage* was published posthumously.

Carr's own writing career began when she was twelve. She took a six-month play-writing course, along with her mother and her brother Donald, then wrote a three-act play. "It was terrible," she recalled in an unpublished interview (6 February 1989). "I must have gotten my plot from my mother's society columns, for I called the play 'The Debutante.' The only line I can remember is 'Mother, you're a brick.' It seemed a perfectly marvelous line at the time." Later, for her high-school newspaper, *The Frond*, Carr wrote a regular feature column. She did layouts for the yearbook, sold advertisements, wrote the high-school column for the local newspaper, and won the senior journalism award, which prompted her to consider a career in journalism.

In 1947, after graduation from high school, Carr entered Florida State University in Tallahassee, where she exempted freshman composition and majored in physical education for a year, then shifted to English and journalism. She minored in journalism, wrote for the *Flambeau* (the

campus newspaper), joined a sorority (Alpha Omicron Pi), and became a trapeze artist and charter member of the FSU "Flying High" Circus. She received her B.A. in 1951 and enrolled in graduate school at the University of North Carolina. "I had realized late in my junior year that there was so much I didn't know that I mistakenly thought a college education might logically have provided me, and I wanted more. I had already fallen in love with the poetry of [Robert] Browning and decided to write a master's thesis on his theory of success in failure," she explained. Carr titled her thesis "Robert Browning and the Philosophy of the Imperfect" ("a philosophy that has stood me in good stead ever since," she added), and received her M.A. in English in 1952.

By this time Carr had met her future husband, Roger Alton Carr, a fellow student from Plymouth, North Carolina, to whom she became engaged while back in her hometown teaching seventh-grade English at the same school from which she had graduated a decade earlier (Central Junior High). She and Carr were married in the First Baptist Church in West Palm Beach on 14 June 1953.

Roger Carr had enlisted in the U.S. Marine Corps as soon as he finished school, and they moved immediately after their wedding to his new assignment as a supply officer at Camp Lejeune near Jacksonville, North Carolina, where Virginia taught English and social studies at the U.S. Marine Corps Base School. When he was sent to Camp Pendleton, California, for "overseas staging" before a year's duty in Korea, she went with him and stayed on the West Coast to await his return. During this time, she taught English and social studies at Benjamin Franklin High School in Los Angeles.

When Carr's husband returned home from Korea in December 1954, they made their home in California, living first in San Mateo, where he sold insurance and she did substitute teaching in the public schools until their first child, Karen Susan, was born on 1 October 1955. Then they moved to Menlo Park, and Carr worked for a time as a personnel interviewer at Varian Associates, an electronic manufacturing firm. They moved again when they bought their first house in San Jose, and Carr took a teaching position for two years at the Elvira Castro Middle School, where she also served as dean of girls. In December 1957 she and her husband returned to West Palm Beach, Florida, in time for the birth of their second daughter, Catherine Lynn, on 11

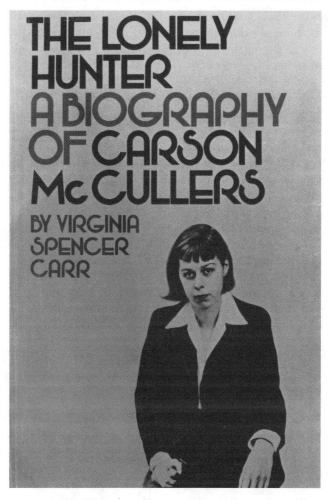

Dust jacket for Carr's first book, for which she received Pulitzer Prize and National Book Award nominations

May 1958. Carr went back into the classroom soon after Catherine's birth, this time at Forest Hill High School, where she chaired the Department of English and advised the yearbook staff. Two years later, she began teaching English and journalism at Palm Beach Junior College. She was also director of public relations at the college and the faculty advisor of the student newspaper and the literary magazine.

The family moved again in 1962, to Savannah, Georgia, where Carr's third daughter, Kimberly Claire, was born on 11 March 1963. By this time Carr was teaching at Armstrong State College and directing the freshman composition program. The Carrs' decision to go back to school together caused still another move in 1967 when both Carr and her husband began graduate work at Florida State University, he to study Spanish and she to pursue a Ph.D. in English. When FSU gave her a teaching fellowship and her husband a graduate research assistantship, they sold their

home in Savannah and moved with their three daughters to Tallahassee, thus beginning a vital stage in Carr's career as a biographer.

"What affected my career most—and my life, ultimately—was having chosen to write a critical paper for my modern American literature class on the work of Carson McCullers," said Carr. "I was reading voraciously everything she had written and was puzzling over what it all meant when my husband came home one day and handed me McCullers's obituary in the *New York Times*. I knew then—at that very moment—that McCullers would become the subject of my dissertation, although I had no idea that I would eventually move to her hometown and write her biography."

Carr received her Ph.D. in 1969 and moved to Columbus, Georgia, to teach at Columbus College. Her husband had already decided to return to banking, and now, for the first time, Carr's move to a new location was independent of her husband's career. "I suppose that I learned a great deal from McCullers herself—though we never knew each other personally—regarding the practicalities and rewards of being one's own person." Carr and her husband were divorced on 1 January 1975, shortly before her biography of McCullers was published (having been based on her dissertation).

She had hoped, after signing a contract with Doubleday to do the biography, to have unrestricted access to McCullers's literary archives at the University of Texas Humanities Research Center, as well as the cooperation of the literary estate, but the executors wanted an established author to write the authorized biography and recognized that Carr was virtually unpublished at the time. Moreover, one of McCullers's literary executors wrote Carr that he was asking everyone who knew McCullers to save their materials and reminiscences for the official biographer, whom they expected to appoint soon. Carr gathered, too, that the executors ultimately wanted no one to write the biography until some twenty-five years after McCullers's death, when everyone connected with her life presumably would be deceased. Carr said that it would be untenable to delay her own considerable research and writing of McCullers's life on the "off-chance that the Estate might change its mind"; thus she proceeded without their cooperation.

Meanwhile, she became an expert interviewer, persuading those who had loved McCullers, as well as those who did not like her—and there were many—to share their impressions, relationships, and anecdotes for the biography. Carr's personal charm and friendliness, her dedication to her subject, and her confidence in her own abilities won her the respect and trust of McCullers's friends and acquaintances, as well as the information she needed. Lamar Smith, McCullers's brother, and Jordan Massee, her cousin from Macon, Georgia (who lived in New York), were especially helpful. The research was thorough, the material gathered painstakingly. As Williams writes in his introduction to Carr's biography, "I knew at once that this lady from Georgia, Carson's native state, was someone who valued the spirit and the writing of Mrs. McCullers as deeply as I did, and it seemed to me that this biographical and critical work had been undertaken by Mrs. Carr much in the way that the devout once made pilgrimages to devout places."

In addition to Williams, whom Carr interviewed extensively, she talked to, or corresponded with, some five hundred people, including such literary and theater figures as Truman Capote, Katherine Anne Porter, Elizabeth Bowen, W. H. Auden, Janet Flanner, Muriel Rukeyser, Louis Untermeyer, Joshua Logan, Anne Baxter, Julie Harris, John Huston, Edward Albee, Arthur Miller, Ethel Waters, June Havoc, Lotte Lenya, José Quintero, Lillian Hellman, Mary Rodgers, and David Diamond. Diamond, a renowned composer and key figure in the lives of both McCullers and her husband, made available his letters and papers, and many others contributed generously in a variety of ways.

Three of the most rewarding interviews, Carr recalled, were with "octogenarians whose memories were vivid." Untermeyer, who told Carr that he "had shared with Carson a platonic love and some not so platonic embraces," was the first important literary figure in America to recognize McCullers's genius. Flanner, who knew McCullers in both New York and Paris, remembered her as "standing out even among New Yorkers as an eccentric of the first water. Carson was always so eager and so full of the energy of affection—she was enough to drive any town right off its rocker."

When Carr knocked on Porter's door in College Park, Maryland, one Sunday afternoon without an appointment (since Porter had not answered her letters), Porter chided Carr—through the closed door—for not having called her first. "Miss Porter, I've come eight hundred miles to see you because you have an unlisted telephone number," replied Carr. "Let me give it to you," said Porter. "You must call me some time."

When Carr explained—still through the closed door—that she realized Porter "did not particularly want to talk about McCullers," but that she, Carr, was an admirer of Porter's work and would like to meet her, Porter invited her in for a glass of sherry. "Miss Porter could hardly wait to talk about McCullers, for whom she felt considerable animosity," said Carr. It seems that McCullers had been so struck by the fame and beauty of "the legendary Porter" that, when she met her at Yaddo Artists Colony in 1941, she reportedly followed her about with "puppy-dog infatuation" and made a nuisance of herself, according to Carr. After being rebuffed repeatedly by Porter, McCullers—confident of her own worth and ability as a writer—observed to Newton Arvin, a fellow writer and board member at Yaddo, "Well, she may be the most important female writer in America today, but just wait until *next* year."

Carr circa 1975 (photograph by Al Alexander)

A major responsibility for Carr as a biographer of McCullers was to present the truth, and in establishing that truth, to be rigorously skeptical about the information she was given. Before artist Henry Varnum Poor would cooperate, he demanded to know what kind of biography Carr intended to write. If it were to be a "goody-two shoes" portrait of his friend, he could not approve the project. "Nor would Carson have approved," he continued. "She would have been the first to laugh it right off the shelf, for no one respected the truth more than Carson, even when she did not always tell it herself." Carr assured Poor that her book would be as honest a portrait as she could make it. McCullers's friends reported repeatedly that the novelist's "flights of imagination" were more interesting to her than the truth, and so far as she was concerned, they became the truth. McCullers loved to fantasize, to exaggerate, or, as her cousin Virginia Storey put it, "to take the truth between her teeth and run

with it." McCullers used to say, "Why tell the truth when fiction makes a much better and truer story?"

Upon reading *The Lonely Hunter*, many of McCullers's friends and acquaintances wrote or telephoned Carr to say that they felt she had dealt honestly, sensitively, and compassionately with all aspects of McCullers's complicated—and complicating—life. Her bisexuality (formerly unknown to her friends and family in the South), her excessive drinking, her husband's suicide, her relationship with her parents, the alcoholism in her immediate family—all presented "thorny problems," said Carr, who usually points out in her lectures that it is much easier for a biographer to present an accurate portrait if the subject is no longer living and has no close family survivors. Oliver Evans, an earlier biographer and McCullers's friend who wrote *The Ballad of Carson McCullers* (1965), acknowledged to Carr that his own book contained many inaccuracies simply because they were "Carson's own." He said that he "had, unfortunately, recorded facts and events as she chose to see them," and that having his friend's cooperation and publishing the book while she was alive was to his "great disadvantage," although he was hardly aware of it at the time.

As her research progressed, Carr saw that there were many contradictions in the life and personality of her subject. McCullers was either the "wounded sparrow" or the "iron butterfly," depending on whom she was with and what she wanted to be at the time. McCullers suffered from ill health most of her life, and people usually perceived her as childlike and vulnerable. Yet at the same time she was resilient and amazingly strong-willed. When Carr asked Williams how he saw McCullers, the playwright pounded his fist on a marble-topped table. "Just like this table," he said. "Indestructible!"

Arnold Saint Subber, another close friend of McCullers and the producer of her second play, *The Square Root of Wonderful* (1958), called her "the most innocent angel in the entire world," as well as "the reddest, most bitchy devil." To many who knew McCullers, she seemed to have no philosophy of life or religious orientation, yet she often feared that she had lost the presence of God: "she needed God in *this* world, for to her there was no other," said Saint Subber. She reserved her most intense feelings for her art. Charismatic, she drew people to her, yet also repelled them. She loved to hear stories of small-town southern life, yet could not tolerate living in a small town.

Carr's biography of McCullers begins with a short scene in which ten-year-old Lula Carson Smith (McCullers) is viewing the midway freaks at the Chattahoochee Valley Fair: the Rubber Man, the Pin Head, the Lady with the Lizard Skin. She gazes at them with "terror and fascination." This opening is especially effective since McCullers seemed aware throughout her life of the aloneness and spiritual isolation of all kinds of people, especially those with physical deformities, and she felt a kinship with them. She understood isolation because she was a lonely, deeply sensitive young girl who was neither liked nor appreciated by most of her peers. Her novels and short stories are peopled with lonely characters who are starved for love and communication with others but thwarted in their efforts to relate to anyone around them.

Carr's biography elicited an enthusiastic response from private readers and reviewers alike. In a 26 June 1975 letter to Carr, Untermeyer called *The Lonely Hunter* an "extraordinary" book and said what many others were also saying, that he could not "remember reading a biography in which research is so exact, so rich, and so rewarding." He claimed, too, that Carr was successful in disclosing "the contrarieties and ambiguities, the prevarications and provocations—in essence the many sides of Carson's difficulties and demands, all the appeals and burdens of her childishly dependent and yet destructive personality." Untermeyer also praised Carr's depiction of McCullers's husband and the "contradictions of the liar and the lover. The indispensable yet cast-off mate . . . the pathetic somebody-nobody." In an 11 November 1976 letter James Dickey called Carr's book "a masterpiece," and wrote: "I think that your biography of Carson McCullers is superior to her work. And that is high praise indeed. I am an avid reader of biographies, but few have equaled and none surpassed this one." Robert Phillips in the *New York Times Book Review* (7 July 1975) described *The Lonely Hunter* as "a fascinating, albeit orthodox biography of a highly unorthodox life. For all its length, it seems not too long, for the focus throughout is the highly complex personality of her subject. . . . Ms. Carr not only re-creates the legend of McCullers, but gets behind it—no small feat when one recognizes that, like Faulkner, Mrs. McCullers was a constant prevaricator, a self-dramatizer for whom no reality was quite so real as her own fantasized version of it. And what a life it was!"

After this impressive debut in the field of literary biography, Doubleday editor Ken McCormick asked Carr in 1976 if she would be interested in writing a biography of Dos Passos and suggested that since she was on her way then to Yaddo Artists Colony to work on another project, she might find other writers there who had known Dos Passos personally and who could give her a few anecdotes that might influence her decision. Carr did indeed discover several people at Yaddo who knew Dos Passos, and she also discovered his memoirs, *The Best Times* (1966), in the Yaddo library. The more she read his work and talked with others about him, the more enthusiastic she became about writing his biography. It seemed to Carr that Dos Passos was one of the most underrated major authors of the twentieth century, and when she returned to New York

129

sat cross-legged in purple pajamas, sipped exotic liqueurs in rooms heavily

hung with brocades and silks, and burned incense before curious bronze

figures under dim lights. Dos Passos thought such posturing inane and

satirized it in a tale he later wrote for the Harvard Monthly,

"An Aesthete's Nightmare," ~~though he did find The Yellow Book humorous.~~

He relished Gilbert and Sullivan's satire of Wilde in the play, Patience,

~~and~~ was bored by most of the decadent verse associated with imitators of

but found The Yellow Book humorous.

the Pre-Raphaelites, The editorial staffs of both The Harvard Advocate

and the Harvard Monthly tried to shake off the surviving vestiges of effete

romanticism by declaring they would publish nothing that smacked of

preciosity. ~~For the most part, they succeeded.~~

~~The magazine~~ Dos Passos ~~yearned most~~ *preferred* ~~to be published in was the~~

to the Advocate ~~and got up he nerve~~

Harvard Monthly ~~Near~~ the end of his freshman year ~~he ventured the~~

entitled

~~To submission of~~ a short story, "The Almeh." ~~Though~~ the piece contained no

conventional

well-made plot or development of character, *but* ~~in a conventional sense,~~ it was

an effective slice-of-life tale, low-keyed and rich in sensory detail. In

James Joyce's

tone and revelation, it compared to ~~an earlier published story,~~ "Araby,"

~~by a writer whose work Dos Passos had begun to take note of, James Joyce.~~

which evolved from his journey to

"The Almeh," ~~spun out of~~ his ~~"Grand Tour"~~ of North Africa and the Middle East,

concerned two ~~school~~ boys ~~probably in~~ (prep school) on tour in Cairo. ~~One,~~

a crass athletic American, Jack Hazen, had little patience with his friend,

with

a sensitive British youth (Dick Mansford,) ~~who had~~ a newly discovered bent

Mansford

for painting ~~and~~ was enamored of the ~~more~~ picturesque, romantic aspects of

and to

the ancient city, ~~When~~ Mansford accidentally ~~caught a~~ glimpse ~~of~~ the face

of a voluptuous, dark-eyed Arab maiden, he was smitten with love and combed

in search of   *upon*   *ing*

the city, ~~for~~ her. His dreams were shattered ~~when he found her and~~ discover

On this and the following two pages, part of a draft for Dos Passos: A Life *(by permission of Virginia Spencer Carr; John Dos Passos Collection, Archives and Special Collections Department, Otto G. Richter Library, University of Miami, Coral Gables, Florida)*

130

~~to be~~
~~she was~~ not the woman of class he had fantasized, but a cheap bazaar dancer.

was
Even more distressing was learning that she ~~had been purchased~~ to be the

That evening the boy
bride of his donkey boy. ~~The British youth~~ captured her beauty in oils

during a night-long orgy of painting, but his disenchantment was reinforced

the next day when he saw her again, this time in his donkey boy's fly-infested

~~mud~~ hut. The story's theme of disillusionment was telescoped in the final

boy   her
scene when the ~~youth~~ observed ~~the girl~~ squatting in the doorway of the hut

cooked   heard her
as she ~~prepared~~ the mid-day meal and , shouting shrewishly to her naked nephews

~~at play outside.~~

to July 1913
"The Almeh" was accepted by the <u>Harvard Monthly</u> for ~~the final~~ issue ,
The final issue   back
~~(July)~~ of the ~~1912-13~~ academic year. By then Dos Passos was ~~already on~~

holding
~~vacation~~ in Virginia with his mother and ~~father, and~~ had no ~~idea~~ that the

a
piece was to be published until ~~his~~ friend from Choate, (John Walcott,) wrote:

"Allow me to offer my congratulations to the distinguished new writer of

the <u>Harvard Monthly</u>!. . . . It is really fine, and now with your volumes

of manuscripts written during the summer you will be an editor by Christmas."

~~I have read it again and shall make everyone else in Concord do so."~~
proud of his accomplishment
Dos Passos was ~~elated~~ because freshman ~~writing was~~ rarely ~~accepted for~~
shed by
publi~~cation in~~ the <u>Harvard Monthly</u>. His only regret was that the story

left
appeared after most students had ~~abandoned~~ Cambridge for the summer.
He stayed in Virginia for less than a month this time,   later
~~Dos Passos left the farm in mid July~~ to spend the remainder of his
with Walcott
holidays in Canada , ~~He boarded a train in Washington, D.C., then journeyed~~

~~across New York to Sackets Harbor on Lake Ontario, where he caught a~~

~~steamboat. From there he went to Kingston, Ontario, then up the Rideau~~

~~Canal to Ottawa. By boat he continued up the Ottawa River to Montreal and~~

~~took a cruise ship to Quebec and Tadlussac, a little town at the mouth of~~

131

~~the Saguenay. Accustomed to being by himself, Dos Passos seldom admitted~~

~~to loneliness.~~ He enjoyed being on his own, took pleasure in practicing

his French on the natives (in the spring he had passed the required oral

examination in French for a baccalaureate degree in liberal arts, another

unusual accomplishment for a freshman), liked the feel and steady hum of

the motors underfoot and the scenery moving continuously, ~~before him,~~ and

scrutinized his fellow-passengers~~, with keen delight~~. Snatches of ~~dialogues~~ conversations

~~with other travellers~~ and ~~his innermost thoughts~~ were set down in his ~~diary~~ journal

~~once or twice daily~~ to become grist for his creative mill ~~once back at~~

Harvard.

By early September Dos Passos was impatient to ~~return~~ to Cambridge,

having concluded that life there was not such a netherworld after all. Over

the summer he had put on weight and now blended into his college environment

with new self-assurance. He had improved his lot considerably by being

published in the Harvard Monthly. Students who read ~~the Harvard Monthly~~ it

were ~~also~~ alert to the names and faces of ~~the~~ contributors and made sociable

overtures. The fledgling author also benefited by moving from the

Harvard Yard to 32 Ware Hall, a private dormitory on Harvard Street at the

edge of the campus. ~~Here~~ residents were a homogeneous mixture of

underclassmen. Every day he saw people with whom he had classes. ~~He could~~

~~talk with them about professors and assignments and readings.~~ They dropped

in upon one another for tea, ~~went to~~ dinner together, and ~~to~~ the ballet or

theatre. ~~Their~~ weekend activities usually included a ~~Saturday night~~ concert

at Symphony Hall.

Most Harvard men took their weekday meals on campus at Memorial Hall.

City at the end of the summer, she agreed to write it for Doubleday.

The overall project took considerably longer than Carr had anticipated (five years altogether), in part because she interrupted her work in the fall of 1980 to accept a Fulbright fellowship to teach at the University of Wroclaw in Poland. She took her Dos Passos materials along, intending to write some ten years of his life there, but the political situation became so critical in Poland early in her stay that the American embassy warned U.S. citizens that they might be forced to leave the country on twenty-four hours' notice, taking with them only one suitcase. Carr could not risk jeopardizing the years of work already finished, and as soon as possible she sent the manuscript and papers back to America by diplomatic courier. She said later that her year in Poland, during which she experienced socialism as an inept way of life and communism as a frightening political knife, helped her "plumb the depths of the young Dos Passos's ambivalences with a subjectivity" she could not have gained otherwise. A reviewer of Carr's biography wrote later (in the *Washington Times Magazine*, 4 September 1984) that "it may be that a year spent as a Fulbright lecturer in Poland gives an added edge to Miss Carr's writing when she touches on the subject of liberty—an edge that 'Dos' would have understood and appreciated."

The question of Dos Passos's identity and the mystery surrounding his illegitimate birth were important issues that Carr had to investigate early in her research. Dos Passos was born in a hotel room in Chicago, but existing records do not show this. His father and mother, both from prominent families, were married, but not to each other, nor were they free to marry until their young son had matriculated to Harvard. In fact, most of his mother's aristocratic southern family preferred to avoid all mention of the name Dos Passos even after he acquired fame as one of America's leading writers. A cousin on his mother's side urgently requested Carr to leave the "entire Sprigg line out of the book." To them Dos Passos would always be the "adopted child" of Lucy Addison Sprigg Madison, not her son by birth. Dos Passos's mother already had one son from her marriage to Ryland Randolph Madison, a direct descendant of President James Madison, and she herself was descended from Joseph Addison, the eighteenth-century poet, essayist, and playwright.

To avoid scandal, Dos Passos's father, John Rodrigues Dos Passos, a prominent New York attorney of Portuguese descent (who changed his middle name to Randolph when he became an avid anglophile), arranged for Mrs. Madison and their young son to spend most of their time in Europe. Consequently, Jack Madison, as the writer was then known, learned to speak French before he spoke English, lived a "hotel childhood" throughout western Europe, and went to private schools in England. When he finally entered Choate, he seemed more like a foreigner than a native-born American because of his strange accent and European mannerisms. This ambiguity about identity extended years later even to his father's obituary in 1917, which noted Louis Dos Passos, the older son from his first marriage, but did not mention the younger Dos Passos—who was then his namesake—as surviving kin. John Dos Passos had, however, been named as an heir in the will, having been fully acknowledged by Dos Passos, Sr., when the older man was free to marry Lucy Madison.

The issues of name and identity were reflected in Carr's organization of the major sections of the book, which corresponded with the distinct stages of Dos Passos's life. Book 1, "Jack Madison 1896-1912," addresses the childhood and schooling of Dos Passos when he knew himself only as Jack Madison and called his father "Didi," whom his mother identified as his "guardian." Book 2, "Dos" (subtitled John R. Dos Passos, Jr., 1912-1947), deals with the Harvard years, with the war years (World War I, the Spanish Civil War, and World War II), and with his first marriage, a period that spanned the most productive and active years of his professional career. Book 3, the shortest section ("Mr. Jack, Squire of Spence's Point, 1949-1970"), covers the last twenty years, the stage of Dos Passos's life when he returned to his boyhood vacation retreat on the Northern Neck of Virginia to live with his second wife and to farm his land. He was still writing prolifically, both fiction and nonfiction, but was more interested in early U.S. history than in writing fiction against a background of current events, which had characterized much of his fiction previously. Dos Passos became less the novelist and more the writer of history and biography, which in part accounted for his diminishing literary audience. History, rather than "pure fiction," as Dos Passos termed it, was more alive and fascinating for him. He once said that he would "rate a good historian higher than a novel-

Dust jacket for Carr's 1984 biography, for which she began research in 1976

ist," and that he considered himself only a second-rate historian.

Dos Passos's widow, formerly Elizabeth Hamlin Holdridge, cooperated fully with Carr during her research for the biography, granting interviews and making available her husband's letters, manuscripts, and other papers. Available to Carr, too, were Dos Passos's literary archives that had been donated to the Alderman Library of the University of Virginia. His close friends included Robert Hillyer, Zelda and F. Scott Fitzgerald, Ernest Hemingway, E. E. Cummings, Gerald and Sara Murphy, James T. Farrell, Theodore Dreiser, Archibald and Ada MacLeish, Edmund Wilson, William F. Buckley, and others from his Harvard years, from his ambulance-driving days in Europe during World War I, and from his life in Provincetown and in Westmoreland, Virginia, with whom he kept up over the years.

Dos Passos was a remarkably sensible and in-

telligent man, keenly idealistic and passionate about the need to preserve the dignity and freedom of the ordinary man. Early critics called him a romantic radical because he spoke out against injustice and threats to individual liberty. Others called him a liberal, a Marxist, a fellow traveler, and comrade (Carr points out that he was never a Communist). When Dos Passos was on the political left, he thought Marxism to be inspired by honorable social and economic needs, but after witnessing the cruel and total disregard of human rights while traveling in Russia and Spain, he became disillusioned with the left and stopped writing for *New Masses*, a strong leftist publication, and before long was contributing to William F. Buckley's *National Review*. Many American writers and critics were affronted by Dos Passos's desertion of what was then a popular and, to many, a just cause. Evidence supports the theory that

Dos Passos's literary reputation suffered because of his increasingly unpopular political stances.

Another intriguing aspect of *Dos Passos: A Life* is Carr's treatment of the long-standing friendship between her subject and Hemingway, which was ruptured in 1937 when they went to Spain to make a documentary film about the Spanish people. Hemingway had wanted to use the film to raise money in America on behalf of the Loyalists, but Dos Passos saw atrocities committed in the name of the Loyalists whose cause he had heretofore espoused, and he also discovered that his friend José Robles—a professor from Johns Hopkins University on leave to serve as an official in the Loyalist Ministry of War—had been arrested, accused of treason as a Fascist spy, and shot without a trial. Hemingway bitterly condemned Dos Passos for leaving the film project and for "stirring up trouble," as Hemingway saw it. Carr's colorful depiction of the relationships of the various Lost Generation writers in Paris and in America in the 1920s makes fascinating reading, too.

In 1954 there was much speculation about whether an American would win the Nobel Prize for literature. When Carson McCullers was told that she was in the running, she said that the prize should rightfully go to Dos Passos (instead, it went to Hemingway and neither Dos Passos nor McCullers received a Nobel Prize). Northwestern University awarded Dos Passos an honorary doctorate of humane letters, and in 1962 he traveled to Rome to accept the prestigious international literary prize, the Feltrinelli. Dos Passos's reputation throughout his life was greater in Europe and Asia than in the United States. In 1938 French writer Jean-Paul Sartre had said of him, "Dos Passos had invented only one thing, an art of storytelling. But that is enough. . . . I regard Dos Passos as the greatest writer of our time."

Writing for the *Boston Herald* (7 October 1984), Albert Duhamel called Carr's biography a "thorough, detailed analysis of the reasons why Dos Passos was once the darling of the international literary set and why he was later stricken from the lists of required reading in this country. That part of her book is an interesting documentation of how literary reputations are made and lost. But the book also succeeds in its re-creation of an unusually sensitive man, a writer who felt as deeply for the mistreated Harlan County coal-

miners in the 20s as he did for the victims of Soviet aggression in the 40s."

Reviewers in general praised Carr for her absorbing, stylishly written, and superbly organized biography, as well as for her diligent research and scholarship, citing the book as a valuable reference work in American studies. Some spoke of the gross or benign neglect Dos Passos had suffered in the past and contended that readers of Carr's biography would find themselves wanting to read all of Dos Passos's works. George Core informed readers of the *Washington Post* (14 October 1984) that the "figure who emerges" from Carr's biography is "thoroughly human and is a sensible and likable and even admirable person who stands in stark contrast to the egomaniacs among the artists who were acquaintances and friends such as Hemingway, Fitzgerald, and Hart Crane."

As a biographer Carr has given readers a finely tooled and balanced presentation of the lives of her subjects and furnished the careful detail necessary to make them both human and impressive. She said that she learned to write biography by "simply doing it" and by believing in it as an art form and as an eminently worthwhile scholarly project. "I could never be a successful biographer," she continued, "if I did not feel passionate about my subjects and have great respect for their work, and if I did not feel that my own involvement with them was time and creative energy well spent." Carr's technique in writing about McCullers and Dos Passos was, in a sense, to live with them, to discover their milieu, to walk in their footsteps, to enter into their psyches, and thus to re-create them so that they came up off the page, inviting Carr's readers as well to enter into their lives, to interact with them, and to discover, perhaps, something of themselves in the process.

Papers:
The archives of Virginia Spencer Carr pertaining to Carson McCullers and the research and writing of *The Lonely Hunter* are in the Virginia Spencer Carr Collection, Manuscript Department, William R. Perkins Library, Duke University. The actual manuscripts for *The Lonely Hunter* and for *Dos Passos* are at the University of Miami.

Scott Donaldson
(11 November 1928 -   )

Robert A. Morace
Daemen College

BOOKS: *The Making of a Suburb* (Bloomington, Minn.: Bloomington Historical Society, 1964);

The Suburban Myth (New York & London: Columbia University Press, 1969);

Poet in America: Winfield Townley Scott (Austin: University of Texas Press, 1972);

By Force of Will: The Life and Art of Ernest Hemingway (New York: Viking, 1977; Harmondsworth, U.K.: Penguin, 1978);

American Literature: Nineteenth and Early Twentieth Centuries, by Donaldson and Ann Massa (Newton Abbott, U.K.: David & Charles/ New York: Barnes & Noble, 1978);

Fool for Love: F. Scott Fitzgerald (New York: Congdon & Weed, 1983);

John Cheever: A Biography (New York: Random House, 1988).

OTHER: Thomas Low Nichols, *Forty Years of American Life: 1821-1861,* introduction by Donaldson (New York: Johnson Reprint Series in American Studies, 1969), pp. v-xxii;

William Douglas O'Connor, *Harrington,* introduction by Donaldson (New York: Johnson Reprint Series in American Studies, 1969), pp. v-xxxv;

"The Book of Scattered Lives," in *Edwin Arlington Robinson Centenary Essays* (Athens: University of Georgia Press, 1969), pp. 42-53;

Harlan Paul Douglass, *The Suburban Trend,* introduction by Donaldson (New York: Johnson Reprint Series in American Studies, 1970), pp. v-xv;

" 'No, I Am Not Prince Charming': Fairy Tales in *Tender is the Night,*" in *Fitzgerald/Hemingway Annual 1973* (Washington: Microcard Editions, 1974), pp. 105-112;

"Booth Tarkington," in *Dictionary of American Biography,* supplement 4 (New York: Scribners, 1974), pp. 815-817;

"Ridgely Torrence," in *Dictionary of American Biography,* supplement 4 (New York: Scribners, 1974), pp. 840-841;

"The Machines in John Cheever's Garden," in *The Changing Face of the Suburbs,* edited by Barry Schwartz (Chicago: University of Chicago Press, 1976), pp. 309-322;

Jack Kerouac, *On the Road,* edited, with an introduction, by Donaldson (New York: Viking Critical Library, 1979);

" 'Irony and Pity'—Anatole France Got It Up," in *Fitzgerald/Hemingway Annual 1978* (Detroit: Gale Research, 1979), pp. 331-334;

"John Cheever," in *American Writers,* supplement 1, part 1 (New York: Scribners, 1979), pp. 174-199;

"F. Scott Fitzgerald," in *Dictionary of Literary Biography 9: American Novelists, 1910-1945,* part 2 (Detroit: Gale Research / Columbia, S.C.: Bruccoli Clark, 1981), pp. 3-18;

"Ernest Hemingway," in *Dictionary of Literary Biography: Yearbook 1981* (Detroit: Gale Research / Columbia, S.C.: Bruccoli Clark, 1982), pp. 89-93;

"Fitzgerald and Hemingway," in *American Literary Scholarship 1980* (Durham: Duke University Press, 1982), pp. 173-191;

"Money and Marriage in Fitzgerald's Stories," in *The Short Stories of F. Scott Fitzgerald: New Approaches in Criticism,* edited by Jackson R. Bryer (Madison: University of Wisconsin Press, 1982), pp. 75-88;

"Fitzgerald and Hemingway," in *American Literary Scholarship 1981* (Durham: Duke University Press, 1983), pp. 171-180;

"Frederic Henry and the Pose of Passivity," in *Hemingway: A Revaluation,* edited by Donald R. Noble (Troy: Whitston, 1983), pp. 165-185;

Critical Essays on F. Scott Fitzgerald's The Great Gatsby, edited, with an introduction and an essay, by Donaldson (Boston: G. K. Hall, 1984);

"Fitzgerald and Hemingway," in *American Literary Scholarship 1982* (Durham: Duke University Press, 1984), pp. 167-182;

Harold Frederic, *The Damnation of Theron Ware,* edited, with an introduction, by Donaldson

Scott Donaldson (photograph by Hans Lorenz)

(New York: Penguin Classics, 1985);
"Americans in Italy: The Clash of Cultures in John Cheever's Stories," in *Letture anglo-americane in memoria di Rolando Anzilotti* (Pisa: Nistri-Lischi, 1986), pp. 113-126;
Conversations with John Cheever, edited, with an introduction, by Donaldson (Jackson: University of Mississippi Press, 1987);
"Humor in *The Sun Also Rises,*" in *New Essays on The Sun Also Rises,* edited by Linda W. Wagner-Martin (New York: Cambridge University Press, 1987), pp. 19-41.

SELECTED PERIODICAL PUBLICATIONS—
UNCOLLECTED: "The Alien Pity: A Study of Character in the Poetry of E. A. Robinson," *American Literature,* 38 (May 1966): 219-229;

"Minding Emily Dickinson's Business," *New England Quarterly,* 41 (December 1968): 574-582;
"Appointment with the Dentist: O'Hara's Naturalistic Novel," *Modern Fiction Studies,* 14 (Winter 1968-1969): 435-442;
"Scott Fitzgerald's Romance with the South," *Southern Literary Journal,* 5 (Spring 1973): 3-17;
"Preparing for the End: Hemingway's Revisions of 'A Canary for One,'" *Studies in American Fiction,* 6 (Autumn 1978): 203-211;
"F. Scott Fitzgerald, Princeton '17," *Princeton University Library Chronicle,* 40 (Winter 1979): 119-154;
"The Crisis of Fitzgerald's Crack-Up," *Twentieth Century Literature,* 26 (Summer 1980): 171-188;

"The Wooing of Ernest Hemingway," *American Literature*, 53 (January 1982): 691-710;

"Woolf vs. Hemingway," *Journal of Modern Literature*, 10 (June 1983): 338-342;

"F. Scott Fitzgerald: The Remaking of a Reputation," *William and Mary Alumni Gazette* (Winter 1983): 2-8;

"Dos and Hem: A Literary Friendship," *Centennial Review*, 29 (Spring 1985): 163-185;

"Frost, Dickinson, and the Strategy of Evasion," *Concerning Poetry*, 19 (1986): 107-116;

"Supermarket and Superhighway: John Cheever's America," *Virginia Quarterly Review*, 62 (Autumn 1986): 654-668;

"The Bifurcated Cheever: An Approach to His Life," *William and Mary Alumni Gazette* (Winter 1987): 2-6.

There has been a surprising, even paradoxical interest in literary biography since the publication of Roland Barthes's apparently premature announcement of "The Death of the Author" (in the 1968 essay of that name, collected in *Image Music Text*, 1977). Much biography has been written by academics who have confused the art of biography with the massive accumulation of information and who have often managed to exhaust their readers as well as their subjects with works that seem less literary than archival in nature. In this regard, the work of Scott Donaldson stands apart. His biographies of Winfield Townley Scott, Ernest Hemingway, F. Scott Fitzgerald, and John Cheever are not only meticulously researched but forcefully narrated. Even as he provides a wealth of detail about each writer, Donaldson does more, offering knowledge of the man and insights into the relationships among that man, his work, and his world. Neither trifling nor tendentious, Donaldson seems determined to understand not only the lives and writings of his subjects but through them the very nature of the American literary experience. Starting from a certain admiration for the works themselves and a vague sense of "fellow feeling" for the authors who wrote them, he has discovered in his subjects a pattern he believes may well be true of many, perhaps even all, the major male American writers. It is a pattern that derives from the influence of strong, dominant mothers and weak or absent fathers, all within the larger context of the anxieties, aspirations, and values of middle-class American life. Blending biography, literary criticism, and a measure of cultural analysis, yet all the while managing to avoid the pitfall of psy-

choanalytical reductiveness to which his larger thesis would seem to make him prone, Donaldson has produced in less than two decades four major biographies.

Donaldson was born on 11 November 1928 in Minneapolis, Minnesota, the son of manufacturer Frank D. Donaldson and his wife, the former Ruth E. Chase. After earning his B.A. from Yale (1951) and his M.A. from the University of Minnesota (1952) and serving three years in the United States Army's Security Agency, Donaldson embarked upon a career in journalism, first as a reporter for the *Minneapolis Star* (1956-1958), then as editor-publisher of the *Bloomington (Minnesota) Sun-Suburbanite* (1958-1961), and finally as executive editor for all the *Sun* newspapers in the Twin Cities area (1961-1964). He then returned to the University of Minnesota, completing his Ph.D. in 1966. That same year, he joined the faculty of the College of William and Mary, where he is currently Louise G. T. Cooley Professor of English. He has also been a Fulbright lecturer in Finland (1970-1971) and Italy (1979), visiting professor at the University of Leeds (1972-1973), visiting research fellow at Princeton (1978), a Rockefeller Foundation fellow (1982), and the recipient of a Phi Beta Kappa award for the advancement of scholarship (1971) and a National Endowment for the Humanities grant (1984). Although best known for his biographies, Donaldson's first major book, *The Suburban Myth* (1969), quickly established his reputation as an Americanist, which his subsequent work as biographer, critic, and editor, including a four-year tenure on the editorial board of *American Literature* (1984-1988), has served to consolidate. He also served as consultant for public television documentaries on Hemingway and Fitzgerald and a dramatization of the lives of Gerald and Sara Murphy. Donaldson married Vivian Breckenridge on 5 March 1982 and is the father of three sons by his second wife, Janet K. Mikelson, from whom he was divorced in February 1982. His first marriage, in 1953, ended with the death of his wife, the former Winifred M. Davis, one year later.

Published in 1972, *Poet in America: Winfield Townley Scott* had its genesis nearly a decade earlier during Donaldson's days as a doctoral student. He read the poems anthologized in George P. Elliott's *Fifteen Modern American Poets* (1956) in a course in American poetry and immediately felt "an extraordinary kinship with Scott," whom he has described—by no means pejoratively—as "a minor poet . . . of great sensitivity and wonderful economy of expression." The letter of appreciation Donaldson contemplated but never wrote, the visit he considered but continued to put off until it was too late, metamorphosed following Scott's death (perhaps a suicide) in 1968 into what was to have been a critical analysis of the poetry. But even this plan underwent revision as Donaldson found himself becoming as fascinated by the poet as he was by the poems. Scott seemed an apt subject for biographical study: talented, interesting yet largely neglected, and ripe for critical revaluation; furthermore, his widow and children were willing to give Donaldson their full support.

That Scott is an interesting literary figure is certain; however, some reviewers questioned whether he merited a full-scale biography. Scott certainly aspired to major literary status. Although under his guidance the book page of the *Providence Journal* became one of the best in the country, Scott wanted to be a "poet," to be able, as John Greenleaf Whittier and Edwin Arlington Robinson had been, to give to common speech a poetic power. To realize his aim, Scott believed that he had to devote himself to his art. Made financially secure thanks to his second wife's wealth, he resigned from the *Journal* and went to live in New Mexico, where his writing alternated with fits of drinking and brooding over the recognition he believed he deserved but failed to receive. Scott not only felt neglected, he also felt guilty for living a life that ran so clearly counter to the values of the middle class in which he had been raised. He could hardly conceive of writing poetry as a real job when it brought him little recognition and even less money. He saw himself as a failure both as a husband and as a poet (not surprisingly his artistic and sexual powers declined together, doubling the anxieties of a man Donaldson says was already sufficiently insecure).

Scott published ten books during his lifetime, nine of them poetry, but the number of works he abandoned was greater still. His ambition to be a major American poet in the age of T. S. Eliot and Wallace Stevens came up against the indifference of publishers, reviewers, and critics, and, perhaps more important, against his own lack of self-esteem. If Scott "escaped greatness," George P. Elliott told Donaldson a year after the poet's death, "it was by the margin of his fears, his self-doubts, and extraordinary modesty and gentleness. . . . If he had written the things he said when drunk, he would have been

as good as Frost, as good as you could get." However, reviewers rejected Donaldson's double bid to redeem Scott's reputation not only by writing and analyzing his life but by turning the biography into a partial anthology of Scott's best poems. *Choice* (July 1973) was the most emphatic: "Scott seems to stand no chance whatsoever of being resurrected." L. S. Dembo, writing in *American Literature* (May 1973), was less abrupt but no less adamant: *Poet in America* does not make a case for Scott's importance; although intelligent and at times even "poignant," according to Dembo it is nonetheless superfluous. Donaldson had contended that "The life of any poet deserves attention, just as his death diminishes us all." Dembo and others felt no diminishment whatsoever; they felt instead that Scott simply did not deserve this kind of attention, and neither *Poet in America* nor Scott's journals, also published by the University of Texas Press that same year, did much to change Scott's critical fortunes.

Donaldson, however, had hoped to do more than revive interest in Scott; he saw Scott not only as a talented poet but, as the biography's title suggests, as a representative one as well. "Winfield Townley Scott was bitched by [American] culture, first through a middle-class, female-dominated childhood in which he was pampered, protected, and provided with enough phobic tendencies to ruin several lives, and then as an adult in whose work 'most people' . . . found little to value and about whose willingness to be supported by his wife they were disposed to shake their heads. Or so it seemed to Scott himself, inescapably a creature of his time and place and hence prone to share judgments and wonderings he knew should not matter." Reviewers proved as resistant to Donaldson's vision of Scott's representativeness as they were to his revisionist claim of Scott's importance as an individual poet. Writing in the *Washington Post Book World* (5 November 1972), William Stafford, himself a poet, wondered whether the failure had been more the poet's than the country's; the poet, Stafford speculated, and his biographer may be too willing to project the poet's own misgivings about himself onto society in order to expiate his sense of guilt. Though Scott's poetry does not quite manage to support Donaldson's large claims for it and while the book's thesis finally seems more provocative than proven, one may still find in *Poet in America* much to admire. It is, after all, precisely the kind of biography Scott claimed could not be written, one that is both accurate and fair. *Poet in America*

Dust jacket for the critical biography that advances the thesis that Hemingway's life and work were determined by the same competitive drives

is exhaustive, authoritative, sympathetic, and candid, raising as many disturbing questions about Scott's character as it does about the literary establishment. Just as important, Donaldson comes as close as a biographer can to that "combination of psychologist, sociologist, literary historian and critic, as well as expert in alcoholism" that Scott, in his review of Mark Schorer's 1961 biography of Sinclair Lewis, believed was needed in order to explain why "it seems our saddest stories are biographies of 20th Century American writers."

Poet in America faced much the same difficulty Scott himself had: lack of recognition. With the next two biographies—*By Force of Will: The Life and Art of Ernest Hemingway* (1977) and *Fool For Love: F. Scott Fitzgerald* (1983)—Donaldson faced the opposite problem. Hemingway and Fitzgerald were subjects about whom it seemed too much had been written. Could any biographer possibly have anything new to say just nine years after the publication of Carlos Baker's voluminous bestseller, *Ernest Hemingway: A Life Story*? Reviewers of *By Force of Will*, both in the popular press and the scholarly journals, felt that Donaldson did. Although he presents little in the way

of new material, Donaldson revaluates the old from a new and illuminating perspective, "rereading the fiction," as George Wickes pointed out in *Modern Fiction Studies* (Winter 1978), "in the light of Hemingway's personal drives and fears." Selden Rodman, writing in the *National Review* (25 November 1977), and Richard B. Hovey, in *American Literature* (January 1978), considered Donaldson's book superior to Baker's. Donaldson "accomplishe[s] . . . something more difficult and rewarding: he has managed," according to Rodman, "to relate the life to the art without blurring the enormities of the first or denigrating the achievements of the second"; he has done what most biographers cannot, linking, says Hovey, "the outward with the inward, the facts of the artist's life with the puzzles and mystery of his creativity," and making clear how this particular writer came to write his particular works. Walter Sullivan, in the *Sewanee Review* (October 1977), sums up Donaldson's achievement: *By Force of Will* "gives us the most vivid and complete picture of Hemingway that has yet been drawn"; Donaldson "comes as close as any is ever likely to come to a final answer concerning the connection between

Hemingway's complex personality and the characters and actions of his novels. I know of no way to overpraise this excellent book."

Such high praise is entirely merited yet rather ironic, given the book's humble origin in Donaldson's senior thesis on Hemingway's short stories (which Yale tried to dissuade Donaldson from doing). His interest increased as he began teaching Hemingway, and eventually it led him to consider writing a scholarly study of morality in Hemingway's work. As the idea developed, it also broadened. From Donaldson's important early analysis of the financial metaphor in *The Sun Also Rises* ("Hemingway's Morality of Compensation," *American Literature*, November 1971), he began to explore Hemingway's ideas on other subjects. Donaldson eventually spent four years researching and another eighteen months organizing and writing. Meanwhile he began circulating a sample chapter. The book was accepted by Viking Press on the recommendation of Malcolm Cowley, whom Donaldson has called "the best words editor I ever had. Write more straight sentences, he told me. Drop so many qualifying clauses."

By Force of Will is less a conventional biography than a compilation of Hemingway's ideas on twelve topics—fame, money, sports, politics, war, love, sex, friendship, religion, art, mastery, and death—and of Donaldson's analysis of Hemingway and his art in relation to these ideas in order "to construct a mosaic of his mind and personality." Donaldson's work did not please all reviewers. *Kirkus Reviews* (January 1977) judged Donaldson "a master gatherer" but complained that the twelve essays never do coalesce to form a single thesis about either Hemingway or his work. George Monteiro, on the other hand, much preferred Donaldson's "series of related but discrete essays" to Baker's "thousand pictures" (*Novel*, Spring 1978). The twelve chapters do in fact coalesce, though perhaps not as straightforwardly and single-mindedly as the *Kirkus* reviewer would have liked. The unity of *By Force of Will* derives from Donaldson's conviction that it is far too easy to take Hemingway at face value and that it is therefore necessary to penetrate the facade of Hemingway's public persona, which has come to dominate all discussion and criticism of Hemingway and his work. "A born story-teller with a flair for self-aggrandizement," Hemingway "was driven to master not only his craft but every aspect of his life in order to live up to an impossible ego ideal of himself he'd erected to replace

that of his somewhat ineffective father." For example, the impossible standards of courage or sexual prowess that Hemingway's heroes set for themselves and about which Hemingway himself often boasted were manifestations of this compulsion and were curiously at odds with the life Hemingway actually lived.

The sources Donaldson mines in order to uncover Hemingway's ideas and values are his fiction, nonfiction, letters, interviews, reminiscences, and the criticism about him. Donaldson emphasizes the importance of the stories and novels, but he does so without blurring the distinction between fact and fiction. Rather, he accomplishes just the reverse. He makes amply clear that, appearances to the contrary, no simple equation can be made between the life and the art, the author and his characters, who form a decidedly angled, often idealized version of their creator that the critic or biographer may choose to equate with Hemingway only at the risk of losing sight of the actual author altogether. Donaldson punctures the myths created by Hemingway and his critics not merely to debunk the myths and their makers but in order to recover the actual writer as best he can. The gap he opens between the real Hemingway and the idealized figure of the fiction and of the biographical legends points to that division, or self-contradiction, that Donaldson posits at the center of Hemingway's personality, a split evidenced in, for example, demanding loyalty from others while offering none himself; in his seeking the friendship of older writers only to repudiate them later; in his Emersonian love of nature coupled with his "concurrent sense of the blank, dark meaninglessness of our existence"; and in that strange division between Hemingway the author for whom writing was everything and Hemingway the celebrity for whom writing was not enough.

Donaldson's discussion of Hemingway and money is typical of the way in which, and of the extent to which, his approach illuminates the man and his fiction. Noting both obvious similarities between Hemingway and Jake Barnes as well as significant differences, Donaldson astutely points out that in money matters Hemingway had less in common with the novel's hero, a physical cripple, than he did with its moral cripples. *The Sun Also Rises* (1926), Donaldson shrewdly concludes, "proposes an extremely high standard of financial responsibility and is organized around a strict morality of compensation which, on the evidence, its author had been unable to achieve during his period of apprenticeship in Paris." This is not to say that the fiction is mere pretense and self-glorification. If Jake is the man Hemingway wanted to become, then Mike Campbell and, in *A Farewell to Arms* (1929), Frederic Henry are the men he condemned himself for being.

Donaldson's topical approach to Hemingway's life and art proved doubly advantageous. It yielded certain insights that had not merely escaped the notice of earlier critics and biographers but that had resisted their modes of inquiry, and it helped to distinguish *By Force of Will* from the mountain of Hemingway criticism. It also had its weaknesses, not the least of which was forcing Donaldson to go back in time whenever he began a new chapter. His use of lists proves just as distracting. Occasionally Donaldson offers a biographical tidbit without verifying its authenticity; this occurs infrequently but manages to stand out in a work in which the aim is to expose the man beneath the myth. Lastly one may note from the privileged position of the early 1990s the assurance with which Donaldson, ever on the lookout for the evidence of Hemingway's middle-class values, claims that "Hemingway found abhorrent any sexual arrangement which slipped off the proper path into unnatural byways"; in light of the 1986 publication of a version of Hemingway's *The Garden of Eden*, the claim appears a bit off the mark. These, however, are minor quibbles, and *By Force of Will* remains today what reviewers said it was then, one of three indispensable books on its subject, the other two being Baker's biography and Philip Young's *Ernest Hemingway: A Reconsideration* (1966), and a major contribution not only to the study of Hemingway but to the art of biography as well.

By the time Donaldson's *American Writers* essay on John Cheever and his Critical Library edition of Jack Kerouac's *On the Road* were published in 1979, he was already deeply involved in researching the life of Fitzgerald. Even as he began, he understood the risks involved in tackling yet another writer about whom so much had already been written. Undaunted, he proceeded, increasingly fascinated by Fitzgerald's life and convinced, as he explained to Dennis Brown of the *St. Louis Post-Dispatch*, that he had "found the hidden drive behind [Fitzgerald's] life and his work" and that he "had something new to say about him that was supported by a lot of new material." Donaldson spent the spring 1978 semester as visiting fellow at Princeton University, poring over the Fitzgerald collection and related materials. Fol-

lowing a half-year Fulbright professorship in Italy, two month-long residencies at the MacDowell Colony in Peterborough, New Hampshire, and his Rockefeller Foundation fellowship, again in Italy, Donaldson completed *Fool for Love*. Andre LeVot's Fitzgerald biography, with its distinctive European slant, appeared the same year (1983), which is to say two years after Matthew J. Bruccoli's *Some Sort of Epic Grandeur: The Life of F. Scott Fitzgerald*. Both books were soon republished in paperback. *Fool for Love* fared less well. Its publisher, Congdon & Weed, folded soon after publication.

Despite its inauspicious beginning and the overabundance of biographical and critical works on Fitzgerald, *Fool for Love* emerged, in the words of James L. W. West III, as "The best study of Fitzgerald's life . . . since Arthur Mizener's and . . . the most penetrating examination of the author ever written" (*Studies in American Fiction*, Spring 1986). Donaldson succeeds because he focuses his study so sharply, surveying Fitzgerald's entire life and career in terms of a lifelong insecurity. Donaldson analyzes Fitzgerald as a man "driven to please other people, especially rich and prominent people," a trait he got from the woman "largely responsible for his social insecurity," his mother. "Fitzgerald didn't belong anywhere. He never had a permanent home or secure position" and so attempted "to prove his worth by exercising his charm."

According to Donaldson, Molly Fitzgerald not only spoiled her son but her efforts to launch him in St. Paul's higher social circles left him emotionally crippled. He came to resent her efforts, as he resented his weak, ineffectual father, and to hate himself for the sense of inadequacy her ambitions had instilled in him. As he matured, he began to court women, particularly wealthy women, in order to prove that he had indeed arrived: Ginevra King, Lois Moran, Emily Vanderbilt, Zelda Sayre, of course, and others. Donaldson's portrait deepens and becomes far more disturbing when he details how Fitzgerald's efforts at Princeton to become an insider only served to accentuate what he was and always would be, an outsider. Donaldson's careful examination of university records shows that Fitzgerald was never well liked and that his metaphorical courtship of Princeton added to his already formidable store of self-doubts. He "courted Princeton's approval, ardently and unsuccessfully," not only during his student days but afterward as well. Like "an ardent suitor" he sought to make amends for earlier mistakes only to be met with continued rebuffs. Donaldson's Fitzgerald is the unrequited lover but in a modern mode: intellectually he knew what he was doing even if emotionally he had no choice other than to act out his compulsion. Fitzgerald had what psychologist Avodah K. Offit has termed a "histrionic personality," and "no amount of sympathy or attention or love is ever enough to satisfy such a person" (quoted in *Fool for Love*).

The chapters Donaldson devotes to Fitzgerald's years at Princeton show Fitzgerald's compulsion in its most elementary and, therefore, most perverse form. However, it is the two chapters devoted to Fitzgerald and Zelda, situated at the center of Donaldson's narrative, that prove the most harrowing. Donaldson's method is no different from that employed throughout the rest of the book, but it is more intensely focused. The result is that the reader comes to see Fitzgerald and Zelda with a new purity and intensity. They emerge as cruel in their dealings with one another but understandably so. Insecure, nearly tragic figures, they do not so much cause as cooperate in one another's destruction, with an inexorableness that Donaldson makes dramatically clear.

As he had in his study of Hemingway, Donaldson shows the deep division in Fitzgerald's personality and in the often oblique ways in which the man and his art reflect one another. He could enter into adulterous relationships yet nonetheless portray adultery in his stories and novels as a sin, "because public mores demanded it and because he shared those mores." He could, for example, idealize Zelda yet become increasingly "apprehensive about her morally," and even as he entered into his relationship with Sheilah Graham, the only relationship in which he did not feel like a social inferior, the same self-loathing that turned him into an alcoholic compelled him to judge her an immoral woman for the simple reason that she was living with him. As Donaldson perceptively shows, the way Fitzgerald felt about women was essentially the same way he felt about social class, for the same insecurity motivated his responses to both. He was at once admiring yet critical, desirous yet doubtful. Self-divided, Fitzgerald was also self-aware; he understood what the worst in him was. "At the last crisis . . . [he] had no real courage, perseverance or self-respect," and in *Tender is the Night* (1934) he came as close as he ever could "to confronting what he most disapproved of in himself." Donaldson details Fitzgerald's shortcomings so that

the reader experiences the intensity of a man who never found the security and approval he sought but one who did finally manage to redeem his life by becoming in the last year of his life "a writer only." The achievement of *Fool for Love* is that despite, or perhaps because of, its narrow focus, it "comes close to what the inner man must have been"—as close as any biography probably can.

Donaldson edited the well-received *Critical Essays on F. Scott Fitzgerald's The Great Gatsby* in 1984 and Harold Frederic's *The Damnation of Theron Ware*, one of Fitzgerald's favorite realist novels, for Penguin Classics one year later, by which time Donaldson had already begun his life of John Cheever. Donaldson's interest in Cheever can be traced back at least as far as his first book, *The Suburban Myth*, in which he briefly discusses Cheever as at once a defender and a critic of suburban life. He developed this thesis in two later essays, "The Machines in John Cheever's Garden" (1976) and "John Cheever" (for Scribners' *American Writers* series). As his research progressed, Donaldson published more analyses of Cheever and his art—"Supermarket and Superhighway: John Cheever's America" in *Virginia Quarterly Review* and "Americans in Italy" in an Italian festschrift, both in 1986—and he edited *Conversations with John Cheever* (1987) for the University of Mississippi's Literary Conversations series. *John Cheever: A Biography* was published in 1988, putting Cheever studies for the first time on a solid factual foundation. The affinities between Cheever and the only writer on whom Cheever ever wrote, Fitzgerald (in a short but illuminating essay for *Atlantic Brief Lives*, 1971), made Cheever as logical a choice for Donaldson after Fitzgerald as Fitzgerald had been after Hemingway. However, the Cheever biography differs from *Fool for Love* in that Donaldson does try to tell "the whole story" and to distinguish the man from the myths he had promoted.

Although Donaldson met Cheever only once, his portrait is sensitive as well as candid and authoritative. Like so much of Cheever's fiction, it is also generous, both in spirit and in the abundance of material presented. The thesis is simple: "Eventually I came to see his complicated and difficult life as a triumph. Hurt in childhood, he grew up a man divided against himself. A battle raged inside him between light and dark, celebration and sorrow, love and hate." The approach is straightforward: twenty-two chro-

Dust jacket for the first biography of the writer whose "complicated and difficult life" Donaldson eventually saw "as a triumph"

nologically arranged chapters, most dealing with periods of from one to four years. And it is also humble: "All biographers know that theirs is an impossible task, for we really cannot understand one another," though in fact Donaldson's reader may come close to understanding Cheever, certainly closer than the reader of Susan Cheever's memoir of life with father, *Home Before Dark* (1984). Donaldson's book is more detailed and more objective, of course, but also deeper, fairer, more human, and eventually more triumphant. Donaldson does not alter the basic pattern of Cheever's life in any significant way. Instead he fleshes out the pattern, correcting errors, adding information, and demystifying the writer to get at the troubled man behind the mask Cheever himself helped create. Author of five novels and more than 180 short stories, this "story-telling machine," as his *New Yorker* editor William Maxwell once called him, was similarly adept and prolific

in altering and embellishing his life to suit his psychological needs.

Fiction, Cheever liked to say, is not crypto-autobiography; rather, it is the most exalted form of human communication. Cheever's fiction was both, as Donaldson makes clear, while valuing the fiction too highly to use it as just another document, grist for the biographer's mill. He values it in large part because it "tells us more about people in the American middle class during that half century [1930-1982] than any other writer's work has done or can do." It tells a good deal about Cheever, too, though in a decidedly angled way. Writing allowed him, for example, to resolve in fiction the conflicts and crises he continued to struggle with throughout his life. Often, as in a discussion of the "patently autobiographical" story, "The Brothers" (1937), Donaldson persuasively calls attention to the ways the ambivalence and self-contradictions within the text re-

fever 5

The exchange rates were such that they were able to afford the apartment

and to hire both a maid and a cook

"After two moves," Ada wrote Maurice Firuski, "we fell heir to a lovely

aprt

¶The apartment was ~~loctad~~ located directly opposite the Luxembourg

gardens, and ~~with the~~ the exchange rates were such that they were able to

                        in addition to Kathy
hire both a cook and a maid, ~~The particular joy of~~ "I never have had such

freedom before," Ada wrote Maurice Firuski in Cambridge. "The particular

joy of ~~medin~~ mid mending Archie's socks is taken from me by Marie who

doesn't fancy seeing Madame do anything useful." Mornings, Ada dropped

Kenny off at school on her way to her studio, ~~where Poyla Frijeh~~ while

Archie went upstairs to ~~a tea~~ the bonne's room ~~under the skylight and~~
                                          under a leaky skylight
~~a leaky skylight~~ and tried to write poems‸ At noon he picked Kenny up
Archie
from school, and ~~lunches were~~ brought him home. ~~Then he wen At lunc~~,
                                                           at lunch,
~~he~~ tried ~~not to drink wine , in order to keep his mind clear tried~~ (without

much success) not to drink ~~the~~ wine‸ in order to keep his mind clear for the
                  ~~at the Bibliotech~~ at the Bibliothèque Nationale "where you can't
~~reading~~ afternoon's reading. ~~Once a week, Ada and Archie met for a~~
possibly find the book you want and they have no artificial lighting."
~~long lunch together Knowingly~~ Twice a week he went to a gym to pull weights
"‸and be sprayed by a fire hose afterwards.X Once a week, he and Ada met for
                                       Aux   a bourgeois restaurant
a long lunch at ~~a restaurant called the~~ Petits Riches‸ where the butter and the

veal were excellent and they did not ~~worry about t~~ stint themselves on the wine.
                                                                     They
~~Both of them took long walks to explore the   And t They took also   took long~~
   Occasionally there would be a dinner party, usually involving the Myerses‸, *but*
~~walks along the Seine.~~ Most evenings, they dined ~~at home and~~ quietly at home.
Weekends, they took long walks along the Seiner
"Think of us as most dreadfully happy," Ada wrote Firuski.
            ~~whoxx~~ a lifelong worrier, worried about)
   Archie ~~naturally had some worries about worries, for he was a natural~~
~~worrier. He worried about~~ expenses, but concluded that as long as the franc

stayed down ~~he was all right.~~   they would be all right. When the weather turned
                                          worked
cold, he found out why so many artists ~~wrote   write~~ in cafes: to keep warm.

The gray Paris winter, relieved by "about ~~two some   a~~ two" sunsets a month,

Not everything was perfect, of course.

Pages from the revised typescript for "Fever of Greatness," a chapter in Archibald MacLeish: An American Life, scheduled for publication in May 1992

fever 6

~~invited ill spirits~~ tended to depress him. ~~Above all, he could not~~ **Darkest** ~~Worst~~ of all,
were the days
~~there were times~~ when he doubted himself. To avoid these, ~~he stuck to his~~
                                      schedule. XXXXXXXXXXXXXXXXX
~~routine almost~~ co compulsively stuck to his ~~routine.~~ "He must learn to waste
               observed,
time, mustn't he?" Ada ~~Time," time," Ada insisted, commented~~ but that was
a lesson ~~Archie could never~~ beyond Archie's capacity, ~~to learn~~ ~~luckily~~ **The vagabonding** Phelps
                             in the late fall,
Putnam turned up in ~~Paris in the late fall,~~ Paris, and managed to ~~tear him loose~~
~~from his carefully planned routine~~ ~~occasionally to~~ tear him loose from his
             It was not easy,   **for Archie would not**
carefully planned ~~routein~~ routine now and then. ~~But~~ letting time slip through
his hands ~~was never something Archie could do~~ without discomfort.

   ~~Christmas Day dawned bright and sunny~~

¶For their first Christmas abroad, the weather was bright and sunny. Archie
         early
and Ada went to ~~high~~ mass at Notre Dame, sitting high up **in** the gallery opposite
the rose window and listening to the full choir of male voices ring through
    ~~Then they walked for miles along the quays, marvelling at their good fortune.~~
the grey stone arches. ~~Then they walked~~ At home there was a Christmas tree,
and Kenny sang ~~carols in perfect French, but without French accent~~ French
carols ~~in with a perfect accent, but~~   "with a perfect accent and not one idea
    They were touched when a ~~cable~~ cable arrived from Amy Lowell. " I should have
what it was all about." ~~After dinner, Amy Lowell sent a wire, and~~ After dinner,
sent her some cigars," Ada thought.
Archie and Ada walked for miles along the quays, marveling at their good fortune.

But he could not help thinking of his sister Ishbel, who ~~was spending~~ he knew
                    alone and far from home,
was spending Christmas day in a sanitarium ~~in~~ Colorado. ~~Short~~ Earlier that
fall, she ~~had found~~ was found to have tuberculosis, and ~~was~~ sent to ~~a~~ Colorado
                (In the end, she spent nearly three years
Springs ~~sanitarium~~ to aid her recovery. ~~In the end, she Ishbel spent nearly~~
there)
~~three years in the sanitarium before making~~ You couldn't be cheerful on Christmas
day in a sanitarium, could you?

flect similar divisions within the man. Because Donaldson is as discerning a critic as he is a biographer, one wishes that *John Cheever* included more critical analysis than it does. What Donaldson does provide in abundance are facts and insights, including the sources for some of the most bizarre characters and situations in Cheever's fiction. Donaldson also provides an excellent discussion of the composition history of Cheever's third novel, *Bullet Park* (1969).

Readers of Donaldson's first three biographies will not be surprised by his emphasis on Cheever's early years, particularly the influence of Cheever's weak, unsuccessful father, whose part he often took, and the domineering mother he came to despise. Together they left their son "the most unfortunate legacy of all: the conviction that he was not loved." Cheever's insecurity was not only emotional but financial and professional as well. He felt like an outsider in the suburbia he both extolled and criticized, and also in the literary world, where the short stories he wrote in order to bring in quick money led reviewers to label him a minor talent. Donaldson's analytical summaries of the critical response to Cheever's fiction and of their effect on an already insecure writer help put the critical and commercial success of *The Stories of John Cheever* (1978) in perspective.

Emotional insecurity led Cheever to attach himself to several surrogate parents: his older brother Fred; literary patron Hazel Hawthorne; Yaddo Artists Colony director Elizabeth Ames (to whom Cheever was fiercely loyal); his first editor, Malcolm Cowley; and Cheever's wife, Mary, who in his final illness became in fact what she had figuratively been all along, the mother Cheever both loathed and longed to love. There were numerous affairs with lovers both male and female, all of which Donaldson recounts in the most straightforward, uncensorious manner possible: "He stayed in the closet and made his confessions in the fiction, where most readers chose to ignore them," not, however, without a good deal of help from Cheever, who used comic hyperbole to defuse the potential explosiveness of his subject.

Donaldson's handling of Cheever's life through the early 1970s is thorough and persua-

sive. His telling of the last ten years is harrowing at first but then, despite the alcoholism, the cancer, and finally the death, triumphant as well. As always, much of Donaldson's effectiveness derives from the way he uses seemingly minor matters to make a larger point: for example, Cheever, on a week-long visit to Stanford with his son Fred, a prospective freshman, suddenly found himself overshadowed by the arrival of Saul Bellow, whose wife was being recruited by the university's mathematics department. Judicious use of largely unknown facts such as this evoke the inner Cheever, especially the inner anguish he continued to experience throughout his life. All the comic rebuffs suffered by the characters in his stories and novels take on an added significance and intensity in the light of such revelations. The art and the life serve to illuminate one another, as they did in *Poet in America*, *By Force of Will*, and *Fool for Love*, yielding a different and certainly darker portrait of the artist "bitched" by middle-class America.

The air of intimacy and immediacy surrounding *John Cheever: A Biography* derives not only from the sympathetic understanding with which Donaldson approaches his subjects but also from the cooperation he received from Mary Cheever. She was, however, also responsible for the year-long delay in publication, as Donaldson and Random House struggled with her sudden decision not to grant them permission to quote from her husband's works. It was a labor made all the more difficult as a result of a U.S. Circuit Court of Appeal ruling in favor of author J. D. Salinger and against Salinger's biographer, Ian Hamilton, which made it impossible even to paraphrase unpublished writings without infringing on the owner's copyright—a decision that would seem to make it possible for authors and literary executors to influence what biographers and others write. Although the Salinger decision may have a potentially chilling effect on literary biographers, the difficulties have not kept Donaldson from beginning his next biography, his fifth, this time of the "poet-patriot" Archibald MacLeish.

John William Halperin

(15 September 1941 -   )

Anne-Marie Foley
University of Missouri

BOOKS: *The Language of Meditation: Four Studies in Nineteenth-Century Fiction* (Ilfracombe, U.K.: Stockwell, 1973);

Egoism and Self-Discovery in the Victorian Novel: Studies in the Ordeal of Knowledge in the Nineteenth Century (New York: Franklin, 1974);

Plots and Characters in the Fiction of Jane Austen, the Brontës, and George Eliot, by Halperin and Janet Kunert (Hamden, Conn.: Archon / Folkstone, U.K.: Dawson, 1976);

Trollope and Politics: A Study of the Pallisers and Others (London: Macmillan, 1977; New York: Barnes & Noble, 1977);

Gissing: A Life in Books (Oxford & New York: Oxford University Press, 1982);

C. P. Snow: An Oral Biography (Brighton, Sussex, U.K.: Harvester, 1983; New York: St. Martin's Press, 1983); index by Paul W. Boytinck (Lewisburg, Pa.: Boytinck, 1985);

The Life of Jane Austen (Baltimore: Johns Hopkins University Press, 1984; Brighton, Sussex, U.K.: Harvester, 1984);

Jane Austen's Lovers and Other Studies in Fiction and History from Austen to le Carré (New York: St. Martin's Press, 1988);

Novelists in Their Youth (New York: St. Martin's Press, 1990).

OTHER: Henry James, *The Golden Bowl*, edited by Halperin (New York: Meridian/Popular Library, 1972);

The Theory of the Novel: New Essays, edited by Halperin (Oxford & New York: Oxford University Press, 1974);

Jane Austen: Bicentenary Essays, edited by Halperin (Cambridge: Cambridge University Press, 1975);

George Gissing, *Denzil Quarrier*, edited, with an introduction and notes, by Halperin (Hassocks, U.K.: Harvester, 1979);

Anthony Trollope, *Lord Palmerston*, edited by Halperin (New York: Arno, 1981);

Trollope, *Sir Harry Hotspur of Humblethwaite*, edited by Halperin (New York: Arno, 1981);

Trollope Centenary Essays, edited by Halperin (London: Macmillan, 1982; New York: St. Martin's Press, 1982);

George Meredith, *The Ordeal of Richard Feverel*, edited by Halperin (Oxford & New York: Oxford University Press, 1984);

Trollope, *Dr. Wortle's School*, edited by Halperin (Oxford & New York: Oxford University Press, 1984);

Gissing, *The Emancipated*, edited by Halperin (London: Hogarth, 1985);

Gissing, *Will Warburton*, edited by Halperin (London: Hogarth, 1985);

Trollope, *The Belton Estate*, edited by Halperin (Oxford & New York: Oxford University Press, 1986);

Trollope, *The American Senator*, edited by Halperin (Oxford & New York: Oxford University Press, 1986);

Gissing, *In the Year of Jubilee*, edited by Halperin (London: Hogarth, 1987).

In his introduction to *Novelists in Their Youth* (1990) John William Halperin defends the importance of biography in an age when critical appraisal often turns away from social, historical, and biographical evidence toward such approaches as deconstructionism: "We live in the midst of our own historical moment, of course; our values, our thoughts, our prejudices, our perceptions, are products of that historical moment and of the accumulated wisdom of social history, as inevitably as they are products of our unique psyche. Whatever a person may choose to do, two of the reasons for that choice must always be found in the personality and in the moment." Halperin asserts that the role of the author must never be forgotten: "All fiction emerges from the consciousness of the writer and is therefore shaped in the way that consciousness perceives." What the author perceives and the way in which he arranges it to create the work of art tell much about his personality and his moment in history. Without an understanding of these factors, accord-

John Halperin circa 1985 (Vanderbilt University, Office of News and Public Affairs)

ing to Halperin, one cannot fully understand the work.

Halperin was born in Chicago on 15 September 1941 to S. William Halperin, a historian, and Elaine Philipsborn Halperin, a translator. He received his A.B. from Bowdoin College in 1963; his M.A. from the University of New Hampshire in 1966; and another M.A. in 1968 and a Ph.D. in 1969 from Johns Hopkins University. In 1963 he had worked as a reporter for the *Wall Street Journal* and in late 1963 and 1964 as an editor for the Associated Press. Halperin became assistant professor of English, director of summer school, and assistant to the academic vice-president of the State University of New York at Stony Brook in 1969; in 1972 he became associate professor of English and director of graduate studies at the University of Southern California.

In his first two books, *The Language of Medita-*

tion: Four Studies in Nineteenth-Century Fiction (1973) and *Egoism and Self-Discovery in the Victorian Novel: Studies in the Ordeal of Knowledge in the Nineteenth Century* (1974), Halperin traces different aspects of selected nineteenth-century fictional heroes' quests for self-knowledge. *The Language of Meditation* examines meditative moments in seven novels by Jane Austen, George Eliot, George Meredith, and Henry James. The study reveals the similarities in the authors' expressions of instants of self-awareness in their protagonists. By examining the language, imagery, and syntax of the meditative passages, Halperin seeks to show "what the analysis of such a passage may tell the reader about the novel . . . and about the author who wrote it." The similarities Halperin finds among Austen, Eliot, Meredith, and James in their fictional descriptions of the meditative moment reveal "the image of the human mental processes" at work. Ira Bruce Nadel wrote in a *Nineteenth Century Fiction* review (1976) that Halperin's first work is of particular value in its "close attention to imagery as it appears in the excerpted passages, the identification of narrative voice, and the description of 'vision' as a persistent metaphor in all the selections."

Egoism and Self-Discovery in the Victorian Novel presents insights, as Halperin says in his introduction, into the "moral and psychological expansion of protagonists who begin in self-absorption and move, through the course of a tortuous ordeal of education, to more complete self-knowledge." Halperin's second book takes up where *The Language of Meditation* leaves off, further examining moments of self-revelation in the nineteenth-century novel, considering characters from Austen, William Makepeace Thackeray, Charlotte Brontë, Anthony Trollope, Charles Dickens, Eliot, Meredith, James, and Thomas Hardy, and placing into high relief what the author demonstrates as a central concern in Victorian fiction, the development of selflessness and self-knowledge, often through suffering.

Jane Austen: Bicentenary Essays (1975), edited by Halperin, was a part of the commemoration of the two hundredth anniversary of Austen's birth in 1775, presenting new articles "written especially for the occasion by some of the most distinguished scholars and critics" in the field of Austen studies, including Robert B. Heilman, Karl Kroeber, Barbara Hardy, A. Walton Litz, Marvin Mudrick, and Alistair M. Duckworth. Covering "many twentieth-century approaches to Jane Austen and characteristic areas of critical concern," the essays are divided into three categories, including backgrounds, close analyses of the novels themselves, and comments on Austen in reference to her fiction. For the collection, Halperin supplied an introduction that traces the "nineteenth-century context out of which modern and contemporary criticism have grown."

In 1976 Halperin became an honorary fellow at Wolfson College, Oxford. His *Trollope and Politics: A Study of the Pallisers and Others*, published in 1977, describes the political novels of Trollope, and what they tell "about the politics of the time, the role of individuals in politics and of politics in the lives of individuals, and the ways in which political systems interact and interdepend. They also tell us a good deal, should we care to know it, about Anthony Trollope himself—his political ideas, prejudices, aversions—and an under-

standing of these in turn helps to illuminate some previously dark corners of the novelist's mind, art, and life." To this end, Halperin includes discussions of each of the six Palliser novels and illuminates the historical events and characters that inform these works. Janet Egleson Dunleavy thought that the study would "fascinate nonprofessional readers of Trollope; no serious student of Victorian literature can afford to be without it. Carefully researched, painstakingly documented, clearly organized, and exceptionally well written, it synthesizes existing scholarship on the subject and contributes persuasive new arguments to a continuing discussion" (*Studies in the Novel*, Summer 1978).

To commemorate the centennial of Trollope's death, Halperin collected essays considering many aspects of a newly emerging critical interest in this important Victorian novelist. *Trollope Centenary Essays* (1982) includes an introduction by Halperin, in which he discusses Trollope's eminence among the Victorian reading public, his fall from popularity, and the recent resurgence of critical interest in his life and works.

Halperin's first full-length biographical study, *Gissing: A Life in Books* (1982), is a fresh appraisal of one of late-Victorian England's premier, though often underappreciated, novelists. Halperin asserts that "More than any other body of work with which I am familiar, Gissing demands of the reader an awareness of biographical matters for fullest understanding." Halperin's biographical method takes into account the obscurity and inaccessibility of many of Gissing's works, tracing the history of his publications along with the events of his life. The study includes descriptions and critical readings of Gissing's fiction, in the light of biographical evidence, giving the reader an overall sense of the progress of Gissing's career and artistic accomplishments.

Halperin organizes his approach around Gissing's most engrossing and central themes in both his life and works: sex, money, and class—all three of which dovetail into a single, encompassing examination of the theme of marriage. For Gissing the subject of marriage brought with it most of the creative considerations in his fiction: the exile theme, in which individuals of intellect, education, and aspirations are unable to become part of their natural intellectual class because of poverty; exogamy (marriage outside one's class); and the "pulverizing effects of poverty and the money-race on the sentient spirit . . .

Dust jacket for the biography in which Halperin dispels some of the myths about Austen that were created by her family after her death

the ways in which human feelings can be degraded by economic pressures." Halperin continues: "The things that Gissing wrote about both obsessed him and happened to him. Written directly from life, his novels are almost without exception parts of a spiritual autobiography, extracts from the story of his own existence."

Halperin draws on unpublished letters, the author's diaries, and other private papers to provide extensive evidence of the autobiographical nature of the novels. He discusses the ways in which Gissing "acted out in life things he wrote about first, and provided a bizarre example of how art and life can interact and each have its impact upon the other."

Gissing: A Life in Books traces his academic progress as a young man until the disgrace that ended his university studies and paved the way to both his career in fiction and his later personal dif-

ficulties. Gissing was caught stealing from his classmates at Owens College in order to support the alcoholic habit of his future wife, a prostitute named Nell Harrison. He was expelled from school and lost his scholarship to the University of London and all his hopes for an academic career: "This disaster—which led to others in Gissing's life, though none quite like this—deprived the world of a brilliant classical linguist, but it just as surely guaranteed, by forcing him to begin earning a living almost immediately, that a significant contribution to English fiction would be made instead. Literature has prospered rather than suffered from this arrangement."

Halperin details the series of later financial and marital disasters that became the primary sources for Gissing's works, and he concludes that "Gissing's books are about aspects of himself and his own experience, that we cannot study them without studying *him*, and that . . . the gloomier the ironies of his life made him the better his writing was likely to be. Gissing himself paired 'art' and 'misery.' So the personality of Gissing is dramatized in his fiction." Charles J. Burkhart, in a 1983 review of the biography for *English Literature in Transition*, writes: "It is as man and author that Halperin approaches Gissing; his subtitle, *A Life in Books*, means what it says, that the best guide to Gissing's life is his books. . . . Halperin's research is supremely meticulous and methodical; every statement is made with care."

Halperin became the Centennial Professor of English at Vanderbilt University in 1983. In that same year, he again turned his talents to biography. *C. P. Snow: An Oral Biography* presents the career, personality, and literary techniques of Snow, using a transcription of tape-recorded interviews with him that Halperin began in March 1978. The interviews with Snow fill eleven ninety-minute cassettes. The final interview took place on 13 June 1980, eighteen days before Snow's death. Though Halperin rearranged the order of the interviews somewhat to achieve overall coherence, he says that "the transcript published . . . is in fact very close indeed to what is on the tapes now in the Huntington Library."

In his interviews, Halperin was able to cover all sixteen of Snow's published novels, though the author's nonfiction is not as well represented. Many of the interviews focus on the relation between Snow's life and his art. Halperin groups the transcribed interviews around the titles of five of Snow's novels: *Time of Hope* (1949), *The Search* (1934; revised, 1958), *The Light and the Dark* (1947), *Corridors of Power* (1963), and *Last Things* (1970)—each of which, as the interviews reveal, is autobiographical. Snow admits that his protagonist in these novels, Lewis Eliot, is fashioned after himself. *Time of Hope* describes Eliot's early years; *The Search* fictionalizes Snow's decision to become a writer. *The Light and the Dark* depicts the war years, and *Corridors of Power* shows the political struggles brought about by the problem of nuclear armaments. In *Last Things* Eliot suffers cardiac arrest during surgery, much like Snow himself. Halperin provides a threefold portrait for his readers: a biography of Snow, a detailed look at the evolution of his fiction, and an account of a half century of British history. As Halperin says, "The novels together cover more than fifty years of British history; their relevance lies not only in the chronicle they give of a distinguished man's life, but in the cultural and intellec-

tual history they provide of a part of the twentieth century. For many of these problems, issues, and quandaries Lewis Eliot faces are those of the sentient modern man; the parade of them in the novels traces his evolution from a relatively hopeful creature to an increasingly pessimistic one. All of this is in the books."

Halperin's next major project, *The Life of Jane Austen* (1984), is arguably his most significant work, a detailed and exhaustive analysis of the author's life, attempting to fill in many of the gaps left by other Austen biographies. Portraying Austen has always been a great difficulty; many of her letters, especially those that shed the most light on her personal life, were destroyed by her sister Cassandra after Jane's death. The Austen family conspired to create a persona of the author that, though pleasant and practically angelic, was obviously an inaccurate account of her personality and her relationship with those she knew closely. Halperin's account dispels many of the family-created Austen myths and penetrates into the evidence of her life, uncovering an individual who was brilliant but often difficult.

Like Halperin's other biographical works, his life of Austen attempts to demonstrate the essential interrelatedness of life and art, and by doing so it reveals much about both. Halperin writes: "My interest here, as elsewhere, is in the relation between the life of the artist and the work produced rather than in either by itself. . . . I perhaps read the works more 'biographically' than my predecessors; this has been intentional." By approaching the fiction in this way, Halperin is able to reconstruct Austen's character and life; he solves some of the mysteries surrounding her suitors, disappointments, and tragedies. To a great extent he demystifies Austen, revealing the negative along with the positive elements of her character.

Halperin draws more extensively on Austen's letters than any previous biographer, uncovering evidence of personal events, and of her likes and dislikes, from seemingly trivial correspondence. He often paraphrases letters, adding commentary and constructing a believable portrait. Halperin deftly moves from fiction to correspondence and other evidence, allowing his biographical readings of her texts to modulate and add to the compilation of data, which builds, better than any other biography, a sense of Austen's personality.

The Life of Jane Austen is organized around her fictional career, with sections of the biography dedicated to juvenilia; to the first "trilogy,"

Dust jacket for the book in which Halperin examines the early lives of six writers, who shared a "community of interests as well as a chronological period," in order to demonstrate the connection of "literature and the historical, cultural, and biographical moments in which it is composed"

which includes *Sense and Sensibility* (1811), *Pride and Prejudice* (1813), and *Northanger Abbey* (1818); to the years in which, because of personal tragedy, Austen produced nothing; and to the second "trilogy," comprising *Mansfield Park* (1814), *Emma* (1816), and *Persuasion* (1818). A central biographical theme is that, even as an adolescent, Austen showed a critical detachment from the world, often tending toward mockery and irony in her fiction, letters, and relationships with others. This tendency was exacerbated by what became her marginal status in the world: she was an unmarried woman without establishment and with scant financial means. Her place as, in many ways, an outsider in society allowed her the distance to penetrate and understand many evils and insensitivities.

In a review of the Austen biography, Catherine S. Green wrote: "This first full-scale critical biography since Elizabeth Jenkins' of 1938 is an engaging redaction of the biographical materials, limitations, and unresolved questions that have characterized all non-familial biographies of Austen, critical or otherwise. Like his predecessors

(Elizabeth Jenkins, Lord David Cecil, and Joan Rees), Halperin deplores the bowdlerization of the author's life, a practice which began when sister Cassandra scissored out objectionable parts of the letters and persisted with later family members who labelled the life uneventful" (*Southern Humanities Review*, Summer 1985).

In 1988 Halperin published a collection of fourteen of his essays—with such diverse subjects as Austen, Barbara Pym, and John le Carré—entitled *Jane Austen's Lovers and Other Studies in Fiction and History from Austen to le Carré*. The collection reflects Halperin's widespread interests and critical methodologies. The title piece, "Jane Austen's Lovers," examines again the contradiction between the smooth picture that Austen's relatives tried to paint of her, and the stuff of which her novels were made. Halperin goes on to discuss the different romantic interests in Austen's life, both harmless flirtations and bitter disappointments.

In 1988 and 1989, supported by a second grant from the John Simon Guggenheim Memorial Foundation (he had held one for 1978-1979),

Halperin wrote a collection of six biographical essays entitled *Novelists in Their Youth*, in which he demonstrates the connection between "literature and the historical, cultural, and biographical moments in which it is composed." Halperin included pieces on Henry James, Thomas Hardy, George Gissing, Joseph Conrad, Edith Wharton, and Somerset Maugham because they shared a "community of interests as well as a chronological period." They all knew each other and each other's works. They also shared, Halperin asserts, a feeling of being an anomaly, of being marginal or isolated in society: "I have tried to link that psychic wound, whatever its nature, to creative power [to show] that the wound that never heals both allows and explains . . . the creative process."

As Halperin says, "Give me the first twenty or thirty years of an author's life, and I think I can explain, through examination of them and of various influences (historical, psychological, geographical, familial, social, or whatever) exerted upon them, some of the reasons why the texts produced during the author's maturity came into being. Familiarity with an artist's formative years can help us to interpret and understand what he produces throughout his career." Halperin traces Hardy's concerns with class to his discomfort at his humble beginnings, and he theorizes that James's unsettling youth caused him to live and express himself through his fiction: "Throughout his early years, and indeed well beyond them, James found it difficult to decide—culturally, philosophically, geographically, and sexually—what he was. Many of these questions he never resolved. His mind was nourished on antithesis: past and present, experience and innocence, power and passiveness, masculine and feminine, Europe and America, tradition and experimentation. Whenever he managed, temporarily at least, to solve some of his dilemmas, this was accomplished by his living vicariously—in the lives of others, either in real life or in his fiction."

Halperin's interpretations of his biographical data are provocative, shedding new light on the artistry of his subjects. An anonymous reviewer for the *Economist* wrote, "familiar territory is made refreshingly new by the astuteness of many of Mr. Halperin's perceptions; an agreeably readable style is enhanced by his flair as a raconteur and quoter of comic lines" (14 April 1990).

Throughout his career Halperin has sought to illuminate the historical, social, and biographical factors that help create the work of art. As Halperin writes in *Novelists in Their Youth*, "Insofar as the origins of art may be understood, biography may help us to understand them. The artist produces what he produces for the liberation of his soul, as Maugham puts it in *Ten Novels and Their Authors*. It is his nature to create, and it is the role of biography to illuminate his nature and thus that which is created."

Walter Harding

(20 April 1917 -   )

Steven Serafin
Hunter College of the City University of New York

BOOKS: *A Centennial Check-List of the Editions of Henry David Thoreau's Walden* (Charlottesville: University of Virginia Press, 1954);

Thoreau's Library (Charlottesville: University of Virginia Press, 1957);

A Thoreau Handbook (New York: New York University Press, 1959);

A Thoreau Profile, by Harding and Milton Meltzer (New York: Crowell, 1962);

Henry David Thoreau's Walden and Civil Disobedience, a Study Guide (Bound Brook, N.J.: Shelley, 1962);

The Days of Henry Thoreau (New York: Knopf, 1965; enlarged edition, New York: Dover, 1982);

Emerson's Library (Charlottesville: University Press of Virginia, 1967);

Theo Brown and Henry Thoreau (Rochester, N.Y.: Gaudeamus, 1968);

A Thoreau Iconography, by Harding and Thomas Blanding (Geneseo, N.Y.: Thoreau Society, 1980);

The New Thoreau Handbook, by Harding and Michael Meyer (New York & London: New York University Press, 1980).

OTHER: *Thoreau Society Bulletin,* edited by Harding (Geneseo, N.Y., October 1941-   );

Roland Wells Robbins, *Discovery at Walden,* introduction by Harding (Stoneham, Mass.: Barnstead, 1947);

Charles Mayo Ellis, *An Essay on Transcendentalism,* edited, with an introduction, by Harding (Gainesville, Fla.: Scholars' Facsimiles & Reprints, 1954);

Thoreau: A Century of Criticism, edited, with a preface, by Harding (Dallas: Southern Methodist University Press, 1954);

The Correspondence of Henry David Thoreau, edited by Harding and Carl Bode (New York: New York University Press, 1958);

Amos Bronson Alcott, *Essays on Education, 1830-1862,* edited, with an introduction, by Har-

ding (Gainesville, Fla.: Scholars' Facsimiles & Reprints, 1960);

"Hound, Bay Horse, and Turtledove," in *Literary Symbolism,* edited by Maurie Beebe (San Francisco: Wadsworth, 1960), pp. 59-62;

Thoreau: Man of Concord, edited by Harding (New York: Holt, Rinehart & Winston, 1960); revised and enlarged as *Thoreau As Seen by His Contemporaries* (New York: Dover, 1990);

Thoreau's Minnesota Journey: Two Documents, edited by Harding (Geneseo, N.Y.: Thoreau Society, 1962);

"Five Ways of Looking at *Walden*," in *Thoreau in Our Season,* edited by John H. Hicks (Amherst: University of Massachusetts Press, 1962), pp. 44-57; reprinted in *Critical Essays on Henry David Thoreau's Walden,* edited by Joel Myerson (Boston: G. K. Hall, 1988), pp. 85-96;

Henry David Thoreau, *The Variorum Walden,* annotated, with introduction and notes, by Harding (New York: Twayne, 1962);

Thoreau, *A Week on the Concord and Merrimack Rivers,* edited, with an introduction, by Harding (New York: Holt, Rinehart & Winston, 1963);

Thoreau, *A Yankee in Canada: Anti-Slavery and Reform Papers,* edited, with an introduction, by Harding (Montreal: Harvest House, 1963; New York: Haskell House, 1968);

Thoreau's Journals, edited by Harding (New York: Dover, 1963);

The Thoreau Centennial, edited, with an introduction, by Harding (Albany: State University of New York Press, 1964);

Sophia Thoreau's Scrapbook: From the Collection of George L. Davenport, Jr., edited by Harding (Geneseo, N.Y.: Thoreau Society, 1964);

"Recent Scholarship on Emerson and Thoreau," in *The Teacher and American Literature,* edited by Lewis Leary (Champaign, Ill.: National Council of Teachers of English, 1965), pp. 81-88;

Walter Harding

The Collected Poems of William Ellery Channing, the Younger: 1817-1901, edited, with an introduction, by Harding (Gainesville, Fla.: Scholars' Facsimiles & Reprints, 1967);

Thoreau, *The Variorum Civil Disobedience,* annotated, with an introduction, by Harding (New York: Twayne, 1967);

Thoreau's Turtle Nest, edited, with a preface, by Harding (Worcester, Mass.: St. Onge, 1967);

Thoreau, *The Variorum Walden and The Variorum Civil Disobedience,* edited by Harding (New York: Washington Square Press, 1968);

"Thoreau's Fame Abroad," in *The Recognition of Henry David Thoreau,* edited by Wendell Glick (Ann Arbor: University of Michigan Press, 1969), pp. 315-323;

"Henry David Thoreau: *Walden: or, Life in the Woods,*" in *Landmarks of American Writing,* edited by Hennig Cohen (New York: Basic Books, 1969), pp. 134-143;

Henry David Thoreau: A Profile, edited, with an in-

troduction, by Harding (New York: Hill & Wang, 1971);

A Bibliography of the Thoreau Society Bulletin Bibliographies, 1941-1969, edited, with an introduction, by Harding, compiled by Jean Cameron Advena (Troy, N.Y.: Whitston, 1971);

Eugene F. Timpe, ed., *Thoreau Abroad,* foreword by Harding (Hamden, Conn.: Archon, 1971);

Henry David Thoreau: Studies and Commentaries, edited by Harding, George Brenner, and Paul A. Doyle, with a foreword by Harding (Rutherford, N.J.: Fairleigh Dickinson University Press, 1972);

The Selected Works of Thoreau, edited, with an introduction, by Harding (Boston: Houghton Mifflin, 1975);

"In Wildness Is the Preservation of the World," in *Population and the Environmental Crisis,* edited by Stephen White (Johnson City: East

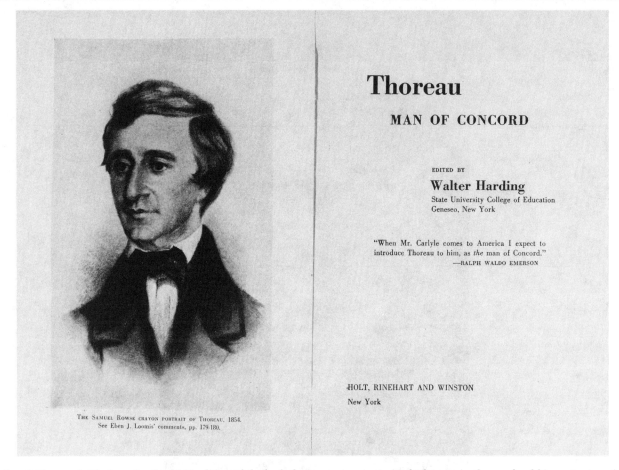

THE SAMUEL ROWSE CRAYON PORTRAIT OF THOREAU, 1854.
See Eben J. Loomis' comments, pp. 179-180.

Thoreau

MAN OF CONCORD

EDITED BY

Walter Harding
State University College of Education
Geneseo, New York

"When Mr. Carlyle comes to America I expect to
introduce Thoreau to him, as *the* man of Concord."
—RALPH WALDO EMERSON

HOLT, RINEHART AND WINSTON
New York

*Frontispiece and title page for the 1960 edition of the book that presents a portrait of Thoreau in the words of his contemporaries
and near contemporaries*

Tennessee State University Press, 1975), pp. 92-104;

"Henry David Thoreau," in *The American Renaissance in New England,* edited by Joel Myerson, *Dictionary of Literary Biography,* volume 1 (Detroit: Gale Research, 1978), pp. 170-182;

Christopher Childs, ed., *Clear Sky, Pure Light,* introduction by Harding (Lincoln, Mass.: Penmaen, 1978);

Thoreau, *In the Woods and Fields of Concord,* edited, with an introduction, by Harding (Salt Lake City: Smith, 1982);

"Thoreau and Children," in *Thoreau Among Others,* edited by Rita K. Gollin and James B. Scholes (Geneseo, N.Y.: State University College, 1983), pp. 86-101;

"Thoreau and Eros," in *Thoreau's Psychology,* edited by Raymond D. Gozzi (Lanham, Md.: University Press of America, 1983), pp. 145-159;

"A New Checklist of Books in Thoreau's Li-

brary," in *Studies in the American Renaissance: 1983,* edited by Myerson (Boston: G. K. Hall, 1983), pp. 151-186;

The Journals of Henry David Thoreau, edited by Harding (Salt Lake City: Smith, 1984).

SELECTED PERIODICAL PUBLICATIONS—
UNCOLLECTED: "A Bibliography of Thoreau in Poetry, Fiction, and Drama," *Bulletin of Bibliography,* 18 (May-August 1943): 15-18;

"The Significance of Thoreau's *Walden,*" *Humanist,* 5 (August 1945): 115-121;

"Thoreau's Feminine Foe," *PMLA,* 69 (March 1954): 110-116;

"The Early Printing Records of Thoreau's Books," *American Transcendental Quarterly,* 11 (1971): 44-60;

"Thoreau in Jail," *American Heritage,* 26 (August 1975): 36-37;

"*Walden*'s Man of Science," *Virginia Quarterly Review,* 57 (Winter 1981): 45-61.

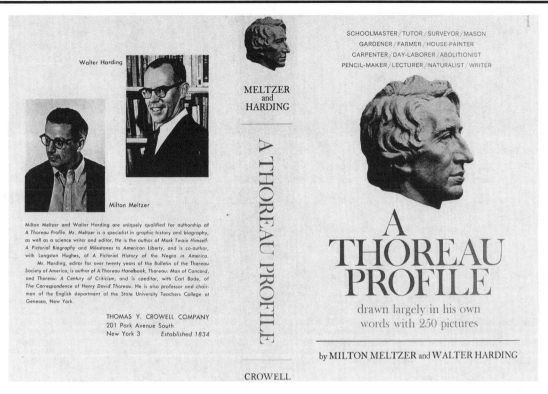

Dust jacket for Meltzer and Harding's attempt to assemble a portrait of Thoreau from "a steady alternation of extracts"
from his writings

"He is a singular character—a young man with much of wild original nature still remaining in him; and so far as he is sophisticated, it is in a way and method of his own. He is as ugly as sin, long-nosed, queer-mouthed, and with uncouth and somewhat rustic, although courteous manners, corresponding very well with such an exterior"—so Nathaniel Hawthorne described Henry David Thoreau after their first meeting, an inauspicious beginning to their friendship and a subtle understatement of Thoreau's stoic image. Generally unrecognized by his contemporaries and often dismissed as "little more than a second-rate imitator" of the more celebrated Ralph Waldo Emerson, Thoreau emerged during the twentieth century to secure a permanent position in American literature as well as modern thought. His influence has been universally acknowledged and his message embraced by young and old alike, by Mahatma Gandhi and Martin Luther King, Jr., Frank Lloyd Wright, N. C. Wyeth, Charles Ives, and writers as disparate as Robert Frost, Sinclair Lewis, and Henry Miller. Yet, as observed by literary critic Carl Bode in the *New York Times Book Review*, it would be hard to find "a more devoted dis-

ciple of Henry Thoreau than Walter Harding" (26 December 1965).

Known as a preeminent Thoreau scholar, Harding has devoted much of his life and academic career to the study of the man he has deemed "one of the giants in the American pantheon." As a founder and lifelong member of the Thoreau Society, Harding has been instrumental in helping to shape and solidify Thoreau's literary reputation and to ensure the accuracy and validity of Thoreau's biography and works. His personal Thoreau collection numbers over thirteen thousand items, including a copy of nearly every edition of each of Thoreau's works, both in English and foreign languages, every known book about Thoreau, and more than eight hundred reviews and critical articles on *Walden*. Throughout his long and distinguished career, Harding has written extensively on Thoreau: numerous articles, monographs, annotated editions, and critical studies. Yet for many readers his most important contribution to Thoreau scholarship has been his biography, *The Days of Henry Thoreau* (1965). The book was immediately recognized as the most thorough and complete portrait of Thoreau published to that time and remains one of the major biographical treatments of the author who, Har-

Henry David Thoreau was born in Concord, Massachusetts, on July 12, 1817,

in what he thought "the most estimable place in all the world, and in the very

nick of time, too."[1]   His birthplace was the easternmost upper chamber of a gray, un-

painted woods frame an old-fashioned, winding, almost deserted pathway

house on Virginia Road on the eastern outskirts of the village, a house that

his friend Ellery Channing has described as:

> a perfect piece of our New England style of building, with its
> gray, unpainted boards, its grassy, unfenced dooryard. The
> house is somewhat isolate and remote from the thoroughfares; the
> Virginia road, an old-fashioned, winding, at-length deserted
> pathway, the more smiling for its forked orchards, tumbling walls,
> and mossy banks. About the house are pleasant, sunny meadows,
> deep with their beds of peat, so cheering with its homely, heath-
> like fragrance; and in front runs a constant stream through the
> centre of that great tract sometimes called "Bedford levels."[2]

in the centre of a great tract known as Bedford level.

Concord, some twenty miles northwest of Boston, is located on the plains

where the Assabet and Sudbury Rivers join to form the Concord, one of the

major tributaries of the Merrimack. In 1817 it was a quiet little town of

two thousand, devoted chiefly to agriculture, although the fact that it then

shared with Cambridge the seat of Middlesex County meant that its village square

was often enlivened at the time of court sessions, as Edward Emerson has recalled:

and its stopping center was stopping place for and
stores and hotels were the stopping places for
farmers and travelers en route from Boston to
southern New Hampshire or northwestern Massachusetts

[Thoreau and Women]

Henry David Thoreau could hardly be called a ladies man. He was apparently twenty-one years old before he ever looked at a member of the opposite sex as such--and not many years later he stopped looking. But for the shy bachelor that most have supposed him, he managed to look fairly seriously at a surprisingly large number of young ladies in that short period of time.

The first and best known of these was Ellen Devereux Sewall, of Scituate, Massachusetts. She was the daughter of the Rev. Edmund Sewall, a Unitarian minister, and the former Caroline Ward. Her maternal grandmother, Mrs. Joseph Ward, and aunt, Prudence, boarded for a number of years with the Thoreaus in Concord. The Sewalls, the Wards, and the Thoreaus had long been friends. Indeed Aunt Maria Thoreau had been instrumental in first introducing Rev. Mr. Sewall to Caroline Ward. And the three families had visited back and forth and corresponded at length for years,

Ellen, ### the oldest of the three Sewall children, was seventeen and her brothers Edmund and George eleven and five respectively when on July 20, 1839, she arrived in Concord for a two-week visit. Although Thoreau had unquestionably met her before-- he suddenly saw her as though for the first time. From all accounts she was a strikingly beautiful young lady--a beauty she was to retain all her life. And Thoreau, at twenty-two, was ripe for such an encounter. The previous winter he had had what was probably his first brief fling at love, the only record of which is a poem in his Journal which begins:

> We two that planets erst had been
>
> Are now a double star,

ding said, "speaks more to our day than to his own."

Walter Roy Harding was born on 20 April 1917 in Bridgewater, Massachusetts, to Roy V. and Mary Alice MacDonald Harding. He attended Bridgewater State Teachers College (now Bridgewater State College) and earned his B.S. in 1939. Pursuing a career in education, he was for the next two years principal of Center School in Northfield, Massachusetts. Then in the summer of 1941 Harding joined with other Thoreau enthusiasts on a "Thoreau Birthday Mecca" trip to Concord, Massachusetts, an event that resulted in the establishment of the Thoreau Society. Since that time Harding has been secretary and editor of its publications and was president from 1963 to 1964. As Harding became increasingly more involved in Thoreau studies, he entered graduate school at the University of North Carolina, earning his M.A. in 1947. On 7 June 1947 he married Marjorie Brook and in that same year became an instructor in English at Rutgers University, where in 1950 he received his Ph.D. His unpublished dissertation, "The Correspondence of Henry David Thoreau, 1836-1849," demonstrated his systematic and orderly approach to research and foreshadowed his comprehensive edition of Thoreau's correspondence (1958).

In 1951 Harding joined the faculty of the University of Virginia, where he was assistant professor for the next five years. During this time he became identified with an emerging school of Thoreau scholarship inspired by the renewed interest in Thoreau following World War II. In order to provide a realistic appraisal of Thoreau's influence, it became increasingly important to verify the accuracy of information concerning his life and works and to address the prevalence of misconception and distortion. This provided Harding both opportunity and direction. In addition to his contributions to the *Thoreau Society Bulletin*, he published his first full-length works in 1954: *A Centennial Check-List of the Editions of Henry David Thoreau's Walden*, an edition of Charles Mayo Ellis's *An Essay on Transcendentalism*, and, most important, Harding's edition of *Thoreau: A Century of Criticism*.

Harding left the University of Virginia in 1956 to accept a position as an associate professor at the State University of New York at Geneseo, where he has spent the remainder of his academic career. In 1959 he was promoted to professor and appointed chairman of the English department. Subsequently he served as chairman

of the humanities division from 1965 to 1966. Harding became university professor in 1966 and distinguished professor in 1973. In 1982 he was named distinguished professor emeritus. In addition Harding was an American Council of Learned Societies fellow (1962-1963) and a Special Program lecturer for the United States Department of State in Japan (1964) and in Iceland, Norway, Spain, France, and Germany (1967). He has also served as director of the Concord summer seminars and the National Endowment for the Humanities summer seminars on transcendentalism.

A major addition to Thoreau scholarship was the appearance in 1958 of Harding's *The Correspondence of Henry David Thoreau*, which he edited with Carl Bode. Although there were previous attempts to assemble Thoreau's letters, most notably Emerson's *Letters to Various Persons* (1865) and F. B. Sanborn's *Familiar Letters of Henry David Thoreau* (1894), Harding and Bode attempted for the first time, as they say in the introduction, "to print in one collection every available surviving letter written by and to Thoreau." An immense undertaking, aided in part by Thoreau's practice of writing on the reverse side of letters he received, the edition confirmed the opinion of the editors that relatively little in Thoreau's life was not reflected in his correspondence: "You can understand him better after looking at the letters he wrote and the letters he received. . . . Many of a person's letters are answers to those received; few are best understood purely by themselves. Almost equally important is the fact that the letters someone receives help to make clear the kind of world he is involved in." Harding and Bode emphasize that, when both sides of a correspondence are included, the result is "a kind of biography. It is a life in letters, not in any limited sense, but a life in letters nevertheless." At the time, Harding gave no impression he was contemplating a biography of Thoreau, yet his work with Bode seemed to emphasize the need for one.

The Correspondence of Henry David Thoreau was followed the next year by the publication of Harding's *A Thoreau Handbook*. Modeled in part on Gay Wilson Allen's *Walt Whitman Handbook* (1946), Harding's *Handbook* attempts to summarize the scholarship on Thoreau and in so doing demonstrates the breadth of Harding's command of his subject. It provided Harding the opportunity to present a brief version of Thoreau's life as well as an analysis of his development as a writer and thinker. Harding offers astute observations of the critical interpretations of Thoreau's

Harding with a bust of Thoreau (State University of New York at Geneseo)

work and presents an overview of all previous biographical treatments. Perhaps anticipating the dilemmas he would later confront in his own work, Harding devotes a section of the *Handbook* to a discussion of the problems facing biographers of Thoreau, such as the lack of primary source materials, the complexity of Thoreau's character, and the diversity of his interests: "Many of his biographers and critics have been satisfied to accept opinions he expressed in one period of his life as definitive of his ideas for his entire lifetime, forgetting that his viewpoints often developed and changed." In essence, Harding claims, "we do not yet have a really satisfactory biography of Thoreau," and he advocates "a detailed, factual account of his day-to-day life." He adds, not without some degree of irony, "There are several scholars in the field who have expressed interest or intentions of producing a new biography of Thoreau. Perhaps one of these will fulfill our need." In reponse to his own request, Harding offered *The Days of Henry Thoreau.*

Prior to the publication of his biography, Harding produced two works that supplemented its development: *Thoreau: Man of Concord* (1960) and *A Thoreau Profile* (1962), the latter co-authored by Milton Meltzer. Both books show extensive use of primary sources and present Thoreau in a realistic manner. *Thoreau: Man of Concord* is a collection of documents or "eyewitness reports" on Thoreau by his contemporaries and near contemporaries, notable for including unfavorable as well as favorable opinions. *A Thoreau Profile* provides a portrait of Thoreau by assembling "a steady alternation of extracts" from his journals and other works as well as the writings of his contemporaries, illustrated with a collection of photographs, maps, reproductions of handbills, newspaper clippings, and private letters. The work is particularly successful, as noted by one anonymous reviewer, in its attempt "to show, as far as possible, Thoreau as a human being, for he has too often been a man buried beneath legend" (*Christian Science Monitor*, 21 November 1962).

The Days of Henry Thoreau is in many ways an extension of this premise: "I have tried to present Thoreau as he really was," Harding declares in his introduction. "Here I am writing about Thoreau the man." The biography was a significant addition to Thoreau scholarship and earned for Harding critical as well as popular recognition. Written out of a "single-minded devotion," the biography begins on the day of Thoreau's birth and ends on the day of his burial. Throughout Harding's career he has always been diligent, persistent, and exact—attributes of the scribe, the collector, and the cataloguer. He essentially came to biography by way of methodology. "I have not attempted to prove any particular thesis in this book," he writes, "but rather to present the facts and let them speak for themselves." The result, as noted by Bode in the *New York Times Book Review* (26 December 1965), is "patently exhaustive" research and meticulous scholarship: "He wanted to provide the amplest possible record of Thoreau. He has found out the facts, certainly as fully as any current biographer could ... [and] has unearthed data that was only suspected of existing."

In *The Days of Henry Thoreau*, Harding avoids offering subjective examination of Thoreau's written work as well as interpretation of the events of Thoreau's life. In addition Harding cautiously tempers the issue of Thoreau's sexuality, which provided cause for in-depth analysis for later biographers. Instead he provides, as noted by Sterling North in the *Saturday Review* (15 January 1966), a "neighborly portrait of Thoreau." Yet North echoes what other critics considered the strength as well as the weakness of the biography. For some the "plethora of detail" too often clouds the emergence of the life. "The writing is plain, clear, familiar," said Bode. "The vocabulary, furthermore, seems nearly neutral." This, however, is Harding's stated intention. "As I have said, in writing this book I have had no thesis to present, no axe to grind." The result, as Bode would emphasize, is "the best biography [of Thoreau] we have."

In 1965 Harding was named editor in chief of the Princeton University Press edition of *The Writings of Henry D. Thoreau*, sponsored by the National Endowment for the Humanities and the Modern Language Association. He served in this capacity until 1973, when he became a member of the executive committee. In 1967 he published

three books: *Emerson's Library*, an edition of *The Collected Poems of William Ellery Channing, the Younger: 1817-1901*, and *The Variorum Civil Disobedience*. Harding's next major work was *Henry David Thoreau: A Profile* (1971), a collection of Thoreau criticism.

In 1972 Harding published *Henry David Thoreau: Studies and Commentaries*, a collection of criticism commemorating the life and works of Thoreau, which he edited with George Brenner and Paul A. Doyle. Echoing his pronouncement in *The Days of Henry Thoreau*, Harding reiterates in his foreword the impact of Thoreau on modern society: "His works are far more alive, far more pertinent today than they were in his own day." Harding has used the classroom as a practical means to communicate Thoreau's message, and he further comments on Thoreau's relevance: "A college generation that liked to boast that they trusted no one over thirty suddenly discovered that someone born one hundred and fifty years ago could be meaningful to them." Designed with this college audience in mind, Harding published *The Selected Works of Thoreau* (1975); *The New Thoreau Handbook* with Michael Meyer (1980); a new edition of Thoreau's *Journals* (1984); and *Thoreau As Seen by His Contemporaries* (1990), a revised and expanded edition of *Thoreau: Man of Concord*. Since 1990 Harding has devoted much of his time and energy to a new edition of Thoreau's correspondence, to be published by Princeton University Press.

Harding claims there is no precise moment when he "chose" Thoreau as the subject of his lifework. His own family upbringing and his love of nature must surely be partly responsible. Yet the decision seems to have been made by the time he was twenty-four, at the first meeting of the Thoreau Society in Concord, and he is still certain of his choice. Yet he has managed also to have a life apart from Thoreau. He and his wife are the parents of four children: David, Allen, Lawrence, and Susan. Harding is inherently a simple man who dedicated himself to what he found meaningful and practical. In his journal for 25 March 1842, Thoreau wrote, "Great persons are not soon learned, not even their outlines, but they change like the mountains in the horizon as we ride along." In Thoreau, Harding realized, as he says in the introduction to *The Days of Henry Thoreau*, "the opportunity of riding by and observing a particularly notable mountain."

Park Honan
(17 September 1928 -   )

Kirk H. Beetz
National University, Sacramento

BOOKS: *Browning's Characters: A Study in Poetic Technique* (New Haven: Yale University Press, 1961);

The Book, the Ring, & the Poet: A Biography of Robert Browning, by Honan and William Irvine (New York: McGraw-Hill, 1974; London: Bodley Head, 1975);

Matthew Arnold: A Life (New York: McGraw-Hill, 1981; London: Weidenfeld & Nicolson, 1981);

Jane Austen: Her Life (London: Weidenfeld & Nicolson, 1988; New York: St. Martin's Press, 1988);

Authors' Lives: On Literary Biography and the Arts of Language (New York: St. Martin's Press, 1990).

OTHER: Percy Bysshe Shelley, *Shelley,* edited by Honan (New York: Dell, 1962);

Edward Bulwer Lytton, *Falkland,* edited by Herbert Van Thal, introduction by Honan (London: Cassell, 1967);

The Complete Works of Robert Browning, 4 volumes, edited by Honan and others (Athens: Ohio University Press, 1969-1973);

"Sterne and the Formation of Jane Austen's Talent," in *Laurence Sterne: Riddles and Mysteries,* edited by Valerie Grosvenor Myer (Totowa, N.J.: Barnes & Noble / London: Vision, 1984), pp. 161-171;

"Richardson's Influence on Jane Austen," in *Samuel Richardson: Passion and Prudence,* edited by Myer (Totowa, N.J.: Barnes & Noble, 1986), pp. 165-177;

The Beats: An Anthology of "Beat" Writing, edited, with an introduction, by Honan (London: Dent, 1987);

"Arnold, Eliot and Trilling," in *Matthew Arnold in His Time and Ours,* edited by Clinton Macham and Forrest D. Burt (Charlottesville: University Press of Virginia, 1988), pp. 171-182.

SELECTED PERIODICAL PUBLICATIONS—
UNCOLLECTED: "A Note on Matthew Arnold in Love," *Victorian Newsletter,* 39 (Spring 1971): 11-15;

"Factuality, Self-Consciousness, and Biography," *Browning Society Notes,* 6 (March 1976): 23-28;

"Matthew Arnold, Mary Claude, and 'Switzerland,'" *Victorian Poetry,* 16 (Winter 1978): 369-375;

"The Theory of Biography," *Novel,* 13 (Fall 1979): 109-120;

"The Young Matthew Arnold," *Contemporary Review,* 245 (October 1984): 191-198;

"Jane Austen and Marriage," *Contemporary Review,* 245 (November 1984): 253-259.

Park Honan's goal when writing each of his biographies has been to be definitive—that is, to create biographies that will be the standard references in their fields. In his biographies of Robert Browning, Matthew Arnold, and Jane Austen he has succeeded, with most scholars and critics agreeing that each biography reveals more about its subject than has any previous one. Honan combines a multitude of previously unpublished facts about the personal lives and careers of his subjects with a narrative style that presents details in a coherent and fluid manner, thus pleasing general as well as scholarly readers. In so doing he has become a significant theorist about the function of literary biography and has reshaped modern views of the personalities of his subjects.

Leonard Hobart Park Honan was born on 17 September 1928 in Utica, New York, and was raised in Bronxville. His father was William Francis Honan, a thoracic surgeon, and his mother was Annette Neudecker Honan, a journalist. Although life in Bronxville was essentially comfortable, at night Park and his brother would sneak water snakes into one another's beds, and the animals would bite when disturbed. Although Honan was a typical youngster in his playing of pranks and boisterous spirits, he was already devel-

Park Honan

oping a powerful intellectual engagement with literature.

In 1945, at the age of seventeen, Honan went to Deep Springs College in California. Two years later he entered the University of Chicago, from which he received his M.A. in 1951. From 1951 to 1956 he held a wide variety of jobs, as a clerk, a baseball player, and a dump-truck driver. The last was his favorite job, but he lost it when he backed his truck into a millpond because he was immersed in reading Johann Wolfgang von Goethe and not paying attention to his driving.

On 22 December 1952 Honan married Jeannette Colin, a Frenchwoman. They eventually had three children: Corinna, Matthew, and Natasha. In 1956 Honan moved, with his wife and first daughter, Corinna, to England, where he entered the doctoral program at the University of London. In 1959 he received his Ph.D.;

his thesis formed the basis for his first book, *Browning's Characters: A Study in Poetic Technique* (1961). From 1959 to 1961 Honan was an instructor in English at Connecticut College and an assistant professor there from 1961 to 1962. During these years he began work on a biography of Browning.

Honan has written extensively about his theories of biography. He seems to be trying to resolve in his own work one of the major divisions of twentieth-century literary biography, the division between interpretive biographies, which emphasize evaluations and explanations of the deeds of the subject, and academic biographies, which emphasize detail and objectivity over interpretation. Critical of academic biographers, Jeffrey Meyers in *The Craft of Literary Biography* (1985) refers to such "encyclopedic accumulation of facts" without interpretation as a

Dust jacket for the biography that Honan completed after William Irvine's death in 1964

"defeatist approach" because the biographers seem to deny that any meaningful interpretation of a life is possible. On the other hand, some academic biographers believe that interpretation cannot recapture the essence of someone who is dead, but an accumulation of the facts of someone's life can at least tell a reader reliably about how that person lived. A first glance at any of Honan's biographies would suggest that he is an academic gatherer of facts. He is proud of his ability to uncover new information: "Three-quarters of the biographical data in this book," he declares in his preface to *Matthew Arnold: A Life* (1981), "has not appeared in a previous study of Arnold." Such a reference to "data" makes Honan sound like a dry pedant, but instead his writing is often exciting and at times moving.

In his biographies Honan plainly hopes to reach a wide, diversified audience. Thus he has developed narrative strategies that invite the reading of his books simply for pleasure. In "Some Poli-

tics" (in *Authors' Lives*, 1990) Honan asserts that "not only its [a biography's] research but its *writing* necessitates painstaking effort, that twenty rewritings of a single sentence may be needed, and that unless every chapter reflects an appropriate sense of the subject's presence, the biography at best has value as an academic reference book." Thus biography should not only reflect high standards of research techniques but should convey an understanding of the character of the subject. Honan sees the resolution of the need for the facts of a subject's external life and the desire to know the inner life of the subject as an aesthetic one. "Good or intelligent biography uses language that brings the sense of the evidence about the biographee before the reader"; that is, the manner in which language is used—the biographer's style—can present the necessary details of a subject's life while still allowing the subject's character to be the focus of discussion.

In "The Theory of Biography" (*Novel*, Fall 1979) Honan asserts, "There is—and should be—

no fixed rule as to temporal contraction in biography, but there is an implicit rule that an account of all years is necessary." He argues that there should be no gaps in time in a biography—each year must be accounted for; but a biographer may choose to emphasize the most significant periods of his subject's life by devoting more space to those periods than to others. For instance, in *The Book, the Ring, & the Poet: A Biography of Robert Browning* (1974), Honan and coauthor William Irvine devote approximately 40 percent of the book to Browning's fifteen-year marriage to Elizabeth Barrett Browning, even though Browning lived seventy-seven years. The short marriage profoundly affected Browning's life and work and is part of one of the world's most interesting love stories. As Honan's inspiration for using the expansion and contraction of time as one of his narrative strategies, he cites James Boswell, author of *The Life of Johnson* (1791), who "brilliantly grasped the principle that accuracy, or fidelity to history, is in no way compromised by narrative tactics which ride over time, playing with time and even ironically playing with everyone's normal stolid image of the biographee." In Boswell's literary strategies and the Enlightenment's view of the individual person, Honan finds the basis for the resolution of the conflict between the need for copious facts and the need to allow the subject's personality to float above the great sea of details. Boswell, he says, uses novelistic strategies to highlight significant moments of Johnson's life and to build suspense. Essential to the success of Boswell's presentation is the allowing of Johnson to reveal himself through his own words. This Honan calls "expressivism."

Honan says that medieval people defined themselves completely in relation to God; religion defined the thoughts and deeds of people. In the eighteenth century this God-centered view had become untenable. People were focused on earthly life, not the afterlife. In writing a biography, the biographer could no longer convincingly use God as the source for interpreting the merits of a life. Therefore, Honan says, "Now man's *authentic words* are all that clarify his psyche." Extensive research into what a subject said and wrote becomes essential to understanding his inner self. By this reasoning Honan argues that the minute details of academic biographies become in and of themselves interpretive when emphasis is given to the biographee's self-expression. Further, he argues, "If we accept an expressivist anthropology, then neither the words of the self-revealing biog-

raphee, nor the words of the biographer which point out, heighten and explain the revelations, are to operate simply at a literal level. Expressivism demands that the biographer not only be aware of style but *exploit* its potentials in his presentation." This suggests that the successful presentation of facts should be anything but a dry recitation; it should involve the biographer's active working on the shape and order of the facts.

Of the many challenges involved in the writing of biography, Honan sees two as especially important to his own expressivist approach. One is that "I may need to include so many expository facts . . . that I find my narrative a clotted string of evidence." The danger is clutter—too many facts ordered chronologically but not logically, thereby losing whatever meaning they might have. On the other hand, Honan believes that "professorial biographers, favoring what is positive and finite, have tended to remove from biography what Roy Pascal has called the impredictable nature of life." How does one present the biographee's life as it was, with events and data swarming in seemingly random ways, while at the same time making rational sense out of the biographee's experience? The unpredictability of experience, when presented in a biography, can give a reader a sense of immediacy—of being there with the biographee as he experiences his life—but of what good is the immediacy if it is purchased at the cost of clotted strings of evidence? What is the good of sharing the immediacy of a life if no meaning for that life can be perceived? These questions, Honan implies, haunt twentieth-century biography: "Biographers have made too little use of style varieties in any attempt to achieve immediacy probably because they have thought too little about the properties of narrative." Novelistic strategies can shape the order of the presentation of facts, thus giving them understandable logic, while maintaining suspense—the understanding that each new day, each turn around a corner, brings with it the unknown. In *Matthew Arnold*, Honan forms the suspense into high drama: the unknown future brings with it literary triumph, heroic ordeals, and profound tragedy. In *Jane Austen: Her Life* (1988), the unknown brings with it surprises and comedy; Austen's own delight in the quirks and prejudices of people makes Honan's biography a deep and heartfelt comedy.

This is not to say that Honan's emphasis on style as a solution to some of the problems of writing biography means that he believes that a biogra-

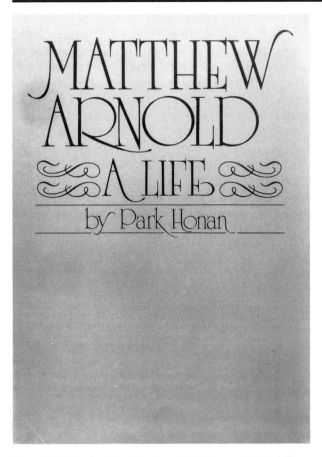

Dust jacket for the biography in which Honan attempts to correct the impression that Arnold was strictly an apologist for "high culture"

phy is primarily an entertainment. "Myths," he says in "Some Politics," "cling to personalities, and . . . the biographer's first duty is to peel them away." The truth, for good or ill, is the biographer's primary objective, and everything, even "his own emotional, intellectual, and moral relationship with his subject," which "gives life to biographical works," should be focused on truth. Thus a biography "must be rigorously factual," even while full of life. Honan's views on the function of biography and of its need to be truthful have evolved over many years and continue to evolve, and his desire for factuality as well as narrative excitement continues to emerge in his writings. As he said in a 1986 interview, "A biographer should add nothing, of his or her own, but study and integrate the evidence so well that the evidence in effect writes the book. . . . The biographer, anyway, deconstructs a life only to reassemble it with a slightly better understanding of reality than he or she had before." The friction between his desire for objective truth and the subjective reconstruction of truth is found in all of Honan's biographical writings. It may be that Honan has come to think that lives are works of art and that truth is found by making that art, those lives, part of oneself.

In "Factuality, Self-Consciousness, and Biography" (*Browning Society Notes*, March 1976) Honan writes: "The first attraction was the poetry [of Robert Browning]: I was interested in the man who could write 'Fra Lippo Lippi' and 'The Bishop Orders His Tomb.' " Thus Honan's first book is a critical study of Browning's poetry, but in it may be found significant elements of Honan's biographies. In *Browning's Characters* Honan demonstrates that much of the murkiness of imagery and rough versification that previous critics have complained of in Browning's poetry can be explained and illuminated by understanding that his first purpose in poetry is to develop and examine characters.

The book is organized as a history of Browning's creative life—a pattern reminiscent of biography. Honan begins with Browning's earliest works, noting that he was writing credible poetry by age fourteen, and Honan follows the development of Browning's techniques to his last writings. In the process Honan reacts against the critical consensus of the 1950s, which held that Browning was a careless versifier. Honan shows that Browning was a conscientious craftsman who spent his life perfecting techniques for poetically examining lives both of characters drawn from his imagination and of historical figures. The crudities cited by some critics in Browning's verse can be explained as techniques he used to develop the characters of the speakers—who are often not skilled users of language.

As a logical consequence of his desire to explore people's characters through dramatic expositions, Browning early in his career wrote several plays, *Strafford* (1837) and the *Bells and Pomegranates* series of eight plays (1841-1846). These dramas were failures, which can be puzzling—the writer of great dramatic monologues should have been able to write good plays. Even though the exact reason for Browning's unsuccessful stage career remains to this day a controversial subject, Honan's study of the plays suggests an explanation that is in harmony with Browning's own character and with the thesis of *Browning's Characters*. Browning's focus was on the development and analysis of characters, to the detriment of plot; action and conflict unnecessary to character development were left out—thus the plots lack coherence. Honan makes a strong case for the importance of the plays to Browning's artistic growth, arguing that the writing of the plays helped the poet learn what his talent was unsuited for, as well as helping him practice his techniques for revealing character through dramatic exposition. Further, from Honan's analysis of them, the plays are shown to have literary merit when *read*, if not when *staged*.

In the first part of *Browning's Characters* Honan discusses the growth of Browning's personality and art, and in the second part he shows an understanding of Browning's artistic achievement; both of these would serve him well in his first biography. Critics warmed to *Browning's Characters* slowly, but it is now regarded as a standard, valuable work.

In 1962 Honan journeyed to London on a Guggenheim Fellowship to research his biography on Browning. While there he met William Irvine, who was also doing research for a Browning biography. Irvine was much further along in his research than was Honan, and he shared his expertise with the less experienced scholar. Irvine was impressed by Honan; after Irvine's death in 1964 his wife wrote to Honan that Irvine had wanted him to finish the biography of Browning that Irvine had started.

Returning to the United States, Honan became assistant professor of English at Brown University (1962-1965), and then associate professor (1965-1968). During his years at Brown, Honan helped found the scholarly journal *Novel: A Forum on Fiction*, which became one of the most important publications devoted to fiction and reflected Honan's strong interest in the theories of narrative technique. In 1968 Honan moved to England and became a lecturer in English at the University of Birmingham. In 1972 the university promoted him to senior lecturer. During this time Honan continued to work on his biography of Browning.

Irvine had completed chapters 1 through 21 of *The Book, the Ring, & the Poet: A Biography of Robert Browning*. Honan rewrote much of chapters 10 and 17 (covering the years 1844 to 1845 and 1851 to 1852); wrote the last six chapters, 22 through 27 (covering the years 1860 to 1889); and edited the entire book into its final form for publication. Browning had long been regarded as a mystery; the difference between his private persona—gentle and kindly—and his public one of being a loud boor was so contradictory and seemingly so absolute that some scholars thought only one or the other image had to be the real

Browning. Browning compounded the mystery by carefully destroying letters and other documents that could have revealed his true nature, a practice that Charles Dickens had followed before him. Further, Browning did not bother to correct misconceptions about himself when he came across them, allowing misinformation to stand as if it had his approval. It was the goal of Irvine and, later, Honan to cut through the mystery and to resolve the contradictions that seemed inherent in Browning's two personas.

It must have been difficult for Honan to graft his view of Browning onto Irvine's, and his later Browning seems more gloomy than Irvine's, but as William S. Peterson points out in the *New Republic* (9 March 1974), the difference between Irvine's and Honan's portraits may be explained by Elizabeth Barrett Browning's death. The loss of his wife cast a pall over Browning's later life. Irvine shows Browning as a man of many moods: always a little adolescent in his impulsiveness, selfishness, and desire for attention, Browning was nonetheless a man of unyielding artistic integrity who committed himself wholeheartedly to his poetry and to his wife. Thus the public and private personas of Browning are resolved into one complex personality. The loud, boisterous public Browning was a manifestation of his diffident, even shy, response to strangers; always a bit immature, he overcame his shyness in public by being overly demonstrative, speaking so vigorously and relentlessly that he sometimes seemed too boorish to be the author of sensitive poetry about people facing life's crises. On the other hand, the publicly awkward Browning loved with an adolescent's passion, throwing a youthful energy into his work, marriage, and friendships that charmed those who knew him well and that brought him devoted friends, who saw in him the poet who could care deeply enough about people to reveal their essential humanity.

It fell to Honan to deal with what in some ways was the hardest part of Browning's life. Critics in general believed that Browning's poetry after the death of his wife was inferior to his earlier writings, so they tended to neglect studying the poet's last twenty-eight years. Further, the critics were put off by the overly sentimental adulation Browning received in his later years. In addition the then-standard biography of Browning, W. H. Griffith and H. C. Minchin's *The Life of Browning with Notices of His Writing, His Family, and His Friends* (1910), slighted Browning's later years.

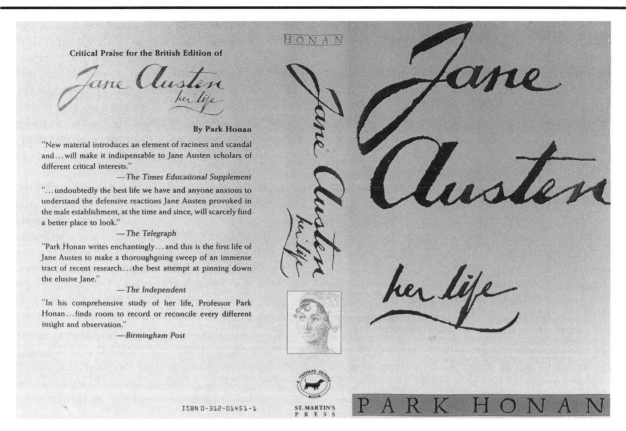

Dust jacket for Honan's 1988 book, for which he drew on recently discovered materials, including manuscripts he found in British and American attics

Honan asserted in an interview (*Studies in Browning and His Circle*, 1986) that *The Book, the Ring, & the Poet* "has no main theme, slant, or aim—except to be true to evidence," yet his section of the biography suggests that he brought to it strong points of view, all of which could have been engendered by his research. One "slant" would be his view that Browning was an inconsistent man—that his moods could shift day by day, and that as he aged, he changed, becoming more thoughtful and developing a mature poetic style that reflected endless experimentation with his craft. This craftsmanship would seem to make Browning's later poetry worthy of study. Honan presents the poetic works of the last years as high examples of Browning's art. In this he echoes his *Browning's Characters,* which emphasizes Browning's worthiness of close study. Honan also echoes his earlier book by emphasizing poems that reflect on Browning's artistic growth.

When discussing Browning in "Factuality, Self-Consciousness, and Biography," Honan asserts that Victorians and people of the modern age shared an important problem: "to preserve the life of the imagination at a time hostile to it," and he says that Browning followed Goethe's solution to the problem, "that the artist 'isolate himself by main force.' " The Victorians, according to Honan, saw this "force of character . . . as force to resist company, friends, social life—to retreat steadfastly into the inner self." If Browning held such a Goethean view, as Honan believes, it would have profound biographical implications. It would mean that Browning's shyness was not just the result of timidity but was also a manifestation of his effort to isolate himself so that he could better exercise his imagination without hostile interference. His living in Italy then becomes an artistic exile, a place where, he said, "I felt alone with my own soul." For Honan, Browning's attitude created a special tension, because "the writer has no other subject *but* life; isolation preserves individuality but separates one from one's material." Honan reveals a deeply troubled man in his portrait of Browning—a man devastated by his wife's death, mired in thoughts of guilt about his failures to her, and emotionally and intellectually committed to living isolated, as if his mind were an island far from the rest of the world. At the same time, England and much of the rest of the world was in a spiritual crisis. Darwinism had opened to question every traditional notion about existence; the faith and prejudices of Victorians were shaken and were falling to ruin. Browning's carefully developed art offered a consistency of philosophy to its readers. Although Browningites went too far in their worshipful praise of him as a prophet and supremely Christian poet, his poetry had, over decades, shown a common humanity among peoples; the poetry implicitly suggested that people were important in and of themselves, whatever the turmoil in society. Browning plainly enjoyed the adulation and was drawn into an engagement with the public and with life.

Honan's research into Browning's active and complicated last years is exhaustive. The organization, which Honan says is the major part of a biographer's presentation, is straightforward and clear, emphasizing reactions to Browning and his poetic response to his new fame. *The Book, the Ring, & the Poet,* when it was published in 1974, was praised for being a unified whole, with credit being given to Honan's editing the entire book as well as writing a significant portion of it. Honan said in 1986, "I *had* no style. . . . Irvine's style was dazzling, shimmering, and also exact." Some reviewers of *The Book, the Ring, & the Poet* took the tack exemplified by Ralph A. Bellas's comments in *Thought* (March 1975), noting that the book recreates Browning's times well and features good criticism of the poetry, but that Griffin and Minchin's biography was still the standard one. A few critics took the view of A. S. Byatt, in the *New Statesman* (11 April 1975), that the new biography failed to capture the authentic personality of Browning and was therefore a failure. The great majority of critics differed from these views; William S. Peterson, for example, proclaimed *The Book, the Ring, & the Poet* to be a "remarkable achievement" whose thoroughness, literary style, and insightful portrait made it not only far and away the best biography on Browning but a triumphant literary achievement. After more than a decade of reconsideration by critics, Irvine and Honan's book is almost universally recognized as the standard biography of Browning and is highly regarded for its thorough research and incisive presentation.

Tall, redheaded, and loud, Honan was a popular teacher, and in 1976 he was promoted to reader in English by the University of Birming-

ham. By this time he had already begun work on a biography of Matthew Arnold; his first significant article on Arnold, "A Note on Matthew Arnold in Love," had been published in spring 1971. Arnold is for Honan the most important of the Victorian essayists, as well as a notable poet, because he possessed a modern sensibility and was deeply interested in the same sort of social problems that most concern people in the late twentieth century.

In *Matthew Arnold: A Life* Honan sees him as enmeshed in the lives of others—schoolchildren, teachers, politicians, bureaucrats, and his family—and believes this involvement in the lives of others led to Arnold's quest for meaning in those lives and to his sophisticated political and social philosophy. Honan complains that scholars have inaccurately portrayed Arnold as strictly an apologist for "bookish" or "high" culture; Arnold, he says, wrote about popular newspapers, popular styles, and popular and second-rate literature. "Who is this Arnold who neglects popular culture?" he asks. Arnold, Honan asserts, saw culture as an "openness-of-mind," and "Arnold insists that those who never read books may enter into this condition, which involves a growing, a becoming . . . whereby a person moves towards realizing his full mental, emotional, and creative potential." Arnold sought this full realization of mental, emotional, and creative powers not only for himself, but for everyone. The crushing misery of the lives of poor schoolchildren moved him deeply, and out of his frustration—born of his inability to persuade England's educational bureaucracy to help the children—came his moralistic view of culture: to deny people the opportunity to reach the fullness of their potential was immoral; to help them to that fulfillment was morally right. Honan sees Arnold's view of culture as constantly evolving; it was a "continual quest in his thought."

During the years Honan researched and wrote *Matthew Arnold,* his theory of biography was evolving. In "Factuality, Self-Consciousness, and Biography" he declares, "The biographer can only penetrate the carapace of a psychic Outer Self by accepting the Inner Self of his subject on the subject's terms, and this is why something more than sympathy and interest is required of the biographer of an important modern writer." By the 1980s this "something more" was taking a deconstructionist bent—the breaking down and reassembly of the subject from the inside out. *Matthew Arnold* reflects the transition from "sympathy" to an interpretation of the internal life.

From the biography's beginning it is evident that Honan admires his subject. This does not stop Honan from revealing the young Arnold's self-centered and irresponsible foolishness, nor from pointing out the older Arnold's affected mannerisms and sometimes insensitive behavior toward his wife. But the tone and narrative of *Matthew Arnold* tend to be like those of an epic: the world of the Victorians is one Arnold perceives as in darkness; it is a world of injustice inflicted on those least able to bear it; and after the publication of Charles Darwin's *On the Origin of Species* (1859), it is an insecure world without a moral center. In this "epic," Arnold is a heroic figure who internalizes and then expresses the era's greatest problems, all the while developing ideas that point the way to a better world. He is more than Achilles, he is Hector, too, waging a conflict within himself between the best and worst qualities of his time; at a terrible personal cost, he makes his life a continuing effort to resolve the major problems of the modern world.

Although Arnold's career is given mythic proportions, Honan strives to show his humanness. Honan shows him to be a sensitive son who spends his life trying to satisfy his parents, especially his father, Thomas Arnold, the Rugby headmaster who after his premature death became a larger-than-life figure for Victorians. Matthew Arnold was the son of the ideal teacher, and he never seemed to live up to expectations. By portraying Arnold's effort to live up to his father's image, Honan reveals his own effort to penetrate the "Inner Self" on Arnold's terms, showing the "boy-in-the-man" who strives perpetually to do for the world what his father had done: to engage actively in life and in the process of making it better. An example of how Honan tries to break down then rebuild Arnold is Honan's handling of women in Arnold's life. Arnold is depicted as an anxious, insecure man who was buoyed by the women around him, particularly by his sister Jane and his wife, Frances Lucy; the psychologically troubled man seems to have been dependent on the admiration and encouragement of women.

The style of *Matthew Arnold* is overtly complicated, making it the most difficult to read of Honan's books. Even so, Arnold emerges as a fully believable, complete human being as well as a mythic figure who "is the Victorian who matters most." Integrating the major elements of Arnold's life, Honan shows how Arnold shifted from writing beautiful lyric poetry to wideranging essays: Arnold was always sensitive to the crises of his time—his poetry spoke of the anxiety of the industrial age. Too much work, personal tragedy, and deep anxiety eventually silenced his poetic voice, but the Arnold of the essays is shown to be the same as the Arnold of the poetry. The interconnections between Arnold's private life, career as a school inspector, and literary life are shown in thorough detail, revealing how one man could be so much all at once.

Honan's stature as the coauthor of *The Book, the Ring, & the Poet* probably helped him obtain access to materials that Arnold's literary heirs had previously kept private—reflecting Arnold's distrust of biographers. With the publication of *Matthew Arnold*, Honan's stature increased even more. Most critics, even some of those who find fault with *Matthew Arnold*, deemed the biography a praiseworthy effort, calling it indispensable. Reviewers noted some errors, such as Honan's referring to Laura Ward as Arnold's niece when she was instead his cousin. Some critics complained that Honan's views are overstated, particularly those expressed in his literary criticism, and others claimed that, as Richard D. Altick stated in *Modern Philology* (November 1982), "Matthew Arnold remains an elusive figure." Although Honan stated that his desire was to write a "definitive" biography of Arnold, some critics believed that he failed to reach his goal because of the vagueness of the link between the public Arnold and the private Arnold. Nevertheless, since its publication in 1981, *Matthew Arnold* has supplanted previous biographies to become the standard one—the first reference for scholar and general reader alike.

The publication of *Matthew Arnold* solidified Honan's reputation as one of the outstanding Victorianists of his generation. He then turned his attention to Jane Austen, one of literature's most enigmatic figures. In 1984 he took the prestigious position of professor of English and American literature at the University of Leeds, England. During the years between the publication of *Matthew Arnold* and *Jane Austen: Her Life* (1988) Honan uncovered new sources of information on Austen's private life and her methods of literary composition—literally finding manuscripts in American and British attics, as well as having materials sent to him from new sources.

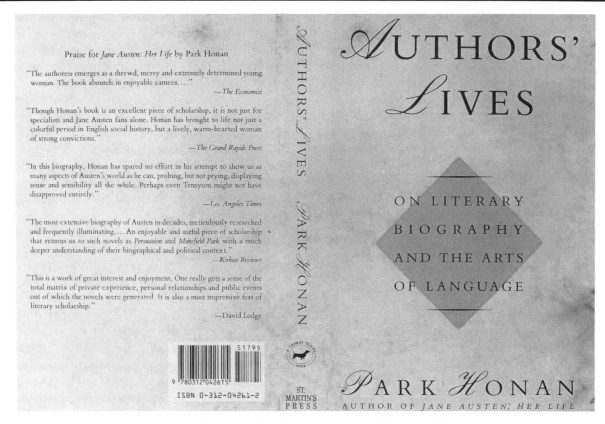

Praise for *Jane Austen: Her Life* by Park Honan

"The authoress emerges as a shrewd, merry and extremely determined young woman. The book abounds in enjoyable cameos...."
—*The Economist*

"Though Honan's book is an excellent piece of scholarship, it is not just for specialists and Jane Austen fans alone. Honan has brought to life not just a colorful period in English social history, but a lively, warm-hearted woman of strong convictions."
—*The Grand Rapids Press*

"In this biography, Honan has spared no effort in his attempt to show us as many aspects of Austen's world as he can, probing, but not prying, displaying sense and sensibility all the while. Perhaps even Tennyson might not have disapproved entirely."
—*Los Angeles Times*

"The most extensive biography of Austen in decades, meticulously researched and frequently illuminating.... An enjoyable and useful piece of scholarship that returns us to such novels as *Persuasion* and *Mansfield Park* with a much deeper understanding of their biographical and political context."
—*Kirkus Reviews*

"This is a work of great interest and enjoyment. One really gets a sense of the total matrix of private experience, personal relationships and public events out of which the novels were generated. It is also a most impressive feat of literary scholarship."
—*David Lodge*

ISBN 0-312-04261-2

AUTHORS' LIVES
PARK HONAN

AUTHORS' LIVES

ON LITERARY
BIOGRAPHY
AND THE ARTS
OF LANGUAGE

PARK HONAN
AUTHOR OF *JANE AUSTEN: HER LIFE*

ST.
MARTIN'S
PRESS

Dust jacket for Honan's 1990 collection of essays on his theory of biography

Jane Austen captures the complexities of Austen's life while being readable. Honan enables Austen, whose private life had for over a century been thought by scholars to be forever lost in obscurity, to come alive as a full personality. Those who love Austen's writings will likely find Honan's detailed revelations about her love life, family life, and social life to be exciting and meaningful. Honan tries to show that the popular notion of Austen as a quiet, subdued woman is incompatible with the woman who wrote the biting satire found in her novels. With the presentation of much background information on the conformity expected of women of her social class, Honan reveals Austen to have had an active inner life that went against society's expectations. Intellectually gifted, astute in judgment, and perceptive in her insights not only into society but into the hypocrisies, ironies, and truths of human existence, Austen had an impressive creative spirit.

Austen has long seemed to be an example of the self-effacing, even submissive, woman. Among her family and friends, her sister, Cassandra, was considered the brighter and more gifted of the two; memoirs from the period seem to confirm this view. On the other hand, Honan reveals Austen to have been a tough-minded woman who coped successfully with harsh realities such as unfair debts, cruel social restrictions, and deadly illness. Further, his readings of her letters show her to be humorous and given to self-deprecating ironic remarks that may suggest the origin of the notion that she suffered from an excess of humility. Honan shows Austen's ironic sense of humor to be part of her effort to express her incisive observations of people. Whereas Arnold received valuable support from the women in his life, Austen was supported and encouraged by her brothers. Her stories were written, in part, to entertain her family and to receive the admiration of her brothers, two of whom, James and Henry, had as young men established themselves as talented writers. Honan shows how Jane Austen, responding partly to her family's pressing financial needs and partly to her own need for self-expression, reworked her early stories into complicated novels; he shows her struggle to publish them in spite of the indifference of publishers and against the restrictions, even hostility, of a male-oriented profession.

In *Jane Austen*, Honan fulfills his objective to absorb, deconstruct, and reassemble a life with a "better understanding of reality" than he had before, in the process reconstructing a life so that it is full, well rounded, and believable—so that it seems real. His Austen has failings, such as a tendency to act without thinking, thus sometimes hurting people, but her failings are integrated with her other qualities, showing how Jane Austen could not be Jane Austen without her weaknesses; this makes for a creditable re-creation of a full person. She is admirable in her humanness.

Throughout his career Honan has been concerned about producing biographies that are literature in their own right. To this end, he has striven to develop a sophisticated narrative style that would have the advantages of the novel while maintaining a rigorous adherence to the facts of a biographee's life and times. Interested in revealing truths about life in general, he has emphasized his subjects' engagement with the major issues and ideas of their times, and in so doing he has shown how their responses to life can illuminate the human condition. His views of how to realize his artistic aims have deepened during his career, from a desire to lay out all the facts of a life, to an effort to penetrate and reveal the inner life of a subject, to the deconstructing and reassembling of a subject so that the subject's inner life, outer life, and world may be revealed in a fully integrated form. In his efforts to write definitive biographies, Park Honan has written the standard references in their fields. His reputation among scholars and critics is high, reflecting their admiration of his erudition, careful and extensive research, and evocation of the subjects' spirits and characters.

Interview:

"Deconstruction and Literary Biography?: An Interview with Park Honan," *Studies in Browning and His Circle,* 14 (1986): 7-15.

References:

Denis Donoghue, "The General Critic's Business," *Times Literary Supplement,* 28 August 1981, pp. 971-972;

Arthur Kincaid, "A Profile: Two Park Honans?," *Studies in Browning and His Circle,* 3 (Fall 1975): 144-147;

William Myers, "Literature and Dogma: Newman and Arnold," *Sewanee Review,* 91 (Spring 1983): 275-282.

Donald R. Howard
(18 September 1927 - 2 March 1987)

Sondra Miley Cooney
Kent State University

BOOKS: *College Workbook of Composition* (Boston: Heath, 1960);

The Three Temptations: Medieval Man in Search of the World (Princeton: N.J.: Princeton University Press, 1966);

The Idea of the Canterbury Tales (Berkeley, Los Angeles & London: University of California Press, 1976);

Writers and Pilgrims: Medieval Pilgrimage Narratives and Their Posterity (Berkeley, Los Angeles & London: University of California Press, 1980);

Chaucer: His Life, His Works, His World (New York: Dutton, 1987); republished as *Chaucer and the Medieval World* (London: Weidenfeld & Nicolson, 1988).

OTHER: "Structure and Symmetry in *Sir Gawain*," in *Sir Gawain and Pearl: Critical Essays*, edited by Robert J. Blanch (Bloomington: Indiana University Press, 1966), pp. 195-208; and in *Twentieth Century Interpretations of Sir Gawain and the Green Knight: A Collection of Critical Essays*, edited by Denton Fox (Englewood Cliffs, N.J.: Prentice-Hall, 1968), pp. 44-56;

Critical Studies of Sir Gawain and the Green Knight, edited by Howard and Christian Zacher (Notre Dame, Ind.: University of Notre Dame Press, 1968);

"Chaucer the Man," in *Chaucer's Mind and Art*, edited by A. C. Cawley (Edinburgh & London: Oliver & Boyd, 1969), pp. 31-45;

The Canterbury Tales: A Selection, edited by Howard and James Dean (New York: New American Library, 1969);

Pope Innocent III, *On the Misery of the Human Condition*, translated by Margaret Mary Dietz, edited, with an introduction, by Howard (Indianapolis: Bobbs-Merrill, 1969);

"Experience, Language, and Consciousness: *Troilus and Criseyde*, II, 596-931," in *Medieval Literature and Folklore Studies*, edited by Jerome Mandel and Bruce A. Rosenberg (New Brunswick, N.J.: Rutgers University Press, 1970), pp. 173-192;

"Lexicography and the Silence of the Past," in *New Aspects of Lexicography: Literary Criticism, Intellectual History, and Social Change*, edited by Howard D. Weinbrot (Carbondale & Edwardsville: Southern Illinois University Press, 1972), pp. 3-16;

"Renaissance World-Alienation," in *The Darker Vision of the Renaissance: Beyond the Fields of Reason*, edited by Robert S. Kinsman (Berkeley & Los Angeles: University of California Press, 1974), pp. 47-76;

"Flying Through Space: Chaucer and Milton," in *Milton and the Line of Vision*, edited by Joseph Anthony Wittreich, Jr. (Madison: University of Wisconsin Press, 1975), pp. 3-23;

"Chaucer's Idea of an Idea," in *Essays and Studies, 1976*, edited by E. Talbot Donaldson (London: Murray, 1976), pp. 39-55;

Geoffrey Chaucer, *Troilus and Criseyde and Selected Short Poems*, edited by Howard and Dean (New York: New American Library / London: New English Library, 1976);

Incipits of Latin Works on the Virtues and Vices, 1100-1500 A.D., edited by Howard and others (Cambridge, Mass.: Medieval Academy of America, 1979);

"The Philosophies in Chaucer's *Troilus*," in *The Wisdom of Poetry: Essays in Early English Literature in Honor of Morton W. Bloomfield*, edited by Larry D. Benson and Siegfried Wenzel (Kalamazoo: Medieval Institute Publications, Western Michigan University, 1982), pp. 151-175.

SELECTED PERIODICAL PUBLICATIONS—
UNCOLLECTED: "The Conclusion of the Marriage Group: Chaucer and the Human Condition," *Modern Philology*, 57 (May 1960): 223-232;

"Literature and Sexuality: Book III of Chaucer's *Troilus*," *Massachusetts Review*, 8 (Summer 1967): 442-456.

Donald R. Howard circa 1976

In the closing sentence of *Chaucer: His Life, His Works, His World* (1987), Donald Roy Howard writes: "One must think of the world while one is in the world; facing eternity, our thoughts become closed within the self, our words become silence, and all our works upon this little spot of earth seem like the waves of the sea." Howard might well have been writing about the close of his own life instead of Geoffrey Chaucer's, for Howard did not live to see the publication of the biography—the capstone of his career. Howard's lifetime of study and his keen mind enabled him, according to a memorial tribute in *Speculum* (July 1988), to "come as close as anyone could to knowing—what Chaucer did think and experience." In all Howard's writing, whether for specialized or general audiences, he endeavored to recreate fourteenth-century England because he was convinced that in that world lay the meaning of Chaucer's poetry, for readers in his time as well as in ours.

Howard was born on 18 September 1927 in St. Louis, Missouri, to Albert and Emily Louise Johnson Howard. He grew up in Swampscott, Massachusetts, and attended Tufts University, graduating summa cum laude with an A.B. in 1950. He then began graduate study at Rutgers University, which granted him his M.A. in 1951; he completed his graduate studies at the University of Florida, receiving the Ph.D. in 1954. In his dissertation, "The Contempt of the World: A Study in the Ideology of Latin Christendom with Emphasis on Fourteenth-Century English Literature," he investigated both a century and a theme on which all his subsequent scholarship would focus.

Howard began his teaching career at the University of Florida, serving as an instructor from 1954 to 1955. The following year he joined the English department faculty at Ohio State University. While there he successively held appointments as instructor, assistant professor, and associate professor. Awarded a Fulbright Research Fellowship, he worked in Italy from 1959 to 1960 on a proposed study of the "contempt of the world" theme. Meanwhile his first book, *College Workbook of Composition*, was published in 1960. In 1963 Howard left Ohio State for California. He taught first (from 1963 to 1966) at the University of California, Riverside, as an associate professor of English.

His first critical book, *The Three Temptations: Medieval Man in Search of the World*, was published in 1966. Although not a biography and not exclusively a study of Chaucer's poetry, it is noteworthy because themes and methodology characteristic of all Howard's later writing appear in it. *The Three Temptations* examines *Troilus and Criseyde*, *Piers Plowman*, and *Sir Gawain and the Green Knight*. These three poems, written within less than twenty years of each other, are "very different from one another in genre, style, and content: yet they all explore the conflict between the ascetic spirit of medieval Christianity and the claims which the World makes upon men." Howard places each poem into its cultural context so that modern readers can understand not only how the poems were read but also how the world was understood in the fourteenth century. The final chapter discusses the style of the poems; Howard defines style as "not . . . mere verbal elegancies but the whole range of forms and qualities which characterize a work." To support both his thesis and his definition of style, Howard draws upon a wide variety of illustrations and allusions. Within just two pages, for instance, he cites Robert Frost, Erich Fromm, Erwin Panofsky, Tennessee Williams, and the elder Pieter Brueghel.

The first California stage of Howard's career ended at UCLA, where he spent one year (1966-1967) before returning to the East Coast academic world. From 1967 until 1977 Howard was a professor of English at Johns Hopkins University; from 1973 to 1977 he was Caroline S. Donovan Professor of English. Awarded a Guggenheim Fellowship for 1969-1970, he worked on *The Idea of the Canterbury Tales* (1976), which he had begun earlier with a *PMLA* article, "Chaucer the Man" (September 1965; collected by A. C. Cawley in *Chaucer's Mind and Art*, 1969). Concentrating on *The Canterbury Tales*, Howard refines and expands the concepts and methodology he introduced in *The Three Temptations*. First he reconstructs the world in which Chaucer's tales were written, for "the intention—like the form, unity, structure, style, or 'world'—of a literary work is identifiable in the work and shares in the culture

of the author's time." Howard proposes that Chaucer had an idea for his work that came from the "conventions, attitudes, and myths of his culture, and expressed it through them." Only by sharing in this experience can contemporary readers explain that idea, and they can do so without removing from their minds "those styles or ways of thinking that have developed since."

The most innovative section of *The Idea of the Canterbury Tales* is chapter 4, in which Howard postulates that *The Canterbury Tales* has an outer and an inner form based upon medieval schemes of *memoria*. The outer form comes from the narrator's remembering the pilgrimage, the pilgrims remembering their own worlds, and the characters in the tales remembering their worlds. The inner form evolves from the series of tales and their relationship to each other. Howard suggests that the tales are related to each other according to the medieval artistic interlace principle, most familiar in the illuminated initials of medieval manuscripts; it "was a model of the mental life itself, of remembered experience and free-floating thought."

In *The Idea* what was to become a distinctive feature of Howard's own style emerges. Still highly allusive, moving back and forth between modern and classical writers, and citing eruditely from a variety of sources, Howard in *The Idea* becomes a participant, an interlocutor, offering arguments and counterarguments. *The Idea* won the Melville Cane Award of the Poetry Society of America in 1977.

Howard returned to California in that same year, becoming professor of English at Stanford University, where from 1984 until his death he was Olive H. Palmer Professor of Humanities. During this period he published two books besides working on his Chaucer biography. One, *Incipits of Latin Works on the Virtues and Vices, 1100-1500 A.D.* (1979), was a collaborative edition with Morton Bloomfield and others. The second, *Writers and Pilgrims: Medieval Pilgrimage Narratives and Their Posterity* (1980), was the outgrowth of work he had done as a resident scholar at the Bellagio Study and Conference Center while on a National Endowment for the Humanities Fellowship for Independent Study and Research (1978-1979). A second Guggenheim Fellowship, for 1983-1984, enabled him to continue research and writing on the Chaucer biography.

As late as 1968 Howard thought that no one could write a biography of Chaucer. Not that factual information was wanting: *Chaucer Life-*

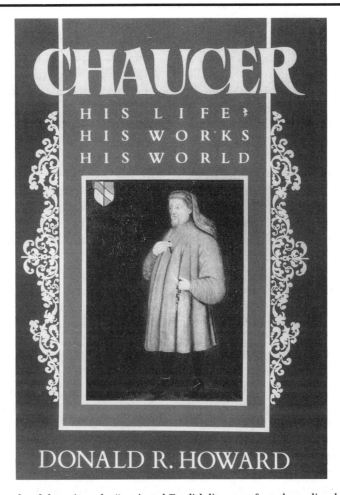

Dust jacket for Howard's biography of the writer who "extricated English literature from the medieval, instituted in English those accomplishments and effects that have meant *literature to us since"*

Records, edited by Martin M. Crow and Clair C. Olson, had been published in 1966. Other evidence was missing, however. As Howard says in his preface to *Chaucer:* "To have a biography, even a 'portrait,' we need to know about a man's family and education, his marriage and domestic life, his beliefs, his attitudes, his friends, his work and amusements. . . ." But by 1976 Howard began to doubt his earlier beliefs. John Gardner's and Derek Brewer's biographies of Chaucer, which Howard thought had not resolved the problem of balancing life, works, and world, stimulated him to write one himself. Behind his decision lay several changes in thinking. Brewer's book, in particular, showed how important Chaucer's world was to his biography. According to Howard, Chaucer's poems "reflect events of his time and of his life, both public and private." Second, Howard concluded that it was not all that necessary to know about the private or secret life of a public figure to have a real biogra-

phy. What Chaucer did—his poetry—was more real than any details of his life. His place in history had been made by the fact that he "extricated English literature from the medieval, instituted in English those accomplishments and effects that have *meant* literature to us since." And Howard had discovered that "a self is a hopeless jumble of selves and . . . a life moves, shapeless, from day to day." The biographer, therefore, "must find a figure in the carpet whether there is a figure there or not."

Howard determined that the appropriate figure to give shape to Chaucer's life was both chronological and topical. He divided the life into three parts. The first, "Into the King's Service—1342-1372," introduces the fourteenth-century world and looks at Chaucer developing his technique and writing the *Book of the Duchess*. Part 2, "To Italy—1372-1380," traces Chaucer's developing court career, his acquaintance with the poetry of Boccaccio and Dante, and his writing of the *House of Fame.* Part 3, "Into Our Time—1380-1400," continues following Chaucer the public figure, as he writes *Troilus and Criseyde* and *The Canterbury Tales.* The result is a full and illuminating picture of Chaucer's world, which sets Chaucer's accomplishments in relief. Hence the contemporary reader can better appreciate the originality of Chaucer's poetry even when it is most derivative.

A topically organized biography such as *Chaucer* can also be fatiguing for the reader. As the writer moves ahead for a period of years with one topic, then backs up and takes another topic through the same period, he inevitably repeats himself; just as inevitably the narrative line becomes confused, particularly when it involves England's royalty and aristocracy, and international politics of the 1300s. In the first chapter alone there are divisions headed "Birth and Childhood," "The Black Death," "Early Education," "The Old Humanism and the New," "Memories at Fourteen," and "The Ulster Household." And, given that *Chaucer* was intended for a broad audience and that notes are relegated to the end of the book, the narrative often stops for parenthetical explanations. Finally, since so much in a Chaucer life must be conjectural, Howard's use of the tags "may have been," "appears to be," "so far as we know," and "might have believed" create a hazy picture not unlike the dreams Chaucer so often used in his own writing. (Howard recalls in his acknowledgments Christopher Isherwood's suggestion when writing about a time long ago and about a writer for whom there is little personal record: "Make it [the writing process] like a seance.")

Attempting to clarify and explain contradictory evidence, conflicting interpretations, and complexities of political and social history, Howard draws extensively upon contemporary allusions. Franz Kafka, J. R. R. Tolkien, Alain Robbe-Grillet, and Vladimir Nabokov are all cited, for instance, in interpretations of Chaucer's Squire's and Manciple's tales. Howard cites Winston Churchill's belief that writing a book is initially "an adventure, a toy, and an amusement" to explain Chaucer's attitude toward his creative task. As before, Howard includes himself and his thinking and writing situation in the narrative.

There is general agreement that Howard's *Chaucer* significantly supplements, even surpasses, all previous biographies. Reviewers have praised its vivid portrayal of the age. However, Derek Brewer, in the *Times Literary Supplement* (15 April 1988), says that for all the information provided, the book lacks "vivid detail" and has little "social or cultural generalization." Claude Rawson in the *New York Times Book Review* (13 December 1987) surmised that Howard's death precluded his revising and tightening the text (his graduate assistants read the references and reference notes in proof). This is probably not so. Even in his earliest books, Howard's prose style manifested the same conversational features. Moreover, his readings of Chaucer's poetry do not move beyond his interpretations in earlier critical work.

One wonders how much more Donald R. Howard could have done for medieval and Chaucer studies had AIDS not prematurely shortened his life. He has left a legacy of articles and books that will continue to challenge, stimulate, and engage scholarly and general readers. Scheduled for publication in 1992 is "The Idea of Medieval Literature: Essays on Chaucer and Medieval Culture in Honor of Donald R. Howard," edited by Christian K. Zacher and James M. Dean.

Reference:
Theodore M. Anderson, John W. Baldwin, and Larry D. Benson, "Donald R. Howard," *Speculum: A Journal of Medieval Studies,* 63 (July 1988): 762-763.

Fred Kaplan

(4 November 1937 -   )

Murray Baumgarten
University of California, Santa Cruz

BOOKS: *Miracles of Rare Device: The Poet's Sense of Self in Nineteenth-Century Poetry* (Detroit: Wayne State University Press, 1972);
Dickens and Mesmerism: The Hidden Springs of Fiction (Princeton, N.J.: Princeton University Press, 1975);
Thomas Carlyle: A Biography (Ithaca, N.Y.: Cornell University Press, 1983; Cambridge: Cambridge University Press, 1983);
Lectures on Carlyle & His Era (Santa Cruz: University of California, 1985);
Sacred Tears: Sentimentality in Victorian Literature (Princeton, N.J.: Princeton University Press, 1987);
Dickens: A Biography (New York: Morrow, 1988; London: Hodder & Stoughton, 1988).

OTHER: *Dickens Studies Annual*, edited by Kaplan and others (New York: AMS, 1980-   );
Charles Dickens' Book of Memoranda, edited by Kaplan (New York: New York Public Library, 1981);
John Elliotson on Mesmerism, edited, with an introduction and bibliography, by Kaplan (New York: Da Capo, 1982);
The Reader's Advisor: A Layman's Guide to Literature, edited by Kaplan (New York: Bowker, 1985).

SELECTED PERIODICAL PUBLICATIONS—
UNCOLLECTED: "The Tyger and Its Maker: Blake's Vision of Art and the Artist," *Studies in English Literature*, 7 (1967): 616-627;
"Dickens' Flora Finching and Joyce's Molly Bloom," *Nineteenth-Century Fiction*, 23 (December 1968): 343-346;
" 'Our Short Story': The Narrative Devices of Clarissa," *Studies in English Literature*, 11 (1971): 549-562;
"Victorian Modernists: Fowles and Nabokov," *Journal of Narrative Techniques*, 3 (May 1973): 108-120;

"Fielding's Novel About Novels: The Prefaces and Plot of Tom Jones," *Studies in English Literature*, 13 (Summer 1973): 108-120;
"Victorian Biography," *Dickens Studies Newsletter*, 12 (June 1981): 59-62;
"Victorian Gossip," *Dickens Studies Newsletter*, 14 (December 1983): 151-154;
"Carlyle's Marginalia and George Henry Lewes' Fiction," *Carlyle Newsletter*, 5 (Spring 1984): 21-27;
"The Real Dickens, or The Old Animosity Shop," *New York Times Book Review*, 2 October 1988, pp. 15-16.

Fred Kaplan's biographies of Thomas Carlyle and Charles Dickens are part of a projected biographical quartet charting the sweep of Anglo-American culture from the Romantic to the modern era. Kaplan is committed to biography as a literary form and draws upon the techniques of narrative art; he aspires to combine the power and dramatic resources of narrative prose and the rigorous intellectual requirements of historical literary scholarship and cultural analysis.

Born in New York on 4 November 1937, the son of an attorney, Isaac Kaplan, who was the first member of his family to go to college, and of Bessie Zwirn Kaplan, Fred Kaplan grew up in the lower-middle-class environment of third-generation Jewish Ashkenazic immigrant culture, first in the Bronx and then in Brooklyn, where his family moved when he was ten. He was one of four sons, the other three of whom became lawyers. His avid reading of novels and other books at home, in the public library, in the public schools of Brooklyn, and at Brooklyn College, where he majored in classics and philosophy (B.A., 1959), led to his partial assimilation into Anglo-American culture; he then earned an M.A. (1961) and a Ph.D. (1966) in English literature from Columbia University. Kaplan's continuing interest in and relationship to his Jewish origins remain strong, and perhaps to some extent have allowed him to have a useful, almost anthro-

Fred Kaplan

pological, perspective on Anglo-American history and culture.

On 28 May 1959 Kaplan married Gloria Taplin, from whom he separated in 1985; they have three children: Benjamin, Noah, and Julia. In 1962 he accepted the first of a series of academic positions, becoming an instructor at Lawrence University from 1962 to 1964; then an assistant professor at California State University at Los Angeles (1964-1967); and an assistant and later full professor at Queens College and the Graduate Center of the City University of New York, from 1967 to the present. He has also held a Fulbright lectureship in Denmark (1973-1974); a Guggenheim Fellowship in England (1976-1977); a Huntington Library Fellowship (1981-1982); a National Humanities Center Fellowship (1985-1986); and a visiting professorship at the University of Paris (1986-1987).

The first of his planned quartet, his 1983 biography of Carlyle, has introduced Kaplan's major topics: the movement in England from sectarian religion to free thought and from objective to subjective values; the rise of literary groups and

families; the social and economic determinants of modern culture; the special relationship between Great Britain and America; the problems of marriage and sexuality; the role of women; the uses of narrative; autobiographical and biographical fictions; and biography as cultural exemplar. His 1988 treatment of Dickens dramatizes the life and art of the major British literary figure of the mid nineteenth century, the high Victorian period. The third of the quartet is a biography-in-progress of Henry James, whose life will further exemplify and deepen the topics Kaplan sees as central to Anglo-American society in the movement from the eighteenth to the twentieth century. The volume completing the quartet will probably be a biography of a twentieth-century American writer.

In addition to their importance as biographies of major figures and their thematic overview, Kaplan's biographies of Carlyle and Dickens (and his work on James) are important as revisionary biographies. They quite purposely, systematically, and self-consciously rewrite the lives of major figures about whom substantial biogra-

Dust jacket for the first book of the projected "biographical quartet" in which Kaplan plans to examine the evolution of Anglo-American culture from the Romantic era to the twentieth century

phies have already been written by Victorian contemporaries and by biographers of the mid twentieth century. Kaplan's books are attempts to present the lives of their subjects in a way that reflects late-twentieth-century views of human nature, social and economic realities, literary and sexual sensibilities, and private and public decorum. Each generation, Kaplan believes, must rewrite and re-create the lives of the great cultural figures of the past to give contemporary life to cultural inheritance. These biographies place special emphasis on portraying sympathetically the inner lives of their subjects, of getting as close as possible to their sensibility and their emotional life. They are based on the premise that the biographer is not a judge; he is a dramatizer for the purpose of vivid portrayal and intellectual communication. The overall interest is in total artistic portrayal, capturing the feel of the subject and his world as much as possible from the inside, while at the same time remaining scrupulously faithful to the historical record—the base from which dramatic presentation, embodied in psychological and social re-creation and analysis, proceeds. But

biography is a narrative art, Kaplan believes, and all storytelling involves imaginative projection. Thus a modern biography of a Victorian literary figure is just as much a story about the biographer and modern culture as it is about the subject and Victorian culture.

Kaplan has explored varied aspects of the Victorian world in three major works of scholarly analysis that define the context for his biographies of Carlyle and Dickens. His emphasis on the crucial distinctions between Victorian and modern culture has led him to illuminate key Victorian patterns and themes embedded so deeply in Victorian values as to make them accessible only to historical study. This aspect of his work began with his analysis of poetic self-consciousness in *Miracles of Rare Device: The Poet's Sense of Self in Nineteenth-Century Poetry* (1972), which focuses on the sense of the literary personality articulated in major nineteenth-century narrative poems, and the psychological anxiety about the status of the self that drives particular poets to reveal, hide, and express it. This exploration is carried forward in *Dickens and Mesmerism: The*

Hidden Springs of Fiction (1975), which documents Dickens's fascination with hypnotism. Tracing Dickens's increasing knowledge of mesmerism and his amateur practice of its techniques, which produced therapeutic results in at least one instance, Kaplan shows how Dickens made the subject an important theme in his fiction. Kaplan also draws upon biographical material to suggest how Dickens's writing process drew upon processes parallel to those of mesmerism—an issue Kaplan would develop later in his biography of Dickens.

He articulates the all-encompassing presence and overwhelming force of the moral sentiments in Victorian culture in *Sacred Tears: Sentimentality in Victorian Literature* (1987), charting the ways in which they define the central complexities of the Victorian era. As Kaplan notes, Dickens and his contemporaries "believed that there was an instinctive, irrepressible need for human beings to affirm both in private and in public that they possessed moral sentiments, that these sentiments were innate, that they best expressed themselves through spontaneous feelings, and that sentimentality in life and in art had a moral basis." This was not a mere latent presence but a dynamic force. "People—all people, except those who had been the victims of perverse conditioning or some misfortune of nature—instinctively felt . . . pleasure, *moral* pleasure, when those they thought of as good triumphed and those they thought of as bad were defeated." This definition of human nature led the Victorians to believe that "the human community was one of shared moral feelings, and that sentimentality was a desirable way of feeling and of expressing ourselves morally." The implications that follow from these beliefs lead to an emphasis on emotion, for men as well as women, and to feeling as an index of character, issues that Kaplan has put into practice in his biographies.

Furthermore, Victorian sentimentality served as "a fundamental, purposeful opposition" to and protest against the "increasingly powerful forces of philosophical and scientific realism that the intellectual community advanced but popular opinion rejected." Thus Victorian literature "defended the vision of the ideal against the claim that the universe and human history are governed by mechanical, or rational, or deterministic, or pragmatic forces; that we cannot maintain metaphysical or religious ideals; that all human nature is flawed; and that literature should not falsify life by depicting ideal characters and happy endings." At the same time, Puritan and Hobbesian pessimism, utilitarianism, rationalism, scientific determinism, and "a weakening though still powerful Calvinism," arguing "strongly against the moral sentiments," were opponents pressing their claims and had to be contended with. In addition to its value as an illuminating study of one of the fundamental Victorian values, *Sacred Tears* also outlines the atmosphere in which Dickens and Carlyle functioned. The treatment of death as a topos in Victorian literature in Kaplan's book is one of the most important critical discussions of the subject and echoes the ways in which Kaplan represents the responses to the deaths of several individuals in the biographies of Carlyle and Dickens.

His analysis of the moral sentiments forms the spine of both the biographies and will figure prominently in the life of James on which he is currently working. Unlike Dickens and Carlyle, whose moral rhetoric ranges throughout human experience, James's morality focuses primarily on aesthetic concerns. In Kaplan's view, James translated the Victorian legacy of the moral sentiments, reinforced by his American Puritan heritage, into a philosophy of art—thereby articulating central aspects of the cultural transition from the Romantic to the modern era. Part of the originality of Kaplan's biographical quartet lies in the links he establishes between English and American culture, as he marshals the details of the lives of his subjects.

Among the most powerful shapers of the institution of English and American literature in the nineteenth century, all three were highly self-conscious about their ability to affect their reading public and articulate a community's sense of the value and force of moral sentiments in and through their work. As literary virtuosos they kept their eyes on the sources of their emotion as representative of wider cultural sentiments. In writing the lives of Carlyle and Dickens, Kaplan has also provided the fundamental materials for an interpretation of their writings (as will also be the case with James) as defining aspects of Anglo-American culture. These biographies set the intellectual context of their protagonists; they provide vivid sketches of the major members of the circle of friends of these men; and in the analyses of the psychological springs of their action Kaplan breaks down the boundaries between biographical portraiture, psychological case study, English and American literature and culture, and anthropologically oriented communal life histories.

Kaplan shows an awareness of late-twentieth-century views of the psychological structure of personality. Aware that much of modern psychoanalytic thought is prefigured in Dickens's fiction, Kaplan also deploys it carefully. His description of Dickens's response to his father, including the severe impact of his father's death, is highly dramatic yet psychically consistent. Similarly Carlyle's response to his father's death, including the section in Carlyle's *Reminiscences* (1881) in which he evokes his father's life as a personal elegy, reveals the manner in which Carlyle had to find a different way of being in the world. The tension between his father's staunch faith and his own skepticism serves to differentiate the father from the son.

Though both Dickens and Carlyle inquired into the nature of heroism, Kaplan does not regard either as moral exemplars; they did not make great art simply because they were good men. Rather, the differences between Kaplan's and earlier biographies lie in his willingness to explore the anger, passion, vindictiveness, illiberality, and even meanness of Carlyle and Dickens (and of James, too) in order to show how the sources of their anger, resentment, and intemperateness became the resources of their art. Both Carlyle and Dickens were passionate, desperate men, making their own "wild way." Both grew up in relative poverty, and both achieved financial and literary success.

As Carlyle struggled to discover his vocation, trying his hand at teaching, journalism, translation, fiction, and historical narrative with little success for the first forty years of his life, the question that haunted him was whether there would be any literary career or any success as a writer at all. His difficult courtship of Jane Welsh and their complicated marriage defined the conditions of the success that came first with the publication of *The French Revolution* (1837); from the beginning Jane was his partner in his intellectual and social success. The extent of that partnership is revealed in Carlyle's comments on his wife in the *Reminiscences*—as Kaplan's discussion makes clear—and even more fully documented in their letters, on which Kaplan draws and whose telling phrases he weaves into his narrative. Throughout his account Kaplan focuses on and analyzes the ways in which the Carlyles' relationship centered both their lives. Thus the early years of Carlyle's life are seen as a preamble to his courtship and marriage; and the years after Jane's death found him numb and at times almost sleepwalking.

Kaplan's presentation of the shaping power of place in Carlyle's life has a Wordsworthian tone: "In the quiet twilight the hoarse cawing of the rooks over Ecclefechan filled the young boy with sensations of mystery and beauty." The narrative moves outward to articulate the force of this Scottish place for its native son: "Ecclefechan in southwestern Scotland was the spot on earth his feelings and imagination most identified with throughout his life. Deeply a man of place, he hated wanderers and wandering, the nomadic obsessions. In his mind and in his words he strained always to reproduce the movement of the rooks whose great circles gave form to mystery and established boundaries to the place he called home." Other places receive their due in the biography, including Edinburgh, London, Chelsea, and the domestic setting of Carlyle's home on Cheyne Walk.

Readers are made aware of the shaping presence of the biographer as someone profoundly sympathetic to Carlyle, seeking to understand why and how this awkward, self-taught Scotsman could have had such a world-defining impact. This characteristic aspect of Kaplan's biography is expressed in the chapter titles, which in most cases are Carlylean phrases taken either from the letters, reported conversation, or his writing. This feature of the biography received wide critical praise. Furthermore, Michael Goldberg claims in *Albion* that "Kaplan's superb work is both the most ambitious biographical study of Carlyle undertaken in this century and the most successful." Compared to earlier accounts, Kaplan's "has the weighty detail found in [David Alec] Wilson presented with a good deal more scholarly precision, and the narrative elegance of [James Anthony] Froude enriched by the advantages of modern perspectives and research."

Though the biography has theatrical elements, its dominant tone is that of a brooding inner life. Kaplan describes the ways in which Carlyle depended upon the external moment, showing how his most lasting work emerged from the interaction of personal sympathy, complex historical conflict, and a dialectical sense of past and future. Kaplan's biography—avoiding the easier interpretation of Carlyle's career either from the liberal or conservative perspective and choosing instead to map the currents that swept Carlyle in given moments to extraordinary insight or stupefying blindness—becomes controversial and pathbreaking. Overall the biography has a tragic cast, revealing what the effort to uncover the sources

Dust jacket for Kaplan's 1988 book, in which he attempted to relate Dickens's life and work suggestively, leaving the reader to discover their reciprocal impact

of heroism and then live up to them cost Carlyle as he made himself into a Victorian sage.

By contrast, the biography of Dickens resembles a romance: it is the story of overwhelming success. This narrative shares the method of scenic construction of the Carlyle biography—part of the originality of both works—but as is appropriate to Dickens's highly theatrical personality, it dramatizes Dickens's self-presentation. Again Kaplan's ability to select telling phrases from letters and conversations makes the chapter titles into focusing elements of his narrative. Dickens's passion for molding and shaping his environment parallels Carlyle's; the effort of both to define their worlds as they wanted them to become, through a subtle and powerful exertion of will that brings the imagination and the external world into mutual and reciprocal discourse, is one of the ways that Kaplan charts their Victorian qualities. Both men take the inheritance of the romantic world and reshape it. These issues are

embedded in the narrative account and revealed in the details of their lives.

Dickens the impresario figures prominently in Kaplan's story. To those who see the literary enterprise as part of the wider sphere of human life, it is illuminating to question the meaning of the frenetic energy and overwhelming industriousness of this characteristic and yet extraordinary writer. Unlike James, who disguised his fundamental moral assumptions about human nature, or Carlyle, who was continuously conflicted about their contradictions, Dickens put them into dramatic play: "Dickens's notion of the ideal was nontheological," and he shared Carlyle's view "of natural supernaturalism, of finding the sacred in everyday life. He needed to distinguish between a realism that enhanced the ideal and a realism that devalued hope, beauty, art, and human nature." Thus Dickens "was radically conservative in his combination of realistic psychological portraiture and moral idealism." Kaplan's narrative

Kaplan circa 1988 (photograph by Alan Dehmer)

thereby touches on difficult issues of literary interpretation by focusing them continuously on the interplay between the writer's life and work. Dickens seems to have played the role of parent to his parents once he became a success. Nevertheless, they constantly threatened his own sense of status and power. Bitterly complaining in a letter that "his father and the rest of the family 'look upon me as a something to be plucked and torn to pieces for their advantage,'" he responded to his own seven sons as if they were "ghostly incarnations of his father's incapacity." Dickens was "terrified by the thought that his sons had inherited their mother's laziness and his father's tendency toward chronic indebtedness. Part of his pain resulted from his sensitivity to the financial burden" of supporting them by the chancy business of writing. In retrospect it seems that literary and financial success were inevitable accompaniments of Dickens's genius, but "there has been a long-standing tendency," Kaplan notes, "to underplay

his obsession with money, as if it devalued his accomplishments."

Late in life Dickens realized that "his father was a better human being than he had previously given him credit for." Dickens, however, never was able to forgive his mother: Kaplan's discussion of the traumatic episode when Dickens was apprenticed to the blacking factory is a subtle and brilliant treatment. Kaplan recognizes the ways in which the blame Dickens places on her echoes back upon himself. Furthermore, Kaplan's analysis makes clear the ways in which the episode influenced Dickens's depiction of many of the befuddled mothers of his fiction.

With the separation from his wife, Catherine, and his relationship with the young Ellen Ternan, Dickens brought a new vitality to many of the female characters in his novels. Kaplan brings together the life and the work in important and suggestive ways, and the reader discovers their reciprocal impact and influence. Psychological analysis, historical understanding, and cultural patterns work together to provide a more complete portrait.

The epigraphs to the Dickens biography define its three central strands. Kaplan quotes an 1858 letter by Dickens: "Constituted to do the work that is in me, I am a man full of passion and energy, and my own wild way that I must go is often—at the best—wild enough." This is followed by Carlyle's comment on his friend: Dickens's "steady practicality withal; the singularly solid business talent he continually had, and deeper than all, if one has the eye to see deep enough, dark, fateful, silent elements, tragical to look upon; and hiding amid dazzling radiances as of the sun, the elements of death itself." The last word is Sigmund Freud's: the goal of biography is "to bring a grand figure nearer to us." And it is unavoidable that "if we learn more about a great man's life, we shall also hear of occasions on which he has done no better than we, has in fact come nearer to us as a human being."

Rather than commenting directly, Kaplan follows Dickens's own method, and embeds these issues in his narrative. "For Dickens," as he notes, "plot revelation needed to rise organically from the interaction of characters in a narrative pattern in which suggestion and symbol appealed to the reader's intuition." As a result, both the Dickens and the Carlyle biographies engage the reader in ways that echo the achievement of the nineteenth-century novel. *Thomas Carlyle* was nominated for the 1983 National Book Critics Circle Award; it was also a jury nominee for the 1984 Pulitzer Prize in biography. In nine months the Dickens biography sold twenty-five thousand copies in England and America.

Kaplan's biographical efforts have led him to reflect upon the differences between Victorian and modern views of biography. In a paper delivered at the 1988 M.L.A. convention, he noted that "for the Victorians the public record tended to embody a sacred ideal. It was a privileged space, like the playing fields at Rugby, with rules and regulations created for the greater good of the society. What mattered was that the individual life affirm the public values of the community. Private life was another matter." Even modern biography tends to be conservative in form and must respond to "the community's expecta-

tions about the relationship between genius and goodness, between art and life, and especially by assumptions about the relationship between community values and narrative forms." Nevertheless, contemporary biographers challenge these assumptions, "and out of the tension between these cultural givens and the biographer's desire for freedom, for increased autonomy and flexibility, some of the distinctive features of modern literary biography emerge." Kaplan summarizes his method and suggests why his biography of James will form the third of his quartet: one of the distinctive features of modern biography is "the uneasy relationship between psychological analysis and conventional storytelling, between personal encounters and letting the so-called facts speak for themselves—let me end with the beginning of an invented extension of a real encounter." When Dickens was visiting America in 1867, "he was lionized, especially in Boston, his American home away from home. Henry James, twenty-four years old, having just recently published his first, very Victorian stories, managed to be introduced to Dickens when the young man was invited to come by after dinner at the home of Charles Eliot Norton," where the "visiting writer was the honored guest. The record suggests that they had only a moment together. It was not a special moment for Dickens. He was tired, and in the noisy room he may not even have heard the young man's name. Apparently Dickens only nodded his head and, so it appeared to James, took in the young man with 'the barest act . . . of the trained eye.' For James, who says almost nothing about the encounter in his letters but who uses it in his *Notes of a Son and Brother* (1914) as an example 'of the force of . . . passion, that may reside in a single pulse of time,' it was a powerful moment." Kaplan dwells upon their encounter to allow the opportunities and the problems of the literary biographer to come forward: "What *did* they say to one another? Let us begin by inventing the answer to that question, and in doing so we may be able to begin to accustom ourselves to the probability that *all* biography dramatizes fictions about ourselves and our world. For the Victorians, the structure that these fictions took was a cultural given. For us, it is both a cultural given and a personal choice."

Justin Kaplan

(5 September 1925 -   )

David Sadkin
Niagara University

BOOKS: *Mr. Clemens and Mark Twain* (New York: Simon & Schuster, 1966; London: Cape, 1967);

Lincoln Steffens: A Biography (New York: Simon & Schuster, 1974; London: Cape, 1975);

Mark Twain and His World (New York: Simon & Schuster, 1974; London: Joseph, 1974);

Walt Whitman: A Life (Franklin Center, Pa.: Franklin Library, 1980; trade edition, New York: Simon & Schuster, 1980);

Born to Trouble (Washington, D.C.: Library of Congress, 1985).

OTHER: *Dialogues of Plato*, edited by Kaplan (New York: Pocket Books, 1950);

With Malice Toward Women: A Handbook for Women-Haters, edited by Kaplan (New York: Dodd, Mead, 1952);

The Pocket Aristotle, edited by Kaplan (New York: Pocket Library, 1958);

Mark Twain and Charles D. Warner, *The Gilded Age*, introduction by Kaplan (New York: Trident, 1964);

Great Short Works of Mark Twain, edited, with an introduction, by Kaplan (New York: Harper & Row, 1967);

Mark Twain: A Profile, edited by Kaplan (New York: Hill & Wang, 1967);

"The Naked Self and Other Problems," in *Telling Lives, The Biographer's Art*, edited by Marc Pachter (New York: New Republic Books, 1979), pp. 36-55;

"The 'Real Life,'" in *Studies in Biography*, edited by Daniel Aaron (Cambridge, Mass.: Harvard University Press, 1979), pp. 1-8;

"Whitman and the Biographers," in *Walt Whitman: Here and Now*, edited by Joann P. Krieg (Westport, Conn.: Greenwood, 1985), pp. 9-21;

The Harper American Literature, 2 volumes, edited by Kaplan and others (New York: Harper & Row, 1987);

Best American Essays, 1990, edited by Kaplan (New York: Ticknor & Fields, 1991).

SELECTED PERIODICAL PUBLICATIONS—
UNCOLLECTED: "Half Song-Thrush, Half Alligator," *American Heritage*, 31 (October/November 1980): 62-67;

"Starting from Paumanok . . . and from Hannibal: Whitman and Mark Twain," *Confrontation*, 27-28 (1984): 338-347;

"Tune that Name," *New Republic*, 190 (7 May 1984): 10-11;

"What Biographies Can't Do," *Boston Review*, 11 (June 1986): 9-10;

"In Pursuit of the Ultimate Fiction," *New York Times Book Review*, 19 April 1987, pp. 1, 24-25;

"A Connecticut Yankee in Hell," *American Heritage*, 40 (November 1989): 97;

"The Biographer's Problem," *Mickle Street Review*, 11 (1989): 80-88;

"Biographies Should Tell All: A Pulitzer Prize Winner's Perspective," *Newsweek*, 117 (22 April 1991): 58.

Justin Kaplan has produced three notable literary biographies: *Mr. Clemens and Mark Twain* (1966), for which he won the National Book Award and Pulitzer Prize; *Lincoln Steffens: A Biography* (1974), a life of the famous muckraking journalist and autobiographer; and *Walt Whitman: A Life* (1980), widely regarded as the best Whitman biography in a long line of superb works on the poet. He is now editing the sixteenth edition of *Bartlett's Familiar Quotations*, to be published by Little, Brown in 1992.

Justin Kaplan was born on 5 September 1925 in New York City to Tobias D. Kaplan, a manufacturer, and Anna Rudman Kaplan. A member of Phi Beta Kappa, the young Kaplan received his B.S. in 1945 from Harvard, where he then pursued graduate studies. He lectured there in 1969, 1973, 1976, and 1978; but he has devoted most of his professional life to editing and, since 1959, to full-time writing, which Kaplan reluctantly decided was incompatible with teaching duties.

Justin Kaplan (photograph by Jerry Bauer)

From 1946 to 1954 Kaplan did free-lance editing and writing for several New York publishers. In 1954 he joined Simon and Schuster, eventually becoming a senior editor. On 29 July of that year, Kaplan married novelist Anne Bernays; they were to have three daughters. During his tenure at Simon and Schuster, Kaplan edited works by Bertrand Russell, Nikos Kazantzakis, and Will Durant. Kaplan's interest in philosophy led him to edit the *Dialogues of Plato* (1950) and *The Pocket Aristotle* (1958). Kaplan learned the principles of good prose as an editor, no doubt influencing the expression and design he brings to his biographies.

In his 1979 essay "The 'Real Life,'" Kaplan defines the literary biography as a work that has literary qualities: the biographer "is essentially a storyteller and dramatist." Thus Kaplan has chosen to write about lives of inordinate interest, about subjects of paradoxical and complicated character. Each of Kaplan's biographies embod-

ies a significant period of American life and represents dominant currents and conflicts of the time. Kaplan notes that readers expect biography to render not only the private and public events of a life, but the "intimate and existential and perceptual textures"—the "real Me" of the subject, as if there *were* such a stable person to be discovered. Kaplan's research and his perceptions gleaned as an editor have led him to the conclusion that such a rendering is impossible. Two of his subjects, Samuel Clemens and Walt Whitman, created conflicting personas. Neither author was in full command of a stable, integrated ego. Both made and remade their public images. Both led disciples far from the truth when dictating their autobiographies. Even Lincoln Steffens had a complex and divided nature and appeared far different "within" and "without." Knowledge of the difficulty of capturing a human essence keeps the biographer "honest" and "writing scared": "It appears that at best biography is only a plausible, inevitably idiosyncratic surmise and reconstruction, severely limited by historical materials that are loaded with duplicities and evasions." Kaplan finds that even psychology is of limited value in dealing with his dead subjects. More important are "tact, empathy, empirical experience, and narrative flair." Biography, then, is "a feat of illusionism, sleight-of-hand, levitation." The more complex the life the less a biographer can "capture" the subject with permanent assurance.

Walter Whitman shortened his name. Samuel Clemens became Mark Twain. In Kaplan's essay "The Naked Self and Other Problems" (1979) he observes that such name changes have been more common than might be supposed. Nathaniel Hathorne added the *w* to his name; David Henry Thoreau reversed his first two names; Zane Grey's real first name was Pearl—he took the Zane from his birthplace, Zanesville, Ohio. Nathaniel Weinstein became Nathan Von Wallenstein Weinstein and, finally, Nathanael West. George Sand, George Eliot, and George Orwell are all self-named writers. All had "written" themselves before they wrote others. How difficult, then, for the biographer to penetrate these shells to find the "real" person beneath. Moreover, the persona often became inseparably fused with the person, as in the case of Clemens/Twain. He often signed both names to autographs, as if he did not quite know where each part of his divided self left off. Whitman insisted (not always successfully) that both his first and last names, "Walt Whitman," be used as a single entity, belying the fact that he was among the most divided selves in literature. Clearly Kaplan was attracted to these dual personalities, perhaps in part for the reason that they *are* impossible to "get down" in any absolute sense and thus give the biographer's novelistic sense much leeway.

Both Twain and Whitman consciously created a persona, but neither was in full control of it. Whitman wrote, "I cannot understand the mystery, but I am always conscious of myself as two—my soul and I." Twain's private life and values were often at diametrical odds with his fictive and public personas. Twain and Whitman became further transformed by others—disciples and biographers who created new identities: William Dean Howells, Twain's lifelong friend and first biographer; Albert Bigelow Paine, to whom Twain dictated his *Autobiography* (1924); and, in the case of Whitman, early biographers and friends William Douglas O'Connor, Horace Traubel, and Richard Maurice Bucke, all of whose works Whitman influenced and even helped write. As Twain noted, biographies "are but the clothes and buttons of the man—the biography of the man himself cannot be written." And Whitman, according to Kaplan, "manages to make nakedness an ultimate disguise, and so he becomes an extraordinarily problematic subject for biography." Thus, Kaplan writes, "the irreducible reality of literary lives may not be the naked self at all, but the sum of a writer's public and verbal acts and ecstasies with language." In turn, the "drama" of the literary biography lies not in "stalking the naked self to its burrow" but with the "tensions between the familiar, shared life of human beings—making it, making out, making a go of it, making waves, making a name—and a vision so singular it deserves to be regarded with awe."

Twain is certainly one of the most "biographied" presences in American literature. He started the process himself by dictating his *Autobiography* to his amanuensis Paine. The book is, in essence, as much a work of fiction as fact—Twain's life as he wished people to know it. Howells's *My Mark Twain* (1910) is an affectionate and reverent portrait. Among later efforts, Van Wyck Brooks's *Ordeal of Mark Twain* (1920) was among the first psychoanalytic biographies, a portrait of defeat and failure, contrasted with the view of Bernard De Voto, who, in several works, created a Twain myth of triumph and high achievement.

Kaplan, having apparently read every scrap extant about and by his subject, takes a panoramic and balanced approach that sees Twain's life as a series of tensions between literary triumph and private torment. Clemens/Twain is a deeply divided personality, an emblem for the divided America of the middle and late nineteenth century, which Twain with friend and collaborator Charles Dudley Warner wrote of in *The Gilded Age* (1873)—their unruly roman à clef about excesses. While Twain treated this period—whose name was coined by him and Warner—with scathing satire, he also devoted his life to joining the very society he abhorred. He established useful friendships with such nineteenth-century notables as Ulysses S. Grant (whose biography Twain published to great financial success); Bret Harte, with whom he had an intense love-hate relationship; George Washington Cable, with whom he toured on the lecture circuit; Howells, with whom he shared a lifelong friendship; and Henry H. Rogers, a vice-president of Standard Oil, who rescued Twain from bankruptcy.

over, without fear——but without it you are speculating upon a dangerous

issue."

~~In commonplace note for journalists~~, The city offered abundant [him]

material for his travel letters. From his rooming house on East Sixteenth

Street he set out daily to cover the sights. He kept to Broadway, he said, so

as not to get lost, and he went on foot, ~~a faster way of travelling than the~~

~~bestial overcrowded~~ The [were overcrowded, often] omnibuses mired in slush and traffic, ~~or swaying~~ [and they swayed] so vio-

lently that passengers had been known to become seasick; ~~and~~ even a veteran ~~of~~ [rider]

~~the more experienced might~~ [could] be flung to the street by a lurch, a whipping up of

the horses. It was a cruel winter; rain and slush gave way to a treacherous

hard freeze during which people crossing on the East River ice from Brooklyn [New York]

to ~~Manhattan~~ might find themselves trapped in mid-passage, the ice flashing

into sudden fragments. Fourteen years earlier, as a wandering printer with

a ten-dollar bill sewn in the lining of his coat, Sam spent a brief summer [had]

in New York. He visited the Crystal Palace at the World's Fair where each [had]

day came six thousand visitors, double the population of Hannibal, and he [had]

~~took~~ [taken] a liking to the city; he found it as hard to leave as Hannibal had been [had]

easy. ~~...~~ It

~~It~~ too big a city [Since then,] he felt, [had become] A business trip or a friendly visit often

took up a whole day, ~~so congested were~~ [were so congested] the streets and so full of distractions.

~~The~~ [They] echoed with the sounds of hammering and building ~~and~~ of that tremendous

~~energy~~ [activity] which the end of the Civil War ~~had~~ [had] unleashed in America. ~~The city was~~

~~all changed now. Away from Broadway he found labyrinths of crooked streets~~

~~turning together at angles ... into that the corner houses were built like the~~

~~bows of steamships ... flatirons; he claimed he could see them only~~

~~by closing one eye.~~ At Fulton Street a pedestrian bridge of cast iron

In chasing after worldly success, Twain owned a subscription publishing house; bought diamond-mine land claims in South Africa; marketed a German health nostrum; invented a pregummed photograph album, several board games, a perpetual calendar, and a bed clamp; attempted to dramatize and produce his novels as plays; invested in a fire extinguisher that worked like a hand grenade; and, most notably, lost a huge fortune backing the infamous Paige Typesetting Machine. While he attempted to escape the role of public platform humorist into the higher calling of man of letters, he was forced to return to the platform again and again to recoup the losses from his failed business ventures.

Kaplan's novelistic approach leads him to begin Twain's story when the author is already thirty-one, on the supposition that Twain's writing is the best source of his "usable past." Twain's formative years are revealed retrospectively and selectively through Kaplan's development of several central theses and motifs.

For those readers wishing a chronological account, Kaplan has written a much shorter, richly illustrated biography, *Mark Twain and His World* (1974), most appropriate for those largely unfamiliar with Twain and his times. It borrows heavily from the larger work but is not nearly as analytic or speculative.

Mr. Clemens and Mark Twain is structured around a series of motifs, the controlling one being twinship, represented by the homonymic Twain/twin and Clemens/claimants. Kaplan reconstructs a series of twinning, or divided, personality patterns that echo the divided self of both Twain and his era. Twenty-six years before he created the notorious twins of *Pudd'nhead Wilson* (1893), Twain was fascinated by the Siamese twins Chang and Eng. Retired from Ringling Brothers' circus, they had been forced by financial reverses to tour again—a precursor to Twain's dilemma. Twain wrote a burlesque of their lives in a sketch called "Personal Habits of Siamese Twins" (1869), embellishing the facts, which were outrageous enough without embellishment. The twins had been slave owners in North Carolina. They had married sisters. One twin abused alcohol, which, of course, made the other drunk. The twins quarreled violently.

Kaplan shows how these grotesques prefigure Twain's life: Clemens and Twain were at enmity with each other; Twain was a child of the slave-holding South who made his fortune in the North; Chang's wife abominated tobacco: so did

Twain's. Twain's burlesque, in which the twins are captured by opposite sides in the Civil War and are exchanged for each other, merely exaggerates the deep conflicts within the author himself. Drunken Chang resembles in personality Twain's brother Orion, whose presence hovers throughout Kaplan's book. Orion was hobbled by alcohol, and he was a dreamer and schemer much like his well-known brother but without his audacity and talent.

Another twin variant is the relationship between Twain and President Grant. Both men had serious reverses, both were beloved by the public, and both were easy pickings for con men and scoundrels. In *The Gilded Age* Twain created the vivid Col. Sellers, who is both the prototypical con man and Southern gentry fallen on hard times, "courtly, hospitable, generous, and broke"—a promoter who sounds like Orion even as he behaves like Twain. Later, Twain returned to this conflicting persona in Hank Morgan, the hero of *A Connecticut Yankee in King Arthur's Court* (1889), which Kaplan regards, rightfully, as one of Twain's masterpieces, and for which he supplies a much-needed reassessment.

Personal and societal boom and bust is another motif that lends coherence to Kaplan's story of Twain's chaotic life. Throughout the book, even when depicting Twain's most prosperous years, Kaplan foreshadows the coming traumatic financial reverses. This specter of failure parallels the fear of failure that haunted Twain, even in times of his greatest success. Kaplan's foreshadowing creates a pervasive feeling of fate, so that, when the reverses arrive, they seem inevitable. Of all the get-rich schemes that brought misfortune to Twain, one in particular becomes symbolic and is invoked throughout the work: his backing of the Paige Typesetting Machine, which becomes a metaphor for Twain's habitual inability to distinguish real gold from fool's gold—echoing a major theme in Twain's work, from his very first fiction.

Other motifs lend fresh insight into Twain's life. The tormented novelist attempted to provide himself a safe harbor with his magnificent Hartford home, and the construction, occupation, and eventual abandonment of this rococo house permeate the biography. The "rise and fall" of the house of Twain takes on as mythic and substantial a role as that of Howells's Silas Lapham and other heroes in world literature, whose houses take on the attributes of the owner and merge with his life.

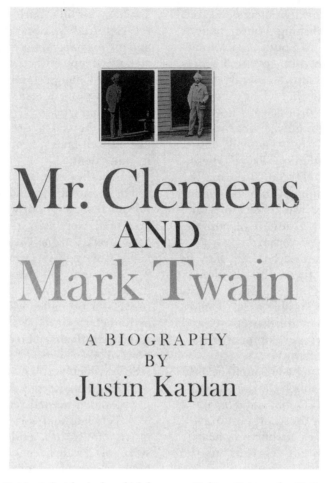

Dust jacket for Kaplan's first book, for which he won a Pulitzer Prize and a National Book Award

Twain's house is described as "permanent polychrome and gingerbread gothic ... part steamboat, part medieval strong-hold, and part cuckoo clock." Kaplan's presentation of life at 351 Farmington Avenue, in the middle of the planned wealthy enclave of "Nook Farm," formerly "Meandering Swine Creek," is a portrait of the emergence of both the American nouveau riche and of an artistic and intellectual colony that prefigured the Hamptons on Long Island. Twain mingled with fellow residents Calvin and Harriet Beecher Stowe, Henry Ward Beecher, Charles Dudley Warner, John and Isabella Beecher Hooker, Senator Francis Gilette, and Howells, who was a frequent visitor. The life-style included a veritable open-door policy and constant rounds of teas, musicales, billiard games, and discussion groups—all with high energy and great financial cost.

The expense of the house, combined with the failure of the Paige typesetter, drove Twain into bankruptcy. While Rogers rescued Twain from total financial ruin, the house, designed to be a haven, became a ball and chain, a cause for continual worry, and, finally, a cause of despair.

Kaplan greatly enlarges the picture formerly available of Twain's beloved wife, Olivia. The old view depicted her as a censor who drained the robustness from her husband's work. The truth, Kaplan finds, is far more complex. Her editing was mostly according to Twain's wishes: she made emendations to make his work more respectable in the world he meant to claim. Moreover, Twain hated to revise. It was not uncommon for him to follow any recommendations by his wife or Howells without question; typically, by that stage, he had turned to other matters of commerce or had lost interest in the book.

While Twain worshiped his wife throughout the marriage, and regarded her early on as morally pure, she soon was more than an ethereal presence; their marriage was one solidly based on the flesh as well as the spirit. Twain probably had more effect on her than the reverse. At the time of her death, she had lost her faith; the teetotaler had turned tippler. During her final decline, Twain was kept from her, partly at his wife's request, because her doctors realized that her illnesses were exacerbated by the tensions of living with Twain. The loving father and husband habitually, and apparently unwittingly, terrorized his children as much as he enervated his wife.

As Kaplan demonstrates how Twain's divided personality affected the themes and content of his fiction and his life, he demonstrates with great cogency how the subscription publication system affected the form of Twain's works. Just as Twain took advantage of the Lyceum Circuit to promote his lectures for ever-increasing fame and profit, so he employed the subscription system, rather than trade publication, to promote his fiction. In fact, Twain was among the first serious fiction writers to employ this mode of publishing, which had served to promote nonfiction as well as utilitarian and inspirational literature. His use of it was another instance of the merging of business and art, to the detriment of art.

In subscription publishing, the prestige of the imprint was commercial. Four principals had to be satisfied: the author; the publisher, who went to press only after enough orders were in place to guarantee commercial success; the subscription agent, who went door-to-door and peddled the book in rural and small-town environments; and the buyer, typically a tradesman or farmer with little intellectual acumen, who was buying a "product," often to display as a parlor artifact.

To meet the tastes of those who equated heft with worth, and to justify the inflated prices of these tomes, subscription books were padded out to six hundred pages, replete with steel engravings and elaborate pictorial devices and tables of contents. According to Kaplan this pre-imposed length forced Twain to develop his books on "purely linear principles, with episode strung after episode until he reached page 600." It forced him to grind out manuscript pages long after he lost interest and "conditioned him to think of his writing as a measurable commodity, like eggs and corn." Kaplan demonstrates that what has often been considered Twain's inability to shape his work was, in fact, conscious decision motivated by commercial considerations.

While Kaplan shows how Twain's milieu and personal conflicts affected his artistic output,

he does not analyze the works as a literary critic might do. Kaplan treats the biography as history refracted through the life of his subject—thus his vivid portrayal of the Gilded Age in *Mr. Clemens and Mark Twain*, the muckraking era in *Lincoln Steffens*, and the ante- and post-bellum periods in *Walt Whitman*.

In awarding *Mr. Clemens and Mark Twain* the National Book Award, the committee cited the book as a "masterly biography of a central figure in the American consciousness—the enigmatic man who was in fact one of its great makers.... Kaplan ... gives us a totally realized portrait—the light and dark and the shadings between—of artist and victim, the time and the place." While Kaplan creates a rich record of source material, and suggests ways by which it might be read, he makes no claim to the "final word."

Kaplan's second major biographical portrait was of the journalist and autobiographer Lincoln Steffens. Unlike the subjects of Kaplan's first and third efforts, Steffens was not a writer of the first magnitude. His impact was historical. He and his fellow crusading journalists—including Ida Tarbell, Upton Sinclair, and John Reed—and the muckraking magazine movement—typified by *McClure's* magazine, for which Steffens did much of his work—engendered reform legislation and social awareness, beginning in 1902 with Steffens's exposure of the Tweed Ring in New York and continuing through the Theodore Roosevelt presidency and beyond.

Steffens's *Autobiography* (1931), while highly popular for a time, is now not often read. *The Shame of the Cities* (1904), Steffens's exposé of the corruption of American municipal government, is more assigned in universities than spontaneously read. Why then was Kaplan attracted to Steffens? The literary biographer being basically a "storyteller and dramatist," the life of Steffens covers a vivid and notorious period in American history, and the dramatic role of the muckraker is a valid focal point from which to view this era.

In his afterword to *Lincoln Steffens*, Kaplan reveals one rationale for restudying Steffens and his era, comparing it to the era of "Ralph Nader, My Lai and Watergate. Never before, perhaps, has there been quite so much to expose or so strong a resistance to exposure.... Never before has muckraking ... been so nakedly recriminated and menaced by men in power." This conflict, Kaplan asserts, is prefigured by the life and career of Steffens. Thus the very last page of the book indicates a political agenda. The placement for this rationale is revealing; one might expect such an agenda in the introduction. Clearly Kaplan means for readers to deduce additional reasons for studying Steffens long before they come to the afterword.

A second rationale for study lies in Kaplan's observation that Steffens's *Autobiography* places its author "squarely in the line of American autobiographers, from Benjamin Franklin on, who have been the conduit of new styles of awareness, radical responses to emergent occasions." Steffens's book and career are both catalytic and representative of an American intellectual tradition that attracts Kaplan.

Further reasons for the attraction can be surmised. There are points of similarity among Steffens, Twain, and Whitman, whose massive biography Kaplan published six years after *Lincoln Steffens*. All three men were autobiographers (even if Whitman's "autobiography" was partly his poetry and partly lodged in books nominally written by others). All three created public personas who only bore partial resemblances to their private selves. All three mined their own lives for the raw materials of their art. All three men, at the end of their lives, became "gurus" who attracted coteries of disciples, true believers who sought to bask in reflected light and carry the reputation of their idols into the future.

Lincoln Steffens is organized chronologically, with occasional "flash-forwards" to the *Autobiography* when Kaplan wishes to compare his view of events with Steffens's refraction of them. *Lincoln Steffens* has little of the fateful foreboding that hangs over *Mr. Clemens and Mark Twain*; nor does it have, at its core, a protagonist as enigmatic as Whitman. Thus the attention shifts more to the world in which Steffens operated.

Through Kaplan's work a new generation of readers can see big-city life from the apex of the Gilded Age, to the Roaring Twenties, to the Depression. Kaplan captures the elegance and decadence of Europe before World War I when he describes the Germany and England where Steffens studied philosophy and met his future wife.

As Kaplan narrates Steffens's life he develops several theses. Steffens's outlook was somewhat determined by the effect of early exposure to evangelical Christianity. As a result Steffens was prone to dogmatic views that often changed to new, no less dogmatic ones when reality was found to be in conflict. It is a tribute to his personality that virtually all who knew him, at least as

Kaplan portrays them, found Steffens irresistible, even when in disagreement with his rigidly held beliefs. Steffens could be zealous without appearing to be a zealot, and this was crucial to his ability to persuade large numbers of influential people of the correctness of his opinions.

Another central thesis is that in all his relationships, including those with his two wives and a longtime mistress, Steffens was "more loved than loving." None of his relationships seemed to be very sexual; repelled by a childhood friend's homosexual advance, Steffens appears to have channeled his erotic drive into politics and reform. Kaplan portrays Steffens as "mother-bound" (as were Twain and Whitman), and his early disillusionment with his rigid, plutocratic father led him throughout his life to find replacements, including S. S. McClure, and, later, Benito Mussolini and Joseph Stalin.

In Germany, Steffens and a fellow student had a close friendship that most who knew them assumed to be homosexual. Such thoughts apparently never crossed Steffens's mind, although the German friend, upon his untimely death, left a considerable fortune to Steffens. Nowhere does Kaplan allege that Steffens was drawn to homosexuality, but the portrayal of his repressed sexual drives, juxtaposed with childhood and youthful experiences, leads the reader to reach his or her own conclusions.

In charting early influences on Steffens and grounding later behaviors and political and philosophical views in them, Kaplan follows unstated Freudian and Ericksonian approaches without being dogmatic or obvious. His interpretations, however, seem more consistently grounded in such theory than those found in *Mr. Clemens and Mark Twain* and *Walt Whitman*. As in the other biographies, though, Kaplan tends to suggest rather than insist.

Although Kaplan does not state it overtly, and may not even have intended it, Steffens's portrait emerges as an indictment of "intellectualism." Steffens became more and more disenchanted with the average citizen's capacity for enlightened self-interest. Much as deeply held, dogmatic religious beliefs often give way to nihilism when challenged by conflicting reality, so Steffens's radical idealism did not withstand the onslaughts of human nature, which refused to conform to the a priori "models" of enlightened behavior presented by the muckrakers. While Kaplan certainly finds much in Steffens's life that is

Dust jacket for Kaplan's 1974 book, a detailed picture of a leading muckraking journalist at the turn of the century

admirable, the subtext seems to compel at least some distancing.

Kaplan's third major literary biography, *Walt Whitman*, follows and makes ample use of a rich tradition of Whitman scholarship even as Kaplan redefines and amplifies his subject. The early biographers, Whitman's passionate disciples and friends, figure heavily in Kaplan's work. William Douglas O'Connor's *The Good Gray Poet* (1866) portrays the mythic Whitman—with Whitman's complicity—as "sage, martyr, redeemer fit to stand with Aeschylus and Socrates and Christ." Equal in spirit was John Burroughs's *Notes on Walt Whitman as Poet and Person* (1867). Whitman actively collaborated in his friend Richard Maurice Bucke's study (1883), much as Twain had done in assisting Paine. In all these works on him, Whitman, directly or indirectly, campaigned for the position of "American Bard."

Bliss Perry's *Walt Whitman* (1906) brought

"higher criticism" to the study of the poet, and was as generally sympathetic as the "hagiographers." But Perry ignored a central fact of Whitman's poetic and private personas: his sexuality. Kaplan has decried later psychoanalytic studies that have attempted to deal with Whitman's homosexuality in terms of neurosis, especially since such studies ignored the centrality of his sexuality in both the subject matter and spirit of his art. That Whitman was ambivalent and sometimes tormented by his homosexual drives there is no doubt. But his *poetic* depiction of all forms of sexuality is joyful and unneurotic. Kaplan would be the first to admit that nobody can say with certainty what Whitman did; furthermore, it is not clear that Whitman himself fully understood his own drives. Kaplan seeks a delicate balance—bringing modern, tolerant attitudes to the subject of Whitman's sexuality, yet allowing the reader to see it in nineteenth-century perspectives—essen-

Justin Kaplan is the author of *Mr. Clemens and Mark Twain*—which was awarded a Pulitzer Prize in biography and a National Book Award—and of *Lincoln Steffens*. Born in Manhattan, he did his undergraduate and graduate studies at Harvard, and worked for several years in a New York publishing house before becoming a writer. He held a Guggenheim Memorial Fellowship while writing *Walt Whitman*. Mr. Kaplan lives in Cambridge, Massachusetts, and is married to the novelist Anne Bernays.

PHOTOGRAPH © BY LILIAN KEMP
0-671-22542-1

SIMON AND SCHUSTER

Dust jacket for Kaplan's 1980 biography of the poet who, according to Kaplan, "manages to make nakedness an ultimate disguise"

tial if the reader is to infer the external as well as internal conflicting forces with which Whitman had to contend.

Whitman saw his sexuality as troublesome; even as he celebrated homosexuality in the "Calamus" poems (in the 1860 edition of *Leaves of Grass*), he rejected British homosexual writers including Edward Carpenter, Edmund Gosse, and John Addington Symonds, who sought unambiguous statements of his preferences. Whitman's private feelings are far too carefully diffused to make any dogmatic interpretation possible. Kaplan treats the whole topic with clarity, tact, and responsibility, tying the issue to the poetry, to the fragmentary details of Whitman's life, and to the time in which he lived, when even heterosexuality was very much a private affair.

Kaplan credits Gay Wilson Allen's *The Solitary Singer* (1955) as an indispensable example of intelligent, systematic, and disciplined biography. That work, along with E. H. Miller's edition of Whitman's letters, *The Correspondence*, published in six volumes (1961-1977), provides much of the documentation for any biographical work on Whitman.

Yet a major problem remained: no work

had yet accounted for the remarkable transformation of the printer/teacher/editor/opera critic/ building contractor/autodidact into the poetically uninhibited "barbaric yawper." Kaplan's work, too, is unable to resolve the unresolvable; but it goes further than any earlier work and perhaps as far as the evidence will allow.

One evidentiary problem Kaplan faced was the disproportionate distribution of source material. The last ten years of Whitman's life, after his creative period was largely over, were the most "public"; he had gathered around him a body of disciples who hung on his every word— some of which were candid words, but many of which were conscious deceptions. Whitman's later years are fully chronicled in letters, daybooks, journals, interviews, public statements, and volumes written by his acolytes.

Conversely, the years prior to the 1855 first edition of *Leaves of Grass* reveal only twelve letters of the three thousand in Miller's *The Correspondence*; and other sources for the first half of Whitman's life are fragmentary. Earlier biographers were overwhelmed by the later material and at a loss to document the early life. Kaplan fills the gap by realizing that there is, in fact, a great deal of material from the earlier years: Whitman's journalism, essays, and public writings, as well as the copiously documented milieu in which Whitman prepared himself to be a poet.

Kaplan begins his biography of Whitman when his subject is an old man, past his creative period, living in the tiny house on Mickle Street in Camden, New Jersey, which had become the mecca for his coterie. Whitman's cottage served partly the same role that the Farmington Avenue house had for Twain: a stable place amid the chaos of his life. The ultimate monument to stability for Whitman was his granite tomb at Harleigh Cemetery, Camden, the design and building of which Whitman had lovingly supervised and which became his final word on death, a central subject throughout his canon. Kaplan uses the tomb as a catalyst for discussion of this subject, a central concern in Whitman's art.

Kaplan chose to begin his biography with a discussion of the end of his subject's life for reasons beyond the imbalance of documentary evidence. The infirm Whitman, at the end of his creative period, while disappearing from the world, is seen making his living "monument" through the work of his friends and biographers, as he made his granite monument. He was creating a lasting persona along with the poetic self he created through the multiple editions of *Leaves of Grass*. As Kaplan put it in his 1985 essay "Whitman and the Biographers," "The man and the bones of his life and personality go into the rendering vat and are steamily absorbed into a sweet-smelling colloidal suspension of disbelief and borax."

By beginning with the "guru of Mickle Street," Kaplan can then go back to the formative years to trace the genesis of the "final product," and to attempt to separate reality from the "borax." Some of the words that were dictated by Whitman or were otherwise taken down by his disciples appear to Kaplan to be authentic and unguarded: Whitman's humor, his earthiness, and his teasing about some great secret he never reveals. His private papers and dictated materials reveal a person much less stuffy and self-important than the persona of some of the poems. For Kaplan, the preoccupations of old age help inform the earlier years, the story of which, by the very dearth of supporting primary source materials, must be speculative. By reading the early life against the heavily documented end of it, abetted by the public writings of the poet-to-be and a discussion of the world in which the poet came to ma-

turity, Kaplan creates a more rounded portrait than any that preceded.

In 1838 when Whitman was the publisher of the *Long Island Democrat*, he was on his own and could work as he pleased. He purchased a mare and rode the countryside of Long Island, frequenting the beach parties that were in vogue at the time: an amalgam of New England clam bake, swimming party, and fishing derby. Kaplan notes that seaside frolic was celebrated by writers such as Gerard Manley Hopkins, in "Epithalamion"; by the painter Georges Seurat in *Une Baignade*; and by artist Thomas Eakins in *The Swimming Hole*. These works are then compared to Whitman's images that appear later in "Song of Myself": "Twenty-eight young men bathe by the shore, / Twenty-eight young men and all so friendly; / Twenty-eight years of womanly life and all so lonesome."

The quotation of this passage also illustrates another important characteristic of Kaplan's work. As in the Twain biography, Kaplan often relegates interpretations of the work to footnotes, especially those possibly controversial interpretations not original with him. While Kaplan's text ties this passage to both Whitman's undisguised life and to artistic traditions of which Whitman was probably aware, the footnote quotes Robert K. Martin's work *The Homosexual Tradition in American Poetry* (1979), in which Martin interprets the passage as "a clear defense of the anonymity of sexual encounter.... The experience could well be repeated in almost any steam bath of a modern large city." Such anonymous sexuality "is an important way station on the path to the destruction of distinctions of age, class, beauty, *and* sex."

By relegating this interpretation to a footnote and quoting without comment, Kaplan has it both ways: he can develop a thesis about sublimated sexuality, yet preserve both his own distance from such interpretations, and maintain "deniability." This might be considered a flaw in his methodology, since it distances the biographer from some major assertions for which he could be asked to take responsibility. Kaplan uses variants of this technique in all his major biographical works.

One of the most apt and useful instances of Kaplan's yoking of the private life to the public poetry is his exploration of Whitman's fascination with phrenology, a nineteenth-century "science" that identified character traits inside the head by means of reading the bumps on the skull. The subject could then work to enhance or suppress those characteristics. Whitman's personality was diagnosed on 16 July 1849 according to a schema developed by the phrenologist Lorenzo Fowler: equally powerful were the traits of "amativeness" (sexual love), "philoprogenitiveness" (parental love and fondness for children and pets), and "adhesiveness" (friendship, attachment, fraternal love). The variety of expressions of love; the ambivalence expressed in the life and the poetry; and the confusion and blending of manly, chaste friendship and sexual longing between males are all seemingly predicted by the diagnosis.

There is no special pleading in the book for any given thesis. Whitman's portrait is derived from the primary evidence of journals, letters, poetry, and prose—all of which Kaplan assumes are products of conscious control, whatever the subconscious components. Whitman was richly connected to his age and sophisticatedly aware of the movements that swept his time, including opera and symphonic music, which he reviewed for several newspapers and whose techniques he incorporated into his poetry.

As in the biography of Twain, Kaplan draws a vivid portrait of the man and his age. Twain, though deeply divided, emerges palpably three-dimensional. Whitman, more subtly divided, appears less substantial. But Kaplan's is as solid a portrait, and as responsible a one, as we are likely to get.

Kaplan brings to the art of biography both the craft of a novelist, in the way he shapes each work, and the care of the scholar who, exhaustively thorough in his research, nevertheless eschews the "scholarly" tendency to inflict either a thesis or a dogmatic methodological approach upon the reader. While Kaplan's organizational strategies and his choice of materials may subtly lead the reader to certain views, the subjects of his books are allowed to stand or fall on their merits. Thus his biographies, while sympathetic, are not "apologies." Kaplan's rigorous research, intellectual honesty, informed perception, and sure and felicitous style virtually guarantee that his major works will remain the standard biographies for years to come.

Richard S. Kennedy
(13 October 1920 -   )

John L. Idol
Clemson University

BOOKS: *The Window of Memory: The Literary Career of Thomas Wolfe* (Chapel Hill: University of North Carolina Press, 1962);
Dreams in the Mirror: A Biography of E. E. Cummings (New York: Liveright, 1980).

OTHER: "Wolfe's Harvard Years," in *The Enigma of Thomas Wolfe*, edited by Richard Walser (Cambridge, Mass.: Harvard University Press, 1953);
"Thomas Wolfe," in *A Bibliographical Guide to the Study of Southern Literature*, edited by Louis D. Rubin, Jr. (Baton Rouge: Louisiana State University Press, 1969), pp. 329-332;
The Notebooks of Thomas Wolfe, edited by Kennedy and Paschal Reeves (Chapel Hill: University of North Carolina Press, 1970);
"Thomas Wolfe's Fiction: The Question of Genre," in *Thomas Wolfe and the Glass of Time*, edited by Reeves (Athens: University of Georgia Press, 1971), pp. 1-44;
E. E. Cummings, *Tulips and Chimneys*, introduction by Kennedy (New York: Liveright, 1976);
Cummings, *The Enormous Room*, introduction by Kennedy (New York: Liveright, 1977);
Cummings, *No Thanks*, introduction by Kennedy (New York: Liveright, 1978);
Thomas Wolfe, *Welcome to Our City: A Play in Ten Scenes*, edited, with an introduction, by Kennedy (Baton Rouge & London: Louisiana State University Press, 1983);
Beyond Love and Loyalty: The Letters of Thomas Wolfe and Elizabeth Nowell, Together with "No More Rivers," A Story by Thomas Wolfe, edited, with an introduction, by Kennedy (Chapel Hill: University of North Carolina Press, 1983);
Etcetera: Unpublished Poems by E. E. Cummings, edited by Kennedy and George James Firmage (New York: Liveright, 1983);
Thomas Wolfe: A Harvard Perspective, edited, with an introduction, by Kennedy (Athens, Ohio: Croissant, 1983);

Wolfe, *The Train and the City*, edited, with an introduction, by Kennedy (Akron, Ohio: Thomas Wolfe Society, 1984);
"Thomas Wolfe," in *Sixteen Modern American Authors*, edited by Jackson R. Bryer (Durham, N.C.: Duke University Press, 1989), pp. 716-755;
Wolfe, *The Starwick Episodes*, edited by Kennedy (Akron, Ohio: Thomas Wolfe Society, 1989).

SELECTED PERIODICAL PUBLICATIONS—
UNCOLLECTED: "Thomas Wolfe at Harvard, 1920-1923," *Harvard Library Bulletin*, 4 (Spring 1950): 172-190; (Autumn 1950): 304-319;
"Wolfe's *Look Homeward, Angel* as a Novel of Development," *South Atlantic Quarterly*, 63 (Spring 1964): 218-226;
"Thomas Wolfe and the American Experience," *Modern Fiction Studies*, 11 (Autumn 1965): 219-233;
"Edward Cummings, the Father of the Poet," *Bulletin of the New York Public Library*, 70 (September 1966): 437-449;
"E. E. Cummings at Harvard: Studies," *Harvard Library Bulletin*, 24 (July 1976): 267-297;
"E. E. Cummings at Harvard: Verse, Friends, Rebellion," *Harvard Library Bulletin*, 25 (July 1977): 253-291;
"Thomas Wolfe at New York University," *Thomas Wolfe Review*, 3 (Fall 1981): 1-10;
"The 'Wolfegate' Affair," *Harvard Magazine*, 8 (September-October 1981): 48-53, 62;
"Thomas Wolfe and Elizabeth Nowell: A Unique Relationship," *South Atlantic Quarterly*, 81 (Spring 1982): 202-213;
"What the Galley Proofs of Wolfe's *Of Time and the River* Tell Us," *Thomas Wolfe Review*, 9 (Fall 1985): 1-8;
"Thomas Wolfe, Coleridge, and Supernaturalism," *Thomas Wolfe Review*, 14 (Spring 1990): 27-32.

Richard S. Kennedy (photograph by Ella Kennedy)

Undaunted by its stature as the winner of a Pulitzer Prize for biography, Richard S. Kennedy said of David Herbert Donald's *Look Homeward: A Life of Thomas Wolfe* (1987): "What troubles me is his [Donald's] seeming reluctance to interpret Wolfe in order to provide understanding of his unusual personality and relate it to his literary achievement or his literary shortcomings. If one's subject is a writer, the countless details of his life are less important than a consideration of why he wrote the kind of books that he did and how they came to be." That principle lies at the core of Kennedy's approach to the lives of Thomas Wolfe and E. E. Cummings and can be traced to Kennedy's first efforts at literary biography as a Harvard graduate student, when he immersed himself in the newly acquired papers of Thomas Wolfe and examined Wolfe's life and writings. The outgrowth of that project, for a seminar with Howard Mumford Jones, was an article entitled "Thomas Wolfe at Harvard, 1920-1923," pub-

lished in two installments in the *Harvard Library Bulletin* (Spring and Autumn 1950).

A native of St. Paul, Minnesota, Richard Sylvester Kennedy was born on 13 October 1920 to William W. Kennedy, a chemist, and Ellen Foley Kennedy. He received his undergraduate training in English at the University of Southern California and at UCLA, where he received a B.A. in 1942. On 31 March 1943 he married Ella Dickinson, a union that produced three children: Elizabeth, Catherine, and James. Following duty with the United States Navy during World War II, including two years in England, France, Belgium, Holland, and Germany, Kennedy enrolled at the University of Chicago, where in 1947 he received his M.A. He studied with several celebrated American scholars, among them Donald Bond, Ronald Crane, Walter Blair, and George Williamson. Bond's course in literary historiography gave Kennedy a "sense in the pleasure of scholarship," while Crane and Blair offered him a strong grounding in aesthetic theory. From Williamson and Blair he gained experience in practical criticism. The intellectual atmosphere of the University of Chicago, as inspired and led by Robert Hutchins and Mortimer Adler, showed Kennedy that "literary study has its place in the march of ideas down through civilization." Writing of this period, Kennedy says, "I developed a kind of intellectual megalomania: I wanted to know everything."

Believing that Chicago's Ph.D. program in English was, at the time, too specialized, Kennedy moved on to Harvard for further studies. The breadth he sought in his studies grew fuller under the tutelage of Douglas Bush, whom Kennedy came to think of as "the greatest scholar of my time for his mastery not only of the whole sweep of English literature but of classical literature as well," and Howard Mumford Jones, "whose enormous range of knowledge encouraged me not to limit my studies to a 'specialty.'" That hunger for knowledge of life and literature, that drive to avoid narrowness, would serve Kennedy well when he began to trace the intellectual and creative lives of Wolfe and Cummings, for the first had sought to devour with Faustian appetite the Widener Library's vast store of books, and the latter had diversified his Harvard training to include American, English, and classical literature. That same regard for breadth and depth would reveal itself in Kennedy's teaching, his papers read, and his essays published following the completion of his Ph.D. at Harvard in 1953. During the next three decades, Kennedy taught courses in Victorian British literature, as well as the whole sweep of American literature, and published or read essays on Charles Dickens, Robert Browning, Aldous Huxley, T. S. Eliot, and Joyce Cary, besides his work on Wolfe and Cummings. His teaching career had begun at Harvard in 1948, where he was named a teaching fellow, and it continued on through the University of Rochester (1950-1957), Wichita State University (1957-1964), and Temple University (1964-1988), where in 1976 he won the Lindback Award for Distinguished Teaching.

Like many college students in the late 1930s and early 1940s, Kennedy had eagerly responded to the pulse, poetic quality, and youthful exuberance of Wolfe's fiction. When Kennedy arrived at Harvard in 1948 and found the newly acquired William Wisdom Collection of Wolfe's papers awaiting exploration, he dug into them for a semi-

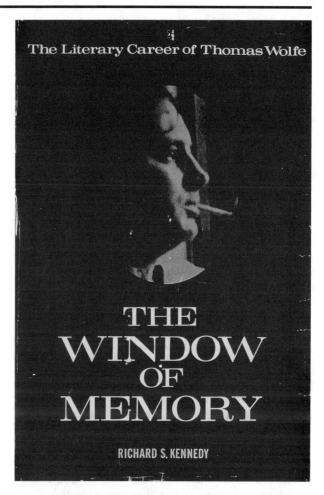

Dust jacket for Kennedy's first book, which he worked on for more than twelve years

nar paper on Wolfe's play writing and intellectual development during his Harvard years. That project led to an important decision, one that would figure prominently in his personal and professional life for many years to come. He decided to write a critical biography up to the point of Wolfe's mid career as the subject of a doctoral dissertation, which was launched in 1950 and completed in 1953. Kennedy then began to look forward to a two-volume critical biography, a dream that ended suddenly when the administrator of Wolfe's literary estate, Edward Aswell, refused to allow him to quote anything from Wolfe's unpublished material, largely the basis of Kennedy's biography. On that projected biography rested Kennedy's hope of earning tenure at the University of Rochester. Not getting the book into print meant a move to Wichita State University and years of frustration and delicate negotiations before Kennedy satisfied all restrictions and limitations and found a publisher, the University of

North Carolina Press. Meanwhile, he had over-hauled the biography three times, mostly because of actions taken by other people. Part of the trouble stemmed from Aswell's decision that no unpublished Wolfe materials could be used until five years after the publication of Elizabeth Nowell's biography of Wolfe, published by Doubleday in 1960. In order to get his book in print, Kennedy had to remove material considered "too biographical," some of which would find its way into print later, a good example being Kennedy's "Thomas Wolfe at New York University" in the *Thomas Wolfe Review* (Fall 1981).

Kennedy brought together over twelve years of work in *The Window of Memory: The Literary Career of Thomas Wolfe* (1962). The result was richly rewarding for students of Wolfe, for it was a search into the familial, social, political, religious, artistic, and philosophical forces shaping Wolfe's mind and art. As a self-proclaimed disciple of Douglas Bush and Howard Mumford Jones and an apt student of Walter Blair and George Williamson, Kennedy had the kind of mind and the range of critical experience needed to bring Wolfe's literary achievements and short-comings into focus.

What could have been a much bigger book turned out to be an eight-part exploration of Wolfe's artistic development with enough biographical detail to string the narrative together. Kennedy moves from Wolfe's formative years in Asheville and Chapel Hill, North Carolina, to his years of apprenticeship at Harvard (the period covered by Kennedy's Harvard seminar paper), then to the shaping of *Look Homeward, Angel* (1929) and on to the frustration of writing *Of Time and the River* (1935). Kennedy next looks at Wolfe's attempts at short fiction and then examines his efforts to find a new hero and more objective forms in the works eventually bearing the titles *The Web and the Rock* (1939) and *You Can't Go Home Again* (1940). The biography ends by revealing how Aswell, with the help and suggestions of Maxwell Perkins and Elizabeth Nowell, fashioned Wolfe's huge stacks of manuscripts into commercially presentable form; Kennedy points out that Aswell permitted himself some "creative editing" as he settled to the "mess" of material Wolfe left behind. Kennedy's demonstration of Aswell's methods and purposes represented pioneering work and led careful scholars to think of Wolfe's posthumously published books as commercial compromises between what might have been and what came to be published. To help readers see what

Aswell had to draw upon, Kennedy added an appendix to his book revealing Wolfe's "rough outline" for his last book. Much later, Kennedy would find himself embroiled in a debate, sensationalized by John Halberstadt, over whether Aswell took improper liberties with Wolfe's materials. The episode, stirred by Halberstadt's article in the *Yale Review* (October 1980), came to be known as "Wolfegate" and called forth rebuttals by Kennedy in *Harvard Magazine* (September-October 1981) and in *Thomas Wolfe: A Harvard Perspective* (1983).

In each of the eight parts of *The Window of Memory*, Kennedy traces stages of Wolfe's literary development, combining approaches from sociology, history, psychology, philosophy, politics, religion, and New Criticism. (The same approaches undergird Kennedy's later biography of Cummings.) Paramount among these are historical concerns and formalistic considerations as practiced by New Critics. Typically, Kennedy, drawing heavily on materials in the Wisdom Collection, sketches the background of a particular work, showing its stages of evolution, then offers probing comments on theme, characters, structure, and literary devices, its relation to other works by Wolfe, influences (if any) by other writers, and public and critical reception. A passage from his discussion of Wolfe's "Proem" to *Look Homeward, Angel* represents this method: "Wolfe announces in rhythmic prose a number of the emotional motifs of his work. He voices directly the problem of human isolation: that man is lost in this world, alone and unable to communicate with his neighbor or with his dearest loved ones. They are akin to him in flesh only." Then Kennedy quotes from the "Proem" and adds: "Introducing his principal symbols, he expresses the longing to return to the former life, to the reality which has been left behind at birth." This prepares the reader for an exploration of themes, symbols, philosophic background, and Wolfe's stylistic practices.

Kennedy's close reading of Wolfe's work in *The Window of Memory*, and the forced exclusion of materials considered "too biographical," provided the best sustained piece of Wolfe criticism yet to appear. The book is looked upon by most students of Wolfe as essential reading for anyone wanting to understand the forces shaping his personality, mind, and art.

His biographical interest in Wolfe did not end, of course, with the publication of *The Window of Memory*. Together with the late Paschal

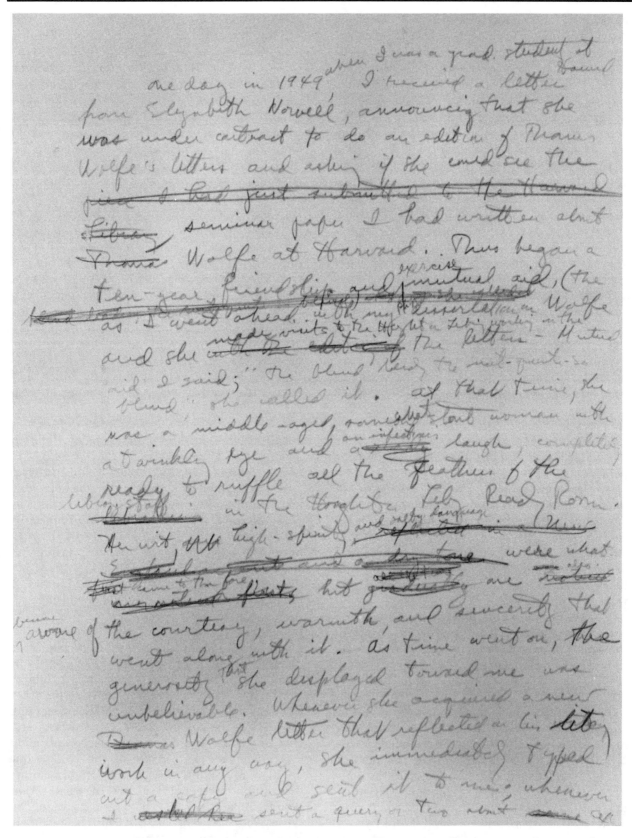

First page from the first draft for Kennedy's introduction to Beyond Love and Loyalty: The Letters of Thomas Wolfe and Elizabeth Nowell *(by permission of Richard S. Kennedy)*

Reeves, he next undertook the task of sorting through Wolfe's pocket notebooks and other jottings, selections of which he and Reeves gathered and edited as *The Notebooks of Thomas Wolfe* (1970). No longer constrained to withhold information out of deference to the work of another biographer, he and Reeves could set forth a fuller and franker image of Wolfe. They offer biographical background and highlighting for the myriad word pictures that Wolfe presented in his notebooks. Further evidence of their biographical work appears in the introduction, in a ten-page chronology, and in numerous footnotes. The notebooks afford a variety of reading experiences, ranging from the totally absorbing to the utterly tedious, but there emerges a Wolfe whom Kennedy must have yearned to represent more fully in his projected biography: a tormented, driven, lusty, poetic, lonely, ambitious, bitter, engaging, romantic, boyish, friendless, art-loving, satiric, jealous, word-drunken, dedicated, and list-keeping man who often turned, Hawthornelike, to his notebooks for space to record some scene or theme he would like to convert later into literary capital. Here were the raw edges and barbaric yawps that Donald was able, later, to work into his 1987 biography. But some passages were excluded from *The Notebooks* because of possible offense to living persons.

The significance of these notebooks to Wolfe studies and to American literature in general can be seen in the decision of the *Saturday Review* syndicate to include *The Notebooks* on its 1970 list of the year's six most important works of nonfiction. The book won the 1970 award of the Georgia Writers' Association as "the best work of nonfiction."

Two other editorial projects by Kennedy regarding Wolfe were published in 1983, one of them an edition of Wolfe's play *Welcome to Our City*, which had been produced at Harvard in 1923. Kennedy had become well acquainted with this experimental and broadly portentous play when he prepared his seminar paper on Wolfe's Harvard years. Never losing faith in its intrinsic merit and its value to students, Kennedy reassembled the play from several texts in the Wisdom Collection and arranged it for publication by the Louisiana State University Press. His eight-page introduction draws upon, and goes far beyond, comments made earlier in *The Window of Memory*.

Beyond Love and Loyalty, also published in 1983, had its origins many years before. During the time he taught at Wichita State, Kennedy finished editing the correspondence between Wolfe and his literary agent, Nowell, whom Kennedy met after she wrote to ask about his seminar paper on Wolfe. Nowell, at work on an edition of Wolfe's letters for Scribners, became a friend. Kennedy quickly saw that her efforts on behalf of Wolfe in finding magazine outlets for his fiction helped Wolfe immeasurably. Not only did she know the literary marketplace but she also had the talent to trim Wolfe's stories and the tact to get him to agree to the wisdom of her suggested cuts. Kennedy wanted her exchange of letters and notes with Wolfe to tell that story. His job was again to write an introduction and provide the notes, which he soon completed. But not until many years later was Kennedy able to convince the University of North Carolina Press to accept the manuscript of *Beyond Love and Loyalty*. David Herbert Donald said of the book, "More fully than any other account it shows just how Wolfe's sprawling stories were edited and compressed for magazine publication. What is equally important, this scrupulously edited book reveals Wolfe at his best, as a serious, careful literary craftsman."

By this time the Thomas Wolfe Society had been formed, one of its founders being Kennedy, and he had been elected its third president, a post he held from 1983 through 1985. In this capacity he planned two conferences, one held in Raleigh and the other in Asheville. He had gained experience for this task by helping to organize the 1982 meeting of the society at Harvard, where he joined with a Harvard dramatics group in a reading of *Welcome to Our City* and where, with the help of the staff of the Houghton Library, he mounted a manuscript exhibition showing how Aswell edited Wolfe's typescript of the play for publication—in an abridged version in *Esquire* (October 1957). This exhibit proved to be one of the quietest, yet most effective, rounds fired in the "Wolfegate Affair." Pages from the exhibition were photographically reproduced for an article Kennedy prepared for the collection of essays published after the conference, *Thomas Wolfe: A Harvard Perspective*. His concluding paragraph about that exhibit speaks directly of the troublesome question of Wolfe's dependence on his editors: the exhibit presented evidence of what serious Wolfe scholars had known for a long time, "because Wolfe, Aswell, Perkins, Nowell, and many others had told them—namely, that editorial influence made its mark on all of Wolfe's published work." Unlike Halberstadt, though, Kennedy did not believe that Aswell overstepped editorial bounds.

The Wolfe Society called on Kennedy to edit its annual publication in 1984, the result of which was *The Train and the City*, published for the first time in the form Wolfe wrote it (portions of it had been used in *The Web and the Rock* and *You Can't Go Home Again*). Kennedy was again chosen to edit the annual publication for 1989. For that project he turned to unpublished sections intended for *Of Time and the River*, material dealing with Eugene Gant's friend and, later, enemy, Francis Starwick. Kennedy called the book *The Starwick Episodes* and wrote an introduction to it, providing both biographical and textual information.

Among other honors bestowed on Kennedy by the Wolfe Society were the 1985 Zelda Gitlin Literary Prize, an annual cash award for the year's best article on Wolfe, and its Citation of Merit Award, a certificate given in recognition of outstanding scholarship or dedicated service to the society. The title of Kennedy's prize-winning essay was "What the Galley Proofs of Wolfe's *Of Time and the River* Tell Us," published in the Fall 1985 issue of the *Thomas Wolfe Review*. The Citation of Merit paid tribute to Kennedy's steady output of pieces on Wolfe since 1950. Most important, the Citation of Merit acknowledged Kennedy's contribution to keeping Wolfe's name before the scholarly world during that time Pamela Hansford Johnson, in *Hungry Gulliver* (1948), says that almost every writer must endure, "The Kicking Season," the period when writers and their works are kicked about to see whether they are good enough to earn a place in the canon. Kennedy firmly kept the faith in a time when "Wolfe-bashing" was in vogue and when many in the academic world went so far as to discourage graduate students from doing research or critical work on Wolfe. Together with the late Richard Walser, C. Hugh Holman, and Louis D. Rubin, Jr., Kennedy can be credited with salvaging Wolfe for the canon of American letters. Kennedy's work has helped Wolfe's fiction find a place in the major anthologies of American literature. That is true perhaps because Kennedy had the critical honesty to admit Wolfe's shortcomings as a man and artist, and had the acumen and tact to present a convincing case for Wolfe's literary successes. The best persuasive analysis of Wolfe's life and art is in *The Window of Memory*. There is little wonder that the book was nominated for the Christian Gauss Prize. Nothing has replaced it as the soundest exploration of Wolfe's literary career.

In the midst of his efforts to get his Wolfe biography revised for publication, Kennedy offered a 1963 honors seminar at Wichita State on "E. E. Cummings and the Poetic Experiment of His Time." Kennedy's hope of writing a book on Cummings had its roots there. Almost six years went by before he could settle once again in the Houghton Library to begin research; another twelve were to pass before he finished *Dreams in the Mirror: A Biography of E. E. Cummings* (1980). That long delay resulted from the wish of Cummings's widow, Marion Morehouse, not to have biographical research begin until five years after Kennedy's initial request to be allowed access to the papers of Cummings (in the Houghton). Meanwhile, Kennedy did have permission to examine the papers of Cummings's father. That is where he began. When he finally gained the right to read the E. E. Cummings papers, he still was almost a decade away from publishing the first biography to draw upon those papers.

Its evolution and conception seem close to the Wolfe biography, for Kennedy explored Cummings's family and upbringing in Cambridge, Massachusetts, then zeroed in on Cummings's Harvard years and early apprenticeship period. These and other periods of Cummings's life would form the first of a planned two-volume treatment and would bear the title "E. E. Cummings: The Years of Innocence." Unsuccessful in his efforts to win a fellowship or research grant, Kennedy had to spend parts of summers and holiday breaks in the Houghton working on the Cummings papers, more extensive than the Wisdom Collection. This pattern was broken in 1973 when he received an award from the National Endowment for the Arts, which allowed him to visit Europe, talk with Cummings's first wife, Elaine Thayer, and see the important sites in Cummings's experiences during World War I. The trip would both enrich his presentation of Cummings's European sojourns and help him write a perceptive, informed introduction to the 1977 edition of *The Enormous Room* (originally published in 1922), Cummings's account of his days in a French detention center. Despite two rejected appeals to the Guggenheim Foundation for support, Kennedy pressed on with his work, doing introductions for other editions of Cummings's work: *Tulips and Chimneys* (1976) and *No Thanks* (1978).

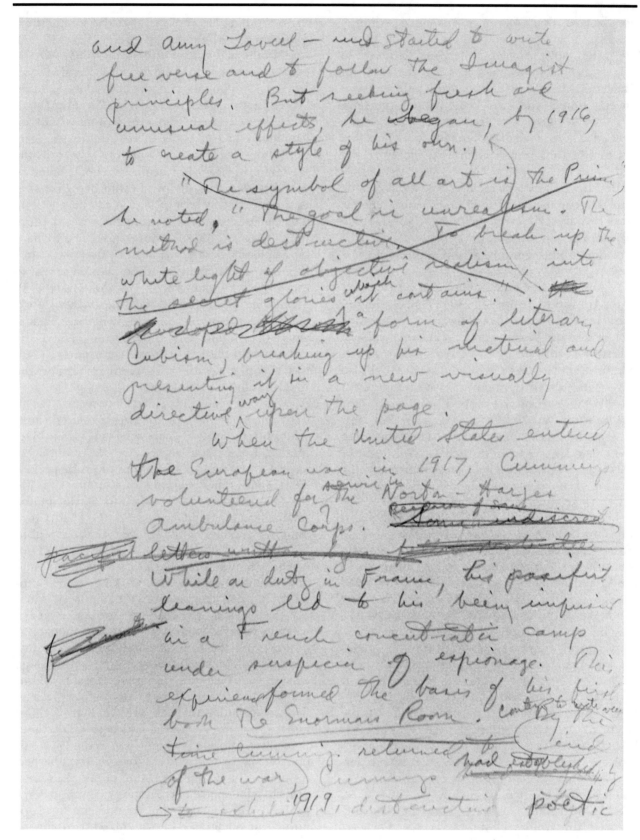

Pages from the first draft for Kennedy's introduction to his Dreams in the Mirror: A Biography of E. E. Cummings *(by permission of Richard S. Kennedy)*

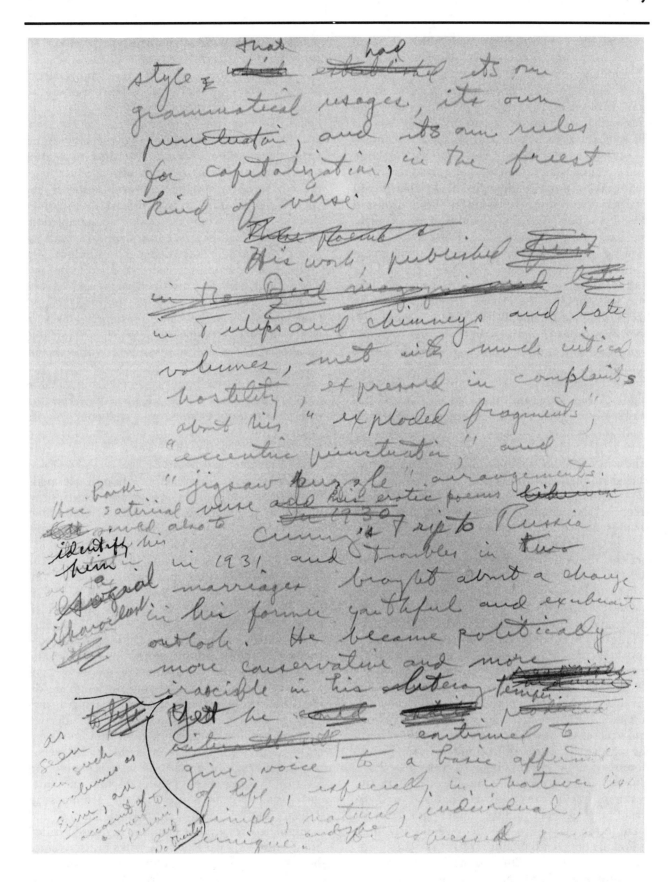

style *that* ~~which~~ ~~established~~ *had* its own
grammatical usages, its own
punctuation, and its own rules
for capitalization, in the freest
kind of verse.

~~This poem to~~
His work, published ~~first~~
~~in the *Dial* magazine and in the~~
in *Tulips and Chimneys* and later
volumes, met with much critical
hostility, expressed in complaints
about his "exploded fragments,"
"eccentric punctuation," and
"jigsaw puzzle" arrangements.
His satirical verse and his erotic poems ~~likewise~~
~~caused also to~~ Cumming's trip to Russia
in 1931, and troubles in two
marriages brought about a change
in his former youthful and exuberant
outlook. He became politically
more conservative and more
irascible in his literary temper.
Yet he continued to
give voice to a basic affirmation
of life, especially in whatever was
simple, natural, individual,
unique and spontaneously expressed.

At the Houghton, Kennedy sifted through letters, drawings, notes, notebooks, volumes from Cummings's library, and manuscripts of poems, plays, and essays. He thought he had worked his way through everything except Cummings's diaries, which were under restriction until 1990, but he learned, along with Harvard, that Cummings's second wife, Morehouse, had kept back a large body of material when Cummings's papers were acquired by the Houghton in 1964. That meant further research just to be certain he had missed nothing important. And, of course, it meant pushing back the publication date. He was also interviewing people who had known Cummings in Cambridge, New York City, New Hampshire, and Europe, including Slater Brown, who had also been held in the French detention center at La Ferté-Macé during World War I because neither Brown nor Cummings, in their roles as volunteer ambulance drivers on the German front, could muster sufficient hatred of the Germans. Kennedy pushed ahead with his planning, writing, and rewriting, and he called on friends, colleagues, and such experts as Josephine Miles to read his manuscript. He finished the book in May 1979, a one-volume biographical and critical study rather than the two-volume project he had earlier outlined for himself.

Kennedy sought to find the roots of forces that helped shape Cummings's talents as a painter and poet. That meant delving into his life in Cambridge, Boston, and at Harvard during the 1890s and the first decade and a half of the twentieth century. It meant looking into the doings and beliefs of Cambridge ladies and gentlemen, and it meant bringing into sharp focus the programs in language and literature at the Cambridge Latin School, which Cummings attended, and at Harvard University. In these early chapters, Kennedy establishes a rhythm and pattern he sustains throughout his study: details about the life and the intellectual and artistic forces shaping that life, then an analysis of paintings, poems, plays, or other writings accomplished during particular phases of Cummings's career. The dominant flow of the book is thus based on Cummings's emergence as an artist, both in the realm of the plastic and the linguistic arts. To make sure readers could see Cummings's development in the plastic arts, Kennedy generously illustrated the book with photographs of sketches, pencil drawings, and paintings done over the course of Cummings's life. Chosen for much the same purpose were several photographs of manuscript pages of Cummings's inventive typographical arrangement of letters, words, and phrases.

Lacking any imposed restrictions from being "too biographical" and eschewing an indulgence in trivia, Kennedy hewed close to the pattern that served him so well in *The Window of Memory*. This approach demands that the biographer spend long, tedious hours of reading note after note, letter after letter, draft after draft, but the secret to arousing intellectual and aesthetic response is presenting a piece of work in a manner that unfolds it from conception to completion. To do that requires great narrative skills and astute critical insight, sacrificing the mundane, liberal use of anecdotes, irrelevant dirty linen and gossip, and hobbyhorses from whatever stable— economic, sociological, religious, political, or psychological. In a sense it means stepping back to that type of biography so pleasant and valuable decades ago, the life, mind, and art of a writer. It also means coming to grips with literature.

Relying on techniques gained from classical scholars and New Critics, Kennedy traced the emerging styles of Cummings, a challenge complicated by the fact that Cummings tried his hand not only at new forms of verse but also fresh ways of creating prose and drama, as in *The Enormous Room* and *Him* (1927). Though Kennedy had a small body of Cummings criticism to draw upon, he preferred to encounter a Cummings piece head-on. That encounter led to his discovery of "three principal styles": "lyric and mythic"; "Satyric"; and "Hephaestian." Kennedy uses the first of these phrases to describe poems "concerned with the cycles of the natural world or the essential rhythms of human life." Such poems treat "sunrise, sunset, snowfall, springtime, the life of plants, the flow of rivers, the changes of the moon, the eternal presence of the stars" and draw upon archetypal mythic images while, at the same time, relying on language directly expressing emotion in words having a singable quality. Cummings's satyric style derives from his practice of revealing both "libidinous energy" and sharp criticism in some of his verse, which can range from naturalistic presentation of life to jolly or wicked mockery of human values and deeds. Poems written in the Hephaestian style are those forged, bent, twisted, shaped, and manipulated verses that Cummings himself called "modernist," a term Kennedy balks at using since the word has come to stand for an early-twentieth-century movement in the arts. Kennedy labeled as Hephaestian those poems taking "the form of elliptical statements, fragmented expression, surprise in the images and shocks in the juxtapositions, wrenches and distortions of diction, and violations of expectations in linguistic usage." These categories or labels adequately cover the range of Cummings's poetry and represent some of the soundest criticism, in relation to individual poems, ever written on Cummings's art and achievement.

Helpful as these discussions of poems are, Kennedy's remarks on Cummings's prose works and plays perhaps stand as a finer critical achievement. The best of these remarks appear in Kennedy's treatment of *The Enormous Room*. Before Kennedy comes to discuss this work in its place in Cummings's literary career, he has retraced Cummings's steps, talked to a fellow prisoner (Brown), and examined notebooks, sketches, correspondence, and official records. When he reaches this powerful and "unique work," as he calls it, Kennedy can count on his earlier details of Cummings's imprisonment to give readers a sense of the oppression, injustice, deprivation, and grim humor of Cummings's experience at La Ferté-Macé. Thus Kennedy is free to explore theme—identified as "romantic individualism"—structure, language, characterization, literary analogues, and style. He finds a three-part structure in the novel: the arrest and journey to La Ferté-Macé, the imprisonment in the Dépôt de Triage, and the concluding section. Kennedy relates this structure to Cummings's allusions to John Bunyan's *Pilgrim's Progress* (1678): Cummings does not "duplicate all the episodes and significances of *Pilgrim's Progress*. He merely employs an accumulation of allusions in order to elevate and intensify the misadventures that befall the narrator." The linguistic variety of Cummings's novel is one of its most noteworthy achievements, in turn grossly naturalistic, imaginatively witty (a gendarme preparing for duty "buckled on his personality"), grimly ironic, and nobly philosophic. Summing up all this variety, Kennedy says, "There is no standard narrative style. Cummings tries out everything." The characters do not become mere allegorical figures representing humanity and inhumanity or vices and virtues in a wartime soci-

ety, but to see them the reader must be capable of seeing them, at times, as "cubistic obliquities." At the end of Kennedy's probing look at this difficult, experimental work, it is easy to agree with him that the linguistic inventiveness, allusions to *Pilgrim's Progress*, and "hints of a mythic dimension" lift *The Enormous Room* "out of the humble category of the war memoir and . . . out of the work-a-day category of the realistic novel. It is then merely a prose work of literary art. There had never been anything quite like it before and there has never been anything like it since."

Reviewing Kennedy's book for the *Christian Science Monitor* (11 February 1980), Rushworth Kidder, the author of *E. E. Cummings: An Introduction to the Poetry* (1979), called it "a labor of love . . . which students can readily trust. . . . [Kennedy] is a refreshingly bright writer. . . . The result is a moving account of a complex, excitable, intelligent, voluble, and not entirely lovable human, grandly generous and sadly pathetic at once. [This book is for] readers who love the arts in this century . . . and those who simply like a well-told story of an essentially noble life."

The accomplishment of *Dreams in the Mirror* makes all the sadder the circumstances that kept Kennedy from publishing his two-volume study of Wolfe. As matters now stand, students of Wolfe must turn to the biographical studies by Richard Walser, Carole Klein, and David Herbert Donald to ferret out those facts that Kennedy would surely have given as he portrayed Wolfe as man and artist. Good as the Cummings book is, one must wonder how much more will be learned of his mind, life, and art when his diaries are studied. Perhaps Kennedy will be the first to tell us just how much they have to add to his portrait and to Cummings's standing as an artist.

Together these two biographical-critical studies reveal much of what can be gained when the biographer can speak to friends, foes, and relatives of the subject, and they also show many of the hurdles the biographer has to leap, or stop before, because of restrictions placed on materials. Without his patience, tact, diplomacy, and charm, Kennedy would not have produced such worthwhile books.

R. W. B. Lewis

(1 November 1917 -   )

Mark Royden Winchell
Clemson University

BOOKS: *The American Adam: Innocence, Tragedy and Tradition in the Nineteenth Century* (Chicago: University of Chicago Press, 1955);

The Picaresque Saint: Representative Figures in Contemporary Fiction (Philadelphia: Lippincott, 1959; London: Gollancz, 1960);

Trials of the Word: Essays in American Literature and the Humanistic Tradition (New Haven & London: Yale University Press, 1965);

The Poetry of Hart Crane: A Critical Study (Princeton: Princeton University Press, 1967);

Edith Wharton: A Biography (New York & London: Harper & Row, 1975; London: Constable, 1975).

OTHER: "John Steinbeck: The Fitful Daemon," in *The Young Rebel in American Literature*, edited by Carl Bode (New York: Praeger, 1959), pp. 121-141;

Herman Melville, edited by Lewis (New York: Dell, 1962);

The Presence of Walt Whitman, edited, with a foreword, by Lewis (New York & London: Columbia University Press, 1962);

Edith Wharton, *The House of Mirth*, edited, with an introduction, by Lewis (Boston: Houghton Mifflin, 1963);

"The Aspiring Clown," in *Learners and Discerners: A Newer Criticism*, edited by Robert Scholes (Charlottesville: University of Virginia Press, 1964), pp. 63-108;

Malraux: A Collection of Critical Essays, edited, with an introduction, by Lewis (Englewood Cliffs, N.J.: Prentice-Hall, 1964);

Herman Melville, *The Confidence Man*, edited, with an afterword, by Lewis (New York: New American Library, 1964);

"The Conflicts of Reality: Cozzens' *The Last Adam*," in *Seven Contemporary Authors: Essays on Cozzens, Miller, West, Golding, Heller, Albee and Powers*, edited by Thomas B. Whitbread (Austin: University of Texas Press, 1966), pp. 1-22;

Wharton, *The Age of Innocence*, edited, with an introduction, by Lewis (New York: Scribners, 1968);

The Collected Stories of Edith Wharton, edited, with an introduction, by Lewis (New York: Scribners, 1968);

Graham Greene, *The Power and the Glory*, edited, with an introduction, by Lewis (New York: Viking, 1970);

American Literature: The Makers and the Making, 2 volumes, edited by Lewis, Cleanth Brooks, and Robert Penn Warren (New York: St. Martin's Press, 1973);

"Hart Crane," in *Reading America*, edited by Denis Donoghue (New York: Knopf, 1987), pp. 242-253;

The Letters of Edith Wharton, edited, with an introduction, by Lewis and Nancy Lewis (New York: Scribners, 1988);

The Selected Short Stories of Edith Wharton, edited by Lewis (New York: Scribners, 1991).

SELECTED PERIODICAL PUBLICATIONS—
UNCOLLECTED: "Crane's Visionary Lyric: The Way to *The Bridge*," *Massachusetts Review*, 7 (1966): 227-253;

"Warren's Long Visit to American Literature," *Yale Review*, 70 (July 1981): 568-591;

"The Courtship of William James," *Yale Review*, 73 (January 1984): 177-198;

"The Names of Action: Henry James in the Early 1870s," *Nineteenth-Century Fiction*, 38 (March 1984): 467-491.

Awarded the Pulitzer Prize for his 1975 biography of Edith Wharton, R. W. B. Lewis established himself first in the field of literary criticism. In fact, his influence can be largely traced to a single seminal work. Since its original publication in 1955 *The American Adam: Innocence, Tragedy and Tradition in the Nineteenth Century* has become acknowledged as one of the major contributions to American literary studies. Coming at a time when many in the academic community

R. W. B. Lewis (photograph by T. Charles Erickson; courtesy of the Yale University Office of Public Information)

were tiring of the aesthetic formalism of the New Criticism, *The American Adam* helped to launch a new era of interdisciplinary cultural analysis. The book's important ramifications have been discovered anew by each succeeding generation of scholars.

Richard Warrington Baldwin Lewis was born on 1 November 1917 in Chicago, Illinois, to Leicester Crosby Lewis and Beatrice Elizabeth (Baldwin) Lewis. After graduating from Phillips Exeter Academy, he entered Harvard University, where he earned his A.B. in 1939. Lewis began his graduate education at the University of Chicago, receiving his M.A. in 1941, before serving four years in the United States Army during World War II and obtaining the rank of major. After the war Lewis returned to Chicago and finished his Ph.D. in 1953. While pursuing his studies, he taught at Bennington College in Vermont (1948-1950), the Salzburg Seminar in American Studies (1950-1951), and Smith College (1951-1952). On 28 June 1950 Lewis married Nancy

Lindau; the couple has two children, Nathaniel and Sophia. From 1953 to 1954 Lewis was a resident fellow in creative writing at Princeton. It was there that he became acquainted with some of the most important American writers of the postwar era. Years later he would recall the time that Theodore Roethke stopped by his house and borrowed his phone for half an hour. Not until the monthly bill arrived did Lewis realize that Roethke was calling Dylan Thomas long-distance in Wales.

Although his book on Edith Wharton is Lewis's only venture into pure literary biography, his criticism has always emphasized the biographical and historical context from which literary narratives emerge. Firmly rooted in the history of ideas, *The American Adam* approaches literary myth not as some arcane branch of folklore or depth psychology but as the storytelling impulse through which a culture strives for self-definition. Particularly during the years 1820 to 1860 America's most important culture-defining story

R. W. Lewis, professor of English and American Studies and former Master of Calhoun College at Yale, is a distinguished and prolific writer on modern literature. He is the author of, among other books, *The American Adam* and *The Picaresque Saint*. A graduate of Harvard (A.B.) and Chicago (Ph.D.), he is the recipient of honorary degrees from Wesleyan University and St. Lawrence College, and of numerous fellowship awards.

"I have been very deeply impressed and delighted by Professor Lewis's lively and engaging life of Edith Wharton. It's as good as a novel by Henry James, who would probably think so, too: beautifully organized, handsomely written, admirably controlled, witty, ironic, subtle, revealing, often astonishing to some of us who had a fixed idea about Mrs. Wharton—in short, a masterful literary biography, at once objective and sympathetic, crowded with memorable scenes and people. It should start a Wharton revival, and I hope it will. What a woman she was!"
                                                                        – Carlos Baker

"If Mr. Lewis has done nothing else, he has made it impossible for us ever again to dismiss Edith Wharton as a remote and minor literary figure. For he has borne witness to her grand and rich passions, which were not only for work, and to her abundant vitality."
                                                                        – Nancy Milford

"At best, there are only three or four American novelists who can be thought of as 'major' and Edith Wharton is one. Due to her sex, class (in every sense), and place of residence, she has been denied her proper place in the near-empty pantheon of American literature. Happily, Mr. Lewis's biography ought to convince the solemn of her seriousness; with much new material, he has illuminated a marvelous figure and her age."
                                                                        – Gore Vidal

ISBN: 0-06-012603-5

Edith Wharton
R·W·B·LEWIS
HARPER & ROW

Edith Wharton
A BIOGRAPHY
R·W·B·LEWIS

Dust jacket for the biography that earned Lewis a Pulitzer Prize

was of a new Adam in a new Eden, "a figure of heroic innocence and vast potentialities, poised at the start of a new history."

This figure was not so much a static image as the focus of a heated cultural debate. As Ralph Waldo Emerson knew, there were at least two voices in this debate—those of "Memory and Hope." According to Lewis, "The key term in the moral vocabulary of Emerson, Thoreau, Whitman, and their followers and imitators . . . was 'innocence.' To the 'nostalgic'—that is to the party devoted to Memory—the sinfulness of man seemed never so patent as currently in America. As the hopeful expressed their mounting contempt for the doctrine of inherited sin, the nostalgic intoned on Sundays the fixed legacy of corruption in ever more emphatic accents."

What makes *The American Adam* more than just a replay of verbal battles between the followers of Emerson and those of Jonathan Edwards is the twist Lewis gives to the conflict. When he listens, Lewis hears not two but three voices, and it is in the nuances of that third voice that he discerns the most complex and authentic rendering of the American experience. Since it had no historically contemporaneous name, he calls that third

voice "the party of Irony"—"the ironic temperament was characterized by a tragic optimism: by a sense of the tragic collisions to which innocence was liable (something unthinkable among the hopeful), and equally by an awareness of the heightened perception and humanity which suffering made possible (something unthinkable among the nostalgic)." No small part of the appeal of *The American Adam* is the case Lewis makes for the relevance of this ironic sensibility to society.

Although Lewis is concerned primarily with imaginative literature, he contends that "the party of Irony" has theological roots in the venerable Christian doctrine of the fortunate fall. This doctrine, which can be traced back almost to the fourth century A.D., found its way into the liturgy of the Roman church in the words of the Holy Saturday hymn—"O happy sin! to deserve so great a redeemer." To a believing Christian this simply means that the joy of life in Heaven will outshine anything that Adam could have imagined in Eden. Hence, the fall of humankind, which was the necessary precondition for the divine mysteries of incarnation and redemption, was a tragic act with immeasurably fortunate consequences.

Obviously such a view would have been regarded as too gloomy by "the party of Hope" and altogether blasphemous by "the party of Memory." But Lewis finds a hint of the paradox of the fortunate fall in the writings of one of the most influential leaders of "the party of Irony"—the philosopher Henry James (1811-1882), father of the well-known novelist.

The elder James's view of human nature was midway between the self-reliant optimism of Emerson and the Calvinistic pessimism of Edwards. James argued that the permanently unfallen condition, "however pleasant, [would] be aimless and 'horticultural'; there would be no rise and no ambition to rise to the nobler condition of genuine manhood." By the same token James was contemptuous of such inveterate doomsayers as Thomas Carlyle, contending that their failure to see beyond the misfortune of the fall was also myopic. According to Lewis, James "escaped the sterilities of both sides—the arrested development of infantile innocence and the premature old age of a paralyzing absorption with sin—by seeing the moral problem in unvaryingly dramatic terms: as a process, a story, with several grand climacterics."

Although James's quasi-theological musings are not nearly as well known as those of transcendentalist and Puritan divines, the transforming experience he imagined for the American Adam is close to what one finds in the fiction of the two most complex and ironic novelists of the American Renaissance—Nathaniel Hawthorne and Herman Melville. Speaking of Hawthorne, Lewis writes, "The characteristic situation in his fiction is that of the Emersonian figure, the man of hope, who by some frightful mischance has stumbled into the time-burdened world of Jonathan Edwards." The results could range from a parable about the danger of innocence in a fallen world to an initiation tale in which expulsion from the garden is itself the rite of passage.

Hawthorne's most explicit use of the *felix culpa* motif was in his last novel, *The Marble Faun* (1860), an equivocal tragedy of enlightenment coming too late. At the end of that novel Hawthorne's character Miriam observes: "The story of the Fall of Man? Is it not repeated in our Romance of Monte Beni? And may we follow the analogy yet farther? Was that very sin—into which Adam precipitated himself and all his race—was it the destined means by which, over a long pathway of toil and sorrow, we are able to attain a higher, brighter and profounder happiness,

than our lost birthright gave?" Although F. O. Matthiessen and others contend that Miriam is simply rationalizing the suffering endured by herself and her friend Donatello, Lewis takes the text of the novel more literally. He argues that despite the uneasiness expressed by the Puritan Hilda and others toward any suggestion of a fortunate fall, the "lingering uneasy impression remains that there has been demonstrated in action what the elder James had argued in theory. . . . Donatello's fall was in many serious respects an upward step—an entrance into the true reality which, for Hawthorne, is measured by time."

In the career of Melville, Lewis sees an evolution from the early hopefulness of *Typee* (1846) through the bleak parables that followed *Moby-Dick* (1851) to a final apotheosis of Adam in the figure of Billy Budd. Of course, this evolution was far from a straight line: the innocent heroes of Melville's early works are constantly bedeviled by an evil that Emerson never dreamt of, and even the most despondent fictions of Melville's dark period are redeemed from nihilism by his pervasive human sympathy. However, the sense of philosophical balance that kept Melville from finally being captured by the forces of either memory or hope is best articulated in "The Try-Works" chapter of *Moby-Dick*. According to Lewis's gloss of that chapter, destruction can come from one of two directions. "On the one hand: an empty innocence, a tenacious ignorance of evil, which, granted the tough nature of reality, must be either immaturity or spiritual cowardice. On the other: a sense of evil so inflexible, so adamant in its refusal to admit the not less reducible fact of existent good that it is perilously close to a love of evil, a queer pact with the devil."

Beyond developing his main argument, Lewis explores the countless other ways in which the image of the American Adam permeated the intellectual culture of mid-nineteenth-century America. His rich cast of supporting characters includes Walt Whitman, Oliver Wendell Holmes, Horace Bushnell, Charles Brockden Brown, James Fenimore Cooper, Robert Montgomery Bird, George Bancroft, Francis Parkman, Theodore Parker, and Orestes A. Brownson. In his epilogue Lewis maintains that the Adamic hero is still a presence in American fiction. From the first half of the twentieth century, he mentions F. Scott Fitzgerald's *The Great Gatsby* (1925) and William Faulkner's "The Bear" (in *Go Down, Moses*, 1942) and then adds that in "the truest and most fully engaged American fiction after the second war, the newborn or self-breeding or orphaned hero is plunged again and again, for his own good and for ours, into the spurious, disruptive rituals of the actual world." That cast of characters includes the protagonists of Saul Bellow's *The Adventures of Augie March* (1933), J. D. Salinger's *The Catcher in the Rye* (1951), and Ralph Ellison's *Invisible Man* (1952).

In 1960, five years after *The American Adam* was published, Lewis began a long and distinguished tenure as professor of English and American studies at Yale. In the years since *The American Adam*, Lewis has written four more books and edited several others. Although this is not an unusually prolific output for a scholarly career that has spanned three and a half decades, some of these books have made ground-breaking contributions to literary study, as is the case with *The Picaresque Saint: Representative Figures in Contemporary Fiction* (1959), a collection of essays by Lewis.

What is obvious from the outset is that *The Picaresque Saint* is more contemporary and less provincial than *The American Adam*. Of the five writers Lewis discusses at length, all belong to what he calls the second generation of the twentieth century, and only one, Faulkner, is an American. However, *The Picaresque Saint* has continuity with the rest of Lewis's work. Although he does not neglect aesthetic values, Lewis's interest in Alberto Moravia, Albert Camus, Ignazio Silone, Graham Greene, and Faulkner is primarily thematic. Moreover, the characteristic that distinguishes this group of writers from the generation of Marcel Proust, Thomas Mann, and James Joyce is a kind of heroic, even desperate, optimism, which affirms the values of life in the face of an unblinking recognition of death. The position of the writers Lewis admires is aptly summed up in the words of the tribune Cherea in Camus's *Caligula*: "To lose one's life is a little thing.... But to see the sense of this life dissipated, to see our reason for existence disappear: that is what is insupportable."

As a stay against nihilism the second generation of twentieth-century writers have looked not to theme or doctrine but to character. What they gave readers is a representative figure who is a kind of cosmopolitan second cousin to the American Adam. Lewis maintains that "it is by means of this figure—this strange recurring, half-hidden or wholly realized, sometimes antic, and in at least one instance godless figure of sainthood— that the sense of life in second generation fiction has been ultimately conveyed.... The figure I am calling the picaresque saint tries to hold in balance ..., by the very contradictions of his character, both the observed truths of contemporary experience and the vital aspiration to transcend them."

Although one is tempted to endorse Lewis's emphasis on the sense of life as a welcome corrective to the overpowering negativism of so much modern fiction and criticism, he seems to overstate his case at times. For example, although Lewis is certainly correct in seeing a more affirmative vision in the later Faulkner (the defiant humanist of the Nobel Prize speech), it is questionable whether this was the essential Faulkner. What T. S. Eliot said of Alfred, Lord Tennyson seems to apply here—that his doubt was more authentic than his faith. Lewis is correct in seeing a definite turning point in "The Bear." Unfortunately, in abstracting "The Bear" from the totality of *Go Down, Moses*, Lewis distorts Faulkner for his own purposes. The image of Ike McCaslin that Lewis presents is of a heroic New World primitive doing penance for the sins of his fathers. However, the context of Faulkner's entire novel reveals Ike to be more a pathetic naif who is destroyed by his own innocence. The most enduring values in *Go Down, Moses* are found not in the patriarchal rites of the forest but in the maternal warmth of the hearth. The salvific figure for Faulkner is neither a picaresque saint nor an American Adam, but a black Madonna.

Lewis's next book, *Trials of the Word* (1965), is unified by his interest in the religious dimensions of literature. That Lewis would explicitly declare such an interest came as no surprise to those who saw religion as the not-so-hidden agenda behind both *The American Adam* and *The Picaresque Saint*. However, in the essay that comes closest to being his theoretical statement on the matter, "Hold on Hard to the Huckleberry Bushes," Lewis stakes out a position different from that of the more doctrinaire literary theologians. He urges readers to see the metaphorical value of Christian elements in the work of secular writers. Citing the novelist Henry James as a representative figure of the post-Christian epoch, Lewis argues that it was "characteristic of James ... to have conveyed his religious sense by intensifying the human drama to the moment where it gave off intimations of the sacred."

The discussion of contemporary American fiction that Lewis seems to promise in the epilogue of *The American Adam* finally arrives in "Days of Wrath and Laughter," the final entry in

Dust jacket for the collection of Wharton's correspondence edited by Lewis and his wife

Trials of the Word and the only one written exclusively for that volume. Lewis is concerned in that essay with the sense of apocalypse that pervades so many mid-twentieth-century American novels. At one level, this apocalyptic sensibility is simply an inversion of the optimistic millennialism of the nineteenth-century "party of Hope." One might be tempted to see the spectre of nuclear holocaust as a powerful literary influence, if it were not for the fact that the atom bomb seems relegated to science fiction and other popular genres. The literature Lewis is concerned with sees the world ending with neither a bang nor a whimper but a kind of maniacal laugh.

Although Lewis's ostensible emphasis is on Ellison's *Invisible Man*, John Barth's *The Sot-Weed Factor* (1960), Joseph Heller's *Catch-22* (1961), and Thomas Pynchon's *V* (1963), most of his essay is devoted to a wide-ranging discussion of apocalyptic writing from the Old Testament to modern times. According to Lewis the tradition to which Ellison, Barth, Heller, and Pynchon be-

long can be traced in America to Melville's *The Confidence-Man* (1857), Mark Twain's *The Mysterious Stranger* (1916), and Nathanael West's *A Cool Million* (1934) and *The Day of the Locust* (1939). "The apprehension of immense catastrophe is close to the heart of their imagination," Lewis writes. "But at the heart itself is a humane perspective rooted not quite in hope but in a hope about hope. The sense of the comic is at once the symptom and the executive agency of that root sensibility. For if there is a large portion of bitterness in the laughter, and if laughter sometimes seems the only response still possible in a radically graceless world, it has served nonetheless to define, to measure and assess the horror, to reveal its sources and make visible its shape."

Prior to his monumental study of Wharton, the closest Lewis came to writing a literary biography was his 1967 book, *The Poetry of Hart Crane: A Critical Study*. Lewis has always believed that criticism should make literature clearer and more accessible rather than less so, and few American poets can profit more from such an approach than Crane. Particularly helpful are the five chapters Lewis devotes to Crane's ambitious, though flawed, epic *The Bridge* (1930). But what makes this study more than just an exercise in textual analysis is Lewis's judicious use of information about Crane's life and literary influences. The image that comes across in these pages is not of the self-destructive American Dionysus, but of a visionary lover of life committed to seeing the miraculous in the mundane.

If Lewis's book has a thesis, it is this: "Crane was not a death-haunted author of death-conscious poetry, any more than he was, in the usual meaning of the phrase, a tragic poet. That false stereotype . . . derives from a muddled view of his life, a consequent misinterpretation of his poetry and a series of misleading associations with some of his genuinely tragic-spirited contemporaries." Of course, too much is known about Crane's life for such a thesis to be supported simply by a reading of his ambiguous body of verse. Lewis's biographical forays are more a matter of argumentative necessity than of critical method. Where others see an urge for self-punishment in Crane's alcoholism and compulsive homosexuality, Lewis finds a hedonistic zest for life. Where others see Crane's drowning at sea as a clear act of suicide, Lewis leaves open the possibility of accidental death. The typical approach to Crane is to allow certain preconceptions about his life to shape the interpretation of his poetry. Lewis uses Crane's poetry to present a revisionist view of his life.

Lewis's interest in the career of Wharton dates back at least to when he wrote the introduction to the 1963 edition of Wharton's 1905 book, *The House of Mirth* (his essay is collected in *Trials of the Word*). Lewis disputes the popular view that Wharton was either a cut-rate imitator of James or a pale precursor of Fitzgerald. Although he concedes that the line leading from James through Wharton to Fitzgerald is one of the clearest in American literary history, he argues that in certain ways Wharton's sensibility is closer to that of the postmoderns than were those of James or Fitzgerald. Like those two, though, Wharton was a historian of manners. However, a few of her books, such as *The Custom of the Country* (1913), are "closer in nature to American novels since the second World War," especially when "her narrative form approaches the picaresque—the episodic ramblings of the morally ambiguous personality through an unstable and discordant world."

Wharton's achievement in *The House of Mirth* consists of a skillful blending of these two disparate modes, with book 1 being primarily a Jamesian history of manners and book 2 a picaresque rite of passage.

Lewis's discussion of Wharton's life and career and his observations about the structure of *The House of Mirth* are all quite sound. It is when he begins discussing theme and character that problems arise. When he rather inelegantly calls Lily Bart "a nymphomaniac of material comfort," he does both Lily and Wharton a disservice. If this characterization were accurate, Lily would be a simpler and far less interesting figure—a sort of aristocratic Sister Carrie. Her problem is actually a reluctance to marry money without love (Simon Rosedale) or love without money (Lawrence Selden). In naively insisting on the possibility of having everything, she ends up with nothing—not even life itself.

What makes Lily more a victim than a fool is the shabby way she is treated by the wealthy society she seeks to join. Her rite of passage in book 2 is the sort of material collapse and moral rise that one would have expected Lewis to identify as a fortunate fall. He offers little convincing support for his contention that Lily might have been saved had the New York aristocracy of an earlier generation remained intact. Her one concrete hope for deliverance is Selden; however, Selden is a self-righteous fop who keeps his distance from Lily when she is ostracized by the beautiful people he hypocritically purports to disdain. The only true image of nurturing love in the novel comes not from the upper classes at all, but from the working-class family of George and Nettie Crane. When Nettie was seduced and abandoned by her employer, George married her and adopted her bastard child. The contrast between his unselfish (and unself-conscious) love for Nettie and Selden's wimpish vacillations toward Lily constitutes Wharton's most withering indictment of those who live in the house of mirth.

As fine a writer as Wharton was, she did not appear to be a prime candidate for a popular biography. Her life was not exactly dull and conventional, but neither did it seem dramatic or exotic enough to interest anyone but a literary historian. She had given her own account of that life in *A Backward Glance* (1934), and many who knew her (notably Percy Lubbock) had already recorded their impressions. Moreover, her most important literary friendship, the one with James, had been well documented by Millicent Bell in

R. W. B. and Nancy Lewis circa 1988

Edith Wharton and Henry James: The Study of Their Friendship (1965). Wharton might make an interesting character in a historical novel by Gore Vidal, but the public record of her life offered little beyond a succession of Atlantic crossings, garden parties, and fat royalty checks. Still, there was a wealth of documents sealed in the Yale University Library. It was always possible that, when those became available to a biographer in 1968, readers would meet someone different from the familiar, slightly stuffy, grande dame of American letters. Such was the case after Lewis studied the documents.

The story he tells of the early life of the woman born Edith Jones is a familiar one. Daughter of a New York family that had been prominent in a world already fast disappearing, Edith was a shy and private girl, devoted to her bookish but distant father and smothered by her domineering mother. After a couple of early romances failed to take her to the altar, she finally married an amiable but doltish aristocrat named Teddy Wharton. A man of little cultivation and of pedestrian interests, Teddy had almost nothing in common with his wife. Moreover, the available evidence suggests that theirs was a celibate marriage. (Edith's premarital sex education had consisted of her mother telling her that by looking at statues she could tell that men and women were built differently.) There was no effort to consummate the marriage until three weeks after the vows, and when that went badly, the couple ap-

parently never tried again. Teddy was kept on for years as a kind of superfluous prince consort until he started using Edith's money to support his debaucheries, including affairs with several dance-hall girls. At that point Edith divorced him, and they rarely saw each other again.

What Lewis discovered in his research that has presented a very different Edith Wharton are the details of a brief but passionate love affair she had in her mid forties. To the extent that this affair was known at all, largely on the evidence of a private diary Wharton kept in 1908, her lover was believed to have been Walter Berry, a lifelong friend (they are buried next to each other) and one of the suitors who failed to marry her in her youth. But, as Lewis demonstrates, the man who actually released Wharton's repressed sexuality was W. Morton Fullerton, an Edwardian dandy whose other paramours included the Ranee of Sarawak. By bringing this affair to light and publishing (in an appendix) a pornographic fragment from Wharton's "Beatrice Palmetto," a projected novel about father-daughter incest, Lewis conclusively shatters the legend of Wharton's sexual frigidity. It is to his credit, however, that he does not use these sensational revelations to manufacture an opposite legend. As Gary H. Lindberg in the *Virginia Quarterly Review* (Winter 1976) rightly points out, "Edith Wharton's erotic nature . . . was not her distinguishing trait, and it deserves emphasis only to correct a false image."

The wealth of information at Lewis's disposal sometimes prompted him to clutter Wharton's story with unnecessary detail. Some reviewers were also dismayed that Lewis devoted only 130 pages to Wharton's first forty years and nearly 400 to her last thirty-five. Moreover, the book's documentation is too general to allow readers to check many assertions that are presented as fact. Finally, in his devotion to telling the story of Wharton's life, Lewis seems constantly to be resisting the tendency to do what he does best—engage in literary criticism. The problem is not that the book lacks literary analysis but that the analysis too often gets lost in minutiae about, for example, what Wharton ate and wore, rather than what she wrote.

Even if one can quibble about the specific emphases and general readability of *Edith Wharton: A Biography*, the importance of the book is unquestionable. In preserving so many letters, diaries, and other documents, Wharton obviously meant to leave a paper trail that would lead to the true story of her life after she and her contemporaries were safely in their graves. Lewis and his staff of research assistants have pursued that trail with enormous energy and professionalism. Furthermore, in 1988 Lewis and his wife, Nancy, published an edition of Wharton's letters, which is more than one hundred pages longer than the biography. Taken together, both volumes have sparked new interest in Wharton as both person and artist.

References:
Elmer Borklund, "R. W. B. Lewis," in his *Contemporary Literary Critics* (New York: St. Martin's Press, 1977), pp. 354-359;
Leon Edel, "A Stone into the Mirror," *American Scholar*, 45 (Winter 1975-1976): 826, 828, 830;
Gary H. Lindberg, "The Making of Edith Wharton," *Virginia Quarterly Review*, 52 (Winter 1976): 139-145;
Cecil F. Tate, "Culture and the Dramatic Dialogue: Lewis's *The American Adam*," in his *The Search for a Method in American Studies* (Minneapolis: University of Minncsota Press, 1973), pp. 87-103.

Maynard Mack

(27 October 1909 -   )

Vicki K. Robinson
State University of New York College at Cortland

BOOKS: *For All Our Fathers, Gentlemen!* (New Haven: Profile, 1932);

Mister Scoggins' Saturday Night (New Haven: City Printing, 1934);

Images of Man, by Mack and Robert Whitney Boynton (New York: Prentice-Hall, 1964);

King Lear in Our Time (Berkeley: University of California Press, 1965; London: Methuen, 1966);

The Garden and the City: Retirement and Politics in the Later Poetry of Pope, 1731-1743 (Toronto: University of Toronto Press / London: Oxford University Press, 1969);

Introduction to the Short Story, by Mack and Boynton (Hasbrouck Heights, N.J.: Hayden, 1965; revised, 1972);

Introduction to the Poem, by Mack and Boynton (Hasbrouck Heights, N.J.: Hayden, 1965; revised, 1973);

Introduction to the Play, by Mack and Boynton (Hasbrouck Heights, N.J.: Hayden, 1969; revised, 1976);

A History of Scroll and Key, 1842-1942 (New Haven: The Society/New Haven Publishers, 1978);

Poetic Traditions on the English Renaissance, by Mack and George deForest Lord (New Haven: Yale University Press, 1982);

Collected in Himself: Essays Critical, Biographical, and Bibliographical on Pope and Some of His Contemporaries (Newark: University of Delaware Press / London: Associated University Presses, 1982);

Alexander Pope: A Life (New Haven: Yale University Press, 1985);

The World of Alexander Pope (New Haven: Yale University Press, 1988).

RECORDING: *Romeo and Juliet* [discussion], De Land, Fla., Everett/Edwards, p1979.722.

OTHER: Henry Fielding, *The History of the Adventures of Joseph Andrews and His Friend Mr. Abra-*

ham Adams, edited, with an introduction, by Mack (New York: Rinehart, 1949);

English Masterpieces: An Anthology of Imaginative Literature from Chaucer to T. S. Eliot, 8 volumes, edited by Mack and others (New York: Prentice-Hall, 1950; revised, 7 volumes, 1961);

Alexander Pope, *An Essay on Man*, edited by Mack (New Haven: Yale University Press, 1951; London: Methuen, 1951);

World Masterpieces, 2 volumes, edited by Mack and others (New York: Norton, 1956; revised, 1965);

William Shakespeare, *The Tragedy of Antony and Cleopatra*, edited by Mack (New York & Baltimore: Penguin, 1960; revised, 1970);

The Morgan and Houghton Library Manuscripts of Alexander Pope's "Essay on Man," compiled by Mack (New York: Roxburghe Club/Oxford University Press, 1962);

Twentieth Century Views [series], edited by Mack (Englewood Cliffs, N.J.: Prentice-Hall, 1962-   );

Essential Articles for the Study of Alexander Pope, edited by Mack (Hamden, Conn.: Archon, 1964; London: Cass, 1964; revised and enlarged, 1968);

Shakespeare, *The History of Henry IV: Part One*, edited by Mack (New York: New American Library, 1965);

The Poems of Alexander Pope: Translations of Homer, edited, with an introduction, by Mack (London: Methuen / New Haven: Yale University Press—volumes 7-8: *The Iliad*, 1967; volumes 9-10: *The Odyssey*, 1967; index, 1969);

Imagined Worlds: Essays on Some English Novels and Novelists in Honour of John Butt, edited by Mack and Ian Gregor (New York: Barnes & Noble, 1968; London: Methuen, 1968);

Twentieth Century Interpretations [series], edited by Mack (Englewood Cliffs, N.J.: Prentice-Hall, 1968-   );

Shakespeare, *The First Part of King Henry the Fourth*, edited by Mack (New York: Hayden, 1973);

Maynard Mack (photograph by Michael Marsland; courtesy of the Yale University Office of Public Affairs)

Shakespeare, *The Tragedy of Hamlet,* edited by Mack (New York: Hayden, 1973);

Shakespeare, *The Tragedy of Julius Caesar,* edited by Mack (New York: Hayden, 1973);

Shakespeare, *The Tragedy of Macbeth,* edited by Mack (New York: Hayden, 1973);

Sounds and Silences: Poems for Performing, edited by Mack and Robert Whitney Boynton (Rochelle Park, N.J.: Hayden, 1975);

Whodunits, Farces, and Fantasies: Ten Short Plays, edited by Mack and Boynton (Rochelle Park, N.J.: Hayden, 1976);

Contexts One: The Beggar's Opera, edited by Mack (Hamden, Conn.: Shoe String, 1976);

Contexts Two: The Rape of the Locke, edited by

Mack and William Kinsley (Hamden, Conn.: Shoe String, 1979);

Rescuing Shakespeare, edited by Mack (New York: Oxford University Press, 1979);

Pope: Recent Essays by Several Hands, edited by Mack (Hamden, Conn.: Archon, 1980; Brighton, U.K.: Harvester, 1980);

The Last and Greatest Art: Some Unpublished Poetical Manuscripts of Alexander Pope, compiled by Mack (Newark: University of Delaware Press / London: Associated University Presses, 1982);

Contexts Three: Absalom and Achitophel, edited by Mack (Hamden, Conn.: Shoe String, 1983);

"Salute to a Three Hundredth Birthday," in *Rheto-*

rics of Order/Ordering Rhetorics, edited by Paul Hunter and Douglas Canfield (Newark: University of Delaware Press, 1989).

SELECTED PERIODICAL PUBLICATIONS—
UNCOLLECTED: "To See It Feelingly," *Publications of the Modern Language Association*, 86 (May 1971): 363-374;
"The Life of Learning," *American Council of Learned Societies Newsletter*, 34 (Winter-Spring 1983): 2-15;
"Alexander Pope: Reflections of an Amateur Biographer," *Modern Language Review*, 79 (January 1984): xxiii-xxxv;
"A Shakespeare Not for Specialists," *Connecticut Council Humanities News* (Winter 1986).

Maynard Mack has accomplished what was thought by twentieth-century scholars to be a Herculean task, a definitive biography of Alexander Pope. *Alexander Pope: A Life* (1985) has been unanimously praised for its remarkable breadth of information, carefully considered suppositions, and graceful style. Yet Mack would probably disdain calling the book his greatest achievement. He has always considered teaching his most important task and has been a teacher at Yale since the 1930s. While he has produced accurate and thorough editions of works by Pope and William Shakespeare, among others; compiled and edited valuable anthologies and collections; and written highly acclaimed books and articles, particularly on the literature of the Renaissance and the eighteenth century, teaching remains the work of which he is most proud, work that carries on the tradition of his father.

Maynard Mack was born on 27 October 1909 in Hillsdale, Michigan, to Jesse Floyd Mack and Pearl Vore Mack. When Maynard was eight, the family moved to Oberlin, Ohio, where his father taught literature at Oberlin College. Along with his sister, Mack grew up in a modest but friendly, open, and intellectually stimulating home. He attended Oberlin High School for two years and, in the summer of 1924, was offered a scholarship to attend the Taft School, an elite preparatory school in Massachusetts, where he spent four years. His Latin master encouraged and assisted him in applying to Yale, where he graduated with a B.A. in 1932.

On 5 August 1933 Mack married Florence Brocklebank, whom he had met in Oberlin during a Christmas holiday. While Mack attended graduate school at Yale, she worked for four years as a blood chemist in cancer research at the Yale Medical School. In 1937 the Macks' first daughter, Prudence (Pam), was born, followed by Sara (Sari) in 1939 and Maynard (Sandy) in 1942. Prudence is a teacher of English composition and a free-lance writer living in Toronto; Sara is a professor of classics at the University of North Carolina at Chapel Hill; and Maynard is a professor of English specializing in Renaissance studies at the University of Maryland and is the author of *Killing the King* (1973), a study of Shakespeare's tragedies. The elder Macks have eight grandchildren and have lived in the same house in New Haven since 1938. Mack chose to remain at Yale both for his graduate degree and his teaching career.

He received his Ph.D. in 1936. His four years of graduate work determined the course of his future scholarship and teaching. In 1932 graduate students at Yale were required to study the history of arts and letters, including philosophy, literature, art, and politics, during the period of history of their choice. Mack selected the eighteenth century and thus began his association with Chauncey Brewster Tinker, whom Mack praises (in an unpublished interview) as a "great teacher" with a "graceful use of language." Mack was also influenced by other scholars, such as Norman C. Torrey in the history of science and George Sherburn, a Pope scholar.

Mack began teaching at Yale early in his graduate career. Because of the sudden illness of a professor, he was asked to teach an introductory English literature class that included three plays of Shakespeare and the works of several Victorian writers. This was an unusual opportunity for a beginning graduate student and helped form Mack's lifelong interests in Shakespeare and the seventeenth century. Among his teaching responsibilities were grading the ten-minute writings from students, then required at the beginning of each class at Yale. Mack maintains that such writings are important to a student's education and were beneficial to him, too.

In his third year of graduate work Mack decided to focus his study on English literature of the eighteenth century and worked closely with Tinker. Drawing from his three-year study of the eighteenth century, Mack wrote his dissertation, "The Intellectual Background of Alexander Pope's *Essay on Man*," a study of philosophical optimism with Pope's long poem as the centerpiece.

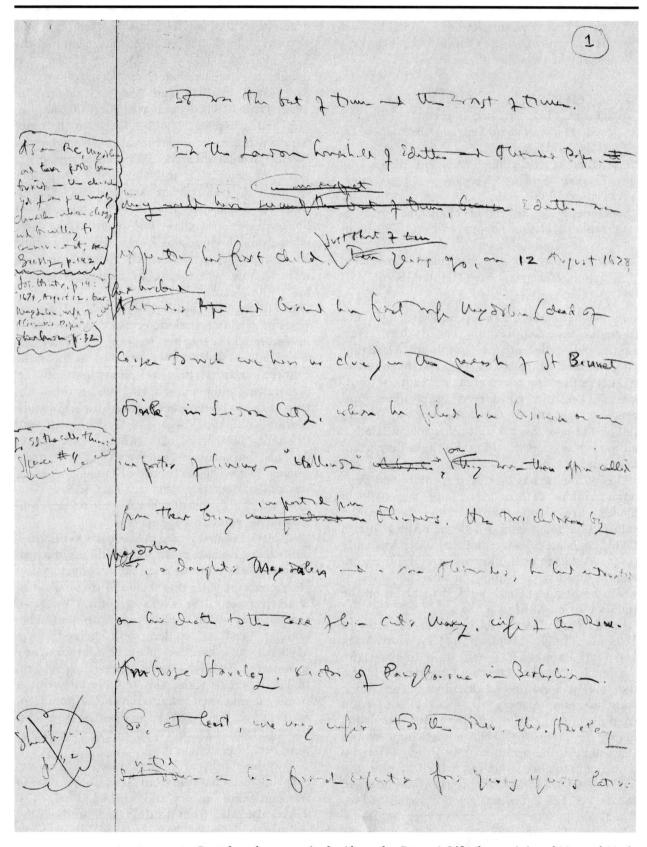

Pages from the manuscript for Alexander Pope: A Life *(by permission of Maynard Mack)*

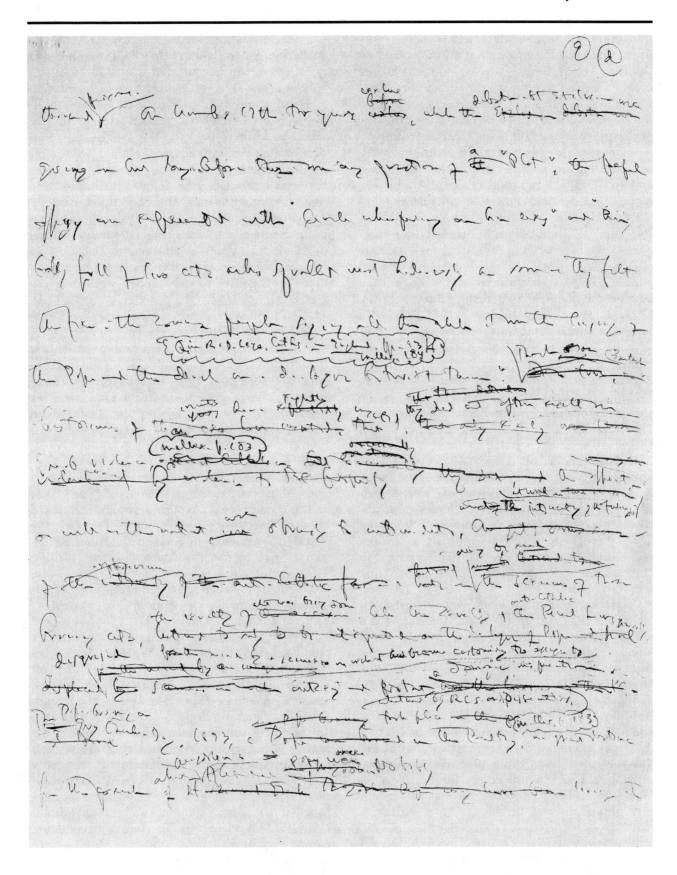

After graduation Mack was invited to join the Yale faculty. He taught a variety of courses, including "World Drama." In 1941 and 1942 he taught the Shakespeare course for the first time, with three lectures per week, twenty-five plays for the school year. Later he taught the graduate Shakespeare course, replacing Charles Proudy.

In 1940 he was named an assistant professor, in 1945 he became an associate professor, and in 1948 a full professor. In 1965 he was named the Sterling Professor of English, and since 1978 he has held the title of Sterling Professor emeritus. In addition, he has been the associate director of the Shakespeare Institute (1953-1962), director of the humanities division at Yale (1962-1964), chairman of the English department at Yale (1965-1968), and director of the National Humanities Institute (1974-1977). He has also held temporary positions at other schools. He was the Walker-Ames Lecturer at the University of Washington in Seattle in 1956, the Alexander Lecturer at the University of Toronto in 1963, the Beckman Visiting Professor at the University of California in Berkeley in 1964 and 1965, and the Lord Northcliffe Lecturer at the University of London in 1972.

Throughout his career, Mack has contended that teaching has been "the main thing. Everything else is so your teaching will be better. . . . We delude ourselves into thinking our discoveries are at the level of Einstein's." Mack believes there is an excessive emphasis on faculty publications, but he agrees that writing is vital in "forcing you to sharpen your ability to present material to students."

Mack's writing has long been successful. In 1932 and 1934 he won the Yale University Prize for his poems *For All Our Fathers, Gentlemen!* and *Mister Scoggins' Saturday Night*, respectively. His first major publication was in 1949, his edition of Henry Fielding's *The History of the Adventures of Joseph Andrews and his Friend Mr. Abraham Adams*. But his most significant early edition was of Alexander Pope's *Essay on Man*, published in 1951 in the Twickenham series. The general editor of the Twickenham Edition, John Butt, had unsuccessfully sought an English editor for the *Essay on Man* who had a background in eighteenth-century philosophy and the history of its ideas. Finally Mack's name was suggested because of his extensive work in this area, particularly in his dissertation. Butt contacted Mack, who agreed to the task, and the resulting edition stands today as the most thorough and complete edition available.

Because of this success Mack was able to persuade the general editors that Pope's *Translations of Homer* should be included in the Twickenham volumes. *The Poems of Alexander Pope: Translations of Homer* was finally published in 1967, with an index in 1969. Mack had argued strongly for the inclusion of these works in the Twickenham Edition because the translations of Homer, representing for Pope a decade's worth of work, gave him the artistic reputation he enjoyed during his lifetime. Dedicated to Butt, Mack's edition includes a six-part introduction, several valuable illustrations, nearly all of Pope's original edition, textual notes on such items as allusions to classical and contemporary authors and critics, and nine appendixes, which serve to show Pope's work in progress.

In 1969 Mack's *The Garden and the City: Retirement and Politics in the Later Poetry of Pope* was published; he had presented the substance of its first three chapters in his Alexander lectures at the University of Toronto in 1963. Focusing on the Twickenham years of Pope's life, from 1731 until his death in 1743, Mack suggests that Twickenham may be seen as a metaphor for the personal and poetic life of Pope. As in a Popean couplet Pope's home is both thesis and antithesis: close to London yet verdant and vegetative, and dedicated to friendships yet the setting of some of Pope's most scathing couplets. It is also a representation of classical harmony, the platonic ideal and the Palladian symmetry so revered by Pope. Benjamin Boyce, in the *Philological Quarterly* (Spring 1970), calls the book "rich and interesting throughout . . . bring[ing] together for unity of understanding the diverse tendencies in Pope's career, personal and literary."

After several more publications on Pope, including *Collected in Himself* (1982), which is an accumulation of Mack's essays on Pope, and *The Last and Greatest Art: Some Unpublished Poetical Manuscripts of Alexander Pope* (also 1982), Mack published in 1985 his 975-page *Alexander Pope: A Life*. Intended for the general reader, the book is the most comprehensive biography of Pope written in the twentieth century. It became a possibility only after certain groundwork had been completed—the critical text of the poems was published in the eleven-volume Twickenham Edition (1938-1969), and George Sherburn's five-volume edition of Pope's correspondence also became available. Mack's extensive background in the eighteenth century and the history of ideas helped to make him especially suited to do a com-

Dust jacket for Mack's biography of the poet whose life he views as "one of the great literary success stories of all time"

prehensive biography. Since Pope was cosmopolitan in his reading, familiar with classical and contemporary writers, his biographer had to possess a similar background.

The book begins with a detailed exploration of Pope's shadowy childhood. Mack describes the pleasures Pope surely enjoyed as the only son of forty-two-year-old Alexander Pope and his second wife, forty-year-old Edith Turner Pope. Undoubtedly doted on by his father, who had already lost one son named Alexander, Pope lived, Mack suggests, within an "adoring" circle, enthralled by "its only man-child." But all was not bliss for the young Pope. The anti-Catholicism, suspicion of papist plots, and laws limiting the freedom of Roman Catholics were a humiliating burden on the child, probably because, as Mack speculates, "injustice seems particularly outrageous to those whom life has not yet hardened to it." Mack describes in detail the strictures placed on Catholics during Pope's youth and the adjust-

ments the family made, such as moving to the largely Catholic Hammersmith area.

The book gives evidence that Pope's severe handicaps were overcome by several personal strengths. The first handicap was, of course, his Roman Catholic religion. Second, he suffered from tuberculosis of the spine (Pott's disease), probably contracted from his nurse when he was an infant. As a result, he stood only four and a half feet tall, had severe kyphoscoliosis (a collapse of the vertabrae both sidewise and backwards), and was continually ill. Yet these difficulties were not his defeat. He nurtured friendships with some of the most innovative people of the eighteenth century, and, while not a true artistic innovator, he was the first writer in English who successfully earned a comfortable living as a poet.

Alexander Pope: A Life received both the Christian Gauss Award from Phi Beta Kappa and the *Los Angeles Times* Book Prize in 1986. Critics were nearly unanimous in their praise: John Wain in the *New York Times Book Review* (2 March 1986) concluded that the "book is a noble effort of research, and all serious readers of Pope will be glad to have it." In the *New York Times* (14 February 1986) John Gross called the book "Maynard Mack's crowning achievement of a life that has been largely devoted to the poet...." Likewise, Ian Donaldson, in the *Times Literary Supplement* (13 September 1985), called the book "magisterial" and Mack "the ideal biographer ... the foremost living authority on Pope and his writings."

Ironically the thoroughness of detail is also the source of the minor criticism of Mack's book. Gross, for example, claims that "some of his digressions and examples could no doubt have been sacrificed." Wain concurs: "The fault is his inability to leave anything out." Wain cites the example of Mack's detailed speculation on the home and destination of the cow that attacked the three-year-old Pope while he was being tended by his sister, Magdalen. "We don't care where the confounded cow came from or was going to," Wain complains. But it is just such material that produces the colorful, albeit leisurely, examination of Pope and his world. Mack is curious about everything, and his enthusiasm for exploring is clearly present in the book.

Mack's contribution to literary biography is significant. With his extensive background in the classics, world literature, and seventeenth- and eighteenth-century ideas, he produced perhaps the finest biography of Pope ever written—a study that illuminates not only the life and works of Pope but also the entire world of eighteenth-century England.

Frank MacShane
(19 October 1927 -   )

Jason Berner
Hunter College of the City University of New York

BOOKS: *Many Golden Ages: Ruins, Temples and Monuments of the Orient* (Tokyo & Rutland, Vt.: Tuttle, 1963);

The Life and Work of Ford Madox Ford (New York: Horizon, 1965; London: Routledge & Kegan Paul, 1965);

The Life of Raymond Chandler (New York: Dutton, 1976; London: Cape, 1976);

The Life of John O'Hara (New York: Dutton, 1980; London: Cape, 1980);

Into Eternity: The Life of James Jones, American Writer (Boston: Houghton Mifflin, 1985).

OTHER: *Impressions of Latin America: Five Centuries of Travel and Adventure by English and North American Writers*, edited by MacShane (New York: Morrow, 1963);

The Critical Writings of Ford Madox Ford, edited by MacShane (Lincoln: University of Nebraska Press, 1964);

The American in Europe: A Collection of Impressions Written by Americans from the Seventeenth Century to the Present, edited by MacShane (New York: Dutton, 1965);

Ford Madox Ford: The Critical Heritage, edited by MacShane (London & Boston: Routledge & Kegan Paul, 1972);

Borges on Writing, edited by MacShane, Norman Thomas di Giovanni, and Daniel Halpern (New York: Dutton, 1973);

"Borges the Craftsman," in *Prose for Borges*, edited by Charles Hamilton Newman and Mary Kinzie (Evanston, Ill.: Northwestern University Press, 1974), pp. 351-354;

The Notebooks of Raymond Chandler; and, English Summer: A Gothic Romance, edited by MacShane (New York: Ecco, 1976; London: Weidenfeld & Nicolson, 1977);

Selected Letters of Raymond Chandler, edited, with an introduction, by MacShane (New York: Columbia University Press, 1981; London: Cape, 1981);

"Two Such Silver Currents," in *The Presence of Ford Madox Ford: A Memorial Volume of Essays,*

Poems and Memoirs, edited by Sondra J. Stang (Philadelphia: University of Pennsylvania Press, 1981), pp. 231-239;

Collected Stories of John O'Hara, selected, with an introduction, by MacShane (New York: Random House, 1984);

"The Teaching of Translation," in *The World of Translation*, edited by Gregory Rabassa and Lewis Galantiere (New York: PEN American Center, 1987), pp. 231-239.

TRANSLATIONS: Miguel Serrano, *The Visits of the Queen of Sheba* (New York & Bombay: Asia Publishing House, 1960);

Serrano, *C. G. Jung and Hermann Hesse: A Record of Two Friendships* (New York: Schocken, 1966);

Serrano, *The Ultimate Flower* (New York: Schocken, 1969; London: Routledge & Kegan Paul, 1969);

Serrano, *El/Ella* (New York: Harper & Row, 1972);

Serrano, *The Serpent of Paradise* (New York: Harper & Row, 1972).

SELECTED PERIODICAL PUBLICATIONS—
UNCOLLECTED: "Dahlberg: Aphorisms & Poetry," *Nation*, 203 (12 September 1966): 225-226;

"New Poetry," *American Scholar*, 37 (Autumn 1968): 642-646;

"Range of Six," *Poetry*, 118 (August 1971): 295-301;

"John O'Hara's Long Concern," *New Republic*, 184 (3-10 January 1981): 22;

"Writing Biographies," *Columbia Library Columns*, 30 (May 1981): 17-27;

"The Fantasy World of Italo Calvino," *New York Times Magazine*, 10 July 1983, pp. 22-23;

"Meeting Ross MacDonald," *New York Times Book Review*, 11 September 1983, p. 14;

"John O'Hara: The Best Conversation in America," *New York Times Book Review*, 3 February 1985, p. 3.

Frank MacShane circa 1980 (photograph by Pamela Griffiths)

As a prolific editor, educator, translator, and biographer, Frank MacShane has dedicated his career to documenting the lives and accomplishments of those writers "with substantial followings and many enthusiastic champions," but who are not "automatically accepted into the highest literary rank" (as he says in "Writing Biographies," *Columbia Library Columns*, May 1981). Feeling that the lives of writers such as Ernest Hemingway and William Faulkner have already been well documented and reported, MacShane chooses as his subjects those authors "who need a little help on the side, the help that a biographer can give," in order to establish more firmly their place in the literary canon. His books include biographies of critically acclaimed writers, such as Ford Madox Ford and John O'Hara, and of more celebrated writers, such as Raymond Chandler and James Jones, whom he feels are somewhat overlooked by literary critics.

MacShane was born on 19 October 1927 in Pittsburgh, Pennsylvania, the son of Frank MacShane, a journalist, and Elizabeth A. Morse

MacShane. He received his A.B. from Harvard in 1949. After receiving his M.A. from Yale in 1951, MacShane left the United States for England to pursue his doctoral work at Oxford. He earned his Ph.D. in 1955 and then returned to North America for a lectureship in English at McGill University in Montreal (1955-1957), immediately followed by a one-year Fulbright professorship at the University of Chile. It was at this time that MacShane became familiar with the writing of Chilean author Miguel Serrano, some of whose works he would later translate into English. In 1958 he became a visiting lecturer at Vassar College in New York, and on 8 July 1959 he married Virginia Lynn Fry, with whom he was to have a son, Nicholas Morse. Also in 1959 MacShane accepted a position as an assistant professor of English at the University of California at Berkeley. In 1960 MacShane's first book was published, a translation of Serrano's *Las Visitas de la Reina de Saba* (*The Visits of the Queen of Sheba*). This was followed in 1963 by two travel books: *Many Golden Ages: Ruins, Temples and Monuments of the Orient* and *Impressions of Latin America: Five*

Dust jacket for the biography in which MacShane attempted to spark a critical reassessment of the most respected stylist of the hard-boiled detective fiction movement

Centuries of Travel and Adventure by English and North American Writers, the latter edited by Mac-Shane. A well-traveled man, MacShane explained the importance of travel literature in the introduction to the Latin American collection: "Now . . . an understanding of the motives of people in other societies is more vital for the survival of decency in the world than it ever was." This concern for an understanding of motivations would serve MacShane well in his works of literary biography.

In 1964 MacShane edited a collection of the critical writings of Ford Madox Ford, a writer who, according to MacShane, "looked upon all good literature as contemporary, and considered great writers not as dead figures from the past appearing in histories of literature, but as living men who had things to say to modern men even though they had died physically five hundred years before." MacShane shared this viewpoint,

and it inspired him to focus his first literary biography on the prolific Ford.

MacShane was not the first to write a biography of Ford, and his book was not destined to be the authoritative history of Ford's life. That would come later with the publication of Arthur Mizener's *The Saddest Story: A Biography of Ford Madox Ford* (1971). What distinguishes the Mac-Shane biography is that it was an attempt to revitalize the career of a publicly overlooked writer. Ford authored more than seventy books, wrote many short stories, and, as one who stressed aesthetic and stylistic evaluation, was an influential critic of contemporary English literature; yet, due to the often experimental nature of his writing, it was often ignored, and he therefore slipped into relative obscurity among other early-twentieth-century English writers. In his preface to *The Life and Work of Ford Madox Ford* (1965) MacShane writes: "of all the figures of twentieth-

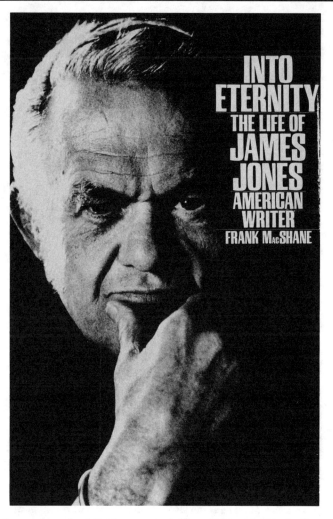

Dust jacket for the biography of an author who, MacShane argued, "deserved to stand in the first rank of American writers of the second half of the twentieth century"

century literature who have exerted powerful influences on its development and who have also been imaginative artists of merit, Ford Madox Ford has perhaps received the least attention and credit for the part he played." Although writing a biography, MacShane stresses that his main purpose is to renew an interest in Ford's writing: "what is important about Ford is his work, and I have always attempted to relate the facts of his life to his writings."

Although it was a scholarly attempt, MacShane's first biography was his least successful. While it does achieve its critical goals, devoting entire chapters to detailed analyses of Ford's major works—*The Good Soldier* (1915) and the *Parade's End* tetralogy (1924-1928)—and giving sensitive evaluations of Ford's poetry, the book fails to generate enough interest in Ford's life. For this reason, MacShane's book met with mixed critical re-

ception. Edward Dahlberg of the *New York Review of Books* (30 September 1965) praised the book, calling it a "Herculean labor" and saying that he could "think of no remarkable memorabilia of a noble figure so faithful to its hero as . . . Frank MacShane's," but other reviews were less favorable. The anonymous critic for the *Times Literary Supplement* (9 September 1965) agreed that the book was "certainly thorough," but he said that "again and again the author has skidded into the bog of Ford's impressionism, repeating fanciful stories as though they were authentic." John Simon, in *Book Week* (26 December 1965), complained, "MacShane has assembled a good many facts . . . but even here much that is of a personal nature is missing. But then, Professor MacShane tells us, his aim was to give us Ford the literary figure and discuss his artistic development. . . . But Professor MacShane, lacking the gift of evocation as much as critical acuity, is not the one to do it."

In fall 1964 MacShane had moved back to the East, where he taught English at Williams College in Williamstown, Massachusetts. During his time there he edited another collection of travel-oriented essays, *The American in Europe: A Collection of Impressions Written by Americans from the Seventeenth Century to the Present* (1965), and translated another of Serrano's books, *C. G. Jung and Hermann Hesse: A Record of Two Friendships* (1966). In 1967 MacShane joined the faculty of Columbia University in New York City, and in the following year he became chairman of the Writing Division. MacShane became a full professor in 1969, and in 1972 he was named chairman of the Translation Center at Columbia. In 1973 he edited *Borges on Writing* with Norman Thomas di Giovanni and Daniel Halpern.

MacShane established himself as a successful literary biographer with the publication of *The Life of Raymond Chandler* (1976). While MacShane was living in California during the early 1960s, as he reports in "Writing Biographies," "someone said, 'if you want to know what California is like, read Raymond Chandler.' " MacShane was attracted to the vivid sense of place evoked in Chandler's novels of the darker side of Hollywood. Chandler is probably best known as one of the originators of the hard-boiled detective story and as the creator of the popular fictional detective Philip Marlowe. As a young man with literary aspirations, Chandler went to Hollywood in the early 1940s to support himself by writing for the screen until he could become a "serious" novelist. Chandler's strategy seems to have backfired, however, as the success and popularity he gained through his career as a mystery novelist and screenwriter caused him to be dismissed by the literary community as little more than a popular hack. MacShane's biography is an example of his desire to validate the work of a popular writer who never received much critical attention as a "serious novelist." The fact that Chandler *was* such a popular figure, however, no doubt generated interest in the biography and helped to solidify MacShane's reputation.

The critical response to this second biography was much more favorable as well. Although some reviewers criticized MacShane for his attempts to make Chandler into a major literary figure—when, according to Leonard Michaels of the *New York Times Book Review* (16 May 1976), "Chandler . . . wasn't deceived about the essential quality of his work. There should be no reason

now to claim more for him than he claimed for himself"—the overall response was that the biography was thorough and engaging. Michaels went on to say that "Chandler emerges . . . as a very powerful and psychologically interesting figure." Peter S. Prescott of *Newsweek* (24 May 1976) said, "MacShane has made an exemplary biography. . . . I think his book is an important addition to our knowledge of how good writers have lived in our society."

At about the same time that the Chandler biography was published, MacShane finished editing *The Notebooks of Raymond Chandler; and, English Summer: A Gothic Romance* (1976). MacShane later resumed his travels, accepting Fulbright professorships at Tribhuvan University in Nepal in 1978 and at Centro di Studi Americani in Rome in 1979. Shortly after returning to the United States, MacShane published his third literary biography, *The Life of John O'Hara* (1980).

Relying heavily on Matthew J. Bruccoli's *The O'Hara Concern: A Biography of John O'Hara* (1975), this is perhaps MacShane's most controversial biography, due to the less-than-universal appeal of the subject. Like Ford, O'Hara was a prolific novelist and short-story writer who was, to an extent, underrated and overlooked. The O'Hara biography, however, generated much more enthusiasm, both among critics and readers, than the book on Ford. O'Hara was a tough-talking, often coarse and abrasive man, best known for his innovative use of prose dialogue in his short stories and novels, his vivid descriptions of New York social life, and his creation of realistic, if somewhat "undesirable," characters (including Pal Joey, on whom the successful Broadway musical was based).

In the introduction to *The Life of John O'Hara* MacShane states that, as was the case with the Ford biography, "the purpose of this book is to renew an interest in O'Hara's work through a look at his life." Though MacShane was aware of the negative reaction that many people would have toward his subject, he maintained his conviction throughout the book that O'Hara was "one of the half-dozen most important writers of his time." At the conclusion of the biography, MacShane writes, "O'Hara's industry—his obsession with writing—was a curse as well as a blessing, for he wrote too much, and the quantity of his work confused his public and caused him to be undervalued. His public statements and vanity turned people against him, and he was resented and underrated, usually by his inferiors and

MacShane circa 1985 (photograph by Joe Pineiro)

often by his own associates." The success of MacShane's biography rests on the fact that he does not apologize for his subject's personal shortcomings but offers a thorough, uncompromising look at the life of an author who deserves more public and critical recognition.

MacShane received his most favorable notices for his biography of O'Hara. Yet this was offset somewhat by the negative reaction of many reviewers to O'Hara himself. Seymour Krim of *Harper's* (February 1981) wrote, "Frank Mac-Shane's new biography of John O'Hara is a hell of a lot more interesting for us today . . . than practically all the fourteen novels O'Hara ever wrote. . . . Mr. MacShane happens to be a very decent, compassionate bloke. . . . But what it [the biography] will do most is confirm the fact that Black Jack O'Hara was a more unsavory character than anything in his fictional shooting gallery, including the classic bastards in his short stories."

Most critics applauded MacShane's scholarship and professionalism, despite the fact that they held some disdain for O'Hara.

In the early 1980s MacShane published *Selected Letters of Raymond Chandler* (1981) and *Collected Stories of John O'Hara* (1984). With *Into Eternity: The Life of James Jones, American Writer* (1985) MacShane seemed to make a slight departure from his earlier writings. Jones was a more familiar figure than either Ford or O'Hara and was more critically acclaimed as a serious novelist than Chandler. MacShane was drawn to Jones as a subject primarily because of his "American to the bone" story. "Born in the heartland of the country," MacShane writes in his introduction, "he was forced by the Depression to join the army, only to find himself trapped in military life for five years by the advent of World War II." MacShane believed that Jones "deserved to stand in the first rank of American writers of the second half of the twentieth century," and, as with Chandler, MacShane wrote this biography to correct what he perceived as an oversight on the part of critics and to help ensure Jones's permanence as an American literary figure.

Into Eternity received almost universal acclaim. Although Jeffrey Meyers in the *National Review* (28 February 1986) criticized Jones as "essentially a one-book author," he praised the biography: "MacShane's lively and interesting narrative is sympathetic to Jones, captures the essence of the man, and offers a fair appraisal of his extremely uneven work." Robert Philips in the *New York Times Book Review* (10 November 1985) wrote, "the biography is chronological and concise, yet Mr. MacShane manages to examine the man from many angles. . . . [It] is a guidebook to the works, accomplishments and failures of an American writer who was not afraid to take chances—a writer for whom the importance of art was that, like the war which was his most successful subject, it took risks."

In "Writing Biographies," MacShane offers some advice for other authors: "Writing biographies is a curious occupation. As you go on . . . you begin to be aware that you are not really writing a biography, you are just writing. The medium happens to be biography, but it is also a personal statement. Your words inevitably reflect attitudes, opinions, values. A scholarly conscientiousness prevents you from turning the biography into fiction, but the vigor of the writing . . . will inevitably be the product of a sensibility and an energy that has shaped the work so that it is more than a mere chronicle of a man's life. I don't like to stress this side of the affair, because it is a mysterious element and probably shouldn't be much discussed. But I also think it is the most important side of the process." MacShane is primarily concerned with revealing the life of a writer through an examination of his work and thereby generating interest in that work, always presented as the axis around which a writer's life turns. MacShane's own unobtrusive style allows the biographies to flow as chronological reports that let readers see the genesis of a writer's work through the episodes of his life. As translator, editor, professor, and writer, MacShane displays a profound respect for the importance of the written word and the writers who utilize its power.

Paul Mariani

(29 February 1940 -   )

Gail Porter Mandell
Saint Mary's College, Notre Dame, Indiana

BOOKS: *A Commentary on the Complete Poems of Gerard Manley Hopkins* (Ithaca, N.Y. & London: Cornell University Press, 1970);

William Carlos Williams: The Poet and His Critics (Chicago: American Library Association, 1975);

Timing Devices: Poems (Easthampton, Mass.: Pennyroyal, 1977; trade edition, Boston: Godine, 1979);

William Carlos Williams: A New World Naked (New York: McGraw-Hill, 1981);

Crossing Cocytus: Poems (New York: Grove, 1982);

A Usable Past: Essays on Modern and Contemporary Poetry (Amherst: University of Massachusetts Press, 1984);

Prime Mover: Poems 1981-1985 (New York: Grove, 1985);

Dream Song: The Life of John Berryman (New York: Morrow, 1990);

Salvage Operations: New and Selected Poems (New York: Norton, 1990).

OTHER: "Breaking Bread," in *The Generation of Two Thousand: Contemporary American Poets*, edited by William Heyen (Princeton, N.J.: Ontario Review, 1984);

William Carlos Williams and John Stanford: A Correspondence, foreword by Mariani (Santa Barbara: Capra, 1984);

"Tomlinson's Use of the Williams Triad," in *Charles Tomlinson*, edited by Kathleen O'Gorman (Columbia: University of Missouri Press, 1988), pp. 57-71.

Paul Mariani's reputation as one of the major literary biographers writing today rests primarily on one book: *William Carlos Williams: A New World Naked* (1981). "This is a biography of days and weeks and months and years carefully recited," wrote Robert Coles in the *New Republic* (25 November 1981). The book presents a multidimensional portrait of the long-lived New Jersey poet and physician, conveying the texture of his everyday life as well as his intellectual and cultural milieu. Mariani also critically appraises Williams's literary achievement, discussing particular poems in their biographical contexts. Generally regarded as "an exemplary biography of a major poet" (*Library Journal*, 1 October 1981), in 1982 the book won the New Jersey Writers Award and was nominated for an American Book Award. In the *New York Times Book Review* (22 November 1981) Gilbert Sorrentino summed up Mariani's purpose in writing Williams's biography and anticipated its importance in securing Williams's place in the forefront of American letters: "The most laudable aspect of Paul Mariani's critical biography of William Carlos Williams is that it largely succeeds in placing him, in his biographer's words, as 'the single most important poet of the twentieth century.'" As Sorrentino noted, "Paul Mariani is relentless in detailing the shabby critical treatment accorded Williams throughout the whole of his career. . . . Mariani shatters these idiocies by a careful examination of Williams's work in poetry, fiction and criticism, setting it against the general somnambulism of the time."

Mariani's interest in Williams exceeds professional bounds; it is intensely personal. In Williams's concern for those without a voice—minorities, the poor—he "spoke for me, for my people," Mariani said in an interview. His first contact with the poet was through Williams's long poem *Paterson* (1946-1958), which attracted him because, as he says in the preface to his biography, "My mother's family had come from that area of New Jersey."

Paul Louis Mariani was born on 29 February 1940 in Astoria, Queens, in New York City. He was the first of seven children born to Paul Patrick Mariani, who ran a gas station and later became a day-camp foreman, and Harriet Green Mariani, a secretary who eventually trained as a nurse. The family moved to Manhattan soon after young Paul's birth, then to various places on Long Island, always living in working-class neighborhoods.

Paul Mariani, February 1991

Raised a Catholic, Mariani decided at age six-teen to study for the priesthood; after a year, how-ever, he changed his mind, completing his second-ary education at Mineola High School. He then attended Manhattan College, earning his B.A. in 1962. He received his M.A. in 1964 from Colgate University and his Ph.D. in 1968 from the City University of New York, where he held an assis-tant professorship in English in 1967 and 1968 at the John Jay College of Criminal Justice. Since 1968 he has taught at the University of Massachu-setts at Amherst, first as assistant professor (1968-1971), then as associate professor (1971-1975), and beginning in 1975 as a full professor. He has been Robert Frost Fellow in Poetry at the Bread Loaf Writers' Conference (1980) and Rob-ert Frost Professor of English at the Bread Loaf School of English (1982). On 24 August 1963 Mariani married Eileen Spinosa, a kindergarten teacher; they have three sons, Paul, Mark, and John.

Mariani's early work included a study of the poetry of Gerard Manley Hopkins (the subject of Mariani's doctoral dissertation) and a survey of published criticism of the work of William Carlos Williams. According to Mariani (in *A Usable Past*, 1984), "Hopkins was my first love, alpha, a fig-ure I needed very much for my own spiritual and intellectual survival. . . . I think now that I de-cided to stay with English—after desultory begin-nings in philosophy and psychology—largely be-cause of Hopkins' marvelous poems." Mariani has traced the beginning of his work on Williams to a course on modern poetry that he taught in au-tumn 1968 at the University of Massachusetts. As Mariani puts it, "If Hopkins had shown me a reli-gious voice creatively countering the growing ag-nosticism and nihilism in the literature, philoso-phy, and politics of the past century, Williams provided for my time what Whitman had pro-vided for the last century: an example of a poet en-gaged in a lifelong struggle to raise my world—

153

--52--

A month earlier ~~he~~ *Williams* had written to the editor of <u>Hika</u> at Kenyon College, *David McDowell,*

that it was important ~~KE~~ for America to stay out of the European mess. "We have

always been Europe's cow," he insisted:

do not indent

    "We are rich in material resources and poor in culture....
    They are civilized. We are barbarians--and shall always be so
    to them. When the war is over we shall be blamed for it <u>all</u>,
    as we were after the last one. ~~Europe is merely working out~~
~~its "cataclysmic fate" which is "typically"~~

Europe was merely working out its *own* "cataclysmic fate," which was a typically

European thing for it to do. It had done it dozens of times in the past and

               It was all a matter of determining who would be
would probably do it again. ~~It was all so "typically European."~~

the new leader~~s~~ *They loved it--all of them.* *But* Americans had to be careful not to

be taken in by *European* claims and counter claims. Language for a European was an ideo-

logical tool, a means of winning, while for Americans it was "still a barrel

of apples." If ~~an~~ *a U.S.* expeditionary force were ever ~~to~~ sent to Europe, Williams

suggested, it would be better to send it over to fight all of Europe and not

just one side or the other. In the coming dialectic it would not be America as

an ally of this country or that, but America against European civilization itself.

But of course to send such an army against Europe was pure insanity. ~~Better than~~
And even though Americans were, after all, transplanted Europeans themselves*, and it was* better

to stay out of *the embroilment* altogether.

insert 52A + B

    Pound*, too* was still sending an occasional letter from Rome, ~~which~~ Williams *where he was now broadcasting his own versions of Roosevelt's fireside chats, and*
worried answer~~ed~~ or refuse~~d~~ to answer as he saw fit. But on the morning of July ~~31st~~
30th, Floss*, had* come running in breathlessly from the *local* bank to tell her husband that *on his short-wave set*
one of the tellers ~~at the Rutherford ban~~ *there* had been listening to Ezra Pound over

Radio Rome the night before and had heard Pound's voice crackling something

about "As my friend Doc Williams of New Jersey would say." That was enough! Pound

had gone absolutely ga-ga, had become merely "a mouthpiece for the disreputable

Mussolini." Williams ~~began~~ *went upstairs and began* writing an essay ~~about his friend~~ to sort out his

own feelings for the man. He'd seen Marianne Moore a few weeks before at Paul
apartment
Rosenfeld's ~~place~~ in the city and had insisted that Pound ~~was a~~ *had become a* "stupid ass,"

another Shaw trying to rewrite Shakespeare's <u>Coriolanus</u>. ~~He~~ *Pound* was one of those

Pages from the typescript for "Clearing the Field: 1938-1942," a chapter in William Carlos Williams: A New World Naked
(by permission of Paul Mariani)

52B

But ^Eaton ~~found himself~~ went to the Little Theatre for Williams' talk and instinctively found himself liking the man. Williams was not imposing in the way Frost could be, but he ~~found Williams a~~ did find him a charming, ~~person and~~ "very generous with his time and enthusiasms," outgoing, and genuinely interested in what others had to say in a way Frost definitely was not. What particularly struck Eaton was that, though his own poetry was so different from Williams', Williams could still take the time to read and to praise it.

Williams did after all have a strong mothering instinct, especially for beginners who could be so easily crushed by the established critics and poets. So, a month after the Breadloaf non-incident, he was consoling Ted Roethke whose first book had been slapped down by R.P. Blackmur. "Weep not, Signor, over the lapses and tortuosities of Blackmur's disappointed mind," Williams wrote. "He is some sort of prince of the book, a latter day collegian." In fact, Williams had himself recently sent Blackmur "a contemptuous letter" for Blackmur's support of second-rate "versifiers" then appearing in Poetry Magazine. Williams offered his own advice, now, telling Roethke to "write more and more fully out of the less known side of your nature if you are to be noticed." It was advice Roethke would brilliantly follow in his next book.

At the end of the year the MacLeish question, which had surfaced at the Puerto Rican conference, surfaced once again, this time in the pages of The Partisan Review, when Dwight Macdonald asked Williams and others to defend or question his own attack on Van Wyck Brooks for supporting and expanding what MacLeish had written in "The Irresponsibles." Would not Goebbels himself, Macdonald wrote, have applauded MacLeish and Van Wyck Brooks' attack on a "degenerate" modern art? Primary literature -- that is, viable, avant garde literature--had of necessity to follow the biological rather than the ideological grain as a "force of regeneration" conducive to race survival. Williams answered Macdonald's letter in late November. Yes, he said, he'd read Brooks' essay, but he'd found it so ridiculous as not to merit serious attention. The problem with Brooks was that he wanted to make literature "safe" for democracy instead of reading what the young were writing. Better to ignore some critics, like this "ignorant sap," bewildered by a "world running away in new and brilliant colors under his nose." A pity, then, that that same world was about to explode, and that the young would soon be carrying rifles rather than pens.

America—to the level of the epic."

At the same time, Mariani was writing poetry himself, although he published little of it until the mid 1970s. His first collection, *Timing Devices*, was published in 1977 and has been followed by three others: *Crossing Cocytus* (1982), *Prime Mover* (1985), and *Salvage Operations* (1990). Autobiographical and frequently confessional in tone, his poetry centers on what he calls "the sacredness of human relationships," which he amplifies through myth. Mariani's poetry reflects the influence of Hopkins in its elevated diction and of Williams in its use of the commonplace. Nevertheless, at its best, the poetry is very much Mariani's own in its narrative intensity and its blend of colloquial and literary language and allusion, as Fred Chappell has noted (*Western Humanities Review*, Autumn 1983). It also conveys, in its visionary quality, his personal religious faith. Indeed, Mariani has written (in "Breaking Bread," 1984) that he found the courage to write poetry only through prayer: "I prayed very hard ... that I might have the courage—and the skill—to do what I by then realized was the most important thing I could ever do: write poetry." According to David Ignatow, "Among contemporary poets, Paul Mariani is almost alone in professing the depth of religion in his life."

Mariani's religious belief also subtly influences his views on biography. A friend of his, a devout Anglican, first suggested to him that his interest in biography could be traced to the reality of the Incarnation in his life, which he therefore sees as informing his understanding of the significance of all life. Consequently, Mariani said in an interview, "a life is not meaningless, and it's more than just a story: its authenticity comes from its spiritual dimension, even if the person is not aware of this." Mariani agrees with his friend's conclusion that he tries "to find the drama, that search for a deeper sense of oneself, in the life." Along these lines, Mariani regards his biography of Williams as his *Purgatorio*. His biography of John Berryman (1990), who had a downward-spiraling struggle against alcoholism, Mariani calls his *Inferno*. The life of Hopkins, he thinks, might someday provide the material for a darkly luminous *Paradiso*.

According to Mariani, his studies of Williams's work and of his reputation as a poet turned out to be "homework" for a biography of the man. Originally intending to write a book about the genesis of *Paterson*, Mariani was convinced in 1976 by James Raimes, then an editor at Oxford University Press, to write a full-scale biography of Williams himself. Although Mariani by that time had already done substantial research on Williams, completing the biography took another five years. The size of the book was impressive: 875 pages. Hugh Kenner in *Harper's* (December 1981) called it a "prolonged bear-hug of a book."

In "Reassembling the Dust: Notes on the Art of the Biographer," first presented by Mariani as the Abernethy Lecture at Middlebury College in the spring of 1982 and collected with various lectures, critical essays, and reviews in *A Usable Past*, he describes the creative process that produced the biography of Williams. The opening passages gave him "more trouble ... than anything else. ... " He finally hit upon the idea of taking up where Williams's autobiography left off, New Year's Eve 1950. Mariani explains, "By beginning just here, then, I would take Williams's own narrative closure and begin all over again for myself ... restructuring Williams's rendering with my own." In spite of this unconventional beginning, however, Mariani organized the rest of the biography chronologically. In fifteen chapters, he recounts the eighty years of the poet-doctor's life, interweaving the many levels of Williams's experience: his family life, which included at times many generations living under one roof; his friends, literary and otherwise, who included Ezra Pound, H. D., Robert McAlmon, and Louis Zukofsky; and his distinct careers as physician and poet. Moreover, Mariani merges literary criticism with his telling of the life, discussing in detail both Williams's writing and his theories about writing.

Unlike most subjects of literary biography, Mariani's was more than the solitary writer at a typewriter; he was also very much a man of action. Mariani moves from narration to exposition and, in telling Williams's life, balances outer and inner worlds. In a passage that describes the oppositions in Williams's life and art, Mariani unwittingly suggests the alternating rhythms that shape his own book: "Force and quiet—the clatter of the falls and the cloistered garden—Whitman's yawp and Keats's silences: these were the two opposed impulses (systole, diastole) that had driven Williams and would continue to drive him for the rest of his life." The biography ends by switching, briefly, from Williams's perspective, which has prevailed throughout the biography, to that of Floss, his wife of fifty years.

Mariani in 1980, the year before his biography of William Carlos Williams was published

As Mariani frankly admits, he modeled his biography of Williams on Richard Ellmann's biography of James Joyce. "I liked [Ellmann's] 'objectivity,' I liked the panoramic range, I liked the epic thrust of [the book]," he has said (in *A Usable Past*). "I see now that what I wanted to give American audiences in particular was a book about Williams peopled with his friends and enemies that would be a counterpart in every way except in tone to what Ellmann had offered in his homage to Joyce. I make no secrets about it. Call it hubris, but my book would be a way of paying homage to the father, of doing for modern American poetry what Ellmann had done for European Modernism."

To dispel the so-called myths that surrounded Williams as a poet—for example, that he was not a serious craftsman but a dabbler in

the art—and to gain critical attention and respect for Williams's often underrated work, Mariani decided that only a large biography would serve. Not only must he fully document the man's life, as Ellmann had done in his biography of Joyce, but he must also show the full range and implications of Williams's experiments with language, the poetic line, and poetic form in general. Thus, Mariani, merging biography and criticism, devoted a large part of five chapters to the creation of *Paterson*. For the most part, however, the form of his biography might be called typical of the academic, or scholarly, biography after Ellmann. Mariani has mastered this form, adapting it to the particular demands of the complex life he tells.

In addition to establishing Williams in the front rank of twentieth-century poets, Mariani de-

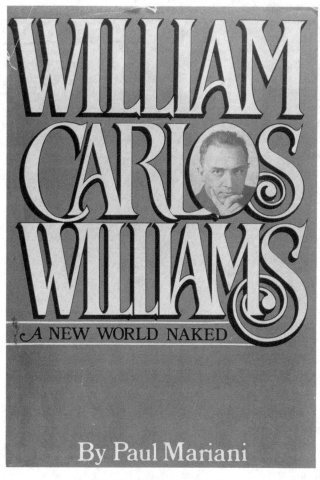

Dust jacket for Mariani's biography of the poet who forced him to reexamine all his " 'classical' assumptions about literature and the Great Tradition"

liberately set out to address certain issues that clouded Williams's reputation: his supposed anti-Semitism, his womanizing, and his attitude toward the black community. Mariani's strategy was to present the full range of Williams's thoughts, language, and actions in the context of his times. Thus, for example, he documents both Williams's derogatory language about black American athletes at the 1936 Olympics in Berlin and also his unprejudiced treatment of and respect for his black patients. Mariani explains the former in part as a consequence of "the reductive image of the black one saw every day in the movies and in the comics," and explains the latter as a result of Williams's characteristic charity (masked though it was at times by testiness and insulting language). Mariani succeeds in establishing Williams's basic humanity, though he does not entirely vindicate Williams's attitudes and behavior. In a man dedicated to healing, whose love was language, Williams's sometimes vulgar,

demeaning actions and words remain anomalous.

When Mariani wrote that he intended to imitate Ellmann's biographical model in all but tone, he referred obliquely to his intention to tell the life of Williams in language suited to his subject. This intention manifests itself in the biography in two ways: in Mariani's simulation in his own prose of Williams's characteristic diction and syntax; and in Mariani's abundant quotations from Williams's letters and other prose as well as poetic documents, so that very often ideas are expressed in Williams's own words. Consequently, Mariani's prose often smacks of the flavor of Williams's: for example, "He [Williams] worked long and hard . . . keeping detailed records and trying to figure what in hell was happening to the poor kids." At times half a line is Mariani's and half Williams's: "Williams steadied himself and then hurled his grandson's hell-cabbage [a large ball of ice], watching it rise slightly before it plunged inevitably 'downward and disappeared

. . . followed almost at once by an explosive bang as it hit the ice below.' "

In *A Usable Past* Mariani offers as a justification for this approach the access that it allows the reader to the conceptual and perceptual framework of the subject. The reader experiences "the world of Subject X by seeing that world through the lens of Subject X's own language." Moreover, Mariani points out, it allows the biographer to "tell the story from the eye and mouth of Subject X, rather than from the outside." The difficulty, which he recognizes, is that this approach makes impossible a "cool, detached stance" on the part of the narrator. As a rule, then, the reader enters into Williams's moral and conceptual framework with relatively little overt mediation from Mariani, as many reviewers have noted, sometimes with disapproval. W. S. Di Piero in the *Sewanee Review* (Fall 1982) objected that "a considerable amount of confusion and distortion can result from a biographer's attempt to ally himself too closely with his subject." In the *Virginia Quarterly Review* (Spring 1983), Raymond Nelson wondered whether "the collapsing of narrative distance . . . threatens the biographer's functions of choice and judgment," leaving both author and reader "at the mercy of Williams's descriptions, interests, and whims." Nevertheless, Nelson concludes that "the biography deserves serious attention as an attempt to imitate the processes of perception, cognition, imagination, memory—the rhythms and proportions of life itself."

However self-effacing Mariani may appear as a narrator, he subtly shapes the reader's response to Williams by the way he structures his material and also by his very silence. For example, by beginning the biography where Williams ends his autobiography, Mariani makes clear that in his opinion Williams's point of view on his own life is inadequate. And by ending the biography with the information, without comment, that Floss chose not to be buried next to her husband, as they had once planned, Mariani causes the reader to reassess Williams's idea of the relationship. In such subtle ways, Mariani conveys his own moral judgments of his subject and provokes the reader to form his or her own. "Just the way I put sequence after sequence is a value judgment," he has admitted.

Both the Williams biography and *Dream Song*, the life of Berryman, underwent extensive revision. Mariani maintains that he enjoys not only the writing but also the rewriting of each book: "Each time I rewrite it, I understand

things I hadn't—I mean, I had the information, but . . . it's only in the actual process of rewriting it that you can see the patterns. . . . Each biography is rewritten four-five-six-seven-eight times." The typescript of the biography of Berryman, for example, which started out in excess of seventeen hundred pages, was trimmed in successive revisions to just over five hundred in the published book. Painful though cutting may be, Mariani finds the give-and-take of working with an experienced editor valuable. In his words, "What I thought was so important, from another person's perspective might not be. And I need that, I need someone else." In retrospect, he wishes that his editor for the Williams biography had "wrestled harder with me."

One of the criticisms of the generally praised biography of Williams has been its bulk, which some see as excessive. The anonymous reviewer for *Booklist* (1 October 1981) objected that "Mariani lets us have it all, no matter how inconsequential, tangential, or tedious many of the tidbits may be." Hugh Kenner complained in *Harper's* (December 1981) that "hardly a sentence couldn't be quickened by excisions." Many others, however, praised the epic quality of the book, calling it, for example, "a heroic piece of reading" (William H. Pritchard in *American Scholar*, Summer 1982) and "a *War and Peace* of literary activity in America" (Phillip Corwin in *Commonweal*, 8 October 1982).

Those who object to the size of the biography often do so on theoretical grounds, resisting what Louis Simpson in the *Washington Post Book World* (3 January 1982) described (and praised) as "the usual method of American biographers . . . [to] put everything in so as not to risk leaving anything out." However, Raymond Nelson leveled more serious criticisms: detail at times overwhelms the narrative, so that the book becomes "less a mediated, shaped biography than a collection of biographical data"; and the uncritical incorporation of available detail results in a certain disproportion in the biography, with the more fully documentable later years dominating the book.

In some cases criticisms of the length come from those who question Williams's place in the forefront of American poets. As Mariani points out in *A Usable Past*, "No one would blink twice if another long life were to appear that dealt with Faulkner or Pound or Eliot or Frost." Williams's eighty years required a long work, Mariani maintains. Furthermore, Mariani says, "In my metapoetics of the biography, I would inundate the

"worth treating." Most of the writers ~~held~~ ^{Berryman had} mentioned were now in

their early thirtys, and all had been set back (like himself)

several years by the war.

At Pound's request, Olson answered Berryman's letter for

him. What Pound had in mind was for five men of Berryman's gener-

ation friendly to Pound to keep in touch with one another to

"fight the fake" and "promote the serious-- ~~his~~ [Pound's] men Kung [Confu-

cius], Frobenius, Ford, Gesell, Fenellosa." Two of the five would

be Olson and Berryman. Was Berryman willing to "do this for EP?"

Again Berryman ignored Olson.

But the thought of getting funding for a new magazine based

on <u>The</u> <u>Criterion</u> ~~still~~ ^{particularly} interested ~~him~~ ^{Berryman.} He wrote Walter Marshall

at the Institute for Advanced Study to see if they might back

such a venture. In his letter, ~~to Marshall he~~ ^{Berryman} specifically ad-

dressed the issue of the Southern critics and the omnipresent

influence of Allen Tate on <u>The</u> <u>American</u> <u>Review</u>, <u>The</u> <u>Southern</u>

<u>Review</u>, <u>The</u> <u>Kenyon</u> <u>Review</u>, <u>The</u> <u>Sewanee</u>. But even <u>The</u> <u>Partisan</u>

<u>Review</u> was slip~~ping~~ ^{beginning to} into "a cult-magazine" which "under an ex-

hausted political impulse" was incapable of understanding ~~his~~ ^{Berryman's}

^{own} brand of ^{radically} conservative thought, ^{in the tradition of Pound and Eliot.}

He was proposing, therefore, a review which he could edit

from New York ~~which would~~ ^{to} be called <u>The</u> <u>Twentieth</u> <u>Century</u>. At the

heart of the magazine would be book-reviewing, "to make known

what is being done out there." Important articles appearing in

the various quarterlies and reviews would be "noted and when

profitable discussed." What he had especially admired about ~~The~~ ^{Eliot's}

<u>Criterion</u> had been the presence of radical and reactionary thin-

kers side by side. ~~His~~ ^{Berryman's own} standards would be as high as those fos-

233

Pages from the typescript for Dream Song: The Life of John Berryman *(by permission of Paul Mariani)*

that he would need an ending ~~which~~ *that* would grow naturally out of the sequence itself. He noted, *too that* he'd written some fairly anti-American government Songs and was afraid they might get him into trouble. To avoid that he would have to scatter ~~those~~ *his political satires* ~~poems~~ throughout the book and be sure to add some patriotic ones.

The theme he had relentlessly pursued in the Bradstreet-- "love for a religious, inaccessible" woman-- he meant to include as well. ~~in the Dream Songs.~~ But he ~~had~~ *would also have* to acknowledge ~~his~~ *Henry's* lusts, ~~as well,~~ the two forces creating their own tension in the sequence, ~~love idealized and simple, uncomplicated lust,~~ as with the fragment he composed on March 7th, ~~nearly fainting~~ *when Henry had nearly fainted* with lust ~~as he watched~~ *watching* the strawberry waitress on the sixth floor of the hospital, "running about on short legs/ with every hair in place, & crystal skin," her speech "laced with intensity."

****

After three and a half weeks in the hospital, ~~he~~ *Berryman* was sent home. Most of that time he'd been able to meet his classes, going to the university by taxi to teach and then returning by taxi to the hospital, sometimes with a stop in between at a local bar for a pick-me-up. When he left Glenwood Hills, he was still uncured, still exhausted, still depressed. He moved into a small apartment at 1917-4th St. South, a block from where he had lived two years before. Once again he was within a few minutes walking distance from his office, and back *again*, in the Seven Corners section of the city with its twenty workingclass bars to keep him company.

It was well he had not read his mother's letter while he was in the hospital, for in it she revealed several upsetting things about John Allyn Smith, Sr. and about John Angus, Uncle Jack. His

431

Dust jacket for the book Mariani has compared to "a detective novel" in which Berryman's poetry "becomes a character, too"

reader with the river of facts surrounding Williams . . . the sense of a life caught in the flux of reality itself, a life that, while in danger of being pulled under by the overwhelming flood of events, dares to question at every turn, responding to the flood of experience as well as it can at every moment."

Mariani's book has also prompted discussion of the controversial question of how explicit the biographer should be, especially about unedifying or unflattering details of the subject's life. Anatole Broyard in the *New York Times* (28 November 1981) comments that "there is something grotesque in the assumption that reading a man's poetry entitles us to learn all the worst things about him. . . . The effect here is to elevate the vulgar rather than the poetry." Karl Shapiro defends Mariani's approach: "Reduction to the human is not only endearing but allows true greatness to come into focus" (*Chicago Tribune Book World*, 15 November 1981).

In writing the lives of Williams and Berryman, both of whom had what Mariani has called "darker" sides to their personalities, he has tried to combine honesty and discretion. He stresses

the responsibility of putting the "little or big secrets" of the subject "in their correct perspective," not emphasizing the "pleasure of the scandal itself." Mariani has said that he regards the biographer as "a kind of confessor and psychiatrist," implying a certain bond of confidentiality. In this connection he has stated that while he would not "whitewash" a life, neither would he gratuitously reveal information that might somehow harm others. For example, he has refused to name those women involved with his subjects who might be hurt, or whose families might be hurt, by the revelation: "I just didn't think I could live with that. It was a moral decision on my part."

Although his biography of John Berryman resembles his life of Williams in several ways—most notably in its scholarly thoroughness (while intended for the general reader), its chronological development, strong narrative line, and sympathetic point of view—Mariani notes significant differences between the two books. Because Berryman's world was more circumscribed than Williams's and also because Berryman was extremely introspective, Mariani has focused more intently

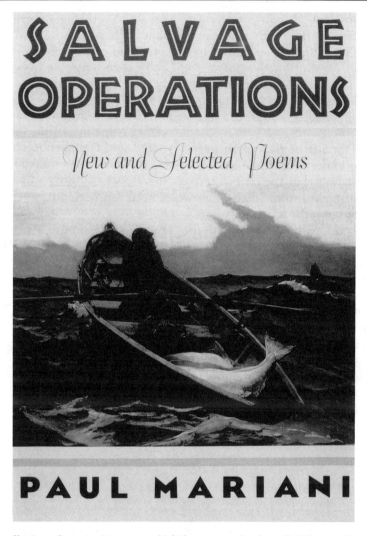

Dust jacket for the 1990 collection of Mariani's poetry, which focuses on what he calls "the sacredness of human relationships"

on Berryman's inner world than he did on Williams's. Describing the book in an interview, he has said that part of its drama is "to watch his [Berryman's] mind as it tries to understand what happens. So I don't give it away—I don't say, 'Here's exactly what happened.' I leave it ambiguous, like a detective novel. We are given only the information that Berryman himself has. We must try to see it through his eyes, through the rest of his life, in his literature." This approach has also influenced the form of the biography, which Mariani calls an "inverted pyramid." According to Mariani, "I try to get through the early years where there's so much unreliable information that I'm leery to use it, and then as he gets older, what happens is his memory kicks in and he begins to rethink the earlier episodes." Mariani's strategy for dealing with Berryman's evolving interpretations of his own experience was "to find

the fascinating ways in which Berryman . . . retells in many forms the same stories, but not just reduce it to *the* story." Berryman's poetry, increasingly autobiographical, becomes central to both Berryman's self-understanding and to his biographer's revelation of him: "The poetry becomes a character, too, in the book."

From the experience of writing the biography of Williams, Mariani has said that he learned much that helped him complete the life of Berryman more expeditiously. In particular he learned to discriminate among types of information, developing for example a better sense of what to record for later use and of when to conduct an interview. As a rule, Mariani has found the papers of the subject to be a more valuable source of information than interviews.

In contrast to writing the earlier biography, when he had the full cooperation of Williams's family, a significant problem Mariani faced in completing the life of Berryman was that he was denied access to a few of his subject's important letters and papers by one of Berryman's former wives and by one of his friends. "I had to fill in with other things," he has admitted. "I had to go to every other source I possibly could and fill in."

Moreover, writing the life of Berryman was a personally harrowing experience for Mariani. "I remember literally trembling at the typewriter as I wrote," he recalls. "I had to stop, I had to go to sleep, then wake up and do it by pages, a page, a page and a half, because literally the goose bumps were raised. I was about to lose the man, and I kept saying, 'John, don't do it.' But it's already history. It's like a Greek tragedy." Because of the intensity of the experience, Mariani found that all work on his own poetry virtually stopped, although he did manage to bring together the poems in *Salvage Operations*.

Consequently Mariani plans to spend the next few years completing another collection of verse. "I have come in the past few years to define myself as a poet," he writes in "Breaking Bread." Even though writing biography is important to him and is now the literary activity for which he is best known, Mariani has said that he chooses to write the lives of poets in part so that he can conduct an "intense meditation" on the craft of poetry itself.

As a biographer Mariani displays great powers of empathy. In his large-spirited understanding of and compassion for his subjects, he carries on the tradition of English biography established by Samuel Johnson and James Boswell. Also inspiring his work, both biography and poetry, is a contemporary fascination with the self as it changes through time and memory, and with language as it reveals the self. Says Mariani of his art, "The prose and the poetry have both been necessary phases of that complex fiction we call the self."

Interview:

Gail Porter Mandell, "Conversation with Paul Mariani," in her *Life into Art: Conversations with Seven Contemporary Biographers* (Fayetteville & London: University of Arkansas Press, 1991), pp. 1-43.

Jay Martin

(30 October 1935 -   )

Donald E. Pease
Dartmouth College

BOOKS: *Conrad Aiken: A Life of His Art* (Princeton, N.J.: Princeton University Press, 1962);

Harvests of Change: American Literature, 1865-1914 (Englewood Cliffs, N.J.: Prentice-Hall, 1967);

Nathanael West: The Art of His Life (New York: Farrar, Straus & Giroux, 1970; London: Secker & Warburg, 1971);

Robert Lowell (Minneapolis: University of Minnesota Press, 1970);

Always Merry and Bright: The Life of Henry Miller (Santa Barbara, Cal.: Capra, 1978; London: Sheldon, 1979);

Winter Dreams: An American in Moscow (Boston: Houghton Mifflin, 1979);

Who Am I This Time?: Uncovering the Fictive Personality (New York: Norton, 1988).

RADIO: *William Faulkner, Sound Portraits of Twentieth-Century Humanists*, National Public Radio, 1980.

OTHER: *Winfield Townley Scott*, edited, with an introduction, by Martin (New Haven: Yale University Press, 1961);

A Collection of Critical Essays on "The Waste Land," edited by Martin (Englewood Cliffs, N.J.: Prentice-Hall, 1968); also published as *Twentieth-Century Interpretations of The Waste Land* (Englewood Cliffs, N.J.: Prentice-Hall, 1968);

Nathanael West: A Collection of Critical Essays, edited, with an introduction, by Martin (Englewood Cliffs, N.J.: Prentice-Hall, 1971);

A Singer in the Dawn: Reinterpretations of Paul Laurence Dunbar, edited, with an introduction and bibliography, by Martin (New York: Dodd, Mead, 1975);

The Paul Laurence Dunbar Reader, edited, with an introduction and bibliography, by Martin and Gossie H. Hudson (New York: Dodd, Mead, 1975);

"Erskine Caldwell's Singular Devotions," in *A Question of Quality*, edited by Louis Filler (Bowling Green, Ohio: Popular Culture, 1976), pp. 40-56;

"The Genie in the Bottle: Huckleberry Finn in Mark Twain's Life," in *One Hundred Years of Huckleberry Finn*, edited by Robert Sattlemeyer and J. Donald Crowley (Columbia: University of Missouri Press, 1985), pp. 56-81;

"Grief and Nothingness: Loss and Mourning in Lowell's Poetry," in *Robert Lowell: Essays on the Poetry*, edited by Steven G. Axelrod and Helen Deese (New York: Cambridge University Press, 1986), pp. 26-50;

"Clinical Contributions to the Theory of the Fictive Personality," in *The Annual of Psychoanalysis*, volume 33, edited by George Pollock (Chicago: Institute for Psychoanalysis, 1986), pp. 267-300;

Economic Depression and American Humor, edited, with an introduction, by Martin (San Marcos: University of Texas Press, 1986).

SELECTED PERIODICAL PUBLICATIONS—
UNCOLLECTED: "A Watertight Watergate Future: Americans in a Post-American Age," *Antioch Review*, 33 (June 1975): 7-25;

"The Deaths of the Novelists / The Lives of the Biographers," *Humanities in Society*, 3 (Fall 1980): 361-376;

"William Faulkner: Construction and Reconstruction in Biography and Psychoanalysis," *Psychoanalytic Inquiry*, 3 (Fall 1983): 295-339;

"The Fictional Terrorist," *Partisan Review*, 55 (Winter 1988): 69-81.

In his literary biographies Jay Martin is concerned with the often-confusing relationship between a writer's life and the alternatives to that life generated out of the writing process. Martin has chosen for his biographies subjects ranging from the unjustly ignored Conrad Aiken and Nathanael West, their art being thus rescued from public obscurity, to such well-known writers as Robert Lowell and Henry Miller, whose creative

165

Jay Martin circa 1988 (photograph by Gordon Burks)

personalities Martin carefully distinguishes from the public's images of them. His biographies examine the dialectical opposition between the life of art and the art of life: the intricate ways in which the activity of writing can either develop or displace a given writer's life, and the no-less-intricate ways in which a writer's invention of an artistic personality can overshadow his artistic accomplishments. Martin's exploration of this dialectic eventually led him to a psychoanalytic understanding of the relationship between the biographical impulse and the life of a culture.

While Martin characteristically emphasizes the vexed relationship between a writer's life and the alternative lives made available in writing, he does not ignore the writer's relationship to his times: the writer is the representative consciousness of his culture. What remains unconscious in the majority of people within any culture becomes conscious, Martin believes, in the writer's struggle for self-expression. The writer, like

other citizens within a culture, does not develop solely within the environment of writing, but the writer distinguishes himself from others in that the history of the age becomes concrete in his character. If writing develops alternative lives for the writer, the culture develops a complex awareness of its condition by way of its writers' evolutions.

Harvests of Change: American Literature, 1865-1914, published in 1967, is Martin's biographical master text. In it he elaborates the relationship between writers' lives and works into what can be described as a biography of the American mind at the turn of the century. He chose the years immediately after the Civil War and just prior to World War I because this was a time of significant transformation in the life of the nation: a time when older forms of life gave way to newer ones but with such rapidity of exchange that only America's best literary talents could give the transition definable shape. Throughout Martin's meticulously documented account of America's dra-

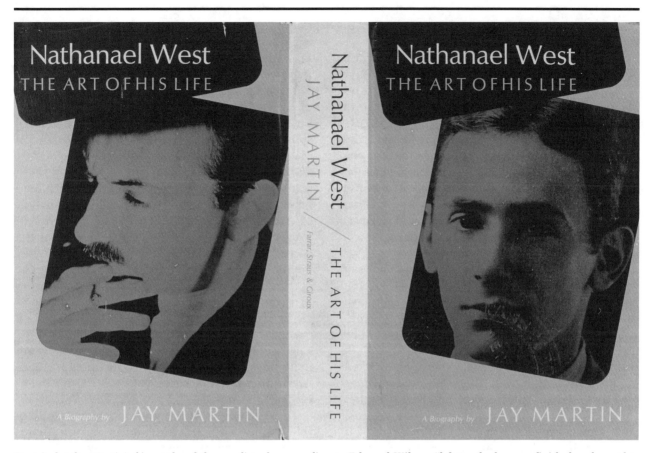

Dust jacket for Martin's biography of the novelist who, according to Edmund Wilson, "left two books more finished and complete as works of art than almost anything else produced by his generation"

matic shift in sensibility, he brings the representatively transitional moments in the culture's history together with writers whose work captured what was importantly involved in these transitions. In *Harvests of Change* Martin takes Ralph Waldo Emerson's observation that "there is properly no history, only biography" and organizes the most confusing period of American history by way of a series of literary biographies. Deploying over thirty biographical sketches of the culture's representative men and women, Martin subordinates historical forces to the biographer's insights. At times he analyzes, with insights into the drama of evolving literary consciousness, the lives these writers develop within the milieu of their writing. At other times he dedicates his analytical skills to an understanding of the psychological resources required to cope with cultural change.

In *Harvests of Change* Martin's use of psychoanalysis occasionally splits off from his strictly bio-

graphical insights, but that division has been present in Martin since his discovery, at age seventeen, of his literary vocation. He describes these two sides of his character in his author's note to *Who Am I This Time?: Uncovering the Fictive Personality* (1988): "When I was seventeen years old, my aim in life was to become a poet. Conrad Aiken, who read some of my poems, arranged for their publication and invited me to live with him in his summer house in Brewster on Cape Cod. He became a second father to me. Aiken's acquaintance with writers was a large one. Allen Tate, say, would come for a lunch one day; the next we might make the trip over to Edmund Wilson's Wellfleet house. A letter from Tom Eliot might appear in the mailbox. Naturally, my own literary ambition grew by leaps and bounds.

"But I also began to learn how interested Aiken was in psychoanalysis. Analysts dropped in at the house almost as often as writers did, and conversations touched on psychological subjects strange and intriguing to me. . . . Conrad Aiken's dual interests, which he passed on to me, led to this doubleness in my own life."

Martin was born in Newark, New Jersey, on 30 October 1935 to Sylvester K. and Ada Mary Smith Martin. His father was an engineer, and Martin grew up in a working-class neighborhood in Brooklyn, whose Irish, German, and Italian residents gave him a glimpse into what he once described in correspondence as "the essence of the modern world." Until his seventeenth year he spent his summers and some holidays in a house near Cranberry, New Jersey; the house, lacking running water, indoor plumbing, and electric lights, afforded insights into premodern America.

Martin graduated from Columbia University with honors in English in 1956. He married Helen Saldini on 9 June of that year, and they have three children: Helen Elizabeth, Laura Ann, and Jay Herbert. Following his marriage, Martin obtained his M.A. (1957) and Ph.D. (1960) from Ohio State University, where he worked on his dissertation with Roy Harvey Pearce as director. Martin interrupted his Ph.D. studies with a one-year instructorship at Pennsylvania State University (1957-1958). After receiving his doctorate, he worked his way up the ranks from instructor to assistant professor and then associate professor in English and American studies at Yale University (1960-1968). He moved from Yale in 1968 to become professor of English and comparative culture at the University of California at Irvine, where he remained until 1979. In 1978 he began the fulfillment of his alternative career when he accepted the positions of lecturer in psychiatry and human behavior and clinical supervisor in the residency program at the California College of Medicine, University of California at Irvine. In 1979 he accepted the Leo S. Bing Professorship of English and American Literature at the University of Southern California. After receiving, in 1983, a Ph.D. in psychoanalysis from the Southern California Psychoanalytic Institute, Martin began a concurrent position as instructor in psychoanalysis at the institute.

Aiken initiated Martin into both of his career identities, and Martin began his career as a literary biographer by trying to establish his surrogate father's credentials as a poet and sage. *Conrad Aiken: A Life of His Art* (1962) elevates Aiken to the status of an exemplary cultural figure. To confirm Aiken in this position, Martin begins with an account of the inadequate reception of Aiken's work. Aiken was the victim, Martin

claims, of critical reaction in the 1930s and 1940s against the elevation of poetic form into an end in itself. Since Aiken's poetry did not call for the improvement of social institutions or elaborate a political agenda, critics misidentified it as an example of art for art's sake. Rightly understood, Martin insists, Aiken's poetry constitutes a perennial spiritual resource able to promote the evolution of human consciousness.

However, Martin organizes his study in terms of Aiken's developing potential rather than his poetic achievement. Martin begins his analysis of Aiken's work with an account of his "work in progress," then treats this unfinished work as the basis for understanding his poetic accomplishments. In his analysis of the work in progress, Martin pays close attention to the relationship between the incomplete work and psychological needs—for alternative selves, fulfilled wishes, changes of mind—registered subconsciously in Aiken's completed poems. In struggling to bring these unrealized drives into adequate expression, Aiken discovered, according to Martin, his deepest poetic resources.

To demonstrate the ways in which Aiken developed his own mind into and by way of poetry, Martin organizes the rest of his study in terms of the interrelationship between poetic and personal growth. He follows his discussion of the unfinished work with successive chapters in which he argues persuasively for the priority of Aiken's poetry over his fiction (which became material for poetry), his intellectual understanding (which gave way to *caritas*, or loving care, as the way of knowing poetically), and his contemporary culture (which depended on poetic wisdom as its own means of evolving in consciousness).

After he subordinates each of these extrapoetic categories to the evolution in Aiken's poetic consciousness, Martin marks the path of that development with cogent analyses of Aiken's major works: *Forslin* (1916) in the chapter entitled "Works in Progress"; *John Deth* (1930) in "The Uses of the Fiction"; *Preludes for Memnon* (1931) in "The Word, the Works, the Wound"; and *A Heart for the Gods of Mexico* (1939) in "Caritas." Accompanying these works was an unrealized poem, the autobiographical masterwork *Ushant* (1952), which Aiken took more than two decades to complete. As Aiken's work in progress, *Ushant* constituted a poetic force insufficiently articulated in his completed works: "Not as a fact but as an ideal, therefore, *Ushant* lay behind two decades of Aiken's work; the intentions

Martin circa 1978

which Aiken examined in *Ushant* governed his poetry and fiction from the early thirties. In this sense, *Ushant* is Aiken's attempt to bring his lifetime of work into the bright focus of consciousness."

In *Harvests of Change* Martin attends to the complicated ways in which novelists realize the dramatic shifts in a culture's sensibility by bodying forth in their works the culture's mind during periods of great cultural upheaval. Martin's chapter headings point to a thematics of cultural upheaval: "The Massing of Forces and the Forging of Masses"; "Paradises Lost"; "The Dream of Drift and the Dream of Delight"; and "The Apocalypse of the Mind." He finds the best articulation of these themes in the works of representative writers. Instead of finding all of these cultural developments clarified within the work of a single writer as he had with Aiken, Martin deploys a two-tiered biographical approach. He finds localized cultural changes represented in the works of minor writers (John William De Forest and George Washington Cable, for example), but he finds enduring cultural changes monumentalized in the work of major writers: Mark Twain transformed the novel of national identity

into the "Great American Novel," while Henry James's novels presented in their international themes the initiation of America into the modern world. In a series of biographical scenarios involving nineteenth-century writers, Martin stages dramatic recognitions of the culture's shifting assumptions against the backdrop of a collective desire for order.

Martin carried over the insights and the approach he developed in *Harvests of Change* into later projects: his introduction to *A Collection of Critical Essays on "The Waste Land"* (1968), *Nathanael West: The Art of His Life* (1970), and *Robert Lowell* (1970). In these works, Martin further developed the implications, for writers and their culture, of the writer's dual loyalties to writing and to life.

In his discussion of *The Waste Land* (1922), Martin finds T. S. Eliot similar to Aiken, his mind always in the process of clarifying confusions into poetry, and similar to the writers in *Harvests of Change* in that his mind came into its own when tested by the forces of anarchy and despair. Living in a time of great cultural upheaval, Eliot had a personal breakdown that made him peculiarly sensitive, Martin asserts, to the possibili-

Dust jacket for Martin's biography of a writer whose "work constitutes the autobiography of his legend, not of his life"

ties of language. His genius was "simply to write a poem which would confront the modern world by 'giving a shape' to the anarchy which contemporary history seems to be." In developing the chaos of modern life into the coherences of his realized poetic form, Eliot gave poetry over to the collective needs of civilization. Through the resources of his poetic form, Eliot rendered intelligible for himself as well as his culture the difficulties of modern life.

With *Nathanael West: The Art of His Life* Martin became increasingly interested in the cultural lives writers must live independently of their writing. To call attention to West's inability to adapt his life to his culture, Martin begins his biography of West with an account of the day of his death. That day left West's biographer with a telling disproportion—an increased interest in West's work combined with misleading information about his life. Tracing the ways, from his early childhood to his early college years, in which West substituted imagination for action, Martin arrives at a composite portrait of West as, by turns, a Jewish outsider and the fantasizing scion of a Russian barony; a rebel against social conventions and a clotheshorse attentive to the lat-

est fashions; and physically lethargic yet capable of rapid-fire mental adjustments.

These and related contradictions within West's character made him a barometer for another period in American history when changes took place too rapidly for adequate assessment. As the conventional society he despised fell apart about him, West, perhaps because he no longer had to consume his energy in rebelling against it, seemed to draw strength from its collapse. Without their anchors within enduring institutions, the social conventions West despised gave way to the fantasies with which he replaced them. As the American Dream was dissolved in the 1930s into a collective nightmare, West explored the alternative values and moralities supportive of that nightmare's victims. West's novels *The Dream Life of Balso Snell* (1931), *Miss Lonelyhearts* (1933), *A Cool Million* (1934), and *The Day of the Locust* (1939) were not about the dissolution of the American Dream so much as they were the enactment of the nightmare.

West's novels did not "harvest" the disruptive experiences of the Depression era and change them into the artist's coherent intellectual vision. Unlike Aiken or the writers covered in *Harvests of Change*, neither West nor his characters wished to adapt to the Depression culture. Indulging his fantasies, West, like his characters, constructed a fictive personality out of imaginative materials. Inventing what Martin calls "a general daydream," West provided a literature of refusal, for himself as well as America's masses, to set against an unlivable culture. Disorders in West's public world were "so immediate and apparent . . . that the crises of self and personality which now became a collective crisis threatened to be ignored altogether." West used his writing neither to evolve within his culture nor to adapt to its conditions. Alert to the many false solutions—which were answering the pervasive need to believe in any remedy no matter how deluded or paranoid— for the general crisis, West undermined collective faith in the artist's ability to salvage order out of chaos. Unlike Eliot's (or Aiken's) poetry, West's fictions were designed to disintegrate back into useless fragments.

West characteristically investigated the complicated ways in which collective fantasies took the place of events. He wrote about this displacement in a style wherein compassion was so intermixed with intelligence that it could fall victim neither to cultural despair nor false hope. "The art of his life" was grounded in that style. Insofar as West embodied a refusal to believe in the writer's ability to transmute chaos into understanding as anything other than a delusion, his life redirected Martin's biographical attention. In his biography of West, Martin was less interested in the self West constructed out of the demands of his writing and more in the inadequacy of the written words.

Martin further pursued his shift in focus in his brief biographical portrait of Robert Lowell. Martin underscores the different selves produced by a poet who, while terrorized and alienated, nevertheless understood the destiny of a personality in culture. Lowell was divided, Martin claims, into a self wholly absorbed within the suprapersonal structure of a culture yet simultaneously split off from any sense that these forms nurtured him: "Like earlier New England poets, his sensibility first found itself in opposition, but unlike them, he has been forced by the rapid changes in American life repeatedly to reconstitute his principles of opposition, and thus always to define freshly his relation to his fellows."

Martin again treats the writer's craft as if it were an adaptive device influential in the evolution of the culture. His biography of Lowell reestablishes adaptation as a cultural ideal. Lowell

also implicitly disclosed the limitations of cultural adaptation.

Partially because of the death in 1973 of Aiken, out of whose art Martin had fashioned his identity as a biographer, and partially due to his formal study of psychoanalysis, Martin, in the years after the Lowell biography, changed his representation of the biographer's mission. When he published his biography of Aiken in 1962, Martin affirmed Aiken's understanding of the popularity of psychoanalytic biographies. Aiken believed this popularity to result from "a passionate desire to know and understand, through the unraveling of these lives, something of ourself." But in an article Martin published in *Humanities in Society* (Fall 1980), "The Deaths of the Novelists / The Lives of the Biographers," he finds the relationship between the biographer and his subject grounded in antagonism, and he says, "a secret assumption still existed—though deeply hidden— that the purpose of biography was to make the final claims for a life, claims that no new act could be allowed to alter. And hence biographical investigation began simultaneously with life's end."

In the first book-length biographical study Martin published after his matriculation at the Psychoanalytical Institute, *Always Merry and Bright: The Life of Henry Miller* (1978), he claims that for both Miller and West writing provided an escape from the demands of culture into the fantasy each projected of himself as a romantic idol. But Miller's fantasy superseded West's in creating an apocalyptic space in which Miller's fictive personality symbolically destroyed society and its neuroses and produced an immortal child (his book) out of that destruction. Since his art told the story of his life, he could not stop writing without losing his life. In writing for this purpose, Miller in a sense echoed sentiments Martin found earlier in Aiken's poetry: "My ultimate purpose as a writer, since it is requested that I state it, is that of every sincere writer—to fulfill myself and thus, inadvertently, enrich the lives of men and women everywhere, now and forever after." But Miller significantly differed from Aiken in claiming for the writer the power to absorb and eradicate the culture's priorities. As the summation and supersession of his previous understanding of the biographer's craft, Martin's *Always Merry and Bright: The Life of Henry Miller* marks a change in his life as a biographer.

Martin's biography of Miller concludes with an account of his fight with the executors of the es-

21

can begin to derive all of Dewey's personal preferences and professional philosophy (which occurred at a time) from this speck of biography, hardly beyond past his conception and birth and even before either of those?

Hermeneutically, I must say "no!" and begin to disassemble this whole cloudy rack and massive edifice which I have built.

Doesn't her

What of the influence of Dewey's mother on his social conception of philosophy? Doesn't the obituary in the Adams Mission Monthly make clear that long before her son she concerned herself with relief of the poor, and protection of the unfortunate? What of the settlement house movement and the influence upon him of Jane Addams? What was the effect upon him of the Herbartian movement in educational philosophy? How was he saved, intellectually, by his teacher Morris's discovery of Hegel, and then how did he work through Hegel by way of Psychology. And what of the undoubted influence of William James upon him?

I could, of course, go on endlessly, but the point is clear: each of these and a hundred other threads need to be followed fully, then utterly doubted and disassembled, before a large picture of Dewey can begin to emerge. Today I have simply followed out as far as I could, in order to illustrate the biographical process, one tiny strand of possibility. Who knows but that not a bit of this elaborately followed thread will lead us into the biographical labyrinth.

Last two pages from Martin's notes for a 21 October 1990 speech, "An Inquiry into Sabino," which addresses some biographical problems with his work in progress on John Dewey and was delivered at a conference called "New Approaches to Biography: Challenges from Critical Theory," held at the University of Southern California (by permission of Jay Martin)

22

into and out of the deep recesses of my subject's life and heart; *Perhaps not a word of replacement children will appear in the completed book.* Doubtless the other 24 linear feet of Dewey's manuscripts will, when consulted, provide dozens of theses just as good. So I could stop here.

But then, ... but then... just as I have fully disassembled my construct, I begin to wonder. Perhaps there *is* something to it. My mind reaches down the years and I remember that, *in 1946,* 19 years after Alice's death, John Dewey was remarried — to a woman, *Roberta Lowitz,* whose family he had known even before he met Alice. Mrs. Sabino Dewey *was matron of honor,* and Sabino, along with Fred and Jane, attended the ceremony. *Previous to the wedding* Jane had lived *with her father* in the Fifth Avenue apartment, but she moved out when the bride moved in.

He was alone now, again, all his children were gone. And what did Dewey *think about?* Why of course, he found himself deeply concerned *this 88 year old man,* with the plight of orphans in post-war Europe. And within *the next* two years *complete, A Noah's Ark family,* he adopted two Belgian orphans. First a boy, then a girl. The *boy was eight* years old. His name was John.

... Perhaps I've got hold of an idea here, after all.

— JAY MARTIN

tate over the biographical rights to Miller's life. For Martin that fight became a metaphor for what he sees as the biographer's task: to take posession of the subject's life as if it were the biographer's own. The lesson Martin learned from that struggle appears in his redefinition of biography (in "The Deaths of the Novelists / The Lives of the Biographers"): "Biography is associated with the psychological mechanism of projective identification. This is a primitive psychological mechanism found in all of us. In this process, a person projects his feelings inside another person both because he wishes to dispose of an unwanted part of himself and because, in the case of a disturbed patient, he is attempting to take revenge on others for the way he feels about himself.

"In a well person, projective identification is also adaptive identification since it can provide a way of observing how the recipient deals with the feelings. . . . Biographies offer invitations to readers to regard the subject as their own identifying project, one whose structure of response chooses and identifies them in their imaginative aspects."

In this passage the focus of Martin's biographical attention has shifted from the drama of consciousness taking place within the writer's mind to the "projective identification" within the biographer's (or reader's) psyche. No longer interested in mediating between the artist's life and art, Martin finds the biographical (projective) impulse the pervasive building block in the construction of every cultural identity.

Instead of remaining secondary to the artist, then, the biographer, as the cultural representative of the psychic process of projective identification, reconstructs both life and art in terms of this process. In turning from biography to psychoanalysis, Martin organized his biographical insights into psychotherapy. *Who Am I This Time?: Uncovering the Fictive Personality* is a series of case histories recast in terms of patients' (and cultural celebrities') successful or unsuccessful projective identifications. Successful identification results in an adaptation of the patient's personality to cultural traumas. When unsuccessful, projective identification, like West's self-invention, alienates the patient.

Martin has also written a forthcoming biography of John Dewey. His works on Aiken, West, Lowell, and especially Miller, along with *Harvests of Change*, have made him a permanent and forceful presence in American biography and literature.

James R. Mellow

(28 February 1926 -)

Jamie Barlowe-Kayes
University of Toledo

BOOKS: *Charmed Circle: Gertrude Stein and Company* (New York: Praeger, 1974; London: Phaidon, 1974);

Nathaniel Hawthorne in His Times (Boston: Houghton Mifflin, 1980);

Invented Lives: F. Scott and Zelda Fitzgerald (Boston: Houghton Mifflin, 1984; London: Souvenir, 1985).

OTHER: *The Best in Arts*, edited by Mellow (New York: Art Digest, 1962);

New York: The Art World, edited by Mellow (New York: Art Digest, 1964).

SELECTED PERIODICAL PUBLICATIONS—
UNCOLLECTED: "Standards of Art," *Commonwealth*, 85 (14 October 1966): 57-59;

"Stein Salon Was the First Museum of Modern Art," *New York Times Magazine*, 1 December 1968, pp. 48-51;

"Matisse: A Celebration of Pleasure," *New York Times Magazine*, 28 December 1969, pp. 16-17;

"Exhibition Preview: Four Americans in Paris," *Art in America*, 58 (November 1970): 84-91;

"A Visit to a Restaurant in France Frequented by Gertrude Stein and Alice B. Toklas," *New York Times*, 5 November 1980, III: 1;

"The F. Scott Fitzgerald and Rosalind Fuller Affair," *New York Times*, 9 November 1984, III: 1.

In *Charmed Circle* (1974), his biography of Gertrude Stein, James R. Mellow says that writing "about the past is like attempting to restore an old house: you can never bring it back to what it once was, but you can hope to make it livable again." Mellow's metaphor aptly describes his three biographies of American authors: in them he restores the lives of Stein, Nathaniel Hawthorne, and F. Scott and Zelda Fitzgerald, providing livable texts where his readers can linger with the authors. Both critically and popularly acclaimed, Mellow's biographies trace in detail the

personal lives and literary careers of his subjects and in each case yield a distinctive portrait of an already well-known author.

James Robert Mellow was born on 28 February 1926 in Gloucester, Massachusetts. His parents, James R. Mellow (a mechanical engineer) and Cecilia Margaret Sawyer Mellow, are indirectly characterized in the dedication to *Charmed Circle*: "For my mother and father, who taught me the quirky realities of life—what was gently funny, what was interesting, what might be beautiful, what was worthwhile."

Mellow served in the U.S. Army Air Force from 1944 to 1946, after which he attended Northwestern University. Since earning his B.S. in 1950, Mellow has been a writer. His work crosses disciplines, especially those of art and literature, but divides generally into two broad categories: art criticism and literary biography. From 1955 to 1965 he worked for *Arts* magazine as a reviewer, production manager, and finally editor in chief; during his tenure there Mellow edited two volumes: *The Best in Arts* (1962) and *New York: The Art World* (1964). From 1965 to 1969 he was editor of *Industrial Design* and an art critic for *Art International*. From 1969 to 1972 he wrote art criticism for the *New Leader*, and from 1968 to 1974 he performed the same function for the *New York Times*. Although he continues to contribute articles on art to these and other publications, since 1974 Mellow has concentrated primarily on writing literary biographies.

In these biographies Mellow places his subjects in their particular personal, cultural, and historical contexts; thus, to say that his subjects are only Stein, Hawthorne, and the Fitzgeralds is to describe his texts inadequately. His projects include an impressive amount of data about other, often well-known, figures whose lives provide part of the context. All these details exist in letters, literary works, journals, memoirs, other biographies, and pictures; but they are subjected by Mellow to a selection process and to interpreta-

James R. Mellow circa 1984

tion that ultimately shapes that material into a coherent portrait.

Mellow's work shows increasing self-consciousness about his position as a "life writer." His relationship to his subjects ranges from his closeness to Stein in *Charmed Circle* to his controlled account of F. Scott and Zelda Zayre Fitzgerald in *Invented Lives* (1984).

Mellow begins each biography with a description of an important event in the life of his subject. By foregrounding this event, Mellow implicitly claims that it profoundly shaped the life. He then moves his reader back to the subject's early childhood. And, throughout the rest of the text, as Mellow follows the chronological progression of the life, the consequences of the event become increasingly evident.

There are some differences, though, in the degree to which Mellow explicitly divulges his plan to his readers. In the biographies of Stein and Hawthorne, Mellow's construction of their portraits is subtle, his method seemingly more in-

ductive than deductive, as he accumulates details confirming the hypotheses implicit in the shaping events. In the biography of the Fitzgeralds, however, Mellow begins with a preface in which he sets forth his thesis about them. The shaping event, then, coming immediately after the preface, is given greater force and specificity than in the biographies of Stein and Hawthorne. In fact, rather than setting aside a full chapter for this event in *Invented Lives*, Mellow combines it with brief accounts of the lives of Scott and Zelda before they meet. All the details—about the Fitzgeralds and about those who provide the context of their lives—thus work deductively to illustrate Mellow's thesis.

Another similarity in Mellow's method is his treatment from book to book of the literary works of his subjects. These artistic products offer Mellow additional means by which to shape his portraits. Mellow chooses not to dwell on the complex layering of the literary works as they present characters, events, and themes through

Mellow in 1974, when his first book, Charmed Circle, *was published (photograph by Augie Capaccio)*

some kind of narrating persona, who may or may not reflect the author's values and beliefs. His method also sidesteps the idea that characters may, like the narrator, hold values very different from the author's, but are included in the text in order to critique those values or to present a plausible fictional world in which there are competing and conflicting values. Nor does Mellow seem to recognize the difficulty of discovering the motivations of the author without using the tools of psychology and psychoanalysis. In other words he does not acknowledge that the reasons an author shapes his materials in a certain way may lie below the surface of the text.

Mellow instead views the literary works as just one more part of his collected data and relates their action, narrators, and characters most often in a one-to-one correspondence with events and people in the lives of the authors. This method allows Mellow to get at what is similar between the author and the literary works but not what is different and complex about the relation

between the life and the literature.

In *Charmed Circle*, which was nominated for the National Book Award in 1974, Mellow makes few negative judgments about Stein, but instead justifies her position and choices. Perhaps his attitude comes from his long-standing interest in her—ever since his days at Northwestern. He writes in the afterword to *Charmed Circle*: "I wanted to hear their voices: [Pablo] Picasso's high, whinnying laugh as Gertrude Stein recalled it; [Henri] Matisse's halting, carefully deliberated pronouncements; the terse self-consciousness of [Ernest] Hemingway . . . and, above all, the surprising, cultivated, contralto voice of Gertrude Stein repeating phrases, sentences, and odd judgments that I have remembered and turned over in my mind for what must be, now, a quarter of a century." Mellow's connection is also powerful because of his experience as an art critic; Gertrude and Leo Stein were inveterate art collectors. In fact, the Steins, with their brother Michael and his wife, Sarah, were strong influences

177

Henry and Clare Boothe Luce and Gertrude (top left); Thornton Wilder and Gertrude (top right); Gertrude and Alice entertain Picasso and his son Paolo and two neighbors (bottom).

Dust jacket for Mellow's biography that was nominated for a National Book Award in 1974. Mellow had been interested in Stein since the 1940s.

on the burgeoning careers of such artists as Matisse and Picasso. Literally covering their walls with the work of new artists, the Steins preached the "gospel of modernism" to the artists and patrons who gathered at the Steins' Paris home on Saturday evenings.

Thus the shaping event of Gertrude Stein's life is the opening of the Steins' studio at 27 rue de Fleurus in 1903, when she was twenty-nine years old. The event began her lifelong association with modern art and literature and established her as an influential presence in the lives of artists and other writers. Opening the studio signified her commitment to the philosophy of modernism, and the commitment becomes the shaping force of Mellow's portrait of her. That commitment, he claims, extended beyond mere taste; it became the core of Stein's being and was apparent in every aspect of her life—from her unconventional life-style to her "eccentric writing-style."

After presenting the shaping event, Mellow moves back to Stein's childhood, filling in the gap between that time and the years in Paris, prior to World War I. He then takes his reader on a remarkably detailed journey through Stein's life, always using those details to fill out and deepen the portrait he begins to shape in the first chapter. Much of that journey, of course, is through Stein's career as a writer. From the early *Three Lives* (1909) to the ponderous but queerly innovative *The Making of Americans* (1925) to *Four in America*, published in 1947, the year of her death, Stein worked against conventions—and thus often against her own acceptance by publishers and the public. Her commitment to modernism was clearly a part of her own work, which ranged through the genres of poetry, drama, "word-portraits," autobiography, biography, lectures, novels, and art and literary criticism. When Mellow describes Stein's most popular work, *The Autobiography of Alice B. Toklas* (1933), he could also be describing features of his own biography: "a crowded canvas, dense wit, personalities, ranging from figures such as Picasso, Matisse, Hemingway, Fitzgerald, [Sherwood] Anderson, who had become world famous, to all the minor but interesting people who had ever moved into Gertrude's orbit . . . it chronicled a quarter of a century of the Parisian art world and the literary world in a historic period. . . . "

Thus Mellow's desire to re-create "the texture of a life, a writer's daily life" is achieved as the pieces—the plethora of details—become the portrait of a remarkable woman.

Mellow's second biography, *Nathaniel Hawthorne in His Times* (1980), won the American Book Award for biography in 1983. According to Mellow the shaping event in Hawthorne's life was his first visit to the Salem, Massachusetts, home of the Peabody sisters, Elizabeth, Mary, and Sophia, on an evening in November 1837. That visit pulled him, for the first time in over a decade, out of his secluded life of recording observations in his journal and turning them into sketches and tales. He made many subsequent visits to Sophia, and in 1842 he married her. In Hawthorne's own terms Sophia was "his salvation," as his relationship with her allowed him to emerge from his "dismal chamber." As Mellow shapes his portrait of Hawthorne, he admits that the relationship with Sophia radically altered the outer texture of Hawthorne's life, yet claims that Hawthorne remained "a man communing with himself, attempting to catch a glimpse of his own identity." Their marriage did not touch the "inmost self" of Hawthorne; thus it did not profoundly affect the stories he would tell nor the manner of his telling.

After re-creating the shaping event, Mellow returns to Hawthorne's birth to trace the path of the man who one day walked into the Peabody house to confront his future as a husband and father. Mellow examines Hawthorne's life from his childhood, spent in Salem and in Maine, to college at Bowdoin, to his twelve years of isolated productivity. Hawthorne's early works are, for Mellow, explorations into the darker places of the human mind. He describes Hawthorne as "the solitary writer and journalizer . . . the student of his own vague dreams and emotions; the man of a sometimes morbid turn of mind. He is the captive of time, the sensitive man. . . . The mystery of sin is what absorbs him." Mellow considers the narrative situation in Hawthorne's story "Monsieur du Miroir" to be paradigmatic of his writings; in it the narrator sees himself in a mirror, a "means of catching some glimpse of his own identity, of distancing himself from his personal ruminations, of attempting to stand outside himself as a concerned, somewhat amused observer."

Thus the mirror image—or variations on it, such as portraits, reflections in water, or daguerreotypes—and the character or narrator as detached observer recur throughout Hawthorne's fiction. "Monsieur du Miroir" is, for Meellow, also representative of Hawthorne's failure ever to come to terms with his own identity; the early tale is a "plain admission of his [Hawthorne's] own disappointed hopes, his sense of failure, neatly woven into the fabric of his allegory on the fateful marriage between the private mind and the public image."

With the same plenitude of detail Mellow offers in the Stein biography, he takes readers through Hawthorne's life, examining his relationships to people, politics, and history, and to his writing. Maintaining a rather detached attitude toward Hawthorne, Mellow remains in control of the way the many details are shaped. The portrait of Hawthorne includes the isolated, disappointed, brooding writer unsuccessfully searching for an identity, and the family man and hardheaded pragmatist, who was sometimes forced to take jobs as desperate measures against financial ruin.

Increasingly unable to write but not always aware of the sources of his creative failures, Hawthorne grew more frustrated. For the final touches on his portrait of Hawthorne, Mellow reintroduces the mirror image he finds so intriguing in "Monsieur du Miroir" to convey Hawthorne's frustration about his later writing: "it is as if Hawthorne had wandered into a hall of mirrors in which fragments of his personal life and pieces of his imaginative fantasies were reflected and repeated in bewildering sequence. . . . All of these elements are picked up, worried over, dropped, reconsidered. . . . The mechanics of his fiction had stalled . . . he could not put his fictional world in order; he remained lost in a thicket of possibilities, unable to find his way out. . . . "

Mellow's word portrait of Hawthorne, then, looks something like the well-known paintings of him by Charles Osgood and Cephas Giovanni Thompson, showing a somewhat stiff, aloof, formal man with a sensuous mouth and eyes burning from the depths within.

Dust jackets for Mellow's second and third books. Nathaniel Hawthorne in His Times *won the American Book Award for biography in 1983.*

The most self-conscious and overtly shaped of Mellow's three biographies is *Invented Lives: F. Scott and Zelda Fitzgerald*. As a work in progress it was titled "Loose Ends" when Mellow intended to write a "brief, brisk, semijournalistic account of the Fitzgeralds' marriage"; however, as he says in the introduction to *Invented Lives*, he began to realize that "the context of their lives was more important than I had allowed for." That context is so important, in fact, that Mellow claims the Fitzgeralds' "circle of friends provided them with alter egos, which they then used as characters in their stories, and with experiences, which they also borrowed for their writings.... What masters of invention they became, creating new versions of themselves, putting themselves into their stories, acting out their stories in real life. Yet *Invented Lives* is also about the hazards of such invention.... *Invented Lives* is about the personal cost of American success and American failure."

Mellow thus exposes his thematic shaping

of the lives of both Scott and Zelda Fitzgerald, and his attitude toward them is aggressively critical: "When I began *Invented Lives*, I felt that the best approach would be not to let the glamorous Fitzgeralds get away with anything. That way, the sense of the real tragedy behind their lives would be all the more apparent in the end." He claims that he became more sympathetic to them—despite his dismay at their waste of energy, money, and talent—recognizing that Scott "was a man who was committed to paying the bills for the mistakes in his life."

The major shaping event, re-created in the first chapter of *Invented Lives*, is the marriage of the Fitzgeralds—the coming together of two immature, selfish people whose own self-destructive bents are twisted more violently and more quickly by their union. Mellow's negative judgment does not extend to the creative potential of these two, especially of Scott; in fact, Mellow's rec-

COPYRIGHT CHECKLIST FOR CHAPTER FIVE: PAGE 4

SL/ (continued)

P.39   "Suppose you want to hear"; EH to Grace Quinlan,
        July 21,1921; SL,51 [30]

        "In your wide and diverse acquaintance" EH to Grace
        Quinlan August 19,1921; SL,55 [44]

P.46   "probably well thumbed correspondence"EH to Y.K.
        Smith, Oct 1,1921; SL,55; [4]

P.46   "You can readily understand" Y.K. Smith to EH, c. 2
        Oct. 1921; SL,56 [26]

SSEH/SCRIBNER'S

P.1213 "His lies were quite unimportant lies": SSEH,244(60) Sold 101, Here
P.13   "A distaste for everything" SSEH,243. Ibid -24
P.14   "all work is honorable" SSEH,249.Ibid -4
P.15   "Don't you love your mother"; SSEH 249-250 Ibid (45)
P.16   "Krebs kissed her hair" SSEH,250 (30)
P.17   "There is a picture"; SSEH,243; ironically the final -[40]
        line has been lifted and adapted from Gertrude
        Stein's "Accents in Alsace," from Geography and Plays
        the bacon grease from FOrd Madox FOrd etc. see..   39
P.17   "complicated word of already defined" SSEH,245 Ibid -(4)

GRIFFIN/AWY

P.20   "It being now decided"; William Horne to EH
        Oct.13,1920; [JFK?]; Griffin.138 [100]

LEWIS/MAKING IT UP

P.13   "In the war that I had known"; Lewis,"Making it
        Up"; Journal of Modern Literature, 236. [30]

COMPLETE POEMS/U NEB.

P.34   "Through the hot pounding rhythm"Complete Poems,33 [24
P.41   "It is cool at night" Complete Poems, 30 [58]
P.41   "At night I lay with you"; Ibid 32 [13]

MONTGOMERY/HEM IN MICH

P.44   "Many telegrams were received"; Montgomery/Hem in
        Mich, 195 [30]

PUL "ylu's words to me" EH to WS c. March 1921 [27]

Page from the list of sources for material quoted in Hemingway: A Life without Consequences *(scheduled for 1992 publication; by permission of James R. Mellow)*

It wasn't any good. He couldn't tell her, he couldn't make her see it. It was silly to have said it. He had only hurt her.

Moments later, full of the mortifying guilt only a mother can induce, Krebs lies. He says he didn't mean it, that he was angry about something else. Having given in, he is then forced to beg his mother to believe that he loves her, that he didn't mean what he had said.

Krebs kissed her hair. She put her face up to him.
"I'm your mother," she said,"I held you next to my heart when you were a tiny baby."
Krebs felt sick and vaguely nauseated.

* .* .*

A river runs through many of Hemingway's stories and novels. Generally, in such a Hemingway story, the river serves as a cleansing baptism, an absolution for past sins, a healing experience, a rite of escape from the outside world as the Big Two-Hearted is for Nick Adams in the story of that name, as the Irati is for Bill Gorton and Jake Barnes in The Sun Also Rises, as the Tagliamento is for Lieutenant Frederic Henry in A Farewell to Arms. But in one of the cleverest touches of any Hemingway story, and in a paragraph that perfectly epitomizes the Hemingway style, he describes Krebs in a souvenir snapshot:

---(5)-16---

An abrupt transition from the previous section. You need to let us know that you're still talking about "Soldier's Home" but not, now, as it applies to the relationship between H. + his mother but to H's life in more general terms.

Typescript pages for Hemingway: A Life without Consequences. *The marginal comment from editor Janet Silver prompted the revision shown on the facing page (by permission of James R. Mellow).*

It wasn't any good. He couldn't tell her, he couldn't
make her see it. It was silly to have said it. He had
only hurt her.
Moments later, full of the mortifying guilt only a mother
can induce, Krebs lies. He says he didn't mean it, that he
was angry about something else. Having given in, he is then
forced to beg his mother to believe that he loves her, that
he didn't mean what he had said.

Krebs kissed her hair. She put her face up to him.
  "I'm your mother," she said,"I held you next to my
heart when you were a tiny baby."
Krebs felt sick and vaguely nauseated.

                        *   *   *

But Harold Krebs's excrutiating confrontation with his
mother is not the only fictional intent of "Soldier's
Home." In every major Hemingway story the human incident
points the way to larger issues that are not, at first, so
apparent. A river, for instance, runs through many of
Hemingway's major stories and his most important novels.
Generally, in such Hemingway fictions, the river serves as a
cleansing baptism, an absolution for past sins, a healing
experience, a rite of escape from the outside world as the
Big Two-Hearted is for Nick Adams in the story of that name,
as the Irati is for Bill Gorton and Jake Barnes in The Sun
Also Rises, as the Tagliamento is for Lieutenant Frederic
Henry in A Farewell to Arms. But in one of the cleverest
touches of any Hemingway story, and in a paragraph that

                        ---224---

                            183

ognition of their creativity is foregrounded, as he sees it complicate their self-destruction through the jealousy and plagiarism between them.

Thus *Invented Lives* looks at the consequences of not knowing oneself well enough to accept shortcomings or limitations, whether they be psychological, genetic, social, educational, or physical. The immediate consequence for the Fitzgeralds was that they "tried on" the lives and experiences of others, often those whose limitations were different from or less apparent than their own. The larger, long-term consequences, though, were destructive—finally deadly: "Zelda's life trailing through mental institutions, Fitzgerald's sliding downhill into alcoholism." Mellow's biography does not, however, examine the psychological causes of the limitations, of the failure to understand and accept them, or of their particular consequences.

Although some reviewers have criticized *Invented Lives* for its failure to have deep psychological or psychoanalytical underpinnings, Mellow was not concerned finally with psychological reasons and causes, nor with psychoanalyzing his subjects. Instead, he was concerned with what he feels are discernible, measurable causes, such as Fitzgerald's embarrassment about his family connections, his academic and athletic failures in school—and the jealousies that resulted—and his dependence on his appearance and later on his ability to write.

Thus Mellow deals, as he does with Stein and Hawthorne, with the accumulated knowledge. When he fills in gaps, he does so with a nod toward the probable—inferred from other behaviors and choices, tracing the patterns of behavior that led to the Fitzgeralds' destruction. An anonymous review in the 23 February 1985 *Economist* sums up Mellow's achievement in the book: "James R. Mellow has managed, in this moving and controlled critical biography, to present an account of Scott's and Zelda's lives, where external circumstances combined with willful folly to destroy two talented people.... The unhappy ending to Scott's and Zelda's lives is rendered the more poignant by its inevitability."

Mellow also set for himself the task of illustrating specifically how their circle of friends—including Ring Lardner, John Dos Passos, H. L. Mencken, Edmund Wilson, George Jean Nathan, John Peale Bishop, Gerald and Sara Murphy, and Ernest Hemingway—provided them with traits, attitudes, life-styles, and experiences to appropriate as their own. Thus Mellow must offer

details about their friends and re-create many of the interactions and interconnections between them and the Fitzgeralds.

Once Mellow sets up the relationship between the Fitzgeralds and the person whose attitudes or life is being appropriated, he uses one of the Fitzgeralds' literary products, usually those of Scott, as the site of the fictional working out of the assumed identity. For example, Scott could never quite reconcile his failed romance with Ginevra King and her subsequent engagement to a very wealthy young man. Again and again in his fiction he re-creates this situation, but takes on the identity of one who could win her affection—for example, in *This Side of Paradise* (1920), *The Great Gatsby* (1925), and numerous short stories. According to Mellow, Dick Diver in *Tender Is The Night* (1934) was based on several of Scott's friends, including Murphy and Hemingway, although Diver's vices were Fitzgerald's. Mellow claims that Scott worked on his marriage in the pages of his book, modeling Nicole Diver after Zelda. Of *Tender Is the Night* Mellow says, "The flaw ... one suspects, was Fitzgerald's search for a suitable identity among the various scrapped idols of his life, the discarded ideals, the roles that had been played and that, in the end, had proven unsatisfactory.... The problem with *Tender Is the Night* is that Fitzgerald tried to solve in literary terms the problems he could not resolve in private life." About *The Great Gatsby* Mellow says, "Like his creator, Gatsby is a man of assumed identities."

Mellow's biography ends by simply describing the deaths of Scott and Zelda, rather than with inferences, conclusions, or implications. Such analysis has been rendered unnecessary because the nature of their deaths and the road they traveled to reach them are, given Mellow's initial presentation of his shaped portraits, predictable.

In all three of Mellow's literary biographies, the notion of context is important. That context—whether it is referred to as a circle of friends, family, and associates or as "circumstantial details"—interacts with a main shaping event to direct the way the lives of Gertrude Stein, Nathaniel Hawthorne, and F. Scott and Zelda Fitzgerald are played out. The individual's life is seen as part of a larger social milieu, thus merging biography with social history. Perhaps, as an anonymous critic put it in a review of *Charmed Circle* in the *New Republic* (2 February 1974), one "can't be sure that everything was as Mellow says it was. . . . It doesn't matter. This is a delightful book and it will enlarge the company of those charmed by the comings and goings of Miss Stein's company." This reviewer is right in saying that it does not matter whether every single detail and inference represents the reality of a historical time, because Mellow is not reporting but interpreting history and shaping portraits of literary figures. Mellow wants to say that things could have happened this way—even, considering the evidence, that things probably happened this way.

Mellow's distinct achievement, in fact, is to take literary figures and set them in their contexts in such a way that readers gain a new perspective on them—one both plausible and significant. Furthermore, Mellow's work creates a new understanding of the relationship between Stein, Hawthorne, and the Fitzgeralds and their literary products. Mellow's work also forces readers to consider his relationship to his biographical subjects and to the portraits of them that he so carefully shapes. Reflecting on that relationship, then, makes one aware that literary biography, as Mellow practices it, is not just finding and reporting biographical facts, not just establishing connections between the life and the literary work, not just describing the larger contexts in which subjects moved, but also interpreting circumstantial details, re-envisioning specific events, and understanding characteristic as well as idiosyncratic behavior as part of some coherent life. Literary biography, then, as practiced by Mellow, is not journalism but history, not chronicle but narrative, and, in that respect, it is potentially as artistic as the fictional narratives by his subjects.

Jeffrey Meyers

(1 April 1939 -   )

Mark Allister
St. Olaf College

BOOKS: *Fiction and the Colonial Experience* (Totowa, N.J.: Rowman & Littlefield, 1973; Ipswich, U.K.: Boydell, 1973);

The Wounded Spirit: A Study of "Seven Pillars of Wisdom" (London: Martin, Brian & O'Keeffe, 1973; revised edition, New York: St. Martin's Press, 1989; London: Macmillan, 1989);

T. E. Lawrence: A Bibliography (New York & London: Garland, 1974);

A Reader's Guide to George Orwell (London: Thames & Hudson, 1975; Totowa, N.J.: Littlefield, Adams, 1977);

Painting and the Novel (New York: Barnes & Noble, 1975; Manchester, U.K.: Manchester University Press, 1975);

A Fever at the Core: The Idealist in Politics (New York: Barnes & Noble, 1976; London: London Magazine, 1976);

George Orwell: An Annotated Bibliography of Criticism, by Meyers and Valerie Meyers (New York & London: Garland, 1977);

Married to Genius (New York: Barnes & Noble, 1977; London: London Magazine, 1977);

Homosexuality and Literature, 1890-1930 (London: Athlone, 1977; Montreal: McGill-Queen's University Press, 1977);

Katherine Mansfield: A Biography (London: Hamish Hamilton, 1978; New York: New Directions, 1980);

The Enemy: A Biography of Wyndham Lewis (London: Routledge & Kegan Paul, 1980; Boston: Routledge & Kegan Paul, 1982);

D. H. Lawrence and the Experience of Italy (Philadelphia & London: University of Pennsylvania Press, 1982);

Disease and the Novel, 1880-1960 (New York: St. Martin's Press, 1985; London: Macmillan, 1985);

Hemingway: A Biography (New York: Harper & Row, 1985; London: Macmillan, 1986);

Manic Power: Robert Lowell and His Circle (New York: Arbor House, 1987; London: Macmillan, 1987);

The Spirit of Biography (Ann Arbor: UMI Research Press, 1989);

D. H. Lawrence: A Biography (New York: Knopf, 1990; London: Macmillan, 1990);

Joseph Conrad: A Biography (New York: Scribners / London: Murray, 1991).

OTHER: *George Orwell: The Critical Heritage*, edited, with an introduction and notes, by Meyers (Boston & London: Routledge & Kegan Paul, 1975);

Katherine Mansfield, *Four Poems*, edited, with an introduction, by Meyers (London: Stevens, 1980);

Wyndham Lewis: A Revaluation, edited by Meyers (London: Athlone, 1980; Montreal: McGill-Queen's University Press, 1980);

Ernest Hemingway: The Critical Heritage, edited, with an introduction and notes, by Meyers (Boston & London: Routledge & Kegan Paul, 1982);

Roy Campbell, *Wyndham Lewis*, edited, with an introduction and notes, by Meyers (Pietermaritzburg, South Africa: University of Natal Press, 1985);

D. H. Lawrence and Tradition, edited, with an introduction, by Meyers (Amherst: University of Massachusetts Press, 1985; London: Athlone, 1985);

The Craft of Literary Biography, edited, with an introduction and one chapter, by Meyers (New York: Schocken, 1985; London: Macmillan, 1985);

"Memoirs of Hemingway: Growth of a Legend," in *Essays by Divers Hands*, volume 44, edited by Angus Wilson (Rochester, N.Y.: Boydell & Brewer, 1986), pp. 125-146;

The Legacy of D. H. Lawrence: New Essays, edited, with an introduction and one chapter, by Meyers (New York: St. Martin's Press, 1987; London: Macmillan, 1987);

Robert Lowell: Interviews and Memoirs, edited, with an introduction and notes, by Meyers (Ann

Jeffrey Meyers circa 1985 (photograph by Inge Morath)

Arbor: University of Michigan Press, 1988; Toronto: Fitzhenry & Whiteside, 1988);

The Biographer's Art, edited, with an introduction and one chapter, by Meyers (New York: New Amsterdam Books, 1989; London: Macmillan, 1989);

T. E. Lawrence: Soldier, Writer, Legend, edited, with two chapters, by Meyers (New York: St. Martin's Press, 1989; London: Macmillan, 1989);

Graham Greene: A Revaluation, edited by Meyers (London: Macmillan, 1989; New York: St. Martin's Press, 1990);

"Giuseppe Tomasi di Lampedusa," in *European Writers*, volume 11, edited by George Stade (New York: Scribners, 1990), pp. 2009-2034.

SELECTED PERIODICAL PUBLICATIONS—
UNCOLLECTED: "The Quest for Katherine Mansfield," *Biography*, 1 (Summer 1978): 51-64;

"The Quest for Wyndham Lewis," *Biography*, 4 (Winter 1981): 66-81;

"The Quest for Hemingway," *Virginia Quarterly Re-*

view, 61 (Autumn 1985): 584-602;

"Ezra Pound and the Russian Avant-Garde," *Paideuma*, 17 (Fall/Winter 1988): 171-176;

"The Quest for D. H. Lawrence," *Virginia Quarterly Review*, 66 (Spring 1990): 249-261.

"A good biographical subject is difficult to find," wrote Jeffrey Meyers shortly after publishing his 1978 book on Katherine Mansfield, his first major biography. Despite his remark, he has since found more "good subjects"—Wyndham Lewis, Ernest Hemingway, Robert Lowell, D. H. Lawrence, and Joseph Conrad—and with their biographies and his essays on the craft of life writing, Meyers has emerged as a leading biographer.

Meyers was born on 1 April 1939 in New York City to Rubin (a clothing-industry worker) and Judith Meyers and grew up in Forest Hills, New York. He attended the University of Michigan, where he completed a B.A. in English in 1959, and then, after a year at Harvard Law School, he did graduate work in English at the University of California, Berkeley, where he earned

Dust jacket for Meyers's biography of a writer whom T. S. Eliot called "a great intellect" and "a great modern writer"

his M.A. in 1961 and his Ph.D. in 1967. From 1963 to 1965 Meyers was an assistant professor of English at the University of California, Los Angeles, and from 1965 to 1966 a lecturer for the University of Maryland's Far East Division in Tokyo. While in Japan, on 12 October 1965, he married Valerie Froggatt, a graduate of Cambridge University and a teacher of English. They have one child, Rachel, born in 1972. After returning from Japan, Meyers was an assistant professor at Tufts University from 1967 to 1971. But weary of student riots and the campus upheavals of the 1960s, and wanting to live in southern Europe, he left teaching to write professionally, which he did in Málaga, Spain, and in London through 1974. In 1975 he returned to the United States, accepting a position as an associate professor at the University of Colorado, Boulder, where he still teaches. He was promoted to full professor in 1978. Meyers has received several grants, including a Fulbright Fellowship (1977-1978) and a Guggenheim Fellowship (1978). In 1983 he was elected a fellow of the Royal Society of Literature.

Meyers began writing primarily as a literary critic who used biography to explicate texts, and he has since become primarily a biographer who occasionally interprets literature. His first four books of literary criticism contain themes, techniques, and subjects that anticipate his later biographical writings.

In *Fiction and the Colonial Experience* (1973) Meyers explicates British-colonial novels by Conrad, Rudyard Kipling, E. M. Forster, Joyce Cary, and Graham Greene, which have in common an exploration of the cultural conflict that arises when Europeans impose their manners, customs, religious beliefs, and moral values on an indigenous way of life. The European hero moves from an ordered to a chaotic world, hostile and difficult to comprehend. In Meyers's book one sees his early fascination with the outsider.

In his next book, *The Wounded Spirit: A Study of "Seven Pillars of Wisdom"* (1973), Meyers again writes about English people in a foreign land, though in this case the Englishman is not a literary character but a real person (T. E. Lawrence). Meyers calls *The Wounded Spirit* a literary analysis and not a biography, but in writing on *Seven Pillars*—Lawrence's spiritual autobiography of his military and political efforts in the Arab struggle for independence during World War I—Meyers moves toward critical biography. He uses the facts of Lawrence's life to suggest motivation, to back an interpretation, and, in general, to explain more convincingly a book Meyers calls "a masterpiece of psychological analysis and self-revelation [that] belongs with the finest books of the modern age."

Before publishing *Painting and the Novel* (1975), Meyers had turned his attention to George Orwell. In addition to editing a collection of essays on Orwell (1975) and compiling with his wife, Valerie, an annotated bibliography of criticism (1977), Meyers wrote *A Reader's Guide To George Orwell* (1975), containing a short biographical sketch, in which Meyers relies too much on Orwell's own claims about his life but uses biography effectively to interpret individual texts.

Meyers's attention to the life of Orwell possibly influenced his next project, because a year later he published *A Fever at the Core: The Idealist in Politics*, a series of six biographical sketches about "romantic idealists" who flourished from 1887 to 1937. While these men were reflective and imaginative, like most writers or artists, they were also political and idealistic. They put their ideas into action—usually doomed but romantically glorious action in which they led followers against the prevailing military and cultural power. For Wilfrid Blunt, R. B. Cunninghame Graham, and Roger Casement, the dream was home rule for Ireland. T. E. Lawrence fought for Arab independence; Gabriele D'Annunzio defied the great powers in 1919, captured the Adriatic city of Fiume, and personally ruled it for sixteen months; André Malraux led a brigade of French aviators during the Spanish Civil War.

These men, writes Meyers, exemplify "the problem of the intellectual as a man of action." All of them charismatically led their followers: they provided oratory, not argument; they made the theatrical gesture, not the politically smart move. They all rode their intense vitality and energy to a moment of triumph, which then led to disillusionment, withdrawal, and renunciation.

In *Married to Genius* (1977) Meyers presents biographical sketches of the marriages of nine modern writers in order to consider "the relation between emotional and artistic commitment." Leo Tolstoy, George Bernard Shaw, James Joyce, Virginia Woolf, F. Scott Fitzgerald, Conrad, Lawrence, Hemingway, and Mansfield all "made a serious commitment to the claims of ordinary life and believed that marriage provided their most profound personal relationship." Meyers argues

that the creative impulse of these authors was indebted to their emotional and intellectual conflicts and ties with their spouses.

For *Married to Genius* and *A Fever at the Core*. Meyers did no primary research, which might have yielded new insights into these various lives. He relies instead on other sources that, in their concentration on one person, are often more interesting. By focusing on specific biographical information and juxtaposing numerous and related examples, Meyers hopes to illuminate an important subject. Biography serves as the vehicle by which to discuss the idealist in politics or the relation of marriage to artistic production. Both books, however, seem somewhat reductive, with Meyers shaping the details of people's lives in such a way as to provide evidence for his viewpoint.

Meyers also published *Homosexuality and Literature, 1890-1930* in 1977; it also examines the connection between sexuality, human relationships, and the creative impulse. Meyers argues that homosexual novelists or novelists dealing with homosexual themes, because of the public taboo against homosexuality, "find a language of reticence and evasion, obliqueness and indirection, to convey their theme." Oscar Wilde's *The Picture of Dorian Gray* (1891), André Gide's *The Immoralist* (1902), E. M. Forster's *A Room with a View* (1908), and Thomas Mann's *Death in Venice* (1912), among others, are subtle, allusive, and symbolic—qualities readers have come to associate with and to praise in the work of great modernists.

After seven books in which he either experimented with using biography for textual explication or grouped together biographical sketches, Meyers published *Katherine Mansfield: A Biography*. In an essay called "The Quest for Katherine Mansfield" (*Biography*, Summer 1978), Meyers lists his "ideal criteria" for selecting a modern biographical subject: the existence of significant and accessible unpublished material, the existence of family and friends to interview, the absence of a recent biography, and, perhaps most important, a subject who will sustain the biographer's attention for several years. Mansfield met the criteria. She also fitted Meyers's interests in the outsider who confronts a "superior" culture and in the sexual rebel whose ideas and feelings are disguised in her art.

The turbulence of Mansfield's short life has been almost matched by the squabbles over the interpretation of her life. In the decades after her death, her husband, the critic John Middleton Murry, published numerous editions of her uncol-

terminated as of April 1, 1943, because of a "general dissatisfaction over the
reports submitted."

Robert Joyce explained why the reports of the Crook Factory were so fantastic and why they
were tolerated at the embassy and in Washington:

> Of course their intelligence was completely fabricated. If their
> reports were sensational they were paid more--$20, instead of $10,
> And most of their reports were contradictory--less than useful, as
> they caused confusion in Washington headquarters at the Pentagon--
> not to speak of the FBI at home and in Havana.

But a major general who headed G-2 in the Pentagon in 1942
said Army intelligence was interested in and welcomed reports from
military attachés on all matters, including educational policy,
sports, etc., everything in short.
The general was a very powerful man at the time and personally overruled Hoover's
attempt to close down the Crook Factory. The best that can be said for the Crook
Factory is that it placed a certain limitation on the activities of the pro-
and did more good than harm at very little cost to the nation.
Nazi Falangists in Cuba by keeping them under surveillance. Only the force
of Hemingway's legend and overpowering personality could have convinced the
ambassador, despite overwhelming evidence from the FBI, that his spy games
had any real value.

Hemingway had replaced writing with spying; he had to justify its worth
to Martha, Braden and the FBI,
and wanted Duran to praise the Crook Factory as he had praised the novel. But
Duran soon became as disillusioned as the FBI about Hemingway's activities. He
had commanded 55,000 troops in battle and felt he was now wasting his time on
that produced unreliable reports.
a foolish enterprise. As Hemingway's rivalry with the FBI intensified, he demanded
absolute loyalty and became hostile when he failed to receive it. Durán was
the only man in Cuba on an equal plane with Hemingway and his defection was
a serious blow. Robert Joyce closely observed the disintegration of the friendship:

> When Durán took over the Crook Factory from Ernesto, he quickly saw
> that its production of "intelligence information" was adding nothing
> of value. He started spending more and more time at the Embassy as

Page from the typescript for Hemingway: A Biography *(by permission of Jeffrey Meyers)*

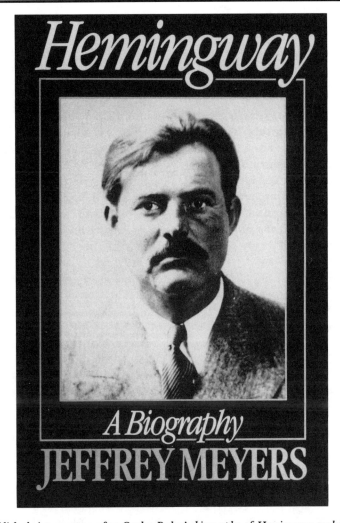

Dust jacket for the book published sixteen years after Carlos Baker's biography of Hemingway and promoted as a corrective to it

lected or unpublished work—poems, stories, journals, and letters. Not only did her work make him substantial money, but his promotion of her as a great writer and a wonderful person (gross misrepresentations) angered many of her friends. He sentimentalized her and romanticized their life together, which was full of betrayal, jealousy, and neglect. He cowrote with Ruth Mantz the first biography, *The Life of Katherine Mansfield* (1931), which is an idealization. The second major biography, Antony Alpers's *Katherine Mansfield* (1954), also failed in this respect.

Meyers was the first biographer to narrate the whole story of Mansfield's life. His chief contribution is that he uncovered information on areas of her life that were unclear. After reading materials unavailable in previous decades and single-mindedly interviewing everyone who knew her, Meyers put together the story of a young woman—cut off from family, critical of societal conven-

tions, and tempestuous and strong-minded—living a life free of the constraints that bound women of previous generations, but paying the high price of guilt and despair. Meyers wrote about her lesbian love affairs when she was eleven and nineteen, about her love affair with Garnet Trowell, which resulted in her becoming pregnant and then being thrown out of the Trowell house by Garnet's father, about her one-day marriage to the singer George Bowden (to provide a father for the baby), and her subsequent miscarriage. Other love affairs, a pregnancy and abortion, her husband's affairs with other women and his failure to provide for her either emotionally or financially when Katherine was suffering greatly from tuberculosis—Meyers describes unrelentingly all the unpleasant details. Staying close to the chronology of her life, he piles up facts, not attempting to render Mansfield's world except as it pertains to her and not attempting extensive interpretations of her stories. Meyers paints the full picture of an inglorious life, but it is a more accurate picture, he maintains, of a life lived with spunk, courage, and artistic endeavor.

The villain of Meyers's book is Murry, who is castigated both for his role as uncaring husband and self-aggrandizing literary executor. In Meyers's biography Mansfield differs radically from the sentimental and idealized portrait that Murry had created and her previous biographers had reinforced; as Meyers portrays her, she is tough, more rebellious and daring, and more cruel and capable. Reviewers of the biography were split on these points. Mary Ellmann (*Yale Review*, Winter 1981) argued that Murry was less a villain than Meyers suggests and more a bumbler, and Hermione Lee (*New Statesman*, 15 December 1978) asserted that Meyers's portrait of Mansfield was unkind and that, despite all the information, neither the life nor the literature was illuminated. Other reviewers, such as V. S. Pritchett (*New Yorker*, 26 October 1981), praised the care and diligence that Meyers showed, and found certain areas he explored—particularly Mansfield's friendship with the Lawrences and her struggles with her disease—to be especially enlightening.

In "The Quest for Katherine Mansfield," Meyers describes the biographer as being part scholar and part detective, someone who delights in "facts for their own sake." The biographer should be one who "enjoys gossip and likes to ferret out secrets." Furthermore, "when he has finished his research, contemplated his discoveries, and understood the intellectual and emotional life of his subject, he must be able to fit everything he has learned into a meaningful pattern and to satisfy his readers' natural curiosity about the life of an extraordinary person." Several years later, in his introduction to *The Craft of Literary Biography* (1985), he modified his approach, saying that the biographer must "effectively portray the social and political background . . . [and] ought to provide a sensitive evaluation of the subject's achievement—which is the justification of the book." It is on these two counts, the providing of a background and the assessment of achievement, that the Mansfield biography is lacking, but the Lewis biography is rich in such details.

The Enemy: A Biography of Wyndham Lewis (1980) tells the story of a man T. S. Eliot called "the most fascinating personality of our time," but who has become the least-known figure of the group known as the "Men of 1914": Joyce, Eliot, Ezra Pound, and Lewis. His lifelong pre-occupations, says Meyers, were sex, health, and money, but he also managed to create a prolific artistic legacy: he wrote 50 books and 360 essays and created 100 paintings and 1,000 drawings. He was the theoretician for vorticism, the revolutionary artistic movement that shook English painting in 1914 and introduced Continental influences to England. With his emphasis on lines, he led English painting toward abstract art. By midlife, however, Lewis began to write more and to paint less. He wrote novels, social and political analysis, philosophical criticism, literary criticism, poems, travel books, and a memoir. Many people disliked or even hated him, because his caustic criticism was likely to be turned on friends as often as enemies. The one constant throughout his life was his skirmishes with other writers and painters. The constant late in his life was his relegation to the fringes of the artistic world.

Lewis has always had a few defenders, and Meyers is one of them. He believes that Lewis was one of the few in his generation deserving of the label "genius": "Lewis's range of knowledge and intellectual vitality, his gale-force energy and daring honesty, his vigorous experimentation and fighting spirit, his caustic wit and analytic ingenuity, his whip-cracking prose and astonishing invention are unmatched in the twentieth century." As a conclusion to the biography, such words ring true, because Meyers demonstrates how essential Lewis has been to modern intellectual thought, whether as a radical champion of a cause or as a reactionary critic. While remaining close to the chronological facts of Lewis's life, while puzzling through the obscured and obscuring details, Meyers shows the intellectual milieu and Lewis's achievement—subjects given less emphasis in his biography of Mansfield.

Meyers gives a shape to Lewis's life, with his several careers and many "turns," without losing the particulars. Meyers's success in telling Lewis's life story—and reviews of *The Enemy* were good, even laudatory—raises an interesting point about the connection between biographer and subject. In his essay on Lewis in *The Craft of Literary Biography*, Meyers reveals that during his research he discovered several characteristics that the two shared: they had "a similar physique, quarrelsome temperament, dislike of publishers, capacity for work and commitment to intellectual life." Perhaps this connection helped Meyers in a most vital way—to treat Lewis both sympathetically and critically, which has been a difficult task for critics because of Lewis's character.

Dust jacket for Meyers's collective biography of "confessional" poets Lowell, Randall Jarrell, John Berryman, Theodore Roethke, and Sylvia Plath

After writing two books of literary criticism—*D. H. Lawrence and the Experience of Italy* (1982) and *Disease and the Novel, 1880-1960* (1985)—and editing a collection of essays, *Ernest Hemingway: The Critical Heritage* (1982), Meyers published his next biography in 1985. This time he chose as a subject a major writer with numerous scholarly books and biographies written on him, unlike Lewis or Mansfield, and, moreover, a writer whose life has become so entangled with a public image that reading his fiction objectively has become problematic. *Hemingway: A Biography* is Meyers's attempt to sort through the true and untrue stories and the myth and reality of Hemingway's life.

Always the diligent researcher, Meyers uncovered new information on Hemingway. He gives a more accurate picture of Hemingway's wounding during World War I and argues that the wounding was less traumatic than Hemingway (and earlier biographers) made it out to be. Meyers writes about Hemingway's affair in the early 1930s with the beautiful and wealthy Jane Mason, who, Meyers suggests, influenced

Hemingway's construction of the character Margot in "The Short Happy Life of Francis Macomber." Meyers's most important discovery, as he explains in "The Quest for Hemingway" (*Virginia Quarterly Review*, Autumn 1985), came when he used the Freedom of Information Act to obtain a copy of the FBI file on Hemingway, which revealed that J. Edgar Hoover "conducted a personal vendetta against Hemingway after the novelist had founded a rival spy network in Cuba during World War II." Hoover had agents track Hemingway for the next eighteen years, even to the doors of the Mayo Clinic, which Hemingway had entered in 1960 because his depression had worsened. Hemingway's claims at the clinic about FBI harassment seemed only to substantiate the diagnosis of extreme depression, and doctors gave Hemingway electroshock therapy treatments (then a common cure for depression) in December of 1960, which impaired his memory, thereby deepening his depression and hastening his slide toward suicide.

As with Lewis the problem when writing about Hemingway is to be sympathetic and critical at the same time. Many people have written about his life and art, and their responses have usually either mythologized or damned him. Meyers attempts to sail a middle course: to discuss directly Hemingway's personal faults—the vindictiveness toward friends, the mistreatment of women, the obsessions with killing animals, and the selection of a scapegoat to relieve his own guilt—while at the same time not losing perspective on Hemingway's accomplishments, as both a person and an artist.

With Hemingway, however, this is dangerous. Most readers, scholars, and writers—particularly those old enough to remember the impact he had on a generation—seem either to revere or despise him, and reviews of Meyers's book reflect this. Raymond Carver in the *New York Times Book Review* (17 November 1985) suggested that the biographer, strongly disapproving of Hemingway, overemphasized the negative and presented unfeelingly Hemingway's self-destruction late in life. (Meyers claims that Hemingway inspired him as a young man, influencing his travels and his values, and that the biography was meant to be positive.) Wilfrid Sheed (*New York Review of Books*, 12 June 1986) claimed that Meyers was not critical enough, particularly about the "bad" novels. But *Hemingway: A Biography* was also praised for its thoroughness, its interpretations of the late novels, and, more particularly, for the discussions of writers who influenced Hemingway: Mark Twain, Stephen Crane, and especially Kipling. In some instances Meyers's book was extravagantly praised. The playwright Tom Stoppard, writing in the *Observer*, chose it as the "Best Book of the Year" in 1986, and Marcel Proust biographer George Painter called it one of the great biographies of the last fifty years.

In "The Quest for Hemingway" Meyers says that he began the biography hoping to write a livelier and more analytical book than the standard biography at that time, Carlos Baker's *Ernest Hemingway: A Life Story* (1969). Meyers also intended to incorporate into a full-length biography what Baker omitted—the revelations (in various memoirs, letters, or interviews) of adultery, lesbianism, impotence, madness, and family feuds within the Hemingway circle. These revelations would not be used to attack Hemingway but simply to explain, to dispel the myths.

Meyers's next biography, *Manic Power: Robert Lowell and His Circle* (1987), recounts the lives of the most prominent "confessional" poets: Robert Lowell, Randall Jarrell, John Berryman, and

Theodore Roethke (Sylvia Plath's life story is also told, in the epilogue). In having multiple subjects, Meyers returned to a format used in *A Fever at the Core* and *Married to Genius*. But, unlike those books, in which the biographical subjects had only slight links to each other, *Manic Power* takes up the story of these poets who were closely bound by similar family backgrounds, a fierce reverence for poetry, and the feeding of their self-destructive lives directly into their art.

In his introduction Meyers calls *Manic Power* both a group biography and a cultural history, which "examines the nourishing effects as well as the destructive dynamics in the interrelated lives of four American poets, and explores ways in which their art reflected contemporary society." Implicit in group biography is not only the belief that one life may illuminate another but also that the whole is always greater than the parts. Meyers describes the life stories of these poets in their connections to each other. By doing so, he explains much about the enormous cost of writing great poetry for the generation that began their careers after World War II, because these poets all saw themselves as victim-heroes of American culture—truth tellers who could only define themselves in opposition to a commercial, crass, and ugly society.

Lowell, Jarrell, Berryman, and Roethke all knew each other well: they corresponded, socialized, taught, and lived together; they encouraged and criticized each other in interviews, reviews, letters, and essays. Each poet had an unhappy childhood, which he attributed to his parents: fathers died or were emotionally absent; strong mothers overcompensated. And each poet led an unhappy adult life, marked by alcoholism, infidelity, or mental breakdowns. Their poetry is characterized by its willingness to engage the madness and desperation of their lives. Yet a life lived on the edge became for these poets a life not wanted: Jarrell and Berryman (and Plath) committed suicide; Roethke and Lowell died of heart attacks, brought on by their reckless ways of life.

After an opening chapter, "The Dynamics of Destruction," which introduces the poets and establishes how they connected madness and art, Meyers alternately pairs in the next three chapters the poets who have the most in common: first Lowell and Jarrell, then Jarrell and Berryman, then Berryman and Lowell. Meyers does not construct their life stories chronologically but shows the similarities of their backgrounds and their apprenticeship to poetry, and how the inter-

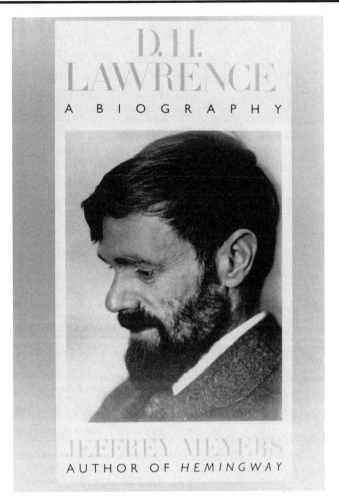

Dust jacket for Meyers's biography of a writer whose marriage is examined in Meyers's Married to Genius

twining of their lives became a crucial element not only in their artistic careers but in their private lives. Meyers does not attempt to illuminate the poetry—he was not allowed to quote lines, and he seldom interprets poems. He assumes that readers know the poems or that they will become interested in the poetry by reading about the lives. In his fifth chapter Meyers focuses on Roethke in relation to the other three. Roethke had German rather than British ancestors, was less intellectual and sophisticated, wrote poetry less cerebral and allusive (rooted instead in nature and the pastoral tradition), and, by teaching in Seattle at the University of Washington, was far removed from the centers of power in the East. Roethke was both a fierce competitor and a friend, and with his similarities to Jarrell, Berryman, and particularly Lowell—with whom he shared the condition and the knowledge that his best poetry came from his manic episodes—Roethke completes Meyers's circle.

In his long epilogue Meyers takes up Plath, who stands both inside and outside the circle. Like the others, Plath had a difficult childhood—with a loved and hated father who died when she was eight, and with a mother who sacrificed herself for her children. Plath was fascinated by German culture and history but identified with the Jews as archetypes of suffering. Though a brilliant student and an immediate literary success when she published her first book of poems, Plath always felt tormented. She first attempted suicide at the age of twenty and succeeded ten years later after feeling betrayed by her husband, Ted Hughes, who was having an affair. In the attempt to stave off that final attempt, to exert control and meaning over her life, she wrote a series of brilliant poems in the final months, published posthumously in *Ariel* (1965), the volume that solidified her reputation. What Meyers shows, in placing her at the end of his group biography, is that the tradition of manic and suicidal poets ful-

341

Chapter Sixteen

Jane Anderson, 1916-1917

I

The vivacious and reckless
Jane Anderson, ignored or neglected by Conrad's biographers, had a ~~profound~~ *significant*
influence on his life. He fell in love with her, met her secretly and--seizing the
last chance for sexual romance--wrote her passionate love letters. She became his
mistress in the summer of 1916 and was the only woman, apart from Jessie, whom we
                          distracted and   *when he was depressed by the war,*
know he slept with. She rejuvenated him and inspired him to engage in the propaganda
effort ~~of World War One~~ by going on sorties in planes and ships, and by writing of
his experiences. (Rebecca West wrote that Jane "was always going up in planes and
down in submarines.") Jane flirted with Borys, who fell for her *in Paris* during his leave
from military service. She also became Joseph Retinger's mistress, broke up his
marriage and, by arousing Conrad's jealousy, ~~seriously~~ damaged their friendship.
                                                          in
Jane stimulated Conrad's interest in journalism, in films and ~~in~~ America. And she
            principal
was the model for the seductive Rita de Lastaola in The Arrow of Gold, the first
novel he published after the war. ~~Later on, Jane's own life exemplified the Conradian~~
~~themes of divided loyalties, imprisonment, degradation, treachery and betrayal.~~
            Jane
~~Jane,~~ an only child, was born Foster Anderson in Atlanta, Georgia, on January 6
                                                            and beautiful
in about 1888. Her mother Ellen Luckie, a ~~fabulous beauty and~~ wealthy socialite,
was the daughter of Foster Luckie, who owned and developed a great deal of property
in Atlanta, and for whom Luckie Street was named. Soon after Jane's birth her
apparently ill-matched parents separated, and her rough, likeable father, Robert
"Red" Anderson, took off for the southwest. Kitty Crawford, Jane's college friend,
described him as "a tall, handsome, reckless-looking man with a humorous quirk to
his mouth and blue-steel sharpness in his eyes." Retinger gave a more colorful
and no doubt exaggerated account of Jane's father:

> When I first met him he was seventy-eight. His breakfast consisted of a
> bottle of whiskey and a 2 lb. steak. Anderson had been an associate of
> Buffalo Bill. He was the head of the police while the Panama Canal was

Page from the typescript for Joseph Conrad: A Biography *(by permission of Jeffrey Meyers)*

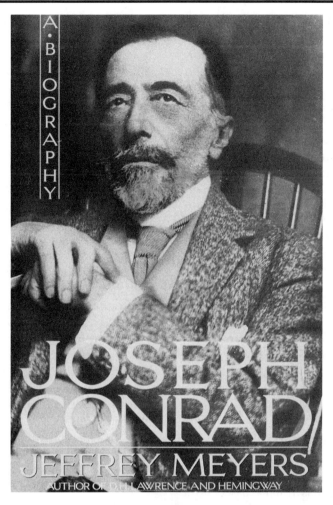

Dust jacket for Meyers's biography of the writer who once commented, "I am not a personage for an orderly biography, either auto or otherwise."

filled itself in the younger Plath, whose joining of poetic power and madness came, at least in part, from the examples of her teachers and masters—Roethke and Lowell.

All these poets have had much written about their lives and art. Meyers found his own niche in that scholarship by focusing *Manic Power* on the relation between madness, power, and the poetic act, and by demonstrating the variations on the same theme by taking up the lives of several poets. But if the book is good as a group biography, it is less so as the cultural history that Meyers claims it to be. Emphasizing the poets' similarities of background and character, Meyers gives scant consideration to their personal and artistic connections to American culture.

Meyers has edited collections of essays on T. E. Lawrence (1989) and Graham Greene (also 1989), a collection of interviews and memoirs on Robert Lowell (1988), a collection of essays on biography (*The Biographer's Art*, 1989), and compiled a selection of his own original essays on biography, *The Spirit of Biography* (1989). After editing and contributing to two collections of essays on Lawrence, *D. H. Lawrence and Tradition* (1985) and *The Legacy of D. H. Lawrence* (1987), Meyers wrote a new biography of him, published in June 1990. The biography enlarges upon work that Meyers had already done—he wrote about D. H. and Frieda in *Married to Genius*, and Lawrence figures centrally in Mansfield's biography.

In April 1991 Meyers published *Joseph Conrad: A Biography*. Meyers's comprehensive study of Conrad's life and works includes details of his relationships with other writers, such as Henry James, H. G. Wells, Stephen Crane, and Ford Madox Ford, and it presents new information on Conrad's suicide attempt, his domestic life, and his 1916 affair with Jane Anderson, an American journalist. There is also a discussion of "The

Strong Man," a little-known and unpublished film scenario by Conrad. *Joseph Conrad: A Biography* is Meyers's attempt to form a complete portrait of a writer who was purposely deceptive and enigmatic, saying at one point, "I am not a personage for an orderly biography." Most reviewers have praised Meyers's book. Roland Wulbert in *Booklist* (1 March 1991) wrote: "Meyers' account . . . is both scholarly and evocative, so that we learn the intriguing trivium that Vladimir Nabokov's grandfather repressed a rebellion incited by Conrad's father, but we also come to understand the political, social, and physical contexts in which the novelist lived."

Meyers's research as a biographer has always been marked by its diligence and care. Perhaps what distinguishes him most is his willingness to confront any difficult issues in the subject's life that his research might uncover. "Contemporary readers," Meyers writes in his introduction to *The Craft of Biography*, "expect to learn the whole truth about the psychological, sexual and medical aspects of the subject." And though "Tell all" might seem Meyers's motto, he has written repeatedly in essays that the "all" should not be told without a careful form. The biographer must compose a story: select, organize, and arrange the facts.

For Meyers that story is usually based on a psychological model; and because he emphasizes familial and other personal relationships and keeps the focus on the subject's life, Meyers writes relatively spare biographies, unlike other biographers who re-create the culture and history within the subject's lifetime. Meyers's biographies suggest the various ways that art comes from or compensates for the wounds in life. Yet he does not stress the art, does not write critical biographies, though he began writing and has continued to write literary criticism. Keeping the focus always on the life, Meyers uses the literary texts to explain the life, not the life to illuminate the subject's writings. Meyers feels no reluctance to move easily from text to life; he remains opposed to the theoretical arguments that insist all texts are fictions, that facts are dependent solely on individual perception, and that no language is purely referential.

Meyers has stated repeatedly that the biographer is an investigative reporter, that hard work and a fondness for facts are essential, and that the task of the biographer is more closely allied to the historian than the novelist. In his introduction to *The Spirit of Biography* Meyers has also stated that his method was captured best in a letter of Jacob Burckhardt's: "My own substitute [for abstract thought] is my effort to achieve with every day a more intense immediacy in the perception of essentials. By nature I cling to the tangible, to visible reality and to history. But I have a bent for incessantly looking for parallels in coordinating facts and have thus succeeded on my own in arriving at a few generalized principles."

Papers:
Meyers's manuscripts are in the Huntington Library; John F. Kennedy Library, Boston; Harvard Library; Harry Ransom Humanities Research Center, University of Texas; and the University of Tulsa Library.

Charles Norman
(9 May 1904 -   )

Bruce Fogelman

BOOKS: *The Far Harbour: A Sea Narrative* (New York: Blue Faun, 1924);

Tragic Beaches: A Book of Narrative Poems About the Sea (New York: Jacobs, 1925);

Poems (New York: Knopf, 1929);

The Bright World and Other Poems (New York: Morrow, 1930; London & Toronto: Dent, 1930);

The Savage Century (Prairie City, Ill.: Decker, 1942);

A Soldier's Diary (New York: Scribners, 1944);

Northwest: Poems (Whitehorse, Yukon: Hanley, 1945);

The Muses' Darling: The Life of Christopher Marlowe (New York & Toronto: Rinehart, 1946; London: Falcon, 1947); republished as *Christopher Marlowe: The Muses' Darling* (Indianapolis: Bobbs-Merrill, 1971);

So Worthy a Friend: William Shakespeare (New York & Toronto: Rinehart, 1947; revised edition, New York: Collier, 1961);

The Case of Ezra Pound (New York: Bodley, 1948; revised and enlarged edition, New York: Funk & Wagnalls, 1968);

The Playmaker of Avon (Philadelphia: McKay, 1949);

The Well of the Past (New York: Doubleday, 1949);

Mr. Upstairs and Mr. Downstairs: Introducing Jane Jonquil and Her Father (New York: Harper, 1950);

The Crumb That Walked: More About Jane Jonquil (New York: Harper, 1951);

Dominick Dragon; or, The Happy Fellow (Drexel Hill, Pa.: Bell, 1951);

Mr. Oddity: Samuel Johnson, LL.D. (Drexel Hill, Pa.: Bell, 1951; London: Murray, 1952);

The Pundit and the Player: Dr. Johnson and Mr. Garrick (New York: McKay, 1951);

Hunch, Munch and Crunch: More About the Jonquils (New York: Harper, 1952);

The Shepherd of the Ocean: Sir Walter Raleigh (New York: McKay, 1952);

Rake Rochester (New York: Crown, 1954; London: Allen, 1955);

To a Different Drum: The Story of Henry David Thoreau (New York: Harper, 1954);

The Genteel Murderer (New York: Macmillan, 1956);

John Muir: Father of Our National Parks (New York: Messner, 1957);

The Flight and Adventures of Charles II (New York: Random House, 1958);

The Magic-Maker: E. E. Cummings (New York: Macmillan, 1958); revised as *E. E. Cummings: The Magic-Maker* (New York: Duell, Sloan & Pearce, 1964); republished as *E. E. Cummings: A Biography* (New York: Dutton, 1967);

Ezra Pound (New York: Macmillan, 1960; revised edition, New York: Funk & Wagnalls, 1969; London: Macdonald, 1969);

Orimha of the Mohawks: The Story of Pierre Esprit Radisson Among the Indians (New York: Macmillan, 1961);

Selected Poems (New York: Macmillan, 1962);

The Long Bows of Agincourt (Indianapolis & New York: Bobbs-Merrill, 1963);

Discoverers of America (New York: Crowell, 1968);

Poets & People (Indianapolis: Bobbs-Merrill, 1972);

The Portents of the Air, and Other Poems (Indianapolis: Bobbs-Merrill, 1973);

The Hornbeam Tree and Other Poems (New York: Holt, 1988);

A Study in Mauve (Middletown, R.I.: Bartlett, 1988).

OTHER: *Boswell's Life of Johnson*, edited by Norman (New York: Collier, 1961);

Poets on Poetry, edited by Norman (New York: Collier, 1962; New York: Free Press / London: Collier-Macmillan, 1965);

Come Live With Me: Five Centuries of Romantic Poetry, edited, with an introduction and notes, by Norman (New York: McKay, 1966);

"The Library is Inside," in *Redwood Papers: A Bicentennial Collection*, edited by Lorraine Dexter and Alan Pryce-Jones (Newport, R.I.: Red-

Charles Norman in Newport, Rhode Island (photograph by Diana Norman)

wood Library & Athenaeum, 1976), pp. 119-129.

SELECTED PERIODICAL PUBLICATIONS—
UNCOLLECTED: "To the Memory of Francesco Bianco, Together with Eleven Poems Translated by Francesco Bianco and Williard R. Trask and a Drawing of the Poet by His Daughter, Pamela Bianco," *Literary Review*, 1 (Winter 1957-1958): 37-50;

"Winston Churchill, Author," *Bulletin of the New York Public Library*, 65 (March 1961): 154-158;

"Portrait of a Nuclear Physicist," *Texas Quarterly*, 5 (Spring 1962): 116-124;

"E. E. Cummings. Notes Toward a Final Chapter," *Texas Quarterly*, 7 (Winter 1964): 87-94.

Charles Norman, a prolific and influential writer, is best known for his biographies of the poets Christopher Marlowe, E. E. Cummings, and Ezra Pound. Norman was born in Russia on 9 May 1904 and was the youngest of six sons. He was brought to the United States when he was three or four years old and raised in New York City. Having enrolled at New York University in 1921, he left in 1924, as he said in an unpublished interview, "to become a full-time poet, and caught poverty," though he was sustained at first by the patronage of James Buell Munn, then a dean at New York University and later head of the Department of English at Harvard. During the summer of 1923 Norman had journeyed to South America as a seaman on a freighter, and a book of poetry based on his experience, *The Far Harbour: A Sea Narrative*, was published the next year, followed in 1925 by another collection, *Tragic Beaches*. He continued his career as a poet in Paris in 1926 and 1927, wrote for the *Paris Times* in 1928, and published two more volumes of poetry by the end of the decade.

Norman's interest in biography had begun in 1925 when, during a visit to London, he picked up a copy of Leslie Hotson's new book,

Norman circa 1940 (photograph by Marion Morehouse)

The Death of Christopher Marlowe, in a small book-shop: "I felt myself being watched and looked up and saw everyone looking at me. I had begun to read Hotson's slender book and had just turned the last page." He began working on his biography of Marlowe during the 1930s while employed as an editor for the North American Newspaper Alliance (1931-1934) and for United Press (1934) and as a staff writer for the Associated Press (1934-1939). He resigned from the Associated Press to finish his book but experienced writer's block, and he went on to work for Time, Incorporated, in 1941 and then for the newspaper *PM*. In 1942 he volunteered for the army and became an infantry lieutenant the following year. He took with him *The Works of Christopher Marlowe* (1910): his first step in writing a literary biography is to read or reread all of the subject's works. In 1944 he published *A Soldier's Diary*, a new collection of poems dealing with his experience in the military.

Upon returning from the service in 1945, Norman resumed his work for *PM* and completed his biography of Marlowe, which was published the following year as *The Muses' Darling: The Life of Christopher Marlowe*. Norman set out to achieve what no earlier biographer of Marlowe

had done: to present him, his friends, and his enemies as people and as "Elizabethans against the background of their time"; and Norman wanted to illuminate Marlowe's life, he says, by "showing how his familiars lived, whenever the records dealing exclusively with him seemed inadequate." Though fully substantiated by extant documents pertaining to Marlowe, Norman's biography shows dramatic intensity as he reconstructs scenes and events in Marlowe's life, in the lives of his family members, and in the lives of his contemporaries. Norman vividly re-creates the setting and atmosphere in which Marlowe dwelt, and he perceptively explores Marlowe's relation to the English court and the role it played in shaping his cynical character. Norman's observations about Elizabethan literary practice contribute to his convincing assessment of Marlowe's achievement. For instance, it was Marlowe who almost without precedent brought out the full dramatic potential of the blank-verse form that dominated Elizabethan drama: "At the very beginning of his career we see him bringing to his work a quality never before found in English verse, a breathless and dramatic lyricism that is all but edged with flame. . . ." Marlowe's refinements of the form, in turn, profoundly influenced William Shake-

Norman at the MacDowell Colony, Peterborough, New Hampshire, 1946 (photograph by Margery Lewis)

speare. Republished in 1971 as *Christopher Marlowe: The Muses' Darling*, Norman's biography remains an important resource.

As Norman shows in *The Muses' Darling*, the relationship between Marlowe and Shakespeare played a crucial role in the literary development of both men. Before Norman's first biography went to press, he—acting on his editor's suggestion—undertook a biography of Shakespeare. Published in 1947, *So Worthy a Friend: William Shakespeare* is a tribute to its subject, though it steers clear of the idolatry that can be a pitfall of such an undertaking. Norman is the first to use source materials to trace the events of Shakespeare's life in sequence and to draw conclusions about his character and motivation and the way they were shaped by his experiences, his background, and his social context. Careful readings of Shakespeare's works, especially the sonnets, provide a major source of insight into his life, yet Norman never plumbs the works for evidence to support preconceived notions about the Bard. Norman's common-sense approach effectively lays to rest some popular notions about Shakespeare, such as the belief that he was a homosex-

ual, and the many conjectures about the "real" authors of his plays. As in Norman's biography of Marlowe, in *So Worthy a Friend* suspense is created by vivid depictions of the subject, his family, and his personal and business relationships. Sidney Cox, a professor of English at Dartmouth, wrote Norman to compliment him on "the first biography of Shakespeare that has something akin to the spirit of its subject in the writing."

In 1946 Norman spent the first of many summers writing at the MacDowell Colony in Peterborough, New Hampshire; occasionally he also lived and wrote at Yaddo Artists Colony. In 1947, at the invitation of Dean Warren Bower, Norman returned to New York University as an instructor in Shakespeare until 1950. Since then he has followed his resolution never to hold down another job and has devoted himself primarily to his work as a biographer and poet. He has also been occupied as a painter since 1937, when he discovered his talent in watercolors. He had a one-man show at the prestigious Julien Levy Gallery in New York in 1940 and has been represented in many exhibits since. He describes himself as a self-taught, lyrical painter.

Self-portrait, Jan. 5, 1938 (oil, 22 x 33 in.)

The Magic-Maker
E. E. CUMMINGS

by CHARLES NORMAN

The Macmillan Company · New York · 1958

Frontispiece and title page for the first biography of Cummings, who became a close friend of Norman in 1925

Norman turned his attention in 1948 to Pound, whom he considers "the greatest single influence on American and British poetry." Pound's wartime radio broadcasts from Rome had caused him to be charged with treason, but then he was found mentally unfit to stand trial and was in 1948 confined at St. Elizabeth's Hospital in Washington, D.C., for psychiatric treatment. Building on an essay about Pound that he had published in *PM* in 1945, Norman compiled *The Case of Ezra Pound* (1948), a short assessment of Pound's life and work, his association with *Poetry* magazine, his ideas on economics, and his radio broadcasts. Norman also collected statements about Pound from Cummings, William Carlos Williams, Louis Zukofsky, Conrad Aiken, and F. O. Matthiessen. The book is intended to present Pound's case impartially: Norman praises Pound's poetry and allows the relevant documents—including excerpts from the radio broadcasts and a transcript of the sanity hearing—to speak for themselves. This brief work on Pound was the prelude to Norman's later, full-length biography of him.

In the late 1940s Norman also began to write for a younger audience and to create fiction for adults. *The Playmaker of Avon*, a young adult's version of *So Worthy a Friend*, was published in 1949 and was followed by works in the same vein on Samuel Johnson (*The Pundit and the Player*, 1951), Sir Walter Raleigh (1952), Henry David Thoreau (1954), John Muir (1957), Charles II (1958), and Pierre Esprit Radisson (1961). Norman's book on Thoreau was translated into Arabic and Spanish. Norman has also written a volume of Americana, *Discoverers of America* (1968), and various volumes of stories and poems for children, from *Mr. Upstairs and Mr. Downstairs* in 1950 to *The Hornbeam Tree and Other Poems* in 1988. His first novel for adults, *The Well of the Past*, was published in 1949; his second, based on his experiences during the 1920s, was *Dominick Dragon; or, The Happy Fellow*, published in 1951.

Norman's next three biographies were to deal with eighteenth- and nineteenth-century subjects. The first, *Mr. Oddity: Samuel Johnson, LL.D.*, was published in 1951. Because Johnson, best-

at first,
To my dismay, I found Professor Brooke's ~~texts;from~~
original
~~accurate~~ texts hard going. Those "u's" and "v's"! The "i"

for "j". ~~(which did not exist)~~ I persisted. From that time on

I could not bear to read Marlowe, ~~in modern spelling, and have~~ or any
in modern
had ~~no difficulty with any~~ other Elizabethan work, spelling.

~~About my first book~~
some   valuable   on
I believe I learned ~~many~~ ~~lessons;on~~ lessons ~~and~~ how to

write ~~biographies~~ biography with my first attempt. What do
had
documents really say to a man or woman who ~~has~~ lived in the
and not chiefly   a
world of men and women, ~~but mainly~~ in the cloister of college

or university, ~~and then in another cloister, of another school,~~

~~teaching.~~ What are the probabilit~~ies?~~ is the first question
undergone varied, a vague or
to ask about any document that has ~~had different~~ interpretations~~?~~.
sensational
The probabilities are ~~that~~ unsensational, ~~Since;writing~~ As
some   at
~~As~~ for "conspiracies," ~~which many~~ writers on Marlowe ~~think;they~~
of them
~~have;discovered;and~~hastened to publish, I ~~always~~ have been

suspicious ~~about conspiracy theories~~ ever since ~~The Muses;~~
For some of them
my work on The Muses' Darling. ~~My advice to writers of biog-~~
alive and
~~raphy is, first and foremost, to write about;if they are truly~~
in Deptford
~~literary, to choos~~
~~from his "mysterious death", to the assertion that he had~~
with,
~~not been killed but hid, somewhere, and wrote under the name of~~

~~William Shakespeare.~~

~~Moral judgments have no place in biography. No biographer~~
hatred
~~should feel superior;shk bring hatred or feelings of superiority~~
a
~~to his subject, as a recent "official" biography;;; biography~~
as
serious
as I am
~~has done.~~

Pages from Norman's notes on biography (by permission of Charles Norman)

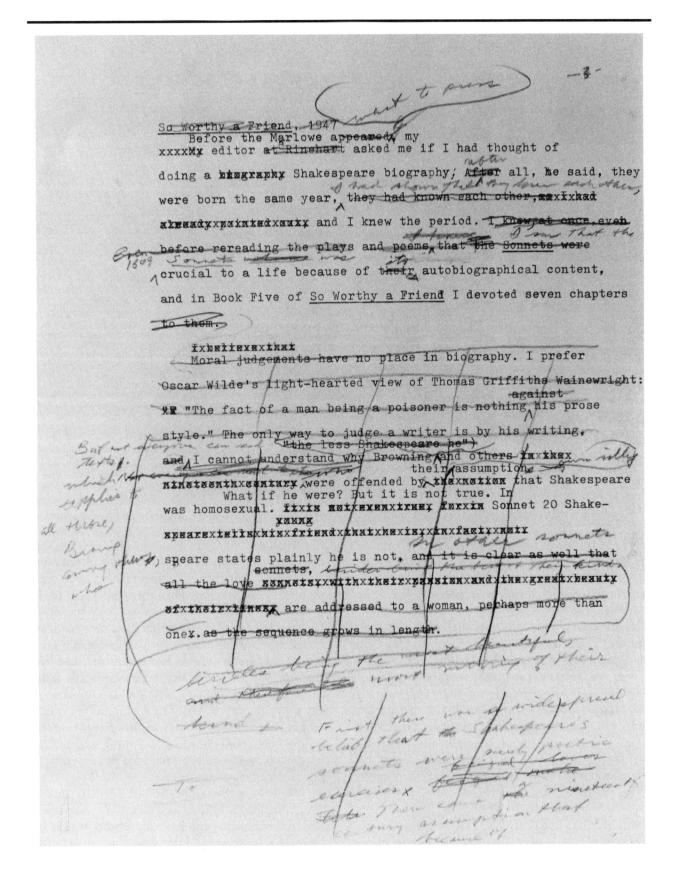

Dust jacket for the 1960 biography of the man Norman calls "the greatest single influence on American and British poetry"

known for his *Dictionary* (1755) and his *Lives of the Poets* (1779-1781), was also reputedly the greatest conversationalist of his day, Norman draws extensively on the dialogue recorded in James Boswell's *The Life of Samuel Johnson, LL.D.* (1791) and in other contemporary records. Norman presents a portrait of Johnson's appearance and his sometimes outrageous manners and demonstrates his impact on other socially prominent members of his circle. Johnson's own journals and diaries provide the material for minute accounts of his daily activities, especially during his tour of Scotland. But perhaps the most striking feature of Norman's biography is its focus on Johnson's inner life, especially the development of his spiritual consciousness.

Rake Rochester, published in 1954, traces John Wilmot, Earl of Rochester's careers as a court figure, as a notorious rake, and most of all as an accomplished and greatly admired poet. Like the biography of Johnson, *Rake Rochester* makes extensive use of conversation to bring to

life its subject and his intrigues. *The Genteel Murderer* (1956) is a detailed and insightful narrative of Thomas Griffiths Wainewright's lives as a painter who was accomplished enough to be praised by William Blake, as a writer admired by Charles Lamb, and as a serial poisoner who was exiled to a penal colony in Van Dieman's Land (now Tasmania), where he spent the last five years of his life; he insisted always on his status as a refined gentleman and on the injustice of his punishment. Norman's treatment of Wainewright, like his biographies of other controversial figures such as Rochester and Pound, appears impartial: "moral judgments have no place in biography," according to Norman.

Following the publication of *The Genteel Murderer*, Norman's editor at Macmillan asked him who the subject of his next biography would be. Norman's reply was: "only E. E. Cummings, if he approves." Norman proceeded to ask Cummings "if your Highness will permit" the project. Cummings replied, "My lowness will be honored." Published in 1958, *The Magic-Maker: E. E. Cummings* was the first biography of the poet, and in it Norman uses his personal experience—he and Cummings met in 1925 and were close friends until Cummings's death in 1962; in fact, the last letter Cummings wrote was to Norman. Norman also drew on his contact with Cummings's friends and relatives, as well as on the poet's works. The biography includes a detailed account of how Cummings's family background and youthful experiences contributed to his development as a poet and as a painter. He learned much, for instance, from his father, who was a sailor, fisherman, woodsman, actor, painter, photographer, carpenter, plumber, preacher, and teacher of English, political economics, and sociology at Harvard; his mother's vivaciousness, joy, and generosity also helped to shape the poet's attitudes, as did the ideas of his neighbor, the psychologist and philosopher William James. Cummings's undergraduate years at Harvard were also formative, especially for his acquaintance there with Foster Damon, John Dos Passos, and Robert Hillyer: "Practically everything I know about painting and poetry came to me through Damon," Cummings once told Norman. Norman's sensitive readings of selected poems offer valuable insights into Cummings's working method and his idiosyncratic punctuation and syntax, and Norman compares the poet's technique with Pablo Picasso's style of painting. The book subordinates chronology to a portrayal of Cummings's character and artistry, and it ends as more than a biography: it is a memoir and a tribute by one who knew Cummings well.

In 1926 Norman met his first wife, Anne Rose Morton, of Asheville, North Carolina, in Paris. With her he had a daughter, Nancy. His second wife was Joy Nicholson, a dancer and actress he met while she was performing with a USO troupe during World War II. In 1960 Norman met and married the painter Diana Louise Marshall, who was born in Vancouver and raised in England. They have had two husband-and-wife exhibits of their art, the first at the Gotham Book Mart Gallery in New York in 1969, the second at the Newport Art Museum in 1979. In 1973 they moved from New York to Newport, Rhode Island, where they currently reside.

Norman's most recent biography for adults is *Ezra Pound* (1960), which includes a penetrating analysis of Pound's early development and especially his college years, an analysis mostly based on recollections solicited from Pound's classmates. Norman convincingly dramatizes the flamboyance of Pound's personality and the excitement of the era when he was an aspiring poet, newly arrived in London and already commanding the attention and exerting the influence that were to help redirect the course of English and American poetry. Norman also provides a clear and well-substantiated assessment of Pound's social and literary impact on his contemporaries, including Cummings, Basil Bunting, T. S. Eliot, Robert Frost, H. D., Ernest Hemingway, James Joyce, Wyndham Lewis, William Carlos Williams, William Butler Yeats, and Louis Zukofsky. Especially important were the compression and intensity Pound brought to modern literature through his conception of imagism and the high degree of control he exerted over the contents of *Poetry* and other major literary journals. As Norman puts it, "one-half of Pound's correspondence is the history of poetry in our time and a curriculum for poets." Norman draws reasonable, objective conclusions about the origins of the anti-Semitism expressed by Pound and some of his contemporaries.

Poets & People (1972) is a memoir of Norman's experiences and acquaintances—among them some of the most prominent figures in art and literature of the period—in Greenwich Village and Paris during the 1920s and 1930s. He continues to paint and write poetry and is currently at work on his "New and Selected Poems." He has read from his poetry and given lectures on Marlowe, Cummings, and Pound at Black Mountain College, New York University, Princeton University, the College of William and Mary, the University of Texas, University of Rhode Island, Providence College, Columbia University, and Salve Regina College in Newport, where he has also taught a course on poetry.

Norman's biographies, in their insight, their lucidity, and their dramatic immediacy, are as much works of art as his poems. What he wrote in reference to Shakespeare applies equally well to him: "The work of an artist is his autobiography," and much of Charles Norman is to be found in his pages on others.

Papers:
Charles Norman's papers are at the Harry Ransom Humanities Research Center, University of Texas at Austin.

William H. Pritchard

(12 November 1932 -   )

Glen M. Johnson
Catholic University of America

BOOKS: *Wyndham Lewis* (New York: Twayne, 1968);

Seeing Through Everything: English Writers 1918-1940 (New York: Oxford University Press, 1977; London: Faber & Faber, 1977);

Lives of the Modern Poets (New York: Oxford University Press, 1980; London: Faber & Faber, 1980);

Frost: A Literary Life Reconsidered (New York: Oxford University Press, 1984);

Randall Jarrell: A Literary Life (New York: Farrar, Straus & Giroux, 1990).

OTHER: "*North of Boston*: Frost's Poetry of Dialogue," in *In Defense of Reading*, edited by Reuben A. Brower and Richard Poirier (New York: Dutton, 1962), pp. 38-56;

"Wildness of Logic in Modern Lyric," in *Forms of Lyric*, edited by Brower (New York: Columbia University Press, 1970), pp. 127-150;

"The Uses of Yeats's Poetry," in *Twentieth-Century Literature in Retrospect*, edited by Brower (Cambridge, Mass.: Harvard University Press, 1971), pp. 111-132;

Profiles in Literature: Wyndham Lewis, edited by Pritchard (New York: Humanities Press, 1972; London: Routledge & Kegan Paul, 1972);

W. B. Yeats: A Critical Anthology, edited by Pritchard (Harmondsworth, U.K.: Penguin, 1972);

"American Prose 1945--," in *The Norton Anthology of American Literature*, edited by Pritchard and others (New York: Norton, 1979; revised, 1985; revised again, 1989);

"Larkin's Presence," in *Philip Larkin: The Man and His Work*, edited by Dale Salwak (Iowa City: University of Iowa Press, 1989), pp. 71-89;

Randall Jarrell: Selected Poems, edited by Pritchard (New York: Farrar, Straus & Giroux, 1990).

SELECTED PERIODICAL PUBLICATIONS—
UNCOLLECTED: "The Grip of Frost," *Hudson Review*, 29 (Spring 1976): 185-204;

"The Six Modern Poets," *Hudson Review*, 30 (Autumn 1977): 451-456;

"Reconsideration: F. R. Leavis (1895-1978)," *New Republic*, 178 (3 June 1978): 36-38;

"The Crisis in Criticism?," *Hudson Review*, 37 (Winter 1984-1985): 637-646;

"Reuben A. Brower," *American Scholar*, 54 (Spring 1985): 239-247;

"The Scholar and the Soap," *New Republic*, 193 (9 September 1985): 37-40;

"West of Boston: Robert Frost," *Yale Review*, 76 (Spring 1987): 380-385;

"Salvos from the Gender War," *Hudson Review*, 41 (Summer 1988): 370-376.

William H. Pritchard once said, "I don't think of myself as a bona fide biographer in either the old-fashioned or recent American sense—I'm not a sleuth or a painstaking researcher nor somebody with a theory about what made Frost or Jarrell go right or wrong"; he believes his books "fall between criticism and biography." His "literary lives" of Robert Frost (1984), Randall Jarrell (1990), and other twentieth-century writers eschew much of what characterizes recent biography. Drawing mainly from published sources, his books do not bulge with archival research. Historical and sociological background is minimal. Freudian speculation is shunned, as are assertions about what an individual "must have thought" in given situations. Feet of clay are not hidden, but Pritchard does not set up standards of behavior or political correctness against which his subject is condescendingly measured. The writer's persona is accepted as an essential element of his literary life.

The biographical chapter of Pritchard's *Wyndham Lewis* (1968) is titled "A Career of Performances," and the life of a writer interests Pritchard primarily in how its "problems and annoyances have been transformed into the energy of a successful literary performance." "Voice" is

William H. Pritchard, 1990

the key term, since it is through the writer's published or otherwise recorded voice that his literary life remains alive. Voice is also a useful notion in understanding Pritchard's "personal approach"—he cites this phrase from F. R. Leavis—to his own writing. Refined in the classroom, Pritchard's reading and commenting voice is at the center of his writing, whether biographical, critical, or essayistic: each of his books is a vade mecum.

Pritchard was born on 12 November 1932 in Binghamton, New York, and grew up in nearby Johnson City. His father, William Harrison Pritchard, was a lawyer for the Endicott Johnson shoe company; his mother, Marion LaGrange Pritchard, was a public-school music supervisor. The young Pritchard began piano lessons before the age of five, and as an adult has performed in recital; his "musical sense" informs his notion of

poetry as vocal performance. He entered Amherst College at sixteen, graduating in 1953 with a B.A. in philosophy and an undergraduate thesis on William James. Accepted into Columbia University's Ph.D. program in philosophy, Pritchard spent most of his year there auditing classes in literature, notably Lionel Trilling's. Deciding not to return to Columbia, he was admitted to Harvard's English program in fall 1954 and stayed to complete the M.A. in 1956 and the Ph.D. in 1960. He married Marietta Perl, a Radcliffe student and later a journalist, on 24 August 1957; they have three sons, David, Michael, and William James Pritchard. Pritchard returned to Amherst in 1958 as an instructor; since 1982 he has been Henry Clay Folger Professor of English.

Pritchard's Harvard dissertation was "The Uses of Nature in Robert Frost's Poetry," but he

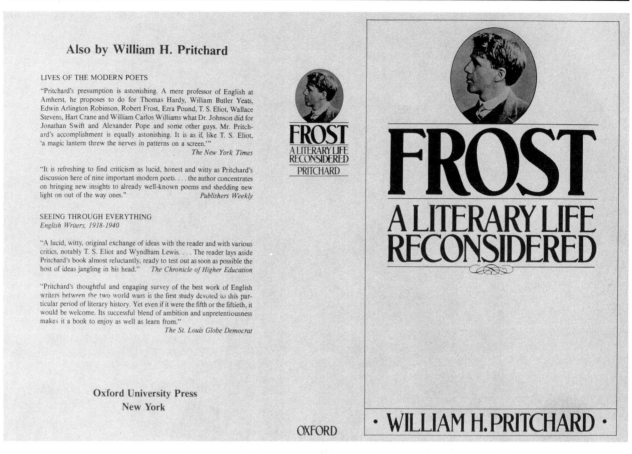

Dust jacket for the book in which Pritchard sought to correct the portrait of a selfish, vindictive Robert Frost that Lawrance Thompson presented in his authorized biography of the poet

waited years to publish "The Grip of Frost" (*Hudson Review*, Spring 1976), which led to the key chapter of his *Lives of the Modern Poets* (1980). Early in his publishing career, Pritchard concentrated on British literature, as in his *Wyndham Lewis* and *Seeing Through Everything: English Writers 1918-1940* (1977). Neither book is, strictly speaking, biographical, but in them Pritchard developed the methods he was to use in three subsequent volumes of "literary lives." *Wyndham Lewis*, in Twayne's English Authors Series, follows Twayne's format of a biographical overview followed by a basically chronological critical discussion of the author's works. Later he began to integrate biographical facts into his critical chapters; this has remained the essential format of Pritchard's books about poets. He later remembered being drawn to Lewis at least partly because he was a significant writer who was outside of—indeed, banished from—Leavis's "great tradition." In terms of Pritchard's later writings, one can see other significance in his choice of Lewis. Like Jarrell, Lewis was a writer whose "career of

performances" in several modes—he was a literary polemicist, a cultural critic, and a graphic artist as well as a novelist—gives him a larger claim to attention than his accomplishment in any specific genre. And, like Frost's, Lewis's reputation was damaged by perceptions of his "churlish self-regard" and by his reactionary political statements. Pritchard's way of dealing with this problem—admitting that life and work cannot be "neatly" separated but holding that the author's works present a valid "best self"—anticipates his handling of the life of Frost.

Seeing Through Everything is a reader's guide to the literature of England between the world wars, in which Pritchard (citing Leavis) risks the "danger" of the "'personal approach' as a *sine qua non* of literary response." A problematical book, its claim to be "neither survey [nor] history" comports uneasily with what Denis Donoghue called Pritchard's "project: to deal in some fashion with 20 years, about 20 writers, perhaps 25 books, and a spirit of the age . . . too much to ask of one critic in a book of 234 pages" (*New*

GUNN 4PIT ALUMNI
4PIT Coover --
[Thurs]

Jarrell's "post-modernism"--spoke about Lowell in these terms.
Nothing magical or superordinary about the poet's situation. He is as other
men, only more so. Jarrell's Wordsworthian notion of what poetry does:

How "A Girl in a Library" is "about" life in distinctive way. Point is to
work yourself into a situation where you are divided, marveling, ironic and
humorous, yet...

Jarrell's attitude toward Reading, librariesPoetry and the Age

106 Children Selecteing Books in a Library: real ambiguity (confusion?) here at
certain points, but the message is clear enough. A Radical thing to believe
and write a poem about.

98-9 "We learn from you to understand but not to change"

War poems and their relation to "Life"
    Losses: what is the loss here?
    Transient Barracks sense orf the "real"
    The Front:

Coover   Nostalgia and importance for Jarrell: "In Those Days" 230
Gunn   Loss and Change in "Woman at Washington Zoo"

    In Those Days: (from Zoo) "In those days everything was better", as the
    fairy tale has it. J. finds these tales revivifying, exclamatory-making.
    Can imagine what sort of tone he'll take toward "these days."

    What is the loss, "losses"--really the fact of Loss
    An early poem (113) 90 North is bleak vision of "the fruit of experience".
    With this vision of life--if we call it that--there is nothing between childhood
    and the cold end

    How much this has to do with being a poet? On the other hand, Jarrell the man
    full of worldly things (cf. Robert Lowell's tribute). But in the poems he wanted
    to speak sadder, more lost, and to rediscover the child within him.

    Many poems celebrate imagined changes, or cry out for their necessity: "Absent
    with Official Leave" (171)--soldier sleeps and dreams into childhood

    Woman at Washington Zoo "aging but /with/ knowledge of the trap?--is this
    about women particularly? (Frost's "Most of It""00==change me, change me.
    But to what? Annihilation? Reincarnation? Jarrell can't say.

    But he can make the lament felt: "Aging"
    Can dream into childhood fantasy (regressive) of changelessness
            "Windows" 232, or "Nestus Gurley"

    The lost World (1965) a continuation of what J. now had discovered were his
    major concerns as a poet. He Had discovered his voice, and often it spoke either
    through himself, or through the voice of a woman, imagined.
            (Frost, dramatic monologues, talk about women in North of Boston).

    "Next Days"

Page from Pritchard's notes for a lecture on Randall Jarrell (by permission of William H. Pritchard)

York Times Book Review, 9 October 1977). Similarly, Pritchard's claim to have no "thesis or over-arching idea" is not fully consistent with his title, which emphasizes the writers' cynical rejection of systems and pieties.

In his introduction to *Seeing Through Everything*, Pritchard acknowledges the origin of his approach in the classroom, "because so much of my own argument about and discussion of books takes place" there. A 1985 tribute in *American Scholar* to Reuben A. Brower, his major professor at Harvard, helps to clarify the importance to Pritchard of his training in the "slow reading" course Brower developed at Amherst (where Pritchard took it) and later moved to Harvard (where it became the well-known "Hum. 6" in which Pritchard taught). Works were chosen for their perceived literary merit—Brower believed that "some works were better than other ones and that an objective account of their value could be given"—and not organized by historical period or theme. Thus one can understand Pritchard's sense that his own books are not surveys and have no thesis, and also his willingness to make literary evaluations and be called "elitist" for doing so. As he says in his tribute, "Brower didn't mind 'privileging' or 'valorizing' certain works of art . . . and that was half the fun." Above all, Pritchard learned from Brower "the centrality of the vocal performance" in teaching, as well as the larger importance of voice in poetry, a notion Brower got at least partly from Frost.

Paul de Man, who also taught in "Hum. 6" at Harvard, later wrote of the difficulty of using Brower's classroom method in written prose. Pritchard acknowledges the problem: "on the printed page, something was assuredly lost: the immediacy, the actuality, the intimacy of reading something aloud with a class— . . . even as skillful a writer as Brower found this a little more than he could get into print." Nevertheless, Brower tried, and so does Pritchard. One useful way to approach Pritchard's books is to see in them the struggle to convey on the printed page the teacher's voice presenting the voice of the poet.

Lives of the Modern Poets deals with nine twentieth-century poets he finds "most interesting and important": Thomas Hardy, W. B. Yeats, Edward Arlington Robinson, Frost, Ezra Pound, T. S. Eliot, Wallace Stevens, Hart Crane, and William Carlos Williams. Pritchard remembers that the "biographical angle" was motivated partly "by

the demands of the market. . . . Oxford [University Press] was eager about a book . . . that wouldn't be 'just' critical." His title's allusion to Samuel Johnson's *Lives of the English Poets* (1779-1781) is useful to Pritchard's project, since, as he points out, Johnson's *Lives* were in fact prefaces, less concerned with biographical narration than with delineation of a poet's "character" and with evaluative discussion of his works. Pritchard's method in *Lives of the Modern Poets* develops that of his earlier books, seeing each life as a creative performance, with the subject's voice sought in his poetry, in critical writings and letters, and in events. The facts of the life interest Pritchard only when their "pressure" results in creative work. Thus Crane's homosexuality is not emphasized, because, Pritchard says, his "distinctive individual consciousness" was "different from the usual notion of personal poetry—in which an 'I' lays bare his inner secrets." On the other hand, the death of Hardy's first wife is central to an extended discussion of the "biographical genesis" of his "Poems of 1912-1913." Somewhere between is Pritchard's handling of Robinson's poem "Eros Turannos," which Pritchard concedes is autobiographical but about which he declines to speculate: "the unknown background, . . . intensely suggestive, [is] an object for us to wonder at, rather than penetrate or understand."

One purpose of *Lives of the Modern Poets* is to define more clearly the central notion of voice as the poet's presence within the poem. Pritchard offers some synonyms: "presence," "temperament," "personality," "personal center," "special posture," "deep personal pressure," the "way of saying" rather than "the truth or relevance or wisdom of the idea communicated." The influence of Frost's "sounds of sense" is clear—the "sense" one paradoxically gets when hearing voices behind a door that obscures the words. Frost's claim (first stated in a 4 July 1913 letter to John Bartlett) that the sounds of sense break their "irregularity of accent across the regular beat of the metre" can be seen as the analogy through which Pritchard understands how a creative performance interacts in complex ways with the facts of biography. For the reader of poetry, Pritchard writes, the task is to begin with "something heard," then "to imagine what it would be like to speak in this voice, in these voices."

Authoritative without being either arrogant or chatty, Pritchard's essays, reflecting "a good memory and musical sense," usually seem less like Johnsonian prefaces than well-shaped class-

-184-

of life was inordinately interested in, girls and libraries.
He had been hard on the species North Carolingian girl, describing to
Lowell her speech as that of an "imbecile trying to be an idiot" and
writing to Hannah Arendt that, for the freshman girls, he might write
a "ballet with a chorus of Peasant Girls." "A Girl in a Library"
both mocks its subject's way of speaking, but goes on to give
her not just a role in the peasant girls' chorus but singled her out
for rather more extended and troubled consideration. The first
section of "A Girl in a Library" is a Jarrellian set-piece which ends
in a tour de force:

> An object among dreams, you sit here with your shoes off
> And curl your legs up under you; your eyes
> Close for a moment, your face moves toward sleep...
> You are very human.
> But my mind, gone out in tenderness,
> Shrinks from its object with a thoughtful sigh.
> This is a waist the spirit breaks its arm on.
> The gods themselves, against you, struggle in vain.
> This broad low strongboned brow; these heavy eyes;
> These calves, grown muscular with certainties;
> This nose, three medium-sized pink strawberries
> ---But I exaggerate. In a little you will leave:
> I'll hear, half squeal, half shriek, your laugh of greeting--
> Then, descrescendo, bars of that strange speech
> In which each sound sets out to seek each other,
> Murders its own father, marries its own mother,
> And ends as one grand transcendental vowel

Already the range of tone and attitude toward the girl is wide, from
a "tenderness" even prepared to risk banality in the words it can
express itself in ("You are very human"), to the jokes about how
solidly this "very human" girl is built, and to the self-delighted
creation of her speech as an Oedipal tragedy that ends up in some
kind of Emersonian or Listzian unity (Jarrell speaks otherwhere
of Wallace Stevens's "transcendental, too transcendtal Etudes). The
most disingenous thing the speaker says is that he exaggerates, after
which he proceeds to high exaggeration of what he hears in her
voice.

Page from the manuscript for Randall Jarrell: A Literary Life *(by permission of William H. Pritchard)*

Dust jacket for the first biography of Jarrell, published simultaneously with Randall Jarrell: Selected Poems, *edited by Pritchard*

room lectures. Beginning with a title that is not quite a thesis—"Yeats: Theatrical Nobility," "Robinson: The Prince of Heartachers," "Eliot: Superior Amusement"—and a brief survey of biographical facts, Pritchard moves selectively through the works, quoting poems (almost never in their entirety) and commenting on them. He does not shy away from evaluation. He can be provocative: Yeats "is probably the modern poet most vulnerable to affectations which are not inevitably amusing"; Stevens is often more "exasperating" than even Pound and needs rescuing from critics who have been "fans rather than discriminators." The teacher's trick is to be provocative without the "aesthetic and cultural bullying" that often characterized Leavis (but never Brower). Reading through the reviews of *Lives of the Modern Poets*,

one is struck by how much opinions of the book reflect the reviewers' reactions to Pritchard's voice. These run the gamut from "good talk," "quite modest," and "deliberately low-pitched" (Richard Ellmann, *New York Times Book Review*, 27 April 1980) to "too much knowingness," "too much superior amusement," and "straining for urbanity" (Alan Jenkins, *Encounter*, July 1981).

In Pritchard's preface to *Lives* he addresses the challenge posed to literary biography by poststructuralist literary theorists with their disdain for the concept of "the author"—that is, for the notion that the individual creative consciousness is the essential element in the production of literature—and for related critical terms such as "self," "individuality," and "voice." The poststructuralist position, as Pritchard summarizes it, attacks "the assumption that a poem has an identifiable author whose life ... these words somehow draw interest from," and it also rejects other "presumed misconceptions," such as the belief that "some opinions are demonstrably better than others [or] that certain appeals to 'words on the page' are possible." In responding, Pritchard notes the difficulty of arguing with theorists who reject one's basic vocabulary: "we are in trouble, but I see no way to 'earn' the validity for such a terminology except by practical demonstration that, in the case of particular authors and their works, the terms take us further into the literary experience."

Several reviewers, including Ellmann and Jenkins, singled out "Robert Frost: Elevated Play" as the finest of the *Lives*, and in his conclusion to the book Pritchard admits that Frost is, with Eliot, one of his favorite poets. He also acknowledges that knowing Frost and having his poems "so well anchored in my head" made "the task of just valuation ... that much more difficult." Pritchard's essay "West of Boston" (*Yale Review*, Spring 1987) recounts the personal relationship between Frost and Pritchard. The young instructor of English was "walked home" by Frost through the night streets of Amherst, and the eighty-six-year-old Frost once took the infant David Pritchard by the hand. Paradoxically, what made Pritchard's "just valuation" and his 1984 "reconsideration" necessary was Lawrance Thompson's three-volume *Robert Frost* (1966-1976), which attacks the self-cultivated image of Frost as (in Pritchard's phrase) "the goodest greyest poet since Walt Whitman." Thompson replaced this with the image of a monster of vanity, manipulation, and vindictiveness.

In *Frost: A Literary Life Reconsidered* Pritchard gives Thompson credit for having exhaustively put on record the facts of Frost's life, but then Pritchard critiques Thompson's "overeager ... explanatory categories" and questions the responses of some prominent reviewers who seemed overeager to accept the revision of Frost into a hateful megalomaniac. In reconsidering Frost, Pritchard does not deny the many examples of unpleasantness (or worse) in Frost's behavior, but rather seeks a new perspective. In *Wyndham Lewis* Pritchard held that literature transforms "problems and annoyances." *Frost* includes a subtler version of this notion: "whatever he did, for better or worse, was done poetically, was performed in a style which must not be pushed

out of the way in order to get at the 'real' or 'deeper' motives."

How this idea works is demonstrated by Pritchard's handling of an incident in 1894, when Frost traveled to St. Lawrence University to present a specially printed book of five poems to his hesitant fiancée Elinor White, who turned him away; then he journeyed southward to the Dismal Swamp, which straddles the Virginia-North Carolina border, where, wandering in darkness, he met a party of convivial duck hunters and ended up on the beach listening to a lifeguard tell legends about Aaron Burr's daughter Theodosia. Thompson treats this episode exhaustively, speculating that Frost intended to punish Elinor with a mysterious suicide; thus Thompson sees an early example of Frost's "bitter" vindictiveness. Pritchard finds that unconvincing. Instead, he thinks the episode is interesting for its "blatantly literary" quality, in two senses: first, "the whole scene feels so beautifully orchestrated in its juxtapositions and incongruities ... that we lose the hero's sufferings in the larger grotesque (or providential) design"; second, the adventure produced, sixty years later, a fine long poem, "Kitty Hawk." Thus, one sees the pattern of Pritchard's *Frost*: if the poems do not transform the events, they share with them a performative design of which they are the highest manifestation. This is the reason for a "literary life": "we care about the life because of the poems which came out of it."

As with *Lives of the Modern Poets*, the main emphasis of *Frost* is on the poems. Reviewers were generally enthusiastic about the result. In the *New York Times Book Review* (14 October 1984) Helen Vendler agreed with Pritchard that, as she put it, "a biographer who relishes and understands the poetic style may have a more accurate sense of the same style as it expresses itself in life." Noting, as did other reviewers, that Pritchard had found new insights by treating Frost's books as wholes, Vendler also praised his sensitivity to the "genuine oddity" of Frost's teasing sense of play, especially his play with language. Vendler's two negative reflections were also found in other reviews. First, she noted that Pritchard's calling it "wild" and theatrical does not adequately deal with an event such as Frost's awakening his six-year-old daughter and, revolver in hand, demanding that the child choose which of her parents would not survive the night. Second, Vendler found that "most of what Mr. Pritchard says about the poems could have

Pritchard at Amherst College, where he is Henry Clay Folger Professor of English

been said without reference to the events of the life." Richard Poirier in the *New York Review of Books* (25 April 1985) made a similar criticism: "Pritchard seems to worry that if he tries to uncover the sources of genius and power in Frost's writing he will compromise his efforts to restore to the man a proper measure of human ordinariness."

Pritchard's next biographical subject was Randall Jarrell, the poet-critic whose mid-century essays on Frost contributed significantly to the older poet's critical reputation. Published in 1990 in tandem with *Randall Jarrell: Selected Poems*, edited by Pritchard, *Randall Jarrell: A Literary Life* is the most conventional in format of Pritchard's "literary lives," since there was no previous factual biography. Jarrell is, in fact, a good test for Pritchard's method, since his life is sparsely fur-

nished with dramatic events. The poet of aerial combat never left the wartime United States, and his death, Pritchard argues, probably was not a suicide as has been widely believed. (Jarrell was hit by a car as he walked alone on a dark road.)

The strength of *Randall Jarrell* lies in Pritchard's conveying of a full sense of the man's accomplishment, which included criticism, editorial work, and teaching as well as verse. Pritchard's approach is displayed in chapter 7, "The Life of Criticism," the center of which is a discussion of Jarrell's poem "A Girl in A Library." The chapter begins by focusing on his prose pieces of the early 1950s, especially the "brilliant lecture-lament 'The Obscurity of the Poet,'" and ends by looking at Jarrell's published appreciations of Walt Whitman and Frost. Pritchard brings out the interrelationships of these works.

The girl in the library is like those whose lack of interest in poetry Jarrell humorously lamented in "The Obscurity," while his ability to share Whitman's reverence for life helps to explain his complex, not just sarcastic, reaction to the girl. As for the essay on Frost, Pritchard sees in the "virtuosity" of Jarrell's appreciation a summation of Jarrell's own richness as a man of letters.

The limitations of Pritchard's method are also illustrated in *Randall Jarrell*. A reader insufficiently predisposed to admire the poem "Lady Bates" is unlikely to be convinced by Pritchard's extolling a "bittersweet . . . voice detached yet pitying," which "seems to be spontaneously discovering what it has to say." And one might wish Pritchard would speculate more about the psychological dimensions of Jarrell's childhood in a broken home, his ambivalent feelings toward his mother, his strong identification with suffering women and with Jews of the Holocaust, and his attraction to children but failure to father any—even his intense devotion to a tomcat named Kit-

ten. Still, Pritchard succeeds in making Jarrell a "sympathetic" character and encouraging more attention to his accomplishments.

Vendler's review of *Frost* brings into focus Pritchard's contribution to literary biography by noting that, having through long acquaintance come to understand and relish a particular poet's works, Pritchard is able to illuminate "the same style as it expresses itself in life." In Pritchard's method, personal appreciation for an artist's works precedes study of the details of the artist's life. That is because there is an essential continuity between biography and creative accomplishment—a continuity in what Vendler calls the poet's "style" and what Pritchard calls "voice." Pritchard's accomplishment has been his ability to provide practical demonstrations of how voice and literary life can be discussed in terms of each other.

William H. Pritchard continues to teach at Amherst College. Among his plans for future writing is "a memoir about teaching."

Arnold Rampersad

(13 November 1941 -   )

Gail Porter Mandell
Saint Mary's College, Notre Dame, Indiana

BOOKS: *Melville's Israel Potter: A Pilgrimage and Progress* (Bowling Green, Ohio: Bowling Green University Press, 1969);
The Art and Imagination of W. E. B. Du Bois (Cambridge, Mass. & London: Harvard University Press, 1976);
The Life of Langston Hughes, Volume I: 1902-1941, I, Too, Sing America; Volume II: 1941-1967, I Dream a World (New York: Oxford University Press, 1986, 1988).

OTHER: "Psychoanalysis and Black Biography," in *Artist & Influence 1986: The Challenges of Writing Black Biography* (New York: Hatch-Billops, 1987), pp. 34-42;
"Langston Hughes," in *Voices and Visions: The Poet in America*, edited by Helen Vendler (New York: Random House, 1987), pp. 353-393;
"Slavery and the Literary Imagination: Du Bois's *The Souls of Black Folk*," in *Slavery and the Literary Imagination*, edited by Rampersad and Deborah McDowell (Baltimore: Johns Hopkins University Press, 1989), pp. 104-124;
"Biography and Afro-American Culture," in *Afro-American Literary Study in the 1990s*, edited by Houston A. Baker, Jr., and Patricia Redmond (Chicago: University of Chicago Press, 1989), pp. 194-224;
"Langston Hughes and Approaches to Modernism in the Harlem Renaissance," in *The Harlem Renaissance: Revaluations*, edited by Amritjit Singh, William S. Shiver, and Stanley Brodwin (New York & London: Garland, 1989), pp. 49-71;
"Langston Hughes," in *African American Writers*, edited by Valerie Smith (New York: Scribners, 1991), pp. 193-204;
Richard Wright, *Works*, 2 volumes, edited by Rampersad, Library of America Series (New York: Literary Classics of the United States, 1991).

SELECTED PERIODICAL PUBLICATIONS— UNCOLLECTED: "W. E. B. Du Bois as a Man of Literature," *American Literature*, 51 (March 1979): 50-68;
"Biography, Autobiography, and Afro-American Literature," *Yale Review*, 73 (Autumn 1983): 1-16;
"The Origins of Poetry in Langston Hughes," *Southern Review*, 21 (July 1985): 695-705;
"Langston Hughes and Amiri Baraka/Leroi Jones," *Steppingstones*, 4 (Summer 1985): 135-143;
"Langston Hughes and His Critics on the Left," *Langston Hughes Review*, 5 (Fall 1986): 34-40;
"Langston Hughes's *Fine Clothes to the Jew*," *Callaloo*, 9 (Winter 1986): 144-158;
"Future Projects on Langston Hughes," *Black American Literature Forum*, 21 (Fall 1987): 305-316;
"Psychology and Afro-American Biography," *Yale Review*, 78 (Autumn 1988): 1-18;
"Biography and Langston Hughes," *Kennesaw Review*, 2 (Summer 1989): 79-92;
"V. S. Naipaul in the South," *Raritan*, 10 (Summer 1990): 24-47;
"Mencken, Race, and America," *Menckeniana: A Quarterly Review*, 115 (Fall 1990): 1-11.

As a scholar, literary critic, and practicing biographer, Arnold Rampersad explores black culture, artistry, and experience. Racial themes dominate his theoretical writings, and in the two volumes of his biography of Langston Hughes (1986 and 1988) and his earlier study of the life and works of W. E. B. Du Bois (1976), Rampersad has narrated the lives of two important black Americans. *The Life of Langston Hughes* has won numerous awards, including the American Book Award in Biography of the Before Columbus Foundation in 1990 and the Clarence Holt Award in 1988, and it was a runner-up for the Pulitzer Prize for biography in 1989; the first volume, *I, Too, Sing America*, was nominated for the National Book Critics Circle Award in 1987.

Arnold Rampersad with one of the two volumes of his edition of the works of Richard Wright (photograph by William Sauro, New York Times News Service)

A native of Trinidad in the West Indies, Rampersad was born on 13 November 1941 in Port-of-Spain and is the only son of Jerome and Evelyn De Souza Rampersad; he is the youngest of their three offspring. His father was a journalist and his mother a telephone operator. Following the completion of his secondary education at Saint Mary's College in Port-of-Spain, Rampersad moved to the United States to attend Bowling Green University in Ohio, where he received a B.A. in English in 1967 and a year later the M.A. In 1969 he received an A.M. degree from Harvard University and obtained his Ph.D. there in 1973, later returning to the Department of Afro-American Studies as a visiting professor for the academic year 1979-1980. On 10 October 1985 he married Marvina White; they have a son, Luke, born in 1987. Rampersad has been a United States citizen since 1985.

Currently Woodrow Wilson Professor of English and director of American studies at Princeton University, Rampersad has also taught at the University of Virginia (1973-1974), Stan-

ford (1974-1983), Rutgers (1983-1988), and Columbia University, where he was Zora Neale Hurston Professor of English from 1988 to 1990. He has held fellowships from the National Endowment for the Humanities, the Rockefeller Foundation, the Center for Advanced Studies in the Behavioral Sciences, and the Guggenheim Foundation. In 1991 he was named a MacArthur Fellow.

In an interview published in *Life into Art: Conversations with Seven Contemporary Biographers* (1991), Rampersad said that, for as long as he can remember, he has been interested in the combination of history and literature. This interest has resulted in his fascination with biography, which he defines as the "history of an individual." Rampersad's two biographies differ markedly in scope, the first focusing closely on Du Bois's work, whereas the second takes a far broader biographical perspective on Hughes's life and work. Nevertheless, they bear certain similarities, among them Rampersad's careful recreation of the geographic, historical, and cul-

 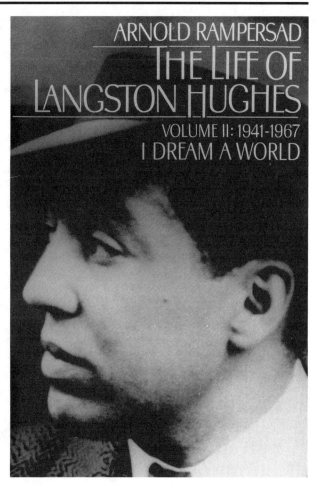

Dust jackets for the biography of a writer who, according to Rampersad, was taught from childhood "that he had a messianic obligation to the Afro-American people, and through them to America"

tural context of each life. Whether it be the nineteenth-century puritanical New England town of Great Barrington, Massachusetts, in which Du Bois spent his first seventeen years, or the "lost Eden" of Lawrence, Kansas, where Hughes lived after its antislavery radicalism had died away, Rampersad creates a nuanced sense of place and time. His gifts as a narrator invigorate each work and support his claim that biography must above all tell a good story.

Rampersad often explores racial themes. With sensitivity and subtlety, he considers the effect of mixed blood on the racial consciousness of American blacks, a topic he implicitly surveys from his vantage point as a native of a culture where those of mixed blood are a majority. As he revealed in *Life into Art*, he has sought to delineate in his biographies, and interpret for white and black readers alike, the cultural life and consciousness of black artists and intellectuals, aspects missing from the work of other writers. He

also examines in both biographies the dilemma of the black American, first identified and described by Du Bois, which results from "the identification of dual souls, American and African." In Rampersad's essay "Biography, Autobiography, and Afro-American Literature" in the *Yale Review* (Autumn 1983), he asserts that this dilemma is central to black consciousness and to Afro-American literature. In his biographies this duality manifests itself as a force that shapes the lives and works of his subjects.

"Being black in America is above all a psychological state," Rampersad says in "Psychology and Afro-American Biography," also published in the *Yale Review* (Autumn 1988). Rampersad affirms his commitment to the use of psychological theory, especially that of Sigmund Freud as developed by Eric Erikson, as a way into the minds of his subjects. Although he eschews the inclusion of psychological terminology, which would disrupt the biographical narrative, he uses the meth-

Rampersad circa 1988 (photograph by Minda Noveck)

ods of psychology to understand the inner lives of his subjects, stating his insights in appropriate language. As he has made clear in various essays, this approach characterizes both his biographies. He has publicly committed himself to "free and frank investigation, within the bounds of reason and the basic rules of evidence," even if it requires the sacrifice of black heroes who are "scrubbed and shining."

"The Du Bois book was a very limited operation," Rampersad admitted in the 1991 interview. Because Rampersad did not have access to the Du Bois papers at the University of Massachusetts, he was limited to relying heavily on the published works, and consequently he explored the life through them. It is no surprise, then, that the events of Du Bois's personal life have secondary importance to the intellectual activity evidenced in his novels and other writings. Therefore, except for the chapters devoted to Du Bois's early life, the biography lacks personal drama. As a character, Du Bois remains abstract, and the account of his private life is minimal. However, the intellectual traits of the subject emerge with clarity and coherence, and the story of the development of his art and of the imagination that shaped it has power. In this biography, Rampersad establishes his ability to illuminate the inner life of his subject and to draw a compelling and finally moving intellectual portrait of a complex man. Du Bois's inner struggle to assert the worth not only of his mind but of his very self comes to symbolize that of all black Americans.

In spite of deserved praise from reviewers, Rampersad remains critical of his first biography. He has come to regard "intellectual biography" or "biography of the mind" as a "poor cousin" of full biography—it is "what you write when you don't have access to the papers." As he says in "Psychology and Afro-American Biography," "there is no real substitute for the full-scale portrait. Terms such as 'literary biography' or 'intellectual biography' are probably, in most cases, confessions of partial portraiture, and partial failure." In spite of his harsh judgment of his own work, it should be remembered that Rampersad wrote the biography of Du Bois early in his career when, by his own admission, he was still learning his craft and proving himself as a scholar—he was as much concerned with producing a work his fellow scholars would respect as in telling the life in an interesting way. Recently republished in a second edition, Rampersad's biography nonetheless offers a careful and thorough consideration of the writings of Du Bois in the context of his life.

In 1979 George Houston Bass, the executor-trustee of the Langston Hughes Estate, asked Rampersad to write a biography of Hughes because he had read *The Art and Imagination of W. E. B. Du Bois* and admired the way in which Rampersad had linked the life and art of his subject. Rampersad would have access to Hughes's papers, unavailable to previous biographers, and would produce the authorized biography. Thus began nearly ten years of research and writing.

The two volumes of *The Life of Langston Hughes* total close to a thousand pages. The first volume traces Hughes's life from his birth in 1902 through 1941, when Hughes was at his lowest point, penniless and sick, artistically eclipsed by younger black writers, and politically ostracized. The second volume carries on Hughes's story from 1941 until his death in 1967, a period during which professional successes and personal satisfactions were fleeting, perpetually threatened by economic and artistic failure.

Originally intending a single volume but with no prior determination of length, Rampersad wrote the draft for the Hughes biography in longhand. When he realized he would have to divide the work into two volumes because of its inordinate length, he faced the difficulties presented by a life whose first half was more interesting than its last half. Determined that the biography would be "dramatic," he made the deci-

sion to end each chapter and the entire first volume at points that would pique the reader's interest. Consequently, as many reviewers have noted, the work, and the first volume in particular, reads like a novel.

The challenge of writing the second volume, once he had settled on it, lay in reshaping the material of Hughes's last twenty-six years. Instead of describing a gradual falling off of the momentum of the life, as originally intended, those chapters had to be expanded and rewritten as a story in themselves so that the second volume would complement and balance the first.

In this endeavor Rampersad only partially succeeded. Perhaps because the last part of Hughes's life, when he was settled and his career established, is less interesting than the first, *I Dream a World* lacks the narrative and imaginative intensity of *I, Too, Sing America*. As Rampersad has said, "[The biographer] really can't be more interesting than the life is interesting." On the other hand, Rampersad acknowledges that it may be unreasonable to expect all parts of a multivolume work to be equally engaging.

The themes of the first volume develop from Hughes's search for the parents who deserted him and the identity that eluded him. Rampersad suggests that, through his art, Hughes fashioned an ideal self that he chased thereafter: a persona who could celebrate his blackness, know where he wanted to be and belong there, and dispel loneliness and sadness with song. The second volume measures the man against the dream he created through his art and which his society as much as he himself "deferred." Rampersad depicts Hughes as a man whose image never quite fit his reality. Therein, Rampersad intimates, lies Hughes's greatness and his tragedy. Whether it was his sexuality, his politics, or his poetry, others misinterpreted and misunderstood Hughes and made of him a scapegoat or a symbol as served their needs. At the end of the complete biography, most readers grasp Hughes's many limitations and failings, both personally and artistically. Nevertheless, Rampersad leaves the reader with a sense both of the man's personal worth and also of his tremendous cultural legacy, not only to blacks but to all Americans. As Darryl Pinckey observed in the *New York Review of Books* (16 February 1989), "The sum of [Hughes's] career is greater than its parts." That the reader realizes this paradox is a tribute to Rampersad's art as a biographer.

Reviewers have praised Rampersad's serious and thorough treatment of Hughes's life and work, and have agreed upon the extent and integrity of his biographical research while lauding the readability of both volumes. The poet Gwendolyn Brooks, whom Hughes encouraged early in her career, commented in the *New York Times Book Review* (12 October 1986), that Rampersad's biography "sparkles when it is involved with Hughes's devotion to his craft, with his eagerness to polish this, to hone that." Brooks as well as other reviewers noted Rampersad's vivid recreation of the times and places in which Hughes lived—the strong component of social history in the biography. The work has been acclaimed as "a near-perfect example of the biographer's art" (*Kirkus Reviews*, 1 July 1986) and "the definitive biography of Hughes" (*Best Sellers*, February 1987). The positive critical reception of the book has enhanced Rampersad's reputation as a biographer, literary scholar, and interpreter of black American culture. In his biography of Hughes, in particular, he has resolved the tension that he asserts all black writers face, of addressing "the double audience, black and white," each of which makes its own demands upon the artist.

Rampersad has recently edited a two-volume edition of the collected works of Richard Wright for the Library of America (1991). His current writing project is a study of race and American literature.

Interview:

Gail Porter Mandell, "Conversation with Arnold Rampersad," *Life into Art: Conversations with Seven Contemporary Biographers* (Fayetteville & London: University of Arkansas Press, 1991), pp. 44-67.

B. L. Reid
(3 May 1918 - 30 November 1990)

William Over
St. John's University

BOOKS: *Art by Subtraction: A Dissenting Opinion of Gertrude Stein* (Norman: University of Oklahoma Press, 1958);

William Butler Yeats: The Lyric of Tragedy (Norman: University of Oklahoma Press, 1961; London: Greenwood, 1979);

The Man from New York: John Quinn and His Friends (New York: Oxford University Press, 1968);

The Long Boy and Others (Athens: University of Georgia Press, 1969);

Tragic Occasions: Essays on Several Forms (Port Washington, N.Y. & London: Kennikat, 1971);

The Lives of Roger Casement (New Haven & London: Yale University Press, 1976);

First Acts: A Memoir (Athens: University of Georgia Press, 1988);

Necessary Lives: Biographical Reflections (Columbia: University of Missouri Press, 1990).

OTHER: "Ordering Chaos: The Dunciad," in *Quick Springs of Sense*, edited by Larry S. Champion (Athens: University of Georgia Press, 1974), pp. 75-96;

"Johnston in Academe," in *Denis Johnston: A Retrospective*, edited by Joseph Ronsley (Totowa, N.J.: Barnes & Noble, 1981), pp. 203-213;

Colin Way Reid, *Open Secret*, edited by Reid (London: Smythe, 1986);

Joyce Horner, *Flag and Feather*, edited by Reid and Elizabeth Alden Green (South Hadley, Mass.: Mount Holyoke College, 1986).

SELECTED PERIODICAL PUBLICATIONS—
UNCOLLECTED: "A Good Man—Has Had Fever: Casement in the Congo," *Sewanee Review*, 82 (July-September 1974): 460-480;

"T. S. Eliot and the Sacred Wood," *Sewanee Review*, 90 (Spring 1982): 227-239;

"Gnomon and Order in Joyce's Portrait," *Sewanee Review*, 92 (Summer 1984): 397-420;

"Works and Days," *Sewanee Review*, 95 (Winter 1987): 61-89.

B. L. Reid's reputation as a biographer and literary critic stands predominantly on the prodigious research for his two full-length biographies. Perhaps his most significant essay, the brief "Practical Biography" (1975; in *Necessary Lives*, 1990), has raised important issues regarding the grounds of biography and has encouraged readers to consider the fundamental differences between narrative history and biographical writing. Reid was awarded the Pulitzer Prize in 1969 for his first biography, *The Man from New York: John Quinn and His Friends* (1968). *The Lives of Roger Casement* (1976), his second full-length biography, was nominated for a National Book Award. Characteristic of both works are the careful selection and presentation of primary source material from an extensive body of research, and the conscientious effort to give priority to facts over interpretation.

Benjamin Lawrence Reid was born on 3 May 1918 in Louisville, Kentucky, to Isaac Errett Reid, a minister, and Margaret Lawrence Reid. When he was six months old, the family moved to Texas, but three years later they returned to Kentucky living first in Crestwood and later in Louisville. He attended the University of Louisville from 1939 to 1943, and on 15 July 1942 he married Joan Davidson, an art and literature scholar. Their marriage produced two children, Jane Lawrence and Colin Way Reid. After receiving his A.B. in English in 1943, Reid served as a conscientious objector in the Civilian Public Service program from 1944 to 1945, where he worked in camps as an outdoor laborer and as an orderly in a mental hospital. From 1946 to 1948 he taught English at Iowa State College of Science and Technology in Ames (now Iowa State University) and at the Camp Dodge campus. While an English instructor at Smith College in Northampton, Massachusetts, from 1948 to 1951, Reid earned an A.M. degree in English from Columbia University. He then taught at Sweet Briar College, Sweet Briar, Virginia, as an instructor (1951-1956) and assistant professor (1956-1957).

B. L. Reid, 1980 (Mount Holyoke College Office of Public Relations)

In 1957 Reid received his Ph.D. in English from the University of Virginia and became an assistant professor at Mount Holyoke College from 1957 to 1959, then associate professor and department chair (1959-1963) and professor (1963-1970). He was named Andrew Mellon Professor in the Humanities in 1970. After retiring from teaching in 1983, Reid continued to live in South Hadley, Massachusetts, and began work on his memoirs, *First Acts* (1988).

Art by Subtraction: A Dissenting Opinion of Gertrude Stein (1958), a nearly verbatim publication of Reid's master's thesis at Columbia, is an attempt to reassess Stein's contributions as a creative writer and theorist of art and literature. It is closely reasoned and reveals an attention to documentation that would later prove the hallmark of Reid's biographies. However, Lloyd Frankenberg in the *New York Times* found Reid's examination of Stein at times too severe and one-

sided, pointing out that his judgments of her "sins" seemed like moralizations rather than discernments of character. Reid contended that Stein was amoral and anti-intellectual, and that her preference for still-life paintings was "not human," because such pictures did not represent people. He claimed she was amoral because she appeared not to be interested in political issues; she was anti-intellectual because she apparently did not believe that concepts influence the visual arts.

Reid's dissertation on William Butler Yeats was the basis for his second book, *William Butler Yeats: The Lyric of Tragedy* (1961). Later, the public availability of the Quinn papers at the Berg Collection of the New York Public Library made possible Reid's 1968 biography of Quinn, a wealthy collector, patron, and New York lawyer. The collection of correspondence was extensive, including letters to and from major figures in twentieth-century art and literature. Reid's choice of

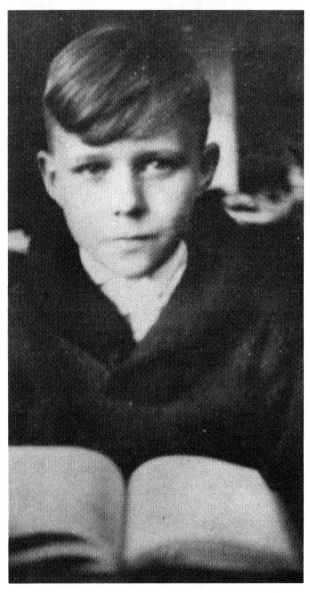

Reid at school in Crestwood, Kentucky

tant organizer of the New York Armory Show in 1913, which helped introduce the modern art movement to America.

Reid's interviews with the Yeats family, with Eliot, and with others enhanced his comprehensive knowledge of Quinn's personal and professional affairs. However, some critics—such as David Dempsey in the *New York Times Book Review* and J. M. Edelstein in the *New Republic*—lamented Reid's reluctance to explore the personality of his subject, pointing out, for example, that a more lively portrait of Quinn had appeared in Aline B. Saarinen's *The Proud Possessors* (1958).

Reid's refusal to embroider Quinn's life partially stemmed from a conscientious attempt "to present evidence for the reader's own induction," as Reid states in the preface. His approach involved a minimum of authorial interpretation, a standard that would be repeated in his biography of Casement. Perhaps the particular nature of Quinn's genius also helped determine this approach for Reid. If Quinn's character remains somewhat obscure despite the prodigious inclusion of correspondence in the biography, this fact is indicative of Quinn's ambition to become adviser, patron, and collector for individuals more creative than himself. Quinn's adept handling of the censorship problems associated with Joyce's publication of *Ulysses* (1922), for example, and his farsighted initiative to secure Eliot's original manuscript of *The Waste Land* (1922), after Pound had radically edited the published version, are indicative of his ambition to advise and support gifted but less practical minds.

Quinn's own personality, although forceful, was to thrive chiefly in the wings rather than on center stage. Reid presents his subject's particular capacity for loyalty and kindness only by inference, as the reader learns of Quinn's accomplishments through the unfolding of selected correspondence. Perhaps the most important previously unpublished letters are to and from Eliot and the Yeats family members. These and other letters are valuable not so much for their elucidation of Quinn's personality but rather as an exposition of important moments in the lives of famous twentieth-century writers.

In *The Lives of Roger Casement* Reid chose another eclectic figure, an Irishman whose life encompassed the different worlds of war, politics, foreign relations, personal choices, and literature. Reid reprised his biographical approach in the Quinn biography: to present the facts of re-

subject was a neglected figure who served as attorney, friend, and confidant to Yeats, T. S. Eliot, Ezra Pound, John Millington Synge, Joseph Conrad, George Russell (Æ), Standish O'Grady, Douglas Hyde, Horace Plunkett, Augustus and Gwen John, James Stephens, Padraic Colum, Maud Gonne, Shane Leslie, Roger Casement, and Isabella Augusta Persse, Lady Gregory. These and others benefited from Quinn's friendship, including James Joyce, whom he helped for years. In the art world of the World War I era Quinn became known as the "noble buyer" among artists such as Pablo Picasso, Henri Matisse, Constantin Brancusi, Paul Gauguin, Georges Braque, and others. He was an impor-

132

~~English beat the Irish solely because they had no music in their souls & were capable of any cold-blooded crime — they are just the same race today."~~ He was constrained to be a British public servant but at least he could be an unwilling one. He was taking the Santos post, he told Mrs. Green, because it was better paid than Bilbao and would give him a bit of extra cash for his "Irishisms."[57]

~~From Ballycastle on September 8,~~ writing with rare economy and point, *to Alice Stopford Green from Ballycastle on September 8,* Casement attacked the English "Devolution" scheme for Ireland as one that would only

create a new "Castle" and class dependent on it. In God's name what Ireland wants is Responsibility. Until the public here feel that they <u>must</u> tackle the state of their own country and abide by their own acts there can be no real improvement. We have to create a governing mind again after 106 years of abstraction of all mind from this outraged land. . . . England destroyed our Constitution, juggled our mind out of our body into hers, and left us only a "corpse on the dissecting table."[58]

At the top of a note he sent Mrs. Green from Cherbourg en route to Santos on September 21, Casement jotted: "Remember my address is Consulate of Great Britain and <u>Ireland</u>, Santos--not British Consulate!!"[59] Just before leaving Southampton on the <u>Nile</u> on the same day he had sent Gertrude Bannister a color postcard of the Euston Hotel in London on which he had blacked out the Union Jack in ink.[60]

From Vigo on September 23 he wrote Gertrude more at length, still saturated with Irish affections and sore irony at his British employment. He asked her to watch for Irish and Congo news and send him cuttings: in Santos

Page from a draft for The Lives of Roger Casement *(by permission of the Estate of B. L. Reid and the Mount Holyoke College Library/Archives)*

9

in the kind of gesture which was to grow habitual, presented
him with four volumes of Yeats's poems and <u>The Celtic Twi-</u>
<u>light</u> and was in due course fervently thanked for reopening
the book of new poetry. From Jack Yeats Quinn bought at once
nearly a dozen paintings, and from his father he bought a
completed portrait of W. B. Yeats and commissioned, at an
agreed price of £20 or roughly $100 each, portraits of John
O'Leary, Douglas Hyde, and George William Russell ("AE").
He was setting out to collect images of his heroes in the
cultural and political life of Ireland.

From London he proceeded to Dublin, where he reveled in
the warm and free flow of Irish talk in the studios, pubs,
and homes, finding John Butler Yeats's description of the
Irish as "a contentious people" accurate and congenial.
"Ireland is most like ancient Athens," J. B. Yeats wrote him
in August, "where all were such talkers and disputants.
England is like ancient Rome with its legions and cohorts
and dull business of conquering the world." In a mere week
in Dublin and Gort Quinn found time to meet, to impress and
to be impressed by, W. B. Yeats and his sisters Lily and
Lollie, Russell, T. W. Rolleston, Douglas Hyde, George Moore,
Edward Martyn, and Lady Gregory. He took part in a Gaelic

At Killeeneen, Craughwell, on the last day of August, Quinn joined
in a Gaelic Feis at the new tomb which Lady Gregory had erected
of the blind Connacht poet Raftery, and Jack Yeats decorated a
program of the day with charming drawings sketches of Quinn, Lady
Gregory, Douglas Hyde, W. B. Yeats, and himself. At Lady Gregory's
great house of Coole Park Quinn heard Hyde read one of his Gaelic
plays; and it must have been at this time that he added his
initials to those carved in the bark of her famous signatory
beech tree. Years later, remembering the occasion in a letter of July
26, 1913, it seemed to her that she had entertained "an angel
unawares."

Page from a draft for The Man From New York: John Quinn and His Friends *(by permission of the Estate of B. L. Reid
and Mount Holyoke College Library Special Collections)*

search for the reader's own judgment with little direct interpretation. The scope of Reid's investigative project was impressive, but critical response repeated the objections raised over the Quinn biography. Some reviewers, including Jeffrey Meyers in the *Nation*, found insufficient analysis of personality and situation and an excessive reliance on detailed description. A further objection was raised to Reid's lack of psychological insight concerning his subject's sexual orientation. Reid left Casement's homosexuality largely unexamined. In spite of Reid's laconic dismissal of it as "abnormal," he generally shows a sympathy for Casement's personal anguish throughout the biography, calling his display of nobility before the public "all the more impressive because it was barely controlling hysteria." Reid gives less attention to the emblematic place Casement held in the Irish national movement, choosing instead to focus on his private life. While the foreground of Casement's life is rendered in great detail, Reid was satisfied to draw the social and political background in broad strokes, leaving much of it unexamined.

The method evident in Reid's two full-length biographies was acknowledged in his "Practical Biography," which sets forth in a personal, almost conversational style three tenets for the art of biography: first, that biography as a form is fundamentally different from other narrative forms, such as the novel, and from literary criticism as well; second, that the biographer must be governed above all by "the ordering of fact within the discipline of time" and that nonessential facts and novelistic embroidering of character and plot should be precluded from consideration; and finally, that biography has a useful, not solely an aesthetic, side, that it is one of the few "efficient lights" into the maze of human experience.

Reid's organizational method in the Quinn biography demonstrates his belief that biographical narration should focus on the judicious selection of documented fact rather than on the elaboration and reordering of character and plot common to novel writing or on the speculative interpretations common to literary criticism. *The Man from New York* is organized by calendar year—1870 to 1924, with a full chapter given to each year from 1910 through 1924, the year of Quinn's death. This strict ordering of time has the effect of de-emphasizing the interpretive aspects of biography in favor of a straightforward sequential account. Moreover, Reid's preference

was for including letters and quotations in place of his own narratives and commentary.

The concentration on fact over opinion in "Practical Biography" is, as Reid admits from the outset, only a personal preference and ought not to be taken as a general epistemological observation. He describes literary criticism as "the literary vestment of opinion," and hence pretentious and at times egotistical. Reid's words reflect a personal mood, what he concedes to be the evolving view of a scholar and not the foundation for a broad literary theory. By "fact" Reid means simply nonfiction, the details of a real person's life. As a literary critic, he felt hampered by New Criticism's injunctions against the personal, biographical approach. He found the lives of writers as interesting as their works. In particular he examined the Irish background of Yeats's writings as a way of getting at their meaning, commenting that "they must be a property of a culture." This outlook seems to have affinity with the New Historicism and Marxist movements, since Reid saw the connection between literary creativity and social structure as important. However, his intention was to make clear the significance of an individual life within the context of a culture, not to uncover hidden social and political agendas within the texts.

Reid's absorption in the subject matter of biography had at bottom a didactic purpose. The study of individual lives "tells us . . . what it has meant to be human, to live a life." Reid regarded subjects worthy of biographical study as "exemplary," either for "illustrious or infamous" reasons. He perceived human life as a process influenced by innumerable circumstances; hence the need to explore the details of individual lives through biography. This orientation helps explain Reid's insistence on the priority given to time divisions throughout his full-length biographies, which he describes as "unforgivingly chronological." Reid sees the order of time in biography as "personality in motion," an "order of linked occurrence"—of actions, events, motives, and feelings.

For Reid, the presentation of time in biography reveals a distinctive form. Biographical prose, he observed, is written in the past tense, as opposed to the "spurious present" of literary criticism. Historical narrative combines a disciplined objectivity with a straightforward narrative style. Reid did not recommend other narrative forms for the writing of biography: novelistic and ideological approaches to biography, he felt, distort

Page from a draft for Reid's First Acts: A Memoir *(by permission of the Estate of B. L. Reid)*

A chronicle of growing up in country and city
in the years between the world wars.

"Life in a southern village felt so pleasant and right that all
the other ways I have lived since boyhood have seemed to me
more or less unnatural, and preferably, temporary. One lux-
uriated in amplitudes of space and time, and in a pace modu-
lated under one's own control—no crowding, no hurry.
There were enough people about for any reasonable purpose,
yet so few that there was nobody one did not know, though
there were a few one did not particularly like. If you saw a
stranger, he was just passing through, or visiting one of your
friends, or, rarely, just moved to town. As most people were
fairly hard up, there was comparatively little class distinction
or snobbery, rivalries were not bitter ones. Such at least was a
small boy's sense of the town."

"Shawnee Park was an immense open-air temple of baseball
where most of the city's amateurs came to perform or to worship. As I remember it, there were eighteen complete baseball
diamonds, each with a number on the backstop, and on a
summer Saturday there might be hundreds of players
watched by thousands of spectators. Some of the diamonds
overlapped a bit, and outfielders in adjoining games might
find themselves face to face; occasionally a game had to be
held up for a moment when a player from the adjoining field
came panting, sweaty and chagrined, after a ball that had
gone over his head, or worse still, through his legs, and
picked it up and heaved it desperately toward his own infield,
while spectators at the invaded diamond craned to see 'who
the heck hit that one.'"

The University of Georgia Press
Athens, Georgia 30602

ISBN 0-8203-1015-8

FIRST ACTS
A Memoir

B. L. REID

Dust jacket for Reid's autobiography (1988). The photo, taken in Texas circa 1918, shows the infant Benjamin Lawrence Reid with his parents—Margaret Lawrence Reid and Isaac Errett Reid, Sr.—and his older brothers, Isaac Errett, Jr., and Joseph Kendrick.

history, since they impose an order of their own. All attempts at authorial intervention "shorten and sweeten and rearrange and simplify."

Given his perception that the sequence of events in human life is its most definitive quality, Reid does not begin the biography of Quinn as an analysis of an unchanging personality, essentialized apart from time. Instead, he presents a series of activities, in causal order, which shape the direction of Quinn's life. Accordingly the style of Reid's full-length biographies, which appears flat-footed and dull to some reviewers, is deliberately straightforward and "plain." This was done, Reid says in "Practical Biography," so as not to impose a writer's personality on the historical ordering of facts.

Reid's method of interweaving extended quotations with simple statements of fact in strict chronological order is grounded in the view that history itself forms its own patterns, which need not be supplanted by the "shapes and excitements of prose fiction." He did not make a closely argued case for this invisible hand of history that is able to set its own patterns upon the raw material of biography. However, he felt strongly that the biog-

rapher needs to "let his material form its own shapes." Presumably, these patterns would only become intelligible after much of the material has been arranged on the biographer's pages. Since these patterns "accumulate one piece at a time," it is folly to attempt to impose upon the known details of a person's life the "preconceived designs" of the scholar. This, Reid warned, can only lead to false perspectives and misguided notions.

In "Practical Biography" Reid recommends that primary sources and documented evidence be presented directly to the reader of biography so that these facts alone will suggest meaning. In other words, Reid would have the reader alone categorize and interpret, based on his or her review of the data. Of course, this material is not entirely inchoate, since the biographer has carefully selected from many sources those facts judged particularly meaningful, which serve to present a comprehensive view of the subject's life. Furthermore, Reid acknowledges a certain duty to treat material in a way that is "honorable and tasteful." However, he does not raise the question whether such treatment could be synonymous with a "preconceived design" imposed by the biographer.

Unlike the objective approach evident in his biographies, Reid's memoir of his formative years as the son of a poor minister contains a store of personal insights. Although the style of *First Acts* was intended to be "historical and lightly monitory . . . deliberately flat," Reid offers a warm and confessional narrative throughout. This change of direction might have been motivated by his desire to explore more fully the underlying forces shaping individual lives. In the preface Reid expresses a certain dissatisfaction with colleagues and students who were content to perceive and report their lives "as a set of accidents within privilege." He characterizes his own life up to the age of twenty-eight as uncertain, often harsh and untidy, but always interesting. Reid reports on his own "strange" life, together with what he remembers of his thoughts and feelings, so that it might prove somehow representative and "worth knowing and feeling." The chapter on his father's continual struggle to follow the contradictory ambition of remaining an evangelical minister while pursuing a series of small business ventures throughout the Midwest evokes the ambience of a Thornton Wilder novel. In the chapter

on Reid's conscientious-objector experience during the war, he presents a view of the social misfits, religious sectarians, and sincere conscientious objectors who constitute the range of war protesters. He reflects on life in the margins of society, where men work under the disdain of their supervisors as field laborers and orderlies in mental hospitals.

The discrete commentary and thoughtful selection of materials in Reid's biographies earned him recognition among scholars. His widely read "Practical Biography" has admonitory value as a statement of general principles for verity in the writing of biography. However, the belief that certifiable truths about human affairs can be pinned down without some form of authorial intervention is a tenet of positivism generally discarded today. In his memoir, however, Reid comes much closer to fulfilling Robert Penn Warren's tenet that "historical sense and poetic sense should not, in the end, be contradictory."

Papers:
The typescript for *The Man from New York* is in the Special Collections Department of the Mount Holyoke College Library, and the typescript for *The Lives of Roger Casement* is in the Mount Holyoke College Archives.

Ernest Samuels
(19 May 1903 -   )

William Over
St. John's University

BOOKS: *Business English Projects* (New York: Prentice-Hall, 1936);

The Young Henry Adams (Cambridge, Mass.: Harvard University Press, 1948; London: Cumberlege, 1948);

Henry Adams: The Middle Years (Cambridge, Mass.: Belknap Press of Harvard University Press, 1958);

Henry Adams: The Major Phase (Cambridge, Mass.: Belknap Press of Harvard University Press, 1964);

Bernard Berenson: The Making of a Connoisseur (Cambridge, Mass. & London: Belknap Press of Harvard University Press, 1979);

Bernard Berenson: The Making of a Legend, by Samuels and Jayne Newcomer Samuels (Cambridge, Mass.: Belknap Press of Harvard University Press, 1987);

Henry Adams (Cambridge, Mass.: Belknap Press of Harvard University Press, 1989).

OTHER: Henry Adams, *Mont-Saint-Michel and Chartres*, introduction by Samuels (New York: New American Library, 1961);

Adams, *Democracy and Esther*, introduction by Samuels (Gloucester, Mass.: Smith, 1961);

"Henry Adams and the Gossip Mill," in *Essays in American and English Literature Presented to Bruce Robert McElderry, Jr.*, edited by Max F. Schulz, William T. Templeman, and Charles R. Metzger (Athens: Ohio University Press, 1967), pp. 59-75;

Adams, *History of the United States of America During the Administrations of Jefferson and Madison*, edited and abridged by Samuels (Chicago: University of Chicago Press, 1967);

Adams, *The Education of Henry Adams*, edited, with an introduction and notes, by Samuels (Boston: Houghton Mifflin, 1973);

The Letters of Henry Adams, I-III: 1858-1892, edited by Samuels and others (Cambridge, Mass.: Belknap Press of Harvard University Press, 1982);

The Letters of Henry Adams, IV-VI: 1892-1918, edited by Samuels and others (Cambridge, Mass.: Belknap Press of Harvard University Press, 1988).

SELECTED PERIODICAL PUBLICATIONS—
UNCOLLECTED: "Confessions of a Biographer," *Quarterly Journal of the Library of Congress*, 38 (Winter 1981): 39-41;

"Henry Adams and Bernard Berenson: Two Boston Exiles," *Proceedings of the Massachusetts Historical Society*, 95 (1983): 100-113.

Henry Adams: The Middle Years (1958), the second volume of Ernest Samuels's trilogy, received the Parkman Award and the Bancroft Award; *Henry Adams: The Major Phase* (1964), the completion of his Adams biography, earned him the Pulitzer Prize and the Friends of Literature Award in 1965. Nominated by Henry Steele Commager and John Barkham for the Pulitzer, Samuels's biography received the unanimous votes of both the biography jury and the Advisory Board. Although he has a literary, not a historical or political background, Samuels gained wide respect for the probing intelligence evident in his work on Adams. Samuels's second full biography is also the result of prodigious research in areas often outside his own training. Comprising two volumes on the art historian and philosopher Bernard Berenson, it was widely praised and received the Carl Sandburg Award in 1981 for the first volume.

Ernest Samuels was born in Chicago on 19 May 1903 to Albert Samuels, a grocer, and Mary Kaplan Samuels. He attended the University of Chicago, where he earned his Ph.B. in 1923. After receiving his J.D. degree from the University of Chicago in 1926, he was admitted to the bar in Illinois and Texas, practicing law in El Paso from 1928 to 1930. He then reentered the University of Chicago, where he earned his M.A. in English in 1931. From 1933 to 1937 he was a lawyer in Chicago. He married Jayne Porter New-

Ernest Samuels, 1988

comer on 24 August 1938, and they were to have three children, Susanna, Jonathan, and Elizabeth. Samuels received his Ph.D. in English from the University of Chicago in 1942, then began a twenty-nine-year teaching career at Northwestern University, where he was Franklyn Bliss Snyder Professor of English until his retirement in 1971. During his tenured career he was chairman of the English department (1964-1966), Leo S. Bing Visiting Professor at the University of Southern California (1966-1967), and Fulbright lecturer and Inter-University Chair in American Studies in Belgium (1958-1959). He was twice a Guggenheim fellow (1955-1956 and 1971-1972). Samuels was a member of the editorial board for *American Literature* (1964-1971) and a member of the publications advisory board for the Adams Papers. From 1966 to 1971 he was a member of the Illinois Community of Scholars and from 1980 to 1981 a member of the Library of Congress Coun-

cil of Scholars. He served on the Pulitzer Prize juries for biography in 1967, 1968, and 1972, and for history in 1969.

For his first volume of biography, *The Young Henry Adams* (1948), Samuels approached his project with the intention of dispelling a prominent misconception of his subject as a writer who remained detached throughout his life from the common current of affairs. Adams himself was partially responsible for this misleading notion, assuming a wry and self-deprecating tone when describing his various contributions to political theory, journalism, education, scholarship, travel, science, and religion. In his autobiography, *The Education of Henry Adams* (1907), there is a conscious attempt to present himself as an isolated individual, sensitive and observant of people and institutions around him but often neglectful of his social duties and prone to solitude. To challenge this view, Samuels reveals the public aspects of

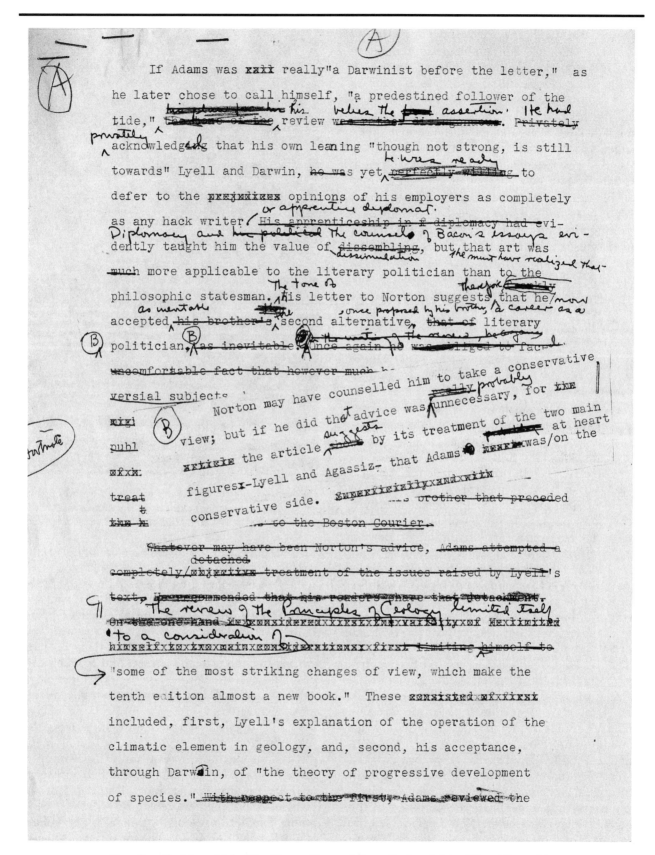

Page from the typescript for The Young Henry Adams *(by permission of Ernest Samuels)*

Adams's discourse: the rhetorical nature of his journal articles; the family ambitions and sibling rivalries evident in his letters; his frustrating attempts to develop a clear prose style in order to enter the influential world of New York journalism; and his stalwart, at times even insulting, polemics in Civil War and Reconstruction politics. In fact Adams's participation in the great events of his day is so well detailed and analyzed throughout Samuels's three volumes that much of the private life of the man is missing, although, especially in volumes two and three, Samuels includes revealing vignettes of Adams's personal behavior and manners, together with glimpses of personal yearnings and anxieties taken from the letters. Samuels's treatment of these more intimate moments is so illuminating that it tends to balance the general emphasis in the biography on civic and intellectual involvements.

In his preface Samuels notes the "self-mockery" and "ironic hindsights" of *The Education of Henry Adams*, written toward the end of Adams's life, and acknowledges the necessity of his own "prosaic spadework" that will uncover the Adams of disciplined determination and social conscience. Seeing Adams as "a very human and ardent idealist," Samuels perceived his study as a corrective for the critical reader of Adams's major works. Concluding the preface, Samuels warns of his attempt to approach objectivity rather than to instill "hero worship." He holds no special reverence for "the Brahman view of life" to which Adams seemed committed.

In *The Young Henry Adams* Samuels carefully situates his subject's conservative idealism and liberal Republican politics within the atmosphere of a Harvard that was undergoing profound and lasting changes regarding scientific methods. Even more influential on Adams was the radical politics of his family, who as lawyers and patriots upheld certain ideals of universal education and the concept of progressive evolution in human affairs. Samuels uncovers many inconsistencies in Adams's autobiography and his early letters: his contemptuous remarks about his early New England schooling, for instance, were contradicted in his 1859 analysis of the much-revered German educational system, which he found excessively regimented and underfinanced compared to the free and open spirit of the New England system. Likewise, Samuels reveals how misleading were Adams's dismissive remarks about his Harvard education by detailing its influential teaching methods, systems of thought, and the personalities

Dust jacket for the third and final volume of Samuels's biography of the writer he called "a very human and ardent idealist"

who directly affected Adams as an undergraduate.

Care is taken to demonstrate how Adams developed his style as a writer—from an awkward and affected form to a concise, flexible prose. Phrases written during his early days as a private secretary are compared to samples from his later journalistic and scientific prose, and Samuels also presents several examples of the development of Adams's political and scientific thought during his formative years.

The intellectual orientation of Adams, his subordination of science to conventional metaphysics, his patronizing dismissal of Darwinism in favor of special creation, his muddled insistence on what he termed the illiberal attitudes of the Darwinists and the new geologists—all these viewpoints Samuels presents within a wider sphere of intellectual debate. At the same time, Adams's rise to permanent contributor and then editor of the *North American Review* is understood as fulfilling his father's precept to avoid the emotionality of light literature and seek instead to transform society through important ideas. Samuels demonstrates the complex motivations of his subject in the role of reformer during the Reconstruction era. While earnest in his abhorrence of "Grantism" and other forms of corruption in institutions, Adams remained disdainful of popular movements, tending to blame the national malaise on the Jacksonian populist turn of Jeffersonian democracy. Samuels offers details of controversies, telling remarks, and excerpts from essays to present Adams as an upholder of enlightened conservativism. Similarly Samuels's handling of the teaching methods and scholarly behavior of Adams as an assistant professor of history at Harvard is documented with details from faculty minutes, student observations, commentaries of friends and family members, and selections from Adams's own colorful anecdotes and evaluations.

Samuels never hesitates to present what would appear to a modern interpreter as his subject's outmoded social beliefs and misconceptions, such as his faith that the remedy for the abuse of economic power lay in private morality alone, or the appeal to reason and higher consciousness as a replacement for the forces of party politics and commercial development in the post-Civil War era. The traditional views of Adams on feminist issues are also presented, though with little critical treatment. A comprehensive range of the great thinkers in mid-nineteenth-century America serves to locate Adams on the cutting edge of an America undergoing profound social and cultural changes. Samuels carefully re-creates the ongoing debates among these people, revealing his subject's lifelong goal to enlist reason and learning to assure the success of mass education and democracy in America. However, Samuels's final assessment of Adams in the first volume is not positive: "Unwilling to apply scientific methods to devise an efficient political system for the new industrial order, he was to drift steadily into the camp of the philosophical idealists who denounced the reality which their ideas disabled them from changing."

For *Henry Adams: The Middle Years* Samuels relied on a wide range of letters, personal testimony, Marian Adams's diary, and other personal accounts to offer a coherent profile of the period when Adams began to forge a solid reputation. Samuels deals in turn with his subject's political, familial, literary, intellectual, and scientific interests; Samuels also describes the social life of Lafayette Square society in Washington, D.C., during

the 1870s and 1880s. His informal writing style in volume two, relaxed substantially from volume one, suits the more intimate material of this phase of his subject's life, from 1871 to 1890. The biographical analysis remains sparing but is often penetrating, as when Samuels assesses Adams's approach to the art of biography, which was to impose a unifying insight on the psychology of his subject, then select details that support this "central perception"; or when he evaluates Adams's revisionist motivations for writing the biography of John Randolph, the proslavery senator from Virginia and the era's most formidable spokesman for secession. Samuels shrewdly observes how Adams came to realize his affinity with Randolph concerning the virtues of small government, even though Randolph had been an enemy of Adams's family and had opposed the antislavery policies of John and John Quincy Adams.

Samuels does not hold Adams responsible in any way for the suicide of his wife, Marian, and Samuels dismisses the view that her husband's pessimism and morbidity led to her emotional downfall. At times Samuels seems to withhold judgmental evaluations of Adams, whose opinions and prejudices are quite evident. For example, the straitlaced fastidiousness of both Marian and Henry Adams—which led them to reject as household guests people such as Oscar Wilde, Sarah Bernhardt, and Adelina Patti, and to accept Lillie Langtry only hesitantly—is conveyed in fine detail but with little critical comment.

Samuels's treatments of *Democracy* (1880) and *Esther* (1884), novels Adams wrote anonymously as romans à clef, apply literary criticism and biographical analysis to stress Adams's social and intellectual motivations. Samuels's insights concern the autobiographical elements of both novels—which reveal portraits of Henry and Marian in the salon atmosphere of Lafayette Square—as well as the literary and political influences on their narrative style and content. Samuels analyzes *Esther* within the context of the general uprootedness of the age, as a particular response in America to the combined forces of Darwinism, positivism, the retreat from religious belief, and the onset of industrial capitalism.

In his discussion of the nine-volume *History of the United States During the Administrations of Jefferson and Madison* (1889-1891), Samuels brings forth the philosophical and historiographical backgrounds influencing Adams's approach to the main currents of American history, and he com-

The Making of a Connoisseur   IV -1-

It was a light-hearted Bernard who packed his books and
papers once more and set out full of anticipation for Geneva
and all the fabled art cities *in Italy* that lay beyond. His letters to
Senda grew longer and more ~~xxx~~ ecstatic, always signed *with the affectionate diminutive* /"B.B."
as from the time of his first arrival in Europe. To Mrs. Gardner
and others, of course, it was still the ~~ceremonially written~~ *formal*
"Bernhard Berenson."   Once again he is fortunate in~~x~~ travelling
companion. The ~~xxxxxxxx~~ personable Clyde Fitch accompanied   [to be checked against letters to Senda]
him to Geneva before departing for England and America. ~~Xxx~~

~~Rxxxxxxxxxx:~~

~~Xxxxxxx~~   (A)   A diaphanous montage *of* ~~xxxxxxxxxxxx~~

~~Withxxx;~~   ~~xxxxxxxxxxx~~ impressions hung like a stage
America
forces with   curtain over all of Italy for the bookish ~~eighteen~~.
and churche   ~~tourist. XxxxXxxxXxxxxxxxxxx Browning~~ One
see in Basl   ~~xxxxxxxxxxxxByxxxxxxxChildexxHarold~~ heard the
The enthral
Lake Zurich   music of Byron's Childe Harold on the inner ear
                  It was ground hallowed by Theophile Gautier and Stendhal.
for him who   or the rugged lyrics of Browning. Hippolyte Taine
Italian lan   helped one see its past in terms of race, time
                  Then to the devotee of Goethe there
on the Ital   and environment, ~~but most compelling of all~~ perhaps
the stars w   ~~to Bernard~~ were the sacred pages of ~~Goethe's~~ *his*
which had i   Travels in Italy ~~(.)~~. ~~Seen~~ The most recent
Hawthorne,   (more)
/Henry James/and William Wetmore Story was all the more intense
                                                       The praises of
for ~~him~~ Bernard for ~~ixxxxxxxxxx~~ its passage through so many
romantic   *from other lands.* (A)   ~~Parroy~~
~~other~~ enthusiasts. ~~XxxLuinoxxxxLakexMaggiore~~/Guidebook in hand
was now prepared to
he challenged every slip of description as he methodically
                 one out-of-the-way *him*
marched from/church to ~~another~~and gallery to gallery. At Luino
                       well
~~on Lake Maggiore~~ there ~~are~~ alterpieces and frescoes to be studied,
especially a decayed fresco by Luini, ~~a pupil of Leonardo~~. In
Milan he began the first of what would be countless visits to
Lake Maggiore and Como sparkled with a lovelier light than
the lakes of Switzerland. His first sight of an Italian cathedral of

Como revealed a beauty more intense than that

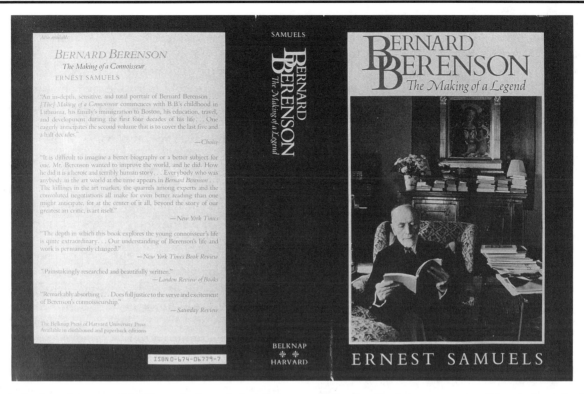

Dust jacket for volume two of the biography Samuels describes as a narrative that "tends to move on parallel and alternating lines somewhat like a Trollopian novel"

bines with them a comprehensive analysis of Adams's personal and familial predispositions. Adams's particular form of historical determinism is described in great detail, based on an exploration of his concept of progress and his underlying materialistic approach to historical causality. Samuels presents the philosophies of dominant thinkers such as Herbert Spencer and Auguste Comte along with a close study of Adams's own evolving views on the nature of democratic societies as they are influenced by industrial capitalism.

The school of determinism that emerged during the post-Civil War era in America was highly mechanistic in perspective, and Adams struggled to come to terms with it. The high level of philosophical discussion does not prevent Samuels from considering Adams's personal apprehensions about the public reception of his *History* nor his elaborate efforts to draw commentary from his most learned friends before publication. Samuels strives to reassess the structure and general trajectory of the *History*, offering an analysis of Adams's attempt to present historical narrative and social science in one form: "One may disregard the science and enjoy the brilliantly written bravura sections in which the artist triumphs over the social scientist, but only at the risk of mis-

reading the total work. The science of it is obviously the indispensible 'myth' of the whole literary structure. Questionable as it may be, it makes the vast array of material cohere."

Making full use of previously unpublished letters, Samuels completed *Henry Adams: The Major Phase* in 1964. This third volume focuses on the writings produced during the last years of Adams's writing career: *Mont-Saint-Michel and Chartres* (1904), *The Education of Henry Adams*, the longer poems, and his memoir of George Cabot Lodge (1911). In the forefront of Samuels's discussion are the ideas in *The Education* and in the essays "The Tendency of History" and "The Rule of Phase Applied to History," which develop Adams's perspective on scientific theories of history and include his apocalyptic predictions of the end of Western civilization in the first half of the twentieth century. Samuels quotes from the prolific correspondence and reminiscences of Adams and his friends to produce a lively narrative of ideas and arguments. Equally impressive is Samuels's presentation of Adams in pursuit of spiritual redress at Chartres.

Samuels indicates the organic relation of *Mont-Saint-Michel and Chartres* to *The Education*, showing Adams's interest in demonstrating thirteenth-century unity in the former while seeking a definition of twentieth-century multiplicity in the latter. Moreover, Samuels finds that the well-known shortcomings of *The Education* in fact support the strengths of its theme: "The unresolved tension between the narrative and didactic elements became itself a dominant motif of the work, an illustration of the very 'mystery of Multiplicity' that the *Education* was to demonstrate, of the unappeasable striving toward Unity of the human mind." Samuels also offers cogent general impressions of his subject during his last years: "He took refuge in the pose of humorous cynicism, counting on his intimates to separate the chaffing wit from the kernel of his instruction."

While sifting through the Adams correspondence at the Massachusetts Historical Society, Samuels came upon letters from Bernard Berenson. His subsequent visit in 1956 to I Tatti, the Berenson villa in Tuscany, and his interview with the ninety-one-year-old Berenson to request his letters from Adams eventually led to a request from Berenson's literary executor that Samuels begin a two-volume life of the legendary art historian and philosopher. Samuels was given, as he says, "a key to the archives, a treasure house of letters from more than twelve hundred correspondents and of masses of untouched papers." *Bernard Berenson: The Making of a Connoisseur* (1979) and *Bernard Berenson: The Making of a Legend* (1987) were well received by both art historians and literary critics. Regarding the first volume, critics praised Samuels's ability to separate fact from rumor in the shadier areas of Berenson's art dealing and attributions, and Ruth Berenson in the *National Review* (8 June 1979) recognized a "beautifully written, objective account, which . . .

seems definitive." Of the second volume, John Updike, in the *New York Times Book Review* (29 March 1987) observed, "Though an 'official' biography . . . the book does not shy from showing its subject as vain, snobbish, ruthlessly romantic and incorrigibly luxury-loving." Commenting on his own narrative form in the Berenson volumes, Samuels felt that the complexities of his biographical approach were needed to match the complexities of his subject's life: "The multiple facets of Berenson's life resisted straightforward chronology, so that the narrative tends to move on parallel and alternating lines somewhat like a Trollopian novel."

The revised and abridged version of the Adams trilogy, *Henry Adams* (1989), received critical praise for its wide-ranging exploration of Adams's life and times, even though Samuels had reduced in size his original three volumes from over fifteen hundred to five hundred pages.

In a lively and provocative article, "Confessions of a Biographer" (1981), Samuels warns future biographers of the temptation to distort the truth for the sake of a pet theory or matter of opinion: "As a biographer one has to submit as gracefully as one can to the illogic of events. One's freedom is limited to those happenings which keep in the foreground the developing identity of the subject. . . . There are often unbridgeable gaps in a life record and one is tempted to throw a line of conjecture across the abyss, especially in the service of an attractive thesis." It is this concern for the integrity of his profession that has made Samuels such a dedicated and rigorous scholar.

Papers:
The Ernest Samuels Papers are in the Northwestern University Archives.

Richard B. Sewall
(11 February 1908 -   )

Timothy Morris
University of Texas at Arlington

BOOKS: *The Vision of Tragedy* (New Haven: Yale University Press, 1959; revised and enlarged edition, New Haven & London: Yale University Press, 1980; enlarged again, New York: Paragon, 1990);

The Lyman Letters: New Light on Emily Dickinson and Her Family (Amherst: University of Massachusetts Press, 1965);

The Life of Emily Dickinson, 2 volumes (New York: Farrar, Straus & Giroux, 1974; London: Faber, 1976).

OTHER: *Short Stories for Study: An Anthology,* edited by Sewall and Raymond W. Short (New York: Holt, 1941; revised, 1950; revised again, 1956);

Tragedy: Modern Essays in Criticism, edited by Sewall and Laurence A. Michel (Englewood Cliffs, N.J.: Prentice-Hall, 1963);

Emily Dickinson: A Collection of Critical Essays, edited by Sewall (Englewood Cliffs, N.J.: Prentice-Hall, 1963);

"Emily Dickinson," in *Voices and Visions,* edited by Helen Vendler (New York: Vintage, 1987), pp. 51-89;

"In Search of Emily Dickinson," in *Extraordinary Lives: The Art and Craft of American Biography,* edited by William Zinsser (Boston: Houghton Mifflin, 1988), pp. 63-90.

When Richard B. Sewall began work on his biography of Emily Dickinson in 1959, there were already several versions of Dickinson's life available, including books by Thomas H. Johnson (1955), Rebecca Patterson (1951), and Genevieve Taggard (1930). Interpretations of Dickinson's life abounded, driven by the need to explain how a reclusive, single Victorian woman could have produced so many poems, several of them among the greatest American lyrics. George Frisbie Whicher's *This Was a Poet,* published in 1939, was the standard work and is still a respected interpretive biography. But Whicher, like all scholars who wrote on Dickinson before 1955,

was hampered by the lack of definitive texts of her poems. When first published, the poems were severely altered by their first editor, Mabel Loomis Todd, to bring them into line with public taste. Before Thomas H. Johnson's *The Poems of Emily Dickinson* (1955) there was no uniform edition and hence no idea of the extent of the corpus, the approximate chronology of the manuscripts, or the status of the variant versions of many of the poems. *The Letters of Emily Dickinson* (1958), edited by Johnson and Theodora Ward, filled in the same gaps of information on her prose.

Sewall's biographical work, which culminated in the publication of his two-volume *The Life of Emily Dickinson* in 1974, was the most important research project to be done on the poet during the 1960s and 1970s, and it became a paradigm for the study of Dickinson.

Sewall's personal history qualified him for the task of writing Dickinson's biography. As he writes in the introduction, he is the descendant of "eleven generations of New England clergymen (all but one Congregational)." The last in this line of clergymen was Sewall's father, Charles Grenville Sewall; the biographer's mother was Kate Strong Sewall. He was born in Albany, New York, on 11 February 1908 and began his education in local public schools. Sewall's higher education, at Exeter, at Williams College, where he received a B.A. in 1929, and at Yale, where he received a Ph.D. in 1933, resembles that of many of Dickinson's male contemporaries; when writing about the Puritan heritage of the Dickinsons, Sewall is also writing about his own heritage. Sewall married Mathilde Parmelee on 18 October 1940; they remained married until her death in November 1974 and had three sons, Stephen, Richard, and David.

In some ways the role of Dickinson biographer seems an unlikely one for Sewall, given his early academic career. His Yale dissertation was on "English Translations of the Discourses of Jean-Jacques Rousseau." After a one-year appoint-

Richard B. Sewall

ment at Clark University (1933-1934), his subsequent teaching career at Yale, from 1934 until his retirement and appointment as professor emeritus in 1976, centered on classical and modern tragedy; in 1959 his critical study *The Vision of Tragedy* was published by Yale University Press. In addition, he was neither an Americanist nor a biographer; he was not an expert on lyric poetry or women writers.

Nevertheless, Sewall's intellectual pursuits during the first half of his academic career foreshadow the approach he was to take in his work as biographer. He was a colleague at Yale of W. K. Wimsatt, Louis Martz, Maynard Mack, René Wellek, and Cleanth Brooks; the formalist approach that characterizes this generation of Yale critics is evident in Sewall's early work. He and Raymond W. Short write in their introduction to *Short Stories for Study* (1941): "A work of

art is an ordered structure, appealing strongly to the same instinct in us that delights in other intricate but well-composed structures, when we find them in nature or in systems of abstract values." The teaching method recommended by Sewall and Short centers on a text and its intrinsic structures, treating the text, however, as "organism," not "mechanism."

Sewall's approach in *The Vision of Tragedy* follows the tenets he and Short expressed eighteen years earlier. Sewall studies texts ranging from the Book of Job, *Oedipus the King*, *Doctor Faustus*, and *King Lear* to modern novels such as *The Scarlet Letter*, *Moby-Dick*, *The Brothers Karamazov*, and *Absalom, Absalom*. (In 1980 Sewall added chapters on *The Trial* and *Long Day's Journey Into Night*; in 1990 he added one on *Death of a Salesman*.) Sewall treats all these texts as manifestations of an underlying tragic vision or spirit. Historical contexts, and even biographical considerations, are pared away from his vision of the central unity of the tragic spirit in these writers. Despite the fact that his book is a major study of a genre, Sewall downplays generic systems and formulae: "In general, the tragic vision is not a systematic view of life. . . . It is an attitude toward life with which some individuals seem to be endowed to high degree, others less, but which is latent in every man and may be evoked by experience." Literary art, for Sewall, is a cross-cultural, instinctive phenomenon.

As a critic, Sewall does not attempt to psychoanalyze authors or to see their work as determined by biographical patterns. His separation of biography from literary analysis made him well-equipped to confront the salient problem of any Dickinson biography: the myths about Emily Dickinson, which were encouraged by the lack of a reliable text and chronology for the poems until 1955—the myth of the lover, male or female, who had tragically altered young Emily's life; the myth of Dickinson as an untutored primitive; the myth of the imperious father and the cipher of a mother; and the myth of the bitter spinster starved for recognition.

Sewall was suspicious of such attempts to explain Dickinson's poems by reference to her life. He has always argued that the poems simply cannot be dated with enough accuracy to allow such interpretations. Most important, though, he was never surprised that Dickinson became a poet. Many of the myths spring from critics' doubts that her drab, sheltered existence could have produced her poetry; some lurid motivation seems to be required. But for Sewall the potential for poetic expression exists in all people; it is not elicited only by certain types of experience. Sewall's belief has always been that artists are essentially artists. As he wrote in his review of the 1958 collection of Dickinson letters in *Saturday Review* (22 March 1958), she was "a poet all the time."

To extend this line of thinking, it is perhaps fair to say that Sewall was a literary biographer all the time: his clear distinction between matters of biography and matters of criticism paves the way for his biographical work. But he makes his specific choice of subject seem almost accidental. "In the beginning," he says, "I didn't go searching for Emily Dickinson; she went searching for me." In 1945 his colleague Stanley Williams suggested that Sewall write a review of the newly published collection of Dickinson poems, *Bolts of Melody*. Sewall's review, in the *New England Quarterly*

(1945), was unfavorable: "In spite of the protest in the Preface that here are poems as fine as she ever wrote, I find very few that rank with her best." Nevertheless, the review attracted the attention of the editor of *Bolts of Melody*, Millicent Todd Bingham. The daughter of Mabel Loomis Todd, Bingham was a link to Dickinson's original publication and reception; her cooperation was essential to any biographer. Perhaps Sewall's forthrightness caught Bingham's eye; certainly his exacting sense of scholarship and his praise of her conservative editorial method appealed to her. Bingham suggested that he write a biography of Dickinson; Sewall protested that he was committed to his work on tragedy. "Tragedy!" he remembers Bingham countering: "What a wonderful preparation for a biography of Emily Dickinson!" Sewall presents himself as being steered, or dragged, into the project by Bingham. After *The Vision of Tragedy* was published in 1959, Sewall devoted his full attention to writing the life of Dickinson. The project involved fifteen years of full-time work for him, culminating in the publication of *The Life of Emily Dickinson*. He retired from the faculty at Yale soon after the publication of the biography, but his teaching career continued with visiting professorships, including a year at Williams College (1976-1977), where he had been awarded an honorary Litt.D. in 1975.

Despite Sewall's picture of himself entering the world of Dickinson almost passively, Bingham's comment certainly shows the attraction that Dickinson had for him: her story, and that of her family, *is* tragic. It is a small domestic tragedy, but in Sewall's narrative it is compelling. His main contribution was to tell that tale realistically rather than assume that Dickinson's life must follow a romantic pattern of love and renunciation. He was tempted to look for such a pattern; at one point in his work Jay Leyda rebuked him: "Do you enjoy being a sleuth?" But ultimately his instincts—and his critical training—won out. He told Dickinson's story in a new way: less a story of someone traumatized into poetry; more a story of a born artist, born into certain social and familial circumstances.

Sewall had the assistance and advice not only of Bingham but also of Leyda, who had assembled a two-volume collection of Dickinson life records, published as *The Years and Hours of Emily Dickinson* (1960). Leyda's collection is still the most valuable single source of biographical data about Dickinson and her family. In a total of more than nine hundred pages, it presents a chronology of events from 1828, when Dickinson's parents became engaged, to 1886, when Dickinson died. Leyda includes not only essential biographical information about the poet and her family, but also a vast range of cultural context: announcements of lectures and entertainments, descriptions of sermons, extracts from local papers—in short, as much information as possible that tends to reconstruct what everyday life in nineteenth-century Amherst was like. Leyda's work—like that of Bingham and Sewall—grew out of the pressure of the myths that surrounded Dickinson's life and was an attempt to set the record straight on matters of fact. But Bingham and Leyda were determined to let Sewall present Dickinson's story in his own way. Bingham revealed the story of her own mother's love affair with Austin Dickinson but laid no conditions on Sewall's presentation of the story. Leyda lent his mastery of the factual record but refused to provide interpretations: "I can collect the facts; it's up to you people to make something of them."

The Life of Emily Dickinson grew during the 1960s in the context of a great burgeoning of Dickinson scholarship. Sewall provided two valuable resources for Dickinson studies during this period: the collection of critical essays on Dickinson that he edited for Prentice-Hall in 1963 and *The Lyman Letters*, published in 1965, an example of Sewall's painstaking approach to Dickinson's life. Following the example of Leyda, who devoted a large section of *The Years and Hours* to "The People Around Emily Dickinson," Sewall set out to assemble as much material as possible about friends and acquaintances who observed Dickinson during her lifetime. The descendants of Joseph B. Lyman, who was a schoolmate of the poet's brother, Austin, and at one time a suitor of her sister, Lavinia, made his letters available for publication, and Sewall wrote a monograph explaining the significance of the letters. Lyman's observations about the Dickinson family and the excerpts he preserved from Emily's letters provide model source material for the approach that Sewall was to adopt in his biography.

Starting with such material, Sewall worked his way in toward the story of the poet's life. He had to strip away the accumulated layers of myth and to extricate her life from the relationships that surrounded her. He was also writing in the context of myths that developed between 1959 and 1974, when his book was finished: new and all-encompassing psychoanalytic approaches and even a claim that Dickinson was essentially not a poet but a plagiarist. Far from being seduced by any of these theories, Sewall became even more resolved to keep approaches to the poet open, rather than seeing his task as one of solving her.

A complicating factor for Sewall's work was that the life of Dickinson was inseparable from her posthumous reception. Before Johnson's 1955 edition, the publishing history of the Dickinson poems had been a piecemeal process, with two large collections of manuscripts belonging to different families providing the basis of several incomplete editions of selected poems. Todd, who edited the first selection of the poems with Thomas W. Higginson in 1890, published four more selections of poems and letters before 1931; Bingham published a final collection of the poems in her possession in 1945. Martha Dickinson Bianchi, the poet's niece, began to publish the manuscripts in her possession in 1914, after the death of her mother, Susan Gilbert Dickinson, and published five additional volumes in the 1920s and 1930s. This publishing feud had originated in what is now one of the most celebrated Victorian love affairs, but which was still unmentioned by Dickinson scholars in the 1950s: the relationship between Mabel Todd and the poet's brother, Austin (Susan's husband). Sewall could not very well pretend that nothing had happened between Emily's death in 1886 and the variorum edition in 1955, and with the encouragement of Bingham he set out to tell the story of the Mabel-Austin affair and the ensuing "War Between the Houses." Sewall, in telling the story of Austin and Mabel for the first time, helped explain the confusing publishing history of Dickinson's poems, which in turn is closely linked to the evolving myths about the poet.

But Sewall's revelations about the Mabel-Austin affair are more than a sidelight on the poet's reception; they are integral to the way he views Dickinson. Her life and poetry were so private that the "problem of the biographer" becomes one of approaching the subject at all. Since the direct approach is ruled out in so many ways, Sewall adopts an indirect method, reaching Dickinson through the people around her. In line with this principle, Austin and Mabel become two "reflectors" of her life, as Sewall puts it, following Henry James's idea.

As Sewall ruefully points out, the poet herself made the indirect approach necessary by thoroughly covering her own tracks. Not only are the usual public records, such as interviews, publishing correspondence, and prefaces nonexistent in

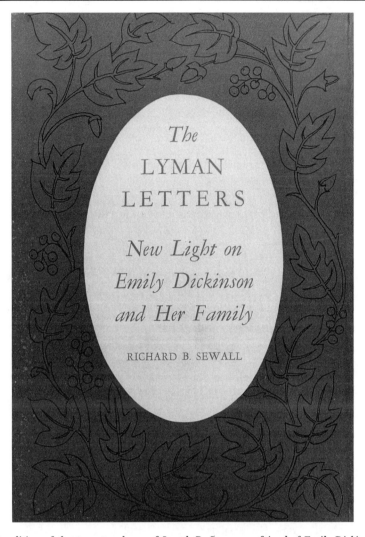

Dust jacket for Sewall's edition of the correspondence of Joseph B. Lyman, a friend of Emily Dickinson's brother and sister

her case, but there are also no intimate records, such as diaries. By Dickinson's request most of the letters she had received were destroyed after her death, so that her correspondence is mainly in the one-sided collections of letters kept by her friends. The manuscript books themselves, luckily saved, present nothing but the bare texts of the poems.

Dickinson made no statement that demands the poems be read through it; she attempted none of the autobiography that clouds the task of the literary biographer. Dickinson, however, lived in a milieu of writers, editors, political and social figures, and most important, of her own talented, ambitious family. She was herself isolated, but the richness of Dickinson's society gave Sewall a ready-made set of reflectors for his biography.

Volume one of Sewall's biography is de-

voted to the Dickinson family; volume two deals with the poet herself, as seen through her education, her relationships with friends and literary contacts, and ultimately her own reading and writing. Volume 1 begins with the story of her paternal grandfather, Samuel Fowler Dickinson, one of the founders of Amherst College; he died when she was seven but shows her immediate connection with her Puritan heritage. He had been born in 1775, and his status as a town father made the old religious culture a living thing to his son and grandchildren. So Dickinson's connections with Puritan thought come to seem less a matter of her reading and her historical interests and more a product of the Connecticut Valley and its strongly conservative families.

Dickinson's relationship with her immediate family had been a fertile field for mythogra-

Wadsworth, famous minister of the Arch Street Presbyterian
Church, the Colemans' church, where Eliza would surely have
taken her visitors.

at Willard's who met the demands of Emily's later fame by ~~searching~~ *searching*

their ~~memories~~ *memories* for whatever they could recall. Thus it is that we hear

about Vinnie's wit as reported by Professor Chickering, *or* of Mrs. *Jeanie*

Greenough's kindly but imprecise memory of Emily:

> My first acquaintance with Emily D. was in Washington
> many years ago. Her father was in Congress. He, with
> his two daughters, my father & mother & myself were
> together at Willard's Hotel. Emily impressed me as a
> girl with large warm heart, earnest nature & delicate
> tastes, & we soon became friends.

Emily's remark to a judge who sat next to her at dinner, when the

flaming plumb pudding was passed, has come down somehow or other:

"Oh, Sir, may one eat of hell-fire with impunity here?" We know

that the girls made the friendship of a certain Mrs. James Brown

and that Vinnie walked with "some ladies here" and got tired out. →OVER→

who later sent them a book, duly inscribed, But, except for the

trip to Mount Vernon, we know nothing more about how the girls

passed their days, whether they visited other monuments, or the

seats of government, whether they saw their father in action, or

what they thought of the whole rugged display of democracy at

work. All we know is that, about March 4, they arrived in Phila-

delphia, probably escorted there by Edward Dickinson on his way

back to Amherst.

¶ It is this second phase of the trip that has long been thought

is supposed to have come the crucial one, for here ~~was~~ the encounter with the Reverend Charles

And yet we know even less about what the girls did ~~in~~

in Philadelphia than in Washington, let alone anything specific about

an encounter with Wadsworth. The only

surviving letter from Philadelphia is the one to Mrs. Holland, and

Emily
in it ~~she~~ makes no mention of having heard

Wadsworth preach or even, for that matter, having gone to church.

curious
The omission is ~~~~ in view of Emily's frequent men-

tion in earlier letters of sermons that impressed her, like Henry

Boynton Smith's when she was at Mt. Holyoke or Edwards Amasa Park's

when he was guest preacher in Amherst in 1853 ("I never heard any-

thing like it, and don't expect to again.") But ~~~~ she must

Pages from the revised typescript for The Life of Emily Dickinson, *volume two (by permission of Richard B. Sewall)*

or anxiety

sorrow about which Emily had written him. The note was first published

in Emily Dickinson's Home, where it is, ~~fully discussed and reproduced~~ *reproduced in facsimile and* ~~fully discussed.~~ ~~in facsimile.~~ It is an earnest but formal pastoral reply. Suggested

dates start at about 1862, *1858 (where Emily's anxiety may have been her mother's health); move on to* to square things with the so-called Master

letters; and go as far as 1877, when Emily was distressed over the

illness of Samuel Bowles. *As to 1858, we must assume that her distress was great enough to make her seek* ~~The first date~~ *1862* must face the many and cogent *beyond Am-* *herst for* *help.* *(The evidence* *is not con-* *clusive.)*

arguments recently made against the theory that Wadsworth was the

Master of the letters, *3* while ~~the latter~~ *1877* reduces to something quite

professional and remote the friendship that Emily described so tenderly,

after Wadsworth's death, in her letters to his friends the Clark

brothers. *4*

~~In this~~ *On the* note, ~~only a few lines,~~ *Wadsworth* begged to hear more about the

"affliction which has befallen, or is now befalling you," and ~~he signed~~ *concluded, "In great haste,"*

"Sincerely and most Affectionately Yours." *It is to be noted that* ~~~~

he misspelled her surname, and failed to sign his own. More important than

any inference that can be drawn from such a document ~~is~~ *is* the ~~history~~ *nature* of

Emily's life for the four or five years after Philadelphia. *in so far as it can be pieced together from scanty knowledge,* ~~The evidence~~ *It seems clear that*

~~that~~ her withdrawal was ~~neither~~ *neither* abrupt ~~or~~ *nor* dramatic. In 1859 and 1860,

she was still going to church, if irregularly, "doing her courtesies," and

enjoying evenings of gaiety at ~~~~ *The Evergreens. Many letters of the period describe moments, at* Vinnie's explanation of *least, of* *laughter and* *delight.*

the withdrawal, though far from the whole truth, seems more likely: "[it]

was only a happen," a ~~habit~~ *way of life* gradually induced by domestic cares and ~~encouraged~~

~~by~~ the needs of her own temperament. As to the immolation in white, it is

well known that she wore white a good deal, but the custom *was probably not* ~~may not have become~~

fixed until after her father's death.

Another view has the Wadsworth meeting growing into an all-encompassing

fantasy in her mind, much as the lovers in the mediaeval Courts of Love

phers, and Sewall devotes a chapter to each family member. Edward Dickinson, her father, had been shaped by myth, as Sewall puts it, into a "Mr. Barrett of Wimpole Street"—not least by some of Emily's own darker hints about his seriousness and closed-mindedness. Of her mother, also named Emily, the poet simply said, "I never had a mother," further skewing the center of the family structure toward Edward.

Sewall accords the parents independent importance, writing separate brief biographies. So much had been written on Dickinson's psychological responses to her father and mother, and she herself had adopted so many poses regarding them, that Sewall felt the need to show what she was posing against. Edward appears as a man of intense passions who was keenly aware that he had many traditional roles to play, and he filled those roles, as squire, treasurer, legislator, and father, with great energy. Emily Norcross Dickinson, by contrast, "made herself dispensable." But the poet shared her mother's aplomb, just as she shared her father's strength. Sewall deliberately steers away from psychoanalyzing Dickinson's reactions to her home life, preferring to establish the picture of how the Dickinsons expressed themselves outwardly. The result is a father less fearsome and a mother more visible than the myths allow.

The poet's brother, Austin, who struggled in his own way with his father's presence, ultimately assumed many of his father's roles—and at last expressed his passions in his love for Mabel Todd. By contrast, Emily's sister, Lavinia, was a "calming influence"—the single person who spent the most time with Emily and was most supportive. Although a target of gentle fun in the poet's letters, she also appears as "heroic," a true friend.

All four of the immediate family members participated in what Sewall calls "the Dickinson Rhetoric," "subtle and circuitous," hyperbolic, evasive. In Austin this rhetoric came out in his agonizing, questioning letters; in Emily it burst into poetry. By studying the lives of her family in such depth, Sewall makes it seem natural that Dickinson should have been a poet—even natural that she should have been the great, enigmatic poet that she was.

Volume one of Sewall's biography closes with the story of Austin and Mabel; volume two goes back to Dickinson's birth and traces her life chronologically by means of many friends who serve as reflectors. Sewall pays some attention to her education but more to her correspondence, drawing heavily on the reminiscences and papers of early friends such as Abiah Root and Joseph Lyman. Several myths are discounted in this volume: Dickinson is shown to have had a considerable education, leaving Mount Holyoke after two terms, less for melodramatic reasons than because her fine primary schooling at Amherst Academy "gave her all the formal education she needed or wanted," and the books and intellectual company she found in Amherst thereafter were sophisticated and stimulating. Nor was her father a dragon, forbidding his daughters to mix with the men from the college. There is no hint of any scene or quarrel that prevented Emily from receiving male suitors—nor any evidence that she was romantically involved with women, though she shared with the women in her life, especially Susan Gilbert, the sort of loving, "homosocial" relationship that has since been explored by Carroll Smith-Rosenberg and other historians.

When discussing Dickinson's adult friendships, Sewall tackles the myth of the "Lover" head-on. The leading candidate for the role of lover was Charles Wadsworth, a married minister Dickinson was supposed to have met in Philadelphia in 1854 and to have loved, hopelessly, until his death in 1882. "This version," says Sewall, "has Emily returning to Amherst in despair, writing her poems of passion and frustration, and, soon after, retiring in white from the world." But even the circumstantial evidence for such a love affair is tenuous. She did know Wadsworth, but the only surviving piece of their correspondence is a brief note from him in which Dickinson's name is misspelled. Better evidence is the sequence of Dickinson's letters to James and Charles Clark, two friends of Wadsworth, that begins after his death in 1882 and speaks of a long and close friendship. But the nature of this friendship remains unknown. Sewall speculates that Wadsworth's sermons attracted Dickinson with their undertone of doubt and their surprising, wry humor. This type of intellectual friendship was certainly the link between Dickinson and Wadsworth.

Dickinson's relationship with Samuel Bowles, the editor of the *Springfield Republican*, poses more problems. Sewall shows that Dickinson was powerfully affected by Bowles, that she sent him many exuberant, emotional letters and poems, that she *may* have intended him to be the recipient of the strange, beautiful love letters addressed only to "Master," that she hoped he would be supportive of her writing—and that he treated her, ultimately, with indifference. He published only a handful of her poems, heavily edited. What either Bowles or Dickinson actually felt, and how far this relationship ever proceeded, is not known. Bowles did not inspire the poetry; he was mainly a potential reader and publisher to the young poet. Sewall shows us Dickinson searching for a reader, preferably one who would always be somewhat shocked and reproving but at the same time play the role of tolerant "preceptor."

Bowles failed in this role on several counts, but Thomas Wentworth Higginson became the perfect foil for Dickinson. By the time she began sending poems and letters to him, in 1862, she had experienced Bowles's coldness to her poetry, and was also to experience Higginson's advice that she "delay to publish." Sewall sums up this important friendship: "He failed her as a critic of her poetry; but at least he answered her letters, came (at last) to see her, and was perceptive enough to see something 'remarkable' in her." Sewall does not show Higginson as patronizing Dickinson or putting her off; in fact, toward the end of her life, Dickinson takes on the decided tone of superior in her relationship with him.

In other friendships, such as the close ones Dickinson had with her cousins Louise and Frances Norcross, and with Dr. and Mrs. Josiah Holland, readers see her in a more familiar setting. In a chapter on Dickinson and Helen Hunt Jackson, Sewall shows the poet enjoying a fruitful correspondence with an important fellow woman writer—and by then, late in her life, avoiding publication as surely as she had sought it before.

Myths surrounding Dickinson's attitude toward publication of her poems are among the most difficult to explore, or to dispel. Before Sewall's biography, several theories pointed toward a decisive event—a rejection by Higginson, say, or a thwarted romantic attachment to Bowles. On one hand, then, a myth grew about her desire to be published and her defeat by prejudice. But Dickinson also made pronouncements against publication in her writing: it was "foreign to my thought, as Firmament to Fin"; it was "the Auction / Of the Mind of Man." Based on these enigmatic, often ironic disclaimers, another myth grew, that Dickinson always shied away from publishing her poetry.

Sewall presents a more complex picture, tracing Dickinson's attitudes toward publication from the start of her poetic career, when she was content with private readers, especially Susan Gilbert Dickinson. As the corpus of her work grew, she naturally enough sought outlets for it and thought that Bowles might provide both private and public readership for her work. When his unhelpfulness became clear, she approached Higginson. In 1882 she was approached by the publisher Thomas Niles and encouraged to submit a volume of poems for publication; Helen Hunt Jackson instigated this contact. Sewall traces the correspondence, which resulted in Dickinson's refusal to send Niles her poems. "We wonder what she was waiting for," comments Sewall; she was middle-aged, still writing, with a vast body of work to draw on, yet she refused to commence a public career. Clearly her attitudes toward publication were ambivalent and changing. Sewall's picture of Dickinson's ambivalence clears away some of the dogmatic assumptions on the issue of publication and helps form a context for later research. Again readers see a dynamic life in Sewall's work, not a set of irrevocable decisions taken at a certain age that predestine the poet to a certain result.

Finally, Dickinson did have a bona fide lover, one who received little attention until Sewall's biography. He was Judge Otis Lord, who became a widower in 1877 and carried on a fervent correspondence and friendship with her until his death in 1884. Sewall doubts if Dickinson and Lord ever really considered marriage; but her frank, personal love letters to him survive and are a startling contrast to the fragmentary, ambiguous evidence for other "lovers."

To complete his picture of Dickinson, Sewall turns to her reading and poems and charts her wide literary experience. The last of the myths start to fall: that she worked "in grand isolation," cut off from literary tradition; that she was somehow a "plagiarist" because so many of her subjects do come from that tradition; and that there is a "figure in the carpet," a central obsession, that explains her work. There is a central theme to her poetry, Sewall writes in his final chapter, "The Poet," but it is a theme of the broadest possible scope: "to mediate to 'every man' the infinitely varied facets and phases of the central 'dazzling' truth as it was vouchsafed her in her moments (she had a hard time defining it) of inspiration." This dazzling truth is, ultimately, that of immortality, "the Flood subject," but its manifestations are various and pervade Dickinson's poetry.

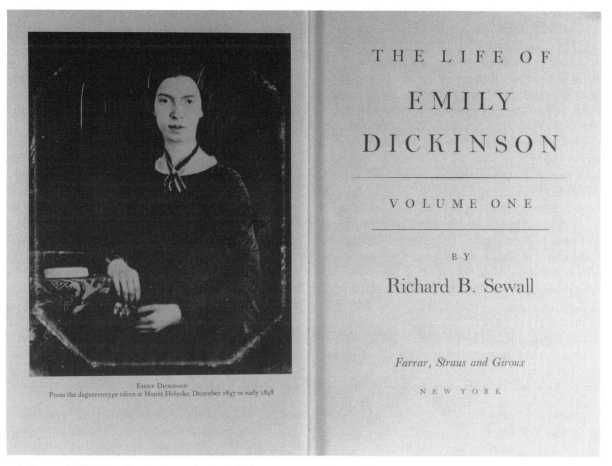

EMILY DICKINSON
From the daguerreotype taken at Mount Holyoke, December 1847 or early 1848

THE LIFE OF
EMILY
DICKINSON

VOLUME ONE

BY

Richard B. Sewall

Farrar, Straus and Giroux

NEW YORK

Frontispiece and title page for the first volume of the biography in which Sewall was faced with two tasks: separating the facts of Dickinson's life from myths created after her death and tracing the complex history of the posthumous publication of her poems

The Life of Emily Dickinson is an unconventional biography, achieving remarkable fullness despite seeming to avoid the life of its own subject. Sewall was strongly influenced by the work of Leyda: his assembly of life records for Herman Melville and for Dickinson extended the use of this biographical tool from the remote past (where it provides, necessarily, most of the material for lives of Geoffrey Chaucer or William Shakespeare) into work on authors just barely out of the reach of living memory. Sewall's inductive method also has affinities with nonliterary biographies, such as Douglas Southall Freeman's life of George Washington. Just as Freeman does not let readers see anything that Washington himself did not experience, Sewall does not fit Dickinson into historical contexts unless they touched her directly. Thus there is a great deal about Samuel Fowler Dickinson, little about "the Puritan heritage" in general, and much about Dickinson's reaction to the death of Frazar Stearns in combat, little about the Civil War as a whole.

The Life of Emily Dickinson received both the Poetry Society of America Award (1974) and the National Book Award (1975). Reviewers were unanimous in commending the biography as a work of scholarship and research. The outstanding feature of the book, for most reviewers, was its demolition of the Dickinson myths: "it disposes of . . . often simplistic theories and . . . romantic claptrap," wrote Herbert Leibowitz in the *New York Times Book Review* (22 December 1974). Striking, too, for many, were the revelations about Mabel Todd and Austin Dickinson; Irvin Ehrenpreis in the *New York Review of Books* (23 January 1975) marveled at the "startling abundance" of new information on this old family scandal. There was a little disappointment, however, that Sewall's research had unearthed nothing startling about the poet herself; Leibowitz wished "that Sewall had probed more boldly into the clandestine emotions, the skein of motives, of his subject." Dorothy Rabinowitz in the *Saturday Review* (22 February 1975) found the book's structure "eccentric"; but more common was Ehrenpreis's realization that Sewall had "really produced three studies": of Dickinson's relationships, of the publication of her poems, and of the family dynamics of her Amherst circle. Such a book was more than, and different from, a narrowly focused life. Probably the most perceptive comment was that of R. W. B. Lewis, Sewall's Yale colleague and fellow literary biographer, in the *New Republic* (8 February 1975): "Like other recent biographers, Sewall tends to make his researches and the problems they raise a continuing part of his narrative. As often as not, he is telling us not so much what happened as why we cannot really be sure what happened. . . . Richard Sewall's biographical version of Emily Dickinson is as complete as human scholarship, stylistic pungency and common sense can arrive at. But it is also, deliberately and gracefully, a covered version as well."

Sewall's book did not have, and perhaps could not have had, the effect of extinguishing Dickinson mythography altogether. Interpreta-

tions continue to be produced that purport to "solve" Dickinson; they propose new candidates for her lover and revive old ones. But Sewall's reasonable, refreshing discussion of all the available "clues" to Dickinson is there to turn to when another theory arises. By placing the focus of Dickinson life studies on her own immediate experience with family, friends, and reading, Sewall opened up many paths for scholarship, paths taken further by Polly Longsworth, Vivian Pollak, and Mary Bernhard in work on the Dickinson and Norcross families; by Barton Levi St. Armand in work on Dickinson and popular culture; and by Joanne Dobson, working on Dickinson and other women writers. The growth of Dickinson studies in the 1970s and 1980s owes much to Sewall's large claims for the poet. He is in large part responsible for the success of his own 1974 prediction (in his introduction), that "within another decade America's two seminal poets will be Whitman and Dickinson."

Kenneth Silverman
(5 February 1936 -   )

Dennis Barone
Saint Joseph College

BOOKS: *Timothy Dwight* (New York: Twayne, 1969);

A Cultural History of the American Revolution: Painting, Music, Literature, and the Theatre in the Colonies and the United States from the Treaty of Paris to the Inauguration of George Washington, 1763-1789 (New York: Crowell, 1976);

The Life and Times of Cotton Mather (New York & London: Harper & Row, 1984).

RECORDING: *The Theater in Early America*, De Land, Fla., Everett/Edwards, p1976 1405.

OTHER: *Colonial American Poetry*, edited, with introductions, by Silverman (New York & London: Hafner, 1968);

Selected Letters of Cotton Mather, edited, with an introduction, by Silverman (Baton Rouge: Louisiana State University Press, 1971);

Literature in America: The Founding of a Nation, edited, with an introduction, by Silverman (New York: Free Press, 1971);

The Autobiography of Benjamin Franklin and Other Writings, edited, with an introduction, by Silverman (Harmondsworth, U.K. & New York: Penguin, 1986).

Kenneth Silverman received both the Pulitzer Prize for biography and the Bancroft Prize in American History for *The Life and Times of Cotton Mather* (1984). Silverman provides both the scholar and the general reader with a true and compassionate account of Mather, "the first unmistakably American figure in the nation's history." As Larzer Ziff wrote in the *New York Times Book Review* (25 March 1984), "Mr. Silverman has a knack for telling the reader with no special knowledge of Puritanism all he need know about the background of an event or the personality of an actor without interrupting the flow of a narrative that engages the specialist as well." It is the compelling narrative and clear analytical prose of *The Life and Times of Cotton Mather* that led John Demos to proclaim in his review for the *New Repub-*

lic (13-20 August 1984) that "what Silverman achieves can well stand as a model for biographers and historians in general."

So indefatigable a researcher is Silverman that, at an auction in Amherst, Massachusetts, he even turned up part of a lawsuit involving Mather. While looking for Mather letters for his edition of the *Selected Letters of Cotton Mather* (1971), Silverman searched libraries and private collections in fifteen states and twenty-one different countries. No mere pedant, however, he can also write colorful, entertaining prose. For example, he describes the myths about Mather as the "gross distortion of so complex a man into a national gargoyle." To describe the prolix style peculiar to his subject he uses the neologism "Matherese."

Silverman was born on 5 February 1936 in New York City to Gustave Silverman, a builder, and Bessie Goldberg Silverman; he did his undergraduate and graduate work at Columbia University, where he received his B.A. in 1956, his M.A. in 1958, and his Ph.D. in 1964. He then became an English instructor at New York University, where he is currently professor of English and graduate adviser in American civilization. Silverman, a fellow of the American Antiquarian Society and a council member of the Institute for Early American History and Culture, has served on the editorial boards of *Early American Literature*, the *William and Mary Quarterly*, and *American Literature*. He has received awards from the Danforth Foundation and the National Endowment for the Humanities.

Silverman's marriage to Sharon Medjuck (whom he married on 8 September 1957) ended in divorce in 1976. He has two children, Willa and Ethan.

Timothy Dwight, (1969) was Silverman's first book-length publication. In little more than 150 pages, he discusses the many complexities of Dwight, a late-eighteenth- and early-nineteenth-century essayist, poet, preacher, and Yale president. In a review for *American Literature* (Novem-

Kenneth Silverman (photograph by Stan Seligson; courtesy of New York University)

ber 1970) Lewis P. Simpson called Silverman's book "a superior biographical and critical study and the best work on his subject yet published."

In five concise chapters Silverman demonstrates that Dwight was more than a voice from an all-but-forsaken Puritan past: Dwight shared much with his contemporaries and looked ahead to America's future. According to Silverman, Dwight envisioned an "America composed of small, promising townships, perpetuating the Connecticut ideal by reproducing the exquisite scale of Connecticut life." The changes, contradictions, and complexities in Dwight's beliefs become apparent. Silverman analyzes why "Dwight could not decide whether the foundation of America's greatness would be the restraints it imposed on human nature, or the restraints it broke."

Yet his analysis rarely moves beyond Dwight's writings. Silverman explains how Dwight's major writings—among them *The Conquest of Canäan* (1785), *The Triumph of Infidelity* (1788), and *Greenfield Hill* (1794)—exemplify his frequently shifting beliefs. But there is little of Dwight's life in the book. Silverman states in his preface that he "tried at all times to maintain contact with Dwight the literary man" and that to understand Dwight fully one would have "to write a history of New England between the Revolution and the War of 1812." Silverman succeeds, though, in showing how Dwight's writings evidence constant change and contradiction. However, Barbara M. Solomon observed in a review for the *William and Mary Quarterly* (January 1971) that by "defining every shift of attitude

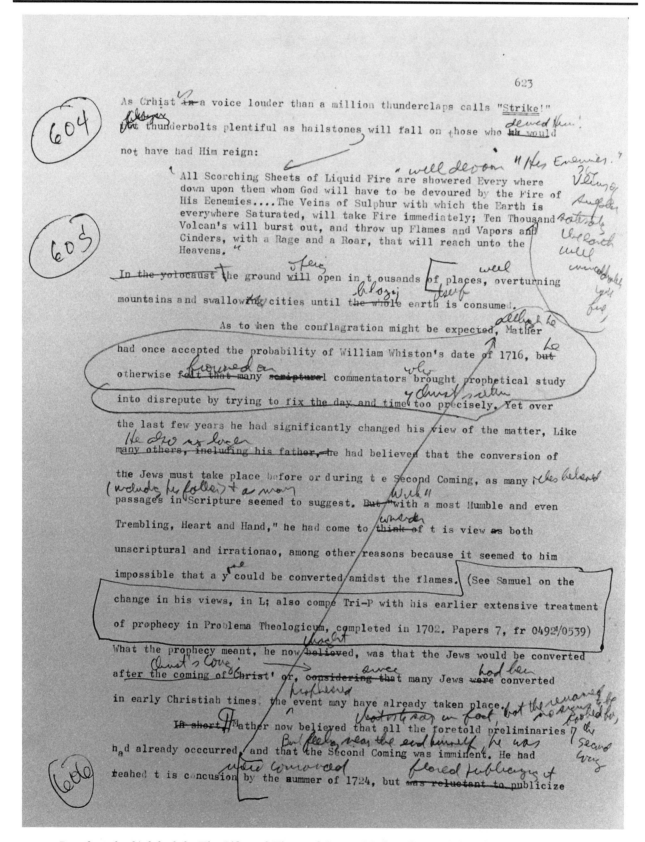

Page from the third draft for The Life and Times of Cotton Mather *(by permission of Kenneth Silverman)*

closely, Silverman stresses Dwight's contradictions but seems to overlook the possible underlying continuity in his views."

Published in 1971, *Selected Letters of Cotton Mather*, Silverman's next book, was a substantial undertaking, for six hundred Mather letters survive (out of over six thousand) in diverse libraries. Rather than fill the book with copious notes, Silverman introduces groups of letters by long commentaries. At the end are brief biographies of Mather's correspondents and other important individuals mentioned in his letters. Approximately one-fourth of the writing in *Selected Letters* is Silverman's; this makes Mather's letters more understandable and more rewarding to read. Since Mather's letters "represent the largest extant correspondence of any American Puritan figure," they tell much about his times as well as his life.

Before undertaking the biography of Mather, Silverman wrote another lengthy and impressive work, *A Cultural History of the American Revolution: Painting, Music, Literature, and the Theatre in the Colonies and the United States from the Treaty of Paris to the Inauguration of George Washington, 1763-1789* (published in 1976). Once again he received praise for his exhaustive research and lively prose. For example, William L. Hedges in *Early American Literature* (Spring 1978) noted that "Silverman's research has a no-stone-unturned definitiveness to it. His command of his sources is virtually total."

In *A Cultural History of the American Revolution* Silverman argues that, at the same time "the country established by war its independence from the British crown," it acquired "the elements of a modern metropolitan cultural life." Dividing the study into three separate parts— "Peace and Learning, 1763-1770"; "Arts and Arms, 1770-1783"; and "Virtue Against Luxury, 1784-1789"—leads to some repetition, but the survey of familiar works and events and the use of new manuscript sources is so rich that the repetitions do little to detract from the value of the book. *A Cultural History of the American Revolution* may well be the best of the books written especially to celebrate the bicentennial of the United States.

Silverman's *Life and Times of Cotton Mather* neither celebrates nor condemns, but rather it offers the first full-length, balanced, analytical portrait of Mather. Silverman is not alone in studying Mather. His biography is part of the modern reappraisal of Mather by Kenneth Murdock,

Perry Miller, Robert Middlekauff, David Levin, Richard F. Lovelace, Sacvan Bercovitch, and others. Silverman's volume is a synthesis and culmination of all modern studies of the Mathers. Cotton Mather may well be the most representative American Puritan. "What makes him fascinating, what makes us keep coming back to him," according to Edmund S. Morgan in the *New York Review of Books* (31 May 1984), "is his palpable display of the tensions and inner conflicts that are evident but more subdued in other Puritans."

Although these tensions and conflicts were obvious in Mather, there are problems in attempting to understand fully both the man and the era he represents. In the preface to *Cotton Mather: The Young Life of the Lord's Remembrancer, 1663-1703* (1978), David Levin notes that the range and sheer number of Mather's works may have done as much to discourage would-be biographers as the poor reputation posterity has afforded him. Levin felt that a full biography should deal with all of Mather's works, avoid a condescending tone, and avoid an argumentative attitude toward other scholars. In these respects, Silverman's work is a success. For example, Silverman and Levin disagree on how the young Mather developed a stammer. Silverman does not insist on his particular view: "Just when and why Cotton Mather's stammer manifested itself is unclear. . . . The affliction may have developed well before 1674. . . . Cotton's several childhood ailments may have contributed. . . . "

Silverman succeeds, too, in maintaining a proper balance between a narrative of the subject's life and an analysis of the subject's writings. He describes and discusses both Mather's life and works, and he explains both continuity and change. For example, he shows that the tension between ambition for fame versus guilt for worldly arrogance was a constant in Mather's life, and yet changes also occurred, such as Mather's coming close, late in life, "to reducing the supernatural experience of grace itself to rational understanding."

Silverman's work on Mather's letters prepared him well for writing the biography. Silverman turns to the letters to fill in the gaps for which there are no surviving Mather diaries. While searching archives for letters, Silverman also found unpublished Mather material in abundance, especially sermons. At the end of his introduction to *Selected Letters of Cotton Mather*, Silverman says that "no comprehensive biography of Mather can be undertaken without these ser-

Silverman circa 1984 (photograph copyright by Jerry Bauer)

mons. . . . Like Emerson, Thoreau, and many later New England writers, Mather wrote very directly out of his immediate experience. All of his sermons, published or unpublished, take their occasion from his life; in debt he preached on debtors; observing his wife's breakdown he preached on insanity."

In *The Life and Times of Cotton Mather* Silverman depicts the major events in Mather's life, such as his involvement in the Salem witch trials and his support for smallpox inoculation, and he discusses Mather's major writings, such as *Magnalia Christi Americana* (1702), *Bonifacius* (1710), and *The Christian Philosopher* (1720). In a review for *Early American Literature* (Fall 1984) Ursula Brumm concluded that "Kenneth Silverman has the talent to keep his readers' attention and to make intricate matters intelligible even to the uninitiated. A splendid achievement in the art of combining excellent scholarship with readability, this book could play a significant role in making the early American period a matter of larger interest."

Cotton Mather was born in 1663, a third generation member of two prominent Boston families of ministers: the Cottons and the Mathers. "He wished to become what he understood his father to have been," Silverman states. "Yet he recognized that his ambitious desire to become a famous preacher like Increase dishonored his sacred obligation to use his ministry to glorify not himself but God alone." These contrasting feelings—pride and self-effacement, a sense of being ignored and a belief in his own place within a divine plan—continued throughout Mather's life and led to his being frequently misunderstood by others. Silverman concludes that the troubles Mather entered into when he took on the administration of the estate of Nathan Howell, who had married his third wife's daughter, typified his life. "He was a man," Silverman says, "whose unique fortune it was to be taken precisely for what he was not. To find himself near ruin for paying the debts of people who despised him was not incidental to his life but of its pervasive substance. . . ." In this instance and many oth-

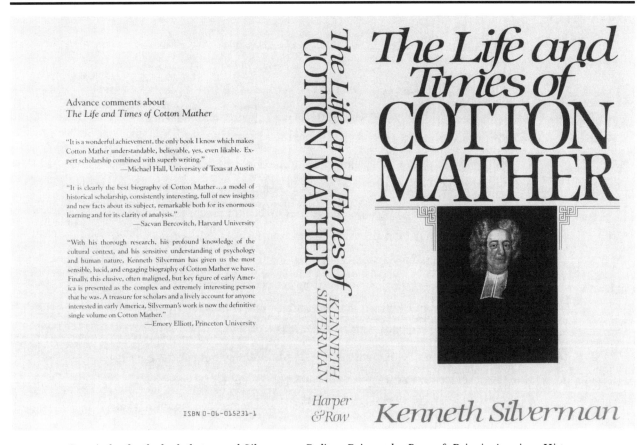

Advance comments about
The Life and Times of Cotton Mather

"It is a wonderful achievement, the only book I know which makes Cotton Mather understandable, believable, yes, even likable. Expert scholarship combined with superb writing."
—Michael Hall, University of Texas at Austin

"It is clearly the best biography of Cotton Mather...a model of historical scholarship, consistently interesting, full of new insights and new facts about its subject, remarkable both for its enormous learning and for its clarity of analysis."
—Sacvan Bercovitch, Harvard University

"With his thorough research, his profound knowledge of the cultural context, and his sensitive understanding of psychology and human nature, Kenneth Silverman has given us the most sensible, lucid, and engaging biography of Cotton Mather we have. Finally, this elusive, often maligned, but key figure of early America is presented as the complex and extremely interesting person that he was. A treasure for scholars and a lively account for anyone interested in early America, Silverman's work is now the definitive single volume on Cotton Mather."
—Emory Elliott, Princeton University

ISBN 0-06-015231-1

Dust jacket for the book that earned Silverman a Pulitzer Prize and a Bancroft Prize in American History

ers it is easy to sympathize with Mather. "When abusive letters arrived," Silverman writes, "he received them emotionlessly, adding them to the large tied bundle on which he had written '*Libels: Father, forgive them!*' "

Before Silverman's biography most Americans knew Mather only as the worst of Puritans, a religious extremist who liked to see witches hang. Silverman provides a more balanced view. Writing in the *Hudson Review* (Winter 1984-1985), Monroe K. Spears observed that readers may still be repelled by the much misunderstood Mather, but they will not be bored. In the *New York Times Book Review* Ziff said that Silverman's "ability to think with Mather never leads him to think like Mather, and his sympathy with his subject never leads him to praise what is dull in Mather's work or condone the deceits Mather sometimes practices on himself as well as on others." Although Silverman's Mather is "hardly less scheming, vain, fork-tongued, or anguished than we have been accustomed to," he is, in Norman Fiering's words, "a figure vastly more understandable" (*Reviews in American History*, December 1984).

Silverman tells of Mather's daily life: "he produced seventy or so formal sermons a year. . . . In preparing each sermon, he reckoned, he usually spent seven hours." Silverman tells of Mather's family life—his three marriages and his fifteen children, only two of whom outlived him.

Silverman's final judgment is that, although the myth of Mather "is simplistic and inaccurate," nonetheless, he was a man of many faults: "His submissiveness that would not grasp that at Salem people were being legally murdered; his meddlesome ambitiousness that stooped or strutted for petty advancement; his guile that wrote self-promoting letters under others' names; his vanity that scented out lurking slurs yet sensed no provocations in himself; his rashness that tendered spite as amity; his envy that sneered at what it could not get." Yet "in his curiousness, epic reach, and quirkily ingenious individualism he was nevertheless the first unmistakably American figure in the nation's history"; "he was the first person to write at length about the New World having never seen the Old"; and he strove "to become conspicuous as an American."

Critics praised Silverman for his thorough research and unobtrusive psychological approach.

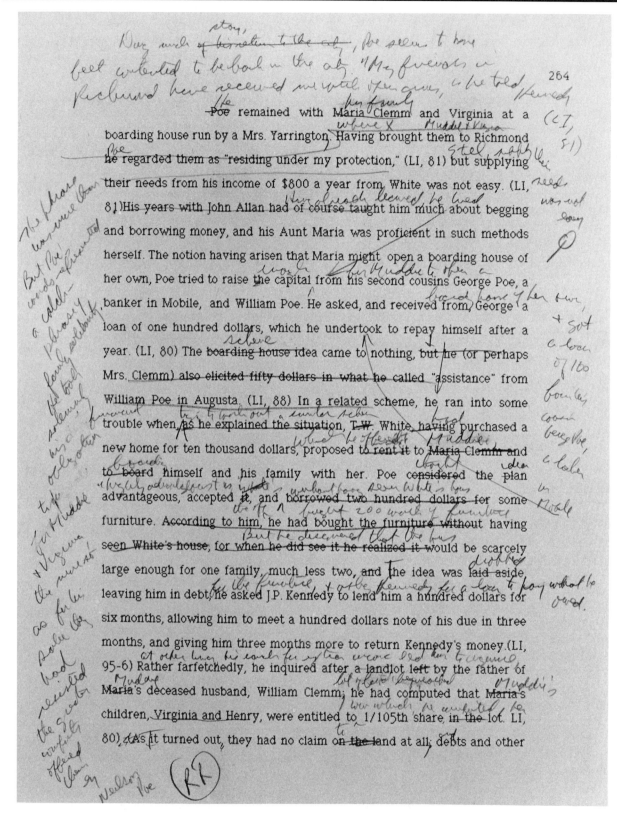

Page from the first draft for Silverman's forthcoming Edgar A. Poe: Mournful and Never-ending Remembrance *(by permission of Kenneth Silverman)*

John Demos in the *New Republic* (13-20 August 1984) said that "this is, above all, a deeply, brilliantly psychological biography. The author seems virtually to have taken up residence inside Mather's head and heart; and the reader is repeatedly invited to see the world as Mather himself would have done—looking out."

The book's faults most often noted by reviewers were that there is too little about theology, that the Mather-as-first-American theme is overstated, that changes in Mather's views are not sufficiently explained, and that the notes are difficult to use. Writing in the *Journal of American History* (December 1984), Charles L. Cohen stated that while "Silverman ably narrates the thrills and pressures that bearing the Mather name imposed . . . he assesses Mather's career as a specifically Puri-

tan thinker less adequately, and he fails to analyze how Mather developed his sense of American identity at a time when sophisticated Bostonians like himself had begun to revel in the culture of metropolitan England."

Recently Kenneth Silverman finished a biography of Edgar Allan Poe. Like his Mather biography, his book on Poe synthesizes recent scholarship and uses a psychoanalytical approach. Publication is planned for 1991. While doing research on Poe, he made several archival discoveries, including two "new" Poe letters and information on the Allan family. Few American authors are more shrouded in myth than Poe. Silverman will no doubt attempt to correct the many falsehoods, to give a complete and accurate portrait of this enigmatic author.

Francis Steegmuller

(3 July 1906 -   )

Robert L. Ross
University of Texas at Austin

BOOKS: *O Rare Ben Jonson*, as Byron Steel (New York: Knopf, 1927);

Java-Java, as Steel (New York: Knopf, 1928);

Sir Francis Bacon: The First Modern Mind, as Steel (Garden City, N.Y.: Doubleday, 1930);

The Musicale (New York: Cape & Smith, 1930);

America on Relief, by Steegmuller and Marie Dresden Lane (New York: Harcourt, Brace, 1938);

Flaubert and Madame Bovary: A Double Portrait (New York: Viking, 1939; London: Hale, 1939; revised edition, New York: Farrar, Straus, 1950; London: Hamilton, 1958; revised again, New York: Farrar, Straus & Giroux, 1968; London: Macmillan, 1968);

A Matter of Iodine, as David Keith (New York: Dodd, Mead, 1940);

A Matter of Accent, as Keith (New York: Dodd, Mead 1943);

States of Grace (New York: Reynal & Hitchcock, 1946; London: Collins, 1947);

French Follies and Other Follies: 20 Stories from "The New Yorker" (New York: Reynal & Hitchcock, 1946);

Blue Harpsichord, as Keith (New York: Dodd, Mead, 1949);

Maupassant: A Lion in the Path (New York: Random House, 1949; London: Collins, 1950);

The Two Lives of James Jackson Jarves (New Haven: Yale University Press, 1951);

The Christening Party (New York: Farrar, Straus & Cudahy, 1960; London: Hart-Davis, 1961);

Apollinaire: Poet Among the Painters (New York: Farrar, Straus, 1963; London: Hart-Davis, 1963);

Cocteau: A Biography (Boston: Little, Brown, 1970; London: Macmillan, 1970);

Stories and True Stories (Boston: Little, Brown, 1972; London: Macmillan, 1972);

Silence at Salerno (New York: Holt, Rinehart & Winston 1978).

OTHER: *Gustave Flaubert, Selected Letters*, edited and translated, with an introduction, by Steegmuller (London: Hamilton, 1953; New York: Farrar, Straus, 1954);

The Grand Mademoiselle (London: Hamilton, 1955; New York: Farrar, Straus, 1956);

Gustave Flaubert, *Madame Bovary*, translated by Steegmuller (New York: Random House, 1957);

Edward Lear, *Le Hibou et la pousiquette* (The Owl and the Pussycat), translated into French by Steegmuller (Boston: Little, Brown, 1959);

Charles-Augustin Sainte-Beuve, *Selected Essays*, edited and translated by Steegmuller and Norbert Guterman (Garden City, N.Y.: Doubleday, 1964);

Eugene Field, *Papillot, Clignot et Dodo*, translated by Steegmuller and Guterman (New York: Farrar, Straus, 1964; London: Collins, 1965);

Flaubert, *Intimate Notebook 1840-1841*, edited and translated, with an introduction, by Steegmuller (Garden City, N.Y.: Doubleday, 1967; London: Allen, 1967);

Flaubert in Egypt: A Sensibility on Tour, edited and translated, with an introduction, by Steegmuller (London: Bodley Head, 1972; Boston: Little, Brown, 1973);

Your Isadora: The Love Story of Isadora Duncan and Gordon Craig, Told Through Letters and Diaries Never Before Published, edited, with a commentary, by Steegmuller (New York: Random House, 1974; London: Macmillan, 1975);

The Letters of Gustave Flaubert, 1830-1857, edited and translated, with an introduction, by Steegmuller (Cambridge, Mass.: Harvard University Press, 1980; London: Faber & Faber, 1981);

The Letters of Gustave Flaubert, 1857-1880, edited and translated, with an introduction, by Steegmuller (Cambridge, Mass.: Harvard University Press, 1982; London: Faber & Faber, 1984).

A versatile man of letters, Francis Steegmuller has distinguished himself in a variety of lit-

Francis Steegmuller, 1989 (photograph by Attilo Pierelli)

erary forms. He has written novels—some of them detective stories, some comic works—as well as short fiction, much of which has appeared in the *New Yorker*; in 1940 he received the Red Badge Mystery Prize for *A Matter of Iodine*. As a critic and essayist, he has contributed regularly to the *New York Times Book Review* and other major periodicals. His 1957 translation of Gustave Flaubert's *Madame Bovary* (1856) has become a standard edition, widely used in the classroom. He has also translated Flaubert's letters into English, as well as the letters of other French literary figures. His 1939 critical study of Flaubert's writing of *Madame Bovary* is still widely available and still an authoritative and useful book. As an editor Steegmuller has shown originality by linking documents and letters together with a lively commentary that transforms what might be tedious and sterile into a stimulating record of real lives, as in *Your Isadora* (1974) and other collections. In a review of *The Letters of Gustave Flaubert, 1857-1880* (1982) V. S. Pritchett praised the richness of Steegmuller's "connecting narrative" and "annotations," noting that "for once, Flaubert is seen alive and enacting himself." Pritchett then paid Steegmuller a compliment and at the

same time summed up the quality that has always characterized Steegmuller's work: "No dubious academic analysis obscures the commentary" (*Atlantic*, November 1982).

Steegmuller has received the greatest recognition for his biographical works on Flaubert, Guy de Maupassant, and Jean Cocteau. *Cocteau* (1970) earned Steegmuller the National Book Award in 1971.

This American who has done so much to help make nineteenth- and twentieth-century French culture accessible to the English-speaking world was born on 3 July 1906 in New Haven, Connecticut, the son of Joseph F. and Bertha Tierney Steegmuller. He attended Dartmouth College for one year in 1923, then completed his B.A. in 1927 at Columbia University; a year later he received his M.A. there. Shunning an academic career, Steegmuller set out to become an independent "man of letters" and published his first book in 1927. On 1 July 1935 he married Beatrice Stein. Two years after her death in 1961, Steegmuller married the novelist Shirley Hazzard (on 22 December 1963), author of the widely acclaimed *The Transit of Venus* (1980). Never a public person, he has for many years

Dust jacket for Steegmuller's 1972 translation of travel notes and letters by Flaubert

lived quietly in New York City; but, as much at home in Europe as in the United States, Steegmuller has always spent time abroad, especially in France and Italy.

Steegmuller published *O Rare Ben Jonson* (1927) under the pseudonym Byron Steel. Then two more Steel books appeared: *Java-Java* (1928) and *Sir Francis Bacon: The First Modern Mind* (1930). Possibly Steegmuller wanted to be sure of his work before attaching his own name to it. Although the two early books on literary figures have been forgotten and are generally unavailable, they do foreshadow Steegmuller's abiding interest in the lives of creative and influential artists. Again, in the 1940s, he was to use a pseud-

onym when, as David Keith, he published three crime novels.

Flaubert and Madame Bovary: A Double Portrait was published in 1939 and helped to establish Steegmuller's reputation as a serious critic, translator, and biographer. The book was followed by several others on Flaubert; noteworthy in particular are Steegmuller's original translations of the French novelist's notebooks and letters. In the foreword to a later book, *Flaubert in Egypt* (1972), Steegmuller calls *Madame Bovary* "the Realist masterpiece that was to change the course of the novel throughout the western world." In the first section of his 1939 biography he addresses Flaubert's longing for Romanticism and his writing of a book in that tradition, *The Temptation of Saint Anthony* (1874), which was not altogether successful. Part 2 of Steegmuller's 1939 book, "The Purge, The Oriental Journey," consists of Flaubert's travel notes and letters written during his travels in Egypt. This section Steegmuller was to expand into *Flaubert in Egypt*, in order to show more fully how the Egyptian experience helped to "purge" Flaubert of Romantic ideals and to lead him into the realist thinking that produced *Madame Bovary*.

Part 3 of *Flaubert and Madame Bovary* traces the day-to-day writing of the novel that was to become Flaubert's most widely known work, even if the author himself resented its fame and later wished he had the money to buy up all the copies in circulation. This section is abundant in detail, full of facts about the people Flaubert knew, revealing in its depiction of the writer's romantic entanglements, and precise in its scholarship. When the book first appeared, English-language sources on *Madame Bovary* were scarce, so Steegmuller's work might be credited in part for introducing the great French novel to the English-reading public. In spite of the abundant criticism now available, Steegmuller's account is still valuable.

The 1980 and 1982 volumes of Flaubert's letters translated by Steegmuller are augmented by introductory passages and annotations in such a way that the letters bring Flaubert to life, along with his circle of friends, including George Sand, and their milieu. Critics have praised this quality, the anonymous reviewer in *Choice* (February 1983) noting that "Steegmuller connects the letters with a masterful narrative that provides a real biography of Flaubert."

Flaubert also figures prominently in Steegmuller's *Maupassant: A Lion in the Path* (1949).

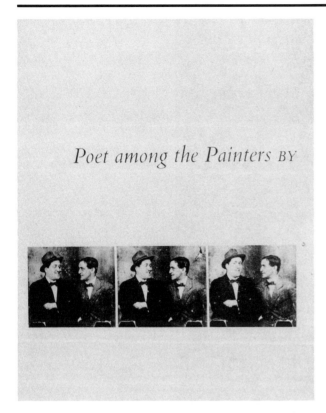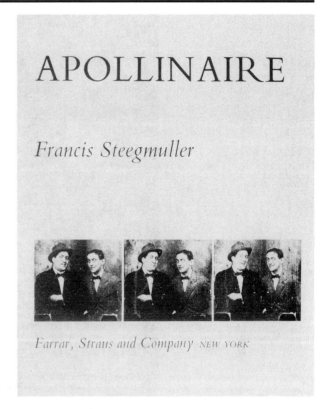

Two-page title for Steegmuller's biography of a poet and art critic who was part of the avant-garde in Paris during the decade be-
fore World War I. The photographs, of Guillaume Apollinaire and illustrator André Rouveyre, were taken on 1 August 1914, the
day after mobilization notices were posted in Paris.

The first third of the book is devoted to the friendship between Flaubert and Maupassant, fully documented by Steegmuller's own translations of letters and diary entries. The remainder focuses on
Maupassant's personal life, career, and writing,
as well as the social, political, and artistic environment in which he lived. Steegmuller laments that
Maupassant is known primarily among English-
speaking readers for his short story "The Neck-
lace," and Steegmuller tries to correct—through
astute biocritical insights—what he sees as an injustice to a writer of such ability. The book continues to be a standard in Maupassant criticism.

The Two Lives of James Jackson Jarves (1951)
presents an American life. During the mid nineteenth century Jarves introduced early Italian
paintings to a bewildered and generally unappreci-
ative American audience; he also lived for a time
in the Hawaiian Islands and is considered the islands' first historian. The son of the inventor of
Sandwich glass, Jarves had been reared in a typical New England atmosphere, much like Steegmuller, who had grown up in New Haven and
must have been familiar with Jarves's collection
in the Yale art gallery. But Jarves had expanded
his horizons to embrace European culture, again

much like Steegmuller, whose interests have always been more European than American.

In his next biographical work, *Apollinaire:
Poet Among the Painters* (1963), Steegmuller traces
the development of Guillaume Apollinaire, the
early-twentieth-century French poet who suffered a severe head wound during World War I
and died in 1918. Apollinaire was not only one
of the most original poets of his time but also an
important and innovative art critic. Through his
critical writings on the avant-garde movement
that was developing at the start of the century,
he helped to formulate the principles of cubism.
While not one of Steegmuller's major works, the
study of Apollinaire does in many ways preface
his later biography on Cocteau. Apollinaire was a
forerunner of Cocteau, and they both shared the
fervor so apparent in French culture during the
early twentieth century. To a degree, *Cocteau* continues the story begun in Steegmuller's book on
Apollinaire.

Cocteau may well be Steegmuller's crowning
achievement. Writing in the *Saturday Review* (19
September 1970), Tom Bishop called the Cocteau
that emerges from this biography "demythified,"
"a complex, fascinating, exasperating, and all in

Dust jacket for Steegmuller's biography of the writer, artist, and filmmaker who created "invisibility-by-autobiography"

all very human figure who must resemble the 'real' Cocteau closely." Mark Schorer in the *New York Times Book Review* (27 September 1970) praised Steegmuller for never glossing over Cocteau's "limitations either as man or artist," but communicating "sharply his irrepressible wit and charm."

As poet, novelist, playwright, and filmmaker, Cocteau played a central role not only in the course of modern French culture but also in the development of modernism. While some have called him a minor artist, no one can question his impact on twentieth-century art, whatever his own personal artistic contribution. Steegmuller shows how Cocteau's work in various mediums has played a part in the formation of twentieth-century artistic expression. But the biography also captures the contradictory personal nature of the man himself, described on one hand as an "opium-addicted homosexual," on the other as a sophisticate at home in the art salons.

His perversity and cruelty, his flashes of kindness, wit, and brilliance, his personal obsessions, and his sexual extravagance are all revealed to form a composite. At the same time, his artistic pursuits are in no way slighted; for example, the section devoted to Cocteau's films, which may eventually be considered his most lasting achievement, adds importantly to the considerable amount of material available in English on Cocteau's filmmaking.

Like all of Steegmuller's previous biographies, *Cocteau* chronicles the era in which the subject lived and worked. Whether in the 1920s or after World War II, the state of the arts—dance, film, theater, literature, painting, and music—is explored. But most of all Steegmuller profiles the people who made the art, for Cocteau encountered the major figures of his time: Marcel Proust, André Gide, Isadora Duncan, Igor Stravinsky, Sergey Diaghilev, Vaslav Nijinsky, Jean Anouilh, Pablo Picasso, and others.

Thus *Cocteau* offers the English reader an intricate picture of one part of twentieth-century history along with an analysis of an influential artist's successes and failures. For Steegmuller the biography of Cocteau represents fully his idea that the art produced makes the artist's life worth remembering. This approach to biography has always guided Steegmuller, who has never subscribed to fashionable critical theory but has consistently looked at the art in the context of the artist's personality, associates, and social milieu. Steegmuller's exploration of the artistic process in terms comprehensible to the layperson and informative to the expert is one of his major accomplishments.

Another of Steegmuller's important books is *Your Isadora: The Love Story of Isadora Duncan and Gordon Craig* (1974), a collection of letters and other documents with brief narrative notes by Steegmuller. The personal documents of Duncan and her lover Gordon Craig were made available for the first time in 1962; Steegmuller also includes other people's letters, press reports, and interviews to round out the story of the Duncan/Craig romance. The book is an important, authoritative addition to the extensive material available on Duncan. As Steegmuller points out, less is known about Craig, but *Your Isadora* brings him out of Duncan's shadow and traces the development of his career in art and scene de-

sign as well as the role he played in the personal and public life of Duncan, whom he once described as someone "who interpreted no one at all—she positively created."

While the book does reveal the intimate details of Duncan and Craig's tempestuous love affair, Steegmuller avoids any tinge of gossip for the sake of gossip. Still, the principals emerge as the passionate, unpredictable, self-centered, obsessed people they must have been. *Your Isadora* also offers views of their artistic aspirations and achievements and places them among the European artistic society of that time. For example, their relationships with such people as Eleanora Duse and Konstantin Stanislavsky are fully detailed. The spirit of the time becomes tangible through Steegmuller's commentary and careful selection and placement of documents.

Whatever the future judgment of Steegmuller's particular approach, his offering of priceless background material—through translation of personal documents, tireless and exacting research, and interviews—will never be questioned. His translations of literary works will also endure, for they have always been praised for their exactness and sensitivity. Steegmuller has stayed somewhat in the background throughout his long and productive career, content to be a conveyor of European culture and an interpreter of those who made it.

Madeleine B. Stern
(1 July 1912 -   )

Sondra Miley Cooney
Kent State University

BOOKS: *We Are Taken* (New York: Galleon, 1935);

The Life of Margaret Fuller (New York: Dutton, 1942; revised edition, Westport, Conn.: Greenwood, 1991);

Louisa May Alcott (Norman: University of Oklahoma Press, 1950; London & New York: Nevill, 1952);

Purple Passage: The Life of Mrs. Frank Leslie (Norman: University of Oklahoma Press, 1953);

Sherlock Holmes: Rare-Book Collector (New York: Schulte, 1953);

Imprints on History: Book Publishers and American Frontiers (Bloomington: Indiana University Press, 1956);

We the Women: Career Firsts of Nineteenth-Century America (New York: Schulte, 1963 [i.e., 1962]; revised edition, New York: Franklin, 1974);

So Much in a Life-Time: The Story of Dr. Isabel Barrows (New York: Messner, 1964);

Queen of Publishers' Row: Mrs. Frank Leslie (New York: Messner, 1965);

The Pantarch: A Biography of Stephen Pearl Andrews (Austin & London: University of Texas Press, 1968);

Heads and Headlines: The Phrenological Fowlers (Norman: University of Oklahoma Press, 1971);

Old and Rare: Thirty Years in the Book Business, by Stern and Leona Rostenberg (New York: Schram / London: Prior, 1974); revised and enlarged as *Old and Rare: Forty Years in the Book Business* (Santa Monica, Cal.: Modoc, 1988);

Between Boards: New Thoughts on Old Books, by Stern and Rostenberg (Montclair, N.J.: Allanheld & Schram / London: Prior, 1978);

Books and Book People in 19th-Century America (New York & London: Bowker, 1978);

The Game's A Head: A Phrenological Case-Study of Sherlock Holmes and Arthur Conan Doyle (Rockville Centre, N.Y.: Greene, 1983);

Antiquarian Bookselling in the United States: A His-

tory from the Origins to the 1940's (Westport, Conn.: Greenwood, 1985).

OTHER: *Women on the Move*, 4 volumes, edited by Stern (Nieuwkoop, Netherlands: De Graaf, 1972);

The Victoria Woodhull Reader, edited by Stern (Weston, Mass.: M & S, 1974);

Behind a Mask: The Unknown Thrillers of Louisa May Alcott, edited, with an introduction, by Stern (New York: Morrow, 1975; London: Allen, 1976);

Louisa's Wonder Book: An Unknown Alcott Juvenile, introduction and bibliography by Stern (Mt. Pleasant: Central Michigan University, 1975);

Plots and Counterplots: More Unknown Thrillers of Louisa May Alcott, edited, with an introduction, by Stern (New York: Morrow, 1976; London: Allen, 1977);

Publishers for Mass Entertainment in Nineteenth Century America, edited by Stern (Boston: G. K. Hall, 1980);

A Phrenological Dictionary of Nineteenth-Century Americans, compiled by Stern (Westport, Conn. & London: Greenwood, 1982);

The Hidden Louisa May Alcott: A Collection of her Unknown Thrillers, edited by Stern (New York: Avenel, 1984);

Critical Essays on Louisa May Alcott, edited by Stern (Boston: G. K. Hall, 1984);

Louisa May Alcott, *A Modern Mephistopheles and Taming a Tartar*, introduction by Stern (New York: Praeger, 1987);

The Selected Letters of Louisa May Alcott, edited by Joel Myerson and Daniel Shealy, associate editor Stern, with an introduction by Stern (Boston: Little, Brown, 1987);

A Double Life: Newly Discovered Thrillers of Louisa May Alcott, edited by Stern, Myerson, and Shealy, with an introduction by Stern (Boston: Little, Brown, 1988);

Madeleine B. Stern (right) with her business partner, Leona Rostenberg, at the auction of the Thomas W. Streeter Collection, Sotheby Parke-Bernet Galleries, New York City, late 1960s (Sotheby Parke-Bernet Galleries, Inc.)

The Journals of Louisa May Alcott, edited by Myerson and Shealy, associate editor Stern, with an introduction by Stern (Boston: Little, Brown, 1989);

Louisa May Alcott: Selected Fiction, edited by Stern, Shealy, and Myerson, with an introduction by Stern (Boston: Little, Brown, 1991).

SELECTED PERIODICAL PUBLICATIONS—
UNCOLLECTED: "Margaret Fuller's School-Days in Cambridge," *New England Quarterly*, 13 (June 1940): 207-222;

"Margaret Fuller and *The Dial*," *South Atlantic Quarterly*, 40 (January 1941): 11-21;

"The House of the Expanding Doors: Anne Lynch's Soirées, 1846," *New York History*, 23 (January 1942): 42-51;

"Louisa Alcott, Trouper: Experiences in Theatricals, 1848-1880," *New England Quarterly*, 16 (June 1943): 175-197;

"The Witch's Cauldron to the Family Hearth: Louisa M. Alcott's Literary Development, 1848-1868," *More Books: The Bulletin of the Boston Public Library*, 18 (October 1943): 363-380;

"Louisa M. Alcott's Contributions to Periodicals: 1868-1888," *More Books: The Bulletin of the Boston Public Library*, 18 (November 1943): 411-420;

"Approaches to Biography," *South Atlantic Quarterly*, 45 (July 1946): 362-371;

"Louisa M. Alcott: An Appraisal," *New England Quarterly*, 22 (December 1949): 475-498;

"Poe: 'The Mental Temperament' for Phrenologists," *American Literature*, 40 (May 1968): 155-163;

"William Henry Channing's Letters on 'Woman in her Social Relations,' " *Cornell Library Journal*, 6 (Autumn 1968): 54-62;

"Mark Twain Had His Head Examined," *American Literature*, 41 (May 1969): 207-218;

"Elizabeth Peabody's Foreign Library (1840)," *American Transcendental Quarterly*, 20 (Fall 1973): 5-12;

"A Biographer's View of Margaret Fuller: 30-Year Survey," *AB Bookman's Weekly*, 53 (4 February 1974): 427-430;

Dust jacket for Stern's first biography (1942), a project suggested to her by Rostenberg

"Louisa M. Alcott in Periodicals," *Studies in the American Renaissance* (May 1977): 369-386;

"The Alcotts and the Emerson Fire," *American Transcendental Quarterly*, 36 (Fall 1977): 7-9;

"Louisa Alcott's Feminist Letters," *Studies in the American Renaissance* (November 1978): 429-452;

"Margaret Fuller and the Phrenologist-Publishers," *Studies in the American Renaissance* (May 1980): 229-237;

"The English Press and Its Successors, 1793-1852," *Papers of the Bibliographical Society of America*, 74 (October-December 1980): 307-359;

"A Feminist Association," *Manuscripts*, 35 (Spring 1983): 113-117;

"Louisa Alcott's Self-Criticism," *Studies in the American Renaissance* (1985): 333-382;

"A Calendar of the Letters of Louisa May Alcott," *Studies in the American Renaissance* (1988): 361-399.

Madeleine B. Stern, as a rare-book dealer, specializes in French, Italian, Latin, and English books of the sixteenth, seventeenth, and eighteenth centuries; as a writer, Stern specializes in the work and lives of nineteenth-century American women and publishers. She regards her endeavors as complementary, finding herself "drawn irresistibly to literary and biographical detective work." She is not interested in facts for their own sake but for what they can tell about the time and place in which a person lived and worked. The results of Stern's half century of literary detective work are accurate, vivid accounts of nineteenth-century American life and people.

Madeleine Bettina Stern, the daughter of Moses R. and Lillie Mack Stern, was born on 1 July 1912 in New York City. She became fascinated with the written word at an early age. When she was only seven years old, she took on the running of a newspaper stand at Lenox Avenue and 126th Street, despite her parents' reservations. At the age of thirteen, during her first trip abroad, she began to give serious consideration to her own writing. She diligently kept a journal in which she made conscious efforts to develop her writing style. By the time she was a student at Hunter High School, she was writing at least one poem a day. After matriculating at Barnard College, where she enrolled in the honors course in English literature, she continued to write, contributing to the *Barnard Bulletin*. Graduating Phi Beta Kappa in 1932, she had little hope of find-

The A Half Century of MF Scholarship ~~1942 — 1990~~ since 1942

In reviewing my Life of Margnret Fuller upon its initial appearance, George

F. Whicher generously commented: "Her work may be supplemented by criticial studies

still to be written, but in its own kind it will hardly be surpassed." ①

~~It is the supplemental~~

zkkak biograpgy
Now that nearly 50 years have passed since my ~~MF~~ made its bow, ~~it is fitting that~~

~~those critical studies that supplemented my biography be~~   it is fitting

~~it is fitting that its supplementation be~~ appraised ~~for those critical studies to be~~

~~that those critical studies be assembled and appraised.~~

for that supplemented them ②

~~that the~~ critical studies ~~that followed and supplemented it~~ be re/viewed and appraised.

Mkskksxxx

The first full-lenth study of MF ~~did not appear until 15 years to follow~~

took 15 years ~~did not appear until~~

A 15-year period intervened between publication of the Stern Life and the

first full-length study of ~~MF~~. ~~Perhaps, the between Wa Mason Wade's Whetstone of~~
that followed
subject
~~Genius and~~   Perhaps the public had been saturated with the ~~public~~, having been

regaled in close succession with Mason Wade's Whetstone of Genius and Stern's Life ③

of MF. Perhaps the ~~intervention of~~ World War II ~~had~~ deflected interest ~~in the one~~
events of
in her various progressions.
~~xxkjxxkxxxRxxkxpxxxkxx~~x who "eluded categories." And perhaps too, there was still

a ~~large readership who number of reader~~ were still ~~was still a~~ multitude ~~of~~
had been taught for most about much
~~potential readers~~ who, having been ~~"to busy learning~~ about Emerson and Thoreau
knew little & cared less about
had ~~xxyxx scarcely heard~~ of Margaret Fuller.   At all event,s it was not until 1957

that Faith Chipperfield published her book romantically entitled In Quest of Love: The

Life and Death of Margaret Fuller. ④
marred
enhanced
Whatever virtues and whatever faults the Chipperfield volume were occasioned
who
by ~~its~~ purpose which was ~~instead~~ to evoke the emotional life of a woman was in effect

a great intellectual. The biographer asked, "Is it not strange that no biographer

has searched the story of MF's heart? Is it not time...to forget the MF of Victorian

legend and remember the MF who lived and longed for love?" And so Chipperfield
and
~~xmbxxkxdx~~ set out to trace Fuller's "lifelong quest for love," In the course of

Page from a draft for an essay added to the 1991 edition of The Life of Margaret Fuller *(by permission of Madeleine B. Stern; Brigham Young University Department of Special Collections)*

ing employment. As she says in the memoir *Old and Rare* (1974), "For any Baccalaureate, class of 1932, few fields were open. For a Baccalaureate, Female, Jewish, still fewer." So she enrolled at Columbia University for graduate studies in English. At about the same time, she met Leona Rostenberg, who was to become her lifetime friend and business associate. Within the years from 1932 to 1934 the course of Stern's life was set. Her master's thesis—a study of Mary Magdalene in literary history—involved Stern in the excitement of literary research, and while on a trip to Europe with her mother, she began looking at and buying books. Although she became a high-school English teacher in New York City in 1934, after earning her M.A. from Columbia, she did not find teaching a congenial profession. All the while she continued writing and experimenting with literary techniques. Rostenberg—during a sight-seeing trip to Concord, Massachusetts—said to her, "There's really no good biography of Margaret Fuller. Why don't you write one?" Stern was ready and eager for the challenge, so she took on the task.

Fuller, considered by many the first American feminist, was a friend of most of the leading transcendentalists and was editor of the *Dial*. She later became the first female correspondent and first arts critic for Horace Greeley's *New York Tribune*. When she fulfilled a lifelong dream and toured Europe, she met leading revolutionary figures of the day, notably those of the Italian revolution. Prior to the 1940s Fuller was known primarily on the basis of *Memoirs of Margaret Fuller Ossoli* (1852), by Ralph Waldo Emerson, William Henry Channing, and James Freeman Clarke. Drawing on their own recollections as well as Fuller's papers, they presented accurately enough the facts of her life (except for her relationship with Giovanni Angelo Ossoli) but misunderstood her emotional nature and intellectual life. The most modern biography of Fuller had been Mason Wade's *Margaret Fuller: Whetstone of Genius* (1940). Its psychoanalytic approach resulted in a better, deeper assessment of Fuller; however, according to John Garratty in *The Nature of Biography* (1957), that type of biography was already passing out of style by 1940.

Stern's *Life of Margaret Fuller* (1942) was altogether different. As Stern stated in *AB Bookman's Weekly* (4 February 1974), her "principal purpose was to reanimate a personality and her time...." Drawing upon Fuller materials at the Houghton and Boston public libraries, Stern attempted to as-

semble them "without lengthy quotations or the biographer's intrusive comments...." She wanted "to create an artistic mosaic out of the bits and pieces of verified detail." Some called this fictionalized biography, but Stern preferred to call it "chronological biography." Acting as something of an omniscient narrator, Stern allows the reader to see Fuller teaching in Bronson Alcott's school and transcribing his conversations, insinuating herself into the home and friendship of Ralph Waldo Emerson, visiting Brook Farm, nursing wounded revolutionaries in Rome, and being washed into the sea and drowning. What the account gains in immediacy, it loses in chronological coherence. Passage of time or movement from one place to another is often not clear; names and places are not always fully identified.

Some critics were not convinced that Stern's "artistic" method was effective. Van Wyck Brooks, who had read the manuscript and encouraged Stern, praised it for its re-creation of Fuller's time (his comments appear on the dust jacket). Other reviewers acknowledged that the highly detailed account created a vivid picture but found the reading difficult because there were no notes incorporated into the text. Instead they were placed at the end of the book, the sources for each chapter in a long, alphabetical paragraph. One contained a hundred titles. Stern's treatment was praised, however, for the absence of psychoanalytic analysis.

Because of Stern's revolutionary—or at least controversial—approach to Fuller's life, she was invited to address a session of the Modern Language Association's 1942 annual meeting. World War II travel restrictions necessitated canceling the session; her paper—"Approaches to Biography"—subsequently appeared in the *South Atlantic Quarterly* (1946). In it Stern contrasts her book with earlier biographies, specifically histories, memoirs, and "life and times." None, she feels, presented a "written history of a person's life." Distinguishing between "fictionalized biography" and "chronological biography," she notes that the latter includes nothing for which there is not record; nothing is included that did not happen. Such material of record is essential if the times of a person are to be re-created. There is an overabundance of such information for nineteenth-century literati, for they were inveterate correspondents and journal writers. The biographer, therefore, must select only that material actually seen by the subject. Then it must be interrelated

Stern circa 1949 at Kettle's paper store in New Oxford Street, London, where she has often bought paper for use in binding rare pamphlets

with the biography. If it is not, both life and times are "meaningless for the reader."

The research on Fuller had, according to Stern, "provided little opportunity for literary detection. The episodes of her life . . . needed not discovery but reconstruction. Louisa May Alcott, on the other hand, seemed to offer far more incentive for sleuthing" (*Old and Rare*). Although in the sixty years following Alcott's death in 1888 several biographies had been written—all by women—the standard ones were those by Ednah Dow Littlehale Cheney: *Louisa May Alcott: The Children's Friend* (1888) and *Louisa May Alcott: Her Life, Letters, and Journals* (1889). Cheney was well acquainted with the Alcotts and the Concord circle. She had been a young—and very impressed— participant in many of Fuller's conversations. Not only had Cheney known Bronson Alcott but she

also had been an object of his passionate fantasies before she married. In writing the life of Louisa May Alcott, she felt that she was doing a service by memorializing the "children's friend." Consequently she excised unfavorable material in letters and journals. She could not report events or people about which Alcott had been secretive, such as the name of the family in whose home she had gone to do maid service. In addition, Cheney was unaware of some materials revealing the darker side of Alcott's life and work. The resulting unanswered questions about Alcott's experience piqued Stern's curiosity; she was determined to answer them if she could. In the course of her research, she and Rostenberg called on Carroll Atwood Wilson, an Alcott collector. The visit, recounted in *Old and Rare*, was valuable on more than one count. He recommended that

Dust jacket for the biography of the writer whose life offered Stern an "incentive for sleuthing." Rostenberg aided Stern in her research.

Stern apply for a Guggenheim Fellowship to support her research and writing. She was awarded one for the years 1943 to 1945. Wilson suggested that Rostenberg try to find out Alcott's pseudonym and to locate the fiction she had written under that name. While working through the Houghton Library's Alcott holdings, Rostenberg came upon letters revealing the pseudonym and was thus able to identify Alcott's lurid thrillers.

Stern, using the same chronological-biography approach of her Fuller biography, tells of Alcott's life from the time she was three until her death. The contemporary world of Boston, Concord, and Washington, D.C., of the Civil War, Brook Farm, and the publishing world, of Ralph Waldo Emerson, Henry David Thoreau, and Nathaniel Hawthorne, the arts, the theater, and nature—all of which would become the stuff of Alcott's writing—are seen through her eyes. And, for the first time, the less-pleasant aspects of being Bronson Alcott's daughter are presented for the reader to understand.

Stern's chronology of events in *Louisa May Alcott* (1950) is clear, and the substantial chapter notes are better organized than in Stern's book on Fuller. Despite the opportunity for psychoanal-

ysis Alcott's life presented, reviewers praised Stern for not taking that approach. However, as they quickly pointed out, there is no significant interpretation of Alcott's life or works in the book. There is, as usual for Stern, the highly detailed and thoroughly factual story. Odell Shepard, biographer of Bronson Alcott, regarded it as the best biography of Louisa May Alcott to that time, but noted that it left unanswered questions.

After her Guggenheim Fellowship expired, Stern returned to teaching and promptly found the work even less to her liking than before. But thanks to her friendship with Rostenberg she had become fascinated by the rare-book business. In spring 1945 she resigned from her teaching position and joined Rostenberg as junior partner in Leona Rostenberg Rare Books. Once the Alcott biography was published, Stern did not abandon her interest in research and writing. Writing was for her a "compulsive discipline," and she spent several hours a week at her typewriter. Following the Alcott book was *Purple Passage: The Life of Mrs. Frank Leslie* (1953). Alcott had written some of her more sensational stories for *Frank Leslie's Illustrated Newspaper* and *Frank Leslie's Chimney Corner*. In 1956 Stern's first work on publishing

272

history, *Imprints on History: Book Publishers and American Frontiers*, was published.

In the early 1960s Stern turned to other nineteenth-century women who had been remarkable and original in varied fields. The women whose biographies are included in her *We the Women: Career Firsts of Nineteenth-Century America* (1963) had to meet three criteria, as she notes in *Between Boards* (1978): "priority firmly established; a colorful career; adequate available and preferably heretofore unused source material." Their importance for the 1960s audience, according to Stern's introduction to *We the Women*, was that "their sexual revolution had to be fought before the current sexual revolution could be launched." In the mid 1960s Stern published two books for juveniles, the first book being about a subject in *We the Women*, Dr. Isabel Barrows (1964), and the other on Mrs. Frank Leslie (1965).

By the 1970s the emergence of women's studies and the feminist movement drew Stern's attention to Fuller and Alcott once again. Invited to discuss Fuller at the December 1973 Modern Language Association meeting, she surveyed work done on Fuller since 1942 (in "A Biographer's View of Margaret Fuller," published on 4 February 1974). Noting that little new material of significance had been made public, she cited the collected letters being prepared and the reissued texts of Fuller's work as materials most valuable to the biographer. But sources alone are not enough for a biographer, she observed: "A wise reading is beholden not only to the definitive annotated edition but to the imagination of the reader. If the scholar is without that imagination, he should not involve himself in biography. Without it, current scholarship will produce only the so-called monumental biography so popular today containing a mass of multitudinous detail offered up in a gray-flannel style."

Her work in the 1970s on Alcott involved editing and making available previously undiscovered or unpublished Alcott materials, both her fiction and personal writing. For each volume Stern wrote introductory material that assesses the stories, their themes and conflicts, and their charac-

ters, showing Alcott's early feminism and her enthusiasm for the unconventional and the extreme in fiction. *Behind a Mask: The Unknown Thrillers of Louisa May Alcott* (1975) includes the stories Rostenberg had unearthed in the 1940s. The stories had not been published since the nineteenth century. A collection of children's tales, *Louisa's Wonder Book: An Unknown Alcott Juvenile* (1975) also contains an updated Alcott bibliography. The stories in *Plots and Counterplots* (1976), on the other hand, are not children's reading material, dealing as they do with issues of violence, mind control, and drug experimentation, among others. This newly revealed side of the "children's friend" has resulted in reexamination of Alcott and her work by other biographers. Most notably, May Saxton uses characters and situations drawn from these stories to illuminate Alcott's life in *A Modern Biography of Louisa May Alcott* (1977).

Stern's activities continued in much the same vein during the 1980s. She edited a collection of nineteenth-century and modern critical essays on Alcott (1984). In association with Joel Myerson and Daniel Shealy, she edited and wrote introductions for a selection of Alcott's letters (1987) and journals (1989), and more undiscovered thrillers (1988). Following up on her book on phrenology, *Heads and Headlines* (1971), Stern compiled *A Phrenological Dictionary of Nineteenth-Century Americans* (1982), which includes phrenological readings of several writers, public figures, and even the whale Moby-Dick. Also during the 1980s she received the Medaile Award from Barnard College (1982) and the American Printing History Association Award (1983). The latter she shared with Rostenberg for "their important services in advancing understanding of the history of printing and its allied arts."

Madeleine Stern continues to bring to life the worlds of nineteenth-century America, of Alcott, and of Fuller. *Louisa May Alcott: Selected Fiction*, edited in association with Myerson and Shealy and with an introduction by Stern, and a revised *Life of Margaret Fuller*—with an essay surveying Fuller scholarship from 1942 to 1990—were published in 1991.

Jean Strouse

(10 September 1945 -)

Lynn Z. Bloom
University of Connecticut

BOOKS: *Up Against the Law: The Legal Rights of People Under Twenty-One* (New York: New American Library, 1970);

Alice James: A Biography (Boston: Houghton Mifflin, 1980; London: Cape, 1981).

OTHER: *Indian Resistance: The Patriot Chiefs*, compiled by Strouse and Alvin Josephy (New York: Grossman, 1972; London: Jackdaw, 1972);

Women and Analysis: Dialogues on Psychoanalytic Views of Femininity, edited, with an introduction, by Strouse (New York: Grossman, 1974);

"Semiprivate Lives," in *Studies in Biography*, edited by Daniel Aaron (Cambridge, Mass.: Harvard University Press, 1978), pp. 113-129;

Response to Frank E. Vandiver's "Biography as an Agent of Humanism," in *The Biographer's Gift: Life Histories and Humanism*, edited by James F. Veninga (College Station: Texas Committee for the Humanities/Texas A&M University Press, 1983), pp. 37-41;

"The Real Reasons," in *Extraordinary Lives: The Art and Craft of American Biography*, edited by William Zinsser (Boston: Houghton, 1986), pp. 161-195;

"Private Strife: Some Social Consequences of the Anatomical Distinction Between the Sexes," in *Women and Higher Education in American History*, edited by John M. Faragher and Florence Howe (New York: Norton, 1988), pp. 3-17.

Jean Strouse's *Alice James: A Biography* (1980) was awarded the Bancroft Prize in American History and Diplomacy in 1981. The book presents Alice James as worthy of a biography of her own, rather than as a footnote to the lives of her well-known brothers William and Henry.

Born on 10 September 1945, Jean Strouse, daughter of Carl David Strouse, a physician, and Louise Friedberg Strouse, grew up in Los Angeles, attended Verde Valley School in Sedona, Arizona, and graduated with honors from Radcliffe College in 1967. Pursuing a career in journalism, she was an editorial assistant for the *New York Review of Books* (1967-1969) and an associate editor at Pantheon Books (1972-1975). From 1979 to 1983, Strouse was a book critic and general editor at *Newsweek*. Her articles and reviews have appeared in the *New Yorker*, the *New York Times*, *Ms.* magazine, and *Commonweal*, among others. *Alice James* was supported by fellowships from the Radcliffe Institute (1976-1977), the Guggenheim Foundation (1977-1978), and the National Endowment for the Arts (1979). She is currently writing a biography of Pierpont Morgan (1837-1913). "It's not an accident," Strouse told an audience in 1985 at the New York Public Library, "that I've chosen two such opposite kinds of stories: after spending five interesting years thinking and writing about a powerless female invalid in a family of intellectuals, I wanted a complete change—and ended up with the most powerful man of the late nineteenth century. Morgan's story leads along very different paths—into the worlds of international finance, politics, art and rare-book collecting . . . and it presents very different kinds of biographical questions" ("The Real Reasons," 1986).

Even though Alice James's only published writing consists of a brief, anonymous letter to the editor of the *Nation* in 1890 (signed "Invalid") and a 193-page diary, published posthumously (four copies printed in 1895; reprinted as *The Diary of Alice James* in 1964, edited by Leon Edel), her writing can stand on its own, according to Strouse: "Alice James's journal and letters display a rare gift for language, sharp wit, psychological acumen, and an intuitive grasp of political and economic realities. F. O. Matthiessen compared her 'wealth of inner resources' with Emily Dickinson's, and Henry James wrote to William that their sister's journal constituted a 'new claim for literary renown.' "

This assessment justifies publishing Alice James's diary, as well as her letters (collected and

Jean Strouse, 1987 (photograph by Thomas Victor)

published by Ruth Bernard Yeazell in 1981), but it does not address the matter of a biography. Strouse offers a complex explanation of—but not a defense of—James's life, typical of many upper- and middle-class Victorian women, "dominated by mysterious illnesses for which no organic cause could be discovered and no cure found," illnesses variously labeled "neurasthenia, hysteria, rheumatic gout, suppressed gout, cardiac complication, spinal neurosis, nervous hyperesthesia, and spiritual crisis." In Strouse's work the history of the individual becomes social history.

As a study of the phenomenon of neurasthenia in nineteenth-century America, *Alice James* has considerable relevance for contemporary readers who are impelled to analyze the lives of sensitive, suicidal twentieth-century women writers such as Virginia Woolf, Sylvia Plath, and Anne Sexton. With restraint and a welcome absence of technical jargon, Strouse's biography demonstrates the interrelationship between James's pro-

gressive invalidism and her imposed roles as "small sister" (younger than all four brothers) and the embodiment of "the passive virtues of genteel femininity." As a teenager she was trying to decide whether to become a serious student and thereby—violating the feminine norm of the day—to compete with Henry, William, and Henry, Sr. However, had she turned to "the womanly sphere" of domestic duties and become the ideal female, "mindless, selfless, and effortlessly good," she would have been competing with her mother and aunt. The "escape route" was hysteria—"a way out of having to choose between a safe boring life of devotion to others and a dangerous assertion of intellectual competence. It justified her failure to achieve while allowing her to preserve a sense of potent capacity."

Strouse offers other justifications for a biography of Alice James. Her life certainly possessed considerable dramatic potential: "Here was an extraordinary family of characters—two real geniuses, a couple of other, ne'er-do-well brothers,

ALICE JAMES
A BIOGRAPHY

Jean Strouse

Houghton
Mifflin
Company

ALICE
JAMES
A BIOGRAPHY

Jean Strouse

*Awarded a Houghton Mifflin
Literary Fellowship*

The Life of the
Brilliant Younger Sister of
William and Henry James

"The interpretation of 'woman in the nineteenth century' begun by Margaret Fuller in 1845 reaches a culmination of perspicuity in Jean Strouse's *Alice James*; a superb biography."
—Gay Wilson Allen

"Alice James has waited a long time for a biography, but she has not waited in vain. Jean Strouse has painted a brilliant portrait that places her and her brothers in a proper perspective."
—Louis Auchincloss

"A psychological portrait of surpassing excellence. Exquisitely written. One comes to care terribly about Alice James, ensnared though she was in a web of invalidism woven at least as much by her parents and two famous brothers as by herself."
—Fawn M. Brodie

"An honor in every way to the difficult, elusive, inimitable Alice James."
—Elizabeth Hardwick

"Jean Strouse's thorough-going, deeply committed biography gives Alice James at last her due as a remarkable woman in her own right and as a member (and captive) of a remarkable American family."
—Justin Kaplan

"In Jean Strouse's skillful hands the life of Alice James, which was one of extraordinary limits, and of barbarous suffering, touches us in ways we had not expected to be touched. Here is a woman's life that was like a knot: as it drew tighter, diminishment and physical pain were its range and its ground. But within those diminished circumstances Alice James became, finally and somewhat fiercely, entirely herself. She held fast against her losses. And Jean Strouse has managed, with a rare ability, to make us see and feel and care."
—Nancy Milford

ISBN 0-395-27787-6
6-96735

Dust jacket for the book that earned Strouse the Bancroft Prize in American History and Diplomacy in 1981

a father who was something of a genius himself—and they were all absorbed with one another and with their own experiences, so they wrote all the time, and you had a wonderful record of what was going on because they were amazingly articulate." Thus Strouse's biography of Alice, embedded as she was in the enveloping though not always comfortable matrix of the James family, becomes for twentieth-century readers what a novel was for a nineteenth-century audience—what Strouse calls a "large slice of life in which questions of character, motivation, morality, social pressure, and internal conflict [are] explored in great depth." Strouse wrote a dynamic biography that moves energetically forward, in spite of the passive, redundant, and—in later years—withdrawn life of its central character. The book reflects Strouse's ability to focus on those aspects of life that dominate Henry James's novels. Indeed, Strouse's *Alice James* illustrates an affinity with the mentality of both William James (said to have written psychology like a novelist) and Henry (said to have written novels like a psychologist).

Strouse interprets her subject in her social, intellectual, familial, historical, and medical contexts. For, as Strouse says in "Semiprivate Lives" (1978), "Private trouble is not a sufficient subject for fiction or biography, though it often passes for one. . . . Semiprivate lives . . . offer new ways of looking at the intersections of public and private experience without the obfuscation of myth. They give us not an official version of history as the chronicles of wars and kings . . . they provide instead glimpses of ordinary life, private drama, personal success and failure, sometimes heroism, sometimes the underside of fame—and a sense of the past as no more confined to a single version than the present is."

Most reviews of *Alice James* were laudatory, epitomized by Joan Lidoff's judgment: "Strouse's careful history lets us see that Alice's nervous sickness was . . . part of 'a collective response to the changing shape of late-nineteenth-century American life, in particular to the changing social positions and functions of women. . . .' What sets up the chemistry for self-destruction or success? Her own tone unflawed, with the right balance of insight and reserve, Jean Strouse does a masterful job of assessing the historical, cultural, and familial conditions that gave Alice James's life its particular shape, and allowed her, finally, a measure of intellectual strength to begin to articulate her own sense of that shape" (*Essays in Criticism*, July 1982). Yet, as Strouse points out, even though the Civil War left sixty-six thousand "surplus" women in Massachusetts alone by 1880, illness was not the inevitable or only alternative to marriage; many other single women became teachers, social reformers, or nurses. Although Strouse's feminism led to her choice of subject and to her sensitive interpretations of James's enriched, restricted life, it—wisely—did not lead her to castigate the rest of the James family for enabling the invalidism that Alice ultimately chose. Alice had other options.

Despite having devoted five years to writing the biography, Strouse candidly admits that Alice "was extremely difficult to live with, both for her contemporaries and for me, virtually 'living' with her long after her death." "At one point in the writing," says Strouse (in "The Real Reasons," 1986), "I got so mad at her that I just got completely stuck. Alice was in her late twenties and early thirties, and she was systematically closing down every option that might have led her away from a life of invalidism. She wasn't doing any intellectual work, although she had some that she could have been doing. She was being awful to every man who approached her and wasn't even very nice to her female friends. She was turning into a tyrannical invalid who collapsed in order to get people to take care of her. And I hated it. I really got so mad that I couldn't continue writing. . . . I just didn't want [the story] to have such a sad ending. So I put it aside for a while. . . . What I eventually came to was a fuller understanding of the conflict in her, based on my own intense reaction to it. I also came to see clearly that the interesting story was what *did* happen, not the way either she or I would have liked it to happen, and that who she was, rather than who she might have been, was the important thing. The unhappy ending was the real point of the story."

Patricia Meyer Spacks commented in the *Yale Review* (Summer 1981) on the accuracy of Strouse's biographical interpretation: "Significant to herself, she [Alice] decided not to attempt significance for many others. The disturbing power of the figure Strouse evokes reflects the challenge such a decision offers to the values of the larger world. Alice James implicitly rejects the standards by which we might readily judge her. She refuses to accept the status of 'neurotic' as sufficient explanation for her way of life; she takes responsibility for her eccentricities and denies her interpreters the comfortable recourse of patronizing her as her brother [William] did. Her biographer, in this dignified, judicious, and controlled assessment, illuminates her subject brilliantly. And the subject does not vanish when we close the book: Alice James, as here evoked, remains a haunting presence, exemplifying the ambiguities of a willed vocation of *being* rather than *doing*."

Pierpont Morgan is virtually the antithesis of his contemporary Alice James. In choosing to write his biography as her next major project, in making another commitment of four or five years of intense effort, Strouse has set for herself a new set of biographical challenges. The distinction with which she resolved the manifold problems in writing *Alice James* leads one to expect a similar interpretation of the life of an exceptionally successful man, externally directed, who exceeded the boundaries of his time and place.

Interview:
"Conversation: Geoffrey Rips with Jean Strouse," in *The Biographer's Gift: Life Histories and Humanism*, edited by James F. Veninga (College Station: Texas Committee for the Humanities/Texas A&M Press, 1983), pp. 107-113.

Aileen Ward
(1 April 1919 -   )

John C. Shields
Illinois State University

BOOKS: *John Keats: The Making of a Poet* (New York: Viking, 1963; London: Secker & Warburg, 1963; revised edition, New York: Farrar, Straus & Giroux, 1986; London: Faber & Faber, 1986);

The Unfurling of Entity: Metaphor in Poetic Theory (New York: Garland, 1987).

OTHER: *Confessions of an English Opium-Eater, and Other Writings by Thomas De Quincey*, edited by Ward (New York: New American Library, 1966);

The Poems of John Keats, edited by Ward (New York: Heritage, 1966; Cambridge: University Printing House, 1966);

"William Blake," in *Atlantic Brief Lives*, edited by Louis Kronenberger (Boston: Little, Brown, 1971);

"The Forging of Ore: William Blake and the Idea of Revolution," in *Literature in Revolution*, edited by Charles Newman and G. A. White (New York: Holt, Rinehart & Winston, 1972);

The Poems of William Blake, edited by Ward (Cambridge: University Printing House, 1973);

" 'That Last Infirmity of Noble Mind': Keats and the Idea of Fame," in *The Evidence of the Imagination: Interactions Between Art and Life in English Romantic Literature*, edited by D. H. Reiman, M. C. Jaye, and B. T. Bennett (New York: New York University Press, 1978);

"The Spirits of '76: William Blake's America," in *From Mt. San Angelo*, edited by William Smart (London: Associated University Presses, 1984);

" 'Sr. Joshua and His Gang': William Blake and the Royal Academy," in *William Blake and His Circle*, edited by Guilland Sutherland (San Marino, Cal.: Henry E. Huntington Library, 1989).

SELECTED PERIODICAL PUBLICATIONS—
UNCOLLECTED: "The Date of Keats's 'Bright Star' Sonnet," *Studies in Philology*, 52 (January 1955): 75-85;

"Keats's Sonnet, 'Nebuchadnezzar's Dream,' " *Philological Quarterly*, 34 (April 1955): 177-188;

"Christmas Day, 1818," *Keats-Shelley Journal*, 10 (Winter 1961): 15-27;

"Keats and Burton: A Reappraisal," *Philological Quarterly*, 40 (October 1961): 535-552.

When Aileen Ward's *John Keats: The Making of a Poet* was published in 1963, the praise was immediate. Carlos Baker, writing for the *New York Times Book Review* (8 September 1963), called it "the best-informed, most thoroughly thought through and certainly the most engaging of the modern biographies of Keats." David Daiches concluded that the book displayed "the kind of unobtrusive sympathy that is one of the best gifts of the biographer." *John Keats* earned for Ward the 1963 Duff Cooper Memorial Prize (awarded for the first time to a woman and an American) and the 1964 Rose Mary Crawshay Prize in England; in the United States it garnered the 1964 National Book Award in Arts and Letters.

Aileen Ward was born on 1 April 1919 in Newark, New Jersey. The daughter of Waldron Merry Ward, an attorney, and Aline Coursen Ward, she received her B.A. from Smith College in 1940, taking highest honors in English and classics. (Her preparation in classical languages and literatures aided her when she later studied the influence of ancient Roman and Greek authors on Keats.) After a year as an instructor at New York City's Dalton School, Ward continued her studies at Radcliffe College of Harvard University, completing her M.A. in 1942.

Following another year of teaching at the Dalton School, Ward was for two years a teaching fellow and tutor at Radcliffe, pursuant to her doctorate. A Marjorie Hope Nicolson Fellow during the school year 1945-1946, Ward was able to devote full time to her studies. Serving one year as an instructor at Wellesley College (1946-1947) and two

278

Aileen Ward

years as an instructor at Barnard College (1947-1949), Ward was fortunate enough to receive a Fulbright Fellowship to Girton College of Cambridge University for 1949-1950; this fellowship enabled her to make considerable progress toward completion of her dissertation. Perhaps of equal importance to her career was the association she began with the Institute of International Education; in 1952 she was named an associate to the Fulbright Program and in 1953 an associate to the Far Eastern Program's Fund for the Advancement of Education. Also in 1953 she received her Ph.D. from Harvard University.

Ward joined the faculty of Vassar College as assistant professor from 1954 to 1958. For the school year 1958-1959 Ward received a Shirley Farr Fellowship from the American Association of University Women, which permitted her to consolidate much of her early research for *John Keats* and to begin writing. From 1960 to 1964 Ward

was a member of the faculty of Sarah Lawrence College. For the remainder of her career she served as professor of English, first at Brandeis University and then at New York University, where she was named Albert Schweitzer Professor of the Humanities in 1980; she retired in August 1990. Ward has received many awards, including a Guggenheim Fellowship (1966-1967), a Radcliffe Institute Fellowship (1970-1971), a doctorate of literature from Skidmore College (1974), a New Virginia Review Fellowship from the Virginia Center for the Creative Arts (1983), and a National Humanities Center Fellowship (1986-1987). In 1983 the Keats-Shelley Association honored her with its Distinguished Scholar Award.

In 1980 Ward founded at New York University the Biography Seminar of the New York Institute for the Humanities. According to Ward this ongoing seminar "is a workshop for biographers

JOHN KEATS

DATES	LIFE	POETRY	PEOPLE	PLACES	THEMES
1795.10 1811.6	I. A Laughing Schoolboy (1-15) Childhood happiness: "sensations" Boyhood: father's death, mother's remarriage, death Transformation of puberty: "thoughts"	Early imagery	Family Uncle, Mother Grandmother	England, 1803 Enfield school	Role of hero "knowledge of light and shade"
1811.7- 1815.8	II. The Apothecary's Apprentice (16-19) "Happy time": reading, discovery of Spenser Rebellion: against master, against orthodoxy Crisis: break with Hammond, declaration as poet	Imitation of Spenser On Hunt's Leaving Prison	Clarke Abbey Mathew	Edmonton England, 1812-14	Role of doctor Liberalism
1815.9- 1816.10	III. Dresser to Mr. Lucas (20) Early success in medical school Alienation from fellows: first poem published Recognition as poet: introduction to Hunt	Calidore Chapman's Homer	Stephens Severn, Haslam Hunt	Guy's Hospital Margate: the sea	Role of poet Poetry as escape
1816.11- 1817.3	IV. The Green Shore (21) Discipleship to Hunt: gives up medicine, plans Poems Widening horizons: influence of Haydon; Elgin Marbles Move toward independence: leaves London, Hunt's circle	"I Stood Tiptoe" Sleep and Poetry	Hunt's circle Shelley	Vale of Health Cheapside Well Walk	Poetry as "luxuries" Poetry as vocation "Something more naked and Grecian"
1817.4- 1817.11	V. A Leap into the Sea Doubts about real poetic ability Discipline to poetry: achieves plan Self-transcendence: discovers "philosophy"	Endymion I Endymion II-III Endymion IV	Taylor Isabella Jones Reynolds family Bailey	Isle of Wight Hastings Oxford, Hampstead Burford Bridge	"Self-creation" Shakespeare as Presidor "Truth of the imagination"
1817.12- 1818.4	VI. Soundings and Quicksands (22) "Cavalier days": disillusionment with literary life Rededication: redefines his ambition: dramatic poetry "A look into the sea": Tom's illness, his own immaturity	Theater reviews What the Thrush Said Isabella	Wordsworth Reynolds Tom Keats	Literary London Devon	"Negative capability" "Creative indolence" "Chambers of Life"
1818.5- 1818.8	VII. Mist and Crag Depression: George's marriage, departure for America Adventure in Scotland: new experience, self-knowledge Anxiety: old problems of women, identity	"This mortal body" Sonnet on Ben Nevis	George and Georgiana Keats Brown Jane Reynolds	Scotland	Love of brothers Foreboding of death Relations with women

Pages from an early outline for John Keats: The Making of a Poet *(by permission of Aileen Ward)*

DATES	LIFE	POETRY	PEOPLE	PLACES	THEMES

1818.8–
1818.12
	VIII. The Shores of Darkness (23)
	Disaster: Tom's relapse,
	  hostile reviews of End.
	Conflict: "Tom, poetry,
	  and that woman": Tom's death
	Emergence into new life: in
	  love with Fanny Brawne
		Hyperion I–II
		
		Fancy
			Bailey's
			betrayal
			"That woman," Charmian,
			and "the lady from Hastings"
			"The Went-
			worthians"
				
				Wentworth
				Place
					Identification
					with Milton
					"Annihilation
					of Identity"

1819.1–
1819.3
	IX. The Melancholy Storm
	First joys of shared love:
	  declaration, secrecy
	Reversal: rejection? refuge
	  with Isabella Jones?
	Rebirth: the "struggle to
	  know myself"
		Eve of St.
		Agnes
		"Why Did I
		Laugh?"
		Hyperion III
			Fanny Brawne
			and mother
			Fanny Keats
			Woodhouse
			Hazlitt
				Chichester
				Bedhampton
					Love
					
					"The agony of
					ignorance"
					"Dying into
					life"

1819.4–
1819.6
	X. The Temple of Delight
	Acceptance of predicament:
	  love and poetry
	Expression of balance:
	  "light and shade"
	Resolution: love through
	  poetry: Chancery suit
		On a Dream
		La Belle Dame
		Odes
			The Brawnes move to
			Wentworth Place
			
			Abbey's
			deception
					"Vale of Soul-
					Making"

1819.7–
1819.9
	XI. Between Energy and Despair
	Tension: exile from Fanny:
	  love versus poetry
	Renunciation: love rejected
	  for poetry
	Frustration of both hopes:
	  farewell to poetry
		"Bright
		Star"
		Lamia
		
		To Autumn
			Rice
			
			Brown vs.
			Fanny
				Shanklin
				
				Winchester
					Marriage
					vs. Love
					The Poet vs.
					the Public

1819.10–
1820.1
	XII. The Siege of Contraries (24)
	Resolution to try journal-
	  ism: return to F.: collapse
	Struggle to keep writing: vs.
	  disillusionment, disease
	Defeat: George's return,
	  first hemorrhage
		Lines to
		Fanny
		The Fall of
		Hyperion
			Henry Hunt
			
			George Keats
				England
				in 1819
					"Public Good"
					
					The Poet vs.
					the Dreamer

1820.2–
1820.8
	XIII. The Wreck of Life
	Struggle against illness:
	  slow recovery
	Struggle against jealousy
	  of Fanny: relapse
	Ironic achievement: success
	  of Lamia, reassurance of
	  love—sentence of exile
			Brown's
			betrayal
			Reconciliation
			with Hunt
			Friends'
			farewells
				Kentish Town	Conviction of fail-
					ure vs. "The Prin-
					ciple of Beauty"

1820.9–
1821.2
	XIV. The Last Voyage
	Struggle for life: journey
	  to Italy: attempted suicide
	Struggle against despair:
	  Naples, Rome: relapse
	Tragic achievement: final
	  assertion of identity in
	  face of death
			Severn	The sea
				
				Italy
				
				Piazza di Spagna,
				Protestant Cemetery	

who meet every several weeks to present their work in progress and discuss practical and theoretical aspects of biography." Ward declares that "all biography is founded on fact." She states in her preface to the Keats biography that her effort was "to work as completely as possible from Keats's own writings and those of his friends." She maintains that the biographer "should work from original sources as much as possible and take a critical or even skeptical attitude toward his predecessors and other secondary sources." Recognizing that the biographer can sometimes be required, for the sake of a smooth narrative for example, to speculate on or interpret events, Ward urges that she or he "must clearly indicate" the relation of these speculations or interpretations "to the known facts."

"But literary biography especially requires more than just a scrupulous regard for fact," Ward insists, "something approaching the subject's own insight and artistry." Any biographer must "provide evidence for any of his statements," but "his work will endure only if he endows his material with significant form." What is significant "is the human meaning and value he finds in his subject's life and work"; the form the biography should take "is the shape that best expresses this significance."

The crowning achievement of Ward's career is, of course, *John Keats*, which has become indispensable reading among scholars of Keats. Perhaps too much emphasis, nonetheless, has been placed on Ward's application of tools from psychology. Leon Waldoff, for example, praises the biography as "still the centerpiece of psychoanalytic work on Keats" (*Keats and the Silent Work of Imagination*, 1985). It is undeniable that Ward seeks support for her argument—that Keats arrived at his identity as a poet only after great labor—from Otto Rank's *Art and Artist: Creative Urge and Personality Development* (1932) and Erik H. Erikson's monograph "The Problem of Ego Identity" (1956); however, her use of these sources hardly overwhelms her text. Typing this biography as the "centerpiece of psychoanalytic work" tends to reduce its value and eclipse the study's other virtues—such as her clever use of chapter headings (mostly quotes from Keats), her finite attention to detail, the sometimes rhapsodic quality of her prose, and her subtle revelation that much of Keats's compulsion to create derived from his capacity to accept the inevitability of an early death while at the same time resolving not to be cheated out of some measure of creative success (if only for himself and on his own terms).

Ward's readers learn that Keats took wing in several intellectual directions, all of which played necessary roles in his miraculous development as a poet. Keats's realization of his essential humanity, the wisdom of which he reminded himself often in his mature years, firmly anchors his best poetry in the real world, not the world of dreams.

Ward provides many details of Keats's contemporary world. For example, early on Ward captures the politically and militarily charged atmosphere of Keats's childhood as she describes the toys common to the boys of England: "Beside their hoops and tops and kites, English lads of 1803 had toy guillotines to play with, toy cannons to fire with real gunpowder, and great English victories to act out in their games." Somehow this image of "lads" releasing imaginary blades on the heads of imaginary enemies of the state and of these same boys armed with "real gunpowder" strikes an unsettling timbre, giving Ward's volume the tone of discord she hoped to achieve. At another point, Ward describes the sardonic manner by which bodies for dissection were obtained for Keats's medical courses: "The subjects were stolen from nearby graveyards, doubled up stark naked in sacks, and smuggled in at the dead of night by body-snatchers—'resurrection men,' as they were called—who were paid three or four guineas for each corpse."

Ward can also capture the intrinsic beauty of a scene. Describing the view from Keats's rooms on the Piazza di Spagna in Rome, she writes: "The windows facing south and west looked down two stories to the steps and the square below, where the Barcaccia, Bernini's boat-shaped fountain, splashed in the sun." This scene becomes especially poignant when the reader realizes that in these very rooms, fronting this lovely view, Keats was to die. In another passage, in which Ward prepares her readers for a consideration of the rich imagery of Keats's *Eve of St. Agnes* (1820), she tells of his seeing in Hampshire a house soon to be consecrated as a chapel: "there was much to catch his gaze. The side windows, high above him, were triple-arched and diamond-paned . . . set with stained-glass scutcheons of the arms [of well-known families]. The sun, flashing out from behind the wind-driven clouds, cast pools of light, blue, amber, and blood-red, on the white lawn of the attendant priests. . . . Wide stairways and long halls with pan-

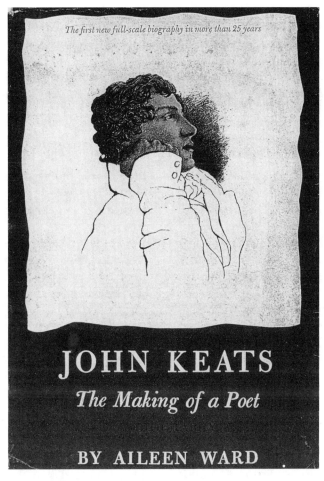

The first new full-scale biography in more than 25 years

JOHN KEATS

The Making of a Poet

BY AILEEN WARD

Dust jacket for the book that earned Ward the 1963 Duff Cooper Memorial Prize, the 1964 Rose Mary Crawshay Prize, and the 1964 National Book Award in Arts and Letters

elling of oak carved in fruits and flowers" were decked with "Arras tapestries and gold-embroidered chairs, fringed with carpets and gold and silver service—it was a banquet for the eye."

All this rich imagery, Ward's and Keats's own language that she often quotes, does not abate the pall of death overhanging much of Keats's life. Such an overwhelming reality could easily cause the book to become maudlin or fatalistic. Yet Ward suggests that it was Keats's awareness that he would meet an early death that empowered his struggle to create. Keats saw his doom as a challenge to be conquered by sheer determination. Keats probably got the notion—that he would die before his time—at the moment of his mother's death in March of 1810; as Ward says, in Keats's time tuberculosis, or consumption, "was thought to be hereditary, and there was no way of diagnosing it with certainty till its final symptoms appeared, when it was too late."

Keats's younger brother, George, remarked

that, shortly after the death of their mother, Keats was given to "bitter fits of hypochondriasm." Ward later suggests that the news that his brother Tom had developed the symptoms of consumption "must have struck Keats with a chill of foreboding." However, Ward is never obtrusive about Keats's premonitions of his premature death; she never presses the issue. But she is careful to demonstrate and to argue that such premonitions rallied Keats to renewed determination to work diligently toward making some worthy contribution to the annals of British poetry. When Ward finally notes Keats's prediction in the spring of 1818 that he had only three more years to live, she relates the occasion of this premonition almost as if it were tantamount to a certainty: "Now the thought seems to have shaped itself with a chilling precision: he had three years—a little more than a thousand days—to live. He knew it was unreasonable; he also knew it was possible." And the regrettable truth is Keats was, for the most part, on target. Now his determination to reach his goal in poetry, Ward maintains, received new and compelling urgency.

Ward argues that Keats's struggle constitutes a successive series of established goals followed, as Keats's genius became more and more manifest, by inevitable refinement of those goals. Ward's analytical narrative of those successive periods of definition and redefinition of Keats's career objectives as poet constitute the lifeblood of her biography. As she states in her preface, "My account of his life . . . is concerned primarily with the development of his character as a poet." In attempting to carry out this objective, Ward insists she has "tried to convey something of the inner drama of his creative life as it is recorded in his poems and letters." Much of the pleasure of reading this biography comes from watching Ward's cogent analytical skills unfold. Early in the volume, for example, Ward makes clear her indebtedness to Otto Rank when she observes that he "has described the psychological mainspring of creative achievement as the 'will to self-immortalization' arising from the universal fear of death—a fear which the average man meets by immersing himself in life through his family and his work." Keats, certainly no "average man," "at twenty found himself . . . increasingly disturbed in his [medical] work by its daily reminders of illness and death. Just as six years before he had escaped from painful reality by retreating into study, now he threw himself into his other life of poetry with the energy almost of despair." Rather than subordinating her thought to Rank's, Ward incorporates his psychological principle and then modifies and extends it.

Ward's treatment of Keats's *Endymion* (1818) is one of the most provocative discussions in the volume. Ward concludes her analysis by stating that "Keats's search for a truth underlying 'the bare circumstance' of his legend [the story line of *Endymion*] is the real significance" of this poem. Keats was "the first English poet to sense the possibility of a human meaning implicit in the myths themselves, rather than to fit them into a preconceived allegorical pattern . . . or merely to use them for decorative effect."

Ward asserts that at the age of fifteen, during a period of intense hero worship, Keats experienced "the first stirrings of a sense of beauty and pathos," which drew him to the world of mythology and notably to the wanderings of Aeneas. It was at this time that Keats embarked upon a translation in prose of Virgil's *Aeneid*, which Keats completed when he was barely sixteen. Ward draws a parallel between Keats and Virgil's prototypical hero. According to Ward, as Keats gradually pulled away from medicine and gravitated toward poetry, he began "to see his life again in terms of the first image he had formed of himself in his battle with the world." The parallel is sustainable throughout the life, for, like Aeneas, Keats endured a seemingly endless train of buffetings. Like his hero, whose primary virtue is his devotion to the gods, to the family, and to his country, Keats struggled almost constantly to live a life ennobled by moral purpose. In the last chapter of her biography, entitled "End of the Voyage," Ward places Keats finally in the country of Aeneas's destiny: "Italy at last, most glorious of all the kingdoms of the earth Keats had dreamed of seeing." The journey for Keats ended in Rome, but for the reader the poet's responsibility to his art continues in Ward's interpretation of his creative life. *John Keats: The Making of a Poet* is both a scholarly biography and an imaginative verbal structure with a kind of poetry of its own.

Stanley Weintraub

(17 April 1929 -   )

John J. Conlon
University of Massachusetts—Boston

BOOKS: *Private Shaw and Public Shaw: A Dual Portrait of Lawrence of Arabia and G. B. S.* (New York: Braziller, 1963; London: Cape, 1963);

The War in the Wards: Korea's Unknown Battle in a Prisoner-of-War Hospital Camp (Garden City, N.Y.: Doubleday, 1964; revised edition, San Rafael, Cal.: Presidio, 1976);

The Art of William Golding, by Weintraub and B. S. Oldsey (New York: Harcourt, Brace & World, 1965);

Reggie: A Portrait of Reginald Turner (New York: Braziller, 1965; London: Allen, 1965);

Beardsley: A Biography (New York: Braziller, 1967; London: Allen, 1967; revised edition, Harmondsworth, U.K.: Penguin, 1972);

The Last Great Cause: The Intellectuals and the Spanish Civil War (New York: Weybright & Talley, 1968; London: Allen, 1968);

Journey to Heartbreak: The Crucible Years of Bernard Shaw, 1914-1918 (New York: Weybright & Talley, 1971); republished as *Bernard Shaw, 1914-1918: Journey to Heartbreak* (London: Routledge & Kegan Paul, 1973);

Whistler: A Biography (New York: Weybright & Talley, 1974; London: Collins, 1974; revised edition, New York: Dutton, 1988);

Lawrence of Arabia: The Literary Impulse, by Weintraub and Rodelle Weintraub (Baton Rouge: Louisiana State University Press, 1975);

Aubrey Beardsley: Imp of the Perverse (University Park & London: Pennsylvania State University Press, 1976);

Four Rossettis: A Victorian Biography (New York: Weybright & Talley, 1977; London: Allen, 1978);

The London Yankees: Portraits of American Writers and Artists in England, 1894-1914 (New York: Harcourt Brace Jovanovich, 1979; London: Allen, 1979);

The Unexpected Shaw: Biographical Approaches to G. B. S. and His Work (New York: Ungar, 1982);

A Stillness Heard Round the World: The End of the Great War, November 1918 (New York: Dutton, 1985; London: Allen & Unwin, 1986);

Victoria: An Intimate Biography (New York: Dutton, 1987); republished as *Victoria: Biography of a Queen* (London: Allen & Unwin, 1987);

Long Day's Journey into War: December 7, 1941 (New York: Dutton/Talley, 1991).

OTHER: *An Unfinished Novel by Bernard Shaw*, edited, with an introduction, by Weintraub (New York: Dodd, Mead, 1958; London: Constable, 1958);

C. P. Snow: A Spectrum, edited, with an introduction, by Weintraub (New York: Scribners, 1963);

The Yellow Book: Quintessence of the Nineties, edited, with an introduction, by Weintraub (Garden City, N.Y.: Doubleday/Anchor, 1964);

The Savoy: Nineties Experiment, edited, with an introduction, by Weintraub (University Park: Pennsylvania State University Press, 1966);

The Court Theatre, 1904-1907, edited, with an introduction, by Weintraub (Coral Gables, Fla.: University of Miami Press, 1966);

Biography and Truth, edited, with an introduction, by Weintraub (Indianapolis: Bobbs-Merrill, 1968);

Evolution of a Revolt: Early Postwar Writings of T. E. Lawrence, edited by Weintraub and Rodelle Weintraub (University Park: Pennsylvania State University Press, 1968);

George Bernard Shaw, *Cashel Byron's Profession*, edited, with an introduction, by Weintraub (Carbondale: Southern Illinois University Press, 1968);

Literary Criticism of Oscar Wilde, edited, with an introduction, by Weintraub (Lincoln: University of Nebraska Press, 1968);

Shaw: An Autobiography, 1856-1898, edited, with an introduction, by Weintraub (New York: Weybright & Talley, 1969; London: Reinhardt, 1970);

Stanley Weintraub, 1978

Shaw: An Autobiography, 1898-1950: The Playwright Years, edited, with an introduction, by Weintraub (New York: Weybright & Talley, 1970; London: Reinhardt, 1971);

Robert S. Hichens, *The Green Carnation*, edited, with an introduction, by Weintraub (Lincoln: University of Nebraska Press, 1970);

Shaw, *Saint Joan*, edited, with an introduction, by Weintraub (Indianapolis: Bobbs-Merrill, 1971);

Bernard Shaw's Nondramatic Literary Criticism, edited, with an introduction, by Weintraub (Lincoln: University of Nebraska Press, 1972);

Directions in Literary Criticism, edited, with an introduction, by Weintraub and Philip Young (University Park & London: Pennsylvania State University Press, 1973);

"Saint Joan": Fifty Years After, 1923/24-1973/74,

edited, with an introduction, by Weintraub (Baton Rouge: Louisiana State University Press, 1973);

Modern British Dramatists, 1900-1945, 2 parts, edited by Weintraub, *Dictionary of Literary Biography*, volume 10 (Detroit: Gale / Columbia, S.C.: Bruccoli Clark, 1982);

British Dramatists Since World War II, 2 parts, edited by Weintraub, *Dictionary of Literary Biography*, volume 13 (Detroit: Gale / Columbia, S.C.: Bruccoli Clark, 1982);

The Portable Bernard Shaw, edited, with an introduction and notes, by Weintraub (New York: Viking, 1977; revised, 1986);

The Portable Oscar Wilde, edited, with an introduction, by Weintraub and Richard Aldington (New York: Viking, 1981; Harmondsworth, U.K.: Penguin, 1981);

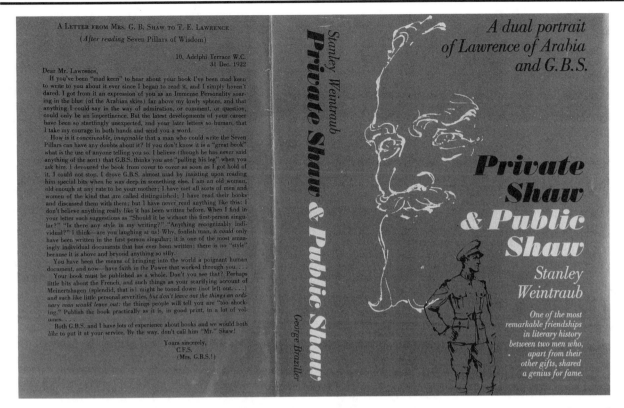

Dust jacket for Weintraub's first book, which grew out of his discovery of the then-little-known friendship between Shaw and Lawrence, who legally changed his last name to Shaw in 1927

Shaw, *Heartbreak House: A Facsimile of the Original Typescript*, edited, with an introduction, by Weintraub and Anne Wright (New York: Garland, 1981);

The Playwright and the Pirate: Bernard Shaw and Frank Harris, a Correspondence, edited, with an introduction, by Weintraub (University Park: Pennsylvania State University Press, 1982; Bucks, U.K.: Smythe, 1982);

Bernard Shaw: The Diaries, 1885-1897, 2 volumes, edited, with an introduction, by Weintraub (University Park & London: Pennsylvania State University Press, 1986);

"Collecting the Quarrels: Whistler and the Gentle Art of Making Enemies," in *Twilight of Dawn*, edited by O. M. Brack (Tucson: University of Arizona Press, 1987), pp. 34-44;

Bernard Shaw on the London Art Scene, 1886-1950, edited, with an introduction, by Weintraub (University Park & London: Pennsylvania State University Press, 1989);

The Annual of Bernard Shaw Studies, Volume 10, edited by Weintraub and Fred D. Crawford (University Park: Pennsylvania State University Press, 1990).

SELECTED PERIODICAL PUBLICATIONS—
UNCOLLECTED: "Humanities Research Center, A Consumer's Report," *Texas Humanist*, 5 (May/June 1983): 6-7;

"Confessions of a Bookworm's Apprentice," *Town and Gown* (September 1984): 24-54.

Stanley Weintraub has, in nearly forty books written and edited over three decades, become one of America's foremost biographers and literary historians. An indefatigable scholar and expositor of George Bernard Shaw, he has edited Shaw's fiction, plays, letters, diaries, and other prose. He has rescued the forgotten (Reginald Turner), elucidated the self-obscuring (T. E. Lawrence), investigated the aesthetic (Aubrey Beardsley and James Abbott McNeill Whistler), and opened visions of Queen Victoria that Lytton Strachey and others had sought to obscure. He has also developed and practiced the art of collective biography in such works as *The Last Great Cause* (1968), *Four Rossettis* (1977), *The London Yankees* (1979), *A Stillness Heard Round the World* (1985), and *Long Day's Journey into War* (1991), the last two detailing worldwide personal responses to historical events, illustrating Ralph Waldo Emerson's dictum that all history is biography.

Born in Philadelphia on 17 April 1929 to Benjamin Weintraub, an insurance agent, and Ray Segal Weintraub, Stanley Weintraub earned his B.S. in 1949 at West Chester State College (now West Chester University) in Pennsylvania and his M.A. in 1951 at Temple University. From 1951 through early 1953 he served in the United States Army in Korea and was admissions officer of a United Nations Hospital with ten thousand beds and eleven thousand patients. He chronicled a six weeks' episode from this experience as *The War in the Wards* (1964), a work of stark, graphic realism. His later collective biographical explorations concern people and events in World War I, the Spanish Civil War, and World War II. His interest in Shaw began during his army service, since his reading consisted of paperbacks his brother Herbert sent him, including Penguin editions of Shaw's works. Returning to civilian life, he began graduate study at Pennsylvania State University, where he has remained since 1953, as a doctoral student (Ph.D., 1956) and teaching assistant, then as an assistant professor (1959-1962), associate professor (1962-1965), professor (1965-1970), research professor (1970-1986), director of the Institute for Arts and Humanistic Studies since 1970, and Evan Pugh Professor of Arts and Humanities since 1986.

On 6 June 1954 he married Rodelle Horwitz, with whom he has edited *Evolution of a Revolt: Early Postwar Writings of T. E. Lawrence* (1968) and written *Lawrence of Arabia: The Literary Impulse* (1975). Their first son, Mark, was born in 1956 and the second, David, in 1958. A daughter, Erica, was born in 1961. In addition to his posts at Penn State, Weintraub has been a visiting professor at the University of California at Los Angeles (1963), the University of Hawaii (1973), the University of Malaya (1977), and the National University of Singapore (1982). He has edited *Shaw, The Annual of Bernard Shaw Studies* (1956-1990) and, since 1987, *Comparative Literature Studies*, and has, among other distinctions, been a Guggenheim fellow (1968-1969), a nominee for the National Book Award (1968) for *Beardsley* (1967), and the recipient of the 1972 George Freedley Award of the American Theatre Library Association for *Journey to Heartbreak* (1971). His *London Yankees* was chosen the 1980 Ambassador Book by Books-Across-the-Sea and earned him an award from the Freedoms Foundation in the same year. In 1985 he received the Pennsylvania

Humanities Council Distinguished Humanist Award.

Weintraub's method of biography, summarized in his introduction to *Biography and Truth* (1968), is to tell a good story, yet a true one; to do so artistically without inventing dialogue or action; and to resist the temptation to tell a good story that cannot be verified. He fixes the biographer's dilemma relative to truth in a double paradox: the facts do not always add up to truth and invention has its own kind of truth. The biographer, according to Weintraub, must wrestle with the several dimensions of truth, may never be able to tell all the truths he discovers or the whole of particular truths for reasons ranging from a sense of propriety to an aversion to litigation. Weintraub is also averse to inventing dialogue in a compellingly told story. Above all, he says, the biographer's facts must be readable: this accounts for the meticulous but unobtrusive scholarship and exact documentation he reserves for his notes, while his lucid, uncluttered prose presents his subjects to his audience.

Like many scholarly findings, some of Weintraub's are the products of curiosity fed by chance. *Private Shaw and Public Shaw* (1963) grew from searching the card catalogue at the Penn State library. There he discovered, while pursuing Bernard Shaw, another "Shaw," Thomas Edward Shaw. Lawrence of Arabia had legally changed his name in 1926 from T. E. Lawrence. From extensive research Weintraub uncovered and presented the little-known relationship between the two. Lawrence became not only somewhat dependent on Shaw to further his lifelong goal of literary fame but also acknowledged that debt in the curious taking of Shaw's name as he sought a strangely public kind of anonymity after World War I. The story of the literary, editorial, and personal relationship extends to Shaw's acute but perhaps cranky advice to Lawrence and Lawrence's occasional, somewhat cranky, acquiescence to it. For Bernard Shaw it also led to a dramatization incorporating tales of Lawrence's second and third careers—as a self-obscuring regular in the Royal Tank Corps and the Royal Air Force—into the background of Private Napoleon Alexander Trotsky Meek in the play *Too True to Be Good* (1932). Weintraub's book remains remarkable, a record of a literary and personal friendship that enriched and influenced the lives of both the old sage and the younger ascetic.

In this early period of Weintraub's career he edited in 1958 *An Unfinished Novel by Bernard*

Dust jacket for Weintraub's book about Shaw during World War I, after Shaw's Common Sense About the War *(1914) provoked charges that he was pro-German because he asserted that Britain and its allies were as culpable as the Germans and called for a negotiated peace*

Shaw—an 1888 fragment—as well as a book on a contemporary novelist, *C. P. Snow: A Spectrum* (1963). In addition, he published his autobiographical *The War in the Wards* and began researching the life of Reginald Turner, a mysterious late Victorian, while preparing, with B. S. Oldsey, *The Art of William Golding* (1965). Turner, however, preoccupied him, and *Reggie: A Portrait of Reginald Turner* was published in 1965. In this work, Weintraub contributed greatly to the nascent interest in the English 1890s, an interest first revived in the late 1940s and championed variously in the 1950s, when a reappraisal of the Victorians, late Victorians, and Edwardians—in the Transitional Age (roughly 1880-1920)—began to receive serious scholarly attention. Like his earlier work on Lawrence, *Reggie* shows evidence of Weintraub's skillful detective work on a life that touched upon the lives of so many twentieth-century literary figures.

A contributor to *The Yellow Book* quarterly, friend of Max Beerbohm, comforter of the dying Oscar Wilde, fixture in the British colony in Florence, and friend to Alfred Douglas, Somerset Maugham, H. G. Wells, D. H. and Frieda Law-

rence, and others, Turner lived among the literary and artistically successful but did not become one of them. Self-characterized as a "futile person," Turner nonetheless brought others together by his generosity and brought others out by his wit, a style of wit that did not translate well from conversation to novels. Apart from the interest Turner's own story provides, Weintraub's exploration of his relationship with those he knew and of their relationships among each other sheds new light upon those—including William Archer, Arnold Bennett, and Robert S. Hichens—who had begun, by the 1960s, to fade from scholarly awareness as they had, in the main, faded from public consciousness.

Weintraub's editing and introducing a collection from *The Yellow Book* (1964), in which there is a Turner story, led him to develop an interest in Aubrey Beardsley and then to produce an edition of *The Savoy: Nineties Experiment* (1966), which led him several steps closer to Beardsley. Weintraub's explorations of the "Imp of the Perverse" led ultimately to one of his most widely recognized biographical achievements, *Beardsley*. His

The afternoon of Wednesday

On/July 2?, 1903 ~~~~~~~~ Jonathan Sturges, Princeton '85, ~~~~~~~ returned by hansom cab to Long's Hotel in New Bond

Street, London, where he lived. Crippled from ~~kirk~~ birth, and stunted he could hardly walk

without a stick to support him, and the stick was always the ~~the~~ silver-headed,

ebony ~~wand~~ one his friend Whistler had given him, after Sturges had admired the

four-foot ebony wand which was as much symbol of Whistler's bellicosity as the

butterfly signature to which the artist often added an anatomically incongruous sting.

~~Onxxx~~ Raised up on a folded blanket, with the glass top of the cab up and the

lower doors closed, his silk hat on his head and gloves in his hand, he looked

impressive and unbent. It was an overcast day, with a persistent drizzle, but

Sturges seemed not to notice. Nor did he seem ready to drag himself from the

puzzling cab when the driver pulled open the doors with his strap. After a pause ~~he~~ Sturges

to himdrag himself signalled the hotel porter, who came forward to the curb and helped ~~Sturges~~ down.

It was the first time anyone had seen him accept assistance, as he took the burly

stickless, in the lobby porter's arm and hobbled into the hotel. ~~He/shifted hixxhand~~ he shifted a shaking hand to the arm of a friend,

Sturges' who noticed that ~~his~~ coat was soaking wet and that under the sodden hat ~~Sturges~~ his

face was pale.

When they were settled in Sturges' rooms, ~~and~~ he had a brandy and soda ~~~~~~~~~~

~~kand~~ brought to him; and after a sip or two he said, "It was dreadful; no one could

lamented have imagined such a thing." Whistler had ~~mourned~~ a few years before, when one of his

long-time adversaries died, that he hardly had a close enemy left in London. The

old and then at the graveyard fact ~~had~~ been demonstrated that day at Chelsea ~~Old~~ Church at Chiswick, where

and Sturges had said his final respects. including Whistler was buried, ~~Hardly a dozen friends were there~~, and several women--his

two sisters-in-law and a lady who kept in the background and was suspected to be

of fifteen years before two wreaths, one his loyal but cast-off mistress, Maud. There were no flowers: only a gilded

one primrose laurel ~~wreath~~ Whistler would have excoriated as in bad taste, and a ~~promise~~ for

mourner open each to drop into the/grave. When it came to ~~Sturges~~ Sturges' turn, after the

The police were out there to restrain the crowd, but there was no crowd. This church had been less than half full, and many ~~~~~ follow to graveside, where a clergyman mumbled vastly through the service. Barely a dozen people remained

passion for verifiable details and his art in telling a good, readable story coalesced into a biography that focuses on one of the more intriguing loners and more accomplished artists of the 1890s. Tracing Beardsley's youth and relationship with his sister Mabel (perhaps his closest lifelong friend), Weintraub follows him from his South Downs origins to his escape to London and his eventual recognition as a gifted, if bizarre, caricaturist and sketcher who cut his artistic teeth by illustrating Sir Thomas Malory's *Le Morte d'Arthur* for the 1894 Dent edition. Awed by James Whistler, contentious with Wilde (he illustrated Wilde's *Salome* also in 1894), and attracted to the erotic, Beardsley turned his artistic practice more and more toward illustration. As art editor for Henry Harland's *The Yellow Book*, Beardsley shocked many, as he had shocked those who had seen his *Salome*; he continued to shock the readership of the *Savoy*, a short-lived venture that he, Leonard Smithers, and Arthur Symons launched. Beardsley's brief life, passed in the service of his art, saw its finest public moments in the sensation caused by his illustrations.

Weintraub captures, as no one before him had done, the "Fra Angelico of Satanism," as Roger Fry called Beardsley. The book won high praise from all quarters, John Russell in the *New York Times Book Review* (16 July 1967) going so far as to proclaim that as a biography it needed no successor. Nominated for a National Book Award in 1968, *Beardsley* was translated into German, Japanese, and Italian. But despite its warm reception, and enthusiasm for it to the contrary, Weintraub knew it did need a successor. In its second edition, published in 1972, he added new information. Yet more information was available, and later, in a more open society, more of Beardsley's daring erotica, chiefly his 1896 illustrations for *Lysistrata*, could be and were included in a new biography based upon the old, *Aubrey Beardsley: Imp of the Perverse* (1976), in which Weintraub notes his first publisher's reticence about Beardsley's more explicit erotica and his own fear of offending "lady librarians." Finally he could use the title he had given his first biography of Beardsley but which his first publisher had thought too provocative.

While editing Shaw's autobiographical works, as well as his own *Biography and Truth*, Shaw's *Cashel Byron's Profession* (1968), and *Literary Criticism of Oscar Wilde* (1968), and continuing his explorations of Lawrence's life—in *Evolution of a Revolt: Early Postwar Writings of T. E. Lawrence*

(1968)—Weintraub was engaged with still other projects, one of which became *The Last Great Cause: The Intellectuals and the Spanish Civil War* (1968). In this work he presents what some might call a chapter in intellectual or literary history but which he would classify as collective biography, as he traces the effects of the ideal and the reality of the Spanish Civil War. Shaw provided one clue: he had written a play (*Geneva*, 1938) about despotism in the late 1930s with characters resembling Adolf Hitler, Benito Mussolini, and Francisco Franco. While Shaw had little otherwise to say about or to do with the war in Spain, other writers said and did much on both the Left and the Right; and Weintraub chronicles the emotional appeal of the war for English and American writers, artists, and intellectuals as evidenced by what they wrote and did. From the British "Platoon of Poets" actively fighting, and mostly dying, on the Left, to Stephen Spender, a committed noncombatant whose Marxist convictions weakened at the Writer's Congress in Madrid (1937), to W. H. Auden, Cecil Day Lewis, and other poets and writers opposing fascism, Weintraub depicts the feeling for liberty and liberation that became necessarily mixed with feelings of failing republicanism and the defeat of sentiment. Ernest Hemingway, George Orwell, and Arthur Koestler take their places as writers who drew intense inspiration from the Spanish experience. Shaw, H. G. Wells, James Joyce, William Butler Yeats, Ezra Pound, and T. S. Eliot join the ranks of Weintraub's "Aloof Olympians" who, in the main, chose to stand apart from the conflict. On the Right, Ray Campbell and Hilaire Belloc, for very different reasons, are leagued with Douglas Jerrold, Wyndham Lewis, and others as a small group siding with Franco.

Weintraub succeeds in rendering widely disparate reactions to the war, reactions that left their marks on literature for decades. He succeeds, moreover, in demonstrating the extent to which those on the Left and Right and those who consciously chose to remain apart from the war were changed by it and how, in turn, these changes wrought further changes upon those who read their works.

Returning his attention to Shaw, Weintraub edited Shaw's self-referential prose and published *Shaw: An Autobiography, 1856-1898* (1969) and *Shaw: An Autobiography, 1898-1950: The Playwright Years* (1970), edited *The Green Carnation* by Hichens (1970)—an 1890s classic—and produced his edition of Shaw's masterpiece *Saint Joan*

Dust jacket for Weintraub's collective biography of Maria Francesca, Dante Gabriel, William Michael, and Christina Rossetti—who together had a major impact on British poetry and painting

(1971). Weintraub deals with Shaw's controversial role as sage and prophet during World War I in *Journey to Heartbreak: The Crucible Years of Bernard Shaw, 1914-1918* (1971). He draws upon his extensive knowledge of Shaw to present the embattled popular philosopher's unpopular *Common Sense about the War* (1914) in the context of Shaw's multifaceted life as playwright, Fabian, and social commentator. Viewing World War I from Shaw's perspective, Weintraub examines its effects, as well as Shaw's troubled relationships with such friends as Wells, his lonely fate as one who voiced unpopular wartime truths, and his difficulties with the prudery of the public and the censorship of the lord chamberlain as he sought to produce newly written plays about the war. Shaw's involvement in debates about war, the trial of Roger Casement (an Irishman who landed in Ireland in a German submarine and sought to have his, and Shaw's, native land join the German war effort), and the everyday events in wartime England form the background against which Shaw's *Heartbreak House* (composed in 1916 and 1917) and *Back to Methuselah* (written between 1918 and

1921) were born. Weintraub's editorial work on Shaw's plays, autobiographical material, and fiction, and his editorship of the *Shaw* annual had established him as an undisputed authority on Shaw. The well-received Shaw biography won for Weintraub the 1972 George Freedley Award of the American Theatre Library Association.

While he continued to edit volumes on Shaw, Weintraub also began to investigate the life of Beardsley's idol, Whistler, and published *Whistler: A Biography* early in 1974. A difficult subject and a difficult personality, Whistler created several fables of his own identity (he chose not, he later remarked, to have been born in Lowell, Massachusetts), which Weintraub unravels. He discusses Whistler's own brief, abandoned autobiography, which Whistler called the fiction of his own biography and which he began in an effort to forestall "the efforts of any mendacious scamp to tell foolish truths about him in the future." Like the wily Shaw who superintended and largely wrote Frank Harris's biography of him, Whistler continued to invent himself and, in the renowned case of *Whistler* v. *Ruskin*, embroidered

292

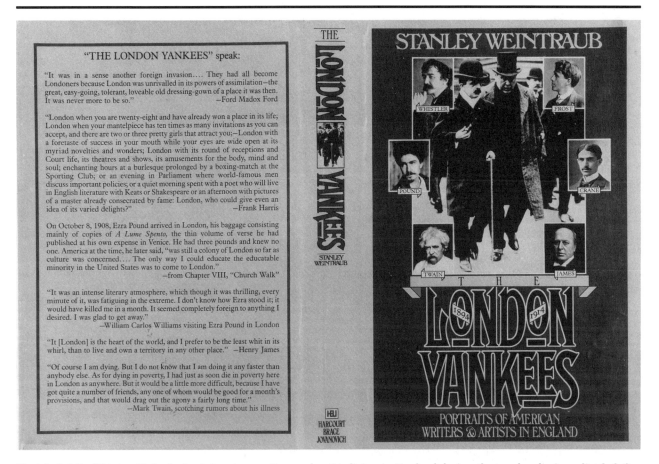

"THE LONDON YANKEES" speak:

"It was in a sense another foreign invasion.... They had all become Londoners because London was unrivalled in its powers of assimilation—the great, easy-going, tolerant, loveable old dressing-gown of a place it was then. It was never more to be so."
—Ford Madox Ford

"London when you are twenty-eight and have already won a place in its life; London when your mantelpiece has ten times as many invitations as you can accept, and there are two or three pretty girls that attract you;—London with a foretaste of success in your mouth while your eyes are wide open at its myriad novelties and wonders; London with its round of receptions and Court life, its theatres and shows, its amusements for the body, mind and soul; enchanting hours at a burlesque prolonged by a boxing-match at the Sporting Club; or an evening in Parliament where world-famous men discuss important policies; or a quiet morning spent with a poet who will live in English literature with Keats or Shakespeare or an afternoon with pictures of a master already consecrated by fame: London, who could give even an idea of its varied delights?"
—Frank Harris

On October 8, 1908, Ezra Pound arrived in London, his baggage consisting mainly of copies of *A Lume Spento*, the thin volume of verse he had published at his own expense in Venice. He had three pounds and knew no one. America at the time, he later said, "was still a colony of London so far as culture was concerned.... The only way I could educate the educatable minority in the United States was to come to London."
—from Chapter VIII, "Church Walk"

"It was an intense literary atmosphere, which though it was thrilling, every minute of it, was fatiguing in the extreme. I don't know how Ezra stood it; it would have killed me in a month. It seemed completely foreign to anything I desired. I was glad to get away."
—William Carlos Williams visiting Ezra Pound in London

"It [London] is the heart of the world, and I prefer to be the least whit in its whirl, than to live and own a territory in any other place." —Henry James

"Of course I am dying. But I do not know that I am doing it any faster than anybody else. As for dying in poverty, I had just as soon die in poverty here in London as anywhere. But it would be a little more difficult, because I have got quite a number of friends, any one of whom would be good for a month's provisions, and that would drag out the agony a fairly long time."
—Mark Twain, scotching rumors about his illness

HARCOURT BRACE JOVANOVICH

Dust jacket for Weintraub's book about American writers and artists living in England during the two decades immediately before World War I

accounts of the trial, which Weintraub sets straight.

Dramatically Weintraub chooses to begin the book with an account of Whistler's funeral from the perspective of an attendee, Jonathan Sturges. Continuing then with Whistler's youth in America, Russia, and England, Weintraub traces his growth in arrogance if not maturity; his stint at West Point, where he began an artist's apprenticeship while neglecting other studies and disregarding the stringencies of military life; his early career with the Coastal Survey, where he began engraving in earnest; and then his bohemian life in Paris. Resettled in London, he took up with Dante Gabriel Rossetti and his circle, went through a Courbet phase and an oriental phase more topical than stylistic, and began going quickly through money he received for his painting and engraving. A public figure who enjoyed being in the public eye, Whistler made hosts of friends and enemies, Wilde among the latter. Impulsive (he once traveled to Valparaiso, Chile, on a whim), self-assured to the point of being self-

centered, articulate, and argumentative, Whistler was an attractively unattractive personality. Yet he was an unquestionably gifted artist who painstakingly painted and rubbed out, repainted and rubbed out until the picture was, to his eye, precisely what he wanted. While this meant delays, some of them infinite, in delivering commissioned work, Whistler asserted and clung tenaciously to the principle that a work of art belonged not to the patron but to the artist who, for a monetary consideration, would let the patron display the work until he needed it for a show. Whistler also asserted that a picture was finished only when all trace of the means used to bring about the end had disappeared. He asserted artistic independence from his subject and codified the antididactic position he had practiced since his Parisian days: a picture did not tell a story; it was, instead, an arrangement of line and color. He carried into painterly practice what Charles Baudelaire had preached in Paris and Walter Pater intimated at Oxford, that all art aspires to the condition of music. One of Whistler's

Dust jacket for Weintraub's 1982 collection of essays on various aspects of Shaw's life and works

points of importance, for Weintraub, is his anticipating the modern conception of the artist, a vision propagandized widely in the course of propagandizing himself as "The Master." Named one of the "Thirty Notable Books of the Year" for 1974 by the *New York Times*, *Whistler* was republished with some updates and corrections in 1988; it remains the most valuable portrait of Whistler.

Weintraub and his wife, Rodelle, decided to collaborate on a study of T. E. Lawrence from a biographical perspective based upon their earlier research into Lawrence's writing and Weintraub's first biography, *Private Shaw and Public Shaw*, and they wrote *Lawrence of Arabia: The Literary Impulse* (1975). Lawrence holds center stage as a figure whose principal ambition was literary and who sought neither military fame nor governmental, commercial, or academic honors but, instead, to write some of the best prose in English and to be recognized as a writer. The Weintraubs provide a detailed view of Lawrence at work as a writer consciously aiming to take his place alongside Herman Melville, Fyodor Dostoyevski, and Friedrich Nietzsche as an "English Fourth." In

his *Seven Pillars of Wisdom* (1926), for which Shaw made copious editorial suggestions, Lawrence may well have achieved that stature. Filled with misgivings, self-doubts, and a sense of literary failure, Lawrence nonetheless persisted in abridging *Seven Pillars* into *Revolt in the Desert* (1927) and in writing and revising *The Mint* from 1922 until his death in May 1935, a work that was not released to the general public until 1955. His translation of the *Odyssey*, however, a long and painstaking effort, did appear in 1932 as a work by T. E. Shaw. The Weintraubs' concluding chapter on the literary impact of Lawrence on his contemporaries and successors contains a perceptive analysis of the popularized Lawrence of Arabia on film and corrects the romantic distortions and factual errors of Robert Bolt's screenplay.

After rewriting portions of *Beardsley* and adding newly discovered data for *Aubrey Beardsley: Imp of the Perverse*, Weintraub completed his *Four Rossettis: A Victorian Biography*, a venture in the collective biography of a remarkable family— friends and neighbors of Whistler in London— whose story had not, prior to Weintraub's volume, been fully told. Dante Gabriel Rossetti, the

Dust jacket for the biography in which Weintraub focuses on the private life of Queen Victoria

second born and elder brother of William Michael Rossetti, has had his biographers, William among the first of them. Christina Rossetti, the youngest, has, likewise had her story told. But of the eldest, Maria Francesca, little had been published, and surely no one had treated the entire dynamic family of an eccentric professor of Italian whose gifted children altered the course of British painting and poetry. Early in life Maria was sent out to be a governess, a station she hated; William became a clerk in the Excise Office; Christina, frail and sickly, remained to write poetry at home; and Gabriel, after a period at the Antique School of the Royal Academy, apprenticed himself to Ford Madox Brown by day and attended classes by night. The patterns of their lives were, in the main, set from these early days. Gabriel's role in the foundation of the Pre-Raphaelite Brotherhood, well known and documented by the secretary, William, is retold with a new emphasis on William's talent for prose writing, but not for painting or, in the main, for poetry. Christina's role as poetess and model, typecast as the demure Virgin for one of Gabriel's early works, has the added dimension of Gabriel's proposing her for membership in the PRB, nearly ending the brotherhood before it was begun. Recounting the

stories of the Rossettis, with Gabriel always at the center, even after his death, Weintraub provides a compelling narrative that includes Christina's early sexual frustration, evident in her *Goblin Market* (1862) and her subsequent religious works; Maria's flight to a convent of Anglican nuns; Gabriel's marriage, affairs, painterly and poetic careers, and gradual death from drugs and drink; and William's seventy-year involvement with the PRB, its history, and his monuments to the monarch of the Rossetti clan, Gabriel. *Four Rossettis* remains the best biography of the family and the clearest candid story of their artistic gifts and their failings.

In 1977 Weintraub introduced and edited *The Portable Bernard Shaw* while at work on *The London Yankees: Portraits of American Writers and Artists in England, 1894-1914*. As in his earlier collective biographies, Weintraub uses a large canvas to situate his portraits in relation to one another. Weintraub touches on the lives of Joseph and Elizabeth Pennell, Henry James, Bret Harte, Pearl Craigie, Stephen Crane, Whistler, Edwin Austin Abbey, Edith Wharton, Ezra Pound, Amy Lowell, Conrad Aiken, Robert Frost and T. S. Eliot, among others. In chronicling the lives and works of Americans in London he demonstrates

Stanley Weintraub in 1991, standing in front of a kamikaze flag (photograph by Greg Grieco)

how the face of literature and art had been profoundly changed by the convergence of the Americans and the English in London. One product was Henry Harland's *The Yellow Book*, publishing the work of such talents as James and Beardsley; another was the Tite Street artists' colony, including, among others, Whistler, Abbey, and John Singer Sargent; a third result was the convergence of Pound and Wyndham Lewis in imagism, in vorticism, and, with the addition of Eliot, in the production of the second issue of *Blast* (1915). James appears to be a uniting force gathering together, in different times and places, most of the expatriates. He asked a telling question of Ezra Pound after being introduced to his bride, Dorothy Shakespear: he wanted to know, in his avuncular way, whether she was a compatriot. James greatly assisted his literary and artistic compatriots in the highly charged 1890s and the Edwardian era. Years later, Weintraub relates, Frost observed to Eliot that they had flown off the pinwheel in different directions; the metaphoric pin-

wheel of the American colony in prewar London hints at the unity that produced the outflying diversity Weintraub so successfully documents. Not only did the book find critical acceptance, but it also won the distinction of becoming the 1980 Ambassador Book, as chosen by Books-Across-the-Sea, and won for him an award from the Freedoms Foundation for an outstanding accomplishment in helping to achieve a better understanding of the American way of life.

Always one to have several projects in hand, Weintraub edited *The Portable Oscar Wilde*, originally edited by Richard Aldington, and edited *Heartbreak House: A Facsimile of the Original Typescript* with Anne Wright, both published in 1981 while he was editing *The Playwright and the Pirate: Bernard Shaw and Frank Harris, a Correspondence* (1982). His next biographical volume, *The Unexpected Shaw: Biographical Approaches to G. B. S. and His Work* (1982), is a foray into Shaw's life that emphasizes the unlikely and unusual elements of his thought and writing, his gestation of a play-

45-12

1600   4:00 PM   8 Dec   Malaya   1620   Thai time

By ~~the~~ late afternoon the
~~The~~ Kota Bharu airstrip was becoming untenable. Several batteries of "Dogra"

artillery had been ordered to the Sabak and Kuala Krai beachheads fronting

Kota Bharu, but mud, rain and swollen streams made rapid movement impossible.

Meanwhile the Japanese landed more troops and nudged forward, no longer

worried about British air strikes, The Australians at the airfield had almost
                                              enduring
nothing serviceable left after several more bombing and strafing runs.

At about four, with stray bullets now reaching the area from the fighting near
                                                        squadron
the airfield perimeter, a rumor reached the that the enemy had broken
                                                           British forces
through. Since the beaches were only two miles to the east, they were, in reality,
                                                        such
close to being within machine-gun range. and From reports the worried
                                             to him
to Air Marshal Pulford was occurring in Singapore it seemed time to put into effect

the "denial scheme" that was the contingency plan for all installations of value
                                                                              too
to the enemy. Second thoughts later were that the evacuation went quickly--

~~and indeed~~ In the panic that gripped ground personnel as bullets landed

around them they abandoned fuel and bombs that should have been destroyed, and
                                                      employed
left the airstrip useable. (The Japanese had used only 150lb bombs only
                                                              remaining   torched,
in order not to damage the runways beyond repair.) But the buildings were
                                crammed with evacuees.
and the flyable planes Peter Gibbs recalled the
                                           his
bullets landing about the field, and being "packed tightly into the fuselage of

a Hudson for the flight to Kuantan some 160 miles south."
              shot-up
One Vildebeeste surviving from 36 Squadron needed only a tire to take off, and
                                                        divots of weedy grass
Flight Lt. G. S. Richardson improvised by stuffing
                                 then clearing
through the bullet hole, the "KB" airstrip. ~~Near Kuantan, the engine~~

~~stalled because its oil had leaked away, but Richardson managed to put the plane~~
                           and wobbling wheel.
~~down with a dead prop. His luck was holding, but it would run out later, at~~

~~Endau, to the south.~~

Page from the typescript for "Hour 45," a chapter in Long Day's Journey into War: December 7, 1941 *(by permission of
Stanley Weintraub)*

297

writing topic (Saint Joan, for example, obsessed him for years before he wrote the play), and the varied influences on some of his works. Chiefly gathered from earlier publications, the selections focus on the spectrum of Shaw's life and works, from his pugilistic training and his thankfully brief venture as an actor, to his career as an art critic and its influence upon his other creative enterprises, to his relationships with Frank Harris, Sean O'Casey, and Mary Kingsley, to possible sources for Shaw's characters. The volume serves as a useful introduction to the multifaceted Shaw and some of his myriad concerns, each portrait advancing a particular aspect of Shaw's universe and the whole acting together to provide a composite, impressionist picture of Shaw based on a sampler of Weintraub's investigations into and discoveries about Shaw spanning more than a quarter of a century.

Weintraub next set himself the exhaustive task of composing a collective biography evoking the five days leading up to the Armistice of 11 November 1918. The result is his most ambitious biography to date, the story of hundreds involved in the Armistice: *A Stillness Heard Round the World: The End of the Great War, November 1918*. The main elements of the work are introduced by the story of the still-little-known False Armistice, which preceded the genuine one by several days, and are concluded by an epilogue, "A Beer Hall in Munich," which describes one reformation of postwar German pride in a thwarted attempt to seize power that resulted in the capture, on 11 November 1923, of Adolf Hitler. Within the main body of the book, Weintraub dramatizes what people were doing, writing, recording, learning, and feeling in the days leading up to 11 November 1918, on the day itself, and in its aftermath.

So, for example, one finds Erich Maria Remarque, a thrice-wounded twenty-year-old conscript at the front, keeping a diary of the horrors he lived, which would be fictionalized as *All Quiet on the Western Front* (1929). The feelings of Siegfried Sassoon and of Alexander Woollcott are recorded by Weintraub as are the exploits of Rudolf Hess, the young Erwin Rommel, and Hjalmar Schacht, who was to be the financial brain of the Hitler regime. The young officer Carl Zuckmayer and army doctor Alfred Döblin would survive the Western Front and go on to write plays and novels, respectively; the latter's *Bürger und Soldaten* (1939) would be published during his exile from Germany. Also featured are Lt. Col. Alfred Dreyfus, Ford Madox Ford, C. P. Snow, V. S. Pritchett, Chaim Weizmann, Evelyn Waugh, Kenneth Clark, and some future heroes of World War II and the Korean War: Jimmy Doolittle, Dwight Eisenhower, and Matthew Ridgeway. And Weintraub notes that, at the front, George S. Patton wrote a poem on the occasion of the Armistice. What the Armistice meant to those in the front lines, in the trenches, and in Paris, Berlin, London, New York, California, and Australia, among other places, is told in many and varied voices drawn from oral histories, newspaper accounts, diaries, letters, plays, novels, poems, and memoirs.

In 1986 Weintraub published his edition of *Bernard Shaw: The Diaries, 1885-1897* in two volumes, originally in Shaw's idiosyncratic Pitman shorthand. While editing the diaries he was also finishing *Victoria: An Intimate Biography* (1987), which was published in England with a more reserved title, *Victoria: Biography of a Queen*. Its American title is more apt since Weintraub interests himself in Victoria's public life as a monarch only to the extent that it concerns her private life. Her relationship with Albert, their intimacy, and her "un-Victorian" enjoyment of sex are three focuses of Weintraub. Her youthful sentiments, her schooling in the role of monarch, her family connections with European rulers, her family history, her years of seclusion after Albert's death, and her relationships with her children and her ministers are also revealed—through the prism of her own personality as seen in her writings and theirs. National tragedies, for example, the losses in the Crimean War and the casualties of the Boer War, are viewed in relation to their personal impact upon her. Reversing the approach taken by Strachey in his biography *Queen Victoria* (1921)—a prime example of anti-Victorian revision of history—Weintraub presents Victoria with a sympathy that does not overlook her foibles and faults but probes the motivation behind, for example, Albert's role in the Crystal Palace Exhibition and, for another, her organizing of her household and management of her children, including her refusal in her old age to cede the throne to Edward, Prince of Wales. Weintraub, long a student of Victorian people and their ideas, achieved a critical and popular success with *Victoria*, a success he won by emphasizing her humanity and revealing the person behind the stereotypes that have grown into myths in the decades since her death.

Much of what contemporary readers know of Shaw and of Whistler, Beardsley, the Rossettis, Lawrence, and Victoria they know thanks to Weintraub's unflagging interest in and able exposition of their lives and works. His steady, scholarly approach to Shaw has made Weintraub a world-renowned expert on the man and his works. Weintraub has said that material in one book often leads him to another, the Beardsley leading to Whistler; Whistler led him back to the Rossettis and forward to the London Yankees. His profound scholarship, his eye for detail, his sense of telling a good (and verifiable) story, and his sense of timing and of audience have produced clear and popular works that have gone beyond the academic libraries and have gained for him a popular readership. Weintraub remains involved with Shaw: *Bernard Shaw on the London Art Scene, 1886-1950*, which contains all 181 pieces of Shaw's writing on art criticism, was published in 1989. Weintraub's *Bernard Shaw: A Guide to Research* is scheduled for publication in 1992.

Weintraub's most recent volume, *Long Day's Journey into War: December 7, 1941* (1991), is a massive collective biography that has been called a microhistory. In it he traces events around the world and through the time zones, providing an hour-by-hour chronicle of Pearl Harbor Sunday. Having traveled the world twice in search of first-hand material, he has produced what he considers may be his most important book to date.

After exactly twenty years at the helm, Weintraub left his post as director of Penn State's Institute for the Arts and Humanistic Studies in 1990, but he remains an active scholar within the institute. He is now at work on a biography of the Victorian politician and writer Benjamin Disraeli.

Interviews:

John F. Baker, "Stanley Weintraub," *Publishers Weekly*, 205 (4 February 1974): 8-9;

Jean W. Ross, "The Practice of Biography: An Interview with Stanley Weintraub," in *Dictionary of Literary Biography Yearbook: 1982*, edited by Richard Ziegfeld (Detroit: Gale / Columbia, S.C.: Bruccoli Clark, 1983), pp. 34-46.

Papers:

Weintraub's manuscripts and other material are in the Stanley Weintraub Room at West Chester University Library.

Stephen E. Whicher

(16 June 1915 - 14 November 1961)

Lynne P. Shackelford
Furman University

BOOK: *Freedom and Fate: An Inner Life of Ralph Waldo Emerson* (Philadelphia: University of Pennsylvania Press, 1953; London: Oxford University Press, 1953).

OTHER: *Bibliographical Materials for the Study of the Reception of American Literature in Sweden, 1920-1952*, compiled by Whicher (N.p., 1956);
Selections from Ralph Waldo Emerson: An Organic Anthology, edited, with an introduction, by Whicher (Boston: Houghton Mifflin, 1957);
The Early Lectures of Ralph Waldo Emerson, 3 volumes, edited by Whicher, Robert E. Spiller, and Wallace Williams (Cambridge, Mass.: Harvard University Press, 1959-1972);
Twelve American Poets, edited by Whicher and Lars Ahnebrink (Stockholm: Almqvist & Wiksell, 1959; New York: Oxford University Press, 1961);
"The Art of Poetry," in *A Time of Harvest, American Literature, 1910-1960*, edited by Spiller (New York: Hill & Wang, 1962), pp. 111-121;
Emerson: A Collection of Critical Essays, edited by Whicher and Milton R. Konvitz (Englewood Cliffs, N.J.: Prentice-Hall, 1962).

SELECTED PERIODICAL PUBLICATIONS—
UNCOLLECTED: "Emerson's Tragic Sense," *American Scholar*, 22 (Summer 1953): 285-292;
"Teaching Emerson," *Emerson Society Quarterly*, 10 (1958): 12-14;
"A Query on the Sources of Emerson's Early Lectures," *Emerson Society Quarterly*, 13 (1958): 31-32;
"Emerson's 'The American Scholar,'" *Explicator*, 20 (April 1962): Item 68.

Stephen Emerson Whicher dedicated his career to exploring the development of Ralph Waldo Emerson's thought, and his 1953 biogra-

phy of Emerson remains an important resource. Whicher was born on 16 June 1915, in New York City. His father, George F. Whicher, was a professor at Amherst College and an eminent Emily Dickinson scholar; his mother, Harriet Fox Whicher, was a professor at Mount Holyoke College. Whicher attended Phillips Exeter Academy and then Amherst College. As a college student he participated in swimming and soccer and won a dozen prizes for scholarship, work in English and the classics, and public speaking. He was elected to Phi Beta Kappa and graduated summa cum laude from Amherst in 1936. The next year he received his M.A. in philosophy from Columbia University. Whicher married in 1940. He and his wife, Elizabeth, were to have four children: Susan, Nancy, Stephen, and John. Pursuing further graduate studies in English at Harvard, Whicher also served as a teaching assistant. In 1942 Harvard awarded him the Helen Choate Bell Prize and the Bowdoin Prize, both for outstanding essays on Emerson. He completed his Ph.D. that same year, with a specialty in American literature.

Later in 1942 Whicher held an instructorship at the University of Rochester. The following year he entered the U.S. Navy, serving as ensign, then lieutenant, and eventually a nightfighter director in the Pacific. He was awarded combat stars at Iwo Jima and Tokyo in 1945. Whicher taught at Harvard in 1946, then held a Rockefeller Post-War Fellowship. In 1947 he joined the faculty at Swarthmore College, where he taught for ten years. From 1952 to 1953 Whicher held a Ford Teaching Fellowship and an appointment as a Fulbright lecturer at the University of Oslo.

Whicher's reputation as a biographer rests upon a single book, *Freedom and Fate: An Inner Life of Ralph Waldo Emerson*. Believing Ralph L. Rusk's *Life of Ralph Waldo Emerson* (1949) to be a definitive study of Emerson's life among his contemporaries, Whicher envisioned *Freedom and Fate* as a complementary volume, a presentation of the

Stephen E. Whicher, Everett L. Hunt, and Frederic S. Klees, faculty members at Swarthmore College, 1952 (courtesy of the Friends Historical Library of Swarthmore College)

"drama of ideas" in Emerson's essays, poems, and journals. It is Emerson's inner life—not the staid Concord existence of the staunch rejector of political activism—that Whicher finds heroic and revolutionary: "His work in the world was to free imprisoned thoughts and bring them to expression.... His life, fuller and more intense than that given to most of us to achieve, was an inner one, the poet's life of the imagination, an adventure of the mind." Whicher covers key events of what he terms Emerson's "outer life" in a simple chronological list following his preface. Then, focusing primarily on the period from 1833 to 1847, Whicher devotes his book to charting Emerson's mental journey from his liberating discovery of God within the soul to an accommodation of skepticism into his philosophy.

Perhaps the most striking feature of Whicher's book, reflected in the title, is its clarity of design. Grouped under the heading "Freedom," the first five chapters examine Emerson's emancipation from history, religious revelation, and social convention after he recognized the divinity within the soul. The latter five chapters, under

the title "Fate," explore how Emerson moved from optimistic egoism to an acceptance of the ultimately mystical, unknowable quality of nature.

To establish the life-altering significance of Emerson's discovery of God within the soul, Whicher begins by describing his subject's poor physical and mental health during the winter of 1826-1827. Tuberculosis, a family affliction, had weakened Emerson, causing him to seek refuge from the harsh New England weather in the South (Charleston and St. Augustine). There he sternly assessed his aspiration to be a great writer and preacher, and found himself lacking discipline, warmth, and unswerving faith. Debilitating self-doubt, catalyzed and transformed by an appreciation of the logic of such skeptical thinkers as David Hume, an enthusiastic reading of German philosophers and Samuel Taylor Coleridge, and a heartfelt need to recapture the Calvinist sense of the vital presence of God, led Emerson to develop the doctrine of self-reliance and to resign from the ministry in 1832.

The foundation of Emerson's philosophy, Whicher believes, is his vision of a "rebirth into

FREEDOM and FATE

An Inner Life of
RALPH WALDO EMERSON

STEPHEN E. WHICHER

Philadelphia
UNIVERSITY OF PENNSYLVANIA PRESS
1953

Title page for Whicher's only book-length biography, which he thought of as a companion volume to Ralph L. Rusk's
Life of Ralph Waldo Emerson *(1949)*

greatness" achieved through recognizing that God and the self are ideally the same. Such a vision empowered Emerson, freeing him from depending on outward circumstances to attain happiness. Yet, as Whicher wisely recognizes in examining passages from *Nature* (1836), "The American Scholar" (1837), and "The Divinity School Address" (1838), there is an underlying tension in Emerson's thought as he moves between the theoretical polarities of "the One and the Many, the Universal and the Individual, faith and the rest of experience, Reason and Understanding" and the temperamental polarities of "pride and humility, egoism and pantheism, activity and passivity, Power and Law." Indeed, throughout the book, by exposing the contradictions within Emerson's thought, Whicher avoids oversimplification.

Whicher defines Emerson's major intellec-

tual dilemma as the attempt to reconcile his dream of the infinite potential of the self with a realistic perception of the limitations imposed by daily life. Emerson recognized that the ecstasy he felt when his soul and God were united was transitory. He also realized, after the harsh public reaction to "The Divinity School Address," that sweeping societal change was unlikely and that any reform he might effect would be personal and moral. As the decade of the 1830s unfolded, Emerson began to see nature as secretive, mysterious, and evolving, and he lost faith in books and friends as sources of truth. Whicher suggests that by 1840 Emerson's thought was clearly unsettled, as he realized that his principles of innovation and insight subverted the permanence of his own beliefs. Emerson's response to this growing skepticism was to view life as an ongoing experiment, an endless series of challenges in an ever-changing present.

To summarize Emerson's final philosophical position, Whicher quotes Emerson's words, written in 1841: "My creed is very simple, that Goodness is the only Reality, that to Goodness alone can we trust, to that we may trust all and always; beautiful and blessed and blessing is it, even though it should seem to slay me." Strongly influenced by Hegelian philosophy, Whicher contends that Emerson reconciled the extremes of self-reliance and fatalism through a humanistic concept of culture, as a means of nurturing and releasing divine energy as the individual strives toward moral betterment. From the thesis of individual freedom and the antithesis of a life subject to time and circumstance, Emerson, according to Whicher, formulated the synthesis of a "necessitated freedom," which he expressed in *The Conduct of Life* (1860).

There is a symmetry to Whicher's book, which begins with a picture of Emerson sick and depressed as a young man and ends with the death of his inner life, as old age diminished his physical and creative powers. Between those two pictures, Whicher presents the metaphysical voyage of a mind ever questing after truths concerning the self, nature, and God. Although highly cognizant of the contrarieties in Emerson's thought and the defeat of his initial vision of divine glory, Whicher nevertheless reveres his subject and defends Emerson's work against charges that it is self-righteous, sentimental, and outdated. Opposing previous biographers and critics who have represented Emerson's inner life as "an eventless and static thing," Whicher finds it charged with dynamism. He reminds his readers that "Emerson believed in the dignity of human life more unreservedly, almost, than any one who has ever written. Man possesses, he felt, an unlimited capacity for spiritual growth and is surrounded by influences that perpetually call on him for the best he has of insight and greatness and virtue and love." That vision, Whicher affirms, is Emerson's invaluable and timeless gift to the world.

Freedom and Fate reflects Stephen Whicher's expanded interpretation of the genre of biography. For him, the story of a life was not merely a compilation of names, dates, and places. He recognized that for Emerson—and, indeed, for many others—thought took precedence over public action. Upholding the principle of organicism that Emerson espoused, Whicher's book offers a valuable account of the evolution of one of the most daring minds in American literature.

Whicher's *Freedom and Fate* earned laudatory reviews. George Genzmer wrote in the *New York Herald Tribune Book Review* (27 December 1953) that the book was "an indispensable companion to every one who explores for himself Emerson's tangled, contradictory, half-obscure half-luminous thought." In an article entitled "Moral Optimism" in the *Nation* (14 November 1953), Joseph W. Krutch praised Whicher for his "detailed and rigorous analysis" of the stages of Emerson's intellectual development, and he observed, "*Freedom and Fate* is probably as complete an exposition and as searching a criticism as we are likely to have." Critics acknowledged two major achievements of Whicher's volume: that it complemented Rusk's definitive factual biography and that it reminded a pessimistic age of the boundless potential of the human spirit.

From 1955 to 1956 Whicher held an appointment as a Fulbright lecturer at Uppsala University in Sweden. Whicher's language skills were notable: he could read Latin, Greek, French, German, Norwegian, Danish, and Swedish. In 1957 Whicher accepted a teaching position at Cornell University, which he held until his death by suicide in 1961. During the last years of his career Whicher edited four works: *Selections from Ralph Waldo Emerson: An Organic Anthology* (1957), *The Early Lectures of Ralph Waldo Emerson* (1959-1972), *Twelve American Poets* (1959), and *Emerson: A Collection of Critical Essays* (1962). As a teacher, biographer, and editor, Stephen Whicher excelled in sharing his intense interest in Emerson with others.

James Leslie Woodress, Jr.

(7 July 1916 -   )

Susan J. Rosowski
University of Nebraska

BOOKS: *Howells and Italy* (Durham: Duke University Press, 1952);

Booth Tarkington: Gentleman from Indiana (Philadelphia: Lippincott, 1955);

A Yankee's Odyssey: The Life of Joel Barlow (Philadelphia: Lippincott, 1958);

Willa Cather: Her Life and Art (New York: Pegasus, 1970);

American Fiction, 1900-1950 (Detroit: Gale Research, 1974);

Willa Cather: A Literary Life (Lincoln: University of Nebraska Press, 1987).

OTHER: "The Dean's Comeback: Four Decades of Howells Scholarship," in *The War of the Critics Over William Dean Howells*, edited by Edwin Cady and David Frazier (New York: Row, Peterson, 1962);

Voices from America's Past, 4 volumes, edited by Woodress and Richard Brandon Morris (New York: Dutton, 1963-1976);

American Literary Scholarship: An Annual, edited by Woodress (Durham: Duke University Press, 1963-1967, 1973-1975, 1977, 1979, 1981);

"The Writing of Biography," in *The Quest for Truth*, volume 2, edited by Martha Boaz (Metuchen, N.J.: Scarecrow Press, 1967), pp. 82-96;

"*Uncle Tom's Cabin* in Italy," in *Essays on American Literature in Honor of Jay B. Hubbell*, edited by Clarence Gohdes (Durham: Duke University Press, 1967), pp. 126-140;

"Popular Taste in 1899: Booth Tarkington's First Novel," in *Essays in American and English Literature Presented to Bruce Robert McElderry, Jr.* (Athens: Ohio University Press, 1967), pp. 108-121;

"John Steinbeck: Hostage to Fortune," in *A Casebook on "The Grapes of Wrath,"* edited by Agnes Donohue (New York: Crowell, 1969);

"Emily Dickinson," in *Fifteen American Authors Before 1900*, edited by R. A. Rees and E. N. Harbert (Madison: University of Wisconsin Press, 1971; revised, 1984), pp. 139-168;

Essays Mostly on Periodical Publishing in America: A Collection in Honor of Clarence Gohdes, edited by Woodress (Durham: Duke University Press, 1973);

"Willa Cather: An American Experience and European Tradition," in *The Art of Willa Cather*, edited by Bernice Slote and Virginia Faulkner (Lincoln: University of Nebraska Press, 1974), pp. 43-62;

"Willa Cather," in *American Novelists, 1910-1945*, 3 parts, edited by James J. Martine, *Dictionary of Literary Biography*, volume 9, part 1 (Detroit: Gale Research, 1981), pp. 140-154;

"William Dean Howells," in *American Realists and Naturalists*, edited by Donald Pizer and Earl N. Harbert, *Dictionary of Literary Biography*, volume 12 (Detroit: Gale Research, 1982), pp. 270-297;

Susannah Mayberry, *My Amiable Uncle: Recollections about Booth Tarkington*, introduction by Woodress (West Lafayette, Ind.: Purdue University Press, 1983), pp. 1-15;

Critical Essays on Walt Whitman, edited, with an introduction, by Woodress (Boston: G. K. Hall, 1983);

The Troll Garden by Willa Cather: A Definitive Edition, edited, with introduction, notes, and textual apparatus, by Woodress (Lincoln & London: University of Nebraska Press, 1983);

"Willa Cather and Her Friends," in *Critical Essays on Willa Cather*, edited by John J. Murphy (Boston: G. K. Hall, 1984), pp. 81-95;

"Willa Cather," in *Sixteen Modern American Authors*, edited by Jackson R. Bryer (Durham: Duke University Press, 1989), pp. 42-72;

"The Composition of *The Professor's House*," in *Writing the American Classics*, edited by James Barbour and Tom Quirk (Chapel Hill: University of North Carolina Press, 1990), pp. 106-124.

SELECTED PERIODICAL PUBLICATIONS—
UNCOLLECTED: "Booth Tarkington's Political

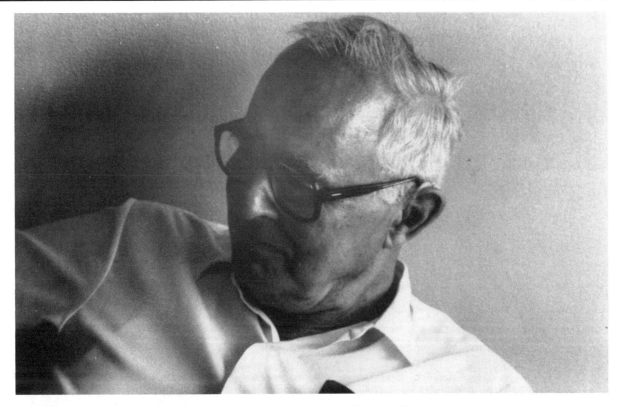

James Leslie Woodress, Jr., 1987 (photograph by Michael-Jean Impressions)

Career," *American Literature*, 26 (May 1954): 209-222;

"Booth Tarkington's Attack on American Materialism," *Georgia Review*, 8 (Winter 1954): 440-446;

"The Tarkington Papers," *Princeton University Library Chronicle*, 16 (Winter 1955): 45-53;

"Willa Cather Seen Clear," *Papers in Language and Literature*, 7 (1971): 96-109;

"Willa Cather and History," *Arizona Quarterly*, 34 (Autumn 1978): 239-254;

"The Genesis of the Prologue of *Death Comes for the Archbishop*," *American Literature*, 50 (November 1978): 473-478.

James Leslie Woodress, Jr., has devoted his distinguished career to scholarship in American literature and has written a series of biographies of American writers culminating in the authoritative biography of Willa Cather (1987). In addition, Woodress was founder and editor of *American Literary Scholarship*, editor of the definitive (1983) edition of Willa Cather's *The Troll Garden*, and author of more than a hundred essays, chapters, and monographs. In 1985 the American Literature Section of the Modern Language Associa-

tion awarded Woodress its Hubbell Medal, given annually to a person "whose total body of work has been a major influence on the study and teaching of American literature."

Woodress was born in Webster Groves, Missouri, on 7 July 1916 to James Leslie Woodress, an electrical engineer, and Jessie Smith Woodress. He obtained his A.B. from Amherst College in 1938, after which he became a radio news editor at station KWK in St. Louis (1939-1940). Woodress married Roberta Wilson on 2 September 1940, and the couple moved to New York City, where Woodress was employed as rewrite man and editor for UPI from 1940 to 1943. Thus Woodress served his literary apprenticeship as a journalist, learning lessons essential to the biographer—including how to select the significant detail and, as Lytton Strachey said, strive toward "brevity which excludes everything that is redundant and nothing that is significant" (quoted by Woodress in "The Writing of Biography," 1967). During his time at UPI Woodress studied at New York University, earning his A.M. in English in 1943. By writing his thesis on the contemporary reaction to Edmund Burke's *Reflections on the Revolution in France* (1790), Woodress extended his journalistic interests into scholarship,

Woodress (left) in Venice, 1946, during his service in the United States Army

reading dozens of pamphlets in that war of words, including Thomas Paine's *The Rights of Man* (1791) as well as pamphlets by Joel Barlow and Mary Wollstonecraft.

During World War II Woodress served in the U.S. Army and rose to lieutenant in field artillery. He was stationed in Italy during 1945 and 1946.

Following the war Woodress continued his scholarly career, entering the Ph.D. program in English at Duke University, where he took courses from Jay B. Hubbell and Lewis Leary and wrote his dissertation under the direction of Clarence Gohdes. While a graduate student, Woodress began teaching as an instructor of English at Grinnell College in Iowa (1949-1950). Upon being awarded his Ph.D. in 1950, he joined the faculty at Butler University in Indianapolis, serving as assistant professor of English from 1950 to 1953, then associate professor from 1953 to 1958, when the Woodresses moved to California; at San Fernando Valley State College Woodress was associate professor of English (1958-1961), professor (1961-1966), chairman of the de-

partment (1959-1963), and dean of letters and sciences (1963-1965). From 1966 until he became a professor emeritus in 1987, Woodress served as a professor at the University of California, Davis, where he was also chair of the department from 1970 to 1974.

The Woodresses also traveled and studied abroad. Appointments to a Guggenheim Fellowship (1958), Fulbright lecturerships in France (1962-1963) and Italy (1965-1966), and visiting professorships at the Sorbonne (1974-1975 and 1983) resulted in Woodress's becoming fluent in Italian and competent in French, having firsthand experience of various cultures and locales, and developing warm friendships that were nurtured by further visits to Europe. In addition the Woodresses have traveled in North Africa, the Middle East, and the Pacific Rim countries.

Experience in journalism, training in history and literature, and personal knowledge of European cultures come together in Woodress's scholarship on American writers. He characteristically chooses his subjects from curiosity about personality in a broad sense. As he already had a strong

Woodress in Indianapolis, 1954

interest in things Italian and a proficiency in Italian, during a 1947 course with Gohdes he became interested in William Dean Howells's Italian years and influences, soon realizing that this was a pristine subject. Perhaps because Woodress, too, was an American who broadened his sympathies by living in Italy, he recognized the importance of the experience to Howells: to the young Howells, "Italy was the laboratory in which he observed life and first began writing of the contemporary scene about him."

In *Howells and Italy* (1952), focusing on the four years Howells was in that country (1861-1865), Woodress demonstrates his curiosity about the interaction of personality, place, and culture. The four-part division of the book presents the biographical details in "Venice, 1861-65"; the writing that came from that experience in "Literary Apprentice"; literary sources of that writing in "Italian Literature"; and later use of the experience in "Italian Life." As the first book on Howells in over a quarter century and the only one to focus on his Italian influences, the Woodress biog-

raphy broke ground in Howells scholarship. Especially noteworthy is Woodress's account of identifying the prototype of Howells's first significant fictional character, Don lppolito in *A Foregone Conclusion* (1875), an account that provides the excitement of a detective story and serves as a model of scholarly method.

Howells and Italy provided, too, an occasion for Woodress's development as a biographer. By tracing the growth of Howells's experiences from accounts in letters, articles, and essays into two of his travel books, *Venetian Life* (1866) and *Italian Journeys* (1867), then interpreting in those books emerging fictional techniques, Woodress refined the methods of the literary biographer who is above all interested in how a writer transforms impressions into art. In working with the voluminous letters written by Howells over nearly sixty-five years, Woodress confronted the interplay of fiction with reality, and he established the rigorous standards of corroboration characteristic of his scholarship. Woodress also exhibited his skills as a bibliographer and textual expert: "Mr. Wood-

Personality traits

Panofsky's tribute for Princeton Lib's exhibition reports
that BT had habit of rising at entrance of any guest, offering guest exactly kind of chair or cigarettes he knew
the guest liked. (This tribute in Ind News 13 Aug 46--ISL-C)

Primarily, says P, BT is interested in human beings, second-
arily their opinions. Respects a conviction however much
it differs from his own. P sees significance in BT's interest and desire to own portraits.

Blank Book (PP) clip Indpls Press 13 Dec 1899:
    In article about BT's 1st two books, anon. friend of
    BT's quoted: "I never knew another man of such infin-
    ite tact. Nor do I know of another a man who is so free
    from enemies. I never knew of Tarkington every hurt-
    ing the feelings of a man, woman or child. His manners
    are exquisite, without being namby-pamby. He can make
    a young girl feel that she is in the seventh heaven,
    by his thoughtful and delicate attentions to her, while
    he completely wins the hearts of the matrons . .."
    Goes on: He never obtrudes himself, but if conver-
    sation lags, he can pull it together. "Men admire
    him becuase he is modest, manly and sympathetic at
    the right time."

BT's extrme kindness and amiability: PP contains two ltrs
from Nicola V. Curinga (see biblio. p. 202), the first asking
if BT would read his MS and make a favorable comment for
jacket blurb. "I work at night as a waiter in a cabaret
and try to write during the day. I am having such a hard
time to get along." earlier: "A few words from you would
help me a great deal financially and morally." So BT read
the MS, not only wrote blurb but sent critique of work.
Total stranger, of course.

Generosity: BT to Daniels 21 Feb 36 Indpls: Reports that
Sue handles most of ltrs, he seeing only Roberts, Daniels,
Streets, and few others. She also handles business. Many
letters in this period came from people asking for money.
Says he seems to have reputation for riches and power. Cites
case of woman, old friend of family, he'd probably not seen
three times since 1890, who'd just written. She wanted to
go to Chile (?) which would use up little money she had, and
would BT take care of her after that. "Of course we temporize--
tell her we'll see her through . . . Sue has a number of
'cases' more or less like it." Then he adds that the poor
souls feel that what BT spends on one picture would take
care of them. He feels a bit guilty to be so prosperous,
but rationalized that he is supporting Silberman's firm
and if he let his boat go, Henry Thirkell and his son would
be on relief.

Recto and verso of a note card Woodress used while writing his biography of Booth Tarkington (by permission of James Leslie Woodress, Jr.; courtesy of the Special Collections Department, William R. Perkins Library, Duke University)

ress's full knowledge of manuscript and printed sources is evident," wrote Howells bibliographer George Arms of *Howells and Italy*; "by enumerating later printings, by citing new reviews, and by closely collating chapters, Mr. Woodress has both added to previous bibliographical work on Howells and corrected it" (*American Literature*, March 1953).

Most important, by interpreting the influence of the Venetian dramatist Carlo Goldoni on Howells's realism, Woodress refined his principles of biography. The Howells-Goldoni literary relationship forms the theoretical heart of *Howells and Italy*, for as Woodress demonstrates, "Between 1861 and 1865 the Goldonian drama helped mold the opinions which later solidified into the Howells doctrine of literary Realism. Through Goldoni's eyes Howells first saw the possibilities of prose fiction based on the commonplace events of contemporary life." As Howells did in fiction, so Woodress was to do in biography, upholding a theory that "is basically simple: . . . 'nothing more and nothing less than the truthful treatment of material.' " In interpreting Howells, Woodress could be describing his own principles of biography: to present men and women as they are rather than "working them by springs and wires"; to gather material from everyday, commonplace events; to distrust the artificial; to respect the importance of environment; and to appreciate a faithful record of the life in a place. Woodress interprets also Howells's criteria for art: "the wonder of the Venetian's [Goldoni's] art lay in the skillful manner in which he recorded the life of the eighteenth century without giving offense to the nineteenth. Those who know that period historically . . . will perceive Goldoni's artfulness." The statement could serve as one of Woodress's criteria for the art of biography.

The historical sense of *Howells and Italy* is evident in specifics as well as in the broad interpretation of American realism against a background of European literature. Woodress sees *Venetian Life*, for example, as "essentially a socioeconomic study of Venice with a prominent thread of autobiography running through it. Unobtrusively added are engaging bits of history, lively anecdotes, amusing incidents, and characterizations which foreshadow the novelist to come."

While *Howells and Italy* provided the historical and theoretical materials for working out his principles of biography, Woodress's turning to Booth Tarkington combined a curiosity about a locale with a personal sympathy for the subject's

writing. Tarkington had been a favorite writer of Woodress's in high school, so when Woodress went to teach at Butler in Indianapolis in 1950, he "decided to reread him to see how his Indianapolis of the 1910's and '20's compared with my Indianapolis." What Woodress found was a "writer of tremendous talent, too popular for his own good, but his ability to evoke urban, middleclass, Midwestern society was still impressive," and Woodress decided to write Tarkington's biography. Circumstances favored the project, as Woodress recalls in "The Writing of Biography": he arranged to meet Tarkington's widow, "who lived only a few blocks away," and who subsequently assisted him. Woodress faced the challenge of immediacy, because Tarkington had died in 1946, and his papers were deposited in Princeton only in 1951. Woodress writes of his experience as "the first person to use a mountainous collection of personal papers, especially a voluminous literary correspondence . . . [and of spending] a winter at Princeton where Tarkington's papers had been deposited but not yet catalogued." There was strenuous physical labor in working with materials so extensive that "Princeton Library had needed a moving van," but "the thrill of discovery was present every day."

The result was *Booth Tarkington: Gentleman from Indiana* (1955), the first biography of Tarkington and still the standard source on his life. Woodress's first full-scale biography, it encompasses the writer's life and takes into account all relevant historical and political details. Woodress found that Tarkington was a popular writer in a multiple sense: one who was genial and widely liked by friends and acquaintances and favored by the general public, and whose works reflected the taste and intelligence of the populace. Woodress's approach was to focus on Tarkington's personality—friendly, optimistic, and generous.

While the appeal of *Booth Tarkington* lies in the presentation of its subject's personality, its drama lies in a counterpoint between that individual personality and a national one. Woodress's method was to establish a sense of an individual in harmony with his time, then to bring out the tension between them. Woodress opens his first chapter, for example, with a long view of the United States "in the ninety-third summer of American independence," then narrows his point of view to the Atlantic seaboard, then to Indiana, to a single street in Indianapolis, to the Tarkington family, and finally to young Tarkington himself. The opening description establishes the har-

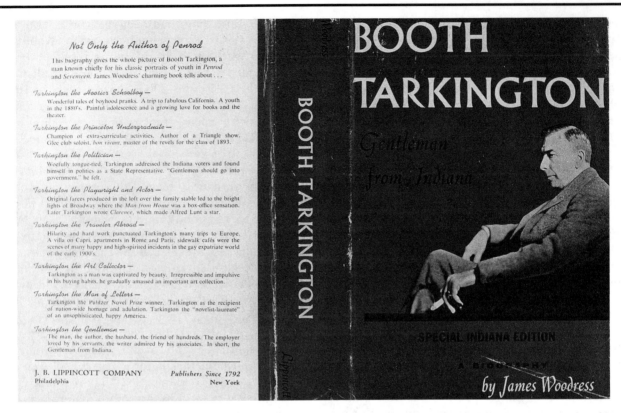

Dust jacket for the biography Woodress began after he moved to Indianapolis in 1950 and reread Tarkington "to see how his Indianapolis of the 1910's and '20's compared with my Indianapolis"

monious optimism of a nation rebuilding after the Civil War, its sense of security reflected in the leisurely life of Indianapolis in 1869 and in the slow pace of Tarkington's apprentice period. His indulgent parents supported him for two years at Phillips Exeter Academy, one at Purdue, two at Princeton, and five back home, jobless but writing. Tarkington was thirty years old by the time he went to New York and saw his first novel published, *The Gentleman from Indiana* (1899), the story of John Harkless, with which Tarkington experienced the beginning of his popularity. Woodress continues the broad historical perspective he established at the outset: opening optimism over the Civil War and the Suez Canal gives way by the end to Tarkington's warnings against the dangers of the atomic bomb and his calls for a global community. Through it all Woodress maintains an ongoing sense of his subject's personal generosity and political commitment. A conservative dismayed by Franklin Delano Roosevelt's New Deal and stung by the New York liberal critics, Tarkington still responded generously when the nation went to war, emerging "from behind the Republican barricades" to write propaganda for the war effort.

In revealing this overall pattern, Woodress demonstrates the juggling that critic James T. Flexner describes as essential to the biographer's art: "Fact and imagination, sober scholarship and dramatic writing, character study and sound history, a sympathetic understanding of his hero and yet a judicial lack of special pleading" (*Saturday Review*, October 1943). All the pieces are kept in motion by Woodress simultaneously—the biography, literature, history, politics, locale, art collecting, and travel. Tarkington's failures are noted, and his dark periods are described (the troubled first marriage and the heavy drinking; later, the threat of blindness), as well as the successes (Tarkington stopped drinking and remarried, this time happily). Through it all there was Tarkington's writing, the compelling activity of his life that resulted in such works as *Seventeen* (1916), *The Magnificent Ambersons* (1918), *Alice Adams* (1921), and the Penrod stories.

As always, Woodress's accounts of European travels and influences are especially good. Woodress recognizes Victor Cherbuliez's influence on Tarkington's experiment with characterization in *The Guests of Quesnay* (1908), for example, and discusses historical analogies central to *The Plutocrat*

310

Woodress with Booth Tarkington's widow, Susanah Robinson Tarkington, in the mid 1950s

(1927): "Tarkington saw America's impact on Western Europe in the twentieth century as similar to Rome's collision with Greek civilization at the beginning of the Christian era. Just as Rome had borrowed, diluted, and overwhelmed Greek culture, so was America repeating the process." Finally, Woodress reveals his sense of the creative, well-selected detail. Woodress's opening description of the smokeless Indianapolis sky of Tarkington's childhood prepares the reader to understand the mature Tarkington's use of smoke as a symbol of change. The result is that the reader becomes acquainted with not only the personality of Tarkington himself but the American character in the early decades of the twentieth century— with its social mobility, particularly seen in the urban middle class.

What is not included in *Booth Tarkington* is as telling about Woodress as what is. Because his work on Tarkington's life was unusually personal (Woodress was working on a boyhood favorite who had died only a few years previously, whose materials he had first access to, and whose widow he knew and respected), *Booth Tarkington* is a show-

case for Woodress's theory and practice of a biographer's relationship to his subject: "the biographer's chief reward is an intimate acquaintance with a significant and vital personality," a carefully worded description that suggests sympathy without approbation. As in his other books, Woodress presents his subject's separate personality as truthfully as he can: he never presumes to speak for his subject, never confuses him with himself, and never reduces him by psychological speculation. Woodress notes Tarkington's restrained treatment of sex, for example, and describes criticism of that restraint, then Tarkington's response to the criticism. He does not, however, attempt psychoanalytic speculation. Instead Woodress maintains the proportions of Tarkington's character and personality as he perceives the man. Therefore, while Woodress describes Tarkington's period of depression and heavy drinking, he does not give such periods undue attention in the life of a man who was, by all accounts, basically optimistic and, after 1911, a nondrinker.

The Tarkington biography illustrates yet another consideration of the biographer, particularly in working on a subject recently deceased. Living family and friends mean ethical considerations, for the biographer must consider not only "the truth of the material" but also its effect upon persons involved in his subject's life. "I could not write a definitive biography with the subject's widow looking over my shoulder," Woodress later recalled in "The Writing of Biography."

He acknowledged that freedom from such constraint "may have been the reason why I went to Joel Barlow for my [next] biography. He died in 1812 and left no direct descendants." In teaching an American literature survey course at Butler in Indianapolis, Woodress was intrigued by the anthology headnote introducing Barlow's *The Hasty Pudding* (1796); the note suggested a life of uncommon interest. "A life that led from Washington's army to Napoleon's retreat from Moscow seemed irresistible," Woodress believed; "it is a truism that minor writers (and historical figures) reflect their times more accurately than the movers and shakers." Unlike Woodress's work on Tarkington materials concentrated at Princeton, his work on Barlow involved visiting nineteen libraries and two private collections located from California to Paris. Again, however, the research provided its own moments of excitement, most dramatically when Woodress discovered in St. Helena, California, the portable writing desk that Barlow was carrying with him when he died in Poland in 1812; it contained "letters from Robert Fulton, Dolly Madison, family members, and even a batch of letters from a college girlfriend."

Writing *A Yankee's Odyssey: The Life of Joel Barlow* (1958) presented in its purest form the biographer's challenge: to convey the interest of his subject's life story. For as Woodress recognized, Barlow was a man who neither shaped history nor created memorable art; he simply—but significantly—lived an interesting life. As the Tarkington book illustrates Woodress's idea of the relationship between a biographer and his subject, the Barlow one illustrates his sense of a biographer's treatment of materials. Where the success of the biography depends completely upon the biographer's ability to bring his materials to life, Woodress writes with a freer narrative style than in his other books:

> The tale is an American success story—the saga of a poor New England plowboy who climbed to wealth and reputation in Europe and America. Horatio Alger's yarns are more prosaic than this

life that spans three continents and the germinal decades of American history. This is a career that leads from the Colony of Connecticut to the American Revolution. It is a tale that unfolds in London and Paris during the French Revolution and continues among the Barbary pirates in Algiers during Washington's presidency. It is a life that touches significantly the career of Robert Fulton and operates backstage in the national capital of Jefferson and Madison, and finally it stops in midflight during one of the great tragedies of history—the shattering winter retreat of the French army from Moscow.

Woodress presents Barlow as a representative American—a "bit player" who was forever on the verge of greatness, an entrepreneur whose "tragedy and triumph lie in his versatility, for he was a preacher of the Gospel, small-city lawyer, land salesman, shipping broker, political pamphleteer, confidant of presidents, diplomat, and finally (most significantly, he hoped) poet."

Woodress frames his subject's odyssey by beginning with Barlow's death. In his opening Woodress describes the political scene of December 1812, with Napoleon Bonaparte's retreat from Moscow—a stream of troops caught in a flood of history, including "the American minister to France, Joel Barlow." Woodress creates the drama of the historical moment, briefly reports Barlow's death in an objective, journalistic style, then switches immediately to his subject's birth: "this story, which ends in the hills of southern Poland, begins inauspiciously on a rocky Connecticut farm in 1754." Completing the frame in his conclusion, Woodress tells again of his subject's death, this time in a full and intensely personal story, by focusing on Barlow himself rather than the large political scene.

With his double focus on history and the individual, Woodress depicts Barlow's America as brash and resilient, an adolescent nation "entering an era of abundant possibilities." Particulars bring the period alive: details of farming in Connecticut in 1750, of American higher education at the time of the Revolution, and of international trade in the era of the Napoleonic Wars. Barlow's transfer to Yale, for example, provides Woodress the occasion to describe Yale as Barlow would have seen it: its treeless campus, regimented student life, and dry, narrow curriculum, by which students were discouraged from independent inquiry; even the rental library was beyond the means of many.

Dust jacket for the biography that Woodress decided to write because "A life that led from Washington's army to Napoleon's retreat from Moscow seemed irresistible"

Again Woodress's restraint in imposing theory on his subject serves his subject well, for
Woodress does not attempt to resolve piquant contradictions: Barlow's marriage to Ruth Baldwin,
kept secret for almost a year and a half, then maintained for thirty years, though they lived apart almost as much as together; his aspiration to be an
epic poet before he had the experience to write
and before his nation had a full story to tell; his
seeking his fortune by selling land for which he
had no title; and his seeking independence while
serving as a pawn for the Ohio Company. Barlow
fulfilled the American goal of success by making
a fortune in France as an agent for American shipping interests; he entered radical intellectual
French circles by writing his pamphlet *Advice
to the Privileged Orders* (1792), assisted Thomas
Paine in publishing the first part of *The Age of Reason* (1794), and eventually faced charges of betrayal in both France and America. Woodress is especially effective in telling of Barlow's diplomatic
mission to Algiers from 1795 to 1797 for the purpose of freeing American seamen held by the Barbary pirates. He opened discussion with the Dey
by offering a new, American-built, thirty-six-gun
frigate. Giving pirates a warship, Woodress com-

ments, was "like offering a gangster a new and
improved machine gun as an inducement to
stop hijacking one's merchandise." Then Barlow secured the release of American prison-
ers by using the Dey's money to pay their ransom.

After he returned from Algiers, Barlow assumed the role of elder, first in Paris, where he
purchased a mansion (in which Fulton lived
while working on his steamboat), then back in
Washington, where, after a seventeen-year exile,
he held state: entertaining in the palatial Kalo-
rama overlooking the Capitol, working on plans
for a national university, and farming. Barlow
chose to rewrite the epic poem he wrote in his
youth, *The Vision of Columbus* (1787), into *The
Columbiad* (1807) rather than to write the history
of the United States that Thomas Jefferson and
James Madison were urging him to do and for
which they were offering official documents and
personal recollections.

The interest of such episodes could easily
overshadow Barlow himself, yet Woodress maintains sympathy for his subject by two means:

James and Roberta Woodress, 1987 (photograph by Michael-Jean Impressions)

first, by the ongoing and extensive correspondence between Barlow and his wife—warm, witty, and personal letters that were the happy result of their long separations. And second, Woodress provides rich historical detail that evokes an understanding of personal circumstances. His description of the primitive state of book publishing in eighteenth-century America enables a reader to see the obstacles to Barlow's literary ambitions, if not his accomplishments.

Again, however, Woodress avoids special pleading in treating a subject for whom he obviously feels sympathy. An example is his treatment of Barlow's writing: he describes Barlow's writing of *The Vision of Columbus* and notes that it "was in a modest way the first American best seller after the Revolution, and Barlow probably was the first American writer anywhere to receive fair pay for a book." But Woodress makes no apology for it, acknowledging that it is "a dinosaur in the clay pits of literary history." *The Hasting Pudding* is Barlow's poem with promise, Woodress notes. Characteristically he provides all the materials necessary for the reader: a full description of the composition and, in an appendix, the poem itself.

The principle of "the truth of the material" found in Howells, the idea of personality worked through with Tarkington, the sense of history illuminated by Barlow, and the regular, close involvement with ongoing scholarship in *American Literary Scholarship*—all come together in Woodress's two biographies of Willa Cather. His work on Cather began with a commission for a brief critical biography and culminated two decades later with a second, full-length one. *Willa Cather: Her Life and Art* was published in 1970, then republished by the University of Nebraska Press in 1975 and again as a Landmark Edition in 1982. During this time Woodress continued work on Cather, teaching and writing about her, as well as presenting talks on her at national and international seminars. By the early 1980s Woodress was concentrating on the research that would result in *Willa Cather: A Literary Life*, the magnum opus of his career.

Each new subject presents particular problems for the biographer. With Cather, these problems concerned neither justification nor emphasis: from the beginning, Woodress saw Cather as of interest because she created art of the first order and was someone of whom he could say (in

Willa Cather: Her Life and Art), "I know of no other American writer of this century who is more likely to go on being read than Willa Cather." Yet he confronted difficulties with access to and use of materials. Partially as a result of her penchant for privacy and partially because she objected to distribution of writing she had not prepared for the press, Cather obscured the record of her published writings, requested that her letters and other personal papers be destroyed, and prohibited in her will the publication or reproduction of any papers that survived. When Woodress wrote his early Cather biography, materials were still being collected and use of them was severely restricted by Cather's will. Recognizing the limitations, Woodress prefaced *Willa Cather: Her Life and Art* by saying that eventually "someone will be able to write the definitive biography of Willa Cather. This book, I hope, will serve until that time comes." *Willa Cather: Her Life and Art* did, indeed, serve well: it supported Cather studies by providing a concise and reliable guide to basic information about Cather, the starting point for serious criticism and scholarship on her. And it suggested directions for that scholarship by revealing Cather as more complex than had been realized: her apprenticeship was longer and slower, she was more determined and ambitious, and her literary output was more extensive.

As Woodress had predicted, eventually Cather studies outgrew the book. The number of letters available increased; interviews, speeches, and public statements surfaced; and criticism on Cather expanded. With *Willa Cather: A Literary Life* Woodress accepted two fundamental challenges: the general one of providing the complete record that a writer of the first rank deserves, and the particular one of adapting the biographer's methods to Cather's exceptionally personal relationship between life and art.

Writing a more comprehensive biography meant weaving into the pattern of the life story all data relevant to his subject; doing so meant maintaining readability while expanding the creative voice of the biographer. Woodress accomplished both in a six-hundred-page book that reads easily, its narrative strong and lively, its scholarly apparatus clear and accessible. By providing a list of names, places, and events relevant to Cather, a chronology of her life, lists of her attitudes toward various subjects, and of her personal characteristics, as well as names of persons and works, the index is invaluable for readers.

By providing a review of scholarship and criticism, the notes serve as another starting point for future work.

Most important, by using all materials available, Woodress corroborates previous speculation, corrects errors, and provides information previously unavailable or unknown: for example, he includes the first reprinting in full of Cather's high-school graduation speech; corrects population figures for Lincoln, Nebraska, during Cather's university years; and identifies prototypes of minor as well as major characters. Woodress also provides materials illuminating her expanding social circles, from the often-cited friendships with Dorothy Canfield Fisher, Isabelle McClung, Edith Lewis, S. S. McClure, and Sarah Orne Jewett to her relationships with Ferris Greenslet, Margaret Deland, Fanny Butcher, Louise Imogen Guiney, Louis Brandeis, Pauline Goldmark, and Laura Hills. For persons interested in gender and lesbianism, subjects of intense critical discussion, Woodress provides detailed information about Cather's adopting male names and dress, her relationships with family and friends, her fictional use of male personae, and her depiction of gender. For the person interested in Cather and business, a subject strikingly slighted in criticism about a writer who spent half her working life in offices, Woodress provides full materials on her Lincoln, Pittsburgh, and New York journalistic periods. And for those interested in her experience of Europe, Woodress provides detailed accounts of her many visits there, including her 1908 trip to Italy—another subject overlooked in the previous criticism.

Yet as Henry James observed in *William Wetmore Story and His Friends* (1903), "to live over people's lives is nothing unless we live over their perceptions, live over the growth, the change, the varying intensity of the same—since it was *by* these things they themselves lived." Woodress's achievement in *Willa Cather: A Literary Life* is that he went beyond compiling massive amounts of information to re-create Cather's mind and life. He did so by responding to the second challenge Cather presented to her biographer when she so intricately wove together her life and art. As Woodress realized, that interweaving poses dangers to the biographer. The most basic criterion of establishing an accurate factual account means remaining on guard, keeping in mind that Cather freely, imaginatively created her own life story: she changed her birth date, claimed that she did not attend primary school in Nebraska,

Dust jacket for Woodress's full-scale biography of Cather (1987), which grew out of his 1970 critical biography of the novelist, published while use of Cather's papers was severely restricted

disclaimed early fiction, and otherwise altered events in ostensibly factual accounts. Yet even as Cather obscured the factual record, she revealed her life in her fiction. "If he can successfully negotiate the minefields, the biographer of Cather has a great deal of autobiographical fiction to help in his task," Woodress concluded. "She turned her own life and experiences into literature to a degree uncommon among writers. I have used many passages from her fiction to document her life, keeping in mind constantly the need for caution." This interweaving of life and art is the approach announced in his subtitle, "A Literary Life," and the one basic to his achievement.

Understanding Woodress's method means understanding Cather's—a taking of experience into herself, carrying it about, then releasing it in art. It is this creative process that lies behind the method of Woodress's biography. He organizes the first half of Cather's life story by her experi-

ence of places and people: childhood and family in Virginia; youth on the Divide; student friendships in Lincoln; meeting and becoming friends with Isabelle McClung in Pittsburgh; and then becoming close to S. S. McClure in New York. Woodress organizes the second half by the literature that came out of her experiences, with a chapter devoted to each of her books. The result is that the biography has its own organic unity: early descriptions of Virginia anticipate fictional locales of *Sapphira and the Slave Girl* (1940); the description of Cather's university years prepares readers for her character Jim Burden's sojourn there; and accounts of Cather's Lincoln friendships foreshadow the character Claude Wheeler's friendship with the Erlichs. Throughout, Woodress's approach reflects that of Cather, which was to reach universals through particulars and ideas through their living representatives. As she began reading the classics with William Ducker in

Red Cloud, for example, so Woodress introduces the subject of the classics and Cather through a look at Ducker.

The result is that *Willa Cather: A Literary Life* can be read on two levels: for the person new to Cather, there is the forward narrative of the biography, of experiencing, as it were, Cather's life. For the person familiar with Cather, however, there is a second level, of recognizing the genesis of art within a scene of the life story. On this second level Woodress most fully realizes the aim of biography described by Virginia Woolf in "The Art of Biography" (1939; collected in *The Death of the Moth*, 1942), which long served as a touchstone for Woodress: "By telling us the true facts, by sifting the little from the big, and shaping the whole so that we perceive the outline, the biographer does more to stimulate the imagination than any poet or novelist save the very greatest. For few poets and novelists are capable of that high degree of tension which gives us reality." In his biographies of Howells, Tarkington, and Bar-

low, Woodress worked out his own principles of sifting. In the process, he refined a method perfectly suited to Cather, an artist who was herself "capable of that high degree of tension which gives us reality."

James Woodress's achievements in biography are best illustrated by *Willa Cather: A Literary Life*. First, by providing all materials relevant to Cather's life, Woodress has provided a full, reliable resource for others interested in its subject. A second strength of the book is more ephemeral—for it involves coming close to the spirit of the writer herself: the art of biography appears artless; the biographer remains in the background, recognizing that his materials contain their own design and that his subject has her own life story.

Papers:

Woodress's papers, including correspondence, notes, and some manuscripts, are in the archives of Duke University.

Checklist of Further Reading

Aaron, Daniel, ed. *Studies in Biography*. Cambridge, Mass.: Harvard University Press, 1978.

Alter, Robert. *Motives for Fiction*. Cambridge, Mass.: Harvard University Press, 1984.

Altick, Richard D. *The Art of Literary Research*. New York: Norton, 1963.

Altick. *Lives and Letters: A History of Literary Biography in England and America*. New York: Knopf, 1965.

Altick. *The Scholar Adventurers*. New York: Macmillan, 1950.

Anderson, James William. "The Methodology of Psychological Biography." *Journal of Interdisciplinary History*, 11 (Winter 1981): 455-475.

Atlas, James. "Literary Biography." *American Scholar*, 45 (Summer 1976): 448-460.

Barzun, Jacques. "Biography and Criticism—a Misalliance Disputed." *Critical Inquiry*, 1 (March 1975): 479-496.

Berry, Thomas Elliott, ed. *The Biographer's Craft*. New York: Odyssey Press, 1967.

Birkets, Sven. *An Artificial Wilderness: Essays on 20th-Century Literature*. New York: Morrow, 1987.

Bloom, Harold, ed. *Dr. Samuel Johnson and James Boswell*. New York: Chelsea House, 1986.

Bowen, Catherine Drinker. *Adventures of a Biographer*. Boston: Little, Brown, 1959.

Bowen. *Biography: The Craft and the Calling*. Boston: Little, Brown, 1969.

Bradford, Gamaliel. *American Portraits, 1875-1900*. Boston & New York: Houghton Mifflin, 1922.

Bradford. *Bare Souls*. New York & London: Harper, 1924.

Bradford. *Biography and the Human Heart*. Boston & New York: Houghton Mifflin, 1932.

Brady, Frank, John Palmer, and Martin Price, eds. *Literary Theory and Structure*. New Haven: Yale University Press, 1973.

Britt, Albert. *The Great Biographers*. New York: McGraw-Hill, 1936; London: Whittlesey House, 1936.

Bromwich, David. *Choice of Inheritance*. Cambridge, Mass.: Harvard University Press, 1989.

Browning, J. D., ed. *Biography in the 18th Century*. New York & London: Garland, 1980.

Cafarelli, Annette. *Prose in the Age of Poets: Romanticism and Biographical Narrative from Johnson to De Quincey*. Philadelphia: University of Pennsylvania Press, 1990.

Clifford, James L. *From Puzzles to Portraits: Problems of a Literary Biographer*. Chapel Hill: University of North Carolina Press, 1970.

Clifford, ed. *Biography as an Art: Selected Criticism, 1560-1960*. New York: Oxford University Press, 1962.

Cockshut, A. O. J. *Truth to Life: The Art of Biography in the Nineteenth Century.* New York: Harcourt Brace Jovanovich, 1974.

Connely, Willard. *Adventures in Biography: A Chronicle of Encounters and Findings.* London: Laurie, 1956; New York: Horizon, 1960.

Couser, G. Thomas. *American Autobiography: The Prophetic Mode.* Amherst: University of Massachusetts Press, 1979.

Daghlian, Philip B., ed. *Essays in Eighteenth-Century Biography.* Bloomington: Indiana University Press, 1968.

Daiches, David. *Critical Approaches to Literature.* Englewood Cliffs, N.J.: Prentice-Hall, 1956.

Davenport, William H., and Ben Siegel, eds. *Biography Past and Present.* New York: Scribners, 1965.

Denzin, Norman K. *Interpretive Biography.* Newbury Park, Cal.: Sage, 1989.

Donoghue, Denis. *Reading America: Essays on American Literature.* New York: Knopf, 1987.

Durling, Dwight, and William Watt, eds. *Biography: Varieties and Parallels.* New York: Dryden Press, 1941.

Edel, Leon. *Literary Biography.* Toronto: University of Toronto Press, 1957; London: Hart-Davis, 1957; revised edition, Garden City, N.Y.: Doubleday, 1959; revised again, Bloomington: Indiana University Press, 1973; revised and enlarged as *Writing Lives: Principia Biographica,* New York & London: Norton, 1984.

Edel. *Stuff of Sleep and Dreams: Experiments in Literary Psychology.* New York: Harper & Row, 1982; London: Chatto & Windus, 1982.

Ellmann, Richard. *Golden Codgers: Biographical Speculations.* New York & London: Oxford University Press, 1973.

Ellmann. *Literary Biography.* Oxford: Clarendon Press, 1971.

Epstein, Joseph. *Plausible Prejudices: Essays on American Writing.* New York & London: Norton, 1985.

Epstein, William H. *Recognizing Biography.* Philadelphia: University of Pennsylvania Press, 1987.

Flanagan, Thomas. "Problems of Psychobiography." *Queen's Quarterly,* 89 (Autumn 1982): 596-610.

Fowler, Alastair. *Kinds of Literature: An Introduction to the Theory of Genres and Modes.* Cambridge, Mass.: Harvard University Press, 1982.

Frank, Katherine. "Writing Lives: Theory and Practice of Literary Biography." *Genre,* 13 (Winter 1980): 499-516.

Friedson, Anthony M., ed. *New Directions in Biography.* Honolulu: University Press of Hawaii, 1981.

Fromm, Gloria G., ed. *Essaying Biography: A Celebration for Leon Edel.* Honolulu: University of Hawaii Press, 1986.

Frye, Northrop. *Anatomy of Criticism: Four Essays.* Princeton: Princeton University Press, 1957.

Frye. *The Well-Tempered Critic.* Bloomington: Indiana University Press, 1963.

Gardner, Helen. *In Defence of the Imagination.* Cambridge, Mass.: Harvard University Press, 1982.

Garraty, John A. *The Nature of Biography*. New York: Knopf, 1957.

Gittings, Robert. *The Nature of Biography*. Seattle: University of Washington Press, 1978.

Greene, Donald. " 'Tis a Pretty Book, Mr. Boswell, But—." *Georgia Review*, 32 (Spring 1978): 17-43.

Hampshire, Stuart. *Modern Writers and Other Essays*. London: Chatto & Windus, 1969; New York: Knopf, 1970.

Havlice, Patricia Pate. *Index to Literary Biography*, 2 volumes. Metuchen, N.J.: Scarecrow Press, 1975.

Heilbrun, Carolyn G. *Hamlet's Mother and Other Women*. New York: Columbia University Press, 1990.

Heilbrun. *Writing a Woman's Life*. New York & London: Norton, 1988.

Hoberman, Ruth. *Modernizing Lives: Experiments in English Biography, 1918-1939*. Carbondale: Southern Illinois University Press, 1987.

Holland, Norman. *The Dynamics of Literary Response*. New York: Oxford University Press, 1968.

Holland. *Poems in Persons: An Introduction to the Psychoanalysis of Literature*. New York: Norton, 1973.

Holmes, Richard. *Footsteps: Adventures of a Romantic Biographer*. New York: Viking, 1985.

Homberger, Eric, and John Charmley, eds. *The Troubled Face of Biography*. New York: St. Martin's Press, 1988.

Honan, Park. *Authors' Lives: On Literary Biography and the Arts of Language*. New York: St. Martin's Press, 1990.

Honan. "The Theory of Biography." *Novel*, 13 (Fall 1979): 109-120.

Horden, Peregrine, ed. *Freud and the Humanities*. New York: St. Martin's Press, 1985.

Hough, Graham. *Style and Stylistics*. London: Routledge & Kegan Paul, 1969; New York: Humanities Press, 1969.

Hughson, Lois. *From Biography to History: The Historical Imagination and American Fiction, 1880-1940*. Charlottesville: University Press of Virginia, 1988.

Hyde, Marietta A., ed. *Modern Biography*. New York: Harcourt, Brace, 1926.

Johnson, Edgar. *One Mighty Torrent: The Drama of Biography*. New York: Stackpole, 1937.

Johnson, ed. *A Treasury of Biography*. New York: Howell, Soskin, 1941.

Kaplan, Justin. "In Pursuit of the Ultimate Fiction." *New York Times Book Review*, 19 April 1987, pp. 1, 24-25.

Kazin, Alfred. *The Inmost Leaf: A Selection of Essays*. New York: Harcourt, Brace, 1955.

Kendall, Paul Murray. *The Art of Biography*. New York: Norton, 1965.

Kenner, Hugh. *Historical Fictions*. San Francisco: North Point Press, 1990.

Kermode, Frank. *The Art of Telling: Essays on Fiction*. Cambridge, Mass.: Harvard University Press, 1983.

Kermode. *The Genesis of Secrecy. On the Interpretation of Narrative*. Cambridge, Mass.: Harvard University Press, 1979.

Kermode. *The Sense of an Ending: Studies in the Theory of Fiction*. New York: Oxford University Press, 1967.

Krupnick, Mark L. "The Sanctuary of Imagination." *Nation* (14 July 1969): 55-56.

Levin, David. *In Defense of Historical Literature*. New York: Hill & Wang, 1967.

Levin, Harry. *Contexts of Criticism*. Cambridge, Mass.: Harvard University Press, 1957.

Lomask, Milton. *The Biographer's Craft*. New York: Harper & Row, 1986.

Mandell, Gail Porter. *Life into Art: Conversations with Seven Contemporary Biographers*. Fayetteville & London: University of Arkansas Press, 1991.

Maner, Martin. *The Philosophical Biographer: Doubt and Dialectic in Johnson's Lives of the Poets*. Athens: University of Georgia Press, 1988.

Mariani, Paul. *A Usable Past: Essays on Modern and Contemporary Poetry*. Amherst: University of Massachusetts Press, 1984.

Marquess, William Henry. *Lives of the Poet: The First Century of Keats Biography*. University Park: Pennsylvania State University Press, 1985.

Maurois, Andre. *Aspects of Biography*. New York: Appleton, 1929.

Merrill, Dana Kinsman. *American Biography: Its Theory and Practice*. Portland, Maine: Bowker, 1957.

Meyers, Jeffrey. *The Spirit of Biography*. Ann Arbor, Mich.: UMI Research Press, 1989.

Meyers, ed. *The Biographer's Art: New Essays*. New York: New Amsterdam, 1989.

Meyers, ed. *The Craft of Literary Biography*. New York: Schocken, 1985.

Nadel, Ira Bruce. *Biography: Fiction, Fact and Form*. New York: St. Martin's Press, 1984.

Nagourney, Peter. "The Basic Assumptions of Literary Biography." *Biography*, 1 (Spring 1978): 86-104.

Nicolson, Harold. *The Development of English Biography*. London: Hogarth, 1928; New York: Harcourt Brace, 1928.

Noland, Richard. "Psychohistory, Theory and Practice." *Massachusetts Review*, 18 (Summer 1977): 295-322.

Novarr, David. *The Lines of Life: Theories of Biography, 1880-1970*. West Lafayette, Ind.: Purdue University Press, 1986.

Oates, Stephen B., ed. *Biography as High Adventure: Life-Writers Speak on Their Art*. Amherst: University of Massachusetts Press, 1986.

O'Neill, Edward Hayes. *A History of American Biography, 1800-1935*. Philadelphia & London: University of Pennsylvania Press, 1935.

Pachter, Marc, ed. *Telling Lives: The Biographer's Art*. Washington, D.C.: New Republic Books, 1979.

Pascal, Roy. *Design and Truth in Autobiography*. Cambridge, Mass.: Harvard University Press, 1960.

Pearson, Hesketh. *Ventilations: Being Biographical Asides*. Philadelphia: Lippincott, 1930.

Petrie, Dennis W. *Ultimately Fiction: Design in Modern American Literary Biography.* West Lafayette, Ind.: Purdue University Press, 1981.

Plagens, Peter. "Biography." *Art in America,* 68 (October 1980): 13-15.

Poirier, Richard. *A World Elsewhere: The Place of Style in American Literature.* New York: Oxford University Press, 1966.

Powers, Lyall H., ed. *Leon Edel and Literary Art.* Ann Arbor, Mich.: UMI Research Press, 1987.

Quilligan, Maureen. "Rewriting History: The Difference of Feminist Biography." *Yale Review,* 77 (Winter 1988): 259-286.

Rampersad, Arnold. "Biography, Autobiography, and Afro-American Culture." *Yale Review,* 73 (Autumn 1983): 1-16.

Rampersad. "Psychology and Afro-American Biography." *Yale Review,* 78 (Autumn 1988): 1-18.

Reid, B. L. *Necessary Lives: Biographical Reflections.* Columbia: University of Missouri Press, 1990.

Rose, Phyllis. *Writing of Women: Essays in a Renaissance.* Middletown, Conn.: Wesleyan University Press, 1985.

Runyan, William McKinley. *Life Histories and Psychobiography: Explorations in Theory and Method.* New York: Oxford University Press, 1982.

Said, Edward W. *Beginnings: Intention and Method.* New York: Basic Books, 1975.

Schaber, Ina. "Fictional Biography, Factual Biography and Their Contaminations." *Biography,* 5 (Winter 1982): 1-16.

Scholes, Robert. *Structuralism in Literature: An Introduction.* New Haven: Yale University Press, 1974.

Shelston, Alan. *Biography.* London: Methuen, 1977.

Siebenschuh, William R. *Fictional Techniques and Factual Works.* Athens: University of Georgia Press, 1983.

Smith, Barbara Herrnstein. *On the Margins of Discourses: The Relation of Literature to Language.* Chicago: University of Chicago Press, 1978.

Sontag, Susan. "On Style." *Partisan Review,* 32 (Fall 1965): 543-560.

Spence, Donald P. *Narrative Truth and Historical Truth.* New York: Norton, 1982.

Stauffer, Donald A. *The Art of Biography in Eighteenth-Century England,* 2 volumes. Princeton: Princeton University Press, 1941; London: Oxford University Press, 1941.

Thayer, William R. *The Art of Biography.* New York: Scribners, 1920.

Vance, John A., ed. *Bowsell's Life of Johnson: New Questions, New Answers.* Athens: University of Georgia Press, 1985.

Veninga, James F., ed. *The Biographer's Craft: Life Histories and Humanism.* College Station: Texas A&M University Press, 1983.

Vernoff, Edward, and Rima Shore. *The International Dictionary of 20th Century Biography.* New York: New American Library, 1987.

Weintraub, Stanley, ed. *Biography and Truth*. Indianapolis: Bobbs-Merrill, 1967.

Wheeler, David, ed. *Domestick Privacies: Samuel Johnson and the Art of Biography*. Lexington: University Press of Kentucky, 1987.

Whittemore, Reed. *Pure Lives: The Early Biographers*. Baltimore & London: Johns Hopkins University Press, 1988.

Whittemore. *Whole Lives: Shapers of Modern Biography*. Baltimore: Johns Hopkins University Press, 1989.

Winslow, Donald J. *Life-Writing: A Glossary of Terms in Biography, Autobiography, and Related Forms*. Honolulu: University Press of Hawaii, 1980.

Woolf, Virginia. *Collected Essays*. London: Hogarth, 1967; New York: Harcourt, Brace & World, 1967.

Zinsser, William, ed. *Extraordinary Lives: The Art and Craft of American Biography*. New York: American Heritage, 1986.

Contributors

Mark Allister...*St. Olaf College*
Jamie Barlowe-Kayes ....*University of Toledo*
Dennis Barone...*St. Joseph College*
Murray Baumgarten...*University of California, Santa Cruz*
Kirk H. Beetz...*National University, Sacramento*
Jason Berner.....................*Hunter College of the City University of New York*
Robert G. Blake...*Elon College*
Lynn Z. Bloom..*University of Connecticut*
Margaret Carter...*Bradley University*
John J. Conlon..*University of Massachusetts—Boston*
Sondra Miley Cooney...*Kent State University*
Bruce Fogelman ....*Knoxville, Tennessee*
Anne-Marie Foley...*University of Missouri*
Warren French..*University of Wales, Swansea*
Lenemaja Friedman..*Columbus College*
John L. Idol ....*Clemson University*
Glen M. Johnson...*Catholic University of America*
Gail Porter Mandell.............................*Saint Mary's College, Notre Dame, Indiana*
Joseph Millichap ....*Western Kentucky University*
Robert A. Morace..*Daemen College*
Timothy Morris ....*University of Texas at Arlington*
William Over..*St. John's University*
Donald E. Pease...*Dartmouth College*
Vicki K. Robinson ....*State University of New York College at Cortland*
Susan J. Rosowski...*University of Nebraska*
Robert L. Ross...*University of Texas at Austin*
David Sadkin ....*Niagara University*
Steven Serafin.............................*Hunter College of the City University of New York*
Lynne P. Shackelford ....*Furman University*
John C. Shields...*Illinois State University*
John C. Ward ....*Centre College*
Mark Royden Winchell ....*Clemson University*

325

Cumulative Index

DLB before number: *Dictionary of Literary Biography*, Volumes 1-111
Y before number: *Dictionary of Literary Biography Yearbook*, 1980-1990
DS before number: *Dictionary of Literary Biography Documentary Series*, Volumes 1-8

A

Cumulative Index

D

F

H

Cumulative Index

Dictionary of Literary Biography, Volumes 1-111
Dictionary of Literary Biography Yearbook, 1980-1990
Dictionary of Literary Biography Documentary Series, Volumes 1-8

Cumulative Index

I

Ivers, M. J., and Company DLB-49

J

Jackmon, Marvin E. (see Marvin X)

Jackson, Angela 1951- DLB-41

Jackson, Helen Hunt 1830-1885 ....DLB-42, 47

Jackson, Holbrook 1874-1948 ....DLB-98

Jackson, Laura Riding 1901- DLB-48

Jackson, Shirley 1919-1965 ....DLB-6

Jacob, Piers Anthony Dillingham (see Anthony, Piers)

Jacobi, Friedrich Heinrich 1743-1819 ....DLB-94

Jacobi, Johann Georg 1740-1841 ....DLB-97

Jacobs, George W., and Company DLB-49

Jacobson, Dan 1929- DLB-14

Jahnn, Hans Henny 1894-1959 ....DLB-56

Jakes, John 1932- Y-83

James, Henry 1843-1916 ....DLB-12, 71, 74

James, John circa 1633-1729 ....DLB-24

James Joyce Centenary: Dublin, 1982 ....Y-82

James Joyce Conference...Y-85

James, P. D. 1920- DLB-87

James, U. P. [publishing house] DLB-49

Jameson, Anna 1794-1860 ....DLB-99

Jameson, Fredric 1934- DLB-67

Jameson, J. Franklin 1859-1937 ....DLB-17

Jameson, Storm 1891-1986 ....DLB-36

Jarrell, Randall 1914-1965 ....DLB-48, 52

Jarrold and Sons DLB-106

Jasmin, Claude 1930- DLB-60

Jay, John 1745-1829 ....DLB-31

Jefferies, Richard 1848-1887 ....DLB-98

Jeffers, Lance 1919-1985 ....DLB-41

Jeffers, Robinson 1887-1962 ....DLB-45

Jefferson, Thomas 1743-1826 ....DLB-31

Jelinek, Elfriede 1946- DLB-85

Jellicoe, Ann 1927- DLB-13

Jenkins, Robin 1912- DLB-14

Jenkins, William Fitzgerald (see Leinster, Murray)

Jennings, Elizabeth 1926- DLB-27

Jens, Walter 1923- DLB-69

Jensen, Merrill 1905-1980 ....DLB-17

Jephson, Robert 1736-1803 ....DLB-89

Jerome, Jerome K. 1859-1927 ....DLB-10, 34

Jerome, Judson 1927- DLB-105

Jerome, Judson, Reflections: After
    a Tornado..DLB-105

Jesse, F. Tennyson 1888-1958 ....DLB-77

Jewett, John P., and Company DLB-49

Jewett, Sarah Orne 1849-1909 ....DLB-12, 74

The Jewish Publication Society...................................DLB-49

Jewitt, John Rodgers 1783-1821...................................DLB-99

Jewsbury, Geraldine 1812-1880 ....DLB-21

Joans, Ted 1928- DLB-16, 41

John Edward Bruce: Three Documents DLB-50

John O'Hara's Pottsville Journalism Y-88

John Steinbeck Research Center Y-85

John Webster: The Melbourne Manuscript Y-86

Johnson, B. S. 1933-1973 ....DLB-14, 40

Johnson, Benjamin [publishing house] DLB-49

Johnson, Benjamin, Jacob, and
    Robert [publishing house] DLB-49

Johnson, Charles 1679-1748.......................................DLB-84

Johnson, Charles R. 1948- DLB-33

Johnson, Charles S. 1893-1956 ....DLB-51, 91

Johnson, Diane 1934- Y-80

Johnson, Edgar 1901- DLB-103

Johnson, Edward 1598-1672 ....DLB-24

Johnson, Fenton 1888-1958.......................................DLB-45, 50

Johnson, Georgia Douglas 1886-1966 ....DLB-51

Johnson, Gerald W. 1890-1980 ....DLB-29

Johnson, Helene 1907- DLB-51

Johnson, Jacob, and Company DLB-49

Johnson, James Weldon 1871-1938 ....DLB-51

Johnson, Lionel 1867-1902.......................................DLB-19

Johnson, Nunnally 1897-1977 ....DLB-26

Johnson, Owen 1878-1952...Y-87

Johnson, Pamela Hansford 1912- DLB-15

Johnson, Pauline 1861-1913.......................................DLB-92

Johnson, Samuel 1696-1772.......................................DLB-24

Johnson, Samuel 1709-1784...........................DLB-39, 95, 104

Johnson, Samuel 1822-1882.......................................DLB-1

Johnson, Uwe 1934-1984...DLB-75

Johnston, Annie Fellows 1863-1931 ....DLB-42

Johnston, Basil H. 1929- DLB-60

Johnston, Denis 1901-1984.......................................DLB-10

Johnston, George 1913- DLB-88

L

N

P

Q

R

W

Y

Z

(Continued from front endsheets)

80: *Restoration and Eighteenth-Century Dramatists,* First Series, edited by Paula R. Backscheider (1989)

81: *Austrian Fiction Writers, 1875-1913,* edited by James Hardin and Donald G. Daviau (1989)

82: *Chicano Writers,* First Series, edited by Francisco A. Lomelí and Carl R. Shirley (1989)

83: *French Novelists Since 1960,* edited by Catharine Savage Brosman (1989)

84: *Restoration and Eighteenth-Century Dramatists,* Second Series, edited by Paula R. Backscheider (1989)

85: *Austrian Fiction Writers After 1914,* edited by James Hardin and Donald G. Daviau (1989)

86: *American Short-Story Writers, 1910-1945,* First Series, edited by Bobby Ellen Kimbel (1989)

87: *British Mystery and Thriller Writers Since 1940,* First Series, edited by Bernard Benstock and Thomas F. Staley (1989)

88: *Canadian Writers, 1920-1959,* Second Series, edited by W. H. New (1989)

89: *Restoration and Eighteenth-Century Dramatists,* Third Series, edited by Paula R. Backscheider (1989)

90: *German Writers in the Age of Goethe, 1789-1832,* edited by James Hardin and Christoph E. Schweitzer (1989)

91: *American Magazine Journalists, 1900-1960,* First Series, edited by Sam G. Riley (1990)

92: *Canadian Writers, 1890-1920,* edited by W. H. New (1990)

93: *British Romantic Poets, 1789-1832,* First Series, edited by John R. Greenfield (1990)

94: *German Writers in the Age of Goethe: Sturm und Drang to Classicism,* edited by James Hardin and Christoph E. Schweitzer (1990)

95: *Eighteenth-Century British Poets,* First Series, edited by John Sitter (1990)

96: *British Romantic Poets, 1789-1832,* Second Series, edited by John R. Greenfield (1990)

97: *German Writers from the Enlightenment to Sturm und Drang, 1720-1764,* edited by James Hardin and Christoph E. Schweitzer (1990)

98: *Modern British Essayists,* First Series, edited by Robert Beum (1990)

99: *Canadian Writers Before 1890,* edited by W. H. New (1990)

100: *Modern British Essayists,* Second Series, edited by Robert Beum (1990)

101: *British Prose Writers, 1660-1800,* First Series, edited by Donald T. Siebert (1991)

102: *American Short-Story Writers, 1910-1945,* Second Series, edited by Bobby Ellen Kimbel (1991)

103: *American Literary Biographers,* First Series, edited by Steven Serafin (1991)

104: *British Prose Writers, 1660-1800,* Second Series, edited by Donald T. Siebert (1991)

105: *American Poets Since World War II,* Second Series, edited by R. S. Gwynn (1991)

106: *British Literary Publishing Houses, 1820-1880,* edited by Patricia J. Anderson and Jonathan Rose (1991)

107: *British Romantic Prose Writers, 1789-1832,* First Series, edited by John R. Greenfield (1991)

108: *Twentieth-Century Spanish Poets,* First Series, edited by Michael L. Perna (1991)

109: *Eighteenth-Century British Poets,* Second Series, edited by John Sitter (1991)

110: *British Romantic Prose Writers, 1789-1832,* Second Series, edited by John R. Greenfield (1991)

111: *American Literary Biographers,* Second Series, edited by Steven Serafin (1991)

Documentary Series

1: *Sherwood Anderson, Willa Cather, John Dos Passos, Theodore Dreiser, F. Scott Fitzgerald, Ernest Hemingway, Sinclair Lewis,* edited by Margaret A. Van Antwerp (1982)

2: *James Gould Cozzens, James T. Farrell, William Faulkner, John O'Hara, John Steinbeck, Thomas Wolfe, Richard Wright,* edited by Margaret A. Van Antwerp (1982)

3: *Saul Bellow, Jack Kerouac, Norman Mailer, Vladimir Nabokov, John Updike, Kurt Vonnegut,* edited by Mary Bruccoli (1983)

4: *Tennessee Williams,* edited by Margaret A. Van Antwerp and Sally Johns (1984)